REACTIONS
OF ORGANIC
COMPOUNDS:
a textbook for the advanced student

REACTIONS OF ORGANIC COMPOUNDS:

a textbook for the advanced student

REYNOLD C. FUSON

Professor of Organic Chemistry and
Member of the Center for Advanced Study
University of Illinois

John Wiley & Sons, Inc.   New York · London

Preface

This textbook is designed for students who have had an introduction to organic chemistry and who seek a mastery of the fundamentals of the subject. As in an earlier book of mine, *Advanced Organic Chemistry*, the reactions of organic compounds constitute the principal topic. This book is organized to take advantage of the great advances that have been made by use of the qualitative electronic theory of organic chemistry. The book consists of three parts. The first part, which is devoted to reactions generally classified as polar, is divided in the conventional manner into two sections according to whether the reagent is considered to be electrophilic or nucleophilic. The second part deals with reactions involving radicals; and the last part is devoted to molecular reactions. Many of the reactions, because information as to their mechanisms is inconclusive, have had to be classified tentatively, of course.

The theoretical aspects of organic chemistry are thus dealt with primarily by implication. For the student who is unfamiliar with the basic concepts the first chapter offers a brief survey. At many points in-the-text references are made to Jack Hine's *Physical Organic Chemistry* (Hine), McGraw-Hill Book Company, Inc., 1956, and to Edwin S. Gould's *Mechanism and Structure in Organic Chemistry* (Gould), Henry Holt and Company, 1959.

Other in-the-text references are to Organic Syntheses (OS), Organic Reactions (OR), Chemical Reviews (CR), Quarterly Reviews (QR), and review articles in Angewandte Chemie (Angew.). Reference has not been made to Organic Syntheses volumes 1 to 29 but rather to the Collective Volumes I, II, and III.

In the preparation of this book I have received help from many organic chemists. Special thanks are due Douglas E. Applequist, Cyrus O. Guss, and H. R. Snyder for critical reviews of the manuscript.

Reynold C. Fuson

University of Illinois
June, 1962

v

Contents

vii

1

Introduction to basic concepts

More than a century has passed since the concept of the tetravalency of carbon was clearly formulated for the first time. This advance in the field of theory may well be the most important achievement of the organic chemist. The names usually mentioned in this connection are those of Kekulé and Couper, who simultaneously and independently arrived at the hypothesis that, in compounds, carbon has four bonds. Great credit goes also to Butlerov, who was among the first to appreciate the possibilities of the new concept and to show how it could be utilized.[1] The basic concept, embracing other atoms as well, was that each atom had a discrete number of valences that enabled it to enter into combination with other atoms. A corollary of the hypothesis was that carbon could unite with itself to form chains; it is this capacity of *catenation* rather than the tetravalency that has proved to be the outstanding characteristic of carbon.

The structural formulas arrived at by use of these ideas continue to be the organic chemist's most valuable tools. Early successes are illustrated by the interpretation of the chemical behavior of the molecules with multiple linkages, which differed in easily recognizable ways from molecules having single bonds only. Ethylenic and acetylenic compounds were known to decolorize solutions of bromine and permanganate, for example.

The new structural theory, which culminated with Kekulé's structure for benzene in 1865, was immediately seen to have overreached itself (Angew., **70,** 37). Kekulé himself recognized that the three double bonds assigned to benzene did not confer upon the molecule the chemical properties characteristic of an olefin. Its "double" bonds were unaccountably unreactive; for example, benzene does not decolorize solutions of bromine or permanganate. Subsequent investigations revealed, moreover, that olefinic bonds in open chain molecules may resemble those assigned to benzene. The central bond in tetraphenylethylene, for example, is not

[1] H. M. Leicester, *J. Chem. Education*, **36,** 328 (1959).

1

attacked by bromine even under conditions that induce nuclear bromination.[2]

$$(C_6H_5)_2C\!\!=\!\!C(C_6H_5)_2 \rightarrow (p\text{-}BrC_6H_4)_2C\!\!=\!\!C(C_6H_4Br\text{-}p)_2$$

Another olefin, 2,4,6-trinitrostyrene, is indifferent to bromine in either water or carbon tetrachloride.[3]

The olefinic bonds in these compounds show the effects of conjugation with other unsaturated functions. The simplest conjugated systems—in which unsaturated functions are connected by single bonds—show the same type of stabilization to a lesser degree and make clear that the classical structural theory cannot be used to represent satisfactorily all types of organic compounds. It serves admirably to depict the framework of molecules but fails to indicate their potentialities for reaction. In the classical structures each atom in the molecule is represented as having the required number of valence bonds, and thus the molecule would be expected to be stable, i.e., unreactive. This expectation is realized to a degree but is in general misleading. And it fails at precisely the points of greatest interest—the functional groups. Eventually it was necessary for organic chemists to recognize that their early enthusiasm for the concept of the constancy of the valence of elements in combination had carried them to a position that was untenable.

The assumption is now made that carbon may abandon the tetravalent state during reactions. The trivalent state, postulated for carbon in many reactions, may conceivably arise in three different ways.

1. Complete removal of the bonding electron pair leaves a carbon atom having only six of the eight electrons that it normally holds. The fragment carries a positive charge and is known as a *carbonium ion*:

$$R$$
$$R\!:\!\overset{\cdot\cdot}{\underset{\cdot\cdot}{C}}{}^+$$
$$R$$

[2] See H. L. Bassett, N. Thorne, and C. L. Young, *J. Chem. Soc.*, 85 (1949).

[3] C. F. Bjork, W. A. Gey, J. H. Robson, and R. W. Van Dolah, *J. Am. Chem. Soc.*, **75**, 1988 (1953).

2. Removal of one electron of the bonding pair leaves a neutral *radical* in which the carbon atom holds seven electrons:

$$\begin{array}{c} R \\ \cdot\cdot \\ R:\overset{\cdot\cdot}{\underset{\cdot\cdot}{C}}\cdot \\ \\ R \end{array}$$

3. In the remaining type the carbon atom retains its octet of electrons, but one of the four pairs is unshared. The fragment has a negative charge and is known as a *carbanion*:

$$\begin{array}{c} R \\ \cdot\cdot \\ R:\overset{\cdot\cdot}{\underset{\cdot\cdot}{C}}:^{-} \\ \\ R \end{array}$$

Carbonium ions, carbanions, and radicals are normally of high energy, and their formation in reactions is often hypothetical; however, stable examples of each species are known.

It is postulated also that reactions at a saturated carbon atom may take place without previous formation of trivalent carbon. One way of explaining this phenomenon has the carbon atom involved with five other atoms simultaneously (S_N2 reactions, Hine, 93).

$$\begin{array}{c} H \qquad H \\ \diagdown \quad \diagup \\ X\cdots C\cdots Y \\ | \\ H \end{array}$$

Another type of intermediate, proposed to account for certain reactions, can be arrived at schematically by removing R^+ from the carbonium ion. The remaining fragment, known as a *carbene* (Angew., **73**, 161), is neutral and has only six electrons in the valence shell of the carbon atom.

$$\begin{array}{ccc} R & & R \\ \cdot\cdot & & \cdot\cdot \\ R:\overset{\cdot\cdot}{\underset{\cdot\cdot}{C}}{}^{+} \rightarrow R^{+} + & :\overset{\cdot\cdot}{\underset{\cdot\cdot}{C}} \\ & & \\ R & & R \end{array}$$

The general idea that carbon may change its valence during reactions has proved to be extremely fruitful. Whereas chemists hail the discovery of the tetravalency of carbon as perhaps the greatest single achievement in the history of organic chemistry, it must be admitted that the most important advances of our time are based on the notion that, at least in many cases, the rule does not hold during the course of reactions.

Electrophiles and Nucleophiles

The characteristic behavior of a carbonium ion is to acquire a pair of electrons to complete the valence shell of the electron-deficient carbon atom. In this respect it resembles the proton furnished by ordinary acids. Belonging to this same category are many other compounds, known as Lewis acids, that contain elements with similarly incomplete valence shells. Prominent among these are certain inorganic compounds such as aluminum chloride, boron fluoride, and ferric chloride.

$$
\begin{array}{ccc}
\text{Cl} & \text{F} & \text{Cl} \\
| & | & | \\
\text{Al—Cl} & \text{B—F} & \text{Fe—Cl} \\
| & | & | \\
\text{Cl} & \text{F} & \text{Cl}
\end{array}
$$

All these substances seek an additional pair of electrons, i.e., are electrophilic, and are known as *electrophiles* (Gould, 115).

Carbanions on the other hand, having an unshared pair of electrons, may be classified as bases. The hydroxide ion, furnished by ordinary bases, and the nitrogen atom of bases such as ammonia, aniline, and pyridine all possess an unshared pair of electrons.

$$
\begin{array}{cccc}
 & \text{H} & \text{H} & \\
 & | & | & \\
:\ddot{\text{O}}\text{H}^- & \text{H—N—H} & \text{C}_6\text{H}_5\text{N—H} &
\end{array}
$$

If the structural formulas are examined it is seen that all trivalent nitrogen compounds and all oxygen compounds similarly have unshared pairs of electrons. Only those that form salts that are stable in water are classed as bases; the others are known as Lewis bases. The distinction is artificial and depends on whether the substance is a stronger or weaker base than water. All such substances can supply the pair of electrons needed by an electrophile and are classed as *nucleophiles*. They seek a nucleus that lacks a pair of electrons in its valence shell.

Certain molecules that contain both electrophilic and nucleophilic functions, properly situated so as to interact, form rings. The copper salt of salicylaldehyde is an example; rings of this type, which are closed by coordination of an atom such as oxygen or nitrogen with a metal atom, are called chelate rings.[4]

---

[4] G. T. Morgan and H. D. K. Drew, *J. Chem. Soc.*, **117**, 1456 (1920).

Types of Reactions

The production of reactive species by rupture of single bonds may occur by heterolytic fission.

$$R : R \quad \xrightarrow[\text{Electron sharing}]{\text{Heterolytic fission}} \quad R:^- + R^+$$

The reverse reaction is seen to be an addition reaction involving *electron sharing*. Reactions of this type, generally referred to as *polar* reactions, are divided into two groups depending on whether the reactant considered to be the reagent is electrophilic or nucleophilic. A modification of the electron-sharing process is *displacement* at the saturated carbon atom; A and B may or may not carry electric charges.

$$R : A + :B \rightarrow R : B + :A$$

This type of displacement is called nucleophilic since the attacking agent (:B) furnishes the electron pair for the newly formed bond and therefore seeks a nucleus that lacks such a pair. If the attacking agent is electrophilic, the reaction takes the form

$$R : A + B \rightarrow R : B + A$$

An analogous change occurs in addition reactions involving multiple linkages, an example being the union of a carbonyl group with cyanide ion.

$$O{=}\overset{|}{C} + :CN^- \rightarrow {^-O}{-}\overset{|}{\underset{|}{C}}{-}CN$$

Rupture of a single bond may also take place by homolytic fission, producing radicals.

$$R : R \quad \xrightarrow[\text{Electron pairing}]{\text{Homolytic fission}} \quad R{\cdot} + R{\cdot}$$

The reverse reaction is an addition involving electron pairing. Another type of addition reaction occurs when a radical attacks a multiple linkage; the electrons of one pair are separated, with the creation of a new radical.

$$R{\cdot} + \overset{\diagdown}{\diagup}C{\cdots}C\overset{\diagup}{\diagdown} \rightarrow R{-}\overset{|}{\underset{|}{C}}{-}\overset{|}{\underset{|}{C}}{\cdot}$$

An electron changes partners.

A substitution reaction occurs when a radical displaces another radical.

$$R{\cdot} + R'{-}H \rightarrow R'{\cdot} + R{-}H$$

A few reactions are known which seem to be neither radical not polar; these are known as molecular. The combination of a carbene with an olefin to give a cyclopropane may sometimes be of this type.

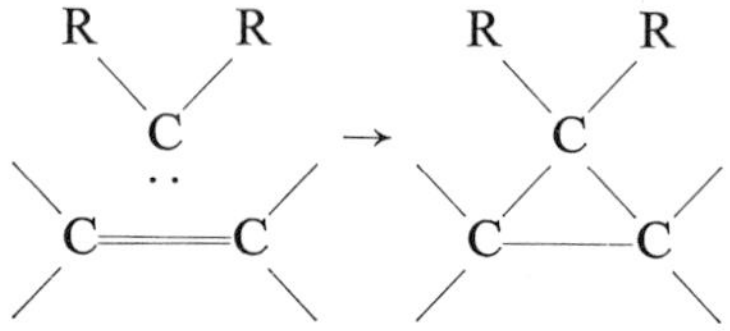

Self addition of olefins to produce cyclobutanes may be similar.

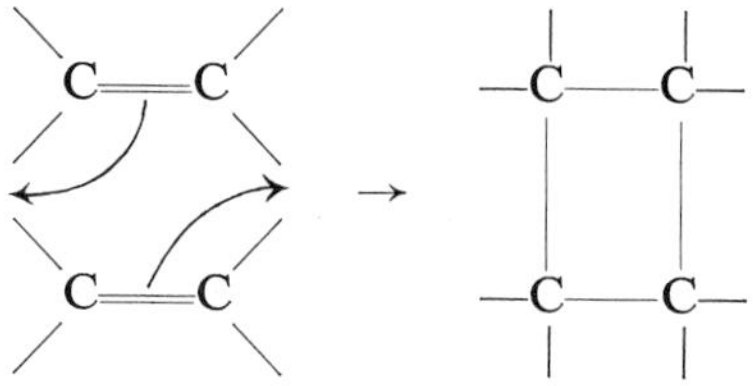

The most common type of molecular reaction is the addition of a conjugated diene to an olefin to give a six-membered ring compound. The addition of 1,3-butadiene to maleic anhydride—a typical Diels-Alder reaction—is illustrative.

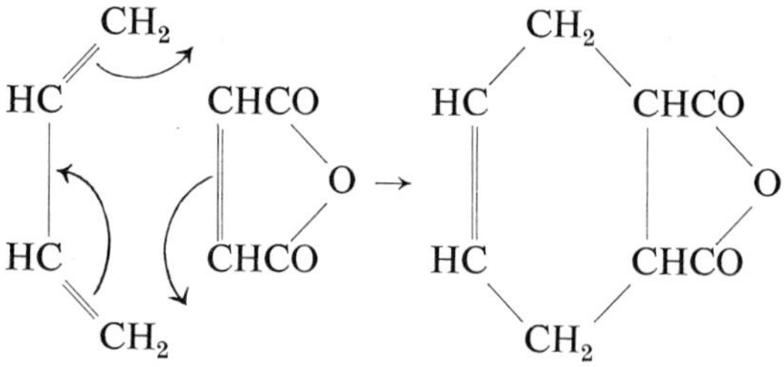

To make use of theoretical concepts in interpreting reactions it is necessary to know whether a particular reactant in a given reaction behaves as an electrophile, a nucleophile, a radical, or in some other way. It may be assumed at the outset that nearly all positive ions and all compounds having an open sextet act as electrophiles and that all negative ions and compounds having unshared electron pairs act as nucleophiles. Moreover, since olefins and aromatic compounds are attacked by such electrophilic agents as NO_2^+, these compounds may be classified as nucleophilic. Carbonyl compounds, sensitive to attack by nucleophiles such as OH^- and CN^-, are to be classed accordingly as electrophilic. The Grignard reagent, which attacks carbonyl compounds but not aromatic hydrocarbons, is then to be placed among the nucleophilic reagents.

If a reaction occurs in the gas phase and is catalyzed by input of energy, the free radical mechanism is suggested. Molecular reactions do not require a catalyst. Diels-Alder reactions are known to be affected but little by catalysts in general. Certain of them, however, are greatly accelerated by the presence of aluminum chloride.[5]

The Inductive Effect

Structural formulas, viewed in the light of the electronic theory, may possess unshared pairs of electrons and thus represent compounds capable of undergoing attack by electrophiles; an electron pair that joins dissimilar atoms is not shared equally but is drawn toward the more electron-attracting (electronegative) one. The bond thus has a corresponding degree of polarity and to that extent is vulnerable to attack by both electrophilic and nucleophilic reagents. In methyl chloride, for example, the carbon atom possesses a partial positive charge and the chlorine atom a partial negative charge. The carbon-hydrogen bonds likewise exhibit a small degree of polarity.

$$H^{\delta+}$$

$$H^{\delta+} : \overset{\cdot\cdot}{\underset{\cdot\cdot}{C}} : Cl^{\delta-}$$

$$H^{\delta+}$$

Any electric charge on an atom induces a dipole in the adjacent bonds. The effect, known as the *inductive effect* (Gould, 200), can be transmitted along a saturated chain but is heavily damped and rapidly becomes small as the length of the chain is increased.

The inductive effect is perhaps best illustrated by the influence of substituents on the strength of saturated acids (CR **25**, 151). The strength of an acid is increased by withdrawal of electrons from the carboxyl group since this facilitates the loss of the proton. Thus the strength of acetic acid is increased by halogen substituents. The following series shows the operation of this effect.

Acid	pK
Cl_3CCO_2H	0.65
Cl_2CHCO_2H	1.30
$ClCH_2CO_2H$	2.86
$ClCH_2CH_2CO_2H$	4.00
CH_3CO_2H	4.80
$CH_3CH_2CO_2H$	4.88

$$\underset{\underset{CH_3}{|}}{\overset{\overset{CH_3}{|}}{CH_3CCO_2H}} \qquad 5.05$$

[5] P. Yates and P. Eaton, *J. Am. Chem. Soc.*, **82**, 4436 (1960).

A chlorine atom in the α-position makes the acid stronger (smaller pK value), but in the β-position has a much smaller effect. Alkyl groups in the α-position cause the acid to be weaker.

Bonds in which the bonding electrons are unequally shared have a dipole moment (Gould, 57); i.e., in an electric field they become less randomly oriented, depending on the magnitude and direction of the field. The dipole of a molecule can be measured and is the vector sum of all the component dipoles.

Dipoles of molecules are partly responsible for the forces that operate to produce the cohesion observed in liquids and solids. Also there are molecular compounds such as the picrates presumably held together at least in part by electrostatic forces. The outstanding example of this type of interaction is known as hydrogen bonding.

Hydrogen bonding

This type of "bonding" is responsible for the association of such compounds as water, alcohols, phenols, and carboxylic acids (Gould, 28). Since the forces appear to be electrostatic in part, the term hydrogen bridge would seem to be more appropriate than hydrogen bond. The association of water may be represented as follows:

$$\begin{array}{cccc}
\text{H—O} & \text{+ H—O} & \rightarrow \text{ H—O} & \cdots \text{ H—O} \\
| & | & | & | \\
\text{H} & \text{H} & \text{H} & \text{H}
\end{array}$$

This remarkable phenomenon is not limited to hydroxyl compounds (O—H—O) but occurs with fluorine compounds (F—H—F, F—H—N, F—H—O), nitrogen compounds (N—H—O, N—H—N, N—H—S), and sulfur compounds (N—H—S, O—H—S). There is evidence that very weak hydrogen bonds are formed by carbon also (C—H—O, C—H—N). Indications are that still other elements likewise may prove to possess this property. For the first short period of the Mendeleeff table the tendency for hydrogen bonding increases in the following order:

$$\text{CH} < \text{NH} < \text{OH} < \text{FH}$$

Association of carboxylic acids does not proceed beyond the dimer, which has been assigned a ring structure (QR **7**, 255).

$$\begin{array}{ccc}
& \text{O} & \text{O} \cdot \cdot \text{H—O} \\
& \diagup\!\!/ & \diagup\!\!/ \qquad\quad \diagdown \\
2\text{RC} & \rightarrow \text{RC} & \quad\quad \text{CR} \\
& \diagdown & \diagdown \qquad\quad /\!\!\diagup \\
& \text{OH} & \text{O—H} \cdot \cdot \text{O}
\end{array}$$

Organic compounds that dissolve in water owe their solubility at least in part to hydrogen bonding with the solvent.

Resonance

The stabilities of the various carbonium ions, as inferred from our knowledge of the reactions supposed to involve them, vary greatly. These differences have been interpreted chiefly in terms of the theories of *resonance* (Gould, 212) and *hyperconjugation*. The crotyl carbonium ion, for example, would be expected to have a high order of stability, since two structures can be written for it by moving electrons and displacing the carbon atoms only slightly.

$$CH_3CH{=}CH{-}CH_2{}^+ \leftrightarrow CH_3\overset{+}{C}H{-}CH{=}CH_2$$

The distances between carbon atoms vary, depending on whether they are joined by single bonds or by the somewhat shorter double bonds. The carbonium ion that is represented by these two structures therefore possesses resonance (Gould, 21). The actual ion is a *resonance hybrid*. Experimentally, ions that possess resonance are more stable than would be expected from their formulas as ordinarily written. An idea of the relative stabilities of two different ions can be arrived at by a consideration of the number of resonance structures that are possible—in general the larger the number of structures, the greater the stability of the hybrid. Also, the stability is greater if the structures are equivalent or nearly so.

The benzyl carbonium ion is analogous to the allyl type of ion; the principal structures are the following.

The first two, the so-called Kekulé structures, retain the aromaticity of the benzene ring and therefore are more important than the others.

In a double bond one pair of electrons forms a *sigma*-bond similar to a single bond. The other pair, the pi-electrons, is held more loosely and is more vulnerable to attack by electron-seeking reagents. The space in which an electron is most likely to be found, i.e., its orbital (Hine, 24), has a dumb-bell shape in the case of the pi-electrons; if the two orbitals are parallel they overlap, forming a more stable system.

Aromatic nuclei represent the extreme case in which the overlapping of orbitals is continuous. One way of representing a resonance hybrid is to indicate the principal structures that can be written for it by use of accepted conventions and connect them by double headed arrows. Benzene has two equivalent structures.

Another way to represent an aromatic ring is to replace the three double bonds by a circle.

A third suggestion is to use only sigma bonds and represent the pi orbitals by circles.[6]

Hyperconjugation

The ethyl carbonium ion is more stable than the corresponding methyl ion but less stable than the isopropyl ion.

$$CH_3^+ < CH_3CH_2^+ < \quad \begin{matrix} CH_3 \\ \diagdown \\ \quad CH^+ \\ \diagup \\ CH_3 \end{matrix}$$

These differences are in agreement with predictions based on the hyperconjugation theory (Gould, 49), which postulates that hydrogen atoms on the adjacent carbon atom can share the electron deficiency. If the ethyl carbonium ion is taken as an example, delocalization of the positive charge is represented by the following structures.

$$H{-}\overset{\overset{\displaystyle H}{|}}{\underset{\underset{\displaystyle H}{|}}{C}}{-}CH_2^+ \leftrightarrow H{-}\overset{\overset{\displaystyle H^+}{|}}{\underset{\underset{\displaystyle H}{|}}{C}}{=}CH_2 \leftrightarrow H^+\ \overset{\overset{\displaystyle H}{|}}{\underset{\underset{\displaystyle H}{|}}{C}}{=}CH_2 \leftrightarrow H{-}\overset{\overset{\displaystyle H}{|}}{\underset{\underset{\displaystyle H^+}{}}{C}}{=}CH_2$$

The isopropyl carbonium has twice as many hydrogen atoms properly placed for hyperconjugative interaction as the ethyl ion, whereas the methyl ion has none. The *t*-butyl carbonium ion, with nine such hydrogen atoms, has a still greater stability just as the hyperconjugation theory predicts.

The Transition State

The ultimate aim of the understanding of reactions is to know completely, including stereochemical factors, the movement of every atom throughout the process and also the energy content of the system at every point. The

[6] R. T. Sanderson, *J. Chem. Education*, **38**, 382 (1961).

path traced by the reactant or reactants in going to the product or products is known as the *mechanism* of the reaction. Of the configurations through which the system must pass the most important is the *transition state* (Gould, 128), the one that possesses the highest free energy. This configuration can break down with equal probability into reactants or into products. The transition state for an S_N2 reaction may be depicted as follows.

$$X + H-\underset{\underset{H}{|}}{\overset{\overset{H}{\diagup}}{C}}-Y \rightarrow X\cdots\underset{\underset{H}{|}}{\overset{\overset{H}{\diagup}\!\!\!\overset{H}{\diagdown}}{C}}\cdots Y \rightarrow X-\underset{\underset{H}{|}}{\overset{\overset{H}{|}}{C}}-H + Y$$

Transition
state

To arrive at a qualitative picture of the transition state is the first aim in the elucidation of a reaction mechanism. Long before such a postulate takes form it is possible to recognize different types of reactions on the basis of mechanistic considerations.

Electron Transfer in Aromatic Compounds

A substituent on the benzene ring may cede electrons to the ring or withdraw them, depending on its nature. Electron transfer may occur by inductive, resonance, and hyperconjugative effects. If the ground state rather than the transition state is considered, the various substituents fall in an order of decreasing power of electron release illustrated by the following series of benzene derivatives.

C_6H_5-ONa	-1.00
$C_6H_5-NH_2$	-0.66
C_6H_5-OH	-0.36
$C_6H_5-OCH_3$	-0.27
$C_6H_5-CH_3$	-0.17
(C_6H_5-H)	
C_6H_5-Cl	$+0.23$
$C_6H_5-\overset{\overset{O}{\|\|}}{C}CH_3$	$+0.52$
$C_6H_5-NO_2$	$+0.78$
$C_6H_5-\overset{+}{N}(CH_3)_3Cl^-$	$+0.86$

Although this order of placement of these compounds on the basis of relative reactivities toward electrophilic reagents has long been known to organic chemists, it was not until 1935 that it was put on a quantitative basis by use of the Hammett equation. The numbers opposite the formulas are the *substituent constants* (Gould, 220) or relative numerical values for release and withdrawal of electrons for a number of functions. The values were arrived at by measurements of the dissociation constants of benzoic acids substituted in the *p*-position (Hine, 69).

The various functional units differ greatly in their power of electron release and uptake. In the following list a number of the more important units are arranged in the order of decreasing power to activate the ring.

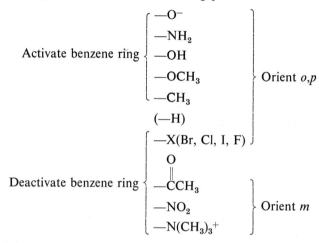

One of the great values of this series lies in the fact that it permits one to predict variations in properties that the substituents undergo when they are joined.

As will be seen when specific reactions are considered, the electronic effect of many substituents may be influenced by other factors such as steric hindrance and the nature of the reaction medium. Thus, in the presence of strong acids, aniline forms salts in which the substituent is the ammonium group. This group falls at the bottom of the list.

It appears that the most strongly *m*-directing groups are those in which the positive poles are attached directly to the benzene ring. The following compounds, for example, yield almost exclusively *m*-nitro derivatives.

$$[C_6H_5N(CH_3)_3]^+NO_3^-$$
$$[C_6H_5IC_6H_5]^+NO_3^-$$
$$[(C_6H_5)_3Sb]^{++}2NO_3^-$$
$$[C_6H_5PbC_6H_5]^{++}2NO_3^-$$

It is held that electron transfer is due in most cases largely to resonance interaction. Aniline, in which the amino group is conjugated with the ring, can be represented by five principal structures—the two Kekulé structures and three secondary structures in which two of the electron pairs of the nitrogen atom are shared with the attached carbon atom.

Another method of formulating conjugative electron transfer makes use of curved arrows. The transfer to the p-position in aniline is represented as follows.

The geometry of the aniline molecule is such that, when the unshared electron pair on the nitrogen atom is utilized to bond the nitrogen atom doubly to the carbon atom of the ring, points of high electron density must be developed in the o- and p-positions.

Phenol, having a hydroxyl group conjugated with the ring, can be represented by similar resonance structures.

The phenoxide ion can be described in like terms. It is to be noted, however, that formation of the secondary structures of phenol, like those of aniline, requires a separation of charges, whereas formation of those of the phenoxide ion does not. To this circumstance is ascribed the tendency of the phenoxide ion to be produced by dissociation of the phenol. It appears then that the reason phenols are more acidic than alcohols is that the phenoxide ion, possessing resonance, is more stable than an alkoxide ion.

Substituents such as —NH_2, —OH, and —OCH_3 are more electronegative than the ring and consequently the inductive effect is opposed to the resonance effect. Usually resonance interaction is so important as to overshadow the inductive effect, however.

Transfer of electrons in the ground state is demonstrated by the physical properties. Reactions that involve the aromatic ring may be interpreted fairly satisfactorily by reference to the ground states of the nuclei involved; this must mean that in most reactions the ground state closely resembles the transition state. For strict accuracy, however, reactions must be considered rather by reference to the respective transition states. Since the competition between the o- , m- , and p-positions on the monosubstituted benzene ring depends on the relative stabilities of the corresponding transition states, the rules of orientation will be discussed later by reference to the structures that can be written as approximations of the transition states.

Aromatic Character

The heat of hydrogenation of benzene, 49.8 kcalories per molė, is less by 36 kcalories per mole than three times that of the hydrogenation of the double bond in cyclohexene. The difference, known as the stabilization energy,[7] is taken as a measure of the aromatic character of the ring. This high degree of stabilization is possible only because the ring is planar. Aromaticity is found in heterocycles such as pyridine and exists also in five-membered heterocycles such as the nuclei of thiophene, furan, and

[7] R. B. Turner, *Theoretical Organic Chemistry* (Kekulé Symposium), Butterworths, London, 1959, p. 69, 1959.

pyrrole in which a carbon-carbon unit of benzene has been replaced by a single atom that possesses a pair of unshared electrons.

Resonance stabilization is found in lower degree in open-chain or alicyclic analogs in which multiple linkages are conjugated with other multiple linkages as in cyclopentadiene, or with atoms having unshared pairs of electrons as in methyl vinyl ether and vinyl chloride.

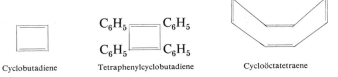

Cyclopentadiene	$CH_2\!=\!CH\!-\!O\!-\!CH_3$	$CH_2\!=\!CH\!-\!Cl$
	Methyl vinyl ether	Vinyl chloride

Since the classical aromatic compounds have cyclic systems that are completely conjugated, much attention has been given to cyclobutadiene and cycloöctatetraene. Efforts to prepare cyclobutadiene have not been successful. Complexes with certain salts have been reported for it and its derivatives; one of these is the complex between tetraphenylcyclobutadiene and nickel bromide.[8]

Cyclobutadiene	Tetraphenylcyclobutadiene	Cycloöctatetraene

Cycloöctatetraene is not aromatic; it is not planar but "tub-shaped." Certain ions have been found to be aromatic. The cyclopentadienyl anion is an example; it has the same number and arrangement of pi-electrons as pyrrole, for example.

Cyclopentadienyl anion	Pyrrole

The character of the cyclopentadienyl anion is illustrated dramatically by a family of organometallic sandwich compounds,[9] notably dicyclopenta-dienyliron, commonly known as ferrocene. In the formation of ferrocene two cyclopentadienyl anions are brought together parallel to each other with an atom of ferrous ion sandwiched between them. When anhydrous

[8] H. H. Freedman, *J. Am. Chem. Soc.*, **83**, 2194, 2195 (1961).

[9] M. D. Rausch, *J. Chem. Education*, **37**, 568 (1960).

ferrous chloride, cyclopentadiene, and sodium ethoxide are allowed to react, ferrocene is formed in 90% yield.[10]

$$2 \underset{\text{Na}}{\diagup\!\!\!\diagdown} \quad + \quad FeCl_2 \quad \longrightarrow \quad \text{Fe} \quad + \quad 2NaCl$$

Ferrocene

Sandwich compounds have been reported also that consist of aromatic molecules such as benzene held together by an atom of a transition element. Furthermore, sandwich complexes of transition metals have been described in which both a cyclopentadiene and an aromatic ring are coordinated with the central metal atom.[11]

Aromatic carbonium ions are known also. In the tropylium ion, for example, the positive charge is uniformly distributed over the seven carbon atoms of the ring, i.e., seven equivalent structures may be written (Angew., **68**, 661).

Perhaps even more remarkable are the cyclopropenyl cations. For the *s*-triphenyl ion the following equivalent structures may be written.

$$C_6H_5C \overset{\overset{+}{C}C_6H_5}{\diagdown_{CC_6H_5}} \quad \leftrightarrow \quad C_6H_5\overset{+}{C} \overset{CC_6H_5}{\diagdown_{CC_6H_5}} \quad \leftrightarrow \quad C_6H_5C \overset{CC_6H_5}{\diagdown_{\underset{+}{C}C_6H_5}}$$

The di-*n*-propylcyclopropenyl[12] and the diphenylcyclopropenyl[13] cations are similar.

The perinaphthenyl cation also is stable; for it six equivalent structures may be written.[14]

(structures) ↔ (structures) ↔ (structures) etc.

[10] W. F. Little, R. C. Koestler, and R. Eisenthal, *J. Org. Chem.*, **25**, 1435 (1960).
[11] T. H. Coffield, V. Sandel, and R. D. Closson, *J. Am. Chem. Soc.*, **79**, 5826 (1957).
[12] R. Breslow and H. Höver, *J. Am. Chem. Soc.*, **82**, 2644 (1960).
[13] D. G. Farnum and M. Burr, *J. Am. Chem. Soc.*, **82**, 2651 (1960).
[14] See R. Pettit, *J. Am. Chem. Soc.*, **82**, 1972 (1960).

Azulene has aromatic properties, which suggest a drift of electrons into the five-membered ring as shown in structure *b*.

a   b

The suggested separation of charge is supported by the observation that azulene has an unusually large dipole moment (Gould, 64). As would be expected, electrophilic substitution occurs preferentially in the more electron-rich ring, i.e., in the five-membered ring. Such substitution has been realized, however, in the seven-membered ring also.[15]

Heptafulvene, which is related to azulene, is unstable and readily forms a polymer.[16]

$=CH_2$

Heptafulvene

A quantum mechanical treatment of conjugated cyclic systems leads to the prediction that aromatic character will be exhibited only by planar rings having $4n + 2$ pi-electrons, where n is an integer. Benzene and other classical aromatic compounds have the so-called aromatic sextet of electrons, i.e., n has the value of 1. The cyclopentadienyl anion and the tropylium cation also have the aromatic sextet of electrons. In the cyclopropenyl cations the number of pi-electrons is 2, i.e., n has the value of 0.

Cycloöctatetraene takes up two electrons readily to form the cycloöctatetraenyl dianion that, having 10 pi-electrons $(n = 2)$, might be expected to be planar and to have aromatic properties.

Cycloöctatetraenyl
dianion

This prediction has been substantiated experimentally.[17]

Hopes of finding aromatic properties in cyclobutadiene and cycloöctatetraene, according to this rule, are vain since the numbers of pi-electrons (4 and 8) do not correspond to any integral value of n.

The eighteen-membered cyclic polyene, cycloöctadecanonaene, seems to

[15] A. G. Anderson, Jr., and L. L. Replogle, *J. Org. Chem.*, **25**, 1275 (1960).

[16] W. von E. Doering and D. W. White, *Tetrahedron*, **11**, 183 (1960).

[17] T. J. Katz, *J. Am. Chem. Soc.*, **82**, 3784, 3785 (1960).

have a near-planar structure and is stable enough to be distilled. In this compound the number of pi-electrons is 18; n has the value of 4.[18]

Cyclooctadecanonaene

The stability of certain chelates suggests that they may possess aromatic character; they also undergo substitution reactions that are characteristic of aromatic compounds. The nitration of the cobalt chelate of acetylacetone is illustrative.[19]

$$\text{CH}_3\text{C}{=}\text{O}\diagdown_{\text{Co}/3} \rightarrow \text{O}_2\text{NC}\diagup^{\text{CH}_3\text{C}{=}\text{O}}\diagdown_{\text{Co}/3}$$
$$\text{HC}\diagup^{}\diagdown_{\text{CH}_3\text{C}{-}\text{O}} \qquad \qquad \text{CH}_3\text{C}{-}\text{O}$$

Dianions of cyclic keto enols having the general formula $\text{C}_n\text{O}_n^{-2}$ seem to possess aromatic character. The ions from diketocyclobutenediol and croconic acid are examples.[20]

Ionization of trichloromethylpentamethylbenzene in 100% sulfuric acid gives a red substance that has been identified as a dipositive carbonium ion.[21]

[18] F. Sondheimer and R. Wolovsky, *Tetrahedron Letters*, No. 3, 3 (1959).

[19] J. P. Collman, R. A. More, S. D. Goldby, and W. S. Trahanovsky, *Chem. and Ind.*, 1213 (1960).

[20] R. West, H.-Y. Niu, D. L. Powell, and M. V. Evans, *J. Am. Chem. Soc.*, **82**, 6204 (1960).

[21] H. Hart and R. W. Fish, *J. Am. Chem. Soc.*, **82**, 5419 (1960).

As has been noted, substitution reactions compete with addition reactions even in olefins. Aromatic compounds generally undergo substitution because in this way the aromaticity of the ring is not lost. At the demand of an electrophilic reagent the aromatic ring supplies a pair of electrons, i.e., behaves as a base. The complex then loses a proton.

$$
\begin{array}{c}
\overset{|}{\underset{|}{C}}=\overset{|}{\underset{|}{C}} + A^+ \rightarrow A-\overset{|}{\underset{|}{C}}-\overset{|}{\underset{|}{C^+}} \\
H \; H \qquad\qquad H \; H
\end{array}
$$

$\xrightarrow{+B^-}$ $A-\overset{|}{\underset{|}{\underset{H}{C}}}-\overset{|}{\underset{|}{\underset{H}{C}}}-B$ Aliphatic behavior

$\xrightarrow{-H^+}$ $A-\overset{|}{\underset{|}{C}}=\overset{|}{\underset{H}{C}}$ Aromatic behavior

The tendency to undergo substitution rather than addition is one of the most important criteria of aromatic character. In the aliphatic series the carbonium ion generally combines with a nucleophile (B^-).

2

Nitration of aromatic compounds

Nitration of aromatic compounds is a typical polar reaction and is generally classified further as an electrophilic reaction because the reagent is an electrophile. The reaction usually is effected by use of a mixture of concentrated nitric and sulfuric acids. Nitrobenzene, for example, is made by treating benzene with this mixture at temperatures not above 60°.

The nitronium ion, the true nitrating agent at least when the nitric acid–sulfuric acid mixture is used, is produced according to the following equation.

$$HNO_3 + 2H_2SO_4 \rightarrow NO_2^+ + H_3O^+ + 2HSO_4^-$$

The accepted mechanism of nitration with this reagent postulates attachment of the nitronium ion to the benzene ring, then loss of a proton by the intermediate positive ion. That the attack of the nitronium ion and the loss of hydrogen cannot be concerted is indicated by the observation that there is no selectivity on the reaction rate due to the breaking of C—H or C—T bonds in the attack of a benzene ring bearing both protium and tritium, i.e., there is no isotope effect (Gould, 192).[1]

The transition state must therefore be similar to the positive ion containing the nitro group; the principal contributing structures are represented by a, b, and c, and the hybrid may be represented by d.[2]

Nitrobenzene

Because of the great stabilizing influence of the nitro group, nitration can be carried out in a controllable manner. Nitrobenzene undergoes nitration

[1] L. Melander, *Nature*, **163**, 599 (1949).
[2] See G. S. Hammond, *J. Am. Chem. Soc.*, **77**, 334 (1955).

satisfactorily at temperatures above 60°. The introduction of the second nitro group proceeds readily at 95°, the chief product being *m*-dinitrobenzene. Attack at a *m*-position produces a species of lower energy than attack at an *o*- or *p*-position because it places the positive charge farther from the positively charged nitrogen atom of the nitro group already a substituent in the ring. The principal resonance structures for the transition state for attack at a *m*-position may be represented as follows.

For attack at the *p*-position the most important resonance structures are the following.

That nitrobenzene is nitrated less readily than benzene means that the nitro group deactivates not only the *o*- and *p*-positions but the *m*-position also, although to a lesser extent. Introduction of a positive charge anywhere in the ring is opposed by the positive charge on the nitrogen atom of the nitro group already present.

It must be recognized that the inductive effect of the nitro group is large; however, because the inductive and resonance effects operate in the same direction it is difficult to interpret the facts in terms of these effects.

The reactivity of the three positions in a monosubstituted benzene is expressed in terms of partial rate factors, which are the values of the rate of substitution at one position in the benzene derivative divided by the rate of substitution at one of the positions in benzene.

1,3,5-Trinitrobenzene can be prepared in good yield by nitrating *m*-dinitrobenzene at 110° with a mixture of anhydrous nitric acid and fuming sulfuric acid.[3] It is made more conveniently from 2,4,6-trinitrobenzoic acid, which is decarboxylated readily (OS I, 541).

---

[3] L. G. Radcliffe and A. A. Pollitt, *J. Soc. Chem. Ind.*, London, **40**, 45T (1921).

Carbonyl Compounds

In acetophenone comparison of the resonance structures for the transition state for attack at a *m*-position with that for attack at an *o*- or *p*-position indicates that *m*-substitution should be favored. Carbonyl compounds undergo nitration at temperatures much lower than the temperature required for nitrobenzene. Nitration of acetophenone is conducted at 0 to 5° (OS II, 434; yield 55%).

$$\text{(COCH}_3\text{)} + \text{HNO}_3 \xrightarrow{\text{H}_2\text{SO}_4} \text{(COCH}_3, \text{NO}_2\text{)} + \text{H}_2\text{O}$$

Benzaldehyde is nitrated at 5 to 10°, the chief product being *m*-nitrobenzaldehyde (OS III, 644; 84% yield). *m*-Nitrobenzoic acid can be made by nitration of benzoic acid. Direct nitration of esters is possible also, an example being that of methyl benzoate (OS I, 372).

$$\text{(CO}_2\text{CH}_3\text{)} + \text{HNO}_3 \rightarrow \text{(CO}_2\text{CH}_3, \text{NO}_2\text{)} + \text{H}_2\text{O}$$

The reaction proceeds more smoothly than the nitration of benzoic acid; at 5 to 15° it gives methyl *m*-nitrobenzoate in 85% yield, hydrolysis of which produces *m*-nitrobenzoic acid. Benzonitrile, which undergoes nitration in much the same way as carbonyl compounds, offers a route to *m*-nitrobenzoic acid by way of *m*-nitrobenzonitrile.

$$\text{(CN)} \rightarrow \text{(CN, NO}_2\text{)} \rightarrow \text{(CO}_2\text{H, NO}_2\text{)}$$

Still another route to this acid is provided by nitration of benzotrichloride; the product is the *m*-derivative, which can be hydrolyzed to the acid.

$$\text{(CCl}_3\text{)} \rightarrow \text{(CCl}_3, \text{NO}_2\text{)} \rightarrow \text{(CO}_2\text{H, NO}_2\text{)}$$

The carbon atom of the —CCl₃ group carries a positive charge and thus favors attack at the *m*-positions.[4] In the preparation of 3,5-dinitrobenzoic acid a mixture of fuming nitric and concentrated sulfuric acids is employed. The reaction begins at moderate temperatures and is completed at 145° (OS III, 337; 60% yield). Nitration of phthalic anhydride, carried out in a

---

[4] J. D. Roberts, R. L. Webb, and E. A. McElhill, *J. Am. Chem. Soc.*, **72**, 408 (1950).

similar way, yields a mixture of 3- and 4-nitrophthalic anhydrides (OS I, 408); the reaction temperature is 110°.

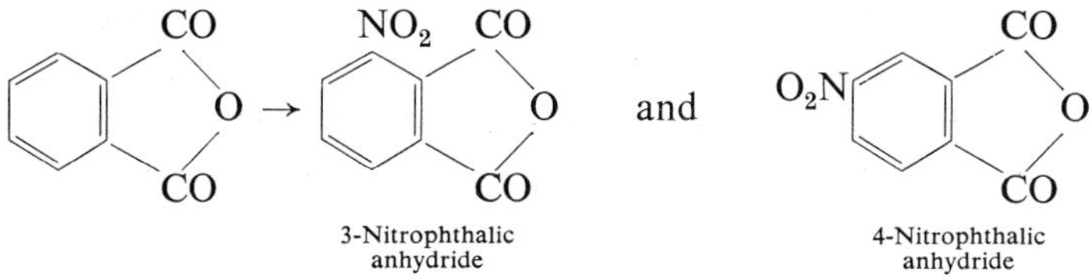

3-Nitrophthalic
anhydride

and

4-Nitrophthalic
anhydride

From phthalimide, 4-nitrophthalimide is obtained (OS II, 459) in 53% yield. The reaction occurs at 10 to 15°, the nitrating agent being a mixture of fuming nitric acid and concentrated sulfuric acid.

Although groups such as NO_2, CO_2H, and CO_2CH_3 are chiefly *m*-orienting, *o*- and *p*-substitution occurs also, of course. A peculiar relationship has been observed in this connection; namely, that the *ortho/para* ratio is generally very large. In other words, these substituents favor *o*- over *p*-substitution. Dinitration of *p*-xylene is illustrative; the *o*-dinitro isomer predominates.[5]

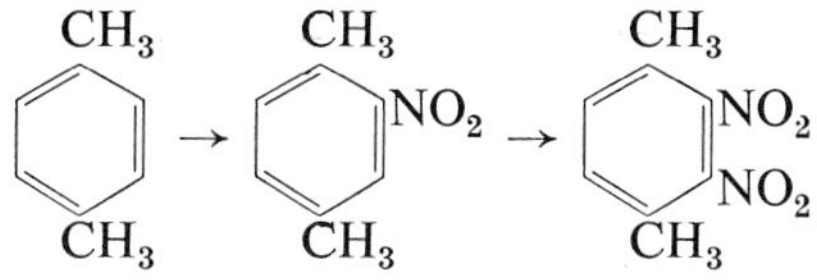

In the nitration of *p*-bromotoluene, also, the position taken by the second nitro group is preferentially *ortho* with respect to the first.[6]

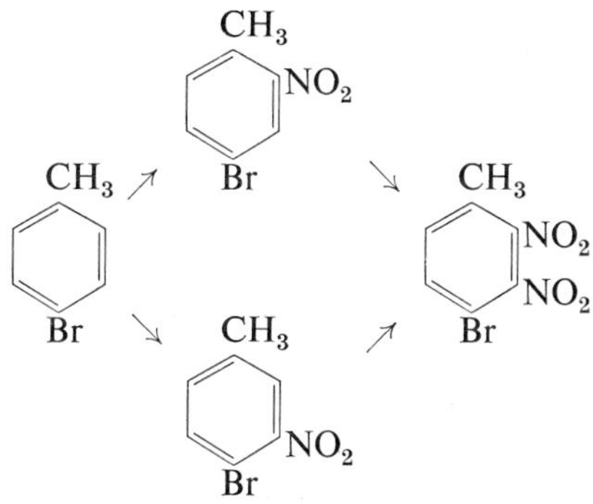

In the nitration of benzonitrile by nitric acid in perchloric acid, the *o*-derivative is formed in an amount more than three times that of the *p*-isomer.[7]

[5] K. A. Kobe and H. Levin, *Ind. Eng. Chem.*, **42**, 352, 356 (1950).
[6] R. D. Kleene, *J. Am. Chem. Soc.*, **71**, 2259 (1949).
[7] G. S. Hammond and K. J. Douglas, *J. Am. Chem. Soc.*, **81**, 1184 (1959).

Aryl Halides

Halogen atoms are *o,p*-directing but are exceptional in that they stabilize rather than sensitize the ring toward electrophilic reagents. The fact that the chlorine atom desensitizes the ring may be accounted for by the withdrawal of electrons to be ascribed to the inductive effect.

Though poorer in electrons than benzene, the aromatic ring, when forced to supply a pair, does so at an *o*- or *p*-position. In other words, the transition state pictured for attack at an *o*- or *p*-position receives contributions from structures in which the chlorine atom carries the positive charge.

Structures of this type are not possible for the transition state for nitration at a *m*-position.

Nitration of chlorobenzene gives a product that consists of about 70% *p*-chloronitrobenzene and 30% of the *o*-isomer.

That the amount of *p*-derivative in this and in most other substitution reactions in the aromatic series is greater than that of the *o*-isomer may seem strange, particularly because there are two *o*-positions and but one *p*-position. An explanation that has been offered is that the *o*-positions are shielded from attack by the substituent already present. It has also been pointed out that the *p*-quinoid structure is thermodynamically more stable than the *o*-quinoid structure, which suggests that attack at the *p*-position may be energetically favored.

Nitration of bromo-, iodo-, and fluorobenzene likewise gives *o*- and *p*-derivatives and can be carried to the dinitro stage without difficulty. 2,4-Dinitrofluorobenzene, for example, is made in a yield of 82% by treating fluorobenzene with a mixture of nitric and sulfuric acids at 70 to 75°.[8]

2,4-Dinitrochlorobenzene is made in a similar way.

Further nitration is difficult but can be accomplished by use of an excess of the usual mixture of concentrated nitric and sulfuric acids and a temperature of 140 to 150°.[9] In practice the product, picryl chloride, is also prepared by an indirect route (p. 380).

When treated with a solution of potassium nitrate in concentrated sulfuric acid, *m*-dichlorobenzene is converted into 1,3-dichloro-4,6-dinitrobenzene (OS **40**, 96; yield 72%).

Iodobenzene is more reactive than bromobenzene, which in turn is more reactive than chlorobenzene. Fluorobenzene, however, does not fall in line; it is more reactive than either the chloro or bromo compound and is almost as reactive as the iodo compound.[10]

Biphenyl

The phenyl radical is *o,p*-directing, as shown by the nitration of biphenyl.[11] The chief product is 4-nitrobiphenyl. Further nitration yields 4,4′-dinitrobiphenyl with lesser amounts of the 2,4′-isomer.

and

[8] *Biochem. Preps.*, **3**, 120 (1953).

[9] P. F. Frankland and F. H. Garner, *J. Soc. Chem. Ind.*, London, **39**, 257T (1920).

[10] J. W. Baker and H. B. Hopkins, *J. Chem. Soc.*, 1089 (1949).

[11] R. D. Brown, *J. Am. Chem. Soc.*, **75**, 4077 (1953).

Biphenyl is more reactive than benzene. The behavior of biphenyl is complicated by the non-coplanarity of the two rings. Because of repulsion between the 2- and 2'-hydrogen atoms the rings in biphenyl itself have an angle of about 45° between their planes; this non-coplanarity greatly diminishes the resonance interaction between the rings. 2,2'-Dimethyl-biphenyl is less reactive than biphenyl because the methyl groups increase the angle between the planes of the rings.

Fluorene, in which the rings are coplanar, is much more reactive than biphenyl.

The terphenyls are nitrated in the terminal rings rather than in the diarylated nuclei. The chief product of nitration of *o*-terphenyl, the least reactive of the three terphenyls, has nitro groups in the *p*-positions of the terminal rings.[12]

As would be expected *p*-terphenyl gives 4-nitroterphenyl, which under-goes further nitration to yield chiefly the 4,4''-dinitro derivative. The nitration is carried out with fuming nitric acid in hot glacial acetic acid.[13]

The influence of a substituted phenyl radical on the position taken by a substituent going into the other ring is independent of the position or nature of the substituent that it holds. Thus 2-, 3-, and 4-nitrobiphenyl

[12] C. F. H. Allen and F. P. Pingert, *J. Am. Chem. Soc.*, **64**, 2639 (1942).
[13] P. Culling, G. W. Gray, and D. Lewis, *J. Chem. Soc.*, 1547 (1960).

suffer nitration in the *o*- and *p*-positions of the unsubstituted ring (CR 7, 407). This result cannot be interpreted satisfactorily on the basis of resonance structures, such as the following, of the ground state.

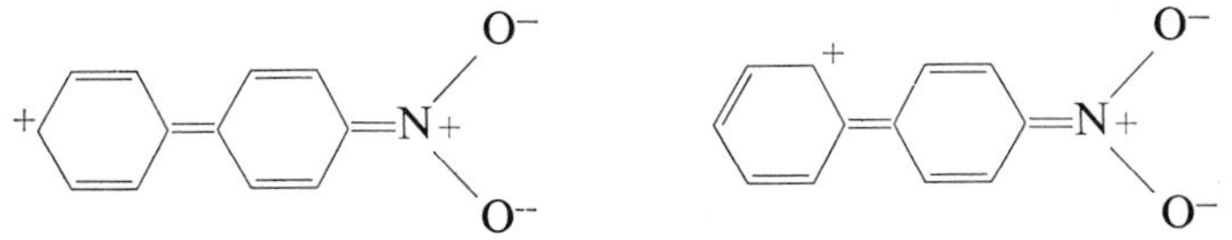

Such structures indicate that *m*-substitution should be favored.

Consideration of the resonance structures that can be written for the transition states, however, affords an interpretation that is in agreement with the facts. In 4-nitrobiphenyl the transition states for *p*- and *m*-nitration may be approximated by *a* and *b*, respectively.

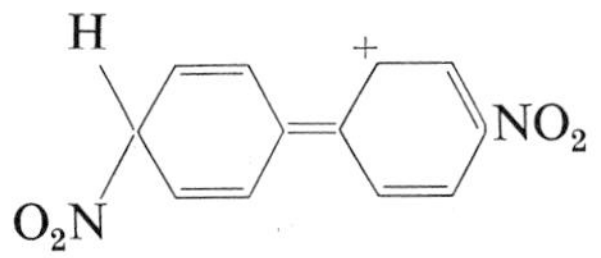

a 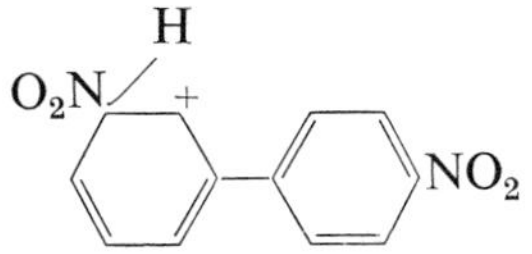   *b*

Although structure *a* contributes little to the transition state for substitution, it shows that the positive charge can be delocalized into the second ring; whereas, as shown by structure *b*, the transition state for attack at a *m*-position can involve only one ring directly.

Alkylbenzenes

Alkylbenzenes are more readily nitrated than benzene, and the products are mixtures consisting chiefly of *o*- and *p*-isomers. Since an alkyl group possesses no unshared pair of electrons, the mechanism by which it releases electrons to the ring in the transition state cannot be the same as that postulated for chlorobenzene. According to the theory of hyperconjugation, however, the positive charge in the transition state can be shared by the hydrogen atoms of the alkyl group. The following structures for the transition state in the nitration of toluene illustrate the concept.

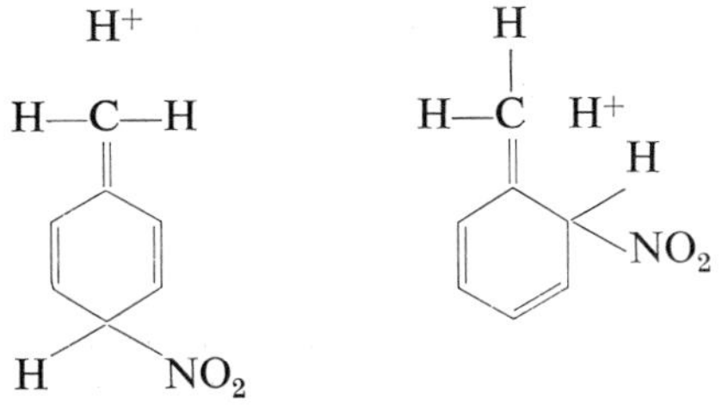

Such structures cannot be written for the transition state postulated for attack at a *m*-position.

In reactions in solution that place a high electron demand on an alkyl group attached to an unsaturated system, toluene reacts faster than ethylbenzene; ethylbenzene undergoes substitution more rapidly than isopropylbenzene; and *t*-butylbenzene is less reactive than isopropylbenzene.

This experimental result, known as the Baker-Nathan effect, has been ascribed to differences in hyperconjugative electron release; alternatively, it has been pointed out that it may be due to steric hindrance to solvation in the vicinity of the alkyl radicals.[14]

It is to be noted that *t*-butylbenzene, which lacks the structure associated with hyperconjugation, is more reactive than benzene, i.e., the *t*-butyl group cedes electrons to the ring. Moreover, like other alkyl groups the *t*-butyl group is an *o,p*-director. It is as though delocalization of the positive charge to a methyl group is possible in the transition state.[15]

Monoalkylbenzenes

Toluene is exceptional in that the yield of the *o*-nitro derivative (59%) is greater than that of the *p*-nitro derivative (36%); the *m*-nitro derivative is produced in yields of 4 to 5%.[16] Continued nitration transforms the *o*- and *p*-isomers into 2,4,6-trinitrotoluene.

[14] W. M. Schubert and R. G. Minton, *J. Am. Chem. Soc.*, **82**, 6188 (1960).
[15] E. Berliner and F. J. Bondhus, *J. Am. Chem. Soc.*, **70**, 854 (1948).
[16] W. W. Jones and M. Russell, *J. Chem. Soc.*, 921 (1947).

$$CH_3\text{-}C_6H_4\text{-}NO_2 \rightarrow O_2N\text{-}C_6H_3(CH_3)\text{-}NO_2$$

$$O_2N\text{-}C_6H_2(CH_3)(NO_2)\text{-}NO_2$$

(toluene) $CH_3\text{-}C_6H_5$

$$CH_3\text{-}C_6H_4\text{-}NO_2 \rightarrow CH_3\text{-}C_6H_3(NO_2)\text{-}NO_2$$

It should be emphasized that the rules of orientation are seldom if ever followed exclusively. In the products of nearly all substitution reactions *o-* , *m-* , and *p*-isomers can be detected; the orientation rules merely indicate the predominant isomer or isomers in the mixtures.

m-Nitrotoluene is an example in which the two substituents oppose each other. It is a rule that an *o,p*-directing substituent is more powerful than any *m*-directing substituent as to the position taken by the entering substituent; the nitration of *m*-nitrotoluene proceeds much as though the nitro group were not present.

$$CH_3\text{-}C_6H_3(NO_2)\text{-}NO_2 \rightarrow CH_3\text{-}C_6H_2(NO_2)_2\text{-}NO_2$$

$$CH_3\text{-}C_6H_4\text{-}NO_2 \rightarrow CH_3\text{-}C_6H_3(NO_2)\text{-}NO_2$$

$$O_2N\text{-}C_6H_3(CH_3)\text{-}NO_2 \rightarrow O_2N\text{-}C_6H_2(CH_3)(NO_2)\text{-}NO_2$$

That nitration at the *p*-position is favored over that at the *o*-position by increase in the steric requirements of the substituent already present is shown by the first column in the following table.

Isomer Ratios

Ratio	o/p	o/m	p/m
Toluene	1.57	13.3	8.45
Ethylbenzene	0.93	6.9	7.45
Cumene	0.48	3.9	8.1
t-Butylbenzene	0.217	1.37	6.32

Since the o- and p-positions are sensitive to both polar and resonance factors, however, this trend alone is not significant. The *para/meta* ratios are sensibly constant, and thus it is apparent that there are no marked changes in the resonance factor in this series. Consequently, the notable diminution in both the *ortho/para* and the *ortho/meta* ratios can only be attributed to a powerful steric influence of the alkyl group on substitution in the o-position.[17]

Nitration of p-bromotoluene is interesting because in this molecule the hyperconjugative influence of the methyl group is pitted against the resonance effect of the bromine atom. It has been observed that, with few exceptions, a group having an unshared electron pair on an atom attached to a benzene ring controls orientation when it is opposed by a methyl group. The chief product (43%) of nitration of o-chlorotoluene is 2-chloro-5-nitrotoluene.[18]

The p-isomer, however, is an exception to the rule; the nitration product is a mixture containing slightly more of the 4-chloro-2-nitrotoluene than of the 4-chloro-3-nitrotoluene.[19]

The importance of the interaction of the two benzene rings in biphenyl, whether it be due to resonance or an inductive effect,[20] becomes clear when

[17] H. C. Brown and W. H. Bonner, *J. Am. Chem. Soc.*, **76**, 605 (1954).

[18] J. P. Wibaut, *Rec. trav. chim.*, **32**, 243 (1913).

[19] F. R. Shaw and E. E. Turner, *J. Chem. Soc.*, 1884 (1932).

[20] V. P. Kreiter, W. A. Bonner, and R. H. Eastman, *J. Am. Chem. Soc.*, **76**, 5770 (1954).

this hydrocarbon is compared with those such as diphenylmethane in which the rings are not interdependent. Whereas mononitration may be made to proceed satisfactorily with biphenyl, diphenylmethane gives dinitrated products, chief of which is 4,4′-dinitrodiphenylmethane.

The *o,p*-orienting influence of the phenyl group is illustrated further by the formation of 2-nitrofluorene by nitration of fluorene, which combines features of biphenyl and of diphenylmethane (OS II, 447; yield 79%).

Diphenylmethane   Fluorene   Biphenyl

The aryl radical is a more powerful director that the methylene group. Further nitration gives 2,7-dinitrofluorene.

It has been pointed out, however, that the methylene group may activate the 2-position by a hyperconjugative effect involving the other ring.[21]

9,10-Dihydrophenanthrene undergoes nitration to yield the 2-nitro derivative (63%) along with a small amount of the 4-derivative.[22]

[21] P. B. D. de la Mare, D. M. Hall, and M. Hassan, *Chem. and Ind.*, 1086 (1958).
[22] J. W. Krueger and E. Mosettig, *J. Org. Chem.*, **3**, 340 (1938).

Phenylacetic acid and its nitrile (OS I, 396) give *p*-nitro compounds primarily. It might be imagined that cinnamic acid, a vinylog (p. 308) of benzoic acid, would undergo electrophilic substitution preferentially at the *m*-positions. The observed predominance of nitration at the *o*- and *p*-positions can be interpreted, as in the case of 4-nitrobiphenyl (p. 27), by reference to the resonance structures of the transition states.

The chloromethyl group like the halogens deactivates the ring but is an *o,p*-director; benzyl chloride yields chiefly the *o*- and *p*-nitro derivatives.[23]

Dialkylbenzenes

In accord with prediction, the xylenes are more reactive than toluene, and mesitylene and durene are still more sensitive to electrophilic attack. The three xylenes differ among themselves in nuclear reactivity; *m*-xylene is the most reactive since the two substituents activate the same positions; in *o*- and *p*-xylene the effects of the groups are opposed; the *p*-isomer is the least reactive of the three since only *o*-activation is possible.

The rule that a *p*-position is substituted more readily than an *o*-position finds another exception in *o*-xylene, which gives a higher yield of *o*- than of *p*-product. Under conditions that bring about mononitration to the extent of 90% the product consists of 58% of 3-nitro-*o*-xylene and 42% of the 4-isomer.[24]

m-Xylene is the source of trinitro-*m*-xylene, usually made by a three-stage nitration. As would be predicted, *p*-cymene is nitrated chiefly at the 2-position.

[23] C. K. Ingold and F. R. Shaw, *J. Chem. Soc.*, 575 (1949).
[24] K. A. Kobe and P. W. Pritchett, *Ind. Eng. Chem.*, **44**, 1398 (1952).

Polyalkylbenzenes

The ease with which polyalkylbenzenes undergo nitration is illustrated by the formation of nitromesitylene, which is produced in 76% yield by treating mesitylene with fuming nitric acid in acetic anhydride at temperatures below 20° (OS II, 449). Mesitylene can be nitrated in such a way as to give the mono-, di-, or trisubstitution product.

Durene, when nitrated by addition of fuming nitric acid to a mixture of the hydrocarbon, chloroform, and concentrated sulfuric acid, gives dinitrodurene in 94% yields (OS II, 254).

3-Nitrodurene is formed but, although less reactive than durene, disappears from the reaction mixture faster. This could be true if the reaction mixture were heterogeneous and the mononitro compound were more soluble than the hydrocarbon in the phase in which nitration occurs.[25]

The tetraethyl analog of durene, 1,2,4,5-tetraethylbenzene, likewise yields only the dinitro derivative.[26]

In this connection it may be mentioned that dipole moment studies indicate that resonance interaction with the ring is practically inhibited when dimethylamino, carboxylate, and nitro functions are placed between two methyl groups on a benzene ring. The infrared absorption frequency of the nitro group in nitromesitylene (1361 cm^{-1}) is higher than that in nitrobenzene (1341 cm^{-1}), which is interpreted to mean that the o-methyl groups prevent the nitro group from lying in the plane of the ring. 2,4,6-Trinitro-t-butylbenzene shows similar impairment of the resonance between the nitro groups and the ring.[27]

[25] G. Illuminati and M. P. Illuminati, *J. Am. Chem. Soc.*, **75**, 2159 (1953).

[26] L. I. Smith and C. O. Guss, *J. Am. Chem. Soc.*, **62**, 2635 (1940).

[27] E. Liss and K. Lohmann, *Chem. Ber.*, **89**, 2546 (1956).

Aryl Ethers

Phenyl ethers such as anisole and phenetole can be nitrated readily, the products being the expected *o,p*-mixtures. Such compounds are generally prepared in other ways, however. Phenyl ether, in which the two benzene rings are not joined directly, nonetheless resembles biphenyl in that mononitration takes place in a controllable manner.

Veratrole, which is readily made by methylation of catechol, yields 4-nitroveratrole, from which 4,5-dinitroveratrole is formed by further nitration.

6-Nitroveratraldehyde is produced in high yield by nitration of veratraldehyde.

These reactions furnish additional illustrations of the rule that *o,p*-directing substituents have greater orienting power than those that direct to the *m*-position. 6-Nitroveratraldehyde, having the oxidizing nitro group adjacent to the readily oxidizable aldehyde function, is remarkably sensitive to light.

Separation of *o*- and *p*-Isomers

From a practical standpoint many substitution reactions are objectionable because they give mixtures of *o*- and *p*-isomers that are hard to separate; as a consequence, neither isomer can be obtained in high yield. In the majority of instances the boiling points of the *o*- and *p*-isomers lie close together, the *o*-compound having the lower boiling point. Separation by distillation is, therefore, difficult. The melting point of the *p*-isomer, however, is generally much higher than that of the *o*-derivative because of the greater degree of symmetry in the molecule. It often happens that the *p*-compound crystallizes and can be separated from the liquid *o*-isomer by filtration. The table on the next page illustrates these points.

Chemical means can be employed also to effect separation of isomers. Dilution of the mixture obtained in nitration of aniline causes hydrolysis of the *o*-nitroaniline sulfate and liberation of the weakly basic amine. If

**Boiling Points and Melting Points of *o*- and
p-Disubstituted Benzene Derivatives**

Substituents	Ortho		Para	
	b.p.	m.p.	b.p.	m.p.
CH_3, Cl	159°	−34°	162°	7.5°
CH_3, Br	182	−28	185	28.5
CH_3, NH_2	200	−16	200	45
CH_3, OH	191	31	202	36
OH, Cl	176	7	217	37
OH, Br	195	5.6	238	63.5
NO_2, Cl	246	33	242	84
NO_2, Br	261	43	259	127
CH_3, NO_2	265	9	258	54

this isomer is removed by filtration and the filtrate treated with soda, in small portions, the *p*-isomer can be isolated. The *m*-isomer, being most basic of the three, is left in solution in the form of its sulfate.

Acidic compounds can be separated in a similar way. In the preparation of saccharin, a mixture of *o*- and *p*-toluenesulfonamides is separated by incompletely acidifying a solution of their sodium salts. The *o*-isomer, being the less acidic, is liberated first.

Naphthalene

The fact that the 3-position of 2-substituted naphthalenes rarely behaves as a true *o*-position is but one of many that reflect the divergence in reaction capacity of condensed aromatic hydrocarbons from the pattern set by benzene and its homologs. In naphthalene, anthracene, phenanthrene, and similar aromatic hydrocarbons the perfect symmetry of the benzene ring is no longer present since the bond common to two rings must do duty in each of them. Such compounds are more reactive than benzene, and the positions of greatest reactivity are those adjacent to the point of juncture of the rings. In naphthalene the α- is much more reactive than the β-position. This difference in reactivity finds an explanation in a comparison of the energies of the transition states; more resonance structures can be written for the transition state for attack at the α-position than for that at the β-position.

The important structures are those in which one ring retains its aromaticity. For α-attack there are four such structures.

The transition state for attack at the β-position has only two structures of this type.

Similar sets of resonance structures can be written for the transition states in nucleophilic substitution, which provides an explanation for the seemingly paradoxical observation that these reagents likewise attack the α-position preferentially.

Naphthalene is more readily nitrated than benzene and yields a mixture that contains about ten times as much 1-nitronaphthalene as of the 2-isomer. Other methods must be used to prepare 2-nitronaphthalene (p. 368).[28] 1-Nitronaphthalene undergoes nitration at the α-positions of the unsubstituted ring, the products being 1,5- and 1,8-dinitronaphthalene. The attack occurs preferentially at the 8-position, the yield of the 1,8-isomer being about double that of the 1,5-isomer.

2-Methylnaphthalene, which is available from coal tar, undergoes nitration readily to give 1-nitro-2-methylnaphthalene in a yield of 57%.[29]

Heterocyclic Compounds

According to the resonance theory, the degree of aromaticity of an aromatic compound is measured by its stabilization energy. This quantity is

[28] M. J. S. Dewar and T. Mole, *J. Chem. Soc.*, 1441 (1956).
[29] J. A. Brink and R. N. Shreve, *Ind. Eng. Chem.*, **46**, 694 (1954).

the difference between the calculated energy of formation, i.e., the sum of the bond energies, and the observed value. The calculated and observed values of energies of formation differ very little for compounds that do not possess resonance. The stabilization energies (kilocalorie/mole) of benzene, thiophene, and furan are given in the following table. According to expectation, the C—C bond lengths fall in the inverse order and likewise the percentage values of double bond quality.

	Stabilization Energy	Lengths of C—C Bonds	% Double Bond Quality
Benzene	36	1.39 Å	50
Thiophene	31	1.44	38
Furan	23	1.46	18

That pyridine would be attacked preferentially at the 3-position can be predicted on the basis of the following resonance structures for the transition states postulated for attack at the 2-, 3-, and 4-positions. The transition states for attack at the 2- and 4-positions is represented in part by structures in which the positive charge is on a divalent nitrogen atom having an open sextet of electrons — structures that would be less stable than those in which the plus charge is on carbon.

Since the stabilization energy of pyridine is not much greater than that of benzene, it is surprising that pyridine is so resistant to electrophilic attack. It seems likely that nitration involves the very stable pyridinium ion. Pyridine does yield 3-nitropyridine but only with difficulty. As in the benzene series nitration is facilitated by the presence of methyl groups. 2,4,6-Trimethylpyridine, for example, gives the 3-nitro derivative in nearly theoretical amounts when heated for several hours at water-bath temperatures with potassium nitrate in fuming sulfuric acid.[30]

[30] E. Plazek, *Ber.*, **72**, 577 (1939).

Electrophilic attack of thiophene occurs more readily at the α- than the β-position. For the transition state in α-attack three structures may be written.

Only two such structures are possible for the transition state in β-attack, and thus this route is less favored.

2-Nitrothiophene can be obtained in good yield by treatment of thiophene with fuming nitric acid in acetic anhydride as solvent, a small amount of the 3-nitro derivative being formed as a by-product.

Orientation in pyrrole and furan follows the same pattern. Since these nuclei are readily destroyed by strong acids, experimental conditions must be relatively mild. Acetyl nitrate, for example, converts furan into 2-nitrofuran.

Furan derivatives undergo α-substitution no matter what substituent may occupy the other α-position.

Examples of nitration of substituted pyrroles have been recorded also. Pyrrole is more sensitive to acids than the other heterocyclic compounds that have been mentioned since it has only one unshared pair of electrons on the hetero atom; protonation robs it of its aromatic sextet.

Nitration Procedures

Use of the usual mixture of concentrated nitric and sulfuric acids is by far the most common method of effecting nitration. As has been noted, however, it may be replaced to advantage in certain cases by other procedures. Dilute solutions of nitrogen pentoxide in carbon tetrachloride bring about nitration and, with a suspension of phosphorus pentoxide, can do so under anhydrous conditions. Benzoyl chloride, for example, can be nitrated without hydrolysis.[31]

$$\text{COCl} \quad \xrightarrow[\text{CCl}_4]{\text{N}_2\text{O}_5} \quad \text{COCl} \quad \text{NO}_2$$

Nitrogen pentoxide, various acyl nitrates, and solutions of nitric acid in acetic anhydride react with certain compounds in what appears to be an anomalous fashion. In particular, they are known to favor the formation of o-isomers. The preparation of 2-acetamido-3-nitrotoluene is accomplished by the nitration of o-acetotoluide with nitric acid in acetic anhydride (OS **35**, 3).

$$\text{CH}_3 \quad \text{NHCOCH}_3 \quad \rightarrow \quad \text{CH}_3 \quad \text{NHCOCH}_3 \quad \text{NO}_2$$

A similar procedure converts biphenyl predominantly into 2-nitrobiphenyl. The amount of the 2-isomer is more than three times that of the 4-isomer.[32]

---

[31] K. E. Cooper and C. K. Ingold, *J. Chem. Soc.*, 836 (1927).

[32] M. J. S. Dewar, T. Mole, D. S. Urch, and E. W. T. Warford, *J. Chem. Soc.*, 3572 (1956).

3

Sulfonation of aromatic compounds

Sulfonation of aromatic compounds is nearly always effected by use of addition products of sulfur trioxide (QR **8**, 40). The most active of these agents is the addition product of sulfur trioxide with itself, known as sulfur β-trioxide, S_2O_6. Oleum is a solution of sulfur trioxide in sulfuric acid. Certain ethers, such as dioxane, form stable addition complexes with sulfur trioxide that are active sulfonating agents. The reactivity of such complexes falls off with increasing basicity of the donor molecule with which sulfur trioxide is combined, the complex with pyridine being among the least reactive. One mechanism that has been suggested for sulfonation with sulfuric acid postulates the ion $^+SO_3H$ as the attacking species.

Sulfonation by sulfur trioxide may be represented as follows.

Sulfonation differs from most other substitution reactions in being reversible. At temperatures between 100 and 200°, for example, benzene and sulfuric acid reach equilibrium when the concentration of the sulfuric acid is 73% (OR **3**, 141). In order to obtain sulfonation products in high yields it is necessary to remove one of the products. Elimination of the water can be accomplished by evaporation or by addition of sulfur trioxide. Sulfonation of benzene on a small scale is carried out by adding the hydrocarbon gradually to ice-cold sulfuric acid containing 5 to 8% of the

40

anhydride. Benzenesulfonic acid forms *m*-benzenedisulfonic acid when heated with 12 to 20% oleum at about 210°. 1,3,5-Benzenetrisulfonic acid can be made in 73% yield by heating the sodium salt of the disulfonic acid with 15% oleum for 12 hours at 275° in the presence of mercury.

Sulfonation is accompanied by sulfone formation, a process that is favored by an excess of the aromatic compound. Sulfone formation, like sulfonation, is reversible. If a reaction is not reversible, as in the case of nitration, it is rate-controlled, i.e., the amounts of isomers are proportional to the rates of the reactions involved. Reversible reactions, on the other hand, may be equilibrium-controlled, the amounts of products being determined by their thermodynamic stabilities.

The effect of temperature is illustrated by the sulfonation of naphthalene, which yields 1- or 2-naphthalenesulfonic acid, depending on whether the sulfonation is effected, respectively, at low (80°) or high (165°) temperatures. Sulfonation takes place reversibly at both positions, but the rate of sulfonation at the 1-position is much greater than at the 2-position. At low temperatures the product is almost exclusively 1-naphthalenesulfonic acid, i.e., the reaction may be said to be rate-controlled. At high temperatures sulfonation at the 2-position becomes appreciable. The reverse reaction at this position is so slow as to make sulfonation at the 2-position virtually irreversible. At high temperatures reversal of the 1-position is rapid. This explains why the 1-isomer, always formed first, is gradually converted into the 2-isomer when heated in the presence of sulfuric acid. In other words, at this temperature the reaction is equilibrium-controlled.

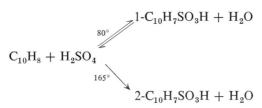

It is to be noted that sulfonation and the Friedel-Crafts acylation reaction (p. 48) are the only substitution reactions that afford a useful entry into the 2-position of naphthalene.

Sulfonation of toluene-1-^{14}C at 25° by 82.3% sulfuric acid under homogeneous conditions gives the corresponding *o*- , *m*- , and *p*-toluenesulfonic acids in yields of 32, 2.9, and 65.1%, respectively.[1]

Sulfonation of anthraquinone normally produces the 2-isomer, but the entering group is directed exclusively to the 1-position by a small amount of mercury. To explain the influence of the metal it has been suggested

[1] L. Vollbracht, H. Cerfontain, and F. L. J. Sixma, *Rec. trav. chim.*, **80**, 11 (1961)

that attack at the 1-position proceeds indirectly by way of a mercury derivative.

Reversal of sulfonation usually is effected by heating with dilute sulfuric acid at temperatures of 135 to 200°. This change may be accomplished by carrying out the reaction in a sealed tube or by passing superheated steam into a solution of the sulfonic acid in dilute sulfuric acid. In a synthesis of 2-bromonaphthalene, for example, 2-amino-1-naphthalenesulfonic acid is converted into 2-bromo-1-napthalenesulfonic acid by the Sandmeyer method (p. 589); the sulfo group is then removed by heating with dilute sulfuric acid.[2]

1-Naphthalenesulfonic acid, as indicated earlier (p. 41), is hydrolyzed much more rapidly than 2-naphthalenesulfonic acid. In fact, the 1-isomer can be removed from a mixture of the two by heating with steam; pure 2-naphthalenesulfonic acid remains. Reversal of sulfonation and other electrophilic substitution reactions calls for protonation of the aromatic ring as the first step. Evidence for this type of reaction is the observation that alkylbenzenes form alkylbenzenonium salts when treated with hydrogen fluoride and boron fluoride.[3]

$$ArH + HF + BF_3 \rightarrow ArH_2{}^+BF_4{}^-$$

Chlorosulfonation

Sulfonyl chlorides may be made by treating the appropriate aromatic compounds with chlorosulfonic acid. Benzenesulfonyl chloride is produced in 77% yield by allowing chlorosulfonic acid to react with benzene at 20 to 25° (OS I, 85).

$$C_6H_6 + 2ClSO_3H \rightarrow C_6H_5SO_2Cl + HCl + H_2SO_4$$

With this reagent toluene gives a mixture of o- and p-toluenesulfonyl chlorides.

[2] W. C. Wolfe and H. M. Doukas, *J. Chem. Education*, **28**, 472 (1951).
[3] G. A. Olah and S. J. Kuhn, *J. Am. Chem. Soc.*, **80**, 6541 (1958).

Another example of chlorosulfonation is encountered in the preparation of p-acetamidobenzenesulfonyl chloride from acetanilide (OS I, 8; yield 81%).

$$\text{NHCOCH}_3\text{-}C_6H_5 + 2\text{ClSO}_3\text{H} \rightarrow \text{NHCOCH}_3\text{-}C_6H_4\text{-SO}_2\text{Cl} + \text{HCl} + \text{H}_2\text{SO}_4$$

4

Acylation of aromatic compounds

Another type of *m*-directing group that can be introduced directly into aromatic rings is the acyl radical. The acylation reaction, like nitration and sulfonation, is formulated as an attack of the ring by an electrophilic agent, which for simplicity is often represented as the acylium ion (R—$\overset{+}{C}$=O). The acylating agent usually is obtained from an acid chloride or anhydride by treatment with a Lewis acid. The resulting Lewis salt, which is the source of the acylating agent, is seen to be analogous to the complex formed by nitric and sulfuric acids, which serves as a source of nitronium ions (NO_2^+), and to the complex produced by combining sulfur trioxide with sulfuric acid, which may serve as source of the sufonating agent.

It seems highly probable that the oxygen atom of the carbonyl group coordinates with aluminum chloride to give a complex in which the electron deficit of the carbon atom of the carbonyl group is enhanced.

$$
\begin{array}{ccc}
R—C{=}O + AlCl_3 & \rightarrow & R—\overset{+}{C}—O{\rightarrow}\bar{A}lCl_3 \\
\quad| & & \quad| \\
\quad Cl & & \quad Cl
\end{array}
$$

Acylium ions formed from acid chlorides are more stable than ordinary carbonium ions because the electron shortage is delocalized to the oxygen and halogen atoms.

$$
\begin{array}{ccccc}
R—C{=}\overset{+}{\underset{}{O}}{\rightarrow}\bar{A}lCl_3 & \leftrightarrow & R—\overset{+}{C}—O{\rightarrow}\bar{A}lCl_3 & \leftrightarrow & R—C—O{\rightarrow}\bar{A}lCl_3 \\
\quad| & & \quad| & & \quad\| \\
\quad Cl & & \quad Cl & & \quad Cl^+
\end{array}
$$

It must be pointed out that, unlike the agents employed for nitration and sulfonation, the acylium ions generally fail to attack aromatic rings that hold a *m*-directing substituent.

The formation of *p*-ethylacetophenone from ethylbenzene may be pictured in the following way.

By treatment of the reaction mixture with water, *p*-ethylacetophenone is obtained in 73% yield.

Although acid chlorides are the most common acylating agents, other acid derivatives and even the acids themselves can be used. On the basis of the known order of increasing electron-releasing power of atoms and groups, these acylating agents might be expected to fall in the following order of increasing effectiveness.

$$\begin{array}{ll}
\text{R—C=O} & \text{Amides} \\
\quad | & \\
\text{NH}_2 & \\
\text{R—C=O} & \text{Acids} \\
\quad | & \\
\text{OH} & \\
\text{R—C=O} & \text{Esters} \\
\quad | & \\
\text{OR} & \\
\text{R—C=O} & \text{Anhydrides} \\
\quad | & \\
\text{OCOR} & \\
\text{R—C=O} & \text{Acid chlorides} \\
\quad | & \\
\text{Cl} &
\end{array}$$

These predictions seem to be in general accord with the facts. The acylation reaction is affected, of course, by many factors other than the character of the reactants themselves; temperature, time, pressure, degree of mixing, and manner of introduction of the reagents have to be considered.

Acids such as sulfuric and hydrofluoric catalyze certain reactions of the Friedel-Crafts type, but the most valuable catalysts are Lewis acids. Of these aluminum chloride is the most useful (OR **3**, 1). Zinc chloride, stannic chloride, boron trifluoride, and many others have been employed also. Aluminum chloride reacts with ketones to form stable complexes that are removed as the reaction proceeds; for this reason it is necessary to use at least one mole of the catalyst. If the product has additional carbonyl groups, an additional mole of catalyst is required for each of them.

Rates of benzoylation of monoalkylbenzenes are in accord with expectation based on the hyperconjugation theory; the relative rates are toluene 1.00, ethylbenzene 0.89, isopropylbenzene 0.82, and t-butylbenzene 0.69.[1]

Orientation

One of the remarkable features of Friedel-Crafts acylation reactions is that, when the p-position is open, the p-isomer is the chief product. Acetylation of t-butylbenzene, an extreme case, has been shown to give the o- , m- , and p-acetyl derivatives in 0, 1.8, and 98.2% yields, respectively.[2]

The production in general of only small amounts of o-isomers has been interpreted to mean that the acylating agent has greater steric requirements than NO_2^+, which gives larger amounts of the o-isomers. In particular, the acetylium ion, $CH_3\overset{+}{C}{=}O$, is so small that it should be able to enter an o-position with facility. That it fails to do so must mean that, if this theory is valid, some other intermediate of larger steric requirements is involved at the substitution stage.[3]

When the p-position is blocked, however, o-derivatives are formed. In the acetylation of p-cymene, as in other substitution reactions (p. 32), the entering group takes a position adjacent to the methyl group (OS II, 3; 55% yield).

Substitution of fluorene, which may be regarded as a biphenyl derivative, has attracted attention because it occurs at the 2- rather than the 3-position

[1] H. C. Brown, B. A. Bolto, and F. R. Jensen, *J. Org. Chem.*, **23**, 414 (1958).
[2] J. C. Butler, L. L. Ferstandig, and R. D. Clark, *J. Am. Chem. Soc.*, **76**, 1906 (1954).
[3] H. C. Brown and W. H. Bonner, *J. Am. Chem. Soc.*, **76**, 605 (1954).

(p. 31). Acetylation is no exception; acetic anhydride in the presence of aluminum chloride affords 2-acetylfluorene in 63% yield (OS III, 23).

This result is in accord with the postulate already discussed that substituents able to supply an electron pair by resonance interaction rather than by the hyperconjugative effect are more effective than alkyl groups in the control of orientation. The behavior of 9,10-dihydrophenanthrene is similar; the 2-acetyl derivative is obtained in 58% yield.[4]

Evidence that the methylene group of fluorene activates the 2-position by a hyperconjugative effect relayed through the other ring (p. 31) is that 9,9-dimethylfluorene is less reactive at the 2-position than is fluorene.

1,3,5-Triphenylbenzene undergoes acylation in the central ring; acetylation gives 2,4,6-triphenylacetophenone.

Influence of Solvents

The Friedel-Crafts acylation often is carried out in the presence of carbon disulfide as solvent. If the aromatic compound is a liquid such as benzene,

[4] J. A. Dixon and D. D. Neiswender, Jr., *J. Org. Chem.*, **25**, 499 (1960).

it may serve as the solvent as well. Petroleum ether is employed frequently also; ethylene chloride and methylene chloride are still better solvents. Molecules that are weak Lewis bases are assumed to owe their solvent power for aluminum chloride to the formation of complexes. Outstanding among them is nitrobenzene, which ameliorates the action of the catalyst.

The course of the Friedel-Crafts acylation in some instances is affected greatly by the solvent. Acylation of naphthalene with acetyl chloride in such solvents as ethylene chloride and carbon disulfide yields chiefly 1-acetylnaphthalene, whereas in nitrobenzene or nitromesitylene the product is predominantly the 2-isomer. This method of obtaining 2-acetyl-naphthalene is very important since it is about the only satisfactory one for the direct introduction of a side chain into this position.

$$C_{10}H_8 + CH_3COCl \xrightarrow[C_6H_5NO_2]{AlCl_3} \text{[naphthalene-COCH}_3\text{]} + HCl$$

The formation of 2-acylnaphthalenes is favored also by use of an excess of the acylating agents; in the benzoylation of naphthalene excess benzoyl chloride causes an increase in the amount of 2-benzoylnaphthalene formed.

When the methyl ether of β-naphthol is condensed with succinic anhydride in carbon disulfide, only the 1,2-isomer is obtained; in nitrobenzene, on the other hand, the 2,6-isomer predominates in the ratio of 9 to 1.[5]

Examination of the transition states for electrophilic attack at the 1-, 6-, and 8-positions places them in the following order of decreasing stability.

[5] W. F. Short, H. Stromberg, and A. E. Wiles, *J. Chem. Soc.*, 319 (1936).

Scope

Acylation stabilizes the ring against further attack and, hence, rarely proceeds beyond the first stage. For this reason monoacyl derivatives usually are obtained uncontaminated with di- or polyacylation products; the condensation of acetyl chloride with benzene produces acetophenone with no appreciable amount of a diacetyl compound. Benzoyl chloride likewise gives the monoketone, benzophenone.

Acylation of a molecule holding an acyl or other m-directing group may proceed, however, if an activating group is present; o-nitroanisole can be acetylated readily.

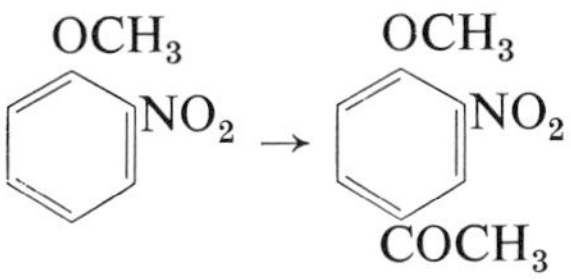

The generalization that a ketone function deactivates the benzene ring so that diacylation does not occur finds exceptions also in mesitylene, durene, and isodurene. When these hydrocarbons are treated with two moles of acetyl chloride in the presence of aluminum chloride, diacetyl derivatives are produced. By contrast m-xylene, which is nearly as reactive as the polymethylbenzenes, gives a monoacetyl derivative.

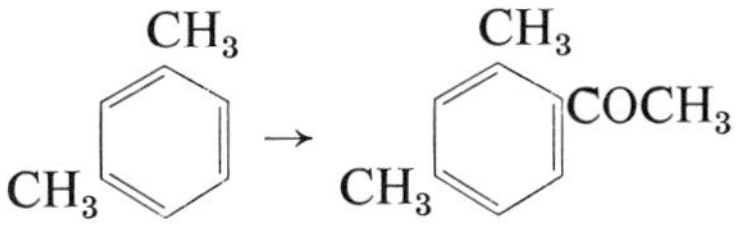

Naphthalene, in spite of its great reactivity, does not undergo diacylation readily (CR **55**, 229). Acenaphthene is acylated first at the 3-position; further acylation yields the 3,6-diacyl derivative. With benzoyl chloride the diketone is 3,6-dibenzoylacenaphthene.[6]

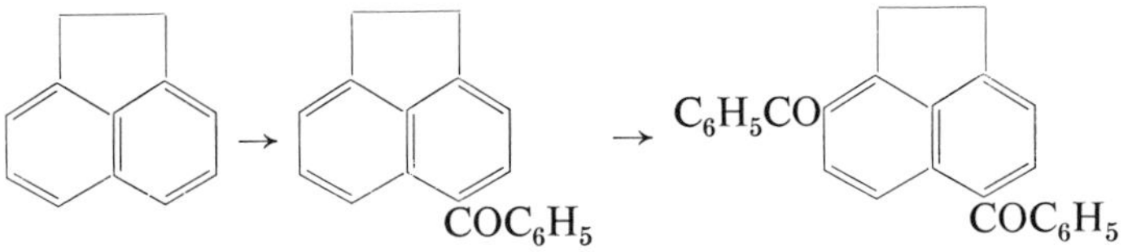

Biphenyl can be diacylated in a stepwise manner also; acetylation gives 4-acetylbiphenyl, then 4,4'-diacetylbiphenyl.

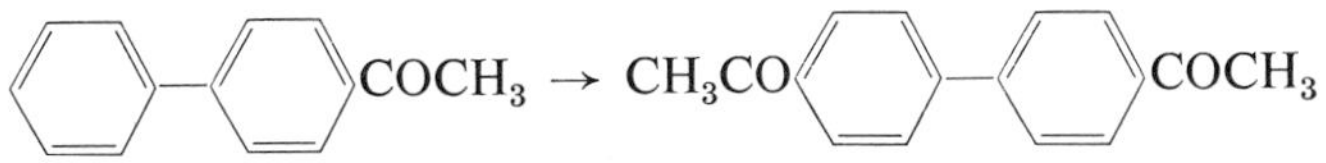

[6] H. J. Richter and F. B. Stocker, *J. Org. Chem.*, **24**, 214 (1959).

Diacylation of diphenylmethane, bibenzyl, and other diaryl derivatives of paraffins is normal; in the dibenzoylation of 1,4-diphenylbutane the yield of diketone is 75%.

$$C_6H_5(CH_2)_4C_6H_5 \rightarrow C_6H_5CO\langle\bigcirc\rangle(CH_2)_4\langle\bigcirc\rangle COC_6H_5$$

Unless there is resonance interaction between the rings as in naphthalene and biphenyl, monoacylation like mononitration (p. 30) is difficult to accomplish controllably.

Ferrocene undergoes acylation in the normal manner; when treated with acetyl chloride in the presence of aluminum chloride it yields a diacetyl derivative.[7]

$$\text{Fe} + 2CH_3COCl \xrightarrow[CS_2]{AlCl_3} \begin{array}{c} COCH_3 \\ | \\ \text{Fe} \\ | \\ COCH_3 \end{array} + 2HCl$$

Acylating Agents

The great versatility of the Friedel-Crafts method of acylation derives from the fact that each component of the acylium ion complex can be varied systematically and through a wide range. As has been seen, the reactivity of the carbonyl group falls off as the chlorine atom of an acid chloride is replaced by more basic groups. Furthermore, the acylating power of the reagent may be altered greatly by choice of catalyst. In certain cases it is possible to gain advantage by modifying the carbonyl group itself, employing its nitrogen analog, the imino group. Success in a particular acylation reaction depends on appropriate manipulation of these various factors.

The radical joined to the carbonyl function may vary greatly in its deactivating power, the greatest effects being exerted by aryl radicals. A nitro group on the aryl radical does not prevent reaction; *m*-nitrobenzoyl chloride has been employed successfully in the synthesis of *m*-nitrophenyl ketones. Acid chlorides of the pyridine series may serve also as acylating agents as is illustrated by the synthesis of 3-benzoylpyridine from benzene and nicotinyl chloride (OS 37, 6).

$$\langle\bigcirc\rangle\text{COCl} + C_6H_6 \xrightarrow{AlCl_3} \langle\bigcirc\rangle COC_6H_5 + HCl$$

_____

[7] R. B. Woodward, M. Rosenblum, and M. C. Whiting, *J. Am. Chem. Soc.*, **74**, 3458 (1952).

A similar procedure converts isonicotinyl chloride into 4-benzoylpyridine in 96% yield (OS **37**, 6).

Even an amino group can be tolerated in the acylating agent if it is protected. This objective may be realized by attaching a *p*-toluenesulfonyl(tosyl) group, which is removed after the Friedel-Crafts reaction has been effected. The synthesis of 2-aminobenzophenone from anthranilic acid is illustrative.

The reaction of acid chlorides that contain an ester group shows that esters are less effective acylating agents than acid chlorides. The difference, as has been noted, must be ascribed to the fact that chlorine is a poorer electron donor than the alkoxyl group; the chloride of ethyl hydrogen adipate affords ethyl δ-benzoylvalerate in 80% yield.[8]

$$\begin{array}{c} CH_2CH_2COCl \\ | \\ CH_2CH_2CO_2C_2H_5 \end{array} + C_6H_6 \xrightarrow{AlCl_3} \begin{array}{c} CH_2CH_2COC_6H_5 \\ | \\ CH_2CH_2CO_2C_2H_5 \end{array} + HCl$$

Acylation, like nitration, is virtually irreversible. Deacylation is comparatively easy to effect, however, in compounds such as acetomesitylene.[9] Heating with polyphosphoric acid converts acetomesitylene into acetic acid and mesitylene. A synthesis of symmetrical ketones involves a cleavage of this type; when duroic acid is heated with *m*-xylene in polyphosphoric acid, duryl 2,4-dimethylphenyl ketone is formed.

Further heating at higher temperatures brings about cleavage of the new

---

[8] S. Grateau, *Comp. rend.*, **191**, 947 (1930).

[9] See H. R. Snyder, *Advances in Chemistry*, Interscience Publishers, New York, Vol. I, p. 35, 1960.

ketone to durene and 2,4-dimethylbenzoic acid. This acid then condenses with m-xylene to produce di-2,4-dimethylphenyl ketone.[10]

$$\text{(CH}_3\text{)(CH}_3\text{)(CH}_3\text{)(CH}_3\text{)} \underset{\text{CH}_3}{\text{CO}} \text{(CH}_3\text{)} + H_2O \rightarrow \text{(CH}_3\text{)(CH}_3\text{)} + CH_3 \text{(CO}_2H\text{)(CH}_3\text{)}$$

$$CH_3 \text{(CO}_2H\text{)(CH}_3\text{)} + \text{(CH}_3\text{)} \rightarrow CH_3 \text{(CO)(CH}_3\text{)(CH}_3\text{)} + H_2O$$

The acid chlorides of dibasic acids offer a number of possibilities in synthetic work. The simplest chloride, phosgene, can serve in the synthesis of symmetrical monoketones; with dimethylaniline it yields Michler's ketone.

$$2(CH_3)_2NC_6H_5 + COCl_2 \rightarrow (CH_3)_2N \text{(CO)} N(CH_3)_2 + 2HCl$$

The chlorides of oxalic, succinic, glutaric, and phthalic acids may behave abnormally (p. 56). The acid chlorides of saturated dibasic acids above glutaric, however, afford the corresponding diketones in satisfactory yields. From adipyl chloride, for example, 1,4-dibenzoylbutane can be prepared in 81% yield (OS II, 169).

Sulfonyl chlorides enter into reactions of the Friedel-Crafts type, yielding sulfones; benzenesulfonyl chloride reacts with benzene in the presence of aluminum chloride to give diphenyl sulfone.

$$C_6H_5SO_2Cl + C_6H_6 \xrightarrow{AlCl_3} (C_6H_5)_2SO_2 + HCl$$

Diphenyl sulfone is obtained in very high yields by the use of benzene-sulfonic anhydride.[11]

$$(C_6H_5SO_2)O + C_6H_6 \xrightarrow{AlCl_3} C_6H_5SO_2C_6H_5 + C_6H_5SO_3H$$

Aromatic sulfonic anhydrides can be prepared by treating sulfonic acids with phosphorus pentoxide; the synthesis of p-toluenesulfonic anhydride is an example (OS **36**, 91; 70% yield).

Anhydrides

The great similarity of acid chlorides and anhydrides is readily appreciated when it is realized that the chlorides are in reality anhydrides also—mixed anhydrides of organic acids and hydrochloric acid. As has been indicated,

[10] R. C. Fuson, B. M. Vittimberga, and G. R. Bakker, *J. Am. Chem. Soc.*, **81**, 4858 (1959).

[11] L. Field, *J. Am. Chem. Soc.*, **74**, 394 (1952).

the anhydrides are excellent acylating agents; acetic anhydride, for example, reacts readily with bromobenzene to give *p*-bromoacetophenone in 79 % yield (OS I, 109).

$$(CH_3CO)_2O + C_6H_5Br \xrightarrow{AlCl_3} CH_3CO\!\!\left\langle\!\!\bigcirc\!\!\right\rangle\!\!Br + CH_3CO_2H$$

Ketene behaves as an anhydride of acetic acid, also yielding acetophenone with benzene. This type of reaction is particularly useful with cyclic anhydrides such as succinic anhydride (OR **5**, 229); with benzene it furnishes *β*-benzoylpropionic acid (OS II, 81; 82 % yield).

$$\begin{matrix} CH_2CO \\ | \qquad\qquad \searrow \\ \qquad\qquad\qquad O + C_6H_6 \xrightarrow{AlCl_3} C_6H_5COCH_2CH_2CO_2H \\ | \qquad\qquad \nearrow \\ CH_2CO \end{matrix}$$

Another example of *succinoylation* is the formation of *β*-(3-acenaphthoyl)propionic acid from acenaphthene (OS III, 6; 81 % yield).

Condensation of aromatic compounds with phthalic anhydride to produce aroylbenzoic acids furnishes a convenient method of preparing derivatives in identification. An example is the synthesis of *o*-benzoylbenzoic acid.

Maleic anhydride can be employed in a similar manner to prepare *β*-aroylacrylic acids. *β*-Benzoylacrylic acid, for instance, can be made in 85 % yield (OS III, 109). With anhydrides it is necessary, of course, to employ at least two moles of aluminum chloride.

$$\begin{matrix} CHCO \\ \| \qquad\qquad \searrow \\ \qquad\qquad\qquad O \xrightarrow{2AlCl_3} C_6H_5COCH\!\!=\!\!CHCO_2H \\ \| \qquad\qquad \nearrow \\ CHCO \end{matrix}$$

$$C_6H_6 + \text{(above)}$$

Acylation of triphenylene is interesting because this hydrocarbon is symmetrical and, like naphthalene, has only α- and β-positions; even when conducted in carbon disulfide, acetylation gives the 2-acyl derivative.[12]

A valuable modification of the benzoylation reaction, developed by Perrier, consists in preparing the addition compound of the acid chloride and the catalyst, which is then allowed to react with the hydrocarbon. The advantage lies chiefly in the fact that the addition compound is soluble in carbon disulfide. The acylation product and the catalyst, however, form an insoluble addition compound that can be removed easily and converted into the ketone by treatment with water, tarry impurities remaining behind in the solvent. The synthesis of 1-benzoyl-naphthalene by this method is particularly to be recommended, since the aluminum chloride addition compound of 2-benzoylnaphthalene, always formed as a by-product, is soluble in carbon disulfide; thus 2-benzoyl-naphthalene does not appear as a contaminant of the product.

Ethers of Phenols

Aryl ethers are so sensitive that acylation may occur in the presence of catalysts that are less powerful than aluminum chloride; even the free carboxylic acids may serve as acylating agents. Anisole, for example, is acetylated by treatment with a mixture of glacial acetic acid and phosphoric anhydride. The high order of reactivity of the ring is revealed also by the fact that, even under these mild conditions, diacetylation occurs (p. 49).[13]

Heterocyclic Compounds

2-Acetothienone is formed in 83% yield when thiophene is treated with acetyl chloride in the presence of stannic chloride (OS II, 8). Another

[12] Ng. Ph. Buu-Hoï, *J. Chem. Soc.*, 941 (1953).
[13] G. M. Kosolapoff, *J. Am. Chem. Soc.*, **69**, 1651 (1947).

procedure for making this ketone is to condense thiophene with acetic anhydride in the presence of phosphoric acid (OS III, 14; 79% yield). Phenyl thienyl ketone can be prepared in 90% yield from thiophene and benzoyl chloride in the presence of aluminum chloride (OS II, 520). By use of phosphorus pentoxide as the catalyst, acylation may be realized with the carboxylic acids themselves; this method gives phenyl thienyl ketone in 66% yield and 2-benzoylfuran in 40% yield.

Attempts to use the Friedel-Crafts reaction with basic nitrogen compounds have met with little success, presumably because the nitrogen atom coordinates with the catalyst.

Formylation with carbon monoxide

In the presence of aluminum chloride and a small amount of cuprous halide, a mixture of hydrogen chloride and carbon monoxide can serve as a formylating agent, acting as formyl chloride would be expected to do. The process, developed by Gattermann and Koch (OR 5, 290), is illustrated by the synthesis of p-tolualdehyde (OS II, 583; 51% yield).

$$C_6H_5CH_3 + [H\overset{\overset{\displaystyle O}{\|}}{C}Cl] \xrightarrow[\text{CuCl}]{\text{AlCl}_3} CH_3 \underset{}{\bigcirc} CHO + HCl$$

Another example is the preparation of 1,2,3,4-tetrahydro-6-naphthaldehyde from tetralin.

Formyl fluoride can be isolated and has been used successfully in formylation.[14]

One of the practical difficulties encountered in the use of this method is obtaining an equimolecular mixture of anhydrous hydrogen chloride and carbon monoxide. A superior procedure consists in dropping chlorosulfonic acid on formic acid.[15]

$$HSO_3Cl + HCO_2H \rightarrow HCl + CO + H_2SO_4$$

If the Friedel-Crafts reaction of aromatic compounds with chloroform could be stopped at the first stage it would provide a route to aldehydes as in the Reimer-Tiemann reaction (p. 269). Closely related to chloroform

---

[14] G. A. Olah and S. J. Kuhn, *J. Org. Chem.*, **26**, 237 (1961).
[15] L. Bert, *Compt. rend.*, **221**, 77 (1945).

are the dichloromethyl alkyl ethers, which do serve as formylating agents. An example is the preparation of 3,4-dimethylbenzaldehyde from o-xylene and dichloromethyl n-butyl ether (p. 150); the yield is 68%.[16]

$$CH_3 \bigcirc \quad and$$
$$CH_3$$

$$Cl_2CHOC_4H_9 \xrightarrow[CS_2]{AlCl_3} \left[CH_3 \bigcirc CHClOC_4H_9 \right] \xrightarrow{H_2O} CH_3 \bigcirc CHO$$
$$CH_3 \qquad\qquad\qquad CH_3$$

This procedure has certain advantages over the Gattermann-Koch method.

Anomalous Acylation Reactions

As has been mentioned, acid chlorides of dibasic acids may behave abnormally. Oxalyl chloride would be expected to condense with aromatic compounds to yield benzils; actually this type of synthesis is realized only with extremely sensitive aromatic nuclei such as the nucleus of anisole, which gives the expected diketone, anisil, in a yield of 90%.

$$2CH_3OC_6H_5 + (COCl)_2 \xrightarrow{AlCl_3} CH_3O \bigcirc COCO \bigcirc OCH_3 + 2HCl$$

Usually oxalyl chloride breaks down to carbon monoxide and phosgene, however, and the condensation products are the acid chlorides or benzophenones derived from phosgene. Since the acid chlorides are normally hydrolyzed during the isolation procedure, a method of carboxylation is provided.[17]

Decarbonylation may occur also with tertiary acid chlorides. It is reminiscent of the loss of nitrogen from certain types of nitrogen compounds.[18] Just as the loss of nitrogen from a diazo compound is ascribed in part to the high order of stability of the nitrogen molecule, decarbonylation must be favored by the great stability of carbon monoxide. It is to be remembered that these molecules are isosters, i.e., they have the same arrangement of electrons, as have the cyanide and acetylide ions.

$$:N:N: \qquad :C:O: \qquad :C:N:^- \qquad ^-:C:C:^-$$

[16] A. Rieche, H. Gross, and E. Höft, *Chem. Ber.*, **93**, 88 (1960).
[17] See T. W. Campbell, *J. Am. Chem. Soc.*, **82**, 3126 (1960).
[18] See E. Rothstein and R. W. Saville, *J. Chem. Soc.*, 1961 (1949).

The tendency of a carbonyl compound to lose carbon monoxide appears to be enhanced by decrease in electron quotient, as in the formation of a carbonium ion from oxalyl chloride.

$$\underset{\text{Cl}}{\overset{\text{O}}{\underset{\parallel}{\text{C}}}}-\underset{\text{Cl}}{\overset{\text{O}}{\underset{\parallel}{\text{C}}}} \longrightarrow \text{Cl}-\overset{\text{O}}{\overset{\parallel}{\text{C}}}-\overset{\text{O}}{\overset{\parallel}{\text{C}}}^{+} \xrightarrow{-\text{CO}} \text{Cl}-\overset{\text{O}}{\overset{\parallel}{\text{C}}}^{+}$$

That such acid chlorides may serve as acylating agents with aromatic compounds that are sufficiently basic is additional evidence that the acylium ion is never really free; otherwise it would lose carbon monoxide.

Phthalyl chloride may behave in an anomalous fashion also; instead of the expected o-diaroylbenzenes it generally yields the isomeric diaryl-phthalides. With benzene, for example, the product is 3,3-diphenyl-phthalide.

The chloride is known to exist in two forms, the normal form being changed to the *pseudo* form by contact with aluminum chloride (OS II, 528). Friedel-Crafts reactions appear to involve the *pseudo* form almost exclusively.

Similar difficulties are encountered with the chlorides of succinic and glutaric acids. Fumaryl chloride, on the other hand, is incapable of existing in a *pseudo* form and reacts normally; with benzene it gives *trans*-dibenzoylethylene in 83% yield (OS III, 248).

Migration of groups sometimes occurs during Friedel-Crafts acylation reactions; whereas acetylation of p-ethyl- , p-propyl- , and p-isopropyl-toluene yields the corresponding 5-alkyl-2-methylacetophenones, acetylation of p-t-butyltoluene gives 4-t-butyl-2-methylacetophenone, the t-butyl group having migrated from the p- to the m-position.[19]

[19] E. P. Taylor and G. E. Watts, *J. Chem. Soc.*, 5054 (1952).

5

Halogenation of aromatic compounds

Halogenation of aromatic compounds has in common with nitration, sulfonation, and acylation the great practical advantage of stabilizing the ring against further attack and thus can be carried out in a step-wise manner without resort to special procedures. The mechanism of the reaction, following the pattern pictured for the other types of electrophilic substitution reactions, would involve attack of the ring by a positive halogen atom followed by loss of a proton.

In most halogenation reactions, however, the reactive species is either molecular halogen or a complex that serves as a carrier of the positive halogen atom. Chlorination and bromination of phenols, anilines, and other compounds possessing sensitive nuclei occur readily in the absence of a catalyst (p. 98). Less reactive compounds, however, require a catalyst, most common of which is the corresponding ferric halide; other Lewis acids may also serve. Pyridine and iodine are likewise effective. The mechanism by which these catalysts operate is probably not the same, but in all cases it must involve polarization of the halogen-halogen bond; in their absence homolytic processes may supervene.

Bromination

In the presence of a catalyst, generally called a carrier, and at suitable temperatures nearly all types of aromatic nuclei undergo halogenation. Bromination in particular has been studied extensively.

Nitro compounds illustrate the less reactive types; the bromination of nitrobenzene, for example, takes place at a useful rate at relatively high temperatures and in the presence of a catalyst. At 135 to 145°, with iron as the carrier, *m*-bromonitrobenzene is produced in 75% yield (OS I, 123). *p*-Nitrotoluene undergoes bromination at 75 to 80° in the presence of iron powder to give 2-bromo-4-nitrotoluene (OS **38**, 11; yield 90%).

Pyridine, which is often compared to nitrobenzene, yields chiefly 3-bromopyridine when brominated at 300° in the absence of a catalyst. At 500°, however, the orientation appears to be anomalous; the chief products are 2-bromopyridine and 2,6-dibromopyridine.

Bromination of quinoline in 98% sulfuric acid containing silver sulfate produces 5- and 8-bromoquinoline and 5,8-dibromoquinoline. The most probable mechanism involves attack of the protonated base by a positively charged brominating species.[1]

Chlorination of pyridine in the presence of 2 moles of aluminum chloride (swamping catalyst conditions) gives 3-chloropyridine.[2]

[1] P. B. D. de la Mare, M. Kiamud-din, and J. H. Ridd, *J. Chem. Soc.*, 561 (1960).
[2] D. E. Pearson, W. W. Hargrove, J. K. T. Chow, and B. R. Suthers, *J. Org. Chem.*, **26**, 789 (1961).

Arylsulfonic acids may be brominated, and they offer the special advantage that the sulfo group can be replaced subsequently by hydrogen. This substituent may serve as a blocking group to aid in achieving bromination at a position not otherwise favored. In the preparation of 3-bromo-*o*-xylene, for example, introduction of a sulfo group into *o*-xylene serves to direct the entering bromine atom to the desired position. The large sulfo group blocks the positions next to it.

Aromatic ketones undergo nuclear bromination, but in synthetic work such reactions do not often offer the route of choice. If the ketone has an active hydrogen atom as in acetophenone, bromination occurs preferentially in the side chain. If the catalyst is taken in an amount sufficient to convert all the ketone to the complex of ketone and catalyst, the entering bromine atom is directed to the *m*-position; under these conditions (swamping catalyst conditions) *m*-bromoacetophenone is obtained in yields of 75% (OS **40**, 7).[3]

Aryl halides are, of course, less reactive than the parent hydrocarbons. Bromobenzene yields a mixture of *o*- and *p*-dibromobenzene, the *p*-isomer being predominant. At 450 to 630°, however, the *m*-isomer is formed in 55 to 60% yield. This result is a striking example of the rule that drastic conditions favor a more nearly random attack, thus increasing the yields of the minor products.

If liquid bromine is used in the presence of iron powder at 0°, bromination proceeds until all nuclear hydrogen atoms are replaced; benzene yields hexabromobenzene.

Chlorobenzene reacts with bromine in the presence of aluminum chloride to give *p*-bromochlorobenzene as the chief product.

[3] D. E. Pearson, H. W. Pope, W. W. Hargrove, and W. E. Stamper, *J. Org. Chem.*, **23**, 1412 (1958).

In a similar way *p*-bromoiodobenzene may be made from iodobenzene.
Biaryls afford interesting examples of the orienting influence of aryl
radicals. As would be expected, biphenyl yields chiefly 4-bromobiphenyl;
the stabilizing effect of the halogen atom causes the second halogen atom
to enter the halogen-free ring preferentially. 4,4'-Dibromobiphenyl is the
predominant dibromide obtained by direct bromination; the reaction may
be carried out by treating the solid hydrocarbon with bromine vapor (OS
31, 29; 77% yield). The high yield of the dibromo compound demonstrates that the phenyl and *p*-bromophenyl groups are predominantly
o,p-directing.[4]

o-Terphenyl is brominated preferentially in the terminal rings. *p*-Ter-
phenyl behaves in a similar way, the chief product being 1,4-*bis*-(4-
bromophenyl)benzene.

m-Terphenyl, on the other hand, gives chiefly 4-bromo-1,3-diphenyl-
benzene, resulting from attack of the central ring.

1,3,5-Triphenylbenzene also suffers preferential attack at the central ring;
2,4,6-triphenylbromobenzene is formed in 91% yield.

Benzene reacts with bromine in the cold, in the presence of iron filings,
to give bromobenzene accompanied by small amounts of dibromobenzenes.
Alkylbenzenes are more readily brominated than benzene. As in the
substitution reactions that have been considered previously, the ease of
bromination of the monoalkylbenzenes increases in the following order.

[4] R. E. Buckles, E. A. Hausman, and N. G. Wheeler, *J. Am. Chem. Soc.*, **72**, 2494
(1950).

The bromination of toluene proceeds according to prediction except that *p*-bromotoluene is brominated preferentially at the position *ortho* to the methyl group.

When treated with liquid bromine in the presence of iron filings, toluene is converted into pentabromotoluene without appreciable attack of the side chain.

Diphenylmethane and other diphenyl derivatives of paraffins undergo bromination preferentially at the *p*-positions; bibenzyl, for example, yields 4,4′-dibromobibenzyl.

Fluorene gives the 2-bromo derivative, which by further bromination goes to the 2,7-derivative.

In electrophilic substitution reactions, biphenylenes (p. 626) behave as derivatives of cyclobutane (*a*) rather than as derivatives of cyclobutadiene (*b*).[5]

a   b

[5] W. Baker, J. E. W. McOmie, D. R. Preston, and V. Rogers, *J. Chem. Soc.*, 414 (1960).

The 2-acetamido derivative undergoes bromination in the 3- rather than the 1-position.

$$\text{(biphenylene)}NHCOCH_3 \rightarrow \text{(biphenylene)}NHCOCH_3, Br$$

Bromination of o-xylene produces 4-bromo-o-xylene in 97% yield; the reaction is carried out at 0 to $-5°$ in the presence of iron or iodine (OS III, 138).

$$\text{(C}_6\text{H}_4\text{)(CH}_3)_2 + Br_2 \rightarrow Br\text{(C}_6\text{H}_3\text{)(CH}_3)_2 + HBr$$

This result is in contrast to that obtained in nitration, in which the 3-nitro derivative predominates (p. 32).

Mesitylene, with three methyl groups so arranged as to provide maximum activation, is so reactive that no carrier is needed, bromomesitylene being formed rapidly at $10°$ in carbon tetrachloride solution; the yield is 82% (OS II, 95).

$$CH_3\text{(C}_6\text{H}_3\text{)}CH_3,\ CH_3 + Br_2 \xrightarrow{CCl_4} CH_3\text{(C}_6\text{H}_2\text{)(Br)}CH_3,\ CH_3 + HBr$$

5-t-Butyl-m-xylene undergoes bromination in the absence of a carrier to give the 2-bromo derivative in 93% yield.

$$CH_3\text{(C}_6\text{H}_3\text{)}CH_3,\ C(CH_3)_3 \rightarrow CH_3\text{(C}_6\text{H}_2\text{)(Br)}CH_3,\ C(CH_3)_3$$

In view of the peculiar behavior of durene toward nitrating agents (p. 33), it is to be noted that monobromination proceeds normally. When durene is treated with bromine in carbon tetrachloride and in the presence of a trace of iodine, bromodurene is obtained in high yield.

$$CH_3,CH_3\text{(C}_6\text{H}_2\text{)}CH_3,CH_3 \rightarrow CH_3,CH_3\text{(C}_6\text{H)(Br)}CH_3,CH_3$$

Condensed aromatic hydrocarbons undergo halogenation as might be expected from their behavior in nitration. Naphthalene can be brominated readily in boiling carbon tetrachloride solution without a catalyst, 1-bromonaphthalene being produced along with lesser amounts of dibromo-naphthalenes (OS I, 121; 75% yield).

When naphthalene and bromine react at higher temperatures, 2-bromonaphthalene is formed also. At temperatures above 500° in the vapor phase over glass wool or pumice, the 1- and 2-isomers are produced in equal amounts, as though attack were random.

9,10-Dibromoanthracene is formed readily when anthracene in carbon tetrachloride is brominated in the cold and without a catalyst (OS I, 207; 88% yield).

Phenanthrene likewise reacts rapidly with bromine; when allowed to occur in the cold and without a catalyst, the reaction yields the addition compound, 9,10-dibromophenanthrene. If the reaction is conducted in the presence of a catalyst or at higher temperatures (OS III, 134), however, substitution takes place, the product being 9-bromophenanthrene. A study of these reactions indicates that the dibromide forms reversibly and is not an intermediate in the substitution reaction (CR **29**, 37).

It should be noted in passing that the 9,10-bond in phenanthrene has a high order of double bond quality for an aromatic linkage.

Aromatic ethers are brominated readily. Anisole, for example, yields chiefly *p*-bromoanisole.

Dibenzofuran, as in nitration and acylation, is substituted preferentially at the 2-position; it reacts with bromine in the absence of a catalyst to give 2-bromodibenzofuran in 80% yield.

Reaction of bromine with furan leads to mixtures of products of addition and substitution. 2-Furoic acid, when treated with bromine in aqueous solution, yields mucobromic acid (OS III, 621; 67% yield). The same product is obtained from furfural under these conditions.

Chlorination

Chlorination of benzene, toluene, naphthalene, and other hydrocarbons is carried out on a commercial scale. Benzene is converted into chlorobenzene by treatment with chlorine at 50° in an iron vessel; the by-products are o- and p-dichlorobenzene. Other aromatic hydrocarbons behave much as they do in bromination.

The use of iodine as a catalyst is illustrated by the chlorination of m-xylene in the preparation of 4-chloro-m-xylene.

Under similar treatment o-xylene yields 4-chloro-o-xylene. From p-xylene 2-chloro-p-xylene is produced. In p-cymene substitution occurs as expected in the 2-position.

With reference to the competition between halogen and alkyl, it is interesting that the second halogen takes the 5-position. The 3-chloro derivative may be made by chlorination of the 2-bromo compound and subsequent removal of the bromine atom with a zinc-copper couple at 200°.

$$(CH_3)_2CH\underset{Br}{\underset{\bigcirc}{}}CH_3 \rightarrow (CH_3)_2CH\underset{Br}{\underset{\bigcirc}{}}CH_3 \rightarrow (CH_3)_2CH\underset{\bigcirc}{}CH_3$$

The difference in reactivity between naphthalene and benzene is illustrated by the fact that benzene may be employed as solvent in the chlorination of naphthalene; technical 1-chloronaphthalene is produced in this way in a yield of about 85%.

As has been mentioned (p. 22), the trichloromethyl group is *m*-directing; an interesting example is the chlorination of 1,3-*bis*(trichloromethyl)-benzene in the preparation of the 5-chloro derivative.

$$\underset{CCl_3}{\overset{CCl_3}{\bigcirc}} + Cl_2 \rightarrow \underset{Cl\quad CCl_3}{\overset{CCl_3}{\bigcirc}} + HCl$$

Iodination

Iodination in general is not carried out in the same way as bromination and chlorination. Iron filings are not effective, presumably because iron does not form ferric iodide. Of the Lewis acids only ferric chloride can be used successfully; the reason for its action is not, however, that it is a Lewis acid, but rather that it is an oxidizing agent. Other oxidizing agents such as nitric acid promote the reaction also; iodobenzene is made in 87% yield by allowing benzene to react with iodine in the presence of nitric acid (OS I, 323). Since nitric acid oxidizes hydrogen iodide to iodine, no iodine is lost to by-products.

$$2C_6H_6 + I_2 + [O] \xrightarrow{\text{HNO}_3} 2C_6H_5I + H_2O$$

2-Iodothiophene can be made from thiophene, yellow mercuric oxide (OS II, 357; 75% yield) serving to remove the hydrogen iodide.

$$2\underset{S}{\overset{\bigcirc}{}} + 2I_2 + HgO \rightarrow 2\underset{S\quad I}{\overset{\bigcirc}{}} + HgI_2 + H_2O$$

That thiophene is more reactive than benzene is dramatized in this procedure in which benzene serves as solvent.

Another general method of iodination consists in treating the organic compound in ether with a suspension of silver perchlorate, iodine, and calcium carbonate; the carbonate neutralizes the liberated perchloric acid.

A modification of this method serves to iodinate veratrole, silver trifluoroacetate being used (OS **36**, 46); 4-iodoveratrole is produced in 91% yield.

$$CH_3O \bigcirc CH_3O + I_2 + CF_3CO_2Ag \rightarrow CH_3O \bigcirc{}^I CH_3O + CF_3CO_2H + AgI$$

In such reactions the silver ion serves as a scavenger for the iodide ion. Iodination is successful also in the presence of iodic acid.[6]

An unusual procedure has been developed for the iodination of phthalic anhydride; the reaction, effected in the presence of sulfur trioxide, gives tetraiodophthalic anhydride (OS III, 796; 82% yield).

$$\bigcirc \begin{matrix} CO \\ \\ CO \end{matrix} O + 4SO_3 + 2I_2 \xrightarrow{H_2SO_4} I\bigcirc{}_I^I \begin{matrix} I & CO \\ \\ & CO \end{matrix} O + 2H_2SO_4 + 2SO_2$$

The iodination procedures that have been cited provide for the removal of hydrogen iodide as though the reaction were reversible. Apparently this is not so, since iodobenzene is recovered unchanged after being heated with hydrogen iodide and red phosphorus for five hours at 182°. Deiodination occurs, however, at 218°.[7] Hydrogen iodide alone effects this change at 250°.[8]

---

[6] H. O. Wirth, O. Königstein, and W. Kern, *Ann.*, **634**, 84 (1960).

[7] A. Klages and C. Liecke, *J. prakt. Chem.*, [2] **61**, 313, 319 (1900).

[8] A. Kekulé, *Ann.*, **137**, 163 (1866).

6

Alkylation of aromatic compounds

The usual methods of direct alkylation of aromatic rings (OR **3**, 1) are formally similar to those employed in acylation. The mechanism involves attack of the ring by a carbonium ion and thus is analogous to the other substitution reactions that have been discussed.[1]

The assumption that carbonium ions are discrete intermediates furnishes a satisfactory basis for interpreting most reactions of the Friedel-Crafts type. This assumption will be made in what follows as a means of simplifying the discussion. Actually, alkylation may be effected not only with alkyl halides, olefins, or alcohols but also with other compounds, among which are esters, ethers, and carbonyl compounds. That paraffinic hydrocarbons may serve as sources of carbonium ions by fragmentation is shown by the fact that 2,2,4-trimethylpentane reacts with toluene in the presence of aluminum chloride to yield *t*-butyltoluene and isobutane.

Carbonium ions are less discriminating than other electrophilic agents, and the tendency to violate the rules of orientation is accordingly more

[1] V. Franzen, *Chemiker Ztg.*, **81**, 68 (1957).

marked. Alkylation occurs most readily with tertiary, less rapidly with secondary, still less readily with primary types of alkyl halides, and least readily with methyl halides.

The relative rates of isopropylation of monoalkylbenzenes fall in the same order as those of bromination, the larger and more complex the substituent alkyl group, the slower the isopropylation. The following compounds are arranged in the order of decreasing speed of isopropylation.

Toluene > Ethylbenzene > Cumene > *t*-Butylbenzene

These differences in rates seem to be a measure of the differences in steric hindrance at the *o*-positions. The rates of isopropylation at the *m*- and *p*-positions are nearly the same for toluene and cumene, whereas the rate at the *o*-position in cumene is about one-sixth of that in toluene.

A possible explanation of the large amount of *m*-substitution observed in the alkylation of toluene and other monoalkylbenzenes is based on the high order of reactivity of the attacking species. Bromination illustrates a mild substitution reaction that is highly selective between benzene and toluene as well as between *m*- and *p*-positions of toluene. Nitration is less selective. Isopropylation shows little selectivity; with toluene it gives 30% of the *m*-isomer. It shows little preference, moreover, for toluene in comparison to benzene. A survey of aromatic substitution reactions in general shows that a correlation can be made between the selectivity between benzene and toluene, on the one hand, and between the *m*- and *p*-positions of toluene on the other. Selectivity in both cases falls off as the reactivity of the attacking species increases.[2] The following table illustrates these points.

	Toluene/Benzene Ratio	Toluene
Bromination	467	(no *meta*)
Nitration	27	4.4% *meta*
Isopropylation	2.1	30% *meta*

Aromatic Components

The aromatic components most often used in Friedel-Crafts condensations are hydrocarbons, aryl halides, phenols, and aryl ethers. The reaction usually is inhibited by *m*-directing groups because of the stabilizing influence that these substituents exert on the ring. This effect may be

[2] H. C. Brown and K. L. Nelson, *J. Am. Chem. Soc.*, **75**, 6292 (1953).

Reactions of organic compounds

offset, however, by the presence of an activating group such as alkoxyl. Nitrobenzene has not been alkylated by this method, but *o*-nitroanisole has been isopropylated in good yield (84%).

$$CH_3O\!\!\left\langle\begin{array}{c}\\ \\NO_2\end{array}\right\rangle + (CH_3)_2CHOH \xrightarrow{HF} CH_3O\!\!\left\langle\begin{array}{c}\\ \\NO_2\end{array}\right\rangle\!CH(CH_3)_2 + H_2O$$

An aldehyde group on an aromatic ring generally prevents Friedel-Crafts reactions from taking place; anisaldehyde has been isopropylated, however, the yield of product being 22%.

$$\begin{array}{c}CHO\\ \left\langle\begin{array}{c}\\ \end{array}\right\rangle\\ OCH_3\end{array} + (CH_3)_2CHCl \xrightarrow[CS_2]{AlCl_3} \begin{array}{c}CHO\\ \left\langle\begin{array}{c}\\ \end{array}\right\rangle\!CH(CH_3)_2\\ OCH_3\end{array} + HCl$$

Benzaldehyde gives very small amounts of *m*-isopropyl and *m-t*-butyl derivatives. Methylation and ethylation of acetophenone have been effected in low yields by conducting the reaction at temperatures in the neighborhood of 180°.[3]

Aromatic heterocycles vary greatly in reactivity; furan is too sensitive to be generally useful. When the furan ring is stabilized by the presence of a carbalkoxyl group, alkylation is possible. Condensation of methyl 2-furoate with *sec*-butyl bromide gives a product made up of 43% of the *t*-butyl derivative and 57% of the *sec*-butyl derivative.[4] Thiophene likewise is sensitive; however, it has been alkylated under properly chosen conditions.[5]

Alkylating Agents

Olefins

Protonation of olefins is the most convenient way of generating carbonium ions; hence olefins are used widely as alkylating agents. They are particularly suitable for sensitive nuclei, such as those of phenols, which call for mild catalysts. Since unsymmetrical olefins are protonated in such a way as to give the more stable of the two possible carbonium ions,

[3] G. Baddeley, *J. Chem. Soc.*, S229 (1949).

[4] C. D. Hurd and G. L. Oliver, *J. Am. Chem. Soc.*, **76**, 50 (1954).

[5] W. G. Appleby, A. F. Sartor, S. H. Lee, Jr., and S. W. Kapranos, *J. Am. Chem. Soc.*, **70**, 1552 (1948).

propylene and isobutylene are converted into the corresponding symmetrical carbonium ions.

$$CH_3CH{=}CH_2 + H^+ \rightarrow CH_3\overset{+}{C}HCH_3 \quad (\text{not } CH_3CH_2CH_2{}^+)$$

$$CH_3{-}\underset{\underset{CH_3}{|}}{C}{=}CH_2 + H^+ \rightarrow CH_3{-}\underset{\underset{CH_3}{|}}{\overset{+}{C}}{-}CH_3 \quad (\text{not } CH_3\underset{\underset{CH_3}{|}}{CH}CH_2{}^+)$$

The Markownikoff rule is thus explained on the basis of hyperconjugative stabilization of carbonium ions. In particular, propylene yields isopropyl derivatives and isobutylene t-butyl derivatives.

t-Butylbenzene is formed when benzene is treated with isobutylene in the presence of sulfuric acid, the use of a stronger catalyst being unnecessary. An unusual condensation takes place between aromatic hydrocarbons and cyclopropane. Here, as in many other reactions, cyclopropane behaves much like its open-chain isomer, propylene. The difference is that the product is a n-propyl rather than an isopropyl derivative.

$$C_6H_6 + CH_3CH{=}CH_2 \xrightarrow{AlCl_3} C_6H_5\underset{\diagdown CH_3}{\overset{\diagup CH_3}{CH}}$$

$$C_6H_6 + \underset{CH_2{-}CH_2}{\overset{CH_2}{\diagup \diagdown}} \xrightarrow{AlCl_3} C_6H_5CH_2CH_2CH_3$$

The condensation may be carried out in the presence of aluminum chloride, small amounts of hydrogen chloride being added. It is as though protonation of cyclopropane yields the normal propyl carbonium ion, which reacts without rearrangement.

$$\underset{CH_2{-}CH_2}{\overset{CH_2}{\diagup \diagdown}} + H^+ \rightarrow CH_3CH_2CH_2{}^+$$

Alkylation has been accomplished also with four- and five-membered cycloparaffins. Cycloalkenes also serve as alkylating agents, an example being the formation of cyclohexylbenzene from benzene and cyclohexene (OS II, 151; 68% yield).

$$C_6H_6 + \hexagon \xrightarrow{H_2SO_4} C_6H_5{-}\hexagon$$

Diolefins are alkylating agents also; of particular interest is butadiene, which reacts with benzene to give 1-phenyl-2-butene.

$$C_6H_6 + CH_2{=}CHCH{=}CH_2 \xrightarrow{HF} C_6H_5CH_2CH{=}CHCH_3$$

At 0 to 40° this is the only monoalkylation product obtained. The carbonium ion involved, which is seen to be a resonance hybrid, reacts as though it had the structure in which the deficient carbon atom is at a terminal position.[6]

$$CH_2=CH-CH=CH_2 + H^+ \rightarrow$$

$$CH_3\overset{+}{C}H-CH=CH_2 \leftrightarrow CH_3CH=CHCH_2{}^+$$

The carbonium ion that would be produced by protonation of a non-terminal carbon atom is less stable because it does not possess resonance, at least so far as the open sextet is concerned.

$$\overset{+}{C}H_2CH_2-CH=CH_2$$

It was to be expected that acetylene would combine with aromatic compounds to produce vinyl derivatives, which in turn would react with the aromatic compounds to yield diarylethanes. Partly because of the tendency of the styrenes to polymerize, this method has given complex products. With mercuric sulfate as a catalyst, however, products are obtainable in satisfactory yields. Toluene and acetylene, for example, furnish 1,1-di-*p*-tolylethane in 64% yield (OS I, 229).

$$2CH_3\!\!\left\langle\bigcirc\right\rangle + C_2H_2 \xrightarrow{\text{HgSO}_4} \left(CH_3\!\!\left\langle\bigcirc\right\rangle\right)_2 CHCH_3$$

The second step of this transformation would appear to be condensation of styrene with toluene; a similar reaction has been realized with styrene and benzene in the presence of sulfuric acid in the preparation of 1,1-diphenylethane.[7]

$$C_6H_5CH=CH_2 + C_6H_6 \xrightarrow{\text{H}_2\text{SO}_4} (C_6H_5)_2CHCH_3$$

The alkylation reaction is not limited to unsaturated hydrocarbons and cycloparaffins but can be effected by a wide variety of unsaturated compounds. Of particular interest are those that contain other functional units also capable of bringing about alkylation. The unsaturated ketones are illustrative. A specific example is the addition of benzene to allylacetone to produce 5-phenyl-2-hexanone; the yield is 82%.[8]

$$CH_2=CHCH_2CH_2COCH_3 + C_6H_6 \xrightarrow{\text{AlCl}_3} CH_3\underset{\underset{C_6H_5}{|}}{C}HCH_2CH_2COCH_3$$

[6] W. Proell, *J. Org. Chem.*, **16**, 178 (1951).
[7] H. H. Szmant and R. Yoncoskie, *J. Org. Chem.*, **21**, 78 (1956).
[8] J. Colonge and L. Pichat, *Bull. soc. chim. France*, 853 (1949).

A few olefinic halides such as the allyl halides react after the manner of simple olefins in the presence of sulfuric acid; allyl bromide combines with benzene to give β-bromocumene in 58% yield. When methallyl chloride is employed under these conditions the product is neophyl chloride (OS **32**, 90; 73% yield).

$$C_6H_6 + CH_2=\underset{\underset{CH_3}{|}}{C}CH_2Cl \xrightarrow{H_2SO_4} C_6H_5-\underset{\underset{CH_3}{|}}{\overset{\overset{CH_3}{|}}{C}}CH_2Cl$$

Alkyl halides

Condensation of benzene with methyl chloride illustrates the difficulty of controlling alkylation; aluminum chloride is required, and it is not possible to prevent the formation of polyalkyl derivatives. The product is a mixture of mono-, di-, tri-, tetra-, penta-, and hexamethylbenzenes. Durene, pentamethylbenzene, and hexamethylbenzene have been made from commercial xylene in this way (OS II, 248).

An interesting use of the Friedel-Crafts method is the condensation of *m*-xylene with *t*-butyl chloride to give 5-*t*-butyl-*m*-xylene. In this process also *m*-substitution predominates. The reason for the anomalous orientation in this case, however, must be that the bulkiness of the *t*-butyl group virtually prevents its entry into an *o*-position.

The formation of 2-*t*-butylnaphthalene, which is similar, takes place readily at 0°.

$$(CH_3)_3CCl + C_{10}H_8 \xrightarrow{AlCl_3}$$ $$+ HCl$$

The high order of reactivity of naphthalene is not an unmixed blessing, however; in the presence of aluminum chloride, for example, it reacts to form binaphthyls. For this reason methylation of naphthalene can be accomplished only in low yields (OR **3**, 1).

Benzyl chloride reacts readily with benzene to produce diphenylmethane (OS II, 232).

$$C_6H_5CH_2Cl + C_6H_6 \xrightarrow{AlCl_3} C_6H_5CH_2C_6H_5 + HCl$$

Even when benzene is taken in great excess, the yield of diphenylmethane is only 52%.

Benzal chloride reacts with two moles of benzene to give triphenyl-methane.

$$C_6H_5CHCl_2 \rightarrow (C_6H_5)_3CH$$

Chloroform is used also in the synthesis of triphenylmethane.

$$CHCl_3 + 3C_6H_6 \xrightarrow[0°]{AlCl_3} (C_6H_5)_3CH + 3HCl$$

The chlorinated carbonium ions, being resonance hybrids, are more easily formed than the methyl carbonium ion.

Diphenylmethane is always produced as a by-product when chloroform is condensed with benzene. This compound would be formed if any one of the postulated intermediate carbonium ions acquired a hydride ion. The dichloromethyl carbonium ion is an example.

The chance that a carbonium ion will take up a hydride ion is, of course, enhanced by the presence of a solvent having a tertiary hydrogen atom. 1,1-Dichloroethane reacts with benzene in the presence of aluminum chloride and methylcyclopentane to give ethylbenzene in 42% yield.[9] In this example either the α-chloroethyl or the α-phenethyl carbonium ion acquires hydride ion from methylcyclopentane. The latter case may be represented as follows.

Carbon tetrachloride can be made to give mono- , di- , or triaryl derivatives. Benzophenone dichloride, obtainable from benzophenone and phosphorus pentachloride, is formed also from benzene and carbon tetrachloride by the Friedel-Crafts procedure (OS I, 95).

$$2C_6H_6 + CCl_4 \xrightarrow{AlCl_3} C_6H_5CCl_2C_6H_5 + 2HCl$$

[9] L. Schmerling, R. W. Welch, and J. P. Luvisi, *J. Am. Chem. Soc.*, **79**, 2636 (1957).

The carbon tetrachloride is taken in excess in order to halt the condensation at the dichloride stage. The yield of benzophenone, produced by hydrolysis of the chloride, is 89%. With three moles of benzene the product is triphenylmethyl chloride, which can be made also from benzotrichloride; tetraphenylmethane does not form.

$$3C_6H_6 \xrightarrow{CCl_4} (C_6H_5)_3CCl \xleftarrow{2C_6H_6} C_6H_5CCl_3$$

The successful condensation of triphenylcarbinol and triphenylmethyl chloride with phenols suggests that the failure with benzene is due to low reactivity of the triphenylmethyl carbonium ion.

$$(C_6H_5)_3COH + \langle\!\!\bigcirc\!\!\rangle OH \xrightarrow{CH_3CO_2H} (C_6H_5)_3C\langle\!\!\bigcirc\!\!\rangle OH + H_2O$$

The ability of a carbonium ion to abstract a hydride ion from a solvent molecule offers an explanation of the observation that the reaction between benzene and carbon tetrachloride may give triphenylmethane. To bring about this result the intermediate triphenylmethyl chloride-aluminum chloride addition product is reduced by ether (OS I, 548); the over-all yield is 84%.

$$3C_6H_6 + CCl_4 + AlCl_3 \rightarrow (C_6H_5)_3CCl \cdot AlCl_3 + 3HCl$$
$$(C_6H_5)_3CCl \cdot AlCl_3 + (C_2H_5)_2O \rightarrow$$
$$(C_6H_5)_3CH + CH_3CHO + CH_3CH_2Cl + AlCl_3$$

Attack of the trityl carbonium ion on the ether molecule produces triphenylmethane and a new carbonium ion that gives rise to ethyl chloride and acetaldehyde.

$$CH_3\overset{+}{C}H\text{---}O\text{---}CH_2CH_3 + Cl^- \rightarrow CH_3CHO + CH_3CH_2Cl$$

Since halogen substituents stabilize aromatic rings to attack by electrophilic agents, it is not surprising that the Friedel-Crafts type of reaction fails with certain polyhalobenzenes. In general it has not been possible to facilitate alkylation by going to higher temperatures.

α-Halogenated carbonyl compounds and nitriles rarely afford alkylation products in good yields. One satisfactory synthesis is the preparation of diphenylacetonitrile from benzene and α-bromophenylacetonitrile (OS III, 347).

$$C_6H_5\underset{\underset{Br}{|}}{CHCN} + C_6H_6 \xrightarrow{AlCl_3} (C_6H_5)_2CHCN + HBr$$

Other such compounds that are useful are α-chlorodesoxybenzoin, α,α′-dibromodibenzyl ketone, and α-bromo-α-phenylacetone; the last-named reacts with benzene to give α,α-diphenylacetone (OS III, 343).

$$C_6H_5\underset{\underset{Br}{|}}{C}HCOCH_3 + C_6H_6 \xrightarrow{\text{AlCl}_3} (C_6H_5)_2CHCOCH_3 + HBr$$

Chloromethylpyridine hydrochlorides react with benzene in the presence of aluminum chloride to give the corresponding benzylpyridines. 2,6-Dibenzylpyridine, for example, may be made in this way in 76% yield.[10]

It seems probable that the success of these alkylation reactions is related to the fact that the carbonium ions involved, being of the benzyl type, are produced readily.

Alcohols

When alcohols are employed as alkylating agents, the water produced reacts with the aluminum chloride, and more of the catalyst is needed. Methanol, ethanol, or isopropyl alcohol may be employed in the place of the corresponding halide in making 1,3,5-trialkylbenzenes if large amounts of aluminum chloride are used. A remarkable feature in alkylation with alcohols with this catalyst is that rearrangements do not occur. This fact permits the direct introduction of normal side chains; with n-propyl alcohol, aromatic compounds yield n-propyl derivatives instead of the isopropyl compounds that are the chief products when a n-propyl halide is employed at ordinary temperatures. When a mixture of one mole of n-propyl alcohol, 1.3 moles of aluminum chloride, and an excess of benzene is maintained for 10 hours at 110°, n-propylbenzene is obtained in 52% yield and m-di-n-propylbenzene in 37% yield. With boron fluoride as the catalyst alcohols may serve as alkylating agents, but rearrangements are common.[11]

Benzyl alcohol may be used as a benzylating agent in the presence of acid catalysts; with benzene, toluene, anisole, p-xylene, and mesitylene benzyl derivatives are obtained in yields of 84 to 97%, p-toluenesulfonic acid

[10] D. Jerchel, S. Noetzel, and K. Thomas, *Chem. Ber.*, **93**, 2966 (1960).

[11] A. Streitwieser, Jr., D. P. Stevenson, and W. D. Schaeffer, *J. Am. Chem. Soc.*, **81**, 1110 (1959).

serving as the catalyst.[12] In the presence of excess aluminum chloride, however, the condensation yields more complex products; benzyl alcohol and benzene under these conditions give anthracene.[13] It may be that benzyl alcohol serves as a source of carbon monoxide in this reaction.

Mandelic acid, a modified benzyl alcohol, combines with mesitylene in the presence of stannic chloride to give mesitylphenylacetic acid in 61% yield.

$$C_6H_5CHCO_2H + CH_3 \underset{CH_3}{\overset{CH_3}{\bigcirc}} \xrightarrow{SnCl_4} \underset{C_9H_{11}}{\overset{C_6H_5}{\diagdown}} CHCO_2H + H_2O$$
$$\underset{OH}{}$$

This type of reaction has proved to be useful in the synthesis of unsymmetrical diarylacetic acids.

Esters and ethers

As has been indicated, esters can be employed likewise to alkylate aromatic compounds, hydrogen fluoride being a superior catalyst for reactions of this type. Diphenylmethane is obtained in 75% yield by treating benzene with benzyl acetate in the presence of this catalyst.

$$CH_3CO_2CH_2C_6H_5 + C_6H_6 \xrightarrow{HF} C_6H_5CH_2C_6H_5 + CH_3CO_2H$$

Alkylation and acylation with hydrogen fluoride are carried out in a copper bomb and at moderate temperatures.

Certain types of ethers can be used also to alkylate aromatic compounds. Ethylene oxide, a cyclic ether, condenses with aromatic compounds to yield the corresponding β-arylethyl alcohols. The reaction with benzene to give phenethyl alcohol is catalyzed by aluminum chloride.

$$C_6H_6 + \overset{O}{\overset{/\diagdown}{CH_2-CH_2}} \xrightarrow{AlCl_3} C_6H_5CH_2CH_2OH$$

Trimethylene oxide (oxetane) condenses with benzene in the presence of aluminum chloride to give 3-phenyl-1-propanol in 71% yield.

$$\begin{matrix} CH_2-O \\ | \quad\quad | \\ CH_2-CH_2 \end{matrix} + C_6H_6 \rightarrow C_6H_5CH_2CH_2CH_2OH$$

[12] E. F. Pratt, R. K. Preston, J. D. Draper, *J. Am. Chem. Soc.*, **72**, 1367 (1950).
[13] H. E. Ungnade and E. W. Crandall, *J. Am. Chem. Soc.*, **71**, 3009 (1949).

By contrast di-*n*-propyl ether, under similar conditions, gives cumene as the principal product.[14]

Carbonyl compounds

Aldehydes and ketones undergo condensation with aromatic compounds in the Friedel-Crafts manner, and in favorable cases the products are carbinols. The synthesis of carbinols by this method is not generally useful, however, because most of them are too reactive to survive under the conditions of the experiment. Formaldehyde reacts with benzene in the presence of sulfuric acid to yield diphenylmethane, benzyl alcohol or the benzyl carbonium ion being the presumed intermediate. *m*-Xylene and acetaldehyde afford the corresponding 1,1-dixylylethane. The product, when pyrolyzed, gives 2,4-dimethylstyrene.

It is possible to use a mixture of *m*- and *p*-xylene and conduct the condensation so as to utilize only the more reactive component. The process thus yields pure *p*-xylene as well as the pure *m*-xylene formed by cracking the diarylethane.

In the reactions with aldehydes the alkylating agent is presumed to be formed by protonation.

$$R—C{=}O + H^+ \rightarrow R—\overset{+}{C}—OH \leftrightarrow R—C{=}\overset{+}{O}H$$
$$\quad\;\; | \qquad\qquad\qquad | \qquad\qquad\quad |$$
$$\quad\;\; H \qquad\qquad\qquad H \qquad\qquad\quad H$$

In the second step of the condensation the ion is of the benzyl type.

$$Ar—\overset{+}{C}—H$$
$$\qquad |$$
$$\qquad R$$

Chloral serves in the preparation of 2,2-*bis*(*p*-chlorophenyl)-1,1,1-trichloroethane or DDT.

$$Cl_3CCHO + 2C_6H_5Cl \xrightarrow{H_2SO_4} Cl_3CCH(C_6H_4Cl\text{-}p)_2 + H_2O$$

[14] S. Searles, *J. Am. Chem. Soc.*, **76**, 2313 (1954).

One way of halting condensation at the carbinol stage depends on the use of glyoxals. The synthesis of p-bromobenzoin from p-bromophenyl-glyoxal and benzene is an example; the condensation, conducted at 0° in the presence of aluminum chloride, gives the benzoin in 70% yield.

$$Br\langle\rangle COCHO + C_6H_6 \rightarrow Br\langle\rangle CO\overset{\overset{\displaystyle OH}{|}}{C}HC_6H_5$$

The benzoin is less reactive than ordinary alcohols of the benzyl type, presumably because of the difficulty of producing an open sextet on a carbon atom joined to a carbonyl group, i.e., to a carbon atom that is itself electron poor.

The use of carbonyl compounds as alkylating agents is limited chiefly to aldehydes and, in particular, rarely proceeds readily with aryl ketones. This circumstance is fortunate since otherwise the Friedel-Crafts ketone synthesis would not be successful. It is, of course, one of the reasons why direct formylation is so difficult.

The stabilizing influence of adjacent carbonyl groups is evident also in the reactions of diethyl mesoxalate with aromatic hydrocarbons. When this ester is treated with p-xylene in the presence of stannic chloride, diethyl 2,5-dimethylphenylhydroxymalonate is produced (OS III, 326; 57% yield).

$$\underset{CH_3}{\overset{CH_3}{\langle\rangle}} + \underset{CO_2C_2H_5}{\overset{CO_2C_2H_5}{\underset{|}{\overset{|}{C}}=O}} \xrightarrow{SnCl_4} \underset{CH_3}{\overset{CH_3}{\langle\rangle}}\overset{}{\underset{OH}{\overset{|}{C}}}(CO_2C_2H_5)_2$$

Conjugate alkylation

α,β-Unsaturated carbonyl compounds combine with acids to give complexes in which the partial positive charge on the carbonyl carbon atom not only is shared by the carbonyl oxygen atom but is also delocalized in part to the β-carbon atom.

$$\overset{\diagdown}{\underset{\diagup}{C}}=CH-\overset{|}{C}=\overset{+}{O}H \leftrightarrow \overset{\diagdown}{\underset{\diagup}{C}}=CH-\overset{|}{\overset{+}{C}}-OH \leftrightarrow \overset{\diagdown}{\underset{\diagup}{\overset{+}{C}}}-CH=\overset{|}{C}OH$$

Such carbonyl compounds may alkylate aromatic rings in the conjugate manner to give β-aryl derivatives. An interesting example is the addition of benzene to benzalacetophenone to produce β,β-diphenylpropiophenone (OS II, 236; yield 85%).

$$C_6H_5CH{=}CHCOC_6H_5 \xrightarrow[AlCl_3]{C_6H_6} (C_6H_5)_2CHCH_2COC_6H_5$$

Acrylyl chloride reacts with two moles of benzene to give β-phenyl-propiophenone; the change occurs in two steps, the second of which is conjugate addition.[15]

$$CH_2{=}CHCOCl + C_6H_6 \xrightarrow{\text{AlCl}_3} CH_2{=}CHCOC_6H_5 + HCl$$

$$CH_2{=}CHCOC_6H_5 + C_6H_6 \xrightarrow{\text{AlCl}_3} C_6H_5CH_2CH_2COC_6H_5$$

Chloromethylation

Another device for stopping the condensation at the first stage is to operate in the presence of hydrogen chloride, which converts the carbinol or the corresponding carbonium ion into the chloride. The resulting chloromethyl compound is less reactive than the carbinol and is able to survive when experimental conditions are controlled carefully. The process is known as *chloromethylation* (OR I, 63). Its great practical importance is due chiefly to the high order of reactivity and great versatility of the chloromethyl group. Chloromethyl compounds are transformed easily into the corresponding alcohols, aldehydes, acids, amines, and a large number of other types of derivatives. By way of the nitrile or the Grignard reagent the corresponding acetic acid can be made. The malonic ester method affords a route to β-arylpropionic acids.

The reagent may be a mixture of hydrochloric acid with formalin, paraformaldehyde, a chloromethyl ether, or a formal. Zinc chloride is commonly employed as the catalyst, although many other compounds, such as stannic chloride and sulfuric acid, may serve. An example of the use of zinc chloride is found in the preparation of benzyl chloride.

$$C_6H_6 + CH_2O + HCl \rightarrow C_6H_5CH_2Cl + H_2O$$

Chloromethylation of alkylbenzenes like other alkylation reactions gives not only *o*- and *p*-derivatives but small amounts of *m*-derivatives as well; *t*-butylbenzene is chloromethylated at the *m*-position to the extent of 5.4%.[16]

Perhaps the most important example of chloromethylation is the formation of 1-chloromethylnaphthalene from naphthalene (OS III, 195; yield 77%).

$$+ CH_2O + HCl \xrightarrow[\text{CH}_3\text{CO}_2\text{H}]{\text{H}_3\text{PO}_4} + H_2O$$

[15] F. Becke and H. Bittermann, *Chem. Ber.*, **93**, 2344 (1960).
[16] S. K. Freeman, *J. Org. Chem.*, **36**, 212 (1961).

This particular reaction is exceptional in that the α-position of naphthalene is attacked whereas alkylation reactions in general occur chiefly at the β-position. It would be expected, of course, that the steric requirements of the alkylating ion ($H_2\overset{+}{C}$—OH $\leftrightarrow$ H_2C=$\overset{+}{O}H$) would be relatively small.

Chloromethylation occurs readily with alkyl derivatives of benzene such as toluene and the xylenes; mesitylene and other 1,3,5-trialkylbenzenes undergo the reaction smoothly. As in bromination and nitration, 5-*t*-butyl-*m*-xylene gives the symmetrical derivative.

A key step in the synthesis of the resolvable [10]paracyclophane-12-carboxylic acid was the chloromethylation of [10]paracyclophane.[17]

Chloromethylation of β-chloroethylbenzene gives a mixture of *o*- and *p*-β-chloroethylbenzyl chlorides. The *p*-isomer by suitable transformations yields *p*-vinylbenzyl alcohol.[18]

Thiophene undergoes chloromethylation when treated with formalin and hydrochloric acid (OS III, 197), the hydrochloric acid serving as the

[17] A. T. Blomquist and B. H. Smith, *J. Am. Chem. Soc.*, **82**, 2073 (1960).
[18] J. G. Abramo and E. C. Chapin, *J. Org. Chem.*, **26**, 2671 (1961).

catalyst; 2-chloromethylthiophene is obtained in 41 % yield. The dichloro-methyl derivative can be made also.[19]

Like other reactions of the Friedel-Crafts group, chloromethylation generally fails with ketones. Highly activated nuclei such as the nucleus in acetomesitylene are exceptional and give chloromethyl derivatives in satisfactory yields.

Bromomethylation appears to be a general reaction also but has not been used widely. Bromomethyl compounds are obtained in excellent yields when sulfuric acid in acetic acid is added slowly to a mixture of the hydrocarbon, paraformaldehyde, acetic acid, and powdered sodium bromide. Under these conditions toluene gives p-methylbenzyl bromide in 87 % yield.[20]

Iodomethylation has been accomplished also.

Attempts to extend the reaction to higher aldehydes have not been very successful. Chloroethylation has been realized with thiophene, thus opening a way to the synthesis of 2-vinylthiophene (OS **38**, 86).

Anisole condenses with aldehydes such as acetaldehyde, propionalde-hyde, isobutyraldehyde, and butyraldehyde. The reaction with acet-aldehyde gives α-chloroethylanisole, which rapidly loses hydrogen chloride, yielding p-vinylanisole.

[19] J. M. Griffing and L. F. Salisbury, *J. Am. Chem. Soc.*, **70**, 3416 (1948).
[20] G. Kubiczek and L. Neugebauer, *Monatsh.*, **81**, 917 (1950).

Interruption of the alkylation at the benzyl stage occurs also if nitriles are present, the over-all process being one of amidomethylation. The change is accomplished by heating an aromatic compound with a mixture of a nitrile and paraformaldehyde in the presence of phosphoric acid or a mixture of acetic and sulfuric acids. Under these conditions *m*-xylene gives *N,N'*-diacetyl-4,6-dimethyl-1,3-di(aminomethyl)benzene when aceto-nitrile is used.[21]

The capture of the benzyl carbonium ion in this way is an example of the Ritter reaction (p. 156).

Dealkylation

Alkylation is accompanied in numerous instances by dealkylation; the final products are not those that would be formed according to the rules of orientation. Dealkylation has been shown in many cases to take the form of transalkylation, i.e., group transfer from one aromatic ring to another. The industrial ethylation of benzene, perhaps the most important of all Friedel-Crafts reactions, illustrates the transfer reaction. Ethylbenzene is distilled and the di- and polyethyl derivatives are added to the next batch. These higher alkylation products can serve as ethylating agents for benzene, and in this way the yield of ethylbenzene is made to be high.

Large amounts of catalyst, while not required for alkylation, may have a pronounced effect on the orientation of the groups in the product. The preparation of mesitylene, 1,3,5-triethylbenzene, and 1,3,5-triisopropyl-benzene is illustrative. These and many other examples indicate that the *m*-arrangement is the most stable one for a dialkylbenzene and that the symmetrical or 1,3,5-isomer is the most stable of the trialkylbenzenes. Monoalkylbenzenes undergo disproportionation in the presence of a hydrogen fluoride-boron fluoride catalyst.[22] Of special interest is the observation that transalkylation is not accompanied by isomerization of the side chain. Studies of the transethylation process show that it is not of the S_N2 type.[23]

[21] C. L. Parris and R. M. Christenson, *J. Org. Chem.*, **25**, 1888 (1960).
[22] D. A. McCaulay and A. P. Lien, *J. Am. Chem. Soc.*, **75**, 2411 (1953).
[23] A. Streitwieser, Jr., and L. Reif, *J. Am. Chem. Soc.*, **82**, 5003 (1960).

When *n*-butylbenzene is heated with aluminum chloride, a similar change is observed; the products are benzene and di-*n*-butylbenzene, of which at least 90 % is the *m*-isomer.[24]

Disproportionation of *t*-butylbenzene in the presence of a hydrogen fluoride-boron fluoride catalyst produces 1,3,5-tri-*t*-butylbenzene.[25] This remarkable hydrocarbon has also been made in low yield by *t*-butylation of *p*-di-*t*-butylbenzene.[26]

In conjugate addition of aromatic hydrocarbons to α,β-unsaturated carbonyl compounds, transalkylation has been observed also. *p*-Bromo-benzalacetophenone reacts with benzene, for example, to give β,β-di-phenylpropiophenone and bromobenzene.

$$BrC_6H_4CH{=}CHCOC_6H_5 + 2C_6H_6 \overset{AlCl_3}{\rightleftharpoons}$$
$$(C_6H_5)_2CHCH_2COC_6H_5 + C_6H_5Br$$

Intermolecular transfer of the *t*-butyl radical takes place so readily as to permit its use as a blocking group. An example is found in the synthesis of hemimellitene from *m*-xylene. The *t*-butylated product, 1,3-dimethyl-5-*t*-butylbenzene, is methylated by way of the chloromethylation product, and the resulting 1,2,3-trimethyl-5-*t*-butylbenzene is treated with *m*-xylene in the presence of a suitable catalyst.[27]

When acetomesitylene is heated with aluminum chloride at 170° for 1½ hours, it is isomerized to 3,4,5-trimethylacetophenone in 87 % yield.

Treatment of mesitylene and pentamethylbenzene with carbon tetra-chloride in the presence of aluminum chloride produces the corresponding

[24] R. E. Kinney and L. A. Hamilton, *J. Am. Chem. Soc.*, **76**, 786 (1954).
[25] D. A. McCaulay, A. P. Lien, and P. J. Launer, *J. Am. Chem. Soc.*, **76**, 2354 (1954).
[26] P. D. Bartlett, M. Roha, and R. M. Stiles, *J. Am. Chem. Soc.*, **76**, 2349 (1954).
[27] M. J. Schlatter, *J. Am. Chem. Soc.*, **76**, 4952 (1954).

trichloromethyl derivatives. Durene under the same conditions suffers methyl migration and gives trichloromethylprehnitene.[28]

$$CH_3 \underset{CH_3}{\overset{CH_3}{\bigcirc}} CH_3 + CCl_4 \xrightarrow{AlCl_3} CH_3 \underset{CH_3}{\overset{CH_3}{\bigcirc}} \underset{CH_3}{CCl_3} + HCl$$

Jacobsen reaction

Many polysubstituted benzenesulfonic acids suffer migration of groups when treated with concentrated sulfuric acid. The phenomenon, known as the Jacobsen reaction, may be illustrated by the behavior of durenesulfonic acid. The main product is prehnitenesulfonic acid, formed apparently by the intramolecular migration of a methyl group. Intermolecular migration also occurs, giving pentamethylbenzenesulfonic acid, pseudocumenesulfonic acid, and hexamethylbenzene (OR I, 370).

Durenesulfonic acid

Prehnitenesulfonic acid

Pentamethylbenzenesulfonic acid

Pseudocumenesulfonic acid

The Jacobsen reaction does not take place with hydrocarbons having fewer than four alkyl groups; mesitylenesulfonic acid, for example, is stable to sulfuric acid. The tetramethyl- , tetraethyl- , and trimethylethylbenzenes of nonvicinal orientation undergo rearrangement. Since the sulfonic acids are readily hydrolyzed to the corresponding hydrocarbons, the Jacobsen reaction affords a way of preparing certain hydrocarbons that would be difficult to obtain in any other manner. Perhaps the most important of these is prehnitene.

Sulfurization

Introduction of sulfur into aromatic rings can be effected readily by the use of sulfur chloride and aluminum chloride, in the manner of typical

[28] H. Hart and R. W. Fish, *J. Am. Chem. Soc.*, **83**, 4460 (1961).

Friedel-Crafts alkylations. Phenyl sulfide, for example, is made from benzene in this way (OS II, 242; yield 83%).

$$2C_6H_6 + S_2Cl_2 \xrightarrow{\text{AlCl}_3} C_6H_5SC_6H_5 + S + 2HCl$$

Similar changes are brought about by the use of elementary sulfur and aluminum chloride. The synthesis of phenoxthin from phenyl ether is an illustration (OS II, 485; 87% yield).

An analogous change is involved in the preparation of phenothiazines such as 2-chlorophenothiazine from secondary aromatic amines.

Direct introduction of strongly activating groups such as hydroxyl or amino would be expected to proceed in an uncontrollable manner since the product would be much more sensitive to electrophilic attack than the starting material. In the presence of strong acids, however, an amino group might lose its activating power by undergoing protonation or by coordinating with a Lewis acid. Amination has been realized, in fact, by use of aluminum chloride and a derivative of hydroxylamine. Hydroxylamine-O-sulfonic acid, for example, aminates toluene to give a mixture of toluidines in 50% yield (51% ortho, 13% meta, and 36% para).[29]

[29] P. Kovacic and R. P. Bennett, J. Am. Chem. Soc., 83, 221 (1961).

7

Electrophilic substitution reactions of aromatic compounds having sensitive nuclei

Phenols and anilines are in general very sensitive toward electrophilic reagents, and for this reason procedures for introducing nuclear substituents into them usually differ widely from those described for other types of aromatic compounds. The great nuclear reactivity has the disadvantage of causing many reactions to be difficult to control; on the other hand, it makes possible reactions with electrophilic agents that are ineffective with less basic aromatic rings.

According to the values of the substituent constants (p. 12) the $-NH_2$ group is a more powerful activator than the $-OH$ group. Since most electrophilic substitution reactions involve acidic media the $-NH_2$ group tends to be transformed to the salt, and its influence is correspondingly weakened. An interesting example is the tritylation of o-aminophenol. When heated with triphenylmethyl chloride in the absence of catalysts it gives 2-amino-4-tritylphenol, i.e., the $-OH$ group under these conditions is a more powerful director than the $-NH_2$ group.[1]

$$\text{OH} \quad \text{NH}_2 + (C_6H_5)_3CCl \rightarrow \text{OH} \quad \text{NH}_2 + \text{HCl}$$
$$C(C_6H_5)_3$$

Nitration

Concentrated nitric acid attacks phenol violently, forming oxidation products as well as nitro derivatives. Controlled nitration is made possible, however, by use of dilute solutions of nitric acid in water or acetic acid.

[1] G. Chuchani, *J. Chem. Soc.*, 325 (1960).

The behavior of phenols and their ethers and esters toward the usual mixture of nitric and sulfuric acids is influenced by the strength of the sulfuric acid. As the concentration of the acid is increased the amount of m-substitution becomes greater. Such effects have been demonstrated for p-cresol and for the carbonate derived from it. Under suitable conditions the carbonate may give di-3-nitro-4-methylphenyl carbonate in yields as high as 65%.

The explanation of this change in orienting power is sought in the protonation of the phenolic oxygen atom, which produces an oxonium compound, i.e., one in which the substituent carries a positive charge. Dilute solutions of nitric acid in water or acetic acid serve to nitrate phenols only if nitrous acid is present; the process is almost certainly one of nitrosation (p. 106) followed by oxidation of the nitroso compound.

Aniline may be nitrated in glacial acetic acid solution or by the use of mixtures of nitric and sulfuric acids that contain no large excess of sulfuric acid. The presence of nitrous acid must be avoided, since it attacks the amino group. A mixture of o- and p-nitroaniline is formed initially; further reaction converts the mononitro compounds to dinitroanilines and finally to picramide. In the presence of large amounts of sulfuric acid m-nitroaniline becomes the chief product, the $-NH_3^+$ group being m-directing. m-Nitroaniline can be made more cheaply, however, by reducing m-dinitrobenzene. m-Nitrodimethylaniline, likewise, has been produced in satisfactory yields (63%) by the nitration of dimethylaniline in concentrated sulfuric acid (OS III, 658).

Another example is the nitration of N,N-dimethyl-p-toluidine, which can be carried out so as to give in good yield either of the two mononitro derivatives.[2]

Aromatic amino groups may be deactivated, to facilitate the control of nitration, by attaching an electron-deficient group. The most usual procedure is to acetylate, the amino group being regenerated subsequently

[2] H. H. Hodgson and A. Kershaw, J. Chem. Soc., 277 (1930).

by hydrolysis of the amide. *p*-Nitroacetanilide is formed in 90% yield when acetanilide is nitrated at 3 to 5°. Higher temperatures increase the amount of the *o*-isomer.

Deactivation occurs also, of course, when a keto or other electron-deficient group is attached to the ring. Nitration of *o*- and *p*-nitroaniline can be carried out without difficulty. The following chart shows various routes to nitro derivatives of aniline.

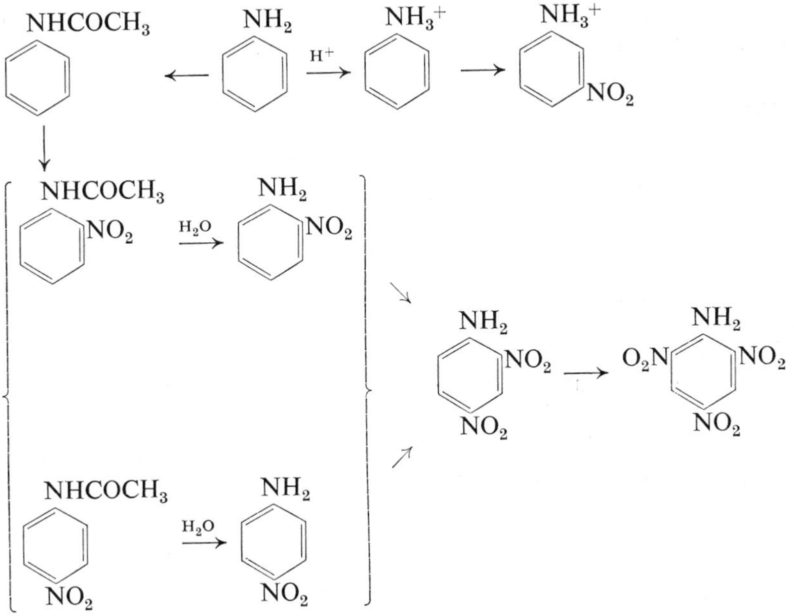

In the nitration of *p*-methoxyacetanilide, the orientation is determined chiefly by the acetamido group (OS III, 661), 4-methoxy-2-nitroacet-anilide being the principal product (79%).

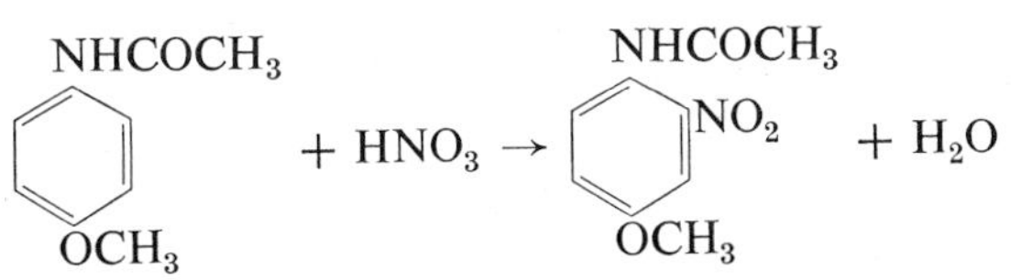

This observation is but one of many that are not in accord with the predictions based on the relative values of the Hammett substituent constants. The value for *p*-methoxyl is -0.268 whereas that for *p*-acetamido is -0.015 (Hine, 72).

Another way of protecting an amino group is to transform the amine to the corresponding urethan by treatment with a chloroformate. An example of this device is involved in a synthesis of 4,5-diethyl-2-nitroaniline from 3,4-diethylaniline. The nitro urethans are more readily hydrolyzed than the corresponding acetamido derivatives.[3]

$$\text{C}_2\text{H}_5\text{—(ring)—NHCO}_2\text{C}_2\text{H}_5 \rightarrow \text{C}_2\text{H}_5\text{—(ring)—NHCO}_2\text{C}_2\text{H}_5,\ \text{NO}_2 \rightarrow \text{C}_2\text{H}_5\text{—(ring)—NH}_2,\ \text{NO}_2$$

2-Acetamidonaphthalene may be nitrated successfully by treatment with concentrated nitric acid in glacial acetic acid solution, the temperature being kept below 40° (OS II, 438). The product, 2-acetamido-1-nitro-naphthalene, is obtained in 49% yield.

$$\text{(naphthalene)—NHCOCH}_3 + \text{HNO}_3 \rightarrow \text{(naphthalene, NO}_2\text{)—NHCOCH}_3 + \text{H}_2\text{O}$$

Sulfonation

Sulfonation of phenols is generally successful and provides a way of desensitizing the ring so that nitration can be conducted satisfactorily. The sulfo group can then be removed, and in this way the desired nitro-phenol is obtained. Successive sulfonation, nitration, and desulfonation serve to convert 3,4-xylenol into 2-nitro-3,4-xylenol.

$$\text{OH, CH}_3, \text{CH}_3 \rightarrow \text{OH, SO}_3\text{H, CH}_3, \text{CH}_3 \rightarrow \text{OH, O}_2\text{N, SO}_3\text{H, CH}_3, \text{CH}_3 \rightarrow \text{OH, O}_2\text{N, CH}_3, \text{CH}_3$$

Sulfonation of aniline and other aromatic amines can be effected in various ways, one of the most useful of which is the "baking process," in which the acid sulfate of the amine is heated at 180° or higher for a period of hours. An illustration of this technique is the production of 4-amino-3-methylbenzenesulfonic acid by heating the acid sulfate of o-toluidine (OS III, 824; 83% yield).

$$\text{CH}_3\text{—(ring)—NH}_2\cdot\text{H}_2\text{SO}_4 \xrightarrow{\text{heat}} \text{CH}_3\text{—(ring, NH}_3{}^+\text{, SO}_3{}^-) + \text{H}_2\text{O}$$

[3] J. P. Lambooy, *J. Am. Chem. Soc.*, **71**, 3756 (1949).

Sulfanilic acid may be prepared conveniently by heating aniline with concentrated sulfuric acid at 200°.

Such amino acids are internal salts or zwitterions and do not form salts with mineral acids.

Acylation

Acyl derivatives of phenols are commonly made by the Fries reaction (p. 96); phenols themselves, however, may react with acylating agents to give phenolic ketones; resorcinol, for example, condenses with acetic acid in the presence of zinc chloride to produce resacetophenone in 65% yield (OS III, 761).

Gallacetophenone is made from pyrogallol by treatment with acetic anhydride in the presence of zinc chloride (OS II, 304; yield 57%).

The orientation problem here is interesting; it might have been expected that the high steric requirement of the acylating agent would favor the unhindered 5-position.

Introduction of the oxalyl group into phenols has been effected by the use of the chlorides of half esters of oxalic acid. Ethoxalyl chloride, for example, reacts with phenols in the presence of aluminum chloride to give the corresponding arylglyoxylic esters. Since the esters undergo hydrolysis readily, it is convenient to isolate the product as the acid. An example is the preparation of 2,4-dihydroxy-3-ethyl-5-methylphenylglyoxylic acid.[4]

[4] R. D. Sprenger, P. M. Ruoff, and A. H. Fraser, *J. Am. Chem. Soc.*, **72**, 2874 (1950).

This type of transformation is successful with aromatic ethers and hydrocarbons that possess sensitive rings; methoxalyl chloride reacts with mesitylene for example, to give methyl mesitylglyoxylate.

Anilines that have hydrogen on nitrogen are converted by acylating agents to anilides, which undergo nuclear acylation. An example is the chloroacetylation of acetanilide; the yield is excellent.

Since the amide is easily hydrolyzed, this procedure provides an indirect route to amino ketones.

Another way to reduce the basicity of aniline is to put a second aryl group on the nitrogen atom. Carbazole, like acetanilide, undergoes nuclear acylation, the orientation being controlled by the amino group. This reaction is peculiar in that the monoacylation product is not isolated. For example, when carbazole is treated with acetyl bromide in the presence of aluminum chloride, 3,6-diacetylcarbazole is formed.

Formylation

Introduction of the formyl group is difficult because formyl chloride and formic anhydride, which would be the normal formylating agents, are unstable. Formamides, on the other hand, are stable and have found important use in the synthesis of aromatic aldehydes. This type of reagent is effective, however, only with very reactive nuclei. Illustrative is the formylation of the ethyl ether of 2-naphthol by the action of N-formyl-methylaniline in the presence of phosphorus oxychloride. 2-Ethoxy-1-naphthaldehyde is made in this way in yields of 84% (OS III, 98).

When 1-methoxynaphthalene is employed, 4-methoxy-1-naphthaldehyde is obtained in 80% yield.[5]

9-Anthraldehyde is prepared in a like manner (OS III, 98; 84% yield).

Formylation of thiophene and certain of its homologs has been accomplished also by this method. For example, when thiophene is heated with N-formylmethylaniline and phosphorus oxychloride, 2-thiophenecarboxaldehyde is formed (OS **31**, 108; 74% yield).

Dimethylformamide also serves as a formylating agent. Dimethylaniline can be converted into p-dimethylaminobenzaldehyde by use of the complex formed by treating this amide with phosphorus oxychloride (OS **33**, 27; yield, 84%).

Pyrrole gives 2-pyrrolecarboxaldehyde (OS **36**, 74; 79% yield).

[5] J. A. VanAllan, *J. Org. Chem.*, **16**, 999 (1951).

Ferrocene, when treated with N-methylformanilide and phosphorus oxychloride, gives ferrocene monoaldehyde in 70% yield.

This reaction shows that ferrocene is more reactive than benzene and that it can be acylated in one ring without the other being attacked.[6]

In the pyrrole and indole series the method has proved to be successful in the synthesis of ketones; indole, for example, condenses with N,N-dimethylpropionamide to give 3-propionylindole in 85% yield.[7]

Formylation with hydrogen cyanide

A number of condensation reactions that resemble the Friedel and Crafts reaction are supposed to involve the formation of unstable imide chlorides. A mixture of hydrogen cyanide and hydrogen chloride appears to be in equilibrium with the unstable formimide chloride.

$$HCN + HCl \rightleftharpoons HC \overset{\displaystyle NH}{\underset{\displaystyle Cl}{\big\langle}}$$

The imide chloride is assumed to condense with aromatic compounds to yield imines, which can be hydrolyzed to aldehydes. The preparation of β-resorcylaldehyde is illustrative.

In a similar way this method, developed by Gattermann, serves to convert 4,5-dimethylresorcinol into 4,6-dihydroxy-2,3-dimethylbenzaldehyde in nearly quantitative yields.[8]

[6] M. Rosenblum, *Chem. and Ind.*, 72 (1957).
[7] W. C. Anthony, *J. Org. Chem.*, **25**, 2049 (1960).
[8] A. Robertson and W. B. Whalley, *J. Chem. Soc.*, 3038 (1949).

A useful modification of the Gattermann method (OR **9,** 37) involves the introduction of zinc cyanide, from which the hydrogen cyanide is generated in the reaction vessel by addition of hydrogen chloride. Zinc chloride, the catalyst, is produced at the same time.

$$Zn(CN)_2 + 2HCl \rightarrow ZnCl_2 + 2HCN$$

The advantage of this procedure is that it obviates the handling of hydrogen cyanide. If the zinc chloride is not a sufficiently strong catalyst, aluminum chloride is added. Mesitaldehyde can be made in 81% yield in this way (OS III, 549).

Hydrolysis of the imine of mesitaldehyde deserves special attention since it is not appreciably impeded by the *o*-methyl groups. It is believed that the attacking reagent must approach at a right angle to the plane of the imino group, which is possible only when the imino group lies in the plane of the benzene ring. Imines of mesityl ketones are, in fact, very difficult to hydrolyze.

Hoesch Synthesis

A method of acylation closely related to the Gattermann synthesis, developed by Hoesch, consists in the condensation of nitriles with phenols in the presence of hydrogen chloride and zinc chloride (OR **5,** 387). An imide chloride presumably is formed as an intermediate; the synthesis of phloroacetophenone from phloroglucinol is an example (OS II, 522); the over-all yield is 87%.

Another example is the preparation of benzyl 4-hydroxy-1-naphthyl ketone from 1-naphthol and phenylacetonitrile.

This reaction is general for phenols and has been used to characterize nitriles.

The use of ethyl cyanoformate makes possible the synthesis of substituted phenylglyoxylic acids, an example being the preparation of 2,4-dihydroxyphenylglyoxylic acid from resorcinol.[9]

Fries reaction

Esters are not often employed to effect acylation since alkylation may occur also. Esters of phenols contain sensitive aromatic nuclei and undergo self-acylation, providing a valuable synthesis of phenolic ketones. The reaction, known as the Fries reaction (CR **27**, 413; OR **1**, 342), occurs when the esters are heated with aluminum chloride, the ester and the catalyst ordinarily being employed in equimolecular amounts. It may be noted in passing that, since phenols are acidic, their esters are comparable to mixed anhydrides.

The mechanism of the Fries reaction has not been fully established. A study of the transformation of *p*-tolyl acetate in the presence of aluminum chloride and nitrobenzene, however, indicates that the chief product, 2-hydroxy-5-methylacetophenone, is formed at least in part by an intramolecular rearrangement.[10]

[9] I. M. Hunsberger and E. D. Amstutz, *J. Am. Chem. Soc.*, **70**, 671 (1948).

[10] N. M. Cullinane, B. F. R. Edwards, and V. V. Bailey-Wood, *Rec. trav. chim.*, **79**, 1174 (1960).

Whether the product is the *o*- or *p*-derivative depends largely on the temperature at which the reaction is carried out. *m*-Tolyl acetate, for example, yields chiefly the *p*-hydroxy ketone at 25° (80%), whereas at 165° the main product (95%) is the *o*-isomer.

Although it is not always possible to obtain either of the two isomers at will, it is generally true that the formation of the *p*-isomer is favored by low temperatures. The solvent and the amount of catalyst also influence the nature of the product. An example is the synthesis of *o*- and *p*-propiophenols from phenyl propionate; at 140 to 150° the yield of the *o*-isomer is 35% and that of the *p*-isomer is 50% (OS II, 543). The use of nitrobenzene as solvent reduces by 80 to 100° the temperature necessary for the reaction to proceed at a useful rate. The reaction takes place with a wide variety of types of esters; the acyl radical may be either aliphatic or aromatic.

Many mixtures of *o*- and *p*-hydroxy ketones can be separated by steam distillation; the *o*-compounds, because of intramolecular hydrogen bonding, are volatile with steam.

2,5-Dihydroxyacetophenone can be made in 77% yield by heating hydroquinone diacetate in the presence of 3.3 moles of aluminum chloride (OS III, 280).

Esters of enols undergo a rearrangement analogous to the Fries reaction, forming 1,3-diketones. An example is the isomerization of isopropenyl acetate to acetylacetone by heating at 500°.

By recycling the enol esters, the β-diketones may be produced in yields of 70 to 85%.[11]

[11] F. G. Young, F. C. Frostick, Jr., J. J. Sanderson, and C. R. Hauser, *J. Am. Chem. Soc.*, **72**, 3635 (1950).

Halogenation

Phenol undergoes bromination readily to yield 2,4,6-tribromophenol.   If the reaction is conducted at 0° and without a catalyst, *p*-bromophenol is formed in 84% yield (OS I, 128), carbon disulfide being employed as the solvent.   If the phenol is taken in 20% excess and the reaction is carried out in ethylene chloride, the yield of *p*-bromophenol is 93%.[12]   In polar solvents such as water, controlled bromination of phenol is virtually impossible since such solvents promote dissociation.

2,6-Dibromo-4-nitrophenol is made satisfactorily from *p*-nitrophenol (OS II, 173).   Bromination is carried out at room temperature in glacial acetic acid; the product is obtained in nearly quantitative yields.

The bromination of guaiacol demonstrates that the hydroxyl group is a more powerful director than the methoxyl group; the chief product is 4-bromo-2-methoxyphenol.

The acetate yields the 5-bromo derivative; evidently the methoxyl group is a more powerful director than the acetoxyl group.

1-Naphthol undergoes bromination readily to yield 4-bromo-1-naphthol, which in turn gives 2,4-dibromo-1-naphthol.

[12] H. E. Podall and W. E. Foster, *J. Org. Chem.*, **23**, 280 (1958).

When 2-naphthol is treated with two moles of bromine in acetic acid in the absence of a catalyst, the product is 1,6-dibromo-2-naphthol; the first bromine atom enters position 1, and the second goes to position 6 (OS III, 132).

The sulfo group serves as a blocking agent in the synthesis of *o*-bromophenol, which can be made in 43% yield by bromination of 4-hydroxy-*m*-benzenedisulfonic acid and hydrolysis of the resulting bromosulfonic acid (OS II, 97).

Bromination of anilines, as would be predicted, is so rapid as to be difficult to control. Tribromoaniline, however, can be made from aniline in this way (OS II, 592). The procedure consists in passing bromine vapors into a solution of aniline in dilute hydrochloric acid.

Amino groups direct preferentially to the *m*-position in bromination if the reaction is conducted in concentrated sulfuric acid. Whereas in acetic acid dimethylaniline gives chiefly 4-bromodimethylaniline, 3-bromodimethylaniline is the chief product (64%) when dimethylaniline is treated with bromine in the presence of concentrated sulfuric acid and silver sulfate.[13]

The difficulty in controlling the bromination of anilines can be lessened by first acetylating the amine; the resulting acetanilide reacts with bromine much more slowly than does the amine itself. 2-Bromo-*p*-toluidine, for example, is made by brominating *p*-acetotoluide at 50 to 55° and then removing the acetyl group by hydrolysis. The acetamido group, although it has a much less powerful directive influence than has the amino group, nevertheless is able to determine the position taken by the entering substituent.

[13] J. H. Gorvin, *J. Chem. Soc.*, 1237 (1953).

The use of blocking techniques to achieve the desired orientation is illustrated by the preparation of 2,6-dichloroaniline from sulfanilamide (OS III, 262). Chlorination gives 3,5-dichlorosulfanilamide (71% yield), which undergoes hydrolysis with steam to form 2,6-dichloroaniline (80% yield).

2,6-Dibromoaniline can be prepared in a similar way, the yields being as high as 79%.

Another way to deal with the problem of chlorinating sensitive nuclei is to employ sulfuryl chloride. This reagent, when used as a chlorinating agent in the aromatic series, generally requires a catalyst; a mixture of sulfur monochloride and aluminum chloride is particularly effective. A solution of 1% of this catalyst in sulfuryl chloride chlorinates benzene rapidly and smoothly in the cold.

$$C_6H_6 + SO_2Cl_2 \rightarrow C_6H_5Cl + HCl + SO_2$$

Stepwise chlorination of benzene to the hexachloro derivative occurs under comparatively mild conditions. Similarly, toluene gives the pentachloro derivative in nearly quantitative yield, the methyl group being unattacked. Sulfuryl chloride chlorinates phenols in about the same way as does chlorine, but the reactions are less vigorous and more easily controlled; it appears that sulfuryl chloride dissociates into sulfur dioxide and chlorine.

Iodination of anilines can be accomplished also. p-Iodoaniline is formed in 84% yield when aniline reacts with iodine; the hydrogen iodide is removed by sodium bicarbonate (OS II, 347).

$$C_6H_5NH_2 + I_2 + NaHCO_3 \rightarrow p\text{-}IC_6H_4NH_2 + NaI + H_2O + CO_2$$

In this procedure only half the iodine is used; the remainder may be recovered by adding a mixture of sulfuric acid and potassium dichromate to the filtrate remaining after the removal of the iodoaniline. The bicarbonate functions to keep the medium from becoming acidic; in acidic media aniline is less sensitive to nucleophilic agents.

A reagent for introducing iodine, especially useful with phenols and anilines, is iodine chloride, which is made by adding chlorine to an equimolecular amount of iodine.

$$I_2 + Cl_2 \rightarrow 2ICl \rightleftharpoons 2I^+ + 2Cl^-$$

Iodine chloride is more reactive than iodine and effects iodination in the absence of a carrier or an oxidizing agent; it reacts with p-nitroaniline to give 2,6-diiodo-4-nitroaniline (OS II, 196; 64% yield). Ionization of iodine chloride would be expected to give I^+ rather than Cl^+ as the attacking agent. The chlorine atom is, in fact, eliminated as hydrogen chloride, the more expensive halogen being utilized completely.

Anthranilic acid can be iodinated in this way to give 5-iodoanthranilic acid in 84% yield (OS II, 349).

Salicylic acid behaves in a similar way to give 2-hydroxy-3,5-diiodobenzoic acid (OS II, 343; 92% yield).

Iodination of phenol with iodine yields 2,4,6-triiodophenol. The same reaction carried out with 2,4,6-trideuterophenol is much slower; the hydrogen isotope effect is in the ratio 1:4.[14]

Introduction of halogen atoms into phenols and other aromatic compounds has been accomplished also by way of mercury derivatives; bromine, iodine, and iodine chloride are used most often. o-Chloromercuriphenol, for example, reacts with iodine to yield o-iodophenol (OS I, 326; 63% yield).

Similarly, p-iodobenzoic acid is formed when p-chloromercuribenzoic acid is treated with iodine (OS I, 325; 81% yield).

[14] E. Grovenstein, Jr., and D. C. Kilby, J. Am. Chem. Soc., **79**, 2972 (1957).

The mercury derivatives generally are made by treating the aromatic compound with mercuric acetate. An example is the mercuration of benzene; the acetoxymercuri group is introduced by adding mercuric acetate in glacial acetic acid to benzene at a controlled rate. At 110° the yield of monomercuration product is 92%.[15]

$$C_6H_6 + Hg(OCOCH_3)_2 \rightarrow C_6H_5HgOCOCH_3 + CH_3CO_2H$$

Mercuration of toluene, phenol, aniline, and other aromatic compounds having an *o,p*-directing substituent gives mixtures consisting chiefly of the *o*- and *p*-isomers. Substitution is abnormal, however, with compounds that have a *m*-directing group. Nitrobenzene, for example, undergoes mercuration in an almost random fashion; and benzoic acid yields exclusively the *o*-substitution product.

One explanation of anomalous mercuration postulates that the mercurating agent is not a positive ion but an undissociated mercuric acetate molecule. In confirmation of this theory, mercuration of nitrobenzene with mercuric perchlorate in perchloric acid solution (in which mercuric ion is the attacking agent) gives orientation effects typical of electrophilic substitution.[16]

The position taken by the acetoxymercuri group can be determined by replacement of the group with halogens. The action of a halogen on a mercurated aromatic compound is involved also in the following conversion of sodium 3-nitrophthalate into 2-bromo-3-nitrobenzoic acid (OS I, 56, 125).

The production of picric acid by the so-called *oxynitration* of benzene—treatment with nitric acid and mercuric nitrate—has been shown to involve mercuration, transforming benzene into phenylmercuric nitrate.

$$C_6H_6 + Hg(NO_3)_2 \rightarrow C_6H_5HgNO_3 + HNO_3$$

[15] K. A. Kobe and P. F. Leuth, Jr., *Ind. Eng. Chem.*, **34**, 309 (1942).
[16] W. J. Klapproth and F. H. Westheimer, *J. Am. Chem. Soc.*, **72**, 4461 (1950).

C-Alkylation

Phenols readily undergo alkylation when treated with olefins in the presence of sulfuric acid, giving the most highly branched alkyl derivative that is possible. Aryl ethers, if formed, undergo isomerization to the corresponding substituted phenols. An example is the preparation of p-t-butylphenol from phenol and isobutylene.

If the alkylation is continued, two and finally three t-butyl groups are introduced.[17]

The commercial mixture of the two diisobutylenes (p. 153) gives a single product, a highly branched octyl phenol. Protonation of the two olefins produces the same carbonium ion.

Similarly, catechol yields p-t-butylcatechol.

Acetone condenses with reactive aromatic compounds, yielding derivatives of the type $Ar_2C(CH_3)_2$. With phenol it forms 2,2-bis(p-hydroxyphenyl)propane.

$$2C_6H_5OH + CH_3COCH_3 \xrightarrow{H_2SO_4} HOC_6H_4\overset{\overset{\displaystyle CH_3}{|}}{\underset{\underset{\displaystyle CH_3}{|}}{C}}C_6H_4OH + H_2O$$

[17] G. H. Stillson, D. W. Sawyer, and C. K. Hunt, J. Am. Chem. Soc., 67, 303 (1945).

The condensation of *o*-cresol with levulinic acid is analogous.[18]

The acid-catalyzed condensation of aldehydes with phenols is a similar reaction. An example is the condensation of 2-naphthol with formaldehyde in the presence of hydrochloric acid. This reaction has been used as a test for the presence of traces of formaldehyde.

Methylenedisalicylic acid is made similarly.

This type of reaction is involved also in the synthesis of phenol-aldehyde resins (p. 527).

Nuclear alkylation of anilines and phenols can be accomplished by the use of the corresponding aluminum derivatives as catalysts. Ethylation of aniline, for example, can be effected in the presence of aluminum anilide and aluminum chloride; the reaction proceeds rapidly at 300° under a pressure of 200 atmospheres.[19] The pi-electrons of ethylene are postulated

[18] A. J. Yu and A. R. Day, *J. Org. Chem.*, **23**, 1004 (1958).

[19] R. Stroh, J. Ebersberger, H. Haberland, and W. Hahn, *Angew. Chem.*, **69**, 124 (1957).

to make up the electron deficit of the aluminum atom, thus creating a carbonium ion that attacks the aromatic ring.

This theory is supported by the fact that ethylation occurs only on the ring and only at the o-positions; N-ethyl-o-ethylaniline is obtained from N-ethylaniline in 86% yield.[20] 2,6-Diethylaniline can be made in 96% yield. Similar results have been obtained with other aromatic amines and with other olefins.

Phenols can be alkylated by the use of aluminum phenoxides; in these reactions also the alkylation occurs predominantly at the o-positions.[21] When phenol, for example, in the form of aluminum phenoxide is treated with isobutylene at 105 to 115° and under a pressure of 30 to 100 pounds per square inch over a 4-hour period, the chief products are 2-t-butylphenol (46%) and 2,6-di-t-butylphenol (36%).[22]

α-Phenethyl chloride alkylates phenols nuclearly and spontaneously without a catalyst. An optically active chloride gives products that are also optically active. o-Alkylation proceeds with retention of configuration, and p-alkylation takes place with inversion.[23]

Chloromethylation of phenols is difficult because of their sensitivity. p-Nitrophenol, however, can be chloromethylated successfully (OS III, 468). When methylal and concentrated hydrochloric acid are used for this reaction, 2-hydroxy-5-nitrobenzyl chloride is obtained in 69% yield.

[20] G. G. Ecke, J. P. Napolitano, and A. J. Kolka, *J. Org. Chem.*, **21**, 711 (1956).
[21] R. Stroh, R. Seydel, and W. Hahn, *Angew. Chem.*, **69**, 699 (1957).
[22] A. J. Kolka, J. P. Napolitano, and G. G. Ecke, *J. Org. Chem.*, **21**, 712 (1956).
[23] H. Hart, W. L. Spliethoff, and H. S. Eleuterio, *J. Am. Chem. Soc.*, **76**, 4547 (1954).

Nitrosation

The high order of reactivity of phenols is reflected in their ability to undergo nitrosation when treated with nitrous acid. Nitroso phenols are tautomeric with the monoximes of the corresponding quinones; *p*-nitrosophenol, in fact, exists in solution as a tautomeric mixture.

The nitrosating species is either the nitrosonium ion (NO^+) or a carrier of it.

Nitrosation, though possible only with aromatic rings having high electron density, is not limited to phenols. Aromatic amines, for example, may be nitrosated, and the reaction is especially useful if the amino group is tertiary. A well-known example is the nitrosation of dimethylaniline to produce *p*-nitrosodimethylaniline (OS I, 214).

A way of stabilizing the ring of an aromatic amine is to introduce into the *o*-positions substituents such as methyl. The classic example is N,N-dimethyl-2,6-xylidine, which fails to undergo nitrosation. The explanation advanced for this and for many similar phenomena is based on the principle that the atoms of a system that possesses resonance lie in a plane, and any departure from strict planarity diminishes the resonance interaction. In the present example it is believed that the *o*-methyl groups prevent the dimethylamino group from being coplanar with the ring, thus virtually inhibiting resonance (Gould, 70). In the structure corresponding to electrophilic attack at the *p*-position, the nitrogen atom must be doubly bound to the ring, and all four methyl groups must occupy the same plane. Examination of a molecular model indicates that this arrangement is not possible.

From dipole moment data it seems certain that the two o-methyl groups do indeed almost completely suppress resonance interaction between the amino group and the ring. A similar explanation has been offered for the observation that 2,6-dimethylacetanilide is nitrated chiefly at the 3-position.

$$\text{(structure of 2,6-dimethylacetanilide)} \rightarrow \text{(3-nitro derivative)}$$

The nitrosation of N-methylaniline yields the N-nitroso derivative. Heating with hydrochloric acid, however, causes the nitroso compound to rearrange to the p-isomer. The isomerization, known as the Fischer-Hepp reaction, is thought to proceed by an intermolecular mechanism with the intermediate formation of nitrosyl chloride, which brings about nuclear nitrosation. In strong sulfuric acid the nucleus may be nitrosated directly.

$$\text{(CH}_3\text{NH / NO structure)} \quad \xleftarrow[\text{Concd. H}_2\text{SO}_4]{\substack{\text{Thermodynamic}\\\text{control}\\\text{HNO}_2}} \quad \text{(CH}_3\text{NH structure)} \quad \xrightarrow[]{\substack{\text{Kinetic}\\\text{control}\\\text{HNO}_2}} \quad \text{(CH}_3\text{N—NO structure)}$$

Primary aromatic amines do not invariably undergo diazotization (p. 540); α-naphthylamine and certain others yield the corresponding p-nitrosoamines by the action of nitrosonium hydrogen sulfate in concentrated sulfuric acid.[24]

Nitrosation of naphthols takes place readily, as is illustrated by the preparation of 1-nitroso-2-naphthol (OS I, 411); the yield is practically quantitative.

$$\text{(2-naphthol)} + HNO_2 \rightarrow \text{(1-nitroso-2-naphthol)} + H_2O$$

N-Nitroso-1-bromo-2-methylaminonaphthalene does not undergo the Fischer-Hepp reaction; this result is in line with other observations indicating that entry into the 3-position is difficult to effect.[25]

$$\text{(structure of N-Nitroso-1-bromo-2-methylaminonaphthalene)}$$

[24] L. Blangey, *Helv. Chim. Acta*, **21**, 1579 (1938).
[25] F. Bell and W. H. Hunter, *J. Chem. Soc.*, 2903 (1950).

Coupling with Diazonium Salts

Another typical electrophilic substitution reaction that proceeds well in the aromatic series only if the nucleus is very electron-rich is coupling with diazonium salts. The attacking species is the positive diazonium cation; the reaction of diazotized aniline with dimethylaniline may be represented as follows.

$$C_6H_5—N{=}\overset{+}{N} + \left\langle\bigcirc\right\rangle—N(CH_3)_2 \rightarrow C_6H_5—N{=}N$$

$${=}\overset{+}{N}(CH_3)_2 \rightarrow$$

$$H$$

$$C_6H_5N{=}N\left\langle\bigcirc\right\rangle N(CH_3)_2 + H^+$$

The failure of certain aromatic amines to undergo coupling has been ascribed to steric inhibition of resonance; benzoquinuclidine is an example.[26]

Benzoquinuclidine

In coupling reactions with phenols and anilines, replacement of hydrogen may occur on oxygen, nitrogen, or carbon. The usual product, however, is an azo compound resulting from attack on the nucleus, the p-position being preferred; another example is the formation of p-hydroxyazobenzene.

$$\left\langle\bigcirc\right\rangle N_2Cl + \left\langle\bigcirc\right\rangle OH \rightarrow \left\langle\bigcirc\right\rangle N{=}N\left\langle\bigcirc\right\rangle OH + HCl$$

1-Naphthol couples with benzenediazonium chloride to give chiefly the 1,4-derivative, the 2,4-bisazo compound being a by-product (OS I, 49).

It is interesting that 4-methyl-1-naphthol undergoes coupling whereas 1-methyl-2-naphthol does not.

[26] B. M. Wepster, *Rec. trav. chim.*, **71**, 1150 (1952).

Methyl red is made in 66% yield by coupling dimethylaniline with diazotized anthranilic acid (OS I, 374).

Diazotized sulfanilic acid couples with 2-naphthol to yield the 1,2-derivative (OS II, 35).

The reaction with phenols involves attack of the phenoxide ion by the diazonium ion. The alkali required to produce the phenoxide ion has an untoward action on the diazonium compound, however, eventually converting it to a form that is ineffective in coupling. The acidity of the solution is therefore regulated by the addition of the salt of a weak acid. Sodium acetate, sodium carbonate, and sodium bicarbonate commonly serve in this capacity in the manufacture of azo dyes.

In acid solution the reactivity of aromatic amines is diminished by salt formation, the positive ammonium ion operating to lower the vulnerability of the ring to electrophilic attack. For this reason amines are coupled in neutral or very weakly acidic solutions.

The formation of azo compounds by coupling occurs not only with phenols and anilines but also with other aromatic compounds that have very reactive nuclei; pyrrole, for example, couples with benzenediazonium chloride in weakly acidic solution to yield both the α- and β-derivatives, the former predominating.

Since coupling involves attack of the aromatic nucleus by the positive ion, $Ar\overset{+}{N}=N$, it is not surprising that nuclear substituents in the ion influence its coupling power. Nitro groups in o- or p-positions, for example, promote coupling; diazotized picramide is able to couple with mesitylene. Electron impoverishment of the ring accentuates the electron deficit of the diazo group.

Introduction of azo groups can be effected indirectly by isomerization of N-azo derivatives. The formation of the N-azo compounds is illustrated by the preparation of diazoaminobenzene from aniline and benzenediazonium chloride (OS II, 163; 73% yield).

$$C_6H_5NH_2 + C_6H_5N_2Cl + CH_3CO_2Na \rightarrow$$
$$C_6H_5NHN{=}NC_6H_5 + NaCl + CH_3CO_2H$$

In the presence of acids diazoamino compounds isomerize to the corresponding aminoazo derivatives, the usual product being the *p*-isomer. Presumably the diazoamino compound undergoes cleavage to the amine and diazonium salt, which then couple.

Cyclic diazoamino compounds may be produced by treatment of *o*-diamino compounds with enough nitrous acid to diazotize one of the amino groups. *o*-Phenylenediamine itself yields 1,2,3-benzotriazole (OS III, 106; 81% yield).

Coupling with an olefinic function occurs in the Widman-Stoermer cinnoline synthesis (CR **37**, 269). An example is the preparation of 4-phenylcinnoline from *o*-amino-1,1-diphenylethylene.

Arsonation

Arsonation occurs when certain highly reactive aromatic compounds are heated with arsenic acid. This reaction, discovered by Bechamp, is practically limited to anilines, phenols, and their derivatives (OR **2**, 428). An example is the action of syrupy arsenic acid (80 to 85%) on aniline to produce arsanilic acid. The reaction is conducted at 155 to 160° (OS I, 70); the yield does not exceed 15%.

Arsonation is analogous to sulfonation in that the introduction of the arsono group proceeds reversibly, the best yields being obtained by removal of the water that is formed. By this method phenol gives *p*-hydroxyphenylarsonic acid in 33% yield.

Hydrogen Exchange

It might be expected that hydrogen exchange would occur when aromatic compounds are treated with acids such as sulfuric acid. Such substitution reactions are observable when deuterium or tritium is employed. Experiment has shown, for example, that phenol is deuterated when treated with deuterium sulfate.

The deuteron attacks the *o*- and *p*-positions; all the tracer element disappears when the tribromide is made. As in other electrophilic reactions of phenols, it is the phenoxide ion that suffers electrophilic attack.[27] Such isotope exchange is not limited to phenols and anilines; it occurs with benzene, in fact (Hine, 333).

Electrophilic displacement of substituents

Many nitration reactions are known in which a substituent is displaced under conditions that would normally lead to the displacement of hydrogen (CR **40**, 117). For example, the sulfo group may be replaced by the nitro group when certain arylsulfonic acids are subjected to conditions for nitration. This type of procedure is of synthetic value, especially in connection with the preparation of nitro derivatives of phenols and naphthols. 2,4-Dinitro-1-naphthol can be made by sulfonating 1-naphthol and replacing the sulfo groups by treatment with nitric acid.

[27] See A. J. Kresge and Y. Chiang, *J. Am. Chem. Soc.*, **81**, 5509 (1959).

The preparation of picric acid may be accomplished also by use of sulfonation. The first step is sulfonation of phenol; the sulfo groups serve to stabilize the phenol molecule and later are replaced by nitro groups.

Although replacement of one substituent by another proceeds most readily with phenols and anilines, it occurs also with compounds possessing less reactive nuclei. Replacement of the sulfo group by halogen has been observed in the treatment of naphthalenesulfonic acids with halogens in aqueous solution. An example is the preparation of 1-bromo-4-methyl-naphthalene by treatment of potassium 4-methyl-1-naphthylenesulfonate with bromine in aqueous solution; the yield based on 1-methylnaphthalene is 28%.

Replacement of an alkyl side chain by the nitro group has been reported many times and in some instances occurs under relatively mild conditions. An example is the conversion of 1,2,4,5-tetraisopropylbenzene to 1,2,4-triisopropyl-5-nitrobenzene by treatment with nitric acid in acetic acid containing enough acetic anhydride to destroy the water that is formed; at 45° the yield is 83%.[28]

[28] A. Newton, *J. Am. Chem. Soc.*, **65**, 2434 (1943).

Replacement occurs with *p*-diisopropylbenzene but not with the *m*-isomer in which the two side chains are not in a position to exert an appreciable influence upon each other. The nitration product of the *p*-isomer consists mostly of 1,4-diisopropyl-2-nitrobenzene and *p*-nitro-cumene.

In the nitration of *p*-cymene to make 2-nitro-*p*-cymene (p. 32) a small amount of the hydrocarbon suffers replacement of the secondary alkyl group, giving *p*-nitrotoluene.

The yield of nitro compounds is 82%, of which about 8% is the toluene derivative (OS III, 653).

Nitration converts both pentamethyl- and hexamethylbenzene into dinitroprehnitene.[29]

Pentaethyl and hexaethylbenzene likewise yield the same dinitro compound, 3,6-dinitrotetraethylbenzene, in which the nitro groups are *para* to one another.[30]

Bromination of aromatic rings that carry side chains resembles nitration in that it does not always proceed normally; bromine may replace an alkyl group attached to an aromatic ring. Cumene, for example, gives hexabromobenzene in good yield when treated with liquid bromine in the presence of iron powder at 0°. Replacement, however, occurs only if the group is secondary or tertiary; *n*-propylbenzene under these conditions yields pentabromo-*n*-propylbenzene.[31]

[29] L. I. Smith and S. A. Harris, *J. Am. Chem. Soc.*, **57**, 1289 (1935).
[30] L. I. Smith and C. O. Guss, *J. Am. Chem. Soc.*, **62**, 2635 (1940).
[31] G. F. Hennion and J. G. Anderson, *J. Am. Chem. Soc.*, **68**, 424 (1946).

Other groups also suffer replacement, especially if they are in *o-* or *p-* positions with respect to a phenolic hydroxyl group. A carbinol group, for example, may be displaced by halogen; the conversion of *p*-hydroxy-benzyl alcohol into 2,4,6-trichlorophenol by the action of chlorine is an example.[32]

$$\text{(structure with } CH_2OH \text{ and } OH) + 3Cl_2 \rightarrow \text{(trichlorophenol structure)} + CH_2O + 3HCl$$

This type of displacement provides an attractive method for making aldehydes when the displacing group is a diazonium ion such as that from sulfanilic acid, and the carbinol group is in the *p*-position of dimethylaniline.[33]

$$\overset{\text{OH}}{\underset{|}{RCH}}\text{—}(C_6H_4)\text{—N}(CH_3)_2 + HO_3S\text{—}(C_6H_4)\text{—N}_2{}^+ \rightarrow$$

$$HO_3S\text{—}(C_6H_4)\text{—N}{=}\text{N}\text{—}(C_6H_4)\text{—N}(CH_3)_2 + R\overset{+}{C}HOH$$

$$R\overset{+}{C}HOH \rightarrow RCHO + H^+$$

The method is general and gives aldehydes in superior yields and in a state of high purity. The by-product (methyl orange) is easily removed because of its insolubility in ether. The carbinols are obtained readily by condensation of Grignard reagents with *p*-dimethylaminobenzaldehyde.

Replacement of nitro groups by chlorine is formally similar. 3-Nitro-phthalic anhydride gives 3-chlorophthalic anhydride when treated with chlorine at 250°; the yield is 76%.[34]

4-Nitrophthalic anhydride reacts in a similar way to give 4-chloro-phthalic anhydride in satisfactory yields.

[32] K. V. Sarkanen and C. W. Dence, *J. Org. Chem.*, **25**, 715 (1960).
[33] M. Stiles and A. G. Sisti, *J. Org. Chem.*, **25**, 1691 (1960).
[34] See A. Heller, *J. Org. Chem.*, **25**, 834 (1960).

8

Ring closure by reactions of the Friedel-Crafts type

In many of the acylation reactions that have been cited, the acylating agent contains an aromatic ring and therefore offers the possibility of self-acylation. Such a reaction is not likely to take place, however, if the carbonyl function responsible for the acylating action is joined directly to the ring, thus defending it from attack. On the other hand, if the acylating function is placed in an alkyl side chain, the ring is vulnerable to attack. Of especial interest are compounds in which the acylating function terminates a three- or four-membered side chain, since such compounds may undergo intramolecular acylation to form cyclic ketones. The usual procedure for cyclizations of this type is to add aluminum chloride to the acid chloride (OR **2**, 114). Better results have been obtained in some instances, however, by adding the acid chloride to the catalyst, i.e., by the *inverse Friedel-Crafts* method. In this way 1-indanone, for example, is formed from hydrocinnamoyl chloride in nearly quantitative yields.[1]

Intramolecular reactions proceed more readily than the corresponding intermolecular changes. If the reverse were true, polymer formation would be observed as is indeed the case with phenylacetyl chloride, ring closure of which is prevented by the strain of the four-membered ring that would be formed.

The explanation of the relative ease of formation of rings is, of course,

[1] W. S. Johnson and H. J. Glenn, *J. Am. Chem. Soc.*, **71**, 1092 (1949).

that the reacting functions are near each other; even the acids themselves may undergo cyclization. 1-Indanone, for example, is formed from hydrocinnamic acid in 73% yield in the presence of hydrogen fluoride.

Under the influence of this catalyst o-benzylbenzoic acid yields anthrone.

1-Tetralone, also a six-membered cyclic ketone, can be made from γ-phenylbutyryl chloride in the presence of aluminum chloride (OS **33**, 90; yield 91%) or from the free acid in the presence of hydrogen fluoride. Polyphosphoric acid, a useful reagent for cyclodehydration, gives 1-tetralone in 66% yield.[2]

Conversion of N-phenylanthranilic acid into acridone occurs in the presence of sulfuric acid (OS II, 15).

If phosphorus oxychloride is employed, the product is 9-chloroacridine (OS III, 53).

The procedure for the formation of 2-methylanthraquinone is similar to that in the acridone synthesis (OS I, 353, 517).

The preparation of quinizarin from phthalic anhydride and p-chlorophenol (OS I, 476; 74% yield) must involve a similar ring closure.

[2] H. R. Snyder and F. X. Werber, *J. Am. Chem. Soc.*, **72**, 2965 (1950).

Intramolecular acylation leading to quinone formation is unusual in that the ring that is acylated already holds a carbonyl group. Similar ring closures are known in which the acylation involves a ring bearing a nitro group; cyclization of o-(4-nitrophenoxy)benzoyl chloride to 3-nitroxanthone may be cited.

Apparently the intramolecular nature of the reaction has a profound effect since the acid chloride of o-nitrohydrocinnamic acid gives 4-nitro-1-indanone in 73% yield.

7-Chloro-4-nitro-1-indanone has been prepared similarly, the yield being 69%.[3]

Another example is the formation of 4-nitrofluorenone by the action of sulfuric acid on o-(o-nitrophenyl)benzoic acid.

When the nitro acid is heated with quinoline and copper chromite, the elements of nitric acid are lost, and fluorenone is formed.[4] The synthesis of fluorenones from o-arylbenzoic acids can be brought about also by the use of polyphosphoric acid.

[3] L. F. Fieser and E. Berliner, *J. Am. Chem. Soc.*, **74**, 536 (1952).
[4] C. Angelini, *Ann. chim. Rome*, **43**, 247 (1953).

Anhydrides may undergo ring closure also as is illustrated by the formation of 4-keto-1,2,3,4-tetrahydro-1-naphthoic acid by treatment α-phenylglutaric anhydride with sulfuric acid; the yield is 57%.

An interesting question is posed by benzylsuccinic anhydride, which can form either a five- or a six-membered ring; actually, the six-membered ketone is produced.

A novel synthesis of 9-aminophenanthrene depends on cyclization of 2-diphenylylacetonitrile.[5]

The *Stobbe condensation* (p. 118) provides a route to γ-arylbutyric acids suitable for ring closure. From methyl *p*-tolyl ketone, for example, it is possible to make 4,7-dimethyl-1-tetralone.[6]

[5] C. K. Bradsher, E. D. Little, and D. J. Beavers, *J. Am. Chem. Soc.*, **78**, 2153 (1956).
[6] W. S. Johnson and A. R. Jones, *J. Am. Chem. Soc.*, **69**, 792 (1947).

A type of closure of unsaturated acids, discovered by Erdmann, is illustrated by the behavior of γ-phenylcrotonic acid, which is transformed by heat to 1-naphthol.

The usual procedure involves an arylparaconic acid, which can be made by the Perkin condensation (p. 499). Presumably the unsaturated acid is formed as an intermediate. The ease with which the ring closure occurs is such that it is sufficient to distil the acid, the temperature of decomposition being between 250 and 300°. This ease of ring closure makes the method especially reliable for synthesizing substituted 1-naphthols of known orientation. The preparation of 7-bromo-1-naphthol is an example.

Rings of more than six members have been closed by the Friedel-Crafts method. 6,9-Dimethylbenzosuberone, for example, is produced in 41% yield by treating δ-(2,5-dimethylphenyl)valeryl chloride with aluminum chloride.

By recourse to high dilution techniques it has been possible to prepare ketones with still larger rings; an example is the closure of 6-phenylhexanoyl chloride to give the corresponding eight-membered ketone in 67% yield.[7]

Many ring closures involve the condensation of an ester group with an aromatic ring; an example is the formation of ethyl 1,3-dihydroxy-2-naphthoate from diethyl phenylacetylmalonate, the reaction being catalyzed by sulfuric acid (OS III, 637).

4-Hydroxy-2-methylquinoline is produced when ethyl β-anilinocrotonate is treated with sulfuric acid or, better, with boiling Dowtherm A, a eutectic mixture of phenyl ether (73.5%) and biphenyl (26.5%) (OS III, 593; 90% yield).

A very similar ring closure is used to make ethyl 7-chloro-4-hydroxy-3-quinolinecarboxylate (OS III, 272).

Lactones are of especial interest since they can bring about both alkylation and acylation. Ring closure of this type occurs, for example, when benzene is treated with γ-butyrolactone in the presence of aluminum

---

[7] W. M. Schubert, W. A. Sweeney, H. K. Latourette, *J. Am. Chem. Soc.*, **76**, 5462 (1954).

chloride; 1-tetralone is obtained in 96% yield (OS **35**, 95). It seems certain that alkylation precedes acylation.

Ring Closure by Alkylation

Ring formation may occur also if an aromatic nucleus holds a side chain containing a function that can serve as an alkylating agent. An example is found in the self-condensation of styrene; at elevated temperatures ring closure may be made to intervene at the dimer stage. The chief product, 1-methyl-3-phenylindane, is formed in 81% yield (OS **35**, 83).

An alkyl halide holding an aromatic ring might likewise be expected to undergo cyclization, and the course of the reaction might be influenced by the size of the ring to be formed. In the synthesis of julolidine, for example, the closure produces a six-membered ring (OS III, 504). The condensation of aniline with trimethylene chlorobromide seems to take the following path.

Alkylation with alcohols proceeds intramolecularly also. The 1,4-ditertiary glycol, 2,5-dimethyl-2,5-hexanediol, is admirably constructed for ring formation with aromatic compounds. "Cyclialkylation" occurs readily with phenol for example.

Many of the methods for making isoquinolines require the condensation of a carbonyl group with an aromatic ring. Especially interesting is the production of dihydroisoquinolines by the dehydration of acyl derivatives of phenethylamines. An example is the formation of 1-benzyl-3,4-dihydroisoquinoline from N-phenethylphenylacetamide; the yield is 84%.

This method, developed by Bischler and Napieralski (OR **6**, 74), has been extended by Pictet and Spengler to the anils formed by condensing aldehydes with phenethylamines (CR **30**, 145; OR **6**, 151).

The Morgan-Walls synthesis of phenanthridines is similar, involving cyclodehydration of o-acylamidobiphenyls, i.e., acyl derivatives of 2-biphenylylamines (CR **46**, 175). Phosphorus oxychloride serves as the dehydrating agent; an example is the synthesis of 9-methylphenanthridine.

The preparation of phenanthridone from 2-biphenylyl isocyanate is another example.[8]

[8] J. M. Butler, *J. Am. Chem. Soc.*, **71**, 2578 (1949).

Certain acyl isothiocyanates undergo ring closure to give monothio-imides, which can be hydrolyzed to dicarboxylic acids. The procedure provides a specific method of o-carboxylation of aromatic acids. An example is the preparation of homophthalic acid from phenylacetic acid. Phenylacetyl isothiocyanate is made by treating the acid chloride with lead thiocyanate.[9]

The ethoxalyl group is especially useful because of its high order of reactivity. The synthesis of 3,4-dihydro-1,2-naphthalic anhydride from ethyl γ-phenylbutyrate requires the intermediate formation of such a derivative (OS II, 194).

[9] P. A. S. Smith and R. O. Kan, *J. Am. Chem. Soc.*, **82**, 4753 (1960).

Ethyl α-phenoxyacetoacetate undergoes ring closure in the presence of sulfuric acid to give ethyl 3-methylcoumarilate (OS **33**, 43).

$$\text{(structure)} \quad \rightarrow \quad \text{(structure)} \quad + H_2O$$

Indene derivatives may be made by a similar ring closure; ethyl α-acetyl-β-(2,3-dimethoxyphenyl)propionate is converted into ethyl 6,7-dimethoxy-3-methyl-2-indenecarboxylate by polyphosphoric acid (OS **40**, 43, yield 86%).

$$\text{(structure)} \quad \rightarrow \quad \text{(structure)} \quad + H_2O$$

Perhaps the best-known example of a ring closure of an aniline derivative is the *Skraup synthesis* (OR **7**, 59). When the reactants are aniline and glycerol, the product is quinoline (OS I, 478; 91% yield). Acrolein is assumed to be an intermediate.

$$\text{(reaction scheme)}$$

A marked reduction of the violence of the Skraup reaction and a substantial increase in the yield of quinolines are achieved if a previously prepared mixture of glycerol, amine, nitro compound, and sulfuric acid is transferred, in portions and at a temperature of 60 to 90°, to a second vessel arranged in such a way that both vessels can be heated to 160 to 170°. After the entire mixture has been transferred, it is heated for 4 to 6 hours longer.[10]

[10] R. H. F. Manske, A. E. Ledingham, and W. R. Ashford, *Can. J. Research*, **27F**, 359 (1949).

When applied to 3-nitro-4-aminoanisole, the Skraup method gives 6-methoxy-8-nitroquinoline (OS III, 568; 76% yield). The same product is formed when acrolein is employed instead of glycerol.

The preparation of lepidine from aniline and methyl vinyl ketone is similar to the Skraup reaction, the closure involving a ketone rather than an aldehyde.

The yields are better if, instead of the unsaturated ketone, one of its progenitors such as 1,3,3-trimethoxybutane is employed.

In connection with the question of the aromaticity of tropolones, it is of interest that 5-aminotropolone undergoes the Skraup reaction.[11]

The Doebner–von Miller quinoline synthesis is very much like that of Skraup. A mixture of an aromatic amine and an aldehyde is treated with hydrochloric acid or zinc chloride. An example is the synthesis of quinaldine from aniline and acetaldehyde. It seems probable that crotonaldehyde, formed initially, condenses with aniline.

[11] J. W. Cook, J. D. Loudon, and D. K. V. Steel, *Chem. and Ind.*, 562 (1952).

When aniline is heated with acetone in the presence of iodine, a trimethyldihydroquinoline forms. By analogy with the Skraup reaction, the following ring closure may be postulated.

The trimethyl compound loses methane when heated at 220 to 230° in the presence of sodium anilide, the product being 2,4-dimethylquinoline (OS III, 329).

It is to be noted that in these examples the nucleus is highly reactive; for this reason success has been achieved also with phenol derivatives. The von Pechmann reaction (OR 7, 1) for the synthesis of coumarins is illustrative. These ring closures are brought about by condensing phenols with malic acid or esters of β-keto acids in the presence of a catalyst such as sulfuric acid. An example is the preparation of 4-methylcoumarin from ethyl acetoacetate and phenol (OS III, 581; 55% yield).

The preparation of 7-hydroxy-4-methylcoumarin (OS III, 281) and that of 6,7-dihydroxy-4-methylcoumarin (OS I, 360) are similar; the yields are excellent. Acetoacetanilide undergoes ring closure in a like manner to give 4-methylcarbostyril (OS III, 580; 91% yield).

$$CH_3C=O$$

The von Pechmann reaction has been accomplished with cationic exchange resins.[12]

In the Pomeranz-Fritsch isoquinoline synthesis, which consists of the condensation of an aldehyde with an aminoacetal (OR **6**, 191), the ring closure depends on condensation of an aldehyde group with an aromatic ring that does not have an activating group. Isoquinoline itself is prepared from benzaldehyde and the ethyl acetal of aminoacetaldehyde.

$$+ H_2NCH_2CH(OC_2H_5)_2 \rightarrow$$

The formation of benzanthrone from anthrone and glycerol (OS II, 62), involving the production of a new carbocyclic ring, is analogous to the Skraup closure; the yield is 65%.

Another synthesis that may be considered here is the preparation of isatin from aniline, chloral hydrate, and hydroxylamine. The isonitroso-acetanilide, formed initially, undergoes ring closure under the influence of sulfuric acid (OS I, 327).

[12] E. V. O. Jones and S. S. Israelstam, *J. Org. Chem.*, **26**, 240 (1961).

Conjugate addition may take place in an intramolecular way to give rings. Aryl vinyl ketones, for example, undergo ring closure in the presence of sulfuric acid to yield indanones. α-Methacrylophenone gives 2-methyl-1-indanone in 88% yield.

The intramolecular cyclization occurs readily in spite of the presence of a ketone group on the ring.

9

Electrophilic reactions
of unsaturated aliphatic compounds

Reactions of olefinic compounds generally lead to products in which the trigonal has been replaced by the tetrahedral type of orbital, i.e., the double bond becomes saturated. In many reactions the olefin accepts a proton or other positive entity to give a carbonium ion. Such ions have trigonal hydridization of their orbitals, i.e., are planar. The carbonium ion generally attacks a base and thus restores the tetrahedral configuration of the carbon atom that held the positive charge. This last step makes the reactions more complex than those in the aromatic series.

Reaction of Olefins with Nitric and Sulfuric Acids

The usual behavior of olefins is to react additively with nitric acid to give derivatives of nitro alcohols; ethylene, for example, yields β-nitroethyl nitrate.

$$CH_2{=}CH_2 \rightarrow O_2NCH_2CH_2ONO_2$$

Better results have been obtained by use of acetyl nitrate in acetic acid–acetic anhydride solution, the principal product generally being the β-nitro acetate. Isobutylene, for example, gives the acetate of 2-methyl-1-nitro-2-propanol in 69% yield.[1]

$$\underset{\overset{|}{CH_3}}{CH_3C}{=}CH_2 + CH_3\overset{O}{\overset{\|}{C}}ONO_2 \rightarrow CH_3\underset{\overset{|}{CH_3}}{\overset{\overset{OCOCH_3}{|}}{C}}CH_2NO_2$$

Concentrated sulfuric acid reacts with olefins as a sulfonating agent;

[1] F. G. Bordwell and E. W. Garbisch, Jr., *J. Am. Chem. Soc.*, **82**, 3588 (1960).

with ethylene it forms ethionic acid and its anhydride, carbyl sulfate, as well
as isethionic acid.

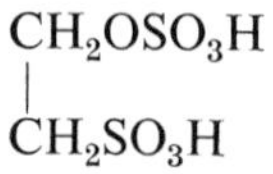

$$CH_2OSO_3H$$
$$|$$
$$CH_2SO_3H$$

Ethionic acid

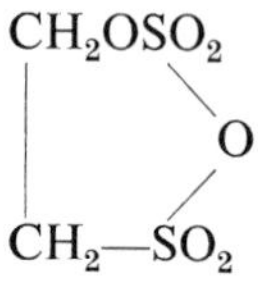

$$CH_2OSO_2$$
$$| \qquad \searrow$$
$$| \qquad\qquad O$$
$$| \qquad \nearrow$$
$$CH_2—SO_2$$

Carbyl sulfate

$$CH_2OH$$
$$|$$
$$CH_2SO_3H$$

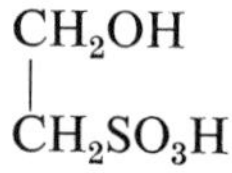

Isethionic acid

Acylation

Acylation occurs with olefins in much the same way as with aromatic
compounds; from cyclohexene and acetyl chloride, for example, 1-
acetylcyclohexene may be obtained in 62% yield.

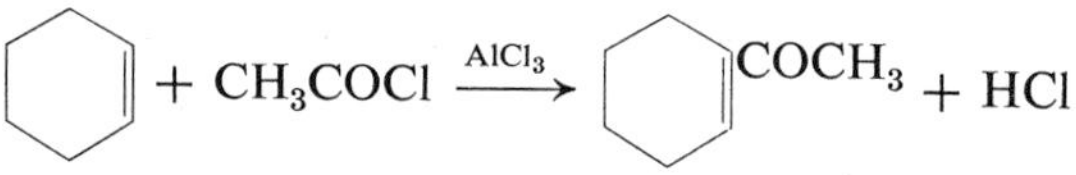

When benzoyl chloride is employed, the product is 1-benzoylcyclo-
hexene; the yield is 40%. A commercial method of a similar type has
been developed for producing unsaturated methyl ketones by condensing
acetic anhydride with olefins.

In many of these reactions the β-chloro ketone, produced as an intermediate, has been isolated. When ethyl vinyl ketone is formed by condensing propionyl chloride with ethylene, for example, the chloro ketone
can be prepared and subsequently dehydrochlorinated; the over-all yield
is 25%.

$$C_2H_5COCl + CH_2{=}CH_2 \xrightarrow{\text{AlCl}_3} C_2H_5COCH_2CH_2Cl \xrightarrow{-\text{HCl}}$$
$$C_2H_5COCH{=}CH_2$$

Apparently such reactions may conform either to the "aromatic" or
"aliphatic" pattern of behavior (p. 19).

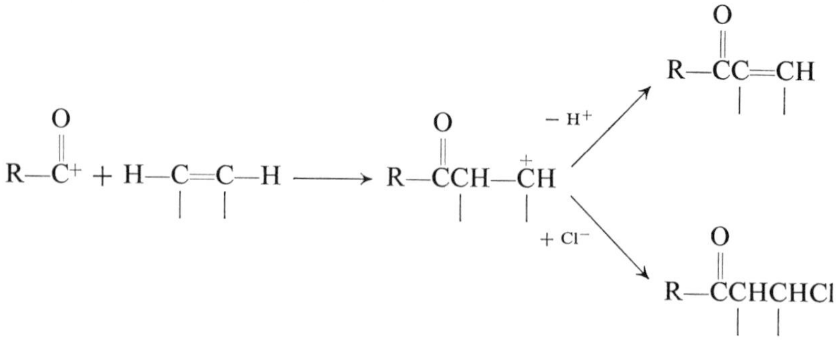

Acid chlorides combine in a similar way with acetylene to yield β-chlorovinyl ketones. The formation of β-chlorovinyl isoamyl ketone is illustrative (OS **32**, 27; yield 64%).

$$(CH_3)_2CHCH_2CH_2COCl + HC\equiv CH \xrightarrow{AlCl_3}$$

$$(CH_3)_2CHCH_2CH_2COCH\!=\!CHCl$$

The production of a carboxylic acid from an olefin, water, and carbon monoxide might possibly be allied to the acylation of olefins with anhydrides. Although carbon monoxide is produced by dehydration of formic acid, preferably in the presence of sulfuric acid, and can be converted to formic acid by hydration by way of the sodium salt (formed by heating carbon monoxide with sodium hydroxide under pressure at 200°), it rarely behaves as an anhydride. One way of formulating the synthesis of carboxylic acids from olefins is to assume attack of carbon monoxide by a carbonium ion and subsequent hydration of the acylium ion. In the case of propionic acid the mechanism would be as follows.

$$CH_2\!=\!CH_2 + H^+ \rightarrow CH_3CH_2{}^+$$

$$CH_3CH_2{}^+ + CO \rightarrow CH_3CH_2\overset{+}{C}\!=\!O$$

$$CH_3CH_2\overset{+}{C}\!=\!O + H_2O \rightarrow CH_3CH_2CO_2H + H^+$$

The process has been used to make acetic and propionic acids commercially.

Carboxylic acids are formed also by treating olefins with sulfuric acid in the presence of formic acid.[2]

Carbonylation of allene in water in the presence of ruthenium catalysts produces methacrylic acid.[3]

One industrial method for propionic acid involves treatment of carbon monoxide with ethylene or ethyl alcohol in the presence of boron trifluoride and water at 125 to 130° and under a pressure of 800 to 900 atmospheres. Acetic acid is made from methanol by a similar procedure.

Glycolic acid is manufactured by a somewhat similar method; formaldehyde, water, and carbon monoxide are condensed in the presence of sulfuric acid and acetic acid, the reaction being complete in about an hour at 160 to 170°. If methanol is employed instead of water, the product is methyl glycolate.

[2] W. Haaf and H. Koch, *Ann.*, **638**, 122 (1960).

[3] T. J. Kealy and R. E. Benson, *J. Org. Chem.*, **26**, 3126 (1961).

In the presence of nickel carbonyl, acetylenic and olefinic hydrocarbons take up carbon monoxide and water to form carboxylic acids. From acetylene, ethylene, and cyclohexene are produced acrylic acid, propionic acid, and hexahydrobenzoic acid, respectively.

$$C_2H_2 + CO + H_2O \xrightarrow{\text{Ni(CO)}_4} CH_2{=}CHCO_2H$$

$$CH_2{=}CH_2 + CO + H_2O \xrightarrow{\text{Ni(CO)}_4} CH_3CH_2CO_2H$$

$+ CO + H_2O \xrightarrow{\text{Ni(CO)}_4}$ CO_2H

If amines or alcohols are employed instead of water, the products are amides or esters, respectively. Examples are the formation of amides and esters of acrylic acid from acetylene.

$$C_2H_2 + CO + RNH_2 \xrightarrow{\text{Ni(CO)}_4} CH_2{=}CHCONHR$$

$$C_2H_2 + CO + ROH \xrightarrow{\text{Ni(CO)}_4} CH_2{=}CHCO_2R$$

When hydrogen is introduced and iron carbonyl is the catalyst, alcohols are formed. From ethylene 1-propanol is produced; the process requires neither high pressure nor high temperature.

$$CH_2{=}CH_2 + CO + H_2 \xrightarrow{\text{Fe(CO)}_4} CH_3CH_2CH_2OH$$

Reaction of Halogens

The addition of bromine and chlorine to olefinic compounds is illustrated by the reaction of bromine with allyl bromide (OS I, 521); 1,2,3-tribromopropane is obtained in 98% yield.

$$CH_2{=}CHCH_2Br + Br_2 \rightarrow CH_2BrCHBrCH_2Br$$

The addition of chlorine to double and triple linkages is illustrated by commercial methods of preparing ethylene chloride, sym-tetrachloroethane, 1,2,3-trichloropropane, and 1,1,2-trichloroethane. Ethylene chloride is made by passing chlorine and ethylene into a liquid, usually ethylene chloride itself. Decolorization of a solution of bromine in carbon tetrachloride, the classical test for unsaturation, is very slow with highly conjugated systems and in extreme cases, as has already been indicated (p. 1), fails entirely.

Iodine combines with ethylene to give ethylene iodide, but the reaction is reversed by heat.

$$CH_2{=}CH_2 + I_2 \rightleftharpoons ICH_2CH_2I$$

Many unsaturated carbonyl compounds readily yield dibromides. Excellent procedures are available for adding bromine to cinnamaldehyde (OS III, 731), ethyl cinnamate (OS II, 270; 85% yield), benzalacetone (OS III, 105; 57% yield), benzalacetophenone (OS I, 205), and fumaric acid (OS II, 177; 84% yield).

The addition of bromine to a double bond is stereospecific and occurs in the *trans*-manner; thus, cyclohexene gives *trans*-1,2-dibromocyclohexane (OS II, 171; 95% yield).

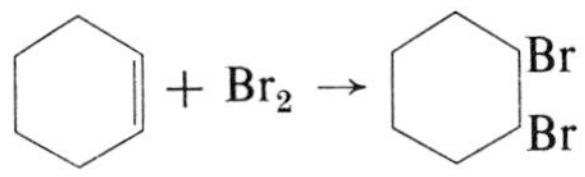

Maleic and fumaric acid yield, respectively, *dl* and *meso* modifications of α,β-dibromosuccinic acid.

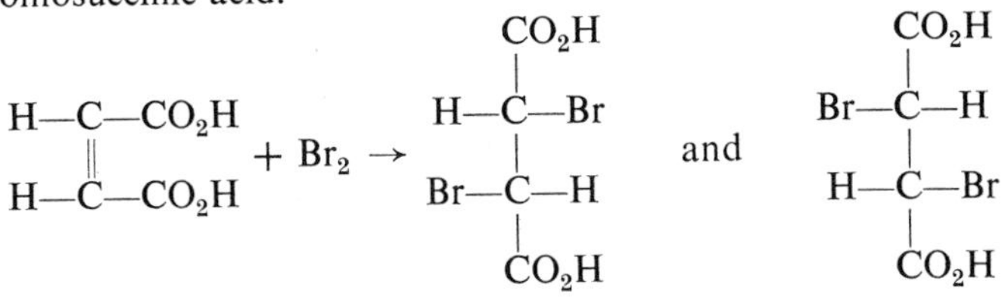

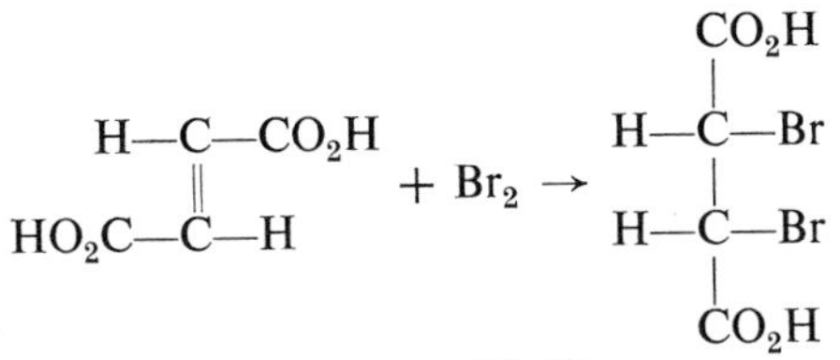

The carbonium ion $BrCH\!-\!\overset{+}{C}HCO_2H$ cannot be an intermediate since, in that case, maleic and fumaric acids would yield the same dibromide. These facts have found a convincing explanation based on the assumption that a bridged ion, a bromonium ion (Gould, 137), is formed initially that is a resonance hybrid of the following structures.

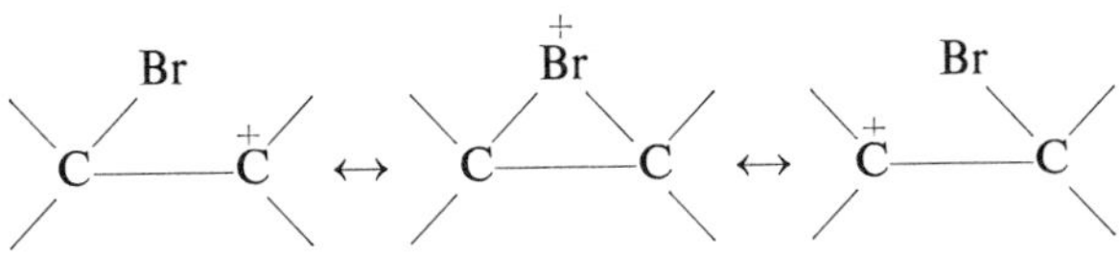

The bromide ion is believed to attack one of the carbon atoms at the face opposite the bond between carbon and bromine, i.e., in the S_N2 manner. The ring opens at the instant the bromide ion becomes attached;

thus, free rotation of one carbon atom with respect to the other cannot occur until their final configurations have been fixed. Moreover, the two halogen atoms are thus added in the *trans*-manner.

A chief postulate of the theory is that the carbon atom "turns inside out" at the moment of attachment of the bromide ion. This theory has been very successful in explaining displacement reactions. As will be seen in the sequel, bromonium ions formed from unsymmetrical olefins react in the way that would involve the more stable carbonium ion. If bromine is added to an olefin in alcoholic solution the bromonium ion may attack the alcohol instead of bromide ion and give rise to an ether. An example is the formation of 1-bromo-2-methoxyhexane by adding bromine to 1-hexene in methanol.

$$CH_3(CH_2)_3CH\!\!=\!\!CH_2 \xrightarrow[CH_3OH]{Br_2} CH_3(CH_2)_3\!\!-\!\!\underset{\underset{OCH_3}{|}}{C}HCH_2Br$$

Lesser amounts of 1,2-dibromohexane and 2-bromo-1-methoxyhexane are produced also.

Reaction of halogens with enols

Replacement of α-hydrogen atoms in carbonyl compounds is thought to proceed by way of the enol form; thus one of the steps would be classified as electrophilic addition of bromine to the olefinic double bond. The bromination of acetone in water solution is an example (Hine, 198).

$$\underset{O}{\overset{\|}{CH_3C}}\!\!-\!\!CH_3 \xrightarrow{+H^+} \underset{\underset{+}{OH}}{\overset{|}{CH_3C}}\!\!-\!\!CH_3 \xrightarrow{-H^+} \underset{OH}{\overset{|}{CH_3C}}\!\!=\!\!CH_2 \quad (slow)$$

$$\underset{OH}{\overset{|}{CH_3C}}\!\!=\!\!CH_2 + Br_2 \rightarrow \underset{O}{\overset{\|}{CH_3CCH_2Br}} + Br^- + H^+ \quad (fast)$$

It is a rule that ketones having an α-hydrogen atom readily yield the corresponding α-halo derivatives. Bromoacetone can be made in this way on a preparative scale (OS II, 88; 44% yield). The chlorination of cyclo-hexanone may be cited also (OS III, 188; 66% yield); the product is 2-chlorocyclohexanone.

2-Methylcyclohexanone reacts with sulfuryl chloride to give 2-chloro-2-methylcyclohexanone (OS 37, 8; 85% yield).

Bromination of acetophenone in the presence of catalytic amounts of aluminum chloride produces phenacyl bromide (OS II, 480; 66% yield).

$$C_6H_5COCH_3 + Br_2 \rightarrow C_6H_5COCH_2Br + HBr$$

The effect of large amounts of aluminum chloride has already been mentioned (p. 60).

The existence of keto-enol equilibria in β-diketones and β-keto esters was demonstrated by Kurt Meyer. In its original form his method consisted of titrating the enol content directly with a standard bromine solution. The procedure has been improved by various changes, one of which is the replacement of bromine by iodine chloride.[4] It is possible to determine such equilibria by measurement of proton resonance with a high-resolution nuclear magnetic resonance spectrometer. By this method, which has the advantage that it cannot affect the equilibrium, acetylacetone was shown to exist in the enol form to the extent of 85%.[5]

Since halogen atoms have a strong attraction for electrons, it might be expected that replacement of one α-halogen atom in an active methylene compound would increase the electron deficit, causing the second α-hydrogen atom to be replaced even more readily than the first. It is known that, in symmetrical ketones such as acetone, the second halogen atom goes on the carbon atom holding the first.

Dibenzoylmethane, which possesses a very reactive methylene group, readily yields a dibromo derivative (OS II, 244; 76% yield).

$$(C_6H_5CO)_2CH_2 + 2Br_2 \rightarrow (C_6H_5CO)_2CBr_2 + 2HBr$$

[4] A. Gero, *J. Org. Chem.*, **19**, 469 (1954).

[5] H. S. Jarrett, M. S. Sadler, and J. N. Shoolery, *J. Chem. Phys.*, **21**, 2092 (1953).

The preparation of α-halo aldehydes by halogenation of aldehydes is not a very useful method. Satisfactory results have been obtained, however, with certain of the lower aliphatic aldehydes under suitable conditions. At high concentrations of hydrochloric acid, acetaldehyde reacts with chlorine to give chloroacetaldehyde at 18 to 20°, dichloroacetaldehyde at 35 to 40°, and chloral at 80 to 90°.[6]

Bromination of paraldehyde yields a tribromo derivative from which bromoacetaldehyde is obtained by distillation in a stream of carbon dioxide. By the use of more bromine, bromal can be made (OS II, 87; 57% yield).

Phenylacetonitrile, as might be expected, undergoes bromination readily to yield α-bromophenylacetonitrile (OS III, 347).

$$C_6H_5CH_2CN + Br_2 \rightarrow C_6H_5\underset{\underset{Br}{|}}{C}HCN + HBr$$

Halogenation of carboxylic acids, however, occurs only with difficulty. This fact is in accord with the expectation that, in carboxylic acids, the electron deficit of the carbonyl carbon atoms is neutralized to a large degree by accession of electrons from the hydroxyl group. Acid chlorides and anhydrides, however, behave as carbonyl compounds and can be halogenated with comparative ease. Chloroacetic acid is manufactured by the chlorination of acetic acid in the presence of a carrier. The chlorination can be carried further to yield dichloroacetic acid; however, this acid is made more satisfactorily in the laboratory by the action of sodium cyanide on chloral in the presence of calcium carbonate (p. 281).

α-Chloropropionic acid may be produced by chlorination of propionic acid. α-Bromo acids are usually prepared by bromination, but the corresponding iodo compounds must be made by indirect methods (p. 249). A superior procedure for producing bromoacetic acid consists in treating acetic acid with bromine in the presence of acetic anhydride and pyridine (OS III, 381; 85% yield). Presumably it is the anhydride that is attacked by the bromine.

The classical procedure for the preparation of α-chloro and α-bromo acids consists in treatment of the acid with the halogen in the presence of phosphorus trichloride. The procedure, known as the Hell-Volhard-Zelinsky method, is illustrated by the synthesis of α-bromocaproic acid (OS I, 115; 89% yield).

$$CH_3(CH_2)_3CH_2CO_2H + Br_2 \xrightarrow{PCl_3} CH_3(CH_2)_3CHBrCO_2H + HBr$$

[6] H. Guinot and J. Tabuteau, *Compt. rend.*, **231**, 234 (1950).

α-Bromoisovaleric acid (OS III, 848; 89% yield) and α-bromoisocaproic acid (OS III, 523; 66% yield) are produced in a similar way. The synthesis of ε-benzoylamino-α-bromocaproic acid illustrates the use of phosphorus tribromide (OS II, 74; 89% yield). If a second halogen atom is introduced by the Hell-Volhard-Zelinsky method, the product is an α,α-dihalo acid. It is sometimes expedient to prepare the acid halide and subject it to halogenation; adipic acid has been converted to the α,δ-dibromo derivative by this procedure (OS III, 623).

Monobromination of derivatives of dicarboxylic acids can be accomplished by treatment of the half ester with thionyl chloride followed by one mole of bromine. The thionyl chloride not only serves to produce the ester acid chloride but also acts as solvent for the bromination. An illustration is the synthesis of diethyl α-bromoadipate.[7]

$$\underset{\underset{CH_2CH_2CO_2C_2H_5}{|}}{CH_2CH_2COCl} \xrightarrow{Br_2} \underset{\underset{CH_2CH_2CO_2C_2H_5}{|}}{\overset{\overset{Br}{|}}{CH_2CHCOCl}} \xrightarrow{C_2H_5OH} \underset{\underset{CH_2CH_2CO_2C_2H_5}{|}}{\overset{\overset{Br}{|}}{CH_2CHCO_2C_2H_5}}$$

As this example shows, simple esters are less easily brominated than acid chlorides. In fact, ethyl acetate has been employed as a solvent in many bromination reactions.

Esters having highly activated methylene groups are brominated without difficulty. Diethyl malonate, for example, is converted readily into diethyl bromomalonate (OS I, 245; 75% yield).

$$CH_2(CO_2C_2H_5)_2 + Br_2 \rightarrow BrCH(CO_2C_2H_5)_2 + HBr$$

Malonic acid and its monoalkyl derivatives, as would be expected, are brominated with ease. Examples for which satisfactory procedures are available are the isopropyl (OS II, 93), benzyl (OS III, 705), and sec-butyl (OS III, 495) derivatives. Since the bromomalonic acids are easily decarboxylated, they offer a route to the corresponding α-bromo monocarboxylic acids. The α-chloro acids can be produced in a similar way.[8]

Alcohols are dehydrogenated by halogens, and thus may yield the products to be expected from the corresponding carbonyl compounds. The commercial production of chloral by treatment of ethanol with chlorine is an example. A few ketones that are unreactive toward bromine can be made in this way. Benzil, for example, is formed by the action of bromine on benzoin.

[7] E. Schwenk and D. Papa, *J. Am. Chem. Soc.*, **70**, 3626 (1948).

[8] R. H. Horn, R. B. Miller, and S. N. Slater, *J. Chem. Soc.*, 2900 (1950).

Positive halogen

Replacement of very active hydrogen atoms by halogen atoms produces halogen compounds in which the halogen atoms, like hydrogen, tend to separate as positive ions. This tendency is, of course, a measure of the electron deficit of the α-carbon atom. Such substances resemble compounds in which bromine is on oxygen or nitrogen, i.e., is "positive" and may actually serve as halogenating agents. Ethyl α-bromoacetoacetate converts phenol into tribromophenol; in the presence of hydrobromic acid, this ester undergoes rearrangement to the γ-bromo ester. The explanation is that bromination at the α-position is reversed more readily than at the γ-position.[9]

$$CH_3COCH_2CO_2C_2H_5 + Br_2 \overset{fast}{\rightleftharpoons} \underset{\underset{Br}{|}}{CH_3COCHCO_2C_2H_5} + HBr$$

$$CH_3COCH_2CO_2C_2H_5 + Br_2 \overset{slow}{\longrightarrow} BrCH_2COCH_2CO_2C_2H_5 + HBr$$

Halohydrin Formation

If a bromonium ion is formed in water, it may be converted into a bromohydrin; the product from propylene, for example, is propylene bromohydrin.

$$\underset{CH_3CH\!-\!-\!-\!CH_2}{\overset{\overset{+}{Br}}{\diagup \ \diagdown}} \overset{H_2O}{\longrightarrow} \underset{CH_3CH\!-\!CH_2}{\overset{OH \ \ Br}{| \quad \ |}}$$

A procedure employed in the formation of 2-chlorocyclohexanol consists in passing chlorine into a mixture of sodium hydroxide and mercuric chloride until the yellow precipitate of mercuric oxide just disappears; nitric acid is introduced and the solution is added to cyclohexene (OS I, 158; 73% yield).

Another procedure, illustrated by an industrial method for making ethylene chlorohydrin, consists in passing chlorine and ethylene into water under carefully controlled conditions.

$$\underset{CH_2}{\overset{CH_2}{\underset{||}{}}} \rightarrow \underset{CH_2OH}{\overset{CH_2Cl}{\underset{|}{}}}$$

[9] A. Becker, *Helv. Chim. Acta*, **32**, 1114, 1584 (1949).

These processes are formulated as being initiated by the attack of Cl_2, the resulting chloronium ion then being hydrated. Allyl chloride gives glycerol α,γ-dichlorohydrin, an intermediate in the synthesis of glycerol from propylene (p. 281).

$$CH_2{=}CHCH_2Cl \rightarrow ClCH_2\overset{|}{\underset{OH}{C}}HCH_2Cl$$

Hydration

The most widely used process for making alcohols from olefins is to absorb the olefin in sulfuric acid and then to add water to hydrolyze any alkyl hydrogen sulfates that are formed. The carbonium ion may attack water to form the alcohol directly. Propylene is much more readily absorbed than ethylene, and isobutylene is taken up with still greater ease. The strength of the sulfuric acid employed is varied according to the nature of the olefin to be hydrated. The mode of hydration of an olefin can be predicted by reference to the relative stabilities of the carbonium ions that it yields when protonated. Propylene and isobutylene yield, respectively, isopropyl alcohol and t-butyl alcohol.

$$CH_3CH{=}CH_2 \xrightarrow{\ H^+\ } CH_3\overset{+}{C}HCH_3 \longrightarrow CH_3\overset{|}{\underset{OH}{C}}HCH_3$$

$$CH_3\underset{CH_3}{\overset{|}{C}}{=}CH_2 \xrightarrow{\ H^+\ } CH_3\underset{CH_3}{\overset{|}{\underset{\ }{\overset{+}{C}}}}CH_3 \longrightarrow CH_3\underset{CH_3}{\overset{|}{C}}{\overset{OH}{\underset{|}{\ }}}CH_3$$

Ethanol is the only primary alcohol that can be made by this method.

Hydration of acetylenes occurs in the presence of mercury salts; acetylene, for example, yields acetaldehyde.

$$HC{\equiv}CH + H_2O \xrightarrow{\ Hg^{++}\ } CH_3CHO$$

1-Acetylcyclohexanol is made in this way from 1-ethynylcyclohexanol (OS **35**, 1; 67% yield).

The formation of alcohols from olefins can be accomplished indirectly to give the product corresponding to non-Markownikoff addition of the elements of water. Diborane is added to the olefin, and the resulting trialkylborane is oxidized to the alcohol. An example is the formation of 2,2-di-*t*-butylethanol from the corresponding olefin.[10]

$$
\underset{(CH_3)_3C}{\overset{(CH_3)_3C}{>}}C=CH_2 \xrightarrow{B_2H_6} \underset{(CH_3)_3C}{\overset{(CH_3)_3C}{>}}CHCH_2B \xrightarrow[(2)\ H_2O]{(1)\ H_2O_2} \underset{(CH_3)_3C}{\overset{(CH_3)_3C}{>}}CHCH_2OH
$$

The hydroboration is accomplished by treating the olefin with sodium borohydride and aluminum chloride in diglyme (dimethyl ether of diethylene glycol).

Formation of Hydroperoxides

Coordination of a carbonium ion with hydrogen peroxide is also possible; in the presence of sulfuric acid certain tertiary olefins absorb hydrogen peroxide, yielding the corresponding alkyl hydroperoxides. An example is the formation of a hydroperoxide from diisobutylene.[11]

$$
\underset{\underset{CH_3}{|}}{\overset{\overset{CH_3}{|}}{CH_3CCH_2}}\overset{\overset{CH_2}{||}}{C} \ \rightarrow \ \underset{\underset{CH_3}{|}\ \underset{CH_3}{|}}{\overset{\overset{CH_3}{|}\ \overset{CH_3}{|}}{CH_3CCH_2COOH}} \ \leftarrow \ \underset{\underset{CH_3}{|}\ \underset{CH_3}{|}}{\overset{\overset{CH_3}{|}}{CH_3CCH}=CCH_3}
$$

Presumably, the formation of 1-phenethyl hydroperoxide from the corresponding alcohol likewise proceeds by way of a carbonium ion.[12]

$$
\underset{\underset{C_6H_5CHOH}{}}{\overset{CH_3}{|}} + H_2O_2 \xrightarrow{H_2SO_4} \underset{\underset{C_6H_5CHOOH}{}}{\overset{CH_3}{|}} + H_2O
$$

This type of reaction takes place most satisfactorily, of course, with alcohols that form relatively stable carbonium ions.

Etherification

When ethylene is absorbed by sulfuric acid, the ethyl carbonium ion that is produced may coordinate with sulfuric acid to form ethyl hydrogen

[10] M. S. Newman, A. Arkell, and T. Fukunaga, *J. Am. Chem. Soc.*, **82**, 2498 (1960).
[11] J. Hoffman and C. E. Boord, *J. Am. Chem. Soc.*, **77**, 3139 (1955).
[12] A. G. Davies, R. V. Foster, and A. M. White, *J. Chem. Soc.*, 1541 (1953).

sulfate (protonated), with water to form ethanol (protonated) (p. 139), or with ethanol to form ethyl ether (protonated). Finally, it may release a proton to regenerate ethylene.

$$CH_3CH_2\overset{+}{O}H$$
$$\overset{|}{\underset{H}{}}$$

$$CH_2{=}CH_2 \rightleftharpoons CH_3CH_2{}^+ \rightleftharpoons CH_3CH_2\overset{+}{O}$$

$$\underset{\overset{|}{H}}{}$$

$$CH_3CH_2\underset{+}{\overset{H}{\overset{|}{O}}}CH_2CH_3$$

All these changes except ether formation are readily reversible; by suitable control of experimental conditions it is possible, at least in theory, to make any of the compounds mentioned from any of the others. This method of making ethers from alcohols is useful with the simpler primary alcohols in the synthesis of symmetrical ethers. Mixed ethers can be prepared also if one of the alcohols forms a relatively stable carbonium ion.

Alcohols of the allyl type form ethers readily, particularly the tri-arylcarbinols, which undergo etherification with great ease. Triphenyl-carbinyl or trityl ethers can be prepared by crystallizing the carbinol from an alcohol containing a trace of acid. The usual method for making trityl ethers is to treat the alcohol with trityl chloride in the presence of pyridine. Presumably because of steric factors, primary alcohol groups react preferentially.

Since derivatives of t-butyl alcohol are prone to undergo elimination reactions, t-butyl ethers cannot be prepared by the Williamson synthesis (p. 284); they can be made by the acid-catalyzed condensation of t-butyl alcohol or isobutylene with the corresponding alcohols. t-Butyl phenyl ether is formed by passing isobutylene into phenol at relatively low temperature in the presence of a trace of sulfuric acid.[13]

A superior method of making t-butyl ethers consists in the interaction of t-butyl esters of peracids with Grignard reagents (p. 457).

[13] D. R. Stevens, *J. Org. Chem.*, **20**, 1232 (1955).

An example of the formation of a cyclic ether by dehydration of a glycol is the preparation of 3-hydroxytetrahydrofuran by heating 1,2,4-trihydroxybutane with p-toluenesulfonic acid monohydrate (OS 38, 37; yield 88%).

$$\begin{array}{cc} CH_2 \!\!-\!\!\!-\!\!CHOH \\ | \qquad\quad | \\ CH_2OH \quad CH_2OH \end{array} \rightarrow \text{(cyclic structure)} OH + H_2O$$

2-Methyl-2,5-decanediol undergoes ring closure in the presence of phosphoric acid; the product is 5,5-dimethyl-2-n-pentyltetrahydrofuran (OS **38**, 25; yield 97%).

$$(CH_3)_2CCH_2CH_2CH(CH_2)_4CH_3 \rightarrow \begin{array}{c} CH_3 \\ \\ CH_3 \end{array} \text{(ring)} O\!-\!(CH_2)_4CH_3 + H_2O$$
$$\quad\; | \qquad\qquad\quad\; |$$
$$\;\; OH \qquad\qquad\; OH$$

By use of a mixture of sulfuric acid and mercuric sulfate hydration of an acetylenic function and etherification of a 1,4-glycol may be accomplished together. 2,5-Dimethyl-3-hexyne-2,5-diol, for example, gives 2,2,5,5-tetramethyltetrahydro-3-ketofuran (OS **40**, 88; yield 82%).

$$\begin{array}{cc} CH_3 \quad CH_3 \\ | \qquad\;\; | \\ HOCC\!\equiv\!CCOH \\ | \qquad\;\; | \\ CH_3 \quad CH_3 \end{array} \rightarrow \begin{array}{c} CH_3 \\ \\ CH_3 \end{array} \text{(ring with } O \text{ and } C\!=\!O) \begin{array}{c} CH_3 \\ \\ CH_3 \end{array}$$

Diazoalkane method

Diazoalkanes may serve as ether-forming agents in the presence of acids, which convert them into nitrogen and carbonium ions. The methylation of phenol with diazomethane, for example, may be represented as follows (Angew. **67**, 439).

$$C_6H_5OH + CH_2\!\!=\!\!\overset{+}{N}\!\!=\!\!\overset{-}{N} \rightarrow C_6H_5O^- + CH_3^+ + N_2$$
$$C_6H_5O^- + CH_3^+ \rightarrow C_6H_5OCH_3$$

Although expensive and hazardous, this method is otherwise highly advantageous and has been used frequently to prepare methyl aryl ethers. The usual procedure is to add the phenol to an ether solution of the methylating agent. The reaction is accompanied by rapid evolution of nitrogen.

Alcohols react with diazomethane only under special conditions, methylation becoming increasingly easy as the acidic character of the hydroxyl group is increased (CR **23**, 193). Oximes yield O-methyl ethers. Ethyl acetoacetate, a typical enolic substance, reacts slowly to yield ethyl β-methoxycrotonate.

Reaction with carboxylic acids is the basis for quantitative determination of diazomethane. Diazomethane is allowed to react with an excess of benzoic acid, and the excess of acid is determined by titration (OS II, 166).

$$C_6H_5CO_2H + CH_2N_2 \rightarrow C_6H_5CO_2CH_3 + N_2$$

Esters from Olefins and Acetylenes

An attractive route to esters is provided by the power of organic acids to combine with olefins. The reaction is catalyzed by acids, a boron fluoride–hydrogen fluoride catalyst being particularly effective. By its use isopropyl acetate may be produced from propylene and acetic acid in 80% yield.[14]

$$CH_3CH{=}CH_2 + CH_3CO_2H \rightarrow CH_3CO_2CH(CH_3)_2$$

In a similar way malonic acid and isobutylene condense in the presence of sulfuric acid to give di-*t*-butyl malonate (OS **34**, 26; yield 60%).

$$
\begin{array}{c}
CO_2H \\
\diagup \\
CH_2 \\
\diagdown \\
CO_2H
\end{array}
+ 2(CH_3)_2C{=}CH_2 \xrightarrow{H_2SO_4}
\begin{array}{c}
CO_2C(CH_3)_3 \\
\diagup \\
CH_2 \\
\diagdown \\
CO_2C(CH_3)_3
\end{array}
$$

Ethyl *t*-butyl malonate is made similarly (OS **37**, 34).

$$
\begin{array}{c}
CO_2C_2H_5 \\
\diagup \\
CH_2 \\
\diagdown \\
CO_2H
\end{array}
+ (CH_3)_2C{=}CH_2 \rightarrow
\begin{array}{c}
CO_2C_2H_5 \\
\diagup \\
CH_2 \\
\diagdown \\
CO_2C(CH_3)_3
\end{array}
$$

In the presence of perchloric acid cyclohexene and formic acid combine to give cyclohexyl formate in 69% yield.[15]

$$\text{cyclohexene} + HCO_2H \xrightarrow{HClO_4} \text{cyclohexyl-OCHO}$$

Suitably constituted unsaturated acids form lactones in the presence of acidic catalysts; γ- and δ-unsaturated acids yield γ-lactones.

$$RCH_2CH{=}CHCH_2CH_2CO_2H \xrightarrow{H^+}$$

$$RCH_2CHCH_2CH_2CO \xleftarrow{H^+} RCH{=}CHCH_2CH_2CH_2CO_2H$$
$$\lfloor\underline{}O\underline{}\rfloor$$

---

[14] R. D. Morin and A. E. Bearse, *Ind. Eng. Chem.*, **43**, 1596 (1951).
[15] H. B. Knight, R. E. Koos, and D. Swern, *J. Am. Chem. Soc.*, **75**, 6212 (1953).

Acetylene condenses with acetic acid in the presence of mercuric acetate to yield either vinyl acetate or the diacetate of acetaldehyde, depending on whether one or two moles of acid are used.

$$HC\equiv CH + CH_3CO_2H \xrightarrow{Hg(OCOCH_3)_2} CH_2\text{=}CHOCOCH_3$$

$$HC\equiv CH + 2CH_3CO_2H \xrightarrow{Hg(OCOCH_3)_2} CH_3CH(OCOCH_3)_2$$

The diacetate may be decomposed thermally into acetaldehyde and acetic anhydride. Vinyl acetate can be made also by condensing acetylene with acetic acid in the vapor phase.

Substituted acetylenes have been employed similarly; vinylacetylene condenses with acetic acid in the presence of boron fluoride to yield acetic anhydride and methyl vinyl ketone; presumably the diacetate is an intermediate.

$$CH_2\text{=}CHC\equiv CH \rightarrow CH_2\text{=}CH\underset{\underset{OCOCH_3}{|}}{\overset{\overset{OCOCH_3}{|}}{C}}CH_3 \quad \rightarrow$$

$$CH_2\text{=}CHCOCH_3 + (CH_3CO)_2O$$

Vinyl methacrylate is formed when methacrylic acid is condensed with acetylene.

$$CH_2\text{=}\underset{\underset{CH_3}{|}}{C}CO_2H + HC\equiv CH \xrightarrow{HgSO_4} CH_2\text{=}\underset{\underset{CH_3}{|}}{C}CO_2CH\text{=}CH_2$$

Acetylene and chloroacetic acid yield vinyl chloroacetate in a similar way (OS III, 853; 49% yield).

The reaction of acetylene with acids illustrates the behavior of acetylene with compounds containing active hydrogen. The products are vinyl compounds, and the type of reaction, vinylation, is very general.

Esterification of Inorganic Acids

Nitrous and nitric acids resemble carboxylic acids in having an oxygen atom doubly bound to the central atom of the functional group. It is not surprising that they react with alcohols to yield esters. Esters of nitrous acid are conveniently prepared by dropping a mixture of an alcohol with sulfuric acid into a flask containing sodium nitrite. The nitrous acid that is generated reacts rapidly with the alcohol. n-Butyl nitrite can be made in 85% yield by this procedure (OS II, 108).

$$C_4H_9OH + HONO \xrightarrow{H_2SO_4} C_4H_9ONO + H_2O$$

Esters of nitric acid are also prepared by the reaction of the acid with alcohols. Another method, employing a mixture of nitric and sulfuric acids, is illustrated by the preparation of methyl nitrate (OS II, 412); the yield is 80% of the theoretical amount. Nitroglycerin is made in this way also.

$$
\begin{array}{l}
\text{CH}_2\text{OH} \qquad\qquad\quad \text{CH}_2\text{ONO}_2 \\
| \qquad\qquad\qquad\qquad\quad | \\
\text{CHOH} + 3\text{HNO}_3 \rightarrow \text{CHONO}_2 + 3\text{H}_2\text{O} \\
| \qquad\qquad\qquad\qquad\quad | \\
\text{CH}_2\text{OH} \qquad\qquad\quad \text{CH}_2\text{ONO}_2
\end{array}
$$

Nitrates of olefinic alcohols are difficult to make because the double bond also reacts with nitric acid. Acetyl nitrate has been used with success.[16]

Esters of sulfuric, phosphoric, and sulfonic acids frequently are made by way of anhydrides or chlorides. A large number of esters of phosphorous and phosphoric acids are produced by alcoholysis of the appropriate chlorides. n-Butyl phosphate is readily formed by the action of n-butyl alcohol on phosphorus oxychloride in the presence of pyridine (OS II, 109; 75% yield).

$$3\text{C}_4\text{H}_9\text{OH} + \text{POCl}_3 + 3\text{C}_5\text{H}_5\text{N} \rightarrow \text{PO(OC}_4\text{H}_9)_3 + 3\text{C}_5\text{H}_5\text{N·HCl}$$

Mono esters of sulfuric acid usually are prepared by the action of sulfur trioxide, chlorosulfonic acid, or sulfuric acid on alcohols. Another method is to add an olefin to sulfuric acid (p. 140). Dimethyl sulfate is produced conveniently by slow distillation of a mixture of methanol and 60% fuming sulfuric acid, taken in the ratio 1 to 4. Under suitable conditions alkyl hydrogen sulfates unite with olefins to form dialkyl sulfates. Diethyl sulfate is prepared readily and cheaply by condensation of sulfuric acid with ethylene under pressure.

A simple and convenient procedure for making dialkyl sulfites consists in dropping thionyl chloride into the appropriate alcohol. Di-n-butyl sulfite can be produced in 83% yields by this method (OS II, 112).

$$2\text{C}_4\text{H}_9\text{OH} + \text{SOCl}_2 \rightarrow (\text{C}_4\text{H}_9)_2\text{SO}_3 + 2\text{HCl}$$

One way to make sulfates is by oxidation of the corresponding sulfites. Di-n-butyl sulfite, for example, is converted into di-n-butyl sulfate by the action of potassium permanganate in glacial acetic acid solution. The same transformation can be effected by the aid of n-butyl chlorosulfonate (OS II, 111; 83% yield).

$$(\text{C}_4\text{H}_9)_2\text{SO}_3 + \text{C}_4\text{H}_9\text{OSO}_2\text{Cl} \rightarrow (\text{C}_4\text{H}_9)_2\text{SO}_4 + \text{C}_4\text{H}_9\text{Cl} + \text{SO}_2$$

[16] M. L. Wolfrom, G. H. McFadden, and A. Chaney, *J. Org. Chem.*, **25**, 1079 (1960).

t-Butyl hypochlorite, which may be looked upon as an ester of hypochlorous acid, is made by the action of a mixture of chlorine and sodium hydroxide on *t*-butyl alcohol (OS **32,** 20).

$$(CH_3)_3COH + Cl_2 + NaOH \rightarrow (CH_3)_3COCl + NaCl + H_2O$$

Hydrohalogenation

The combination of a halide ion with a carbonium ion to give an alkyl halide is thought to be the final step in the addition of hydrogen halides to olefins by an ionic mechanism. This type of reaction has been observed with a wide variety of unsaturated compounds. As in the other reactions that have been discussed, it is held that the first step of the reaction is attack by the electron-poor atom, in this case the hydrogen ion. The evidence in connection with the addition of hydrogen chloride or bromide to certain olefins is convincing. In donor solvents such as ether or dioxane, the addition of hydrogen chloride or bromide is much slower than it is in solvents such as benzene. The tendency of ethers and dioxane to form oxonium compounds by coordination with hydrogen ions offers a satisfactory explanation of the retarding effect.

If the olefin is unsymmetrical, the Markownikoff rule is followed as illustrated by the addition of hydrogen chloride to propylene to produce isopropyl chloride.

$$CH_3CH{=}CH_2 + H^+ \longrightarrow CH_3\overset{+}{C}HCH_3 \overset{Cl^-}{\longrightarrow} CH_3\underset{Cl}{CHCH_3}$$

Vinyl chloride is manufactured by the addition of hydrogen chloride to acetylene in either the liquid or vapor phase. Addition of hydrogen chloride to olefinic compounds is catalyzed by the salts of various metals; the synthesis of ethyl chloride from ethylene, for example, is catalyzed by bismuth trichloride. The use of hydrogen iodide is illustrated by the formation of iodocyclohexane, which may be produced in 90% yield by adding cyclohexene to a solution of potassium iodide in 95% orthophosphoric acid (OS **31,** 66) and heating the mixture for 3 hours at 80°.

Addition of dry hydrogen chloride to 1-methylcyclohexene proceeds in a nearly quantitative manner in the presence of stannic chloride.

Cyclopentadiene combines with hydrogen chloride at temperatures below 0° to give 3-chlorocyclopentene (OS **32**, 41; 90% yield).

Obedience to the Markownikoff rule is not to be expected in α,β-unsaturated carbonyl compounds since protonation should occur in such a way as to place the new positive charge as far as possible from the one already present.

$$CH_2{=}CH{-}\underset{\delta+}{\overset{\overset{\displaystyle R}{|}}{C}}{=}O + H^+ \rightarrow \overset{+}{C}H_2CH_2\underset{\delta+}{\overset{\overset{\displaystyle R}{|}}{C}}{=}O \quad \left(not \quad CH_3\overset{+}{C}H\underset{\delta+}{\overset{\overset{\displaystyle R}{|}}{C}}{=}O \right)$$

Such reactions may, of course, proceed by 1,4-addition followed by isomerization of the resulting enol. The conjugate addition mechanism cannot serve, however, to explain the behavior of the vinyltrimethylammonium ion, which combines with hydrogen iodide to give the corresponding β-iodoethyl derivative. The reaction of 1,1,1-trifluoro-2-propene with hydrogen bromide is similar.[17]

$$CH_2{=}CHCF_3 + HBr \xrightarrow{\text{AlBr}_3} BrCH_2CH_2CF_3$$

Few compounds in which a carbon atom holds both a hydroxyl group and a halogen atom have been isolated (p. 395). In contrast, conjugate addition of hydrogen halides is a general reaction of α,β-unsaturated carbonyl compounds. It is to be supposed that 1,2-addition occurs readily but generally is not favored by the equilibrium.

$$RCH{=}CHC{=}O \atop \underset{R}{|} \Bigg\langle {\begin{array}{l} RCH{=}CH\overset{\overset{\displaystyle OH}{|}}{\underset{\underset{\displaystyle R}{|}}{C}}{-}X \\ \\ RCHCH_2C{=}O \atop \underset{X}{|}\ \underset{R}{|} \end{array}}$$

Since hydrogen halides are capable of combining additively with isolated olefinic bonds (p. 146), the fact that addition of a hydrogen halide to α,β-unsaturated carbonyl compounds always produces the β-halogen derivative justifies the belief that the reactions are correctly classed as conjugate addition. Methyl acrylate and hydrogen bromide, for example, give methyl β-bromopropionate (OS III, 576; 84% yield).

$$CH_2{=}CHCO_2CH_3 + HBr \rightarrow BrCH_2CH_2CO_2CH_3$$

[17] A. L. Henne and S. Kaye, *J. Am. Chem. Soc.*, **72**, 3369 (1950).

In a similar manner hydrogen chloride combines with acrolein to form β-chloropropionaldehyde (OS I, 166).

$$CH_2{=}CHCHO + HCl \rightarrow ClCH_2CH_2CHO$$

Nitroform resembles halogen acids in certain ways; it combines with α,β-unsaturated ethers to give α-trinitromethyl ethers; the reaction can be carried out in dioxane, with which nitroform unites to give a solid complex.

$$O\quad O + 2HC(NO_2)_3 \rightleftharpoons (O_2N)_3CHO\quad OHC(NO_2)_3$$

Ethyl vinyl ether produces ethyl 1-methyl-2,2,2-trinitroethyl ether in 68% yield.[18]

$$CH_2{=}CHOCH_2CH_3 + HC(NO_2)_3 \rightarrow CH_3CHOCH_2CH_3$$
$$\underset{\displaystyle C(NO_2)_3}{|}$$

Alkyl Halides from Alcohols

Alcohols react with hydrogen halides to give the corresponding alkyl halides. The formation of n-butyl bromide by treating 1-butanol with a mixture of sulfuric and hydrobromic acids is illustrative (OS I, 28; 95% yield).

$$C_4H_9OH + HBr \rightarrow C_4H_9Br + H_2O$$

Another method is to heat the alcohol with anhydrous hydrogen bromide. n-Dodecyl bromide (OS II, 246; 88% yield) and decamethylene bromide (OS III, 227; 90% yield) are formed in this way.

This type of reaction is very useful, but the rate and the yield vary considerably with the nature of the reactants. Hydrogen iodide reacts faster than hydrogen bromide, which in turn reacts faster than hydrogen chloride. In a given series tertiary alcohols react fastest and primary alcohols slowest, with secondary alcohols taking an intermediate position. Secondary and tertiary alcohols generally afford halides in lower yields because of loss to side reactions, chief of which is dehydration. The difference in reaction rates has been made the basis of the Lucas test—a test designed to distinguish primary, secondary, and tertiary alcohols.[19] The alcohols are shaken with a solution of zinc chloride in concentrated hydrochloric acid. Under these conditions a tertiary alcohol reacts at once, and the mixture becomes turbid because of the presence of the insoluble alkyl chloride. Secondary alcohols react within 5 minutes, and primary alcohols fail to give the test under the conditions specified. Exceptions are alcohols of the allyl and benzyl types.

[18] H. Shechter and H. L. Cates, Jr., *J. Org. Chem.*, **26**, 51 (1961).
[19] H. J. Lucas, *J. Am. Chem. Soc.*, **52**, 802 (1930).

Preparation of halohydrins from glycols involves replacement of only one of the hydroxyl groups and for this reason is most satisfactory with hydrogen chloride. An example is the conversion of hexamethylene glycol into hexamethylene chlorohydrin or 6-chloro-1-hexanol (OS III, 446). The reaction is conducted in such a manner that the chlorohydrin is removed as it is formed; further reaction is thus prevented. At best, however, the yield does not exceed 55%.

Phosphorus trichloride or tribromide may serve in place of the corresponding halogen acid with very satisfactory results. The use of phosphorus tribromide is illustrated by the preparation of isobutyl bromide (OS II, 358; 60% yield). This reagent serves also to prepare pentaerythrityl bromide from pentaerythritol (OS II, 476; 76% yield).

$$3C(CH_2OH)_4 + 4PBr_3 \rightarrow 3C(CH_2Br)_4 + 4H_3PO_3$$

Monobromopentaerythritol is made by treating pentaerythritol with 48% hydrobromic acid (OS **38,** 68; yield 54%).

Pinacol, a ditertiary alcohol, reacts readily with hydrogen bromide to give tetramethylethylene bromide.

Another example is found in the preparation of β-ethoxyethyl bromide from cellosolve; the yield is 66%, based on the phosphorus tribromide (OS III, 370). A mixture of phosphorus and bromine may be used also. Ethyl bromide can be made conveniently by treating ethanol with this mixture; the yield of product is 90%, based on the bromine (OS I, 36).

t-Butyl chloride is made from *t*-butyl alcohol in 88% yield by a few minutes' shaking with concentrated hydrochloric acid (OS I, 144). *n*-Butyl alcohol, on the other hand, requires heating at 150 to 165° for an hour with the same reagent (OS I, 142). Under these conditions *n*-butyl chloride is formed in 78% yield.

Glycerol reacts with hydrogen chloride to yield glycerol α-monochlorohydrin (OS I, 294; 66% yield) or glycerol α,γ-dichlorohydrin (OS I, 292; 57% yield), the primary alcohol groups being replaced in preference to the secondary. This preferential replacement occurs also with phosphorus and bromine; glycerol α,γ-dibromohydrin is produced (OS II, 308; 54% yield).

Replacement of hydroxyl groups by iodine can be effected by the action of phosphorus triiodide. An example is the conversion of cetyl alcohol into the corresponding iodide, n-hexadecyl iodide (OS II, 322; 78% yield).

$$3C_{16}H_{33}OH + PI_3 \rightarrow 3C_{16}H_{33}I + H_3PO_3$$

The reaction is effected by heating a mixture of the alcohol, phosphorus, and iodine. Methyl iodide can be produced in a similar way in yields of 95%, based on the iodine (OS II, 399).

Constant-boiling (57%) hydrogen iodide can be used to prepare iodides from the corresponding alcohols; the usual procedure is to add the alcohol to an excess of the acid and subject the mixture to slow distillation. A mixture of potassium iodide and phosphoric acid may serve the same purpose. Hexamethylene iodide is formed when hexamethylene glycol is heated with this mixture (OS 31, 31; 85% yield).

Aldehydes and ketones react with phosphorus pentachloride as though they were 1,1-dihydroxy compounds, yielding the corresponding dichlorides.

$$\begin{array}{c} R \\ \diagdown \\ C{=}O + PCl_5 \rightarrow \\ \diagup \\ R \end{array} \quad \begin{array}{c} R \\ \diagdown \\ CCl_2 + POCl_3 \\ \diagup \\ R \end{array}$$

This reaction is general but finds little application; one use is in the preparation of chlorides to be employed in the syntheses of acetylenic compounds (OR 5, 20). When acetophenone is treated with phosphorus pentachloride, the dichloride is obtained readily and loses hydrogen chloride to yield α-chlorostyrene.

Formates resemble aldehydes in their behavior with phosphorus pentachloride, the organic products being dichloromethyl alkyl ethers. The synthesis of dichloromethyl n-butyl ether from n-butyl formate is an example.[20]

$$C_4H_9OCHO + PCl_5 \rightarrow C_4H_9OCHCl_2 + POCl_3$$

A superior reagent for replacing the oxygen atom of a carbonyl group by two fluorine atoms is sulfur tetrafluoride; it converts 5-nitro-2-furaldehyde, for example, into 2-difluoromethyl-5-nitrofuran.

[20] A. Rieche, H. Gross, and E. Höft, Chem. Ber., 93, 88 (1960).

This reagent also transforms carboxyl groups to trifluoromethyl groups; 5-nitro-2-furoic acid, for example, forms 2-trifluoromethyl-5-nitrofuran.[21]

$$O_2N \overset{\text{SF}_4}{\underset{O}{\longrightarrow}} CO_2H \xrightarrow{\text{SF}_4} O_2N \underset{O}{\longrightarrow} CF_3$$

Nitriles from Olefins

Although the addition of hydrogen cyanide in the conjugate manner to unsaturated carbonyl compounds, nitriles, etc., is well known (p. 425), such reactions have been difficult to achieve with simple olefins. Hydrocyanation occurs, however, in the presence of cobalt octacarbonyl at 130° in sealed vessels. Under these conditions propylene, for example, is converted into isobutyronitrile to the extent of 75%.[22]

$$CH_3CH{=}CH_2 + HCN \rightarrow \overset{CH_3}{\underset{CH_3}{\diagdown}}CHCN$$

Since the addition occurs in the Markownikoff sense, it is formally like other electrophilic additions; the mechanism is obscure, however.

Hydrolysis of Imino Compounds

Imino compounds readily undergo hydrolysis to give the corresponding carbonyl compounds. This type of reaction is encountered in the preparation of carbonyl compounds from nitriles and Grignard reagents, in the Hoesch synthesis, and in other transformations in which imino derivatives occur as intermediates.

Nef Reaction

Primary and secondary nitro compounds are capable of undergoing numerous reactions characteristic of active methylene compounds. When treated with alkalis, they form salts, which resemble Schiff bases and oximes in having a nitrogen atom doubly bonded to a carbon atom and undergo hydrolysis in a similar manner. When the salts are added to strong sulfuric acid, aldehydes or ketones are formed; nitroethane yields acetaldehyde.

$$2CH_3CH{=}NO_2Na + 2H_2SO_4 \rightarrow 2CH_3CHO + N_2O + 2NaHSO_4 + H_2O$$

[21] W. R. Sherman, M. Freifelder, and G. R. Stone, *J. Org. Chem.*, **25**, 2048 (1960).
[22] P. Arthur, Jr., D. C. England, B. C. Pratt, and G. M. Whitman, *J. Am. Chem. Soc.*, **76**, 5364 (1954).

In a similar way, acetone can be made from 2-nitropropane.

$$2 \overset{\displaystyle CH_3}{\underset{\displaystyle CH_3}{\diagdown\!\!\diagup}}C\!\!=\!\!NO_2Na + 2H_2SO_4 \rightarrow$$

$$2CH_3COCH_3 + N_2O + 2NaHSO_4 + H_2O$$

This reaction, known as the Nef reaction (CR **55**, 137), is fairly general for primary and secondary nitro compounds. The rate-controlling step seems to be attack of the solvent on the conjugate acid formed by protonation of the *aci*-nitro compound.[23]

$$2HON \rightarrow HON\!\!=\!\!NOH \rightarrow H_2O + N_2O$$

This type of change has served also in the synthesis of certain cyclohexanone derivatives. 4-Nitro-5-phenylcyclohexene, obtained by condensing butadiene with β-nitrostyrene (p. 685), gives 6-phenyl-3-cyclohexen-1-one in 78% yield.[24]

Primary nitroparaffins undergo hydrolysis when heated with strong mineral acids to give hydroxylamine and an organic acid; it seems probable that the corresponding hydroxamic acids are formed as intermediates. 1-Nitropropane with sulfuric acid yields hydroxylamine sulfate and propionic acid, for example.

$$CH_3CH_2CH_2NO_2 + H_2O + H_2SO_4 \rightarrow CH_3CH_2CO_2H + H_2NOH\cdot H_2SO_4$$

[23] M. F. Hawthorne, *J. Am. Chem. Soc.*, **79**, 2510 (1957).
[24] W. C. Wildman and R. B. Wildman, *J. Org. Chem.*, **17**, 581 (1952).

Cationic Polymerization

Attack of a carbonium ion on an olefin produces a new carbonium ion that, in turn, can attack a molecule of olefin. The process is capable of proceeding indefinitely, i.e., is one of polymerization (QR **8**, 88). In the presence of sulfuric acid, isobutylene gives low-molecular-weight products at temperatures that favor release of protons from the carbonium ions. In practice it is found that the reaction can be halted at an early stage; the formation of the diisobutylenes in an example. Commercial diisobutylene consists of about 85% of 2,4,4-trimethyl-1-pentene and 15% of 2,4,4-trimethyl-2-pentene. The reaction product also contains triisobutylenes as well as compounds of still higher molecular weight.

$$(CH_3)_3C^+ + CH_2{=}CCH_3 \longrightarrow (CH_3)_3CCH_2\overset{+}{C}CH_3 \xrightarrow{\ -H^+\ }$$
$$\underset{CH_3}{|} \qquad\qquad \underset{CH_3}{|}$$

$$\underset{\underset{CH_3}{|}}{\overset{\overset{CH_3}{|}}{CH_3C}}{-}CH{=}\underset{\underset{CH_3}{|}}{CCH_3} \quad \text{and} \quad \underset{\underset{CH_3}{|}}{\overset{\overset{CH_3}{|}}{CH_3C}}{-}CH_2\underset{\underset{CH_3}{|}}{C}{=}CH_2$$

At lower temperatures the formation of high-molecular-weight polymers occurs. Isobutylene at $-100°$, for example, gives such a polymer in a fraction of a second. Monomers that are polymerized best by such cationic initiation are those that form relatively stable carbonium ions and include isobutylene, styrene, α-methylstyrene, vinyl alkyl ethers, and 1,3-butadienes. The initiators are Lewis acids such as boron trifluoride and aluminum chloride; they require a cocatalyst to supply hydrogen, and the real catalyst is believed to be the proton. The mechanism, illustrated by isobutylene, may be formulated as follows.

$$BF_3 + H_2O \rightarrow H^+ + BF_3OH^-$$

1. Initiation

$$CH_2{=}\underset{\underset{CH_3}{|}}{C}{-}CH_3 + H^+ \rightarrow CH_3{-}\underset{\underset{CH_3}{|}}{\overset{\overset{CH_3}{|}}{C^+}}$$

2. Propagation

$$CH_3{-}\underset{\underset{CH_3}{|}}{\overset{\overset{CH_3}{|}}{C^+}} + CH_2{=}\underset{\underset{CH_3}{|}}{C}{-}CH_3 \rightarrow CH_3{-}\underset{\underset{CH_3}{|}}{\overset{\overset{CH_3}{|}}{C}}{-}CH_2{-}\underset{\underset{CH_3}{|}}{\overset{\overset{CH_3}{|}}{C^+}}$$

3. Termination

$$CH_3-\underset{\underset{CH_3}{|}}{\overset{\overset{CH_3}{|}}{C}}\left[-CH_2\underset{\underset{CH_3}{|}}{\overset{\overset{CH_3}{|}}{C}}-\right]_{n-1}-CH_2\underset{\underset{CH_3}{|}}{\overset{\overset{CH_3}{|}}{C}}{}^+ \rightarrow$$

$$CH_3-\underset{\underset{CH_3}{|}}{\overset{\overset{CH_3}{|}}{C}}\left[-CH_2-\underset{\underset{CH_3}{|}}{\overset{\overset{CH_3}{|}}{C}}-\right]_{n-1}-CH_2C=CH_2 + H^+$$
$$\underset{CH_3}{|}$$

Alternatively the β-olefin may form.

Acetylene undergoes self-condensation to yield a variety of products. Spongy copper catalyzes a polymerization reaction leading to a highly complex material known as cuprene. In the presence of cuprous chloride and ammonium chloride, acetylene condenses to vinylacetylene and divinylacetylene.

$$HC{\equiv}CH + HC{\equiv}CH \longrightarrow CH_2{=}CHC{\equiv}CH \xrightarrow{C_2H_2}$$
$$CH_2{=}CHC{\equiv}CCH{=}CH_2$$

Condensation of acetylene with itself gives benzene in high yields and other aromatic hydrocarbons in lesser amounts. Acetylene, diluted with an equal amount of carbon dioxide, is heated at about 600°, preferably in the presence of vanadium pentoxide as catalyst. Use of a diluent is equivalent to employing reduced pressure and diminishes the number of intermolecular collisions, thus favoring cyclization. The condensate obtained in this way contains benzene (66%), toluene (8%), xylenes (2%), and styrene (7%). With a catalyst composed of nickel carbonyl and triphenylphosphine ($Ni[CO]_2 \cdot [(C_6H_5)_3P]_2$) not only acetylene but also substituted acetylenes give aromatic compounds in high yields.

When a nickel cyanide catalyst is employed in tetrahydrofuran, cyclo-öctatetraene is formed. The chemistry of eight-membered ring compounds has received much attention, several methods of making cycloöctatetraene having been developed.[25]

Disubstituted acetylenes can be trimerized to the corresponding hexa-substituted benzene derivatives by the use of the catalytic system tri-isobutylaluminum-titanium tetrachloride; 2-butyne, for example, gives hexamethylbenzene.[26]

$$3CH_3C{\equiv}CCH_3 \rightarrow$$

[25] A. C. Cope, *Record of Chem. Progress*, **11**, 115 (1950).

[26] B. Franzus, P. J. Canterino, and R. A. Wickliffe, *J. Am. Chem. Soc.*, **81**, 1514 (1959).

When sodium borohydride and then cobalt nitrate are added to a solution of acetylene in ethanol, a black solid is formed that contains long sequences of conjugated double bonds in the *trans*-arrangement.[27] Catalysts are also known that produce the polymer in the *cis*-arrangement.[28]

Reaction of Alkyl Halides with Olefins

The reaction of alkyl halides with aromatic nuclei has a parallel in the behavior of olefins; chloroform and carbon tetrachloride, for example, can be condensed with chloroölefins in the presence of aluminum chloride. The primary difference in the two series is that the tendency toward aromatization, so pronounced in the dihydroaromatic series, is absent in the aliphatic analogs. The reaction, discovered by Prins, has been extended to simple halides. When ethylene is condensed with *t*-butyl chloride, for example, 1-chloro-3,3-dimethylbutane is formed in 65% yield.[29]

$$CH_2{=}CH_2 + (CH_3)_3CCl \xrightarrow{AlCl_3} (CH_3)_3CCH_2CH_2Cl$$

It is possible to formulate this type of reaction in a manner similar to that postulated for the addition of paraffins to olefins (p. 179). In the example cited the first step would be production of a *t*-butyl carbonium ion.

$$(CH_3)_3CCl + AlCl_3 \rightarrow (CH_3)_3C^+ + AlCl_4^-$$

Combination of the carbonium ion with ethylene would yield a new carbonium ion, which, in turn, would remove a chloride ion from *t*-butyl chloride.

$$(CH_3)_3C^+ + CH_2{=}CH_2 \rightarrow (CH_3)_3CCH_2CH_2^+$$

$$(CH_3)_3CCH_2CH_2^+ + (CH_3)_3CCl \rightarrow (CH_3)_3CCH_2CH_2Cl + (CH_3)_3C^+$$

Especially interesting is the condensation of *t*-butyl chloride with vinyl chloride in the presence of ferric chloride; 1,1-dichloro-3,3-dimethylbutane is obtained in 77% yield.

$$(CH_3)_3CCl + CH_2{=}CHCl \xrightarrow{FeCl_3} (CH_3)_3CCH_2CHCl_2$$

Apparently the carbonium ion, $(CH_3)_3CCH_2\overset{+}{C}HCl$, is more stable than the isomeric ion $(CH_3)_3CCHCH_2^+$. The chlorine atom attached to the carbon
|
Cl
atom carrying the positive charge can assume part of the electron-deficit, as the following resonance structures show.

$$(CH_3)_3CCH_2\overset{+}{C}HCl \leftrightarrow (CH_3)_3CCH_2CH{=}\overset{+}{C}l$$

[27] L. B. Luttinger, *Chem. and Ind.*, 1135 (1960).
[28] M. L. H. Green, M. Nehmé, and G. Wilkinson, *Chem. and Ind.*, 1136 (1960).
[29] F. C. Whitmore, H. E. Whitmore, and N. C. Cook, *J. Am. Chem. Soc.*, **72**, 51 (1950).

Another example is the condensation of chloroform with tetrachloro-ethylene to give *unsym*-heptachloropropane (OS II, 312; 93% yield).

$$CHCl_3 + Cl_2C{=}CCl_2 \xrightarrow{AlCl_3} CCl_3CCl_2CHCl_2$$

A reaction that presents an analogy to this type occurs when acetals and vinyl ethers are brought together in the presence of boron trifluoride etherate. An example is the addition of dimethyl acetal to methyl vinyl ether; the yield of 1,1,3-trimethoxybutane is 79%.[30]

$$CH_3CH(OCH_3)_2 + CH_2{=}CHOCH_3 \xrightarrow{BF_3} CH_3\underset{\underset{OCH_3}{|}}{C}HCH_2CH(OCH_3)_2$$

Ritter Reaction

As was noted earlier (p. 83), combination of a carbonium ion with a nitrile in the presence of water gives an amide. The production of N-*t*-butylacetamide from acetonitrile and isobutylene is an example.

$$CH_3\overset{+}{\underset{\underset{CH_3}{|}}{C}}CH_3 + CH_3CN \longrightarrow (CH_3)_3CN{=}\overset{+}{C}CH_3 \xrightarrow{H_2O} (CH_3)_3CNH\overset{\overset{O}{||}}{C}CH_3$$

The formation of amides in this way is known as the *Ritter reaction*; one valuable feature of the process is that hydrolysis of the products yields *t*-carbinamines, most of which are otherwise difficult to obtain. When the nitrile is replaced by hydrogen cyanide, the products are alkyl formamides, which are hydrolyzed readily to amines. The synthesis of *t*-butylamine is an example.

$$HCN + (CH_3)_3COH \xrightarrow{H_2SO_4} H\overset{\overset{O}{||}}{C}NHC(CH_3)_3 \xrightarrow{H_2O} HCO_2H + (CH_3)_3CNH_2$$

The reaction ordinarily is restricted to olefins and alcohols that can form secondary or tertiary carbonium ions. Alcohols of the benzyl type, which likewise form relatively stable carbonium ions, may serve also; aceto-nitrile and benzyl alcohol, for example, give N-benzylacetamide.[31]

$$CH_3CN + C_6H_5CH_2{}^+ \rightarrow CH_3\overset{+}{C}{=}NCH_2C_6H_5 \xrightarrow{H_2O} CH_3CONHCH_2C_6H_5$$

[30] R. I. Hoaglin and D. H. Hirsh, *J. Am. Chem. Soc.*, **71**, 3468 (1949).
[31] C. L. Parris and R. M. Christenson, *J. Org. Chem.*, **25**, 331 (1960).

The procedure has been applied successfully to dinitriles also; fumaro-nitrile, for example, gives N,N'-diisopropylfumaramide when treated with concentrated sulfuric acid and isopropyl alcohol.[32]

$$\begin{array}{c} CHCN \\ \parallel \\ NCCH \end{array} \xrightarrow[H_2SO_4]{(CH_3)_2CHOH} \begin{array}{c} CHCONHCH(CH_3)_2 \\ \parallel \\ (CH_3)_2CHNHCOCH \end{array}$$

A related type of reaction occurs when nitriles and aldehydes are brought together in concentrated sulfuric acid; the products, methylene-*bis*-amides, are obtained in yields of 90%. The condensation of benzo-nitrile and formaldehyde is an example.

$$2C_6H_5CN + CH_2O + H_2O \xrightarrow{H_2SO_4} C_6H_5CONHCH_2NHCOC_6H_5$$

Applied to dinitriles, this method yields polyamides; an example is the condensation of adiponitrile with formaldehyde.[33]

$$nNC(CH_2)_4CN + nCH_2O + nH_2O \xrightarrow{H_2SO_4} \overset{\displaystyle O \qquad \ \ O}{-[NH\overset{\parallel}{C}(CH_2)_4\overset{\parallel}{C}NHCH_2]_n^-}$$

The conversion of nitriles to perhydro-*s*-triazines is similar (OS **30**, 51); the yields are best when carbon tetrachloride is the solvent. An example is the preparation of 1,3,5-triacrylylperhydro-*s*-triazine from acrylonitrile.[34]

$$3CH_2{=}CHCN + (CH_2O)_3 \xrightarrow{H_2SO_4} \begin{array}{c} CH_2 \\ \diagup \ \diagdown \\ CH_2{=}CHCON \qquad NCOCH{=}CH_2 \\ | \qquad\quad | \\ CH_2 \quad CH_2 \\ \diagdown \ \diagup \\ NCOCH{=}CH_2 \end{array}$$

Prins Reaction

The Prins reaction (CR **51**, 505) takes place when certain ethylenic com-pounds are treated with aldehydes in the presence of an acidic catalyst. Styrene, for example, combines with formaldehyde in the presence of sulfuric acid to yield a glycol, 1-phenyl-1,3-propanediol.

$$C_6H_5CH{=}CH_2 + CH_2O + H_2O \rightarrow \begin{array}{c} C_6H_5CHCH_2CH_2OH \\ | \\ OH \end{array}$$

[32] F. R. Benson and J. J. Ritter, *J. Am. Chem. Soc.*, **71**, 4128 (1949).

[33] E. E. Magat, L. B. Chandler, B. F. Faris, J. E. Reith, and L. F. Salisbury, *J. Am. Chem. Soc.*, **73**, 1031 (1951).

[34] W. D. Emmons, H. A. Rolewicz, W. N. Cannon, and R. M. Ross, *J. Am. Chem. Soc.*, **74**, 5524 (1953).

The mechanism proposed for the Prins reaction involves protonation of formaldehyde followed by attachment of the hydroxymethyl carbonium ion to the double bond and finally solvolysis of the resulting cation.[35]

$$CH_2O + H^+ \rightarrow \overset{+}{C}H_2{-}OH \leftrightarrow CH_2{=}\overset{+}{O}H \xrightarrow{C_6H_5CH=CH_2}$$

$$C_6H_5\overset{+}{C}HCH_2CH_2OH + H_2O \rightarrow C_6H_5\underset{\underset{OH}{|}}{C}HCH_2CH_2OH + H^+$$

Alternatively the carbonium ion may lose a proton to give the unsaturated alcohol. Under appropriate conditions the carbonium ion may also combine with formaldehyde to produce 4-phenyl-m-dioxane (OS **33**, 72; 88% yield). When the formal is reduced with sodium and butyl alcohol, 3-phenyl-1-propanol is produced in 83% yield (OS **33**, 76).

$$C_6H_5\underset{\underset{\diagdown\,\diagup}{\underset{CH_2}{O \qquad O}}}{C}HCH_2CH_2 \xrightarrow[C_4H_9OH]{Na} C_6H_5CH_2CH_2CH_2OH$$

Other styrene derivatives may be converted by this procedure into the corresponding 3-phenyl-1-propanols. Anethole gives 3-(4-methoxyphenyl)-2-methyl-1-propanol in about 80% yield.[36]

Condensation Reactions of Active Methylene Compounds

Condensation reactions of active methylene compounds, when effected with acidic catalysts, have been formulated as attack of a carbonium ion on an olefin, i.e., on an enol. The condensation of acetone with itself would occur as follows (Hine, 257).

$$(CH_3)_2\overset{\underset{OH}{|}}{C}{}^+ + CH_2{=}\overset{\underset{OH}{|}}{C}CH_3 \rightarrow (CH_3)_2\overset{\underset{OH}{|}}{C}CH_2\overset{\overset{+}{O}H}{\overset{||}{C}}CH_3 \xrightarrow{-H^+} (CH_3)_2\overset{\underset{OH}{|}}{C}CH_2\overset{O}{\overset{||}{C}}CH_3$$

[35] V. Franzen and H. Krauch, *Chem. Ztg.*, **79**, 335 (1955).
[36] E. A. Brucker and M. G. J. Beets, *Rec. trav. chim.*, **70**, 29 (1951).

The product actually obtained is mesityl oxide, which is not surprising since diacetone alcohol is readily dehydrated.

$$\underset{\substack{| \\ OH}}{(CH_3)_2C}\underset{}{CH_2}\underset{\substack{|| \\ O}}{C}CH_3 \xrightarrow{-H_2O} (CH_3)_2C{=}CHCOCH_3$$

Acetylation of acetone by acetic anhydride in the presence of boron fluoride may be formulated in a similar way (OS III, 16); acetylacetone is produced in 84% yield.

$$CH_3COCH_3 + (CH_3CO)_2O \xrightarrow{BF_3} CH_3COCH_2COCH_3 + CH_3CO_2H$$

Benzoylacetone has been obtained similarly by acetylation of acetophenone.

$$C_6H_5COCH_3 + (CH_3CO)_2O \xrightarrow{BF_3} CH_3COCH_2COC_6H_5 + CH_3CO_2H$$

When saturated with dry hydrogen chloride and allowed to stand, acetone condenses with itself to yield mesityl oxide, which in turn reacts with acetone to produce phorone.

$$\underset{\substack{\diagdown \\ CH_3}}{\overset{\substack{CH_3 \\ \diagup}}{}}C{=}O + CH_3COCH{=}C(CH_3)_2 \xrightarrow{HCl}$$

$$(CH_3)_2C{=}CHCOCH{=}C(CH_3)_2 + H_2O$$

Another reaction of this type is the condensation of formaldehyde with acetone, which can be carried out satisfactorily with sulfuric acid as the catalyst. Dehydration of the product yields methyl vinyl ketone.

$$CH_3COCH_3 + CH_2O \rightarrow CH_3COCH_2CH_2OH \rightarrow$$

$$CH_3COCH{=}CH_2 + H_2O$$

When diethyl malonate is heated at 95° for 30 hours with acetaldehyde in the presence of acetic anhydride, diethyl ethylidenemalonate is produced (OS **32**, 54).

$$CH_3CHO + CH_2(CO_2C_2H_5)_2 \xrightarrow[95°]{(CH_3CO)_2O} CH_3CH{=}C(CO_2C_2H_5)_2 + H_2O$$

Methyl ethyl ketone is of exceptional interest because it can undergo condensations involving either the methyl or the methylene group. When the catalyst is hydrogen chloride the methylene group is attacked chiefly, whereas sodium ethoxide leads to condensation primarily affecting the methyl group. The condensation with benzaldehyde illustrates this difference.

$$C_6H_5CH=CHCOCH_2CH_3 + H_2O$$

alkali

$$CH_3COCH_2CH_3 + C_6H_5CHO$$

acid

$$CH_3COCCH_3 + H_2O$$
$$\underset{\displaystyle CHC_6H_5}{\|}$$

In alkali both aldols are formed reversibly and both yield the straight-chain unsaturated ketone, the rate-controlling step being the dehydration. With an acid catalyst the hydroxy ketones are rapidly dehydrated, and the rate is controlled by the irreversible addition step.[37]

Coupling of Enols with Diazonium Compounds

Aromatic diazonium compounds react with the enol forms of β-diketones and β-ketonic esters to produce hydrazones. The O-azo compounds, which are formed initially, appear to rearrange to C-azo compounds, which in turn undergo isomerization to hydrazones (OR **10**, 1). An example is the reaction of ethyl acetoacetate with benzenediazonium chloride.

$$\underset{\displaystyle CH_3C=CHCO_2C_2H_5}{\overset{\displaystyle ON=NC_6H_5}{|}} \rightarrow \underset{\displaystyle \underset{N=NC_6H_5}{|}}{\overset{\displaystyle O}{\underset{\displaystyle \|}{}} CH_3CCHCO_2C_2H_5} \rightarrow \underset{\displaystyle NNHC_6H_5}{\overset{\displaystyle \|}{} CH_3COCCO_2C_2H_5}$$

If the azo group is attached to a tertiary carbon atom, one of the acyl groups is removed by cleavage to make hydrazone formation possible. This type of coupling, known as the Japp-Klingemann reaction (OR **10**, 143), is illustrated by the formation of the phenylhydrazone of ethyl pyruvate from ethyl methylacetoacetate.

$$\underset{\displaystyle \underset{N=NC_6H_5}{|}}{\overset{\displaystyle CH_3}{|}} CH_3COCCO_2C_2H_5 \rightarrow \underset{\displaystyle NNHC_6H_5}{\overset{\displaystyle \|}{} CH_3CCO_2C_2H_5}$$

[37] M. Stiles, D. Wolf, and G. V. Hudson, *J. Am. Chem. Soc.*, **81**, 628 (1959).

If the sodium salt is employed, the carboxyl group is lost in preference to the acetyl group, the product being the phenylhydrazone of biacetyl.

Cleavage of Ethers

The ethers may suffer fission of the carbon-oxygen bond; as would be expected, this linkage is not readily attacked by basic reagents but is sensitive to acids. The most common reagent for effecting cleavage is concentrated hydriodic acid. This is the reagent that is employed in the Zeisel method of determining alkoxyl groups.

Constant-boiling hydrobromic acid (48%) (OS I, 26) is a superior reagent for ether cleavage. It serves, for example, to make catechol from guaiacol (OS I, 150; 87% yield).

$$\text{(ring)}\begin{matrix}OH\\OCH_3\end{matrix} + HBr \rightarrow \text{(ring)}\begin{matrix}OH\\OH\end{matrix} + CH_3Br$$

A mixture of 48% hydrobromic acid and acetic acid is widely used in cleavage experiments in which hydriodic acid brings about undesirable side reactions.

The idea that oxonium compounds are formed as intermediates is supported by the fact that strong mineral acids are effective cleavage agents. Also, it is in accord with the observation that zinc and aluminum halides are likewise effective.

A mixture of 95% orthophosphoric acid and potassium or sodium iodide furnishes hydrogen iodide and brings about cleavage of ethers to produce the corresponding iodides. Tetrahydrofuran, for example, gives tetramethylene iodide (OS **30**, 33; 96% yield).

$$\text{(ring)} + 2KI + 2H_3PO_4 \rightarrow I(CH_2)_4I + H_2O + 2KH_2PO_4$$

When benzoyl chloride, tetrahydrofuran, and zinc chloride are heated together, the ether ring is opened and 4-chlorobutyl benzoate is formed (OS III, 187). The yield of chloro ester, based on the benzoyl chloride, is 83%.

$$\begin{matrix}CH_2{-}CH_2\\ | \qquad | \\ CH_2 \quad CH_2 \\ \diagdown \quad \diagup \\ O\end{matrix} + C_6H_5COCl \xrightarrow{ZnCl_2} C_6H_5CO_2CH_2CH_2CH_2CH_2Cl$$

Tetrahydrofurfuryl alcohol yields a triacetate (OS III, 833).

$$\begin{matrix} CH_2\!\!-\!\!CH_2 \\ | \qquad | \\ CH_2 \quad CHCH_2OH \\ \diagdown \;\; \diagup \\ O \end{matrix} \;\; + 2(CH_3CO)_2O \;\xrightarrow{ZnCl_2}\;$$

$$\begin{matrix} CH_2\!\!-\!\!CH_2 \\ | \qquad | \\ CH_2 \quad CHOCOCH_3 \\ | \qquad | \\ CH_3CO_2 \quad CH_2OCOCH_3 \end{matrix} \;\; + CH_3CO_2H$$

Hydrogen chloride alone transforms tetrahydrofuran into tetramethylene chlorohydrin (OS II, 571; 57% yield). Tetrahydropyran is cleaved by a mixture of 48% hydrobromic acid and concentrated sulfuric acid, the product being pentamethylene bromide (OS III, 692; 82% yield).

Under suitable conditions tetrahydrofuran is cleaved by phosphorus oxychloride to give 4-chlorobutyl ether (OS **30**, 27; 54% yield).

$$\boxed{}_{O} \;\xrightarrow[H_2SO_4]{POCl_3}\; Cl(CH_2)_4O(CH_2)_4Cl$$

The disulfonic acid obtained from 4-chlorobutyl ether is cleaved by heating with hydrochloric acid to yield 4-hydroxy-1-butanesulfonic acid sultone (OS **37**, 55).

$$O\begin{matrix}\diagup CH_2CH_2CH_2CH_2SO_3H \\ \\ \diagdown CH_2CH_2CH_2CH_2SO_3H \end{matrix} \;\;\rightarrow\; 2CH_2\begin{matrix}\diagup CH_2CH_2 \diagdown \\ \qquad\qquad SO_2 \\ \diagdown CH_2\!\!-\!\!O \diagup \end{matrix}$$

Vinyl ethers are readily hydrolyzed by acids. 3-Ethoxy-2-cyclohexenol, made by reducing 3-ethoxy-2-cyclohexenone, undergoes hydrolysis in cold 10% sulfuric acid. Ketonization of the enol gives 3-hydroxycyclohexanone, which is dehydrated under the experimental conditions employed; the final product is 2-cyclohexenone (OS **40**, 14).

Opening of the furan ring is analogous; the product is a dicarbonyl compound. Subsequent changes often occur, however. The Marckwald synthesis of diethyl γ-oxopimelate from furylacrylic acid is an example (OS **33**, 25; yield 83%).

Acetals and ketals have two ether linkages attached to the same carbon atom and are much more reactive than simple ethers. In the presence of acidic catalysts they are hydrolyzed readily to the corresponding carbonyl compounds. Aldehydes may be "protected" by transforming them to acetals, which unlike aldehydes are stable in alkaline media.

3,4-Dihydro-1,2-pyrans, readily made by the combination of α,β-unsaturated aldehydes with vinyl ethers (p. 693) undergo hydrolysis to yield the corresponding glutaraldehydes. Glutaraldehyde itself may be prepared from acrolein.

β-Methylglutaraldehyde is made in a similar way from crotonaldehyde.

Certain acetals, notably the dioxolanes, are difficult to cleave even with acidic reagents. s-Trioxane, a cyclic trimer of formaldehyde, is remarkably stable to heat and is hydrolyzed very slowly by boiling, dilute mineral acids.

Ortho esters, as would be expected, are still more sensitive than acetals to acidic reagents, being readily hydrolyzed to carboxylic acids. The interaction of orthoformic ester and carbonyl compounds to produce ketals (p. 399) is another indication of their reactivity. Also, they are attacked readily by Grignard reagents (p. 451), whereas acetals and ethers are generally resistant to this type of reagent.

When certain ethers are treated with alcohols in the presence of p-toluenesulfonic acid, transetherification may occur. Benzohydryl ether reacts with benzyl alcohol to form benzohydryl benzyl ether and benzohydrol.[38]

$$(C_6H_5)_2CHOCH(C_6H_5)_2 + C_6H_5CH_2OH \rightarrow$$
$$(C_6H_5)_2CHOCH_2C_6H_5 + (C_6H_5)_2CHOH$$

[38] E. F. Pratt and J. D. Draper, *J. Am. Chem. Soc.*, **71**, 2846 (1949).

Transetherification occurs readily and reversibly when ortho esters are heated with alcohols. A method of preparing the higher ortho esters from ethyl orthoformate depends on this type of change; an example is the synthesis of *sec*-butyl orthoformate. The ethanol is removed by distillation; the yield is 88%.[39]

$$HC(OC_2H_5)_3 + 3C_4H_9OH \rightarrow HC(OC_4H_9)_3 + 3C_2H_5OH$$

Isopropyl orthoformate can be made in 75% yield by treating methyl orthoformate with isopropyl alcohol in the presence of a little concentrated sulfuric acid.[40]

Displacement of one alkoxyl group by cyano occurs when orthoesters are treated with hydrogen cyanide in the presence of an acid catalyst. Thus ethyl orthoformate and hydrogen cyanide react in the presence of zinc chloride to produce diethoxyacetonitrile.[41]

$$CH(OC_2H_5)_3 + HCN \rightarrow (C_2H_5O)_2CHCN + C_2H_5OH$$

Ethylene oxide

Ethylene oxide is a particularly interesting type of ether because of the size of the ring and the attendant strain. As would be expected, this compound undergoes hydrolysis readily, yielding ethylene glycol. With alcohols, it gives hydroxyethyl derivatives; cellosolve is formed from ethyl alcohol.

$$CH_3CH_2OH + \overset{O}{\overset{/\,\backslash}{CH_2-CH_2}} \rightarrow CH_3CH_2OCH_2CH_2OH$$

Diethylene glycol is produced by condensing ethylene glycol with ethylene oxide.

$$HOCH_2CH_2OH + \overset{O}{\overset{/\,\backslash}{CH_2-CH_2}} \rightarrow HOCH_2CH_2OCH_2CH_2OH$$

Ammonia reacts with ethylene oxide to yield ethanolamine, diethanolamine, and triethanolamine.

$$\overset{O}{\overset{/\,\backslash}{CH_2-CH_2}} \xrightarrow{NH_3} HOCH_2CH_2NH_2 \xrightarrow{\overset{O}{\overset{/\,\backslash}{CH_2CH_2}}}$$

$$(HOCH_2CH_2)_2NH \xrightarrow{\overset{O}{\overset{/\,\backslash}{CH_2CH_2}}} (HOCH_2CH_2)_3N$$

[39] E. R. Alexander and H. M. Busch, *J. Am. Chem. Soc.*, **74**, 554 (1952).

[40] R. M. Roberts, T. D. Higgins, Jr., and P. R. Noyes, *J. Am. Chem. Soc.*, **77**, 3801 (1955).

[41] J. G. Erickson, *J. Am. Chem. Soc.*, **73**, 1338 (1951).

β-Diethylaminoethyl alcohol is made by condensing ethylene oxide with diethylamine in methanol at 40 to 60°.

$$\begin{array}{c} C_2H_5 \\ \diagdown \\ NH + CH_2{-}CH_2 \rightarrow \\ \diagup \\ C_2H_5 \end{array} \overset{O}{\diagup\diagdown} \begin{array}{c} C_2H_5 \\ \diagdown \\ NCH_2CH_2OH \\ \diagup \\ C_2H_5 \end{array}$$

Thiodiglycol is formed by the condensation of ethylene oxide with hydrogen sulfide, β-hydroxyethylmercaptan being an intermediate.

$$CH_2\overset{O}{{-}}CH_2 + H_2S \rightarrow HOCH_2CH_2SH + CH_2\overset{O}{{-}}CH_2 \rightarrow$$
$$HOCH_2CH_2SCH_2CH_2OH$$

Hydrogen halides also open the ethylene oxide ring. When ethylene oxide is passed into a 46% hydrobromic acid solution in the cold, ethylene bromohydrin is produced in 92% yield (OS I, 117).

Many of these reactions can be employed with other epoxy compounds. The conversion of cyclohexene oxide into the corresponding sulfide by the action of potassium thiocyanate illustrates another reaction of epoxy compounds (OS **32**, 39; yield 73%).

Ethyleneimine undergoes ring opening with water, hydrogen sulfide, and similar reagents.

$$CH_2\overset{NH}{{-}\!\!-\!\!-}CH_2 + H_2O \rightarrow HOCH_2CH_2NH_2$$

$$CH_2\overset{NH}{{-}\!\!-\!\!-}CH_2 + H_2S \rightarrow HSCH_2CH_2NH_2$$

γ-Lactones are converted by hydrochloric or hydrobromic acid into the corresponding γ-halo acids. γ-Bromobutyric acid, for example, can be made by treating γ-butyrolactone with hydrobromic acid. In a similar way 5-chloro-2-pentanone is formed when α-acetyl-γ-butyrolactone is heated with concentrated hydrochloric acid (OS **31**, 74; 90% yield), ring opening being accompanied by decarboxylation.

$$\begin{array}{c} CH_3COCH{-}CO \\ | \qquad\qquad \diagdown \\ | \qquad\qquad\quad O + HCl \rightarrow CH_3COCH_2CH_2CH_2Cl + CO_2 \\ | \qquad\quad \diagup \\ CH_2CH_2 \end{array}$$

Dibutyrolactone reacts with hydrochloric acid to give 1,7-dichloro-4-heptanone (OS **38,** 19).

$$CH_2-C\!\!=\!\!=\!\!C-CO$$

$$\begin{array}{ccc} | & \diagdown O & | & \diagdown O + 2HCl \rightarrow \\ CH_2-CH_2 & CH_2-CH_2 & \end{array}$$

$$ClCH_2CH_2CH_2COCH_2CH_2CH_2Cl + CO_2$$

Cleavage of Amines

The Zeisel method for determining alkoxyl groups (p. 161) can serve also to estimate methylamino groups, but the conditions necessary for cleavage of the amines are more drastic than those employed with ethers. To determine N-methyl groups, for example, it is necessary to heat amines with hydrogen iodide at 200 to 300°.

Cyanogen bromide undergoes nucleophilic displacement of the halogen atom by tertiary amines, presumably to form unstable quaternary ammonium compounds, which then break down to give disubstituted cyanamides. The over-all change, the replacement of an alkyl group by cyano, is known by the name of its discoverer, von Braun. An example is the conversion of N,N-dimethyl-α-naphthylamine into methyl-1-naphthylcyanamide (OS III, 608).

The von Braun cyanogen bromide cleavage has been applied successfully to a wide variety of tertiary amines, including many heterocyclic nitrogen compounds (OR **7,** 198).

A similar type of cleavage, likewise discovered by von Braun, is exemplified by the preparation of pentamethylene bromide by the action of phosphorus pentabromide on N-benzoylpiperidine (OS I, 428; 72% yield).

$$C_6H_5CON\!\!\big\langle\;\big\rangle + PBr_5 \rightarrow Br(CH_2)_5Br + C_6H_5CN + POBr_3$$

Certain acid chlorides containing tertiary amino groups have been observed to undergo an intramolecular reaction involving the elimination of an alkyl chloride, the products being pyrrolidones or piperidones. An example is the conversion of δ-diethylaminovaleryl chloride into 1-ethyl-2-piperidone.

Reaction of Mercury Salts

In the presence of alcohols and mercuric halides, olefins take up the elements of alkoxymercuric halides. The addition may be formulated as the aliphatic counterpart of aromatic mercuration, the first step being electrophilic attack of the olefin by a positive mercuric ion.

$$C{=}C + {}^{+}HgX \longrightarrow XHg\overset{|}{C}{-}\overset{|}{C}{}^{+} \xrightarrow{ROH} XHg\overset{|}{C}{-}\overset{|}{C}OR$$

An interesting example is the addition of mercuric acetate to *o*-allyl-phenol; the product, 1-acetoxymercurimethyl-1,2-dihydrobenzofuran, may be formed by the following sequence of changes.

$$Hg(OCOCH_3)_2 \rightarrow {}^{+}HgOCOCH_3 + CH_3CO_2{}^{-}$$

Addition of Nitrosyl Chloride

The formal similarity of the nitroso group to the carbonyl group suggests that nitrosyl chloride might be comparable to acid chlorides. The addition of nitrosyl chloride to olefins, if the analogy is extended to the mechanism, might then be expected to involve initial attack of NO^{+} followed by combination of the resulting carbonium ion with chloride ion. The addition of nitrosyl chloride to trimethylethylene, to take an example, would be formulated as follows.

$$CH_3C=CHCH_3 + NO^+ \rightarrow CH_3\overset{+}{C}\!-\!CHCH_3 + Cl^- \rightarrow CH_3C\!-\!CHCH_3$$
$$\underset{CH_3}{|} \qquad\qquad\quad \underset{CH_3\ NO}{|\quad|} \qquad\qquad\quad \underset{CH_3\ NO}{|\quad|}$$

with a chlorine (Cl) above the rightmost carbon.

When heated or allowed to stand, this nitrosochloride rearranges to the corresponding oxime.

$$(CH_3)_2C\!-\!CHCH_3 \rightarrow (CH_3)_2C\!-\!CCH_3$$
$$\underset{Cl\ \ NO}{|\quad\ |} \qquad\qquad \underset{Cl\ \ NOH}{|\quad\ \|}$$

If the olefin is of the type $R_2C=CR_2$ or $R_2C=CHR$, the nitrosochloride is solid. These derivatives have found extensive use in characterization work, notably in the terpene series. To prepare them it is not necessary to make nitrosyl chloride; a mixture of concentrated hydrochloric acid with a nitrite such as ethyl or amyl will serve the same purpose.

1-Methylcyclopentene nitrosochloride is formed in satisfactory yield by adding concentrated hydrochloric acid slowly to a mixture of the olefin, ethyl nitrite, and acetic acid.[42]

Such nitrosochlorides offer a route to α,β-unsaturated ketones. When the moist nitrosochloride from 1-phenylcyclopentene is heated in pyridine, for example, it undergoes dehydrochlorination and yields the oxime of 2-phenyl-2-cyclopentene-1-one.

In crystalline form nitrosochlorides are dimeric and colorless; in solution or when melted they revert to some extent to the monomers, which are blue. In the dimeric forms nitroso compounds have a double bond between the nitrogen atoms and as a consequence may exist in *cis*- and *trans*-modifications (QR **12**, 321).

[42] A. M. Gaddis and L. W. Butz, *J. Am. Chem. Soc.*, **69**, 1203 (1947).

Addition of Sulfur Compounds

Hydrogen sulfide reacts with olefins to yield mercaptans, the addition taking place according to Markownikoff's rule. Mercaptans and thiophenols, similarly, combine with olefins to produce thio ethers. These reactions are particularly sensitive to the influence of peroxides (p. 583).

The reaction of olefins with sulfur chlorides has been studied extensively because of the unusual properties of the products. A reaction that has received much attention is that between ethylene and sulfur monochloride to produce mustard gas.

$$2CH_2{=}CH_2 \xrightarrow{S_2Cl_2} ClCH_2CH_2SCH_2CH_2Cl$$

Olefins react additively with sulfur dioxide to give linear polymers (p. 601).

Nitration of Amides

The nitrates of urea and guanidine yield nitro derivatives when treated with concentrated sulfuric acid. The procedure for nitrourea is to add dry, powdered urea nitrate in small portions to concentrated sulfuric acid at $-3°$ (OS I, 417; 87% yield).

$$\underset{NH_2}{\overset{NH_2 \cdot HNO_3}{C{=}O}} \xrightarrow{H_2SO_4} \underset{NH_2}{\overset{NHNO_2}{C{=}O}} + H_2O$$

The preparation of nitroguanidine is carried out in a similar way (OS I, 302, 399).

$$\underset{NH_2}{\overset{NH_2 \cdot HNO_3}{C{=}NH}} \xrightarrow{H_2SO_4} \underset{NH_2}{\overset{NHNO_2}{C{=}NH}} + H_2O$$

Nitration of the methylamide of hydantoic acid is interesting because the compound contains three dissimilar amide groups; the primary amide group is nitrated preferentially.[43]

$$H_2NCONHCH_2CONHCH_3 + HONO_2 \rightarrow$$
$$O_2NNHCONHCH_2CONHCH_3 + H_2O$$

This result is in accord with the expectation that the most basic amide group will be nitrated most readily.

[43] W. E. Bachmann and C. E. Maxwell III, *J. Am. Chem. Soc.*, **72**, 2880 (1950).

Halogenation of Amines and Amides

Hypochlorites convert primary and secondary amines into the corresponding N-chloro derivatives, both mono- and dichloroamines being produced. An example is the formation of the N-chloro derivative of di-*n*-butylamine (OS III, 159).

$$(CH_3CH_2CH_2CH_2)_2NH + Cl_2 + NaOH \rightarrow$$
$$(CH_3CH_2CH_2CH_2)_2NCl + NaCl + H_2O$$

Amides likewise yield N-chloro and N-bromo derivatives when treated with the corresponding hypohalites. Acetamide is converted into N-bromoacetamide by the action of bromine in the presence of 50% potassium hydroxide solution (OS **31**, 17; 51% yield).

$$CH_3CONH_2 + Br_2 + KOH \rightarrow CH_3CONHBr + KBr + H_2O$$

N-Bromosuccinimide, employed as a brominating agent (p. 610), is produced by the action of an alkali hypobromite on succinimide.

Sulfonamides undergo halogenation also, the best-known example being the conversion of *p*-toluenesulfonamide into Chloramine-T.

The dichloroamide, which can be formed also under suitable conditions, is transformed into Chloramine-T by the action of sodium hydroxide.

10

Molecular rearrangements involving electron-deficient carbon atoms

A large number of intramolecular rearrangements involve the migration of an atom or a group (M) from one atom (A) to an adjacent atom (B). Such 1,2-rearrangements generally are induced by the development of an electron shortage on B, the migration terminus. The migrating group M acts as a nucleophile and moves because the demand for electrons is greater at the migration terminus than at the migration origin. The generalized statement of the rearrangement take the following form.

$$\begin{array}{ccc} A\!\!-\!\!B & & A\!\!-\!\!B \\ | & \rightarrow & | \\ M & & M \end{array}$$

Electron deficiency at B will mean, in the case of carbon, that we are dealing with a carbonium ion or a carbon atom that has suffered electron impoverishment without actual rupture of a bond. It is customary for ease of discussion to assume, in many instances, the extreme case and represent the reacting species as a carbonium ion. The electron deficit may arise because of the loss from the migration terminus of a group that takes the pair of bonding electrons with it. A good leaving group is water (from a protonated alcohol).

$$\begin{array}{ccc} | \ \ | \ \ \overset{+}{} & & | \ \ | \\ -C-C-\overset{+}{O}H_2 & \rightarrow & -C-C^+ \\ | \ \ | & & | \ \ | \end{array}$$

The electron deficit at the migration terminus may be produced also, of course, by protonation of an olefin.

The problem of devising a suitable mechanism for the rearrangements has been approached by a study of the degree of stereospecificity they exhibit when the three centers involved are asymmetric. To the extent that such 1,2-migrations from carbon to carbon are stereospecific, configuration is retained in the migrating group and inverted at the migration origin and at the migration terminus. Asymmetry can be either retained or lost at the latter sites but is always retained in the migrating group.

The migration of hydrogen (as hydride ion) is illustrated by the rearrangement of isobutyl carbonium ion to t-butyl carbonium ion.

$$CH_3CHCH_2{}^+ \rightarrow CH_3\overset{+}{C}CH_3$$
$$\quad\;\; | \qquad\qquad\quad |$$
$$\quad\;\; CH_3 \qquad\qquad\; CH_3$$

Hydride ion migration is postulated to explain a wide variety of results in reactions that may be formulated as involving carbonium ions. Hydration of certain olefins, for example, leads to the formation of alcohols that are isomeric with those to be expected; 3-methyl-1-butene yields t-amyl alcohol instead of methylisopropylcarbinol.

$$(CH_3)_2CH\overset{+}{C}HCH_3 \longrightarrow (CH_3)_2\overset{+}{C}CH_2CH_3 \xrightarrow{H_2O} (CH_3)_2\overset{\overset{\displaystyle OH}{|}}{C}CH_2CH_3$$

A similar example is encountered in the hydration of the methylcyclohexenes; the 2- and 3-methyl-1-cyclohexenes yield the same alcohol as the 1-isomer—the tertiary alcohol.

The two olefins, 2-methyl-2-butene and 2-methyl-1-butene, give the same alcohol, t-amyl alcohol.

$$
\underset{CH_3}{\overset{CH_3}{\diagdown}}C{=}CHCH_3 \xrightarrow{H^+} \underset{CH_3}{\overset{CH_3}{\diagdown}}\overset{+}{C}{-}CH_2CH_3 \xleftarrow{H^+} \underset{CH_2}{\overset{CH_3}{\diagdown}}C{-}CH_2CH_3
$$

$$\downarrow H_2O$$

$$
\underset{CH_3}{\overset{CH_3\ \ OH}{\diagdown\ |}}C{-}CH_2CH_3
$$

Terminal olefins in the presence of acid catalysts exhibit preferential migration of the double bond into the chain or ring, the product normally being the most highly branched olefin. 1-Methylcyclohexene is formed not only from methylenecyclohexane but also from 3-methylcyclohexene.

Migration of a double bond may occur by protonation followed by loss of a proton from a new site.

Transformation of an olefin to a less highly branched, less stable isomer may be accomplished by hydroboration (p. 140). The borane from 3-ethyl-2-pentene isomerizes when heated, the boron moving to the less hindered position. When the borane is then heated with 1-decene, 3-ethyl-1-pentene is formed in high yield.[1]

$$
(CH_3CH_2)_2C{=}CHCH_3 \xrightarrow{B_2H_6} \left[(CH_3CH_2)_2\underset{CH_3}{\overset{|}{CHCH}}{-}\right]_3 B \longrightarrow
$$

$$
[(CH_3CH_2)_2CHCH_2CH_2]_3B \longrightarrow (CH_3CH_2)_2CHCH{=}CH_2
$$

Many of the observations that have been made in the preparation of alkyl halides from alcohols are in accord with the hypothesis that a carbonium ion is an intermediate. Methylisopropylcarbinol reacts with hydrogen chloride, for example, to yield exclusively *t*-amyl chloride; the result has been ascribed to isomerization of the intermediate carbonium ion.

[1] H. C. Brown and M. V. Bhatt, *J. Am. Chem. Soc.*, **82**, 2074 (1960).

$$\underset{\overset{|}{CH_3}}{\overset{CH_3}{\underset{|}{CH}}}\text{—}\underset{\overset{|}{OH}}{CH}\text{—}CH_3 + H^+ \rightarrow \underset{\overset{|}{CH_3}}{\overset{CH_3}{\underset{|}{CH}}}\text{—}\overset{+}{CH}\text{—}CH_3 + H_2O$$

$$\underset{\overset{|}{CH_3}}{\overset{CH_3}{\underset{|}{CH}}}\text{—}\overset{+}{CH}\text{—}CH_3 \longrightarrow \underset{\overset{|}{CH_3}}{\overset{CH_3}{\underset{|}{\overset{+}{C}}}}\text{—}CH_2CH_3 \overset{Cl^-}{\longrightarrow} \underset{\overset{|}{CH_3}}{\overset{CH_3}{\underset{|}{CH}}}\text{—}\underset{\overset{|}{Cl}}{C}H_2CH_3$$

In a similar way diisopropylcarbinol yields 2,4-dimethyl-2-chloropentane.

$$\underset{CH_3}{\overset{CH_3}{}}\text{CHCHCH}\overset{CH_3}{\underset{CH_3}{}}\text{—}\overset{}{\underset{OH}{}} \rightarrow \underset{CH_3}{\overset{CH_3}{}}\text{CHCH}_2\text{CCl}\overset{CH_3}{\underset{CH_3}{}}$$

Carbonium ion rearrangement offers an explanation of certain lactonizations of unsaturated carboxylic acids. Most unusual of these, perhaps, is the isomerization of oleic acid to γ-stearolactone under the influence of zinc chloride.

$$CH_3(CH_2)_7CH\text{=}CH(CH_2)_7CO_2H \rightarrow CH_3(CH_2)_{13}\underset{\underset{O}{\underline{\qquad}}}{CHCH_2CH_2CO}$$

The double bond in the carbonyl group of lactones belongs to a class known as *exocyclic*, as contrasted with the *endocyclic* double bonds in such compounds as cyclohexene. The preferential formation of five-membered lactone rings is an example of what appears to be a rule; namely, reactions proceed in such a manner as to favor the formation or retention of an exocyclic double bond in a five-membered ring and to avoid the formation or retention of an exocyclic double bond in a six-membered ring.[2]

The formation of a five-membered sultone by sulfonation of propylene corresponds to the intermediate production of a carbonium ion isomeric with that to be expected.

$$CH_3CH\text{=}CH_2 \xrightarrow{H_2SO_4} \underset{\underset{O\underline{\qquad}SO_2}{|\qquad\quad|}}{CH_2CH_2CH_2}$$

Anomalous Friedel-Crafts Reactions

The carbonium ion theory makes it possible to interpret various Friedel-Crafts reactions giving products isomeric with those that might have been

[2] H. C. Brown, J. H. Brewster, and H. Shechter, *J. Am. Chem. Soc.*, **76**, 467 (1954).

expected. In Friedel-Crafts alkylation reactions there is, in fact, a general tendency for an alkyl group to isomerize, when this is possible, from primary to secondary or from secondary to tertiary during alkylation. Rearrangements of a primary to a tertiary carbonium ion is, of course, specially favored. When the alkylating agent is an olefin, the condensation product may be that to be expected of an isomeric olefin, apparently produced by shift of the double bond. Alkylation of benzene with 3-methyl-1-butene in the presence of sulfuric acid, for example, yields *t*-amylbenzene instead of 2-methyl-3-phenylbutane.[3]

$$(CH_3)_2CHCH{=}CH_2 + C_6H_6 \xrightarrow{\text{H}_2\text{SO}_4} C_6H_5\underset{\underset{C_2H_5}{|}}{C}(CH_3)_2$$

A striking example of isomerization is found in the condensation of the methylcyclohexenes with benzene; all yield the same product, 1-methyl-1-phenylcyclohexane. 4-Methylcyclohexene is an example.[4]

With β-naphthol and 2- , 3- , or 4-methylcyclohexanol also a single product is obtained; the remarkable feature of these alkylation reactions, however, is that the tertiary methylcyclohexyl radical *enters the 6-position*.[5]

This behavior recalls the bromination of β-naphthol (p. 99).

That alkylation of benzene produces *t*-alkylbenzenes whenever these are possible has proved to be an overstatement. The amount of secondary and tertiary derivatives formed depends on the catalyst and reaction conditions.[6]

1-Cyclohexenylacetic acid reacts with benzene to give 4-phenylcyclo-hexaneacetic acid, which suggests that the intermediate carbonium ion

[3] V. N. Ipatieff, H. Pines, and L. Schmerling, *J. Am. Chem. Soc.*, **60**, 353 (1938).
[4] V. N. Ipatieff, E. E. Meisinger, and H. Pines, *J. Am. Chem. Soc.*, **72**, 2772 (1951).
[5] Ng. Ph. Buu-Hoï, H. Le Bihan, and F. Binon, *J. Org. Chem.*, **16**, 185 (1951).
[6] B. S. Friedman, F. L. Morritz, and C. J. Morrissey, *J. Am. Chem. Soc.*, **79**, 1465 (1957).

rearranges in such a manner as to place the positive charge at the point that is most remote from the carboxyl group.

$$C_6H_6 + \langle\bigcirc\rangle CH_2CO_2H \xrightarrow{AlCl_3} C_6H_5\langle\bigcirc\rangle CH_2CO_2H$$

This type of behavior is observed frequently. Cyclohexene, acetyl chloride, and benzene react to give, not the expected methyl 2-phenyl-cyclohexyl ketone, but the isomeric ketone in which the phenyl group is in the 4-position, methyl 4-phenylcyclohexyl ketone.[7]

$$\bigcirc\!\! + CH_3COCl + C_6H_6 \xrightarrow{AlCl_3} \overset{\displaystyle COCH_3}{\underset{\displaystyle C_6H_5}{\bigcirc}} + HCl$$

Under similar conditions cyclopentene yields methyl 3-phenylcyclopentyl ketone.

When α-olefins are used the phenyl group is found on the methylene group most remote from the original double bond but never in the terminal position. It would appear that failure of the phenyl group to occupy the end position is to be ascribed to the lower stability of the primary carbonium ion that would be involved. 1-Butene, for example, reacts with acetyl chloride and benzene to give 5-phenyl-2-hexanone.

$$CH_3CH_2CH{=}CH_2 \rightarrow \underset{\displaystyle C_6H_5}{CH_3CHCH_2CH_2COCH_3}$$

Under the influence of acids, triphenylcarbinol undergoes dehydration to yield 9-phenylfluorene. The rearrangement may be pictured as follows, the triphenylmethyl carbonium ion being formed in the first step.

[7] C. D. Nenitzescu I. and G. Gavăt, *Ann.*, **519**, 260 (1935).

A similar transformation occurs when benzilic acid is treated with aluminum chloride in benzene; 9-fluorenecarboxylic acid is produced in 81% yield (OS **33**, 37).

$$(C_6H_5)_2CCO_2H \rightarrow$$
$$\underset{\displaystyle OH}{|}$$

$+ H_2O$

Alicyclic Dienones

Isomerization of alicyclic dienones is a potentially useful method of obtaining phenols (CR **33**, 89). Carvone, for example, rearranges almost quantitatively to carvacrol in the presence of hydrochloric acid.

Another example is 2-methylene-1-tetralone, which rearranges to 2-methyl-1-naphthol.

A much more remarkable illustration is the acid-catalyzed isomerization of 3,7-dibenzal-1,2-cycloheptanedione to 3,7-dibenzyltropolone.[8]

Isomerization of Paraffins

One of the most important types of molecular rearrangement ascribed to carbonium ions is the isomerization of paraffins. The most valuable of these, the formation of isobutane from *n*-butane, occurs in the presence of aluminum chloride or bromide. At room temperature an equilibrium is reached at which the mixture is about 80% isobutane and 20% *n*-butane.

$$CH_3CH_2CH_2CH_3 \xrightleftharpoons{AlCl_3} CH_3\underset{\displaystyle CH_3}{\underset{\displaystyle |}{CH}}CH_3$$

[8] N. J. Leonard and G. C. Robinson, *J. Am. Chem. Soc.*, **75**, 2143 (1953).

Aluminum chloride and other Lewis acids, as was mentioned in connection with cationic polymerization (p. 153), require the presence of a mineral acid or other proton donor to be effective. Boron fluoride, for example, can serve as the catalyst for such isomerizations if used together with hydrogen fluoride.[9] Actually, slight traces of impurities such as olefins or alcohols—substances that can give rise to carbonium ions—serve to initiate reaction. When pure aluminum chloride and a pure paraffin are used, no reaction occurs. Once a carbonium ion is available, the reaction takes the following course.

(1) $CH_3CH_2CH_2CH_3 + R^+ \rightleftharpoons CH_3\overset{+}{C}HCH_2CH_3 + RH$

(2) $CH_3\overset{+}{C}HCH_2CH_3 \rightleftharpoons CH_3CHCH_2{}^+ \rightleftharpoons CH_3\overset{+}{C}CH_3$
$\qquad\qquad\qquad\qquad\qquad\quad |\qquad\qquad\qquad\quad |$
$\qquad\qquad\qquad\qquad\qquad CH_3\qquad\qquad\qquad CH_3$

(3) $CH_3\overset{+}{C}CH_3 + CH_3CH_2CH_2CH_3 \rightleftharpoons CH_3CHCH_3 + CH_3\overset{+}{C}HCH_2CH_3$
$\quad\; |\qquad\qquad\qquad\qquad\qquad\qquad\qquad\qquad |$
$\quad CH_3\qquad\qquad\qquad\qquad\qquad\qquad\quad CH_3$

The essential feature of the isomerization is the rearrangement of the butyl carbonium ion. It is to be noted that, according to the proposed mechanism, one carbonium ion (R^+) is sufficient to bring about the isomerization of many butane molecules, i.e., the reaction is of the chain type.

Under suitable conditions ethylcyclopentane, 1,3-dimethylcyclopentane, and 1,1-dimethylcyclopentane rearrange to methylcyclohexane.[10]

One step in an industrial process for toluene is the isomerization of dimethylcyclopentanes to methylcyclohexane. Benzene is made similarly by passing methylcyclopentane over a molybdena-alumina catalyst in the presence of hydrogen.

[9] E. C. Hughes and S. M. Darling, *Ind. Eng. Chem.*, **43**, 746 (1951).
[10] H. Pines, F. J. Pavlik, and V. N. Ipatieff, *J. Am. Chem. Soc.*, **73**, 5738 (1951).

Isomerization of higher normal alkanes has been accomplished also. Rearrangement of propane containing C^{13} in an end position has been realized as well.

$$CH_3CH_2\overset{13}{C}H_3 + R^+ \rightarrow CH_3\overset{+}{C}H\overset{13}{C}H_3 \rightleftharpoons CH_3CH_2\overset{13}{C}H_2{}^+ \rightleftharpoons {}^+CH_2\overset{13}{C}H_2CH_3$$

$$\overset{+}{C}H_2\overset{13}{C}H_2CH_3 + CH_3CH_2\overset{13}{C}H_3 \rightarrow CH_3\overset{13}{C}H_2CH_3 + CH_3\overset{+}{C}H\overset{13}{C}H_3$$

Condensation of Paraffins with Olefins

The addition of paraffins to olefins, discovered in 1932 by Ipatieff and his coworkers, is the basis of commercial processes for producing alkylate, a primary component of high-test gasolines. Common catalysts are sulfuric acid, aluminum chloride, and hydrogen fluoride. In these processes isobutane is condensed with olefins (CR **37**, 323), the raw materials being the low-boiling hydrocarbons from the cracking process. The transformation may be illustrated by consideration of the C_4 fraction. In one process the mixture of butylenes and isobutane is treated with sulfuric acid, which causes the isobutane to condense with the unsaturated hydrocarbons to give chiefly octanes. The condensation of isobutane with isobutylene may be formulated as follows.

$$(1)\ CH_3C{=}CH_2 + H^+ \rightarrow (CH_3)_3C^+$$
$$\qquad\quad |$$
$$\qquad\quad CH_3$$

$$(2)\ (CH_3)_3\overset{+}{C} + CH_2{=}CCH_3 \rightarrow (CH_3)_3CCH_2\overset{+}{C}CH_3$$
$$\qquad\qquad\qquad\quad |\qquad\qquad\qquad\qquad |$$
$$\qquad\qquad\qquad\quad CH_3\qquad\qquad\qquad\qquad CH_3$$

In the presence of isobutane the newly formed carbonium ion is able to acquire a hydride ion.

$$(3)\ (CH_3)_3CCH_2\overset{+}{C}CH_3 + (CH_3)_3CH \rightarrow (CH_3)_3CCH_2CHCH_3 + (CH_3)_3\overset{+}{C}$$
$$\qquad\qquad\qquad |\qquad\qquad\qquad\qquad\qquad\qquad\qquad\qquad |$$
$$\qquad\qquad\qquad CH_3\qquad\qquad\qquad\qquad\qquad\qquad\qquad CH_3$$

As a consequence of the hydride ion transfer, a new paraffin is produced that corresponds to the condensation of isobutane with isobutylene. The carbonium ion attacks the olefin in such a way as to give the more stable of the two possible carbonium ions. Since the *t*-butyl carbonium ion is regenerated in step 3, the reaction also is of the chain type, one *t*-butyl carbonium ion being sufficient for the formation of an indefinite number of molecules of the new hydrocarbon. In general the condensation reaction is found to yield mixtures that contain not only isomers of the expected paraffin but higher and lower homologs as well. The results can be explained by assuming intermolecular transfer of alkide ions. When isobutane and propylene are the reactants, the chief product is 2,3-dimethylpentane (62 to 66%). A small amount (8 to 12%) of 2,4-dimethylpentane is formed also along with hexanes and octanes. The formation of the chief product is to be ascribed to rearrangement of the original carbonium ion, by a hydride ion shift, followed by methide ion transfer and capture of a hydride ion from a molecule of isobutane.

$$
\begin{array}{c}
\text{CH}_3 \\
| \\
\text{CH}_3\text{—C—CH}_2\overset{+}{\text{C}}\text{HCH}_3
\end{array}
\;\rightarrow\;
\begin{array}{c}
\text{CH}_3 \\
| \\
\text{CH}_3\text{—C—}\overset{+}{\text{C}}\text{HCH}_2\text{CH}_3
\end{array}
\;\rightarrow\;
$$

$$
\begin{array}{c}
\text{CH}_3\overset{+}{\text{C}}\text{——CHCH}_2\text{CH}_3 \\
| \qquad | \\
\text{CH}_3 \;\; \text{CH}_3
\end{array}
\;\rightarrow\;
\begin{array}{c}
\text{CH}_3\text{—CH—CHCH}_2\text{CH}_3 \\
| \qquad | \\
\text{CH}_3 \;\; \text{CH}_3
\end{array}
$$

Friedel-Crafts Reactions with Paraffinic Hydrocarbons

Comparison of the reactions of olefins with those of aromatic nuclei, as has been seen, shows a close parallel. The problem is different with saturated aliphatic or alicyclic hydrocarbons, however; yet these compounds too are capable of undergoing alkylation and acylation by the Friedel-Crafts procedure. As a matter of fact this type of reaction, the first to be encountered, was discovered by Friedel and Crafts in 1877 in a study of the action of aluminum metal on n-amyl chloride. These experimenters found that long-chain alkyl chlorides were produced by the elimination of hydrogen chloride and that the true catalyst was aluminum chloride (CR 17, 327).

$$ 2C_5H_{11}Cl \xrightarrow{\text{AlCl}_3} C_{10}H_{21}Cl + HCl $$

One theory that has been advanced to explain alkylation and acylation of paraffinic hydrocarbons assumes that the first step is dehydrogenation. If we assume the presence of a trace of an olefin, an alcohol, or other molecule capable of reacting with the catalyst to give a carbonium ion, we may imagine the following sequence of changes, taking the acetylation of cyclohexane as a specific example.

It has been established in fact that acetylation of cyclohexane, n-pentane, and n-hexane proceeds by primary isomerization and subsequent dehydrogenation, followed by addition of the acylating agent to the olefinic linkage.[11]

[11] C. D. Nenitzescu and I. Chicos, Ber., 68, 1584 (1935).

(1)
$$\text{H}_2\text{C} \overset{\displaystyle \text{CH}_2\text{CH}_2}{\underset{\displaystyle \text{CH}_2\text{CH}_2}{\diagup\diagdown}} \text{CH}_2 + \text{R}^+ \rightarrow \text{H}_2\text{C} \overset{\displaystyle \text{CH}_2\text{CH}_2}{\underset{\displaystyle \text{CH}_2\text{CH}_2}{\diagup\diagdown}} \text{CH}^+ + \text{RH}$$

(2)
$$\text{H}_2\text{C} \overset{\displaystyle \text{CH}_2\text{CH}_2}{\underset{\displaystyle \text{CH}_2\text{CH}_2}{\diagup\diagdown}} \text{CH}^+ \longrightarrow \overset{\displaystyle \text{CH}_2\text{CH}_2}{\underset{\displaystyle \text{CH}_2\text{CH}_2}{|\qquad}} \text{CHCH}_2{}^+ \longrightarrow$$

$$\overset{\displaystyle \text{CH}_2\text{CH}}{\underset{\displaystyle \text{CH}_2\text{CH}_2}{|\qquad}} \overset{+}{\text{C}}\text{CH}_3 \xrightarrow{-\text{H}^+} \overset{\displaystyle \text{CH}_2\text{CH}}{\underset{\displaystyle \text{CH}_2\text{CH}_2}{|\qquad}} \text{CCH}_3$$

(3)
$$\overset{\displaystyle \text{CH}_2\text{CH}}{\underset{\displaystyle \text{CH}_2\text{CH}_2}{|\qquad}} \text{CCH}_3 + \text{CH}_3\overset{+}{\text{C}}=\text{O} \rightarrow \overset{\displaystyle \text{CH}_2\text{CHCOCH}_3}{\underset{\displaystyle \text{CH}_2\text{CH}_2}{|\qquad}} \overset{+}{\text{C}}\text{CH}_3$$

(4)
$$\overset{\displaystyle \text{CH}_2\text{CHCOCH}_3}{\underset{\displaystyle \text{CH}_2\text{CH}_2}{|\qquad}} \overset{+}{\text{C}}\text{CH}_3 + \text{H}_2\text{C} \overset{\displaystyle \text{CH}_2\text{CH}_2}{\underset{\displaystyle \text{CH}_2\text{CH}_2}{\diagup\diagdown}} \text{CH}_2 \rightarrow$$

$$\overset{\displaystyle \text{CH}_2\text{CHCOCH}_3}{\underset{\displaystyle \text{CH}_2\text{CH}_2}{|\qquad}} \text{CHCH}_3 + \text{H}_2\text{C} \overset{\displaystyle \text{CH}_2\text{CH}_2}{\underset{\displaystyle \text{CH}_2\text{CH}_2}{\diagup\diagdown}} \text{CH}^+$$

Dehydration of Alcohols

Hydration of olefins (p. 139) generally can be reversed and so regenerates the original olefin. In many cases, presumably because of isomerization of the intermediate carbonium ion, rearrangement occurs. The synthesis of phenanthrene by dehydration of 9-fluorenecarbinol is illustrative; the yield of the hydrocarbon is high.

Dehydration of tetrahydrofurfuryl alcohol to give 2,3-dihydropyran is at least formally similar (OS III, 276; 70% yield).

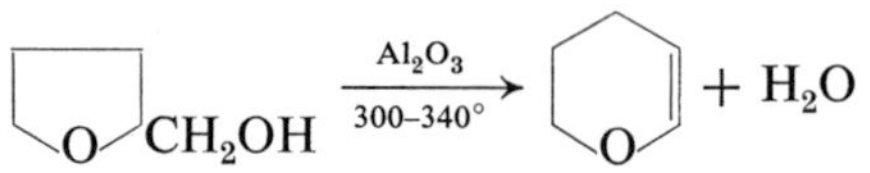

$$\text{(tetrahydrofurfuryl alcohol)} \xrightarrow[300-340°]{Al_2O_3} \text{(2,3-dihydropyran)} + H_2O$$

Certain tertiary acetylenic alcohols rearrange to the corresponding unsaturated ketones, as though the elements of water had been removed and returned to the molecule in a new location. An example is the rearrangement of the condensation product of acetylene and cyclohexanone (OS III, 22); 1-acetylcyclohexene is the chief product (70%). The isomerization of this and other 1-ethynyl-1-cyclohexanols yields also small amounts of the corresponding cyclohexylideneacetaldehydes.

$$\text{(1-ethynyl-1-cyclohexanol)} \xrightarrow{P_2O_5} \text{(1-acetylcyclohexene)} \quad \text{and} \quad \text{(cyclohexylideneacetaldehyde)}$$

This type of isomerization is to be compared with the remarkable rearrangement discovered by Meyer and Schuster, which occurs when acetylenic carbinols of the type $Ar_2CC{\equiv}CAr$ are treated with acids. An

$$\underset{\displaystyle \text{OH}}{|}$$

example is the formation of β-phenylbenzalacetophenone from diphenylphenylethynylcarbinol.

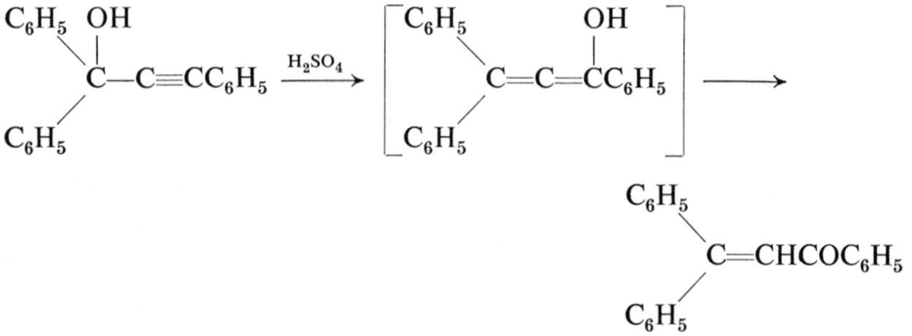

$$\underset{C_6H_5}{\overset{C_6H_5\ \ OH}{\diagdown\underset{\diagup}{C}-C{\equiv}CC_6H_5}} \xrightarrow{H_2SO_4} \left[\underset{C_6H_5}{\overset{C_6H_5}{\diagdown\underset{\diagup}{C}=C}}\overset{OH}{\underset{}{=}}CC_6H_5\right] \longrightarrow$$

$$\underset{C_6H_5}{\overset{C_6H_5}{\diagdown\underset{\diagup}{C}}}=CHCOC_6H_5$$

This curious change probably involves the intermediate formation of an allenic alcohol that ketonizes to form the final product. The shift may be looked upon as a special case of the allylic rearrangement (p. 468) in which the carbonium ion is a resonance hybrid of the following structures.

$$(C_6H_5)_2\overset{+}{C}-C{\equiv}CC_6H_5 \leftrightarrow (C_6H_5)_2C=C{=}\overset{+}{C}C_6H_5$$

1,2-Glycols

Dehydration of simple 1,2- or α-glycols produces aldehydes or ketones by what has been called *vinyl dehydration*. Ethylene glycol, for example, yields acetaldehyde.

$$\underset{\underset{\displaystyle CH_2CH_2}{|\quad\ |}}{OH\ OH} \xrightarrow{-H_2O} CH_3CHO$$

2,3-Butanediol gives methyl ethyl ketone in a similar fashion.

$$\underset{\underset{\displaystyle CH_3CHCHCH_3}{|\ \ \ |}}{OHOH} \rightarrow CH_3COCH_2CH_3 + H_2O$$

1-Phenyl-1,2-cyclohexanediol similarly yields 2-phenylcyclohexanone.

When *trans*-2-butene-1,4-diol is treated with sulfuric acid, crotonaldehyde is produced in 80% yield.

$$HOCH_2CH\!\!=\!\!CHCH_2OH \rightarrow CH_3CH\!\!=\!\!CHCHO$$

1,1,2-Triphenyl-1,2-propanediol, when treated with a solution of iodine in glacial acetic acid, yields methyl trityl ketone.[12]

$$\underset{\underset{\displaystyle C_6H_5}{|}}{\overset{\overset{\displaystyle OH\ \ \ OH}{|\quad\ \ |}}{(C_6H_5)_2C\!\!-\!\!-\!\!CCH_3}} \rightarrow (C_6H_5)_3CCOCH_3 + H_2O$$

The direction of opening of epoxides generally can be predicted on the basis of the relative stabilities of the possible carbonium ions. The more stable ion usually forms, and the migratory aptitudes of hydrogen, alkyl, and aryl fall in the following order.

$$C_6H_5\!\!-\ >\ H\!\!-\ >\ R\!\!-$$

The synthesis of methyl isopropyl ketone from *t*-amyl alcohol or trimethylethylene by way of the halide probably involves vinyl dehydration also. When treated with bromine, *t*-amyl alcohol yields trimethylethylene

[12] J. L. Greene and H. D. Zook, *J. Am. Chem. Soc.*, **80**, 3629 (1958).

bromide, which gives methyl isopropyl ketone when subjected to hydrolysis (OS II, 408; 59% yield).

$$
\begin{array}{c}
CH_3 \\
\diagdown \\
\quad CCH_2CH_3 \xrightarrow{Br_2} \\
\diagup \quad | \\
CH_3 \ OH
\end{array}
\quad
\begin{array}{c}
CH_3 \\
\diagdown \\
\quad C{-}CHCH_3 \longrightarrow \\
\diagup \ | \ | \\
CH_3 \ Br \ Br
\end{array}
$$

$$
\begin{array}{c}
CH_3 \\
\diagdown \\
\quad C{-}CHCH_3 \longrightarrow \\
\diagup \ | \ | \\
CH_3 \ OH \ OH
\end{array}
\quad
\begin{array}{c}
CH_3 \\
\diagdown \\
\quad CHCOCH_3 \\
\diagup \\
CH_3
\end{array}
$$

Substituted ethylene oxides are isomerized readily to carbonyl compounds. Diphenylacetaldehyde, for example, is formed from *trans*-stilbene oxide by the action of boron fluoride etherate (OS **38**, 26; yield 83%).

$$
\begin{array}{c}
C_6H_5 \qquad O \qquad H \\
\diagdown \ \diagup \diagdown \ \diagup \\
C{-\!-}C \qquad \xrightarrow{BF_3 \cdot O(C_2H_5)_2} \quad (C_6H_5)_2CHCHO \\
\diagup \qquad\qquad \diagdown \\
H \qquad\qquad C_6H_5
\end{array}
$$

Pinacol-pinacolone rearrangement

Ditertiary 1,2-glycols, generally obtained by bimolecular reduction of ketones, are called *pinacols* (p. 585). When dehydrated, they undergo rearrangement to ketones known as *pinacolones*. Pinacol and benzopinacol, for example, yield pinacolone (OS I, 462; 72% yield) and β-benzo-pinacolone (OS II, 73; 96% yield), respectively.

$$
\begin{array}{c}
CH_3 \ OH \ HO \ CH_3 \\
\diagdown | \qquad | \diagup \\
C{-\!-}C \qquad \xrightarrow{H_2SO_4} \quad CH_3{-}CCOCH_3 + H_2O \\
\diagup \qquad\quad \diagdown \qquad\qquad\qquad | \\
CH_3 \qquad\quad CH_3 \qquad\qquad\qquad CH_3
\end{array}
$$

$$
\begin{array}{c}
C_6H_5 \ OH \ HO \ C_6H_5 \\
\diagdown | \qquad | \diagup \\
C{-\!-}C \qquad \xrightarrow[CH_3CO_2H]{I_2} \quad (C_6H_5)_3CCOC_6H_5 + H_2O \\
\diagup \qquad\quad \diagdown \\
C_6H_5 \qquad\quad C_6H_5
\end{array}
$$

The reagents most commonly used to bring about this type of molecular rearrangement, usually called the *pinacol-pinacolone* rearrangement (QR **14**, 357), are sulfuric acid, hydrochloric acid, acetyl chloride, and iodine in acetic acid. Pinacol itself can be dehydrated, however, without extensive rearrangement, by a proper choice of conditions. 2,3-Dimethyl-1,3-butadiene is obtained in 60% yield when pinacol hydrate is boiled for 2 hours in the presence of a small amount of hydrogen bromide, the water being removed as fast as it is formed (OS III, 312).

$$
\underset{\underset{CH_3}{|}}{\overset{\overset{OH}{|}}{CH_3-C}}\!\!-\!\!\underset{\underset{CH_3}{|}}{\overset{\overset{OH}{|}}{C}}\!\!-\!\!CH_3 \;\rightarrow\; CH_2\!\!=\!\!\underset{\underset{CH_3}{|}}{C}\!\!-\!\!\underset{\underset{CH_3}{|}}{C}\!\!=\!\!CH_2 + 2H_2O
$$

Only 25% or less of the product is pinacolone. An alternative method is to pass pinacol over activated alumina at 420 to 470°; this procedure may give the diene in yields of 86% (OS III, 313). Pinacolone may be formed as an intermediate; under these conditions it likewise is dehydrated to the diene. In fact, the ketone may be converted to the diene in 77% yields by this procedure (OS III, 315).

$$
(CH_3)_3CCOCH_3 \;\rightarrow\; CH_2\!\!=\!\!\underset{\underset{CH_3}{|}}{C}\!\!-\!\!\underset{\underset{CH_3}{|}}{C}\!\!=\!\!CH_2 + H_2O
$$

Dehydration of pinacolone is of especial interest, since it is accompanied by a rearrangement that regenerates the original carbon skeleton of pinacol. This rearrangement resembles that of pinacolyl alcohol (p. 186).

A very remarkable change of this type occurs when 1-naphthyl triphenylmethyl ketone is treated with sulfuric acid; an acenaphthene derivative is formed.[13]

Especial interest attaches to pinacols containing two different aryl radicals, since rearrangement serves to compare the relative migration tendencies of the radicals. Because the radical is transferred as a carbanion,

[13] W. A. Mosher and M. L. Huber, *J. Am. Chem. Soc.* **73,** 795 (1951).

it would be expected that the migration aptitude would be proportional to its electron donating power. Experimental results are in approximate agreement with this prediction; the following radicals are arranged in the order of relative ease of migration.

The o-tolyl radical migrates about three times as readily as the phenyl radical. It is assumed that the carbonium ions involved have lifetimes long enough to permit the establishment of equilibrium of the various conformational isomers (Gould, 73).[14]

Wagner-Meerwein rearrangement

Dehydration of t-alkylcarbinols frequently is accompanied by rearrangement of the carbon chain. For example, when pinacolyl alcohol is passed over a phosphorus pentoxide-silica gel catalyst at 300°, it yields chiefly the rearrangement products, 2,3-dimethyl-1-butene and tetramethylethylene. Only a small amount of the normal dehydration product, t-butylethylene, is obtained.[15]

Approximately the same mixture of olefins is obtained when any one of them is subjected to the conditions specified for the dehydration of the alcohol. It is presumed that the carbonium ions that undergo rearrangement are formed by combining the olefins with protons from the catalyst.

This type of rearrangement, known as the *Wagner-Meerwein rearrangement*, may serve also to enlarge rings, as is shown by the following synthesis of 1,2-dimethylcycloheptene.

[14] V. F. Raaen and C. J. Collins, *J. Am. Chem. Soc.*, **80**, 1409 (1958).

[15] K. C. Laughlin, C. W. Nash, and F. C. Whitmore, *J. Am. Chem. Soc.*, **56**, 1395 (1934).

When 1,2,2,2-tetraphenylethanol is treated with acetyl chloride, tetraphenylethylene is produced.

$$C_6H_5\underset{\underset{OH}{|}}{C}HC(C_6H_5)_3 \rightarrow (C_6H_5)_2C{=}C(C_6H_5)_2 + H_2O$$

The Wagner-Meerwein rearrangement, as far as the carbon skeleton is concerned, is the reverse of the pinacol-pinacolone change; for this reason it is known also as the *retropinacol* rearrangement.[16] The direction of rearrangement is related to the resonance energy provided by conjugation of the substituents with the various possible carbonium ions or radical centers. For example, $(CH_3)_3CCH_2{}^+$ and $(C_6H_5)_3C\overset{+}{C}HC_6H_5$ rearrange and $(CH_3)_3C\overset{+}{C}HC_6H_5$ does not.

Rearrangement occurs in S_N1 reactions but not in S_N2 reactions of neopentyl bromide. This bromide can be made, incidentally, by treating triethylneopentoxysilane with phosphorus tribromide in the presence of quinoline hydrochloride.[17]

$$(CH_3)_3CCH_2OSi(C_2H_5)_3 \xrightarrow{PBr_3} (CH_3)_3CCH_2Br$$

Reaction of Primary Aliphatic Amines with Nitrous Acid

Salts of nitrous acid and aliphatic amino compounds usually are unstable, undergoing decomposition at ordinary temperatures or when warmed. The reaction is illustrated by the action of nitrous acid on benzylamine, benzyl alcohol being produced.

$$C_6H_5CH_2NH_3NO_2 \rightarrow C_6H_5CH_2OH + N_2 + H_2O$$

This type of reaction has limited usefulness, however, partly because of the formation of by-products. In many instances it gives rise to olefins, showing that the mechanism of the change is more complex than is indicated by the equation; moreover, the alcohol is often accompanied by an isomeric alcohol. Isobutylamine gives a mixture containing three times as much *t*-butyl alcohol as isobutyl alcohol. An explanation of these results is provided by the assumption that a carbonium ion is produced by disintegration of the unstable diazo compound.

$$R{-}N{=}NOH \rightarrow R^+ + N_2 + OH^-$$

As we have seen (p. 19), such ions, failing to unite promptly with a base (in this case water), may eliminate a proton. Also, they may rearrange to

[16] R. B. Scott and J. B. Gayle, *J. Org. Chem.*, **18**, 740 (1953).

[17] L. H. Sommer, H. D. Blankman, and P. C. Miller, *J. Am. Chem. Soc.*, **76**, 803 (1954).

more stable ions according to the postulates of hyperconjugation (p. 10). The isomeric alcohol is formed from the more stable carbonium ion. The origin of the products obtained from isobutylamine, for example, may be accounted for by the following changes.

$$(1) \quad CH_3CHCH_2^+ \rightleftharpoons CH_3\overset{+}{C}CH_3 \overset{OH^-}{\longrightarrow} CH_3\overset{\overset{\displaystyle OH}{|}}{C}CH_3$$
$$\underset{\displaystyle CH_3}{|} \qquad\qquad \underset{\displaystyle CH_3}{|} \qquad\qquad \underset{\displaystyle CH_3}{|}$$

$$(2) \quad CH_3CHCH_2^+ \overset{-H^+}{\longrightarrow} CH_3C{=\!=}CH_2$$
$$\underset{\displaystyle CH_3}{|} \qquad\qquad \underset{\displaystyle CH_3}{|}$$

$$(3) \quad CH_3CHCH_2^+ + OH^- \longrightarrow CH_3CHCH_2OH$$
$$\underset{\displaystyle CH_3}{|} \qquad\qquad\qquad\qquad \underset{\displaystyle CH_3}{|}$$

The action of nitrous acid on amino acids is the basis of the Van Slyke method (p. 542).

Demjanov ring expansion

Alicyclic amines may undergo ring opening or enlargement; cyclo-propylamine yields allyl alcohol as the chief product. It is not surprising, of course, that ring opening occurs, since the allyl carbonium ion is a resonance hybrid.

$$\begin{array}{c} CH_2 \\ | \quad\diagdown \\ \quad\quad CHNH_2 \rightarrow CH_2{=\!=}CHCH_2OH \\ | \quad\diagup \\ CH_2 \end{array}$$

Cyclobutanemethylamine gives cyclopentanol and cyclobutanemethanol, as well as the corresponding olefins.

The ring enlargement can be represented as a rearrangement of the primary carbonium ion.

$$\begin{array}{c} CH_2{-}CHCH_2^+ \\ | \qquad | \\ CH_2{-}CH_2 \end{array} \rightarrow \begin{array}{c} CH_2{-}\overset{+}{CH} \\ | \qquad\quad\diagdown \\ \qquad\qquad CH_2 \\ | \qquad\quad\diagup \\ CH_2{-}CH_2 \end{array}$$

This type of reaction, known as the Demjanov ring expansion (OR **11** 157), has served to enlarge all sizes from three- through eight-membered rings. The rearrangement occurs when a primary alkyl group is converted to a secondary or tertiary one, when strain is relieved in a small (four- or five-membered) ring, or when a benzyl alcohol is produced from a phenethylamine.[18]

There is much evidence that the carbonium ions indicated for these deamination reactions are not free, the transformations often having much S_N2 character.

An extension of the Demjanov method to aminomethylcycloalkanols, known as the Tiffeneau-Demjanov ring expansion (OR **11**, 157), is illustrated by the last step in the synthesis of cycloheptanone from cyclohexanone (OS **34**, 19).

Rearrangements similar to that of pinacols occur when 1,2-amino alcohols are deaminated with nitrous acid.[19] An example is the rearrangement of 1,1-diphenyl-2-amino-1-propanol to give 1,2-diphenyl-1-propanone.

This type of change is known as *semipinacolinic deamination*. The example chosen is of interest because, when an optically active form of the amine is employed, the carbon atom (marked with an asterisk) bearing the amino group undergoes a Walden inversion (Gould, 148) in the reaction. Apparently the phenyl group attacks the carbon at the rear at the moment that the nitrogen atom is released.

[18] P. A. S. Smith, D. R. Baer, and S. N. Ege, *J. Am. Chem. Soc.*, **76**, 4564 (1954).
[19] See H. O. House and E. J. Grubbs, *J. Am. Chem. Soc.*, **81**, 4733 (1959).

Rearrangement of Diazoketones

Diazoketones rearrange with loss of nitrogen in the presence of a catalyst—generally colloidal silver—and in water yield acids. If the base is an alcohol or ammonia, esters or amides are produced, respectively. An example of this reaction, known as the Wolff rearrangement (OR 1, 41), is the preparation of phenylacetamide from diazoacetophenone.

$$C_6H_5COCHN_2 + NH_3 \rightarrow C_6H_5CH_2CONH_2 + N_2$$

An extraordinary result is obtained when o-diazoöxides, made by the action of nitrous acid on o-aminophenols, are decomposed by radiation in the near ultraviolet region. The benzene ring is contracted; the product obtained from o-aminophenol is cyclopentadienecarboxylic acid.[20]

[20] See P. A. S. Smith and W. L. Berry, *J. Org. Chem.*, **26**, 27 (1961).

11

Molecular rearrangements involving nitrogen and oxygen atoms

Many molecular rearrangements are known in which nitrogen and oxygen atoms appear to play a role similar to that attributed to carbon in analogous rearrangements in which carbon is the key element.[1]

Rearrangements Involving a Nitrogen Atom

The most important reactions of this group are the Hofmann degradation of amides, the Lossen rearrangement of hydroxamic acids, the Curtius decomposition of acid azides, the Schmidt reaction of carbonyl compounds with hydrazoic acid, and the Beckmann rearrangement of oximes.

Hofmann degradation

Amides react with bromine and alkali in the presence of water, to give amines of one less carbon atom. The reaction, discovered by Hofmann, is applicable to a wide variety of aliphatic and aromatic amides. The N-bromoamide that forms initially reacts with the alkali to yield an isocyanate, which in aqueous solution is hydrolyzed to an amine (OR **3,** 267).

$$RCONH_2 + Br_2 + OH^- \rightarrow RCONHBr + Br^- + H_2O$$
$$RCONHBr + OH^- \rightarrow [RCONBr]^- + H_2O$$
$$[RCONBr]^- \rightarrow RN{=}C{=}O + Br^-$$
$$RN{=}C{=}O + H_2O \rightarrow RNH_2 + CO_2$$

The rearrangement step is perhaps best represented as a concerted process undergone by the conjugate base of the N-bromo amide.

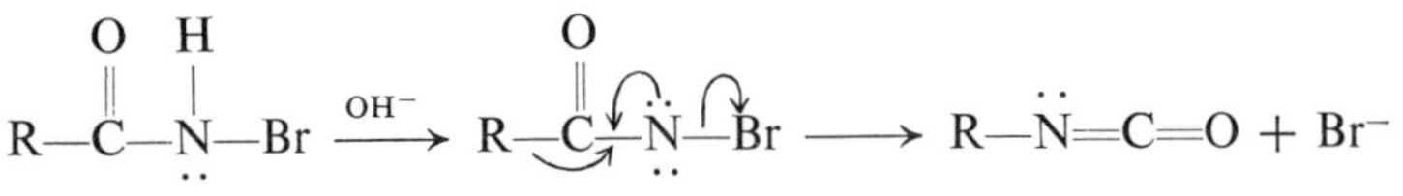

---

[1] F. C. Whitmore, *J. Am. Chem. Soc.*, **54,** 3274 (1932).

191

If R is asymmetric, it is found that optical activity is retained; an example is the rearrangement of α-benzylpropionamide to α-benzylethylamine.

This transformation is useful in the aromatic series in cases in which the amino group cannot be introduced by more conventional methods. An example is the synthesis of 3-aminopyridine from nicotinamide.

In the isoquinoline series the only readily available 3-substituted derivative is 3-methylisoquinoline. 3-Aminoisoquinoline is prepared from it by the following sequence of changes; the yield in the final step is 64%.[2]

Veratramide gives 4-aminoveratrole (OS II, 44); the yield is 82%.

If methanol is employed instead of water, the product is the corresponding carbamate. This modification of the procedure is useful for amides of aliphatic acids above caprylic acid, since these afford amines in unsatisfactory yields in aqueous media. The amine can be obtained, with

---

[2] C. E. Teague, Jr., and A. Roe, *J. Am. Chem. Soc.*, **73**, 688 (1951).

little loss, from the carbamate; the preparation of undecylamine from lauramide is an illustration.

$$C_{11}H_{23}CONH_2 \xrightarrow[Br_2]{CH_3ONa} C_{11}H_{23}NHCO_2CH_3 \xrightarrow[H_2O]{OH^-} C_{11}H_{23}NH_2$$

If one-half the usual amounts of bromine and alkali are used, acyl alkyl ureas are produced by union of the isocyanate with unchanged amide. From acetamide, for example, 1-acetyl-3-methylurea is obtained in yields of 90% (OS II, 462).

$$CH_3CONH_2 + Br_2 + 2NaOH \rightarrow CH_3N{=}C{=}O + 2NaBr + 2H_2O$$

$$CH_3N{=}C{=}O + CH_3CONH_2 \rightarrow CH_3NHCONHCOCH_3$$

The failure of the original Hofmann procedure to be useful with the higher amides is due to the tendency of the hypohalite to dehydrogenate the amine. With an excess of bromine in alkaline solution primary amines yield the corresponding nitriles, the dibromo amine being formed as an intermediate. This method is convenient for the production of the nitriles of aliphatic acids having an odd number of carbon atoms.

$$RCH_2CONH_2 \rightarrow RCH_2NH_2 \rightarrow RCH_2NBr_2 \rightarrow RCN$$

Succinimide undergoes the Hofmann reaction to give β-alanine in yields of 45% (OS II, 19).

$$\begin{matrix} CH_2CO \\ | \quad\quad\quad {\Large\diagdown} \\ \quad\quad\quad\quad NH + KOBr + 2KOH \rightarrow \\ | \quad\quad\quad {\Large\diagup} \\ CH_2CO \end{matrix} \quad\quad \begin{matrix} CH_2NH_2 \\ | \quad\quad\quad\quad + KBr + K_2CO_3 \\ CH_2CO_2H \end{matrix}$$

The method has been used successfully also with phthalimide, anthranilic acid being formed in high yields.

In the reactions with imides the N-bromo derivative is formed first and then decomposed by action of the alkali.

As would be expected, aldehydes are produced from amides of α-hydroxy acids or α,β-unsaturated acids. Phenylacetaldehyde is formed from cinnamamide in satisfactory yield by way of methyl styrylcarbamate.

$$C_6H_5CH{=}CHCONH_2 \rightarrow C_6H_5CH{=}CHNHCO_2CH_3 \rightarrow C_6H_5CH_2CHO$$

In a similar way mandelamide yields benzaldehyde.

$$C_6H_5\underset{\underset{OH}{|}}{C}HCONH_2 \rightarrow [C_6H_5\underset{\underset{OH}{|}}{C}HNH_2] \rightarrow C_6H_5CHO + NH_3$$

The method fails also with urea since the product, hydrazine, is readily oxidized by the reagent. Hydrazine may be obtained, however, if urea is employed in excess. Aryl semicarbazides yield aryl azides, apparently by the following steps.

$$ArNHNHCONH_2 \rightarrow ArN{=}NCONH_2 \rightarrow [ArN{=}N{-}NH_2] \rightarrow ArN_3$$

Lossen rearrangement

Hydroxamic acids and their acyl derivatives undergo a rearrangement that is very similar to the Hofmann reaction (CR **33**, 209); the leaving group in the case of the acyl derivatives is a carboxylate ion instead of a halide ion (Hine, 318).

$$R{-}\underset{\underset{O}{\|}}{C}{-}\underset{\underset{H}{|}}{N}{-}O{-}\underset{\underset{O}{\|}}{C}R' \rightarrow R{-}\underset{\underset{O}{\|}}{C}{-}N{-}O{-}\underset{\underset{O}{\|}}{C}R' \rightarrow R{-}N{=}C{=}O + R'CO_2^-$$

Curtius reaction

A rearrangement discovered by Curtius in 1890 resembles that of Hofmann except that the acid azide is the rearranging species instead of the bromo amide (OR **3**, 337).

$$R\underset{\underset{O}{\|}}{C}{-}N_3 \rightarrow RN{=}C{=}O + N_2$$

The reaction is useful for the preparation not only of isocyanates but also for compounds derivable from them, such as urethans, amides, and amines. The usual route to the acid azides involves the preparation of the corresponding acid hydrazides by the action of hydrazine on esters (p. 342). The hydrazides give azides when treated with nitrous acid.

$$RCO_2R + H_2NNH_2 \rightarrow RCONHNH_2 + ROH$$

$$RCONHNH_2 + HNO_2 \rightarrow RCON_3 + 2H_2O$$

Acid azides may be formed also by the interaction of acid chlorides and sodium azide.

$$RCOCl + NaN_3 \rightarrow RCON_3 + NaCl$$

An example of the Curtius reaction is the formation of undecyl isocyanate from lauroyl azide (OS III, 846; 86% yield).

$$n\text{-}C_{11}H_{23}CON_3 \rightarrow n\text{-}C_{11}H_{23}N{=}C{=}O + N_2$$

Since isocyanates are easily hydrolyzed, the Curtius reaction furnishes a practical procedure for replacing a carboxyl group by an amino group.

Another example is the preparation of benzylamine from ethyl phenylacetate by way of the urethan.

$$C_6H_5CH_2CO_2C_2H_5 \rightarrow C_6H_5CH_2CON_3 \rightarrow$$
$$C_6H_5CH_2N{=}C{=}O \rightarrow C_6H_5CH_2NH_2$$

The preparation of putrescine from diethyl adipate is similar (OS **36**, 69).

$$
\begin{array}{ccc}
\text{CH}_2\text{CH}_2\text{CO}_2\text{C}_2\text{H}_5 & \text{CH}_2\text{CH}_2\text{CON}_3 & \text{CH}_2\text{CH}_2\text{NH}_2 \\
| & \rightarrow \quad | & \rightarrow \quad | \\
\text{CH}_2\text{CH}_2\text{CO}_2\text{C}_2\text{H}_5 & \text{CH}_2\text{CH}_2\text{CON}_3 & \text{CH}_2\text{CH}_2\text{NH}_2
\end{array}
$$

Azides of α,β-unsaturated acids are interesting because they yield vinyl isocyanates; hydrolysis of these or the corresponding urethans or ureas yields aldehydes or ketones. Azides of α-hydroxy acids yield aldehydes; an example is the conversion of lactic acid to acetaldehyde.

$$
\begin{array}{ccc}
\text{CH}_3\text{CHCON}_3 & \rightarrow \quad [\text{CH}_3\text{CHNH}_2] & \rightarrow \quad \text{CH}_3\text{CHO} \\
| & | & \\
\text{OH} & \text{OH} &
\end{array}
$$

Another type of aldehyde synthesis involves the hydrazide of a malonic acid derivative. Diethyl benzylmalonate gives phenylacetaldehyde.

$$
\begin{array}{ccc}
\quad\quad \text{CO}_2\text{C}_2\text{H}_5 & \quad\quad \text{CON}_3 & \\
\quad\quad / & \quad\quad / & \\
\text{C}_6\text{H}_5\text{CH}_2\text{CH} & \rightarrow \text{C}_6\text{H}_5\text{CH}_2\text{CH} & \rightarrow \text{C}_6\text{H}_5\text{CH}_2\text{CHO} \\
\quad\quad \backslash & \quad\quad \backslash & \\
\quad\quad \text{CO}_2\text{C}_2\text{H}_5 & \quad\quad \text{CON}_3 &
\end{array}
$$

The mechanism of the Curtius reaction has been formulated as follows (Hine, 319).

Schmidt reaction

Another method for the preparation of amines consists in treating carboxylic acids with hydrazoic acid in the presence of strong mineral acids.

$$RCO_2H + HN_3 \xrightarrow{H_2SO_4} RNH_2 + CO_2 + N_2$$

Hydrazoic acid produces similar changes with other types of carbonyl compounds; the process has become known as the Schmidt reaction (OR **3,** 307). The most extensive application has been in the preparation of amines from saturated aliphatic acids. Adipic acid, for example, gives putrescine in 83% yield.

$$\begin{array}{ccc}
CH_2CH_2CO_2H & & CH_2CH_2NH_2 \\
| & \rightarrow & | \\
CH_2CH_2CO_2H & & CH_2CH_2NH_2
\end{array}$$

Cinnamamide yields phenylacetaldehyde, as would be expected. Curiously, aniline is produced as a by-product. Applied to ketones, the Schmidt method produces amides; from acetone and benzophenone, for example, N-methylacetamide and benzanilide, respectively, are obtained in high yields. When o-phenylbenzophenone is treated with hydrazoic acid, the product is 9-phenylphenanthridine; presumably the carbonium ion produced by the migration of the 2-biphenylyl group is an intermediate.[3]

The mechanism of the Schmidt reaction, illustrated by the behavior of ketones, has been pictured in the following way.

[3] P. A. S. Smith, *J. Am. Chem. Soc.*, **76,** 431 (1954).

Beckmann rearrangement

The configurations of oximes of ketones usually have been assigned on the basis of the products obtained by subjecting them to the action of certain acidic reagents; an isomerization known as the Beckmann rearrangement occurs, the product (amide) from the *syn*-isomer being different from that obtained from the *anti*-isomer.

The Beckmann rearrangement (OR **11**, 1) may be effected by use of such reagents as phosphorus pentachloride, phosphorus oxychloride, acetyl chloride, and sulfuric acid. A mixture of acetic acid, acetyl chloride, and hydrogen chloride—known as "Beckmann's mixture"—has often been used. The reagent of choice is probably polyphosphoric acid; the rate of rearrangement of oximes of acetophenones, for example, is 12 to 35 times as rapid in polyphosphoric acid as in sulfuric acid.[4]

In this rearrangement the shift of groups is *trans* rather than *cis* (CR **12**, 215). The following scheme has been used to represent the change.

$$R-C-R' \rightarrow R'-C-OH \rightarrow R'-C=O$$
$$\quad \parallel \qquad \qquad \parallel \qquad \qquad \mid$$
$$\quad NOH \qquad \quad RN \qquad \qquad NHR$$

$$R-C-R' \rightarrow HO-C-R \rightarrow R-C=O$$
$$\quad \parallel \qquad \qquad \parallel \qquad \qquad \mid$$
$$\quad HON \qquad \quad NR' \qquad \qquad NHR'$$

Hydrolysis of the amide produces an acid and an amine; from these the structure of the original ketone is deduced. The Beckmann rearrangement serves as a synthetic method for amides, as illustrated by the preparation of ε-caprolactam (OS II, 76, 371).

$$\begin{array}{ccc} CH_2CH_2 & & CH_2CH_2CO \\ H_2C & C=NOH \rightarrow H_2C & | \\ CH_2CH_2 & & CH_2CH_2NH \end{array}$$

Monoximes of α-diketones undergo a type of rearrangement known as a Beckmann rearrangement of the second order, the products being an acid and a nitrile. This reaction is a key step in a method of degrading aliphatic acids that takes the following course.[5]

$$RCH_2CH_2CH_2CO_2H \rightarrow RCH_2CH_2CH_2COCl \rightarrow$$

$$\qquad \qquad \qquad \qquad \overset{NOH}{\parallel}$$
$$RCH_2CH_2CH_2COC_6H_5 \rightarrow RCH_2CH_2CCOC_6H_5 \rightarrow$$
$$\qquad \qquad RCH_2CH_2CN \rightarrow RCH_2CH_2CO_2H$$

---

[4] D. E. Pearson and R. M. Stone, *J. Am. Chem. Soc.*, **83**, 1715 (1961).

[5] See W. G. Dauben, E. Hoerger, and J. W. Petersen, *J. Am. Chem. Soc.*, **75**, 2347 (1953).

A synthesis of the hydrochloride of *dl*-lysine from cyclohexanone involves a second-order Beckmann rearrangement.[6]

$$\text{HON}\!\!=\!\!\overset{\displaystyle O}{\bigcirc}\!\!=\!\!\text{NOH} \quad \xrightarrow[\substack{(CH_3CO)_2O}]{\substack{CH_3CH_2OH \\ CH_3CH_2ONa}} \quad \overset{\displaystyle \text{NOH}}{NC(CH_2)_3\overset{\|}{C}CO_2C_2H_5} \quad \xrightarrow[\substack{(CH_3CO)_2O}]{H_2,Ni}$$

$$\underset{\displaystyle CH_3CONH(CH_2)_4\overset{|}{C}HCO_2C_2H_5}{\overset{\displaystyle NHCOCH_3}{}} \quad \xrightarrow[H_2O]{HCl} \quad \underset{\displaystyle H_2N(CH_2)_4\overset{|}{C}HCO_2H\cdot HCl}{\overset{\displaystyle NH_2}{}}$$

Certain oximes behave anomalously; in the presence of *p*-toluene-sulfonic acid they yield the corresponding α-amino ketones. This transformation, known as the *Neber rearrangement*, is illustrated by the behavior of the oxime of 2,4-dinitrophenylacetone.[7]

$$O_2N\!\!\overset{\displaystyle NO_2}{\underset{\displaystyle \underset{NOH}{CH_2\overset{\|}{C}CH_3}}{\bigcirc}} \rightarrow O_2N\!\!\overset{\displaystyle NO_2}{\underset{\displaystyle CH\!\!-\!\!\underset{N}{C}\!\!-\!\!CH_3}{\bigcirc}} \rightarrow$$

$$O_2N\!\!\overset{\displaystyle NO_2}{\underset{\displaystyle \underset{NH_2}{CHCOCH_3}}{\bigcirc}}$$

The mechanism of the Beckmann rearrangement must be very similar to those already given. In some cases intermediate esters have been isolated and found to undergo rearrangement (Hine, 321). The rearrangement of the acetyl derivative of benzophenone oxime is an example.

$$\underset{\displaystyle \underset{C_6H_5 \quad C_6H_5}{\overset{\displaystyle \|}{C}}}{\overset{\displaystyle \overset{OCOCH_3}{N:}}{}} \quad \xrightarrow{-CH_3CO_2^-} \quad C_6H_5\!\!-\!\!\overset{..}{N}\!\!=\!\!\overset{+}{C}\!\!-\!\!C_6H_5 \quad \xrightarrow{H_2O}$$

$$\underset{\displaystyle C_6H_5\!\!-\!\!N\!\!=\!\!\overset{|}{C}\!\!-\!\!C_6H_5}{\overset{\displaystyle OH}{}} \quad \longrightarrow \quad C_6H_5NHCOC_6H_5$$

[6] A. F. Ferris, F. E. Gould, G. S. Johnson, H. K. Latourette, and H. Stange, *Chem. and Ind.*, 996 (1959).

[7] M. J. Hatch and D. J. Cram, *J. Am. Chem. Soc.*, **75**, 38 (1953).

Stieglitz rearrangement

Triarylmethylhydroxylamines undergo rearrangement when treated with phosphorus pentachloride to produce anils. Triphenylmethyl-hydroxylamine, for example, gives the anil of benzophenone.

$$(C_6H_5)_3CNHOH \rightarrow (C_6H_5)_2C{=}NC_6H_5 + H_2O$$

This type of change, known as the Stieglitz rearrangement, has been used to compare migration aptitudes of aryl radicals.[8] The Stieglitz rearrangement may be compared to the Wagner-Meerwein rearrangement (p. 186).

Isomerization of N-substituted anilines

Substituents attached to the nitrogen atom in aromatic amines show a tendency to migrate to the ring. The isomerization of nitrosamines to nuclear nitroso derivatives has already been mentioned (p. 107). N-Alkyanilines suffer a transfer of alkyl groups when their hydrochlorides or hydrobromides are heated in a sealed tube, *p*-derivatives being produced. Methylaniline hydrochloride gives *p*-toluidine hydrochloride in satisfactory yields. It seems probable that the alkyl group is removed as an alkyl halide, which then alkylates the aniline at the *p*-position. If that position is occupied, the migrating group goes to an *o*- but never to an *m*-position. Isomerization of phenylhydrazine to *p*-phenylenediamine, likewise effected by heating the hydrochloride, illustrates the migration of an amino group.

β-Arylhydroxylamines. Reactions of the general type under discussion might conceivably involve an intermediate containing an electron-deficient nitrogen atom. The deficiency would, of course, be taken over in large degree by the ring. One of the group of reactions that has been formulated in such a way is the rearrangement of phenylhydroxylamines to amino-phenols, which is catalyzed by acids. An example is the formation of 4-amino-3-chlorophenol from *o*-chlorophenylhydroxylamine by treatment with sulfuric acid (OS **35**, 22).

The following mechanism has been proposed for the analogous reaction of *β*-phenylhydroxylamine.[9]

[8] M. S. Newman and P. M. Hay, *J. Am. Chem. Soc.*, **75**, 2322 (1953).
[9] H. E. Heller, E. D. Hughes, and C. K. Ingold, *Nature*, **168**, 909 (1951).

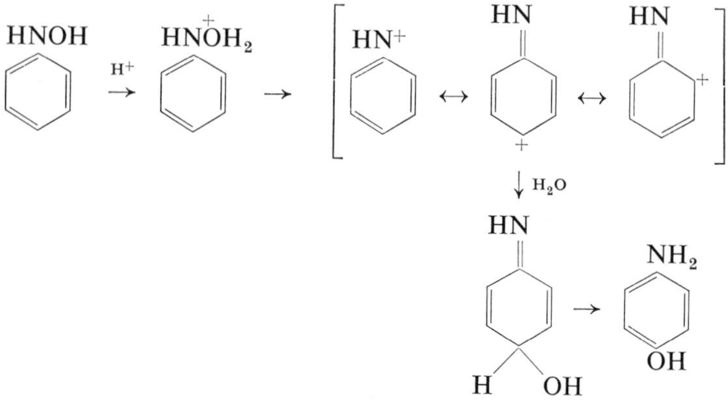

Wallach Rearrangement. A very similar change occurs when azoxy compounds are treated with concentrated sulfuric acid; they undergo rearrangement to the corresponding hydroxyazo derivatives, the *p*-isomers predominating. Azoxybenzene, for example, gives *p*-hydroxyazobenzene.

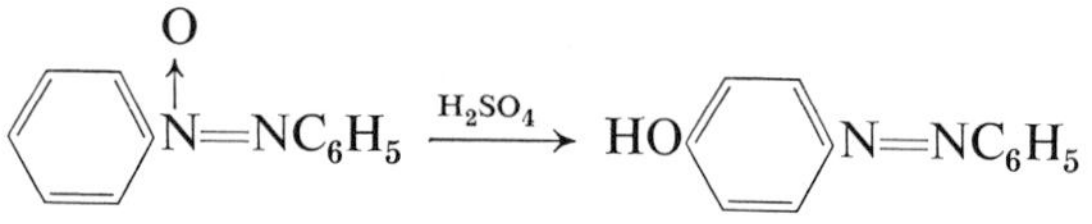

This reaction, known as the Wallach rearrangement, has been made the basis of a generic test for azoxy compounds.[10] The azoxy compound reacts with sulfuric acid to give a bright red solution, which deposits the azophenol when diluted with water. The product is fairly soluble in dilute basic solution.

Benzidine Rearrangement. By far the most important rearrangement of this type occurs when hydrazobenzenes are treated with acids. Hydrazobenzene itself yields benzidine, from which the reaction gets its name.

Benzidine

Semidine is produced also but has been shown not to be an intermediate; when subjected to the conditions that produce benzidine rearrangements, it is recovered unchanged.

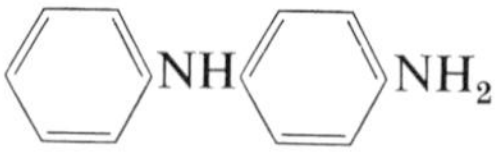

Semidine

[10] R. Gaudry and K. F. Keirstead, *Can. J. Research*, **27**, 897 (1949).

Diphenyline is formed also from hydrazobenzene, but the amount is never more than one-fourth that of benzidine.

Diphenyline

The benzidine rearrangement is of special interest because it is known to proceed intramolecularly.[11] Rearrangement to an *o*-position is observed also, and in the naphthalene series, *o,o*-diamines have been produced. These compounds may undergo ring closure to form pyrroles. 1-Hydrazonaphthalene, for example, yields a dibenzocarbazole.

The formation of a pyrrole derivative from a hydrazine in this way is analogous to the change that occurs in the Fischer indole synthesis.

Fischer indole synthesis

The most important general method of preparing indoles, discovered by Emil Fischer, involves the elimination of ammonia from phenylhydrazones. The phenylhydrazone of acetone, for example, yields 2-methylindole.

The catalyst may be zinc chloride, dilute sulfuric acid, alcoholic hydrochloric acid, or glacial acetic acid.

In a similar way 2-phenylindole may be prepared from the phenylhydrazone of acetophenone (OS III, 725; 80% yield).

[11] See M. D. Cohen and G. S. Hammond, *J. Am. Chem. Soc.*, **75**, 880 (1953).

When phenylhydrazine is added to a boiling solution of cyclohexanone in acetic acid, the phenylhydrazone that forms undergoes ring closure directly, giving 1,2,3,4-tetrahydrocarbazole; the yield is 95%.[12]

A convenient procedure for the synthesis of ethyl 3-indoleacetate involves treatment of ethyl γ,γ-dimethoxybutyrate with phenylhydrazine. The acetal, readily available from the hydroformylation (p. 647) of ethyl acrylate, is converted into the corresponding aldehyde-ester, the phenylhydrazone of which undergoes cyclization.[13]

3-Methyloxindole is formed from β-propionylphenylhydrazine in a similar way (OS **37**, 60; 44% yield).

It has been proposed that the Fischer indole synthesis proceeds by way of a rearrangement analogous to an o-benzidine rearrangement.

[12] C. U. Rogers and B. B. Corson, *J. Am. Chem. Soc.*, **69**, 2910 (1947).
[13] M. W. Bullock and S. W. Fox, *J. Am. Chem. Soc.*, **73**, 5155 (1951).

Rearrangement of Peroxidic Compounds

One way in which an electron-deficient oxygen atom could arise would be by heterolytic fission of the peroxide linkage. The decomposition of cumene hydroperoxide to give phenol and acetone, for example, has been formulated in the following way (Hine, 326). Apparently migration of a methyl group occurs also, since acetophenone and methanol are formed as by-products.

$$
\begin{array}{ccc}
\underset{\underset{C_6H_5}{|}}{\overset{\overset{CH_3}{|}}{CH_3-C-O-OH}} \overset{H^+}{\rightleftharpoons} & \underset{\underset{C_6H_5}{|}}{\overset{\overset{CH_3\quad H}{|}}{CH_3-C-O-O^+-H}} \xrightarrow{-H_2O} & \underset{\underset{C_6H_5}{|}}{\overset{\overset{CH_3}{|}}{CH_3C-O}}
\end{array}
$$

$$
\underset{\underset{C_6H_5}{|}}{\overset{\overset{CH_3}{|}}{CH_3-C-O}} \xrightarrow{H_2O} \left[\underset{\underset{OH}{|}}{\overset{\overset{CH_3}{|}}{CH_3-C-OC_6H_5}} \right] \rightarrow C_6H_5OH + CH_3COCH_3
$$

The conversion of *p*-cymene into acetone and *p*-cresol is similar. Analogous is the formation of acetone and neopentyl alcohol from the hydroperoxide made from the diisobutylenes (OS **40**, 76).

$$
\underset{\underset{CH_3}{|}}{\overset{\overset{CH_3\qquad CH_3}{|\qquad\quad|}}{CH_3C-CH_2-COOH}} \rightarrow CH_3COCH_3 + (CH_3)_3CCH_2OH
$$

The absence of *t*-amyl alcohol among the products is taken to mean that the neopentyl carbonium ion is not an intermediate in the reaction.[14]

In the rearrangement of the 9-decalyl ester of perbenzoic acid the peroxide linkage appears to undergo heterolytic cleavage (Hine, 322).

(Ion-pair)

Experiments with the perester labeled with O^{18} in the carbonyl group show that all the O^{18} remains in this group during rearrangement and lead to the assumption that the ions are not free but held as an ion-pair (Gould, 102).[15]

---

[14] J. Hoffman and C. E. Boord, *J. Am. Chem. Soc.*, **77**, 3139 (1955).

[15] D. B. Denney, *J. Am. Chem. Soc.*, **77**, 1706 (1955).

Baeyer-Villiger oxidation

The transformation of carbonyl compounds by peracids, known as the Baeyer-Villiger oxidation (OR 9, 73), has been represented in the following way (Hine, 324).

$$R'CO_3H + R_2CO \rightarrow R'-\overset{O}{\overset{\|}{C}}-O-O-\overset{R}{\underset{R}{\overset{|}{C}}}-O-H \rightarrow$$

$$R'CO_2^- + RO\overset{}{\underset{R}{\overset{|}{C}}}=O + H^+$$

The oxidizing agent originally employed in this work was monopersulfuric acid, known as Caro's acid; later investigations showed that similar results can be obtained with perbenzoic acid. When acetophenone, for example, is treated at 23 to 26° with perbenzoic acid for ten days in moist chloroform solution, phenyl acetate is obtained in 63% yield.

That the reaction is intramolecular is shown by the fact that optically active 3-phenyl-2-butanone yields optically active α-methylbenzyl acetate with the opposite sign of rotation.[16]

$$\overset{CH_3}{\underset{}{\overset{|}{C_6H_5CHCOCH_3}}} \rightarrow \overset{CH_3}{\underset{}{\overset{|}{C_6H_5CHOCOCH_3}}}$$

The Baeyer-Villiger cleavage of simple aldehydes and ketones is quantitative with peroxytrifluoroacetic acid in ethylene chloride solution and affords a method for determining such compounds.[17] When α-diketones are treated with peracids, anhydrides are produced; biacetyl, for example, yields acetic anhydride.

$$\overset{O \quad O}{\underset{}{\overset{\| \quad \|}{CH_3C-CCH_3}}} \rightarrow \overset{O \qquad O}{\underset{}{\overset{\| \qquad \|}{CH_3C-O-CCH_3}}}$$

o-Quinones behave in a similar way as is illustrated by 1,2-naphthoquinone.

[16] K. Mislow and J. Brenner, J. Am. Chem. Soc., 75, 2318 (1953).
[17] M. F. Hawthorne, Anal. Chem., 28, 540 (1956).

Cyclanones react with perbenzoic acid in chloroform to give the corresponding lactones. The rate of the cleavage is at a maximum for cyclohexanone and falls off as the ring size is either increased or decreased. The products from cyclobutanone and cyclooctanone, isolated as the corresponding ω-hydroxyhydrazides, are obtained in yields of 70 and 61 %, respectively.[18]

This reaction has been applied spectacularly to many-membered cyclic ketones, lactones containing large rings having been produced in this way.

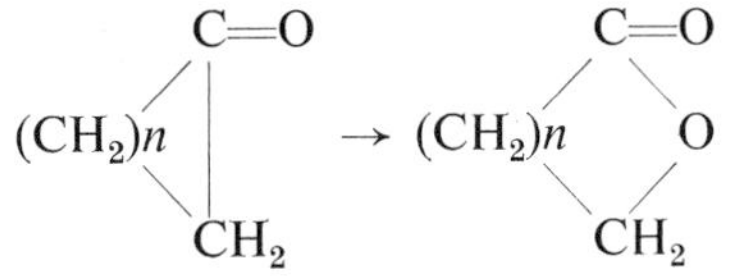

$$(CH_2)n \underset{CH_2}{\overset{C=O}{|}} \rightarrow (CH_2)n \underset{CH_2}{\overset{C=O}{\diagdown}} O$$

Peracetic acid oxidizes β-naphthol to o-carboxycinnamic acid (OS **34**, 8; yield 70%).

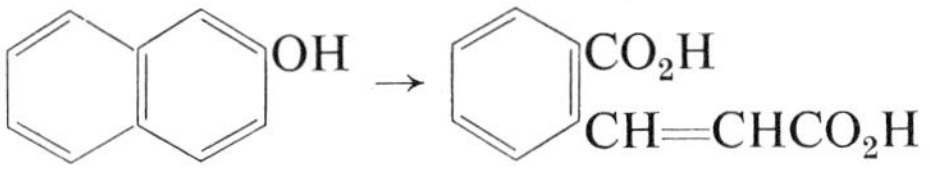

When fluorenone is treated with a mixture of acetic anhydride, hydrogen peroxide, and sulfuric acid, the corresponding lactone is produced in 65% yield.[19]

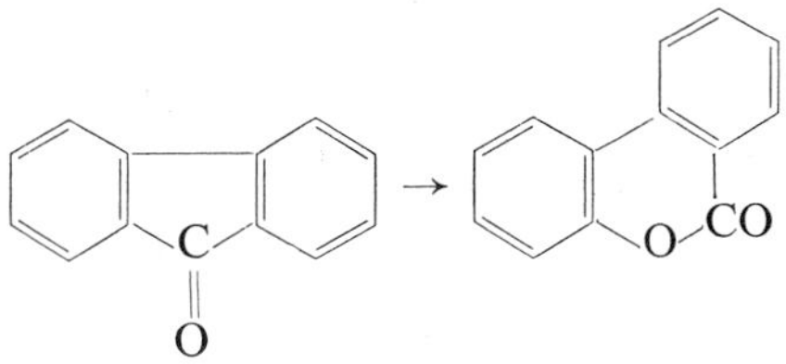

As is well known, α-dicarbonyl compounds are cleaved readily by hydrogen peroxide in the presence of alkali. This reaction is, in fact, a test for the presence of twinned carbonyl groups. The oxidation of benzil to benzoic acid is an example.

$$C_6H_5COCOC_6H_5 + H_2O_2 \rightarrow 2C_6H_5CO_2H$$

Dakin reaction

Dakin found that hydrogen peroxide in the presence of alkali is capable of replacing an acyl group on an aromatic ring with a hydroxyl group. In

---

[18] S. L. Friess and P. E. Frankenburg, *J. Am. Chem. Soc.*, **74**, 2679 (1952).
[19] G. Wittig and G. Pieper, *Ber.*, **73**, 295 (1940).

other words, aromatic aldehydes and ketones yield the corresponding phenols. Salicylaldehyde gives catechol in 73% yield (OS I, 149).

In a similar way, 2-hydroxy-3-methoxybenzaldehyde can be converted into a methyl ether of pyrogallol (OS III, 759; 80% yield).

The Dakin cleavage is limited to aromatic aldehydes and ketones that have a hydroxyl or an amino group in an *o*- or *p*-position. The mechanism by which this cleavage occurs is probably similar to that proposed for the Baeyer-Villiger oxidation (Hine, 324).

12

Oxidation

The rearrangements involving electron-deficient oxygen atoms that have been discussed are steps in oxidative processes and may serve to open the way to a discussion of the broad topic of oxidation in organic chemistry. Attention will be restricted to reactions that produce a new carbon-oxygen bond. Oxidation by oxygen is usually considered to involve radicals rather than ions, and its treatment will be deferred (Chapter 24). Other reagents that operate by a one-electron transfer are ceric sulfate, ammoniacal silver nitrate, Fehling's and Benedict's solutions, and ferricyanide.

Many of the most commonly used oxidizing agents such as dichromate and permanganate, however, may be classified as electrophilic since they attack olefinic bonds and other functions known to be sensitive to the action of electrophiles. In what follows the discussion is organized not by reference to reagents but rather to the type of change that is effected.

Carbonyl Groups from Methylene Groups

The synthesis of ketones by oxidation of a CH_2 group to a carbonyl group is not difficult if the ketone is resistant to attack by the oxidizing agent. Diaryl ketones, which are relatively difficult to oxidize by dichromate, permanganate, and nitric acid, can be made by the action of such reagents on the corresponding diarylmethanes. Benzophenone is formed in 90% yield when diphenylmethane is heated with dilute nitric acid in the presence of lead acetate. 2-Benzoylpyridine is obtained in similar yield by subjecting 2-benzylpyridine to oxidation with permanganate.

Fluorenone has been prepared by oxidizing fluorene with sodium dichromate in glacial acetic acid.

When 2-acetylfluorene is oxidized in a similar manner, both the acetyl and the methylene groups are attacked, the product being 2-fluorenone-carboxylic acid (OS III, 420; 74% yield).

Acenaphthene, when treated with a mixture of sodium dichromate and glacial acetic acid in the presence of a small amount of ceric acetate, gives acenaphthenequinone (OS III, 1; 60% yield).

Oxidation of methyl groups generally is not difficult but is hard to interrupt at the aldehyde stage. One procedure for accomplishing this change involves the use of chromium trioxide in acetic anhydride that contains sulfuric acid. An example of the use of this technique is the synthesis of p-nitrobenzaldehyde from p-nitrotoluene (OS **36**, 58). The aldehyde diacetate is formed, thus preventing the oxidation from going too far; the diacetate is easily hydrolyzed to the aldehyde.

$$p\text{-}O_2NC_6H_4CH_3 \xrightarrow[\text{(CH}_3\text{CO)}_2\text{O}]{\text{(O)}} p\text{-}O_2NC_6H_4CH(OCOCH_3)_2 \xrightarrow[\text{H}_2\text{SO}_4]{\text{H}_2\text{O}}$$

$$p\text{-}O_2NC_6H_4CHO$$

o-Nitrotoluene gives less satisfactory results, the yields of o-nitro-benzaldehyde being only about 18% (OS III, 641). Other examples are p-bromo- and p-cyanobenzaldehydes (OS II, 442). The method is applicable to the preparation of benzaldehydes in which there is no substituent easily attacked by the oxidizing agent.

Chromyl chloride (CrO_2Cl_2) can be used to oxidize many types of organic compounds (CR **58**, 25). For example, it transforms toluene to benzaldehyde, a molecular complex being isolated as an intermediate.

This method has attracted special attention because it serves to oxidize only one methyl group even when others are present; *m*-xylene gives *m*-tolualdehyde in 80% yield.

$$CH_3 \quad\quad\quad CH_3 \; (CrO_2Cl_2)_2 \quad\quad CHO$$

(structure) $+ 2CrO_2Cl_2 \longrightarrow$ (structure) $\xrightarrow{H_2O}$ (structure) CH_3

Another example of this reaction, known as the Étard reaction, is the oxidation of 2-methoxy-6-nitrotoluene to 2-methoxy-6-nitrobenzaldehyde.[1]

$$NO_2 \quad\quad\quad NO_2$$

(structure) CH_3 $\rightarrow$ (structure) CHO
$OCH_3 \quad\quad\quad OCH_3$

Ethyl side chains can be changed to acetyl groups by suitable procedures. *o*-Ethylacetophenone, for example, is oxidized by potassium permanganate in the presence of magnesium nitrate to *o*-diacetylbenzene in 71% yield.[2]

Dimethyl sulfoxide acts upon α-bromo ketones to produce the corresponding glyoxals; phenacyl bromide, for example, gives phenylglyoxal in 71% yield.

$$C_6H_5COCH_2Br \xrightarrow{(CH_3)_2SO} C_6H_5COCHO$$

The method serves also to convert alkyl halides and alkyl tosylates into the corresponding aldehydes.[3]

Nitro groups sometimes act as oxidizing agents, being thereby reduced to amino groups. The use of nitrobenzene in the Skraup synthesis (p. 124) is based on this fact. Intramolecular changes of this sort are not infrequent. In the presence of sodium hydroxide and sodium sulfide monohydrate, the methyl group of *p*-nitrotoluene, for example, is oxidized at the expense of the nitro group, the product being *p*-aminobenzaldehyde (OS **31**, 6; yield, 50%).

$$CH_3 \quad\quad CHO$$

(structure) $\rightarrow$ (structure)
$NO_2 \quad\quad NH_2$

A novel oxidative coupling takes place when certain nitro derivatives of toluene and similar compounds are exposed to air in the presence of

[1] G. R. Pettit, *J. Org. Chem.*, **24**, 866 (1959).

[2] W. Winkler, *Chem. Ber.*, **81**, 256 (1948).

[3] N. Kornblum, W. J. Jones, and G. J. Anderson, *J. Am. Chem. Soc.*, **81**, 4113 (1959).

alcoholic alkali. *p*-Nitrotoluene, for example, gives *p,p'*-dinitrobibenzyl in 76% yield (OS **34**, 35).

$$2CH_3\text{—}C_6H_4\text{—}NO_2 \rightarrow O_2N\text{—}C_6H_4\text{—}CH_2CH_2\text{—}C_6H_4\text{—}NO_2$$

Selenium dioxide

Of unusual value in the oxidation of methyl and methylene groups is selenium dioxide (OR **5**, 331). Aldehydes and ketones that have a methyl or a methylene group attached to the functional group are oxidized by this reagent to the corresponding dicarbonyl compounds (CR **36**, 235). The method is at its best with compounds that have only one methyl or methylene group that can react. Acetophenone gives phenylglyoxal in 72% yield when treated with an equimolecular quantity of selenium dioxide for 4 hours in boiling dioxane (OS II, 509).

$$C_6H_5COCH_3 + SeO_2 \rightarrow C_6H_5COCHO + Se + H_2O$$

2-Naphthylglyoxal is made in a similar yield.

$$C_{10}H_7COCH_3 + SeO_2 \rightarrow C_{10}H_7COCHO + Se + H_2O$$

This method is especially useful in the synthesis of unsymmetrical benzils such as mesityl phenyl diketone, which can be produced from benzyl mesityl ketone in 83% yield.

$$\text{(mesityl)}COCH_2C_6H_5 \xrightarrow{SeO_2} \text{(mesityl)}COCOC_6H_5$$

Methyl phenyl diketone can be prepared in 50% yield from propiophenone.

$$C_6H_5COCH_2CH_3 \xrightarrow[\text{SeO}_2]{\text{12 hours}} C_6H_5COCOCH_3$$

Diethyl malonate gives diethyl mesoxalate in 32% yield. An alternative procedure involves oxides of nitrogen as the oxidizing agent (OS I, 266).

$$CH_2(CO_2C_2H_5)_2 \rightarrow CO(CO_2C_2H_5)_2$$

Ninhydrin, a reagent for amino acids (CR **60**, 39), has been made in 35%
yield by selenium dioxide oxidation of 1,3-indandione.

Selenium dioxide is remarkable in that it ordinarily does not attack
the aldehyde function. Glyoxal, the simplest dialdehyde, is made by
treatment of acetaldehyde with selenium dioxide in an autoclave. A more
convenient laboratory method consists in the oxidation of paraldehyde
with selenium dioxide or selenious acid in a solution of dioxane and acetic
acid.

$$(CH_3CHO)_3 + 3H_2SeO_3 \rightarrow 3\underset{\underset{CHO}{|}}{CHO} + 3Se + 6H_2O$$

The product can be isolated as the bisulfite addition compound in 74%
yield (OS III, 438). Glyoxal is produced commercially by catalytic
dehydrogenation of ethylene glycol (p. 655).

Propionaldehyde and butyraldehyde furnish pyruvaldehyde and
ethylglyoxal in 30 and 40% yields, respectively. Yields are generally lower
with ketones that can be attacked at more than one point. Acetone,
however, is reported to give pyruvaldehyde in 60% yield.

$$CH_3COCH_3 + SeO_2 \xrightarrow{\text{4 hours}} CH_3COCHO + Se + H_2O$$

Cyclohexanone gives 1,2-cyclohexanedione (OS **32**, 35; yield 63%).

Similarly, cycloheptanone furnishes 1,2-cycloheptanedione. Unless
otherwise specified, the foregoing reports of yields are based on the
oxidizing agent.

The methyl groups in quinaldine and lepidine are oxidized to aldehyde
groups by selenium dioxide. Cinchoninaldehyde, for example, is prepared
in this way; it is isolated in the form of a hydrate in 61% yield.

It should be mentioned that active methylene compounds are not the only ones to be oxidized by selenium dioxide. Other types of substances that are sensitive to this reagent include olefinic and acetylenic compounds, alcohols, phenols, and mercaptans.

Oxidation of Alcohols

Oxidation of primary and secondary alcohols to aldehydes and ketones, respectively, may be accomplished by use of a mixture of potassium dichromate and sulfuric acid. This procedure, illustrated by the synthesis of propionaldehyde (OS II, 541; yield 49%), is successful because the aldehyde is immediately volatilized and thus is not allowed to remain in contact with the oxidizing agent. Propiolaldehyde (propargylaldehyde) may be made from propargyl alcohol in a similar way (OS **36**, 66; 41% yield).

$$HC\equiv CCH_2OH \rightarrow HC\equiv CCHO$$

Only the more volatile aldehydes can be produced in this manner.

In work with isopropyl alcohol evidence has been accumulated that supports the assumption of the intermediate formation of the ester $(CH_3)_2CHOCrO_3H$.[4]

Glycerol α,γ-dichlorohydrin is converted into *sym*-dichloroacetone in 75% yield by the action of sodium dichromate and sulfuric acid (OS I, 211). In a similar way 2-cyclopentene-1,4-diol is oxidized to 2-cyclopentene-1,4-dione.[5]

t-Butyl chromate, made by adding chromium trioxide to *t*-butyl alcohol, oxidizes primary alcohols to aldehydes almost quantitatively; it does not attack ordinary double bonds. An example of its use is the oxidation of geraniol to citral.

$$CH_3C{=}CHCH_2CH_2C{=}CHCH_2OH \rightarrow CH_3C{=}CHCH_2CH_2C{=}CHCHO$$
$$\quad\;\; | \qquad\qquad\quad | \qquad\qquad\qquad\quad | \qquad\qquad\quad |$$
$$\quad\;\; CH_3 \qquad\quad\;\; CH_3 \qquad\qquad\qquad CH_3 \qquad\quad\;\; CH_3$$

Primary and secondary alcohols are oxidized also by permanganate to the corresponding carbonyl compounds. In the case of primary alcohols, it is hard to interrupt the oxidation at the carbonyl stage. Secondary alcohols, of course, present less difficulty. An ingenious procedure has been developed for the conversion of ethyl lactate into ethyl pyruvate (OS **31**,

---

[4] A. Leo and F. H. Westheimer, *J. Am. Chem. Soc.*, **74**, 4383 (1952).
[5] C. H. DePuy and E. F. Zaweski, *J. Am. Chem. Soc.*, **81**, 4920 (1959).

59; 54% yield). The oxidation is effected by bringing the hydroxy ester in contact with potassium permanganate in a buffered aqueous solution overlaid by a large amount of petroleum ether. The keto ester, being less polar than the hydroxy ester, passes into the hydrocarbon layer, thus escaping further contact with the oxidizing agent.

$$CH_3\underset{\underset{\textstyle OH}{|}}{C}HCO_2C_2H_5 + (O) \xrightarrow{KMnO_4} CH_3COCO_2C_2H_5 + H_2O$$

The transformation of α-hydroxy ketones and aldehydes to the corresponding dicarbonyl compounds, traditionally carried out with Fehling's or Benedict's solution, has been realized also with the higher members, which are not very soluble in water. Oxidation of sebacoin to sebacil, for example, is effected by copper acetate in acetic acid (OS 36, 77; 89% yield).

$$(CH_2)_8 \underset{\diagdown}{\overset{\diagup}{\begin{array}{c} C=O \\ | \\ CHOH \end{array}}} \rightarrow (CH_2)_8 \underset{\diagdown}{\overset{\diagup}{\begin{array}{c} C=O \\ | \\ C=O \end{array}}}$$

Oxidation of benzoins to the corresponding benzils is accomplished easily with copper sulfate in pyridine. Benzoin gives benzil in 96% yield (OS I, 87). This type of oxidation has also been brought about in high yields by treating benzoins with a boiling solution of ammonium nitrate in glacial acetic acid.

Diphenyl tetraketone can be made by oxidation of the formoin, obtained from phenylglyoxal (p. 430), with ammonium nitrate in glacial acetic acid.

$$2C_6H_5COCHO \xrightarrow{KCN} C_6H_5COCO\underset{\underset{\textstyle OH}{|}}{C}HCOC_6H_5 \xrightarrow{-H_2}$$

$$C_6H_5COCOCOCOC_6H_5$$

A convenient qualitative test for acyloins consists in heating, at 100° (or at its boiling point), a solution of 0.1 g. of the substance in a few milliliters of acetic acid with a little bismuth oxide (Bi_2O_3); a black precipitate of finely divided bismuth is produced almost immediately.[6]

N-Bromosuccinimide is capable of oxidizing primary and secondary alcohols to the corresponding carbonyl compounds, and in many cases the action is highly selective. α-Hydroxy acids are converted by this reagent into the corresponding aldehydes or ketones, with the simultaneous

[6] W. Rigby, *J. Chem. Soc.*, 793 (1951).

formation of bromine and carbon dioxide. An example is the conversion of benzilic acid into benzophenone.[7]

$$(C_6H_5)_2-\underset{OH}{\underset{|}{C}}CO_2H + 2 \quad \underset{CH_2CO}{\overset{CH_2CO}{\diagdown}}NBr \rightarrow$$

$$(C_6H_5)_2CO + Br_2 + CO_2 + 2 \quad \underset{CH_2CO}{\overset{CH_2CO}{\diagdown}}NH$$

Reduction of ketones by the Meerwein-Ponndorf-Verley method (p. 549) can be reversed, serving to transform secondary alcohols to ketones. In this method, known as the Oppenauer oxidation (OR **6**, 207), the aluminum derivative of the alcohol is prepared by means of aluminum t-butoxide and is oxidized with a large excess of acetone or cyclohexanone (OR **2**, 181).

Oxidation of saturated primary alcohols to the corresponding acids may be effected by nitric acid. The conversion of trimethylene chlorohydrin into β-chloropropionic acid is an example (OS I, 168; 79% yield). Here it is important to avoid alkalis, which might dehydrochlorinate the product.

Oxidation of cyclohexanol to adipic acid may involve cyclohexanone as an intermediate. It is known that ketones can be oxidized to acids by strong oxidizing agents. Examples are the conversion of cyclohexanone and cyclopentanone to adipic and glutaric acid, respectively, by treatment with nitric acid. In either case it is possible to employ the alcohol instead of the ketone. Adipic acid may be made (OS I, 18) by oxidizing cyclohexanol with 50% nitric acid at 55 to 60° in the presence of ammonium vanadate; the yield is 60%.

$$\text{(cyclohexanol)} + 4(O) \xrightarrow{HNO_3} HO_2C(CH_2)_4CO_2H + H_2O$$

An interesting synthesis of n-butyl n-butyrate consists of oxidation of n-butyl alcohol with the dichromate-sulfuric acid mixture, the oxidation being conducted in such a manner as to convert the alcohol directly into the ester (OS I, 138; 47% yield). The evidence supports the theory that the aldehyde formed initially combines with the alcohol to produce the corresponding hemiacetal, which in turn is oxidized to the ester.[8]

[7] M. Z. Barakat and M. F. A. El-Wahab, *J. Am. Chem. Soc.*, **75**, 5731 (1953).

[8] J. C. Craig and E. C. Horning, *J. Org. Chem.*, **25**, 2098 (1960).

Caustic alkalis may serve also as oxidizing agents for alcohols. Lauryl alcohol, for example, gives lauric acid when heated at 270° with potassium hydroxide under a pressure of 25 to 30 atmospheres.

$$CH_3(CH_2)_{10}CH_2OH \rightarrow CH_3(CH_2)_{10}CO_2H$$

Manganese dioxide converts allylic alcohols into the corresponding carbonyl compounds and attacks saturated alcohols less readily under similar reaction conditions (QR **13**, 61).

Alcohols of the benzyl type are oxidized by manganese dioxide to the corresponding aldehydes and ketones in high yields.[9]

Oxidation of Aldehydes

Aldehydes are easily oxidized by permanganates, of course. Certain aromatic aldehydes, readily available from natural sources, serve as raw materials in the production of the corresponding acids. An example is piperonal, which can be oxidized to piperonylic acid in 84% yield with potassium permanganate (OS II, 538).

Permanganate oxidation is usually carried out without addition of a base or an acid. Under these conditions the solution in certain cases becomes progressively more basic as reaction proceeds since hydroxide ion is generated. Sometimes, however, it is advantageous to add sulfuric acid. *n*-Heptaldehyde, one of the few aliphatic aldehydes that can be made readily from natural products, is converted into *n*-heptanoic acid in 78% yield by oxidation with acid permanganate (OS II, 315).

$$3C_6H_{13}CHO + 2KMnO_4 + H_2SO_4 \rightarrow$$
$$3C_6H_{13}CO_2H + K_2SO_4 + 2MnO_2 + H_2O$$

The use of this relatively strong oxidizing agent is satisfactory in this instance because the oxidation product, a saturated aliphatic acid, is resistant to further oxidation.

A similar example is the oxidation of β-chloropropionaldehyde to β-chloropropionic acid with nitric acid (OS I, 166).

$$ClCH_2CH_2CHO \rightarrow ClCH_2CH_2CO_2H$$

[9] E. F. Pratt and J. F. Van de Castle, *J. Org. Chem.*, **26**, 2973 (1961).

A method of determining aldehydes involves oxidation with silver oxide followed by titrametric estimation of the acids produced.[10]

$$RCHO + Ag_2O \rightarrow RCO_2H + 2Ag.$$

The method is particularly valuable for aldehydes in the presence of ketones. It serves also in a preparative way as is illustrated by the conversion of 3-thiophenecarboxaldehyde into 3-thiophenecarboxylic acid (OS **33**, 94; 97% yield).

The procedure is suitable for use with aldehydes that contain other easily oxidizable groups. The sodium salt of vanillic acid, for example, can be made in high yield by treating vanillin with silver oxide in the presence of sodium hydroxide.

Glycidaldehyde can be oxidized to glycidic acid by hydrogen peroxide at a pH of 9.[11]

The oxidizing action of fused alkalis (p. 215) is generally effective with aldehydes, being employed for example to convert such diverse substances as acetaldehyde, vanillin, and furfural into salts of the corresponding acids.

Degradation of Side Chains to Carboxyl Groups

Side chain oxidation often is accomplished by the use of a mixture of sodium dichromate and sulfuric acid; an example is the conversion of *p*-nitrotoluene into *p*-nitrobenzoic acid (OS I, 392; 86% yield).

2,4,6-Trinitrobenzoic acid can be made similarly (OS I, 543; 69% yield).

[10] J. Mitchell, Jr., and D. M. Smith, *Anal. Chem.*, **22**, 746 (1950).
[11] G. B. Payne and P. R. Van Ess, *J. Org. Chem.*, **26**, 2984 (1961).

Chromium trioxide in glacial acetic acid is used extensively also. The conversion of 3-bromo-4-nitrotoluene into 3-bromo-4-nitrobenzoic acid is illustrative; the yield is 60%.[12]

Potassium permanganate is perhaps the most widely used reagent for the oxidation of side chains; for example, it converts o-chlorotoluene into o-chlorobenzoic acid in 78% yield (OS II, 135).

$$o\text{-}ClC_6H_4CH_3 + 2KMnO_4 \rightarrow o\text{-}ClC_6H_4CO_2K + 2MnO_2 + KOH + H_2O$$

Oxidation of p-chloromercuritoluene (OS I, 159) gives the corresponding acid in high yield. Picolinic acid, isolated as the hydrochloride, can be produced by the action of permanganate on 2-picoline (OS III, 740; 51% yield). Nicotinic and isonicotinic acids are prepared from the corresponding methylpyridines in a similar way.[13] Mesitylene is oxidized to the tribasic acid, trimesic acid.

Nitric acid has been used also to oxidize side chains; the degradation of nicotine to nicotinic acid is an example (OS I, 385; 74% yield).

Methyl p-tolyl ketone may be oxidized to terephthalic acid conveniently in two stages, the first of which is accomplished with nitric acid. The oxidation is completed with potassium permanganate (OS III, 791); the over-all yield is 88%.

[12] M. Rieger and F. H. Westheimer, *J. Am. Chem. Soc.*, **72**, 28 (1950).
[13] G. Black, E. Depp, and B. B. Corson, *J. Org. Chem.*, **14**, 14 (1949).

In a number of instances methyl groups are oxidized to carboxyl groups by lead dioxide; 2-hydroxyisophthalic acid is produced in 61% yield by treatment of 2-hydroxy-3-methylbenzoic acid with lead dioxide in the presence of potassium hydroxide (OS **40**, 48).

$$\text{CH}_3\text{-C}_6\text{H}_3(\text{OH})(\text{CO}_2\text{H}) \rightarrow \text{CO}_2\text{H-C}_6\text{H}_3(\text{OH})(\text{CO}_2\text{H})$$

An interesting example of differential oxidation is the conversion of *p*-cymene into *p*-toluic acid (OS III, 822; 51% yield). The preparation of *o*-toluic acid from *o*-xylene (OS III, 820; 55% yield) is carried out in a similar way.

Competition experiments with 15% nitric acid show that the ease of oxidation of side chains falls off in the following order: $(\text{CH}_3)_2\text{CH—}$, $\text{CH}_3\text{CH}_2\text{—}$, $\text{CH}_3\text{—}$. As might be expected, the *t*-butyl group is extremely resistant to oxidation.[14]

Controlled oxidation with chromate may convert alkylbenzenes into the corresponding phenylalkanoic acids. *n*-Butylbenzene, for example, gives γ-phenylbutyric acid in 70% yield.[15]

Epoxidation

Epoxidation of olefins can be effected quantitatively by per acids such as perbenzoic acid (OR **7**, 378). This reaction forms the basis of Prilezhaev's method for determining the number of double bonds in a molecule.

$$\text{RCH=CHR} + \text{C}_6\text{H}_5\text{CO}_3\text{H} \rightarrow \text{RCH} \overset{\text{O}}{\underset{}{\diagdown\diagup}} \text{CHR} + \text{C}_6\text{H}_5\text{CO}_2\text{H}$$

The method is valuable also in the synthesis of oxirane compounds. Styrene reacts readily with perbenzoic acid to give styrene oxide in 75% yield (OS I, 494). *trans*-Stilbene is oxidized to the oxide in 75% yield by peracetic acid (OS **38**, 83). Terminal olefinic bonds are attacked much less readily by perbenzoic acid than those located at other points in a chain.

α,β-Unsaturated esters are oxidized readily to the corresponding glycidic esters (p. 495) by the action of peracetic acid. Ethyl α-phenylcrotonate, for example, gives ethyl 2,3-epoxy-2-phenylbutyrate in 95% yield.[16]

[14] L. N. Ferguson and A. I. Wims, *J. Org. Chem.*, **25**, 668 (1960).
[15] R. H. Reitsema and N. L. Allphin, *J. Org. Chem.*, **27**, 27 (1962).
[16] D. L. MacPeek, P. S. Starcher, and B. Phillips, *J. Am. Chem. Soc.*, **81**, 680 (1959).

$$CH_3CH{=}CCO_2C_2H_5 \rightarrow CH_3CH\overset{O}{\overbrace{\qquad}}CCO_2C_2H_5$$
$$\underset{C_6H_5}{\mid} \qquad\qquad \underset{C_6H_5}{\mid}$$

The suggestion has been made that epoxide formation by this method involves a cyclic polar change in which the proton becomes attached to the carbonyl oxygen atom simultaneously with the attack on the olefinic bond.[17]

$$C_6H_5C \underset{O}{\overset{O{-}O}{\diagdown}}\quad \overset{CHR}{\underset{CHR}{\parallel}} \quad H \rightarrow C_6H_5C\overset{O}{\diagup}_{OH} + O\underset{CHR}{\overset{CHR}{\diagup\diagdown}}$$

α,β-Unsaturated ketones such as benzalacetophenone yield oxido compounds when treated with alkaline hydrogen peroxide, a reagent that does not attack isolated double bonds. The epoxidation of mesityl oxide is another example.

$$\underset{CH_3}{\overset{CH_3}{\diagdown}}C{=}CHCOCH_3 + H_2O_2 \rightarrow \underset{CH_3}{\overset{CH_3}{\diagdown}}C\overset{O}{\overbrace{\qquad}}CHCOCH_3 + H_2O$$

In a similar way isophorone gives the corresponding epoxy ketone in 72 % yield (OS **37**, 58).

The simplest epoxyaldehyde, glycidaldehyde, has been made by this method also.[18] The procedure is successful with other aldehydes such as crotonaldehyde and cinnamaldehyde.

$$CH_2{=}CHCHO + H_2O_2 \rightarrow CH_2\underset{O}{\overset{}{\diagdown\diagup}}CHCHO + H_2O$$

[17] P. D. Bartlett, *Record of Chem. Progress*, **11**, 47 (1950).
[18] G. B. Payne, *J. Org. Chem.*, **26**, 250 (1961).

Epoxidation of quinones can be effected also by the alkaline hydrogen peroxide reagent; 2-methyl-1,4-naphthoquinone affords the epoxide in 89% yield.

An interesting feature of this process is that it is highly stereoselective.[19] The following mechanism has been proposed.

The carbon-nitrogen double bond of certain imino compounds is attacked by peracids in a manner analogous to that observed with olefins and yields *oxaziranes*. The transformation of the azomethine compound derived from *t*-butylamine and benzaldehyde is an example.[20]

Hydroxylation of Olefins

Olefins may be changed to the corresponding glycols by a number of methods.[21] If an olefinic compound is treated with a mixture of hydrogen peroxide and formic acid the formoxy hydroxy derivative, which is easily hydrolyzed to the dihydroxy compound, is obtained in high yield. The first step in the reaction is the generation of performic acid, which then oxidizes the olefin to the corresponding oxirane. The reaction of formic acid with hydrogen peroxide is reversible and goes to completion, since the per acid is used in the reaction with the olefin.

$$H_2O_2 + HCO_2H \rightleftharpoons HCO_3H + H_2O$$

[19] H. E. Zimmerman, L. Singer, and B. S. Thyagarajan, *J. Am. Chem. Soc.*, **81**, 108 (1959).

[20] W. D. Emmons, *J. Am. Chem. Soc.*, **79**, 5739 (1957).

[21] See F. D. Gunstone, *Advances in Organic Chemistry*, Interscience Publishers, Inc., New York, Vol. I, p. 103, 1960.

Formic acid then acts upon the oxide to open the oxirane ring, giving the hydroxy formoxy derivative. Acetic acid can replace formic acid in this method if sulfuric acid is present as a catalyst.

trans-1,2-Cyclohexanediol is produced in satisfactory yield by treatment of cyclohexene with 30% hydrogen peroxide in the presence of 88% formic acid (OS III, 217; 73% yield).

Since perbenzoic acid can be prepared conveniently by autoxidation of benzaldehyde (p. 621), peroxidation can be brought about by passing air or oxygen into a solution of benzaldehyde and the olefinic compound. The perbenzoic acid is consumed as it is generated. Monoperphthalic acid is more stable than perbenzoic acid and is advantageous for peroxidations conducted in solvents such as chloroform because the phthalic acid produced is insoluble. Best for this purpose, however, is pertrifluoro-acetic acid, which gives the epoxides in much better yields. With this reagent, oleic acid is rapidly hydroxylated in quantitative yield.

In the presence of osmium tetroxide, vanadium pentoxide, chromium trioxide, or even ultraviolet light, hydrogen peroxide combines with ethylenic compounds to yield glycols. A superior procedure involves treatment of the olefinic substance with hydrogen peroxide in the presence of osmium tetroxide, the hydroxylation being carried out in anhydrous *t*-butyl alcohol. By this method, for example, glycerol and β-phenyl-glyceric acid are obtained in yields of 60 and 56%, respectively.[22]

$$CH_2{=}CHCH_2OH + H_2O_2 \xrightarrow{OsO_4} CH_2CHCH_2$$
$$\underset{\text{OH OH OH}}{}$$

$$C_6H_5CH{=}CHCO_2H + H_2O_2 \xrightarrow{OsO_4} C_6H_5CHCHCO_2H$$
$$\underset{\text{OH OH}}{}$$

An intermediate of the type

OsO₂ has been isolated, which affords an explanation of the observation that the method gives *cis*-glycols (Angew., **51**, 519). Glycols formed by way of chlorohydrins and epoxy derivatives usually have the opposite configuration.

[22] N. A. Milas and S. Sussman, *J. Am. Chem. Soc.*, **58**, 1302 (1936).

Oxidation of olefinic compounds with potassium permanganate is the basis of the well-known Baeyer test, which owes its value to the accompanying discharge of the permanganate color. Olefinic compounds react with dilute permanganate solution to form glycols, and with careful control often give the glycols in relatively high yields. Examples are isobutylene, cinnamic acid, and oleic acid.

$$
\begin{array}{cc}
& \text{OH} \quad \text{OH} \\
& | \qquad | \\
\text{CH}_3\text{C}{=}\text{CH}_2 \;\rightarrow\; & \text{CH}_3\text{C}{-\!-\!-}\text{CH}_2 \\
| & | \\
\text{CH}_3 & \text{CH}_3
\end{array}
$$

$$
\begin{array}{cc}
& \text{OH} \quad \text{OH} \\
& | \qquad | \\
\text{C}_6\text{H}_5\text{CH}{=}\text{CHCO}_2\text{H} \;\rightarrow\; & \text{C}_6\text{H}_5\text{CH}{-}\text{CHCO}_2\text{H}
\end{array}
$$

$$
\text{CH}_3(\text{CH}_2)_7\text{CH}{=}\text{CH}(\text{CH}_2)_7\text{CO}_2\text{H} \;\rightarrow\; \text{CH}_3(\text{CH}_2)_7\text{CH}{-}\text{CH}(\text{CH}_2)_7\text{CO}_2\text{H}
$$
$$
\qquad\qquad\qquad\qquad\qquad\qquad\qquad\qquad | \quad\; |
$$
$$
\qquad\qquad\qquad\qquad\qquad\qquad\qquad\quad \text{OH} \;\; \text{OH}
$$

The synthesis of glyceraldehyde from acrolein can be achieved by such an oxidation. The aldehyde group must be protected, however, since aldehydes are sensitive to permanganate as well as to alkalis. Acetals, as will be seen (p. 401), are cleaved by acids but are not attacked by alkalis. The problem can thus be solved by converting the aldehyde groups into acetal groups, from which they may be regained at a later point in the synthesis. The first step in the preparation of glyceraldehyde is the conversion of acrolein into its diethyl acetal (OS II, 17).

In the oxidation of maleic and fumaric acids by permanganate, the two hydroxyl groups enter the molecule at the points previously united by the pi-bond; i.e., *cis*-addition takes place. Maleic acid yields *meso*-tartaric acid and fumaric acid *dl*-tartaric acid. *cis*-Addition has proved to be general for the conversion of olefinic compounds into glycols by the use of permanganate.

$$
\begin{array}{ccc}
& & \text{CO}_2\text{H} \\
& & | \\
\text{H}{-}\text{C}{-}\text{CO}_2\text{H} & \xrightarrow{\;\text{KMnO}_4\;} & \text{H}{-}\text{COH} \\
\| & & | \\
\text{H}{-}\text{C}{-}\text{CO}_2\text{H} & & \text{H}{-}\text{COH} \\
& & | \\
& & \text{CO}_2\text{H}
\end{array}
$$

As has been seen in connection with the addition of bromine (p. 133), however, addition reactions usually take place in the *trans*-manner; the behavior of permanganate is thus not typical.

In order to account for the formation of *cis*-glycols it has been proposed that, as with osmium tetroxide, a cyclic intermediate is involved. Evidence in support of this postulate is that the oxygen atoms of the glycol are derived from the permanganate.[23]

Compounds containing an olefinic linkage conjugated with an acetylenic linkage are attacked preferentially at the double bond. Vinylacetylene, for example, yields 3-butyne-1,2-diol.[24]

$$CH_2{=}CHC{\equiv}CH \rightarrow \underset{\underset{OH}{|}}{CH_2}{-}\underset{\underset{OH}{|}}{CHC}{\equiv}CH$$

Olefins can be transformed to the corresponding glycols also by the method of Prévost, which requires treatment of the olefins with the complex formed by iodine and silver benzoate. An example is the preparation of 1,2-hexadecanediol from 1-hexadecene.

$$CH_3(CH_2)_{13}CH{=}CH_2 \xrightarrow[I_2]{C_6H_5CO_2Ag}$$

$$\underset{\underset{CH_2OCOC_6H_5}{|}}{CH_3(CH_2)_{13}CHOCOC_6H_5} \longrightarrow \underset{\underset{OH}{|}\ \underset{OH}{|}}{CH_3(CH_2)_{13}CH{-}CH_2}$$

Methyl oleate and methyl elaidate furnish the low- and high-melting forms, respectively, of 9,10-dihydroxystearic acid. Hydroxylation by the Prévost method is stereospecific, yielding *trans*-glycols.

Tetraarylethylenes react with chromium trioxide in glacial acetic acid to yield carbonates of the corresponding pinacols; tetraphenylethylene, for example, gives benzopinacol carbonate.[25]

$$(C_6H_5)_2C{=}C(C_6H_5)_2 \xrightarrow[CH_3CO_2H]{CrO_3} (C_6H_5)_2C\overset{\displaystyle \overset{CO}{\diagup\ \diagdown}}{\underset{O\qquad O}{\rule{0pt}{0pt}}}C(C_6H_5)_2$$

Cleavage of 1,2-Glycols

Aldehydes and ketones are produced also when 1,2-glycols are oxidized with certain reagents, notably periodic acid (OR **2**, 341; **8**, 225) and lead tetraacetate. The reaction affords one of the few ways in which a carbon-carbon single bond can be cleaved readily. Various theories have been

[23] K. B. Wiberg and K. A. Saegebarth, *J. Am. Chem. Soc.*, **79**, 2822 (1957).
[24] V. A. Engelhardt and J. E. Castle, *J. Am. Chem. Soc.*, **75**, 1734 (1953).
[25] W. A. Mosher, F. W. Steffgen, and P. T. Lansbury, *J. Org. Chem.*, **26**, 670 (1961).

proposed to explain the cleavage, one of which postulates that the glycol is changed to a 1,4-zwitterion, which in turn breaks down to form two carbonyl groups. According to this theory the cleavage of 2,3-butanediol with lead tetraacetate may be depicted as follows.

$$
\begin{array}{c}
CH_3CHOH \\
| \\
CH_3CHOH
\end{array}
+ Pb(OCOCH_3)_4 \rightarrow
\begin{array}{c}
CH_3CHO \\
\diagdown \\
| \quad\quad Pb(OCOCH_3)_2 \\
\diagup \\
CH_3CHO
\end{array}
+ 2CH_3CO_2H
$$

$$
\begin{array}{c}
CH_3CHO \\
\diagdown \\
| \quad\quad Pb(OCOCH_3)_2 \rightarrow \\
\diagup \\
CH_3CHO
\end{array}
\begin{array}{c}
CH_3CHO^- \\
| \\
CH_3CHO^+
\end{array}
+ Pb(OCOCH_3)_2
$$

$$
\begin{array}{c}
CH_3CHO^- \\
| \\
CH_3CHO^+
\end{array}
\rightarrow 2CH_3CHO
$$

As in oxidation by permanganates or osmium tetroxide and hydrogen peroxide, a cyclic intermediate is postulated. The first step is an interchange involving the elimination of acetic acid; in the second the lead atom becomes divalent, releasing the unstable zwitterion, which breaks down to give two molecules of acetaldehyde.

2,3-Butanediol can be determined quantitatively by use of periodic acid. The oxidation product, acetaldehyde, is isolated as the bisulfite addition compound and determined by titration of the bisulfite liberated when the addition compound is decomposed with alkali.

$$
\begin{array}{cc}
OH & OH \\
| & | \\
CH_3CH & -CHCH_3
\end{array}
+ HIO_4 \rightarrow 2CH_3CHO + HIO_3 + H_2O
$$

Taken together with a reaction that converts an olefinic compound into a glycol, the cleavage effects the same type of change that is brought about by ozone and affords an alternative route to aldehydes and ketones.

The cleavage procedure has been used to make chloroacetaldehyde by oxidation of glycerol α-monochlorohydrin (p. 149) by periodic acid.

$$
\begin{array}{c}
CH_2CHCH_2Cl \\
| \quad | \\
OH \, OH
\end{array}
\rightarrow ClCH_2CHO
$$

Another example is the formation of the monodiethylacetal of glyoxal from the diethylacetal of glyceraldehyde (p. 222).

$$
\begin{array}{c}
CH_2-CHCH(OC_2H_5)_2 \\
| \quad\quad | \\
OH \quad\quad OH
\end{array}
\rightarrow
\begin{array}{c}
CH(OC_2H_5)_2 \\
| \\
CHO
\end{array}
$$

Cyclic 1,2-diols have been used in the synthesis of dialdehydes; a cyclopentanediol, for instance, yields a 1,5-dial.[26] It is significant that this reaction does not take place with 1,3- or 1,4-glycols; aldehydes and ketones also fail to undergo the cleavage. Even α-hydroxy aldehydes and ketones are unreactive; but this is true only in the absence of water or other hydroxy compounds. When a small amount of moisture is admitted, for example, cleavage occurs. The explanation given for this behavior is that the aldehyde or ketone tends to be hydrated to give a "pseudoglycol," which is sensitive to the reagent.

$$
\underset{\substack{| \\ \text{RCHCOR}}}{\text{OH}} \xrightarrow{\text{H}_2\text{O}} \underset{\substack{|\ \ | \\ \text{RCHCR} \\ | \\ \text{OH}}}{\text{OHOH}} \xrightarrow{\text{Pb(OCOCH}_3)_4} \text{RCHO} \quad \text{and} \quad \text{RCO}_2\text{H}
$$

Cleavage of olefins to aldehydes by way of the corresponding glycols can be accomplished by treatment with periodate in the presence of catalytic amounts of osmium tetroxide.[27]

Both lead tetraacetate and periodic acid react with α-dicarbonyl compounds also. α-Hydroxy acids, however, are cleaved readily only by lead tetraacetate.

1,2-Amino alcohols behave much like 1,2-glycols. The reaction yields ammonia, which permits it to be followed quantitatively. A method for the determination of threonine is illustrative.

$$
\underset{\substack{|\ \ \ | \\ \text{OH NH}_2}}{\text{CH}_3\text{CH}-\text{CHCO}_2\text{H}} + \text{NaIO}_4 \rightarrow
$$

$$
\text{CH}_3\text{CHO} + \text{OCHCO}_2\text{H} + \text{NH}_3 + \text{NaIO}_3
$$

A procedure for making n-butyl glyoxylate involves oxidation of di-n-butyl tartrate with lead tetraacetate (OS **35**, 18; yield 87%).

$$
\begin{array}{c}
\text{CO}_2\text{C}_4\text{H}_9 \\
| \\
\text{CHOH} \\
| \\
\text{CHOH} \\
| \\
\text{CO}_2\text{C}_4\text{H}_9
\end{array}
\rightarrow
\begin{array}{c}
\text{2CHO} \\
| \\
\text{CO}_2\text{C}_4\text{H}_9
\end{array}
$$

Cleavage of glycols can be effected also with sodium bismuthate. Diethyl tartrate, for example, is cleaved by this reagent to ethyl glyoxylate.[28]

[26] G. W. K. Cavill, D. L. Ford, H. Hinterberger, and D. H. Solomon, *Chem. and Ind.*, 292 (1958).

[27] R. Pappo, D. S. Allen, Jr., R. U. Lemieux, and W. S. Johnson, *J. Org. Chem.*, **21**, 478 (1956).

[28] J. Rigby, *J. Chem. Soc.*, 1907 (1950).

$$\begin{array}{c} CO_2C_2H_5 \\ | \\ CHOH \\ | \\ CHOH \\ | \\ CO_2C_2H_5 \end{array} \xrightarrow[CH_3CO_2H]{NaBiO_3} \begin{array}{c} 2CO_2C_2H_5 \\ | \\ CHO \end{array}$$

When sodium bismuthate is used in glacial acetic acid, the reddish-brown color of the reagent is discharged; the color change may serve as a qualitative test.

Iodosobenzene diacetate (p. 248) resembles lead tetraacetate in its action on 1,2-glycols. Isohydrobenzoin, for example, is oxidized to benzaldehyde.[29]

$$C_6H_5I(OCOCH_3)_2 + \begin{array}{c} C_6H_5CHOH \\ | \\ C_6H_5CHOH \end{array} \rightarrow 2C_3H_5CHO + 2CH_3CO_2H + C_6H_5I$$

Cleavage of Olefins

The most general and most reliable procedure for cleavage of olefins with simultaneous location of the ethylenic bond is oxidation with ozone (CR **58,** 925). Ozonolysis usually is carried out by conducting a stream of ozonized oxygen (OS III, 673) through a solution of the olefinic compound. The concentration of ozone may be as high as 14 or 15%. The high concentration is used for oxidation of aromatic rings and compounds containing highly conjugated double bonds. Common solvents are glacial acetic acid, ethyl acetate, methylene chloride, carbon tetrachloride, hexane, petroleum ether, and dichlorodifluoromethane. From the standpoint of resistance to attack by ozone, water, acetic acid, ethyl chloride, carbon tetrachloride, and monofluorotrichloromethane are to be preferred.

Directions have been provided for obtaining aldehydes, ketones, or acids in 60 to 70% yields by oxidation of olefins with ozone. For the preparation of aldehydes the reaction mixture is added dropwise to a hydrolyzing mixture containing zinc and acetic acid. An example is the synthesis of 5-methylhexanal (yield 62%).

$$(CH_3)_2CHCH_2CH_2CH_2CH=CH_2 \rightarrow (CH_3)_2CHCH_2CH_2CH_2CHO$$
6-Methyl-1-heptene   5-Methylhexanal

The function of the reducing agent is to destroy the hydrogen peroxide that is formed in the hydrolysis. The decomposition of the peroxide can be effected catalytically also.

To obtain acids the reaction mixture may be added dropwise to a mixture of acetic acid and hydrogen peroxide. One mole of added hydrogen

[29] K. H. Pausacker, *J. Chem. Soc.* 107 (1953).

peroxide should be sufficient for each mole of olefinic compound, but in practice two moles are added. Cyclohexene, for example, gives adipic acid in 60% yield.

$$\text{cyclohexene} \rightarrow \begin{array}{l} CH_2CH_2CO_2H \\ | \\ CH_2CH_2CO_2H \end{array}$$

If the ozonation mixture is treated with lithium aluminum hydride or sodium borohydride, the cleavage products are obtained as alcohols and in good yields. The procedure is valuable therefore in synthesis and in characterization.[30]

A superior method for preparing aldehydes and ketones is to conduct the ozonolysis at low temperature in a hydroxylic solvent and effect the reduction of the hydrogen peroxide with an alkyl phosphite such as trimethyl phosphite.[31]

Another useful application of ozonolysis is illustrated by the preparation of aldehyde esters from methyl oleate and methyl undecylenate.

$$CH_3(CH_2)_7CH\!=\!CH(CH_2)_7CO_2CH_3 \rightarrow$$

Methyl oleate

$$CH_3(CH_2)_7CHO \quad \text{and} \quad OCH(CH_2)_7CO_2CH_3$$

$$CH_2\!=\!CH(CH_2)_8CO_2CH_3 \rightarrow CH_2O \quad \text{and} \quad OCH(CH_2)_8CO_2CH_3$$

Methyl undecylenate

An industrial method involves ozonolysis of oleic acid to produce pelargonic and azelaic acids.

$$CH_3(CH_2)_7CH\!=\!CH(CH_2)_7CO_2H \xrightarrow{O_3}$$

$$CH_3(CH_2)_7CO_2H \quad \text{and} \quad (CH_2)_7\!\!\begin{array}{l} \diagup CO_2H \\ \diagdown CO_2H \end{array}$$

An unusual example of ozonolysis is the conversion of $\Delta^{9,10}$-octalin into 1,6-cyclodecanedione.[32]

$\Delta^{9,10}$-Octalin   1,6-Cyclodecanedione

[30] J. A. Sousa and A. L. Bluhm, *J. Org. Chem.*, **25**, 108 (1960).
[31] W. S. Knowles and Q. E. Thompson, *J. Org. Chem.*, **25**, 1031 (1960).
[32] W. Hückel, R. Danneel, A. Schwartz, and A. Gercke, *Ann.*, **474**, 121 (1929).

The octalin forms a nitrosochloride (p. 168) from which it can be regained by treatment with sodium methoxide.

The use of ozone in the proof of structure of unsaturated compounds may be illustrated by the diisobutylenes. One of these, 2,4,4-trimethyl-1-pentene, gives methyl neopentyl ketone and formaldehyde; the other, 2,4,4-trimethyl-2-pentene, yields trimethylacetaldehyde and acetone.

The course of ozonolysis of an olefin has been formulated as follows.

$$\underset{}{\ce{C=C}} + O_3 \rightarrow \underset{O_3}{\ce{C-C}} \rightarrow$$

$$\underset{\underset{a}{O^+ \quad O-O^-}}{\ce{C-C}} \rightarrow \underset{\underset{b}{O}}{\ce{C}} \text{ and } \underset{\underset{c}{O-O^-}}{{}^+\ce{C}}$$

The rupture of the carbon-carbon bond is caused by the cationic oxygen atom that takes the bonding electron pair. In addition to the carbonyl compound (*b*) a zwitterion (*c*) results. The zwitterion may dimerize or polymerize. Also, it may combine with a carbonyl compound to give an ozonide.

$$2 \underset{{}^-O-O}{{}^+\ce{C}} \rightarrow \underset{O-O}{\overset{O-O}{\ce{C \qquad C}}}$$

$$n \underset{{}^-O-O}{{}^+\ce{C}} \rightarrow -\ce{C-O-O}\left(\ce{C-O-O}\right)_{n-2}\ce{C-O-O}-$$

The ozonide from 1,2-dimethylcyclopentene probably forms as follows.

$$\underset{\underset{CH_2}{CH_2 \qquad CH_2}}{CH_3C{=}CCH_3} \rightarrow \underset{\underset{CH_2}{CH_2 \qquad CH_2}}{\underset{O-O^-}{CH_3\overset{+}{C} \qquad \overset{O}{\overset{\|}{C}CH_3}}} \rightarrow \underset{\underset{CH_2}{CH_2 \qquad CH_2}}{\underset{O-O}{\overset{O}{CH_3C \qquad CCH_3}}}$$

By ozonolysis of tetramethylethylene in the presence of acetaldehyde it has been possible to isolate an ozonide that involves the aldehyde.

$$
\begin{array}{c}
CH_3 \\
 \diagdown \\
C\!=\!C \\
\diagup \\
CH_3
\end{array}
\begin{array}{c}
CH_3 \\
\diagup \\
 \\
\diagdown \\
CH_3
\end{array}
\longrightarrow
\begin{array}{c}
CH_3 \\
\diagup \\
C^+ \\
\diagdown \\
CH_3 O\!-\!O^-
\end{array}
\xrightarrow{\;O=CHCH_3\;}
\begin{array}{c}
O \\
CH_3 \diagup \diagdown \\
CCHCH_3 \\
CH_3 O\!-\!O
\end{array}
$$

Ozone combines with *trans*-di-*t*-butylethylene at −75° to give an "initial" ozonide that at higher temperatures undergoes isomerization to the normal ozonide.[33]

$$
\begin{array}{c}
(CH_3)_3C H \\
\diagdown \diagup \\
C\!=\!C \\
\diagup \diagdown \\
H C(CH_3)_3
\end{array}
\xrightarrow{\;O_3\;}
(CH_3)_3CCH\!\!\overset{\displaystyle O_3}{\overbrace{}}\!\!CHC(CH_3)_3 \longrightarrow
$$

$$
\begin{array}{c}
O\!-\!O \\
(CH_3)_3CH CH(CH_3)_3 \\
\diagdown \diagup \\
O
\end{array}
$$

Ozonides have been prepared also by trapping zwitterions with ketones; ozonation of *trans*-1,4-dibromo-2,3-dimethyl-2-butene is an example. When conducted at −70° in pentane, the reaction gives the corresponding ozonide in 58 % yield.[34]

$$
\begin{array}{c}
CH_3 CH_2Br \\
\diagdown \diagup \\
C\!=\!C \\
\diagup \diagdown \\
BrCH_2 CH_3
\end{array}
+ O_3 \rightarrow
\begin{array}{c}
CH_3 O\!-\!O CH_2Br \\
\diagdown \diagup \\
CC \\
BrCH_2 \diagdown \diagup CH_3 \\
O
\end{array}
$$

Ozonation of certain tetraarylethylenes gives chiefly cyclic peroxides, which are considered to be dimers of the postulated zwitterions; the behavior of tetraphenylethylene is typical.[35]

$$
\begin{array}{c}
C_6H_5 C_6H_5 \\
\diagdown \diagup \\
C\!=\!C \\
\diagup \diagdown \\
C_6H_5 C_6H_5
\end{array}
\xrightarrow{\;O_3\;}
\begin{array}{c}
C_6H_5 O\!-\!O C_6H_5 \\
\diagdown \diagup \\
CC \\
C_6H_5 \diagup \diagdown C_6H_5 \\
O\!-\!O
\end{array}
$$

[33] R. Criegee and G. Schröder, *Chem. Ber.*, **93**, 689 (1960).
[34] R. Criegee, S. S. Bath, and B. von Bornhaupt, *Chem. Ber.*, **93**, 2891 (1960).
[35] See J. I. G. Cadogan, D. H. Hey, and W. A. Sanderson, *J. Chem. Soc.*, 4897 (1960).

Many other oxidizing agents react with olefins to bring about rupture of the chain at the point of unsaturation. In this type of oxidation the cleavage products normally appear in the form of carboxylic acids; in favorable cases, however, the reaction may be halted at the aldehyde stage. This type of degradation has found use in the preparation of certain aromatic aldehydes from naturally occurring substances containing unsaturated side chains. Anisaldehyde, for example, is formed by oxidation of anethole.

$$CH_3O\langle\bigcirc\rangle CH{=}CHCH_3 \rightarrow CH_3O\langle\bigcirc\rangle CHO$$

The oxidation may be effected by nitric acid, chromic acid, or ozone. Similarly vanillin can be made from eugenol. The first step in this process, the rearrangement of eugenol to isoeugenol, is brought about by heating with alkali.

Eugenol — Isoeugenol — Vanillin

This type of isomerization, general for allylbenzene derivatives, is a 1,3-shift of an allylic system. In the present example the double bond migrates to a position in which it is conjugated with the ring.

Piperonal is made from safrole in a similar way.

Safrole — Isosafrole — Piperonal

Rearrangement of allyl ethers to isopropenyl ethers occurs also under the influence of strong bases; the reaction is stereospecific for the *cis*-isomer.[36]

Molten potassium hydroxide at 300° converts oleic acid into palmitic acid, acetic acid, and hydrogen.

$$CH_3(CH_2)_7CH{=}CH(CH_2)_7CO_2H \rightarrow$$

$$CH_3(CH_2)_{14}CO_2H + CH_3CO_2H + H_2$$

[36] T. J. Prosser, *J. Am. Chem. Soc.*, **83**, 1701 (1961); C. C. Price and W. H. Snyder, *J. Am. Chem. Soc.*, **83**, 1773 (1961).

In this process, discovered by Varrentrapp in 1840, reversible migration of the olefinic double bond along the chain appears to occur until the double bond reaches the α,β-position; chain cleavage of the reverse aldol type would produce acetic acid and palmitaldehyde. Alkali reacts with the aldehyde to give palmitic acid and hydrogen (p. 215). Similar results have been obtained with other olefinic acids.[37]

Oxidative cleavage of the carbon chain serves also in the preparation of azelaic acid from ricinoleic acid (OS II, 53).

$$\underset{\displaystyle CH_3(CH_2)_5\overset{\overset{\textstyle OH}{\textstyle |}}{C}HCH_2CH{=}CH(CH_2)_7CO_2H}{} \xrightarrow{KMnO_4} (CH_2)_7\overset{\textstyle CO_2H}{\underset{\textstyle CO_2H}{<}}$$

A route to glutaric acid has been made convenient by the availability of 2,3-dihydropyran (p. 182). Its hydrolysis product, δ-hydroxyvaleraldehyde, is oxidized to glutaric acid in yields as high as 75% by treatment with nitric acid (OS **30**, 48).

$$\xrightarrow[H^+]{H_2O} HOCH_2CH_2CH_2CH_2CHO \xrightarrow{HNO_3} (CH_2)_3\overset{\textstyle CO_2H}{\underset{\textstyle CO_2H}{<}}$$

Methyl groups attached to carbon, i.e., C-methyl groups, generally survive oxidative degradation and appear among the products in the form of acetic acid. The Kuhn-Roth method of determining C-methyl groups, which depends on oxidation with chromium trioxide in sulfuric acid, has proved to be especially valuable in the examination of aliphatic chains and alicyclic rings.

The last step in the Barbier-Wieland method of degrading an acid to the next lower homolog depends on the same type of oxidation. It is an oxidative cleavage of an olefin prepared by the action of the phenyl Grignard reagent on the ester and dehydration of the resulting alcohol.

$$RCH_2CO_2C_2H_5 \longrightarrow RCH_2\overset{\overset{\textstyle OH}{\textstyle |}}{C}(C_6H_5)_2 \xrightarrow{-H_2O}$$

$$RCH{=}C(C_6H_5)_2 \xrightarrow{oxidation} RCO_2H + (C_6H_5)_2CO$$

[37] R. G. Ackman, P. Linstead, B. J. Wakefield, and B. C. L. Weedon, *Tetrahedron*, **8**, 221 (1960).

An example is the preparation of nordesoxycholic acid from desoxycholic acid (OS III, 234; 68% yield); oxidation is effected by chromium trioxide in glacial acetic acid.

Various modifications of the Barbier-Wieland procedure have been suggested. If the olefin is heated with N-bromosuccinimide, bromination occurs at the allyl position. Oxidation of the diene produced by dehydrobromination of the bromo compound yields an acid having three less carbon atoms than the original.

$$RCH_2CHBrCH{=}C(C_6H_5)_2 \rightarrow RCH{=}CHCH{=}C(C_6H_5)_2 \rightarrow RCO_2H$$

Tertiary alcohols may suffer oxidative cleavage, yielding oxidation products having fewer carbon atoms than the original alcohol. Results of uncommon interest have been obtained with the carbinols resulting from the action of Grignard reagents on cyclopentanone, cyclohexanone, and cyclooctanone. Treatment with chromium trioxide at 30° converts them smoothly into the corresponding keto acids. An example is the preparation of δ-benzoylvaleric acid.

In the synthesis of o-acetylphenylacetic acid from 1-indanone by way of 3-methylindene the oxidation is carried out with dichromate and sulfuric acid. The yield in the oxidation step is 58%.[38]

This reagent converts 2-methylcyclohexanol into ε-oxoheptanoic acid in a yield of 55% (OS 31, 3).

With ketones di-Grignard reagents give dihydroxy compounds, which by dehydration followed by oxidation of the diolefins provide a route to diketodicarboxylic acids. The product from cyclohexanone and the Grignard reagent derived from hexamethylene bromide is an example.[39]

[38] J. O. Halford and B. Weissmann, J. Org. Chem., 18, 30 (1953).
[39] A. Kreuchunas, J. Am. Chem. Soc., 75, 4278 (1953).

The preparation of homophthalic acid by oxidation of indene is another example of oxidative cleavage of a ring (OS III, 449; 77% yield).

Cleavage of Aromatic Rings

Several procedures are available for oxidative destruction of aromatic rings. Ozonolysis of such rings occurs if the ozone is used in sufficiently concentrated solutions. *o*-Xylene, for example, gives a mixture of glyoxal, pyruvaldehyde, and biacetyl. The proportions of these compounds in the mixture indicate that the six bonds of the ring are equivalent and that the methyl groups produce a steric effect.

It has been postulated that ozone attacks aromatic rings by an electrophilic mechanism. In support of this theory is the observation that the rate of ozonation is accelerated by Friedel-Crafts catalysts such as boron trifluoride and aluminum chloride. In the ozonation of Schiff bases and nitrones, however, ozone seems to behave as a nucleophilic agent.[40]

Ozonation of pyrene produces 5-formyl-4-phenanthrenecarboxylic acid in 38% yield (OS **38**, 32).

In many instances oxidative opening of aromatic rings has preparative value. Oxidation of naphthalene with permanganate is an example. Phthalonic acid, an intermediate product, can be converted by loss of carbon dioxide into phthalaldehydic acid. Decarboxylation is brought

[40] A. H. Riebel, R. E. Erickson, C. J. Abshire, and P. S. Bailey, *J. Am. Chem. Soc.*, **82**, 1801 (1960).

about by heating the bisulfite addition compound with hydrochloric acid (OS II, 523).

Phenanthrene is sensitive to oxidation at the 9,10-positions; treatment of the hydrocarbon with 50% hydrogen peroxide in glacial acetic acid gives diphenic acid in yields of 70%.[41]

Triphenylene may be oxidized to mellitic acid in yields of about 45%, the oxidation being initiated with nitric acid and completed with permanganate.[42]

Mellitic acid is formed also from many types of coke, graphite, pitches, and carbon blacks by this procedure. The result is in accord with the belief that such substances contain highly condensed aromatic ring systems. Mention should be made of the oxidation of charcoal to pyromellitic acid; the yield depends considerably on the type of charcoal selected. Powdered pure spruce charcoal is to be preferred (OS II, 551).

Sodium chlorate is a powerful oxidizing agent; by its use it is possible, for example, to degrade furfural to fumaric acid (OS II, 302; 58% yield).

[41] W. F. O'Connor and E. J. Moriconi, *J. Am. Chem. Soc.*, **73**, 4044 (1951).
[42] B. Juettner, *J. Am. Chem. Soc.*, **59**, 1472 (1937).

Quinone Formation

The formation of *p*-benzoquinone as an intermediate in the oxidative cleavage of benzene has been postulated (p. 620). With certain aromatic hydrocarbons direct oxidation furnishes a preparative method for quinones. Benzene is oxidized directly to quinone by electrolysis with an anode of lead or lead alloy and an inactive cathode. The usual procedure in industrial practice is oxidation of aniline sulfate by manganese dioxide or sodium dichromate.

Naphthalene is oxidized more readily than benzene When the oxidation is effected with chromium trioxide in acetic acid, 1,4-naphthoquinone may be obtained (OS **33,** 50; yield 22%). Although the yields are low, the process is less expensive than other methods.

Comparison of toluene and 2-methylnaphthalene toward this oxidizing agent is instructive, since in toluene the methyl group is attacked, whereas oxidation of the methylnaphthalene involves the nucleus, yielding 2-methyl-1,4-naphthoquinone.

Anthracene is oxidized even more readily than naphthalene, being converted into anthraquinone by the action of sodium chlorate in the presence of vanadium pentoxide, glacial acetic acid, and dilute sulfuric acid (OS II, 554; 91% yield).

The usual procedure, however, for making quinones involves oxidation of anilines or phenols, nearly all of which can serve (OR **4,** 305). The best method of making *p*-benzoquinone is by oxidation of hydroquinone; of the many oxidizing agents that are effective, sodium chlorate (OS II, 553; 96% yield) and the sodium dichromate-sulfuric acid mixture (OS I, 482; 92% yield) can be recommended.

1,2-Naphthoquinone is produced from 1-amino-2-naphthol hydrochloride in 94% yield by the action of ferric chloride in acid media (OS II, 430).

The dichromate-sulfuric acid reagent is less satisfactory because it attacks the quinone. It serves, however, to produce 1,4-naphthoquinone in 81% yield from the hydrochloride of 1,4-aminonaphthol (OS I, 383).

Thymoquinone is produced by treatment of the corresponding aminothymol with nitrous acid (OS I, 512; 80% yield).

o-Quinones are made from the corresponding catechols; an example is the oxidation of 4-methylcatechol to 4-*o*-toluquinone by means of silver oxide.

Duroquinone can be made from the corresponding diamine (OS II, 254; 90% yield).

A change similar to quinone formation occurs when pyridinium salts are oxidized electrolytically. The synthesis of 1-methyl-2-pyridone from pyridine (OS II, 419) is such a transformation.

When the oxidizing agent is alkaline potassium ferricyanide solution, the product forms in yields of 70%.

Oxidation of phenols by ferricyanide gives products that indicate the first step to be the formation of aryloxyl radicals; such radicals may couple in the *o*- or *p*-positions and in certain cases lead to quinone formation (CR **58**, 439). *o*-Cresol, for example, undergoes *para-para* coupling, the final product being a quinone.

Glaser Coupling Reaction

Compounds containing an acetylenic hydrogen atom are transformed to diethynyl compounds by oxidation of their cuprous salts. The usual catalyst for the oxidation, known as the Glaser coupling reaction, consists of a mixture of cuprous chloride, ammonia, and ammonium chloride. Amines may serve in place of ammonia. Catalytic amounts of cuprous chloride in pyridine, for example, cause rapid oxidation of phenylacetylene to diphenyldiacetylene; the yield is 86%.[43]

$$2C_6H_5C\equiv CH \xrightarrow[\text{CuCl}]{O_2} C_6H_5C\equiv C-C\equiv CC_6H_5$$

o-Diethynylbenzene gives a tetrayne having a twelve-membered ring.[44]

[43] A. S. Hay, *J. Org. Chem.*, **25**, 1275 (1960).
[44] O. M. Behr, G. Eglinton, and R. A. Raphael, *Chem. and Ind.*, 699 (1959).

Oxidative coupling of octa-1,7-diyne with cupric acetate in pyridine yields the corresponding cyclic "dimer."[45]

$$HC{\equiv}CCH_2CH_2CH_2CH_2C{\equiv}CH \ \rightarrow$$

$$(CH_2)_4 \begin{array}{c} {-}C{\equiv}C{-}C{\equiv}C{-} \\ \\ {-}C{\equiv}C{-}C{\equiv}C{-} \end{array} (CH_2)_4$$

The "trimer," "tetramer," and higher cyclic polyacetylenes are formed also. Application of this method to 1,5-hexadiyne gives highly unsaturated eighteen-membered rings.[46]

Willgerodt Reaction

When alkyl aryl ketones are treated with yellow ammonium polysulfide, a very unusual reaction occurs, the side chain being transformed in such a way as to give the amide of the corresponding ω-aryl carboxylic acid (OR 3, 83).

$$ArCO(CH_2)_nCH_3 \ \xrightarrow{\ (NH_4)_2S_x\ } \ ArCH_2(CH_2)_nCONH_2$$

This transformation, discovered by Willgerodt, occurs not only with ketones of this type but also with aliphatic ketones such as pinacolone and 4-heptanone. In many cases the yields are superior. The reagent is made by saturating concentrated ammonium hydroxide with hydrogen sulfide and dissolving 10% by weight of sulfur in the solution. The addition of 40% of dioxane or of pyridine greatly improves the yield, which falls off as the value of n increases. An example of the use of this method is found in the synthesis of 2-naphthylacetamide.

Although the mechanism of the change is not known with certainty, it appears that a progressive reaction occurs along the chain that will pass a tertiary but not a quaternary carbon atom. Isobutyrophenone, for example, yields α-methyl-β-phenylpropionamide.

$$C_6H_5COCHCH_3 \ \rightarrow \ C_6H_5CH_2CHCONH_2$$
$$\qquad\quad | \qquad\qquad\qquad\quad | $$
$$\qquad\; CH_3 \qquad\qquad\qquad CH_3$$

The Willgerodt method was improved greatly by Kindler, who used sulfur and a dry amine instead of aqueous ammonium polysulfide; a

[45] F. Sondheimer, Y. Amiel, and R. Wolovsky, *J. Am. Chem. Soc.*, **81**, 4600 (1959).
[46] Y. Amiel and F. Sondheimer, *Chem. and Ind.*, 1162 (1960).

thioamide is the principal product. When a mixture of acetophenone, sulfur, and morpholine is heated, the thiomorpholide is obtained in excellent yield.

$$C_6H_5COCH_3 + S + HN\left\langle\begin{array}{c}CH_2CH_2 \\ \\ CH_2CH_2\end{array}\right\rangle O \rightarrow$$

$$C_6H_5CH_2\underset{\underset{\|}{S}}{C}-N\left\langle\begin{array}{c}CH_2CH_2 \\ \\ CH_2CH_2\end{array}\right\rangle O + H_2O$$

The reaction is not peculiar to ketones but occurs also with aldehydes, alcohols, olefins, and acetylenes. When styrene is heated with sulfur and morpholine, phenylthioacetomorpholide is formed. Hydrolysis converts the morpholide into phenylacetic acid; the over-all yield is 84%.

Tracer studies with C^{14} have shown that, when unsymmetrical dialkyl ketones are subjected to the Willgerodt reaction, the functional group shows a preferential tendency to migrate to the nearer end of the chain.[47]

The use of sulfur compounds as oxidizing agents includes aqueous sulfate if it is employed in the presence of a sulfur compound that has a lower valence state. This reagent is widely applicable and in particular serves to convert xylenes to the corresponding dibasic acids.[48]

Oxidation of Nitrogen Compounds

Aromatic amines react with Caro's acid or hydrogen peroxide to yield derivatives in which oxygen is joined to nitrogen. When aniline, for example, is oxidized by one of these reagents, β-phenylhydroxylamine is the first product that can be detected. Further oxidation produces nitrosobenzene.

$$C_6H_5NH_2 \rightarrow C_6H_5NHOH \rightarrow C_6H_5NO$$

Azobenzene and azoxybenzene are formed also. The appearance of these products is understandable, since it is known that nitrosobenzene reacts with aniline to yield the azo compound and with β-phenylhydroxylamine to give the azoxy derivative (p. 531). β-Phenylhydroxylamine reduces the Fehling and Tollens reagents in the cold to form nitrosobenzene, which is made conveniently by oxidation of β-phenylhydroxylamine with a mixture of dichromate and sulfuric acid (OS III, 668).

---

[47] E. Cerwonka, R. C. Anderson, and E. V. Brown, *J. Am. Chem. Soc.*, **75**, 28 (1953).
[48] W. G. Toland, *J. Am. Chem. Soc.*, **82**, 1911 (1960).

Oxidation to the corresponding nitroso derivative with Caro's acid has been effected with many amines. An example is the preparation of 5-nitro-2-nitrosotoluene from 2-amino-5-nitrotoluene (OS III, 334; 71% yield).

Suitably constituted primary amines are oxidized to oximes by hydrogen peroxide in the presence of sodium tungstate, the corresponding hydroxylamines being formed as intermediates. Cyclohexylamine, for example, gives cyclohexanone oxime.[49]

A number of 2,6-dibromo and 2,6-dichloro anilines have been oxidized to the corresponding nitroso compounds by treatment with 30% hydrogen peroxide dissolved in glacial acetic acid.[50]

Oxidation of amino groups to nitro groups has preparative value with aromatic amines that can be made more readily than the corresponding nitro compounds; oxidation of 2- and 4-aminopyridines has been accomplished by use of 30% hydrogen peroxide dissolved in 30% fuming sulfuric acid. 2-Amino-4-methylpyridine gives 4-methyl-2-nitropyridine in 68% yield.[51]

A solution of hydrogen peroxide in trifluoroacetic acid is a superior agent for oxidizing substituted anilines to the corresponding nitrobenzenes.[52]

Sodium perborate in acetic acid oxidizes primary aromatic amines to azo

[49] K. Kahr and C. Berther, *Chem. Ber.*, **93**, 132 (1960).
[50] R. R. Holmes and R. P. Bayer, *J. Am. Chem. Soc.*, **82**, 3454 (1960).
[51] R. H. Wiley and J. L. Hartman, *J. Am. Chem. Soc.*, **73**, 494 (1951).
[52] W. D. Emmons and A. F. Ferris, *J. Am. Chem. Soc.*, **75**, 4623 (1953).

compounds; *p*-aminoacetanilide, for example, gives 4,4'-*bis*(acetamido)-
azobenzene (OS **40**, 18; 58% yield).

$$2CH_3CONH\underset{}{\bigcirc}NH_2 \xrightarrow[H_3BO_3]{NaBO_3}$$

$$CH_3CONH\bigcirc N{=}N\bigcirc NHCOCH_3$$

t-Carbinamines are oxidized to nitro compounds by permanganate;
t-butylamine gives *t*-nitrobutane in 83% yield.[53]

$$(CH_3)_3CNH_2 \rightarrow (CH_3)_3CNO_2$$

Tertiary amines, both aliphatic and aromatic, react with hydrogen
peroxide to yield amine oxides; an example is the oxidation of dimethylaniline.

$$C_6H_5N(CH_3)_2 + [O] \rightarrow C_6H_5\overset{\overset{\displaystyle CH_3}{|}}{\underset{\underset{\displaystyle CH_3}{|}}{N}}{\rightarrow}O$$

The structure assigned to amine oxides is supported by the fact that,
when the three hydrocarbon radicals are different, the compound exists in
optically active forms. Higher aliphatic tertiary amines react sluggishly
with hydrogen peroxide but readily yield oxides with peracetic acid.
Tri-*n*-hexylamine affords the oxide in 84% yield.[54]

$$n\text{-}(C_6H_{13})_3N \xrightarrow{CH_3CO_3H} n\text{-}(C_6H_{13})_3NO$$

Peracetic acid oxidizes pyridine to pyridine N-oxide (OS **33**, 79).

$$\underset{N}{\bigcirc} \rightarrow \underset{\underset{O}{\overset{|}{N}}}{\bigcirc}$$

Nicotinamide N-oxide is made in a similar way (OS **37**, 63; 82% yield).

$$\underset{N}{\bigcirc}CONH_2 \xrightarrow[H_2O_2]{CH_3CO_2H} \underset{\underset{O}{\overset{|}{N}}}{\bigcirc}CONH_2$$

---

[53] N. Kornblum and R. J. Clutter, *J. Am. Chem. Soc.*, **76**, 4494 (1954).
[54] A. C. Cope and H.-H. Lee, *J. Am. Chem. Soc.*, **79**, 964 (1957).

Amine oxides of pyridine and its derivatives have been found useful in connection with the problem of orientation. Thus although pyridine undergoes nitration in the 3-position, its N-oxide yields chiefly the 4-isomer. This method provides a route to 4-nitro derivatives since the oxide can be reconverted to the pyridine compound by reduction. An example of the procedure is the conversion of 3-methylpyridine into 3-methyl-4-nitro-pyridine.[55]

2-Picoline N-oxide reacts with acetic anhydride to give 2-pyridine-methanol acetate.[56]

When hydroxamic acid chlorides are treated with mild alkalis, hydrogen chloride is eliminated and *nitrile N-oxides* result. These compounds likewise have the N→O linkage and are somewhat unstable, showing a marked tendency to dimerize to the corresponding furoxans. The behavior of benzonitrile N-oxide is an example.[57]

Many oxidizing agents do not add oxygen to nitrogen but abstract hydrogen. These reagents never oxidize aniline to β-phenylhydroxylamine or nitrosobenzene but rather to the bimolecular derivatives, azobenzene and N-phenylquinonediimine. The only monomolecular product that can be isolated is benzoquinone, which is produced only under vigorous conditions. It seems to be derived from polymeric materials, which are characteristic products of this type of oxidation.

[55] W. Herz and L. Tsai, *J. Am. Chem. Soc.*, **76**, 4184 (1954).
[56] V. Boekelheide and W. J. Linn, *J. Am. Chem. Soc.*, **76**, 1286 (1954).
[57] See R. H. Wiley and B. J. Wakefield, *J. Org. Chem.*, **25**, 546 (1960).

Hydrazine derivatives are oxidized readily as is illustrated by the behavior of phenylhydrazine. Mild oxidizing agents such as copper sulfate and ferric chloride convert it into benzene, presumably by way of the azo compound.

$$C_6H_5NHNH_2 \rightarrow [C_6H_5N{=}NH] \rightarrow C_6H_6 + N_2$$

Phenylhydrazine reacts with air in alcohol or benzene to give hydrogen peroxide in almost quantitative yield. Semicarbazide gives positive tests with both the Fehling and the Tollens reagents. Hydrazobenzenes are oxidized to azobenzenes with great ease, even air being able to bring about the change.

Aliphatic hydrazine derivatives can be oxidized also, monoalkyl hydrazines yielding nitrogen and hydrocarbons.

$$RNHNH_2 \rightarrow [RN{=}NH] \rightarrow RH + N_2$$

An example of the oxidation of a disubstituted hydrazine is encountered in the synthesis of diethyl azodicarboxylate (OS III, 375). The reagent is hypochlorous acid.

$$\begin{array}{c} NHCO_2C_2H_5 \\ | \\ NHCO_2C_2H_5 \end{array} \xrightarrow{\text{HOCl}} \begin{array}{c} NCO_2C_2H_5 \\ \| \\ NCO_2C_2H_5 \end{array}$$

Hypohalites serve also in the preparation of 2-azo-*bis*-isobutyronitrile from the corresponding hydrazine derivative.

$$\begin{array}{ccc} & CN & CN \\ CH_3 & | & | & CH_3 \\ & \diagdown & \diagup \\ & CNHNHC & \\ & \diagup & \diagdown \\ CH_3 & & CH_3 \end{array} \rightarrow \begin{array}{ccc} & CN & CN \\ CH_3 & | & | & CH_3 \\ & \diagdown & \diagup \\ & CN{=}NC & \\ & \diagup & \diagdown \\ CH_3 & & CH_3 \end{array}$$

In the preparation of the analogous cyclohexyl derivative, 1,1′-azo-*bis*-1-cyclohexanenitrile, the oxidation is carried out with bromine (OS **32**, 16).

Oxidation of *sym*-dimethylhydrazine to azomethane may be accomplished by treatment with dichromate.

$$CH_3NHNHCH_3 \rightarrow CH_3N{=}NCH_3$$

Isohydrazones yield the corresponding azo compounds, which possess the three-membered ring structure originally proposed for aliphatic diazo compounds. An example is the oxidation of the isohydrazone of cyclohexanone.[58]

$$\text{(cyclohexane ring with =NH, NH substituents)} \xrightarrow{\text{KMnO}_4} \text{(cyclohexane ring with N, N substituents)}$$

Benzophenone hydrazone is oxidized by mercuric oxide to diphenyldiazomethane (OS III, 351).

$$(\text{C}_6\text{H}_5)_2\text{C}=\text{NNH}_2 \xrightarrow{\text{HgO}} (\text{C}_6\text{H}_5)_2\text{CN}_2$$

In the oxidation of benzil monohydrazone the intermediate azo compound, azibenzil, can be isolated (OS II, 496). When heated it forms nitrogen and diphenylketene (OS III, 356); the yield of the ketene, based on the hydrazone, is 58%.

$$\begin{array}{l}\text{C}_6\text{H}_5\text{C}=\text{NNH}_2 \\ | \\ \text{C}_6\text{H}_5\text{C}=\text{O}\end{array} \xrightarrow{\text{HgO}} \begin{array}{l}\text{C}_6\text{H}_5\text{CN}_2 \\ | \\ \text{C}_6\text{H}_5\text{CO}\end{array} \longrightarrow (\text{C}_6\text{H}_5)_2\text{C}=\text{C}=\text{O} + \text{N}_2$$

The dihydrazone of benzil, oxidized in a similar way, gives diphenylacetylene (OS **34,** 42). The yield, based on benzil, is 73%. The oxidation has been carried out to advantage by the use of silver trifluoroacetate in triethylamine.[59]

$$\begin{array}{l}\text{C}_6\text{H}_5\text{C}=\text{NNH}_2 \\ | \\ \text{C}_6\text{H}_5\text{C}=\text{NNH}_2\end{array} \rightarrow \text{C}_6\text{H}_5\text{C}\equiv\text{CC}_6\text{H}_5$$

Especially useful in the study of certain alkaloids has been the dehydrogenation of tertiary amines with mercuric acetate. One of the most common results of this treatment is the introduction of a double bond in a position α,β to the nitrogen atom. An example is the transformation of the saturated bicyclic amine, quinolizidine into $\Delta^{1(10)}$-dehydroquinolizidine.[60]

$$\text{(quinolizidine bicyclic structure)} \rightarrow \text{(dehydroquinolizidine bicyclic structure)}$$

[58] E. Schmitz and R. Ohme, *Chem. Ber.*, **94,** 2166 (1961).

[59] M. S. Newman and D. E. Reid, *J. Org. Chem.*, **23,** 665 (1958).

[60] N. J. Leonard, A. S. Hay, R. W. Fulmer, and V. W. Gash, *J. Am. Chem. Soc.*, **77,** 439 (1955).

Nitroso compounds can be oxidized to nitro compounds by a number of reagents. Oxidation of 5-nitro-2-nitrosotoluene with a mixture of sulfuric acid and potassium dichromate, for example, not only converts the side chain into a carboxyl group but also changes the nitroso group to a nitro group, the product being 2,5-dinitrobenzoic acid (OS III, 334; 66% yield).

$$\underset{O_2N}{\overset{CH_3}{\bigcirc}} NO \rightarrow \underset{O_2N}{\overset{CO_2H}{\bigcirc}} NO_2$$

Oxidation of Sulfur Compounds

The capacity of sulfur to unite with itself is demonstrated in a striking way by the behavior of sulfhydryl compounds when exposed to the air; oxidation to disulfides occurs very rapidly, especially in alkaline solutions. Thus thiophenol yields diphenyl disulfide.

$$2C_6H_5SH + (O) \rightarrow C_6H_5SSC_6H_5 + H_2O$$

This type of oxidation can be effected by many oxidizing agents, including ferric chloride, hydrogen peroxide, "positive" halogen compounds (p. 138), and the halogens. The use of hydrogen peroxide is illustrated by the preparation of di-p-aminophenyl disulfide from the sodium salt of p-aminothiophenol (OS III, 86).

$$2H_2N\text{—}\bigcirc\text{—}SNa + H_2O_2 \rightarrow H_2N\text{—}\bigcirc\text{—}SS\text{—}\bigcirc\text{—}NH_2 + 2NaOH$$

Thiol acids are also oxidized to disulfides, an example being the formation of dibenzoyl disulfide from thiolbenzoic acid by the action of iodine on the potassium salt (OS III, 116).

$$2C_6H_5\overset{O}{\overset{\|}{C}}SK + I_2 \rightarrow C_6H_5\overset{O}{\overset{\|}{C}}SS\overset{O}{\overset{\|}{C}}C_6H_5 + 2KI$$

The disulfides may be reconverted into the sulfhydryl compounds by reducing agents. One of the best-known examples of this type of interconversion is that of cystine and cysteine.

$$2HSCH_2\overset{NH_2}{\overset{|}{C}}HCO_2H \rightleftarrows \overset{NH_2}{\overset{|}{S}}CH_2CHCO_2H$$
$$\overset{|}{S}CH_2CHCO_2H$$
$$\overset{|}{N}H_2$$

Cysteine   Cystine

Perhaps the outstanding chemical characteristic of organic sulfur compounds is the capacity of the sulfur atom to take up oxygen. It is a rule, applicable to all classes of sulfur compounds, that oxidation proceeds until the sulfur atom has attained the valence state that it has in sulfuric acid. An important example is the oxidation of thio ethers to *sulfones*, a process that can be carried out stepwise. Sulfones, very stable compounds that occur as by-products in sulfonation (p. 41), may be produced in high yield by treating the corresponding sulfides with a suitable oxidizing agent. Probably the best general procedure is the addition of 30% hydrogen peroxide to a solution of the sulfide in glacial acetic acid or acetone. If equimolecular amounts of reactants are taken, the product is the *sulfoxide*, which is readily oxidized to the sulfone by an additional mole of the peroxide.

This type of reaction has been realized also with certain thiophenes; 2,5-dimethylthiophene is oxidized by perbenzoic acid to the corresponding sulfone.[61]

$$CH_3 \overbrace{}_{S} CH_3 \rightarrow CH_3 \overbrace{}_{SO_2} CH_3$$

Unusual sulfur compounds, analogous to the sulfoxides, have been made by the action of Chloramine-T on certain halogen-containing sulfides. The products are known as *sulfilimines*, an example of which is the sulfilimine from β-bromoethyl ethyl sulfide.

$$[p\text{-}CH_3C_6H_4SO_2Cl]^-Na^+ + S\big\langle{}^{CH_2CH_2Br}_{CH_2CH_3} \rightarrow$$

$$p\text{-}C_6H_4SO_2N{=}S\big\langle{}^{CH_2CH_2Br}_{CH_2CH_3} + NaCl$$

The structures of sulfones and certain related compounds have been written variously. Sulfones are best described perhaps as resonance hybrids.[62]

$$\begin{matrix} O^- & & O \\ \uparrow & & \| \\ R{-}S^+{-}R & \leftrightarrow & R{-}S{-}R \\ \| & & \downarrow{+} \\ O & & O_- \end{matrix}$$

[61] J. L. Melles and H. J. Backer, *Rec. trav. chim.*, **72**, 314 (1953).
[62] E. D. Amstutz, J. J. Chessick, and I. M. Hunsberger, *Science*, **111**, 305 (1950).

Sulfenyl halides may be prepared by the action of halogens on thiophenols (CR **39**, 269). If chlorine is passed into a solution of p-thiocresol in carbon tetrachloride the following reactions occur.

$$CH_3C_6H_4SH + Cl_2 \rightarrow CH_3C_6H_4SCl + HCl$$

$$CH_3C_6H_4SH + CH_3C_6H_4SCl \rightarrow CH_3C_6H_4SSC_6H_4CH_3 + HCl$$

If, on the other hand, the thiophenol is added slowly to a carbon tetrachloride solution of chlorine, the disulfide is largely avoided. By this method p-toluenesulfenyl chloride is obtained in 88% yield (OS **35**, 99).

$$CH_3C_6H_4SSC_6H_4CH_3 + Cl_2 \rightarrow 2CH_3C_6H_4SCl$$

Di-o-nitrophenyl disulfide reacts with chlorine to produce o-nitrobenzenesulfenyl chloride (OS II, 455). The yield is nearly quantitative.

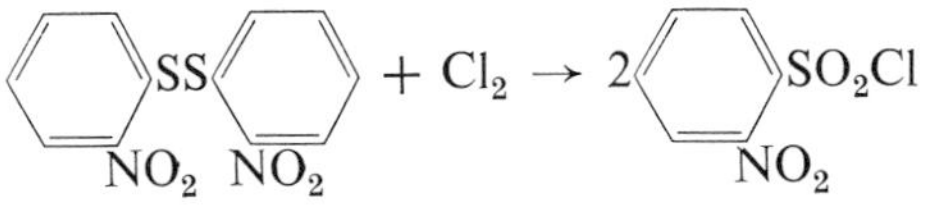

When the disulfide is treated with chlorine in the presence of hydrochloric and nitric acids, the product is o-nitrobenzenesulfonyl chloride (OS II, 471; 84% yield).

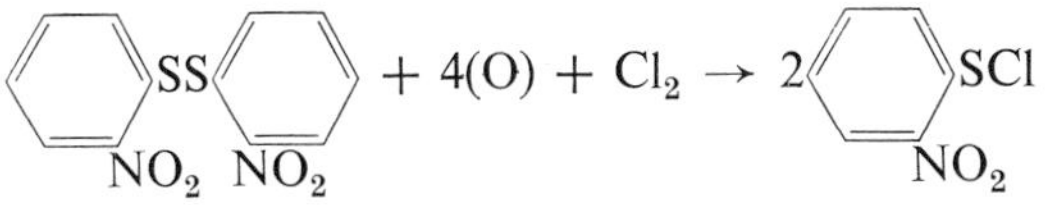

It has been possible to effect chlorinolysis of a few aliphatic disulfides also, notably di-2-chloroethyl disulfide.

$$ClCH_2CH_2SSCH_2CH_2Cl + Cl_2 \rightarrow 2ClCH_2CH_2SCl$$

Three moles of chlorine convert disulfides into alkyl- or arylsulfur trichlorides; dimethyl disulfide yields methylsulfur trichloride. The trichlorides undergo solvolysis to give sulfinyl chloride; methylsulfur trichloride is changed to methanesulfinyl chloride. The yield, based on the disulfide, is 92% (OS **40**, 62).

$$CH_3SSCH_3 \xrightarrow{Cl_2} CH_3SCl_3 \xrightarrow{CH_3CO_2H} CH_3SOCl$$

Oxidation of Iodine Compounds

Aryl iodides and a few alkyl iodides have been oxidized; iodobenzene yields iodosobenzene when treated with ozone or peracetic acid.

$$C_6H_5I \rightarrow C_6H_5IO$$

Iodosobenzene can be made also by hydrolysis of phenyliodochloride, produced by chlorination of iodobenzene.

$$C_6H_5I \xrightarrow{Cl_2} C_6H_5ICl_2 \xrightarrow{H_2O} C_6H_5IO$$

When heated or allowed to stand for extended periods, iodosobenzene undergoes disproportionation to iodobenzene and iodoxybenzene.

$$2C_6H_5IO \rightarrow C_6H_5I + C_6H_5IO_2$$

If the oxidation of iodobenzene is carried out with 30% peracetic acid, iodosobenzene diacetate can be isolated in high yield.[29]

$$C_6H_5I + CH_3CO_3H + CH_3CO_2H \rightarrow C_6H_5I(OCOCH_3)_2 + H_2O$$

The diacetate can be made also by treating iodosobenzene with acetic acid.

13

Nucleophilic reactions
in the aliphatic series

One of the most common types of organic reactions consists in the displacement of one nucleophile by another at a saturated carbon atom.

Halide Ion Interchange

An example is the interchange of halide ions that occurs when certain alkyl halides are treated with a halide ion. The reaction is reversible and may be made to go to completion if one of the reactants is removed as it is formed. Since sodium chloride and sodium bromide are insoluble in acetone whereas sodium iodide is soluble, many chlorides and bromides may be converted into the corresponding iodides by treatment with sodium iodide in acetone solution. This method, discovered by Finkelstein, provides a convenient route to allyl iodide, which can be produced in satisfactory yield from the commercially available chloride.

$$CH_2\!\!=\!\!CHCH_2Cl + NaI \rightarrow CH_2\!\!=\!\!CHCH_2I + NaCl$$

Iodoacetic acid is made from chloroacetic acid in a similar way.

$$ClCH_2CO_2H + NaI \rightarrow ICH_2CO_2H + NaCl$$

A remarkable example is the transformation of pentaerythrityl bromide, which has the neopentyl structure, to the corresponding iodide; however, the reaction requires heating in methyl ethyl ketone for 48 hours (OS II, 477; 98% yield).

$$C(CH_2Br)_4 + 4NaI \rightarrow C(CH_2I)_4 + 4NaBr$$

$\alpha,\alpha,\delta,\delta$-Tetrabromoadiponitrile reacts with sodium iodide in acetone to give the corresponding tetraiodo compound in 24% yield.[1]

$$
\begin{array}{ccc}
\text{CN} & & \text{CN} \\
| & & | \\
\text{CH}_2\overset{|}{\text{C}}\text{Br}_2 & & \text{CH}_2\text{CI}_2 \\
| & \rightarrow & | \\
\text{CH}_2\text{CBr}_2 & & \text{CH}_2\text{CI}_2 \\
| & & | \\
\text{CN} & & \text{CN}
\end{array}
$$

This type of reaction has been made the basis of a test for the degree of reactivity of halogen atoms in alkyl halides. Tertiary halides are less reactive than secondary, which in turn are less reactive than primary halides. Primary bromides give a precipitate of sodium bromide in 3 minutes at 25°, whereas for secondary and tertiary bromides the solution must be heated to 50°. An exchange reaction of the S_N2 type (Gould, 252) would be impeded by radicals that shield the rear of the carbon atom involved in the exchange. The silver nitrate test, which shows the reverse order of reactivity, appears on the other hand to depend on a reaction of the S_N1 type and is favored by attachment of radicals to the carbon atom that is affected.

Further advances in our knowledge of the Walden inversion have been obtained by work with optically active iodides. When l-2-iodoöctane is treated with sodium iodide in acetone solution, for example, racemization occurs. By the use of sodium iodide containing radioactive iodine it was found that the reaction occurs by a bimolecular mechanism and that every individual substitution inverts the configuration of the carbon atom.

$$ \text{C}_8\text{H}_{17}\text{I} + \overset{*}{\text{I}}{}^- \rightleftharpoons \text{C}_8\text{H}_{17}\overset{*}{\text{I}} + \text{I}^- $$

Similar results have been obtained with 1-phenethyl bromide and α-bromopropionic acid.

One of the earliest and most interesting examples of the Finkelstein reaction is the cyclization of $\alpha,\alpha,\alpha',\alpha'$-tetrabromo-$o$-xylene under the influence of sodium iodide; the primary product is 1,2-dibromobenzocyclobutene.[2]

---

[1] W. Treibs, J. Herrmann, and G. Zimmermann, *Chem. Ber.*, **93**, 2198 (1960).
[2] See M. P. Cava and D. R. Napier, *J. Am. Chem. Soc.*, **79**, 1701 (1957).

Alkyl fluorides can be obtained by heating the corresponding alkyl bromides with potassium fluoride in ethylene glycol. n-Hexyl fluoride, for example, may be made in 45% yield by this method (OS **36**, 40).

$$CH_3(CH_2)_4CH_2Br + KF \rightarrow CH_3(CH_2)_4CH_2F + KBr$$

Halogenation of ketones in alkaline media (Gould, 372), illustrated by the haloform reaction (p. 356), may be mentioned in this connection even though it appears to involve nucleophilic displacement on halogen rather than carbon. Thus the bromination of acetone might take the following path.

$$CH_3COCH_2 \quad Br-Br \rightarrow CH_3COCH_2Br + Br^-$$

Reactions that are analogous to halogen interchange occur when alkyl sulfates are treated with halides. The formation of methyl iodide from dimethyl sulfate is an example (OS II, 404).

$$\begin{array}{c} CH_3O \\ \diagdown \\ \diagup \quad SO_2 + KI \rightarrow CH_3I + CH_3OSO_3K \\ CH_3O \end{array}$$

The methyl iodide is allowed to distil as it is formed.

Displacement of p-benzenesulfonyl, p-toluenesulfonyl (tosyl), and similar groups is also known. The preparation of pentaerythrityl bromide, for example, can be accomplished by treating pentaerythrityl benzenesulfonate with sodium bromide (OS **31**, 82; 78% yield).

$$C(CH_2OSO_2C_6H_5)_4 \rightarrow C(CH_2Br)_4$$

An example of the displacement of the tosyl group by bromide ion is the last step in the conversion of 1,1-di-(hydroxymethyl)cyclohexane to 1,1-di-(bromomethyl)cyclohexane.[3]

Displacement of carboxylate ion by halide ion occurs with β-propiolactone; with sodium chloride it gives sodium β-chloropropionate.

$$\begin{array}{c} CH_2CH_2 \\ | \quad | \quad + NaCl \rightarrow ClCH_2CH_2CO_2Na \\ O-C=O \end{array}$$

[3] E. R. Buchman, D. H. Deutsch, and G. I. Fujimoto, *J. Am. Chem. Soc.*, **75**, 6228 (1953).

Similarly, sodium acetate yields sodium β-acetoxypropionate.

$$\begin{array}{c} CH_2-CH_2 \\ | \qquad\quad | \\ O\text{------}C\text{==}O \end{array} + CH_3CO_2Na \rightarrow CH_3CO_2CH_2CH_2CO_2Na$$

C-Alkylation

The formation of a carbon-carbon bond is encountered in the synthesis of nitriles by the nucleophilic displacement of halide and similar ions by cyanide ion. When the entering nucleophile is an enolate, C-alkylation generally predominates. In this category are the alkylation reactions of active methylene compounds. Phenolates undergo O-alkylation chiefly, but C-alkylation is not uncommon.

Nitrile formation

The displacement of a halide ion by cyanide ion is one of the most useful reactions of halogen compounds. It not only provides an important method of synthesis of nitriles but at the same time opens a route to the carboxylic acid having one carbon atom more than the original halide. It is thus a method of lengthening carbon chains. Furthermore, it is applicable to a wide variety of halogen compounds. An example of this type of transformation is the formation of n-valeronitrile from n-butyl bromide.

$$CH_3CH_2CH_2CH_2Br + NaCN \rightarrow CH_3CH_2CH_2CH_2CN + NaBr$$

The product is contaminated with about 1% of the corresponding isonitrile, readily detected by its intense odor.

The formation of nitriles and isonitriles is possible because cyanide is an ambident ion (Gould, 296). In practice this reaction provides a way of making the nitriles of the acids having an odd number of carbon atoms from normal alkyl bromides with an even number of carbon atoms, derivable from naturally occurring fatty acids. From n-dodecyl bromide, for example, the nitrile of n-tridecanoic acid is produced (OS II, 292).

$$CH_3(CH_2)_{11}Br + KCN \rightarrow CH_3(CH_2)_{11}CN + KBr$$

The reaction is especially valuable for benzyl chloride and similar compounds. Many halides of this type are obtained conveniently by chloromethylation (p. 80) and are very reactive. Phenylacetonitrile (OS I, 107; 90% yield) and mesitylacetonitrile (OS III, 558, 93% yield) are made readily from such chlorides.

Anisyl chloride although sensitive gives p-methoxyphenylacetonitrile in

81% yield if the reaction is carried out in dry acetone in the presence of sodium iodide (OS **36**, 50).

$$CH_3O\!\!-\!\!\langle\bigcirc\rangle\!\!-\!\!CH_2Cl \rightarrow CH_3O\!\!-\!\!\langle\bigcirc\rangle\!\!-\!\!CH_2CN$$

Halogen atoms that are situated near an oxygen-containing functional group react also. Chloroacetic acid and α-bromoacetophenone yield cyanoacetic acid (OS I, 181, 254) and benzoylacetonitrile, respectively. β-Hydroxyl and alkoxyl groups do not interfere. Ethylene chlorohydrin and the ethyl ether of ethylene bromohydrin yield, respectively, ethylene cyanohydrin (OS I, 256; 80% yield) and its ethyl ether, β-ethoxypropionitrile (OS III, 372; 58% yield).

$$HOCH_2CH_2Cl + NaCN \rightarrow HOCH_2CH_2CN + NaCl$$

$$C_2H_5OCH_2CH_2Br + NaCN \rightarrow C_2H_5OCH_2CH_2CN + NaBr$$

Ethylene bromide and trimethylene bromide give succinonitrile and glutaronitrile (OS I, 536; 86% yield), respectively. Trimethylene chlorobromide, because of the difference in reactivity of the two halogen atoms, can be converted into γ-chlorobutyronitrile in 70% yield (OS I, 156).

$$ClCH_2CH_2CH_2Br + KCN \rightarrow ClCH_2CH_2CH_2CN + KBr$$

Adiponitrile can be made from tetramethylene chloride.

$$ClCH_2CH_2CH_2CH_2Cl \xrightarrow{NaCN} \begin{array}{l} CH_2CH_2CN \\ | \\ CH_2CH_2CN \end{array}$$

Pimelonitrile is produced similarly from pentamethylene chloride.

$$Cl(CH_2)_5Cl \rightarrow NC(CH_2)_5CN$$

Replacement of halogens by the cyano group in this way is useful only with primary and secondary halides; tertiary halides usually yield dehydrohalogenation products. The use of dimethyl sulfoxide as solvent is advantageous especially with secondary alkyl halides.[4] In this solvent neophyl chloride reacts slowly with sodium cyanide to give the corresponding nitrile.

$$C_6H_5\overset{\overset{\displaystyle CH_3}{|}}{\underset{\underset{\displaystyle CH_3}{|}}{C}}CH_2Cl \rightarrow C_6H_5\overset{\overset{\displaystyle CH_3}{|}}{\underset{\underset{\displaystyle CH_3}{|}}{C}}CH_2CN$$

[4] L. Friedman and H. Shechter, *J. Org. Chem.*, **25**, 877 (1960).

Many halogen compounds that are too sensitive to be heated with alkali cyanides may be converted into the corresponding nitriles by use of cuprous cyanide. Allyl bromide, for example, gives allyl cyanide (OS I, 46; 84% yield) with this reagent, whereas with sodium cyanide the product is crotononitrile. When the method is applied to crotyl or methylvinylcarbinyl halides, the product in either case consists of 92% of 3-pentenonitrile and 8% of 2-methyl-3-butenonitrile. These reactions involve a typical allylic shift (p. 469).

Acid halides react with cuprous cyanide to furnish α-ketonitriles; benzoyl chloride, for example, affords benzoyl cyanide in 65% yield (OS III, 112). In the aliphatic series the acid bromides are reported to be superior to the chlorides; acetyl, propionyl, isobutyryl, and similar bromides give the corresponding α-ketonitriles in good yields.

Displacement of carboxylate ion by cyanide ion occurs when phthalide is heated with potassium cyanide. The product, the potassium salt of o-carboxyphenylacetonitrile, gives the free cyano acid when treated with hydrochloric acid (OS III, 174; 83% yield).

The preparation of glutaric acid from γ-butyrolactone involves a similar ring opening (OS **37**, 47).

Dialkyl sulfates may serve also in the synthesis of nitriles. An example is the formation of propionitrile from diethyl sulfate and potassium cyanide (CR **42**, 189).

Enolates

The familiar condensation reactions by which the alkylation of active methylene compounds is accomplished consist of two steps. The active methylene compound is converted into the corresponding enolate that then, in the case of alkyl halides, displaces a halogen atom at a saturated carbon atom.

Formation of enolates

The usual method of producing enolates is by displacement on hydrogen by a base that is stronger than the enolate being generated (Gould, 365). Methyl acetate yields the corresponding enolate when treated with methoxide ion.

$$CH_3\bar{O} \curvearrowright H \overset{\curvearrowleft}{—}CH_2CO_2CH_3 \rightarrow CH_3OH + \bar{C}H_2CO_2CH_3$$

Even with such esters as those of acetoacetic and malonic acids, which furnish much more stable enolates, it is convenient to employ the alkoxide ion corresponding to the alkoxyl group of the ester. If either or both reactants contain one or more ester groups, the alkoxide selected should correspond to the alkoxyl radical of the ester function. Otherwise alcoholysis may lead to a mixture of esters. Alcoholysis occurs very sluggishly with t-butoxide; a number of successful alkylations have been carried out with t-butoxide in t-butyl alcohol.[5]

The ease of removal of a proton is proportional to the stability of the resulting carbanion; the enolate from acetoacetic ester has the following principal resonance structures.

$$\overset{O^-}{\underset{|}{CH_3C}}=CH—\overset{O}{\overset{\|}{C}}OC_2H_5 \leftrightarrow CH_3\overset{O}{\overset{\|}{C}}—\bar{C}H—\overset{O}{\overset{\|}{C}}OC_2H_5 \leftrightarrow$$

$$CH_3\overset{O}{\overset{\|}{C}}—CH=\overset{O^-}{\underset{|}{C}}OC_2H_5$$

Nitrocyclopropane is exceptional among primary and secondary nitro compounds in that it does not form salts when treated with bases. It seems probable that the formation of the nitronate ion is opposed by the attendant increase in internal strain that would be involved.[6]

[5] M. Kopp and B. Tchoubar, *Bull. soc. chim. France*, 30 (1951).
[6] H. B. Hass and H. Shechter, *J. Am. Chem. Soc.*, **75**, 1382 (1953).

Cyclopentene-3,5-dione also seems to be incapable of forming an enolate.[7]

$$ O=\underset{}{\bigcirc}=O \;\not\!\!\rightarrow\; O=\underset{}{\bigcirc}-O^- \; + H^+ $$

Alkylation

Alkylation (OR 9, 107) generally is accomplished by treating an enolate with an alkyl halide. Alkyl sulfates, alkyl sulfonates, and other types of compounds are employed less often. Primary halides are the most useful. Tertiary halides, as in other types of reactions with nucleophilic agents, tend to undergo elimination reactions preferentially and are of little value as alkylating agents. As an example of the alkylation reaction may be taken the butylation of acetoacetic ester. The enolate is produced by treating the ester with a suitable base.

$$ CH_3COCH_2CO_2C_2H_5 \xrightarrow{base} \underset{a}{CH_3\overset{\overset{O}{\|}}{C}-\overset{-}{C}HCO_2C_2H_5} \leftrightarrow \underset{b}{CH_3\overset{\overset{O^-}{|}}{C}=CHCO_2C_2H_5} $$

The enolate ion is a hybrid, the principal resonance structures being a and b. The alkylation product generally corresponds to structure a; with n-butyl bromide the chief product is ethyl n-butylacetoacetate (OS I, 248; 72% yield). The dialkylation product may be prepared also.

$$ \underset{\overset{|}{C_4H_9}}{CH_3COCHCO_2C_2H_5} \rightarrow \underset{\overset{|}{C_4H_9}}{CH_3CO\overset{\overset{C_4H_9}{|}}{C}CO_2C_2H_5} $$

Diethyl malonate affords similar results, diethyl n-butylmalonate being formed in 90% yield (OS I, 250). Monoalkyl derivatives yield enolates less readily than do the original esters, which is additional evidence that an alkyl group is electron donating. This is fortunate because it permits the alkylation of the original ester in the presence of its monoalkylation product, thus making possible monoalkylation with little dialkylation.

The choice of catalyst for reactions of this type depends on a number of factors. Although sodium metal and sodium alkoxides have been employed most commonly, other catalysts such as sodium hydride offer special advantages.

As would be predicted on this basis, diethyl acetonedicarboxylate yields a symmetrical dialkylation product, the second alkyl group becoming

[7] C. H. DePuy and E. F. Zaweski, *J. Am. Chem. Soc.*, **79**, 3923 (1957).

attached to the unalkylated methylene group. Advantage of this fact has been taken in the synthesis of symmetrical keto acids, the alkylating agents being esters of ω-iodo acids.[8]

$$
\begin{array}{l}
CH_2CO_2C_2H_5 \\
\diagup \\
CO \\
\diagdown \\
CH_2CO_2C_2H_5
\end{array}
\xrightarrow{2I(CH_2)_nCO_2C_2H_5}
$$

$$
\begin{array}{l}
(CH_2)nCO_2C_2H_5 \\
| \\
CHCO_2C_2H_5 \\
\diagup \\
CO \\
\diagdown \\
CHCO_2C_2H_5 \\
| \\
(CH_2)nCO_2C_2H_5
\end{array}
\rightarrow
\begin{array}{l}
CH_2(CH_2)nCO_2H \\
\diagup \\
CO \\
\diagdown \\
CH_2(CH_2)nCO_2H
\end{array}
$$

Ethylene oxide or ethylene chlorohydrin reacts with acetoacetic ester to give a lactone, which can be transformed into γ-acetopropyl alcohol.

$$
CH_3COCHCO_2C_2H_5 + CH_2\text{—}CH_2 \rightarrow CH_3COCH\text{—}CO + C_2H_5O^-
$$

$$
CH_3COCH\text{—}CO
$$
$$
O + H_2O \rightarrow CH_3COCH_2CH_2CH_2OH + CO_2
$$
$$
CH_2CH_2
$$

If diethyl malonate is used instead, the final product is γ-butyrolactone. The condensation can be effected also with aluminum chloride as the catalyst.

Primary and secondary alkyl halides can serve as alkylating agents, allyl and benzyl halides being especially reactive. An example of the allyl type is 3-chlorocyclopentene, which condenses with diethyl malonate to yield diethyl Δ^2-cyclopentenylmalonate (OS **32**, 52; yield 61%).

$$
\bigcirc\text{—}Cl + \bar{C}H(CO_2C_2H_5)_2 \rightarrow \bigcirc\text{—}CH(CO_2C_2H_5)_2 + Cl^-
$$

Diethyl acetosuccinate is made in 62% yield by condensing the sodium derivative of ethyl acetoacetate with ethyl chloroacetate (OS II, 262).

$$
CH_3CO\bar{C}HCO_2C_2H_5 + ClCH_2CO_2C_2H_5 \rightarrow CH_3COCHCH_2CO_2C_2H_5 + Cl^-
$$
$$
| \\
CO_2C_2H_5
$$

[8] N. J. Leonard and W. E. Goode, *J. Am. Chem. Soc.*, **72**, 5404 (1950).

The chief by-product is the ethyl ester of β-acetotricarballylic acid.

$$CH_3CO\overset{|}{\underset{|}{C}}CO_2C_2H_5 \;+\; ClCH_2CO_2C_2H_5 \;\rightarrow\; CH_3CO\overset{CH_2CO_2C_2H_5}{\underset{CH_2CO_2C_2H_5}{C}}CO_2C_2H_5 \;+\; Cl^-$$

with the lower substituent on the left being $CH_2CO_2C_2H_5$.

Diethyl acetonylmalonate is produced when diethyl malonate is condensed with chloroacetone.

$$\overset{-}{C}H(CO_2C_2H_5)_2 + ClCH_2COCH_3 \;\rightarrow\; CH_3COCH_2CH(CO_2C_2H_5)_2 + Cl^-$$

With sodium amide in liquid ammonia phenylacetic acid yields a sodium derivative analogous to the Ivanov reagent (p. 522); alkylation with benzyl chloride converts it into α,β-diphenylpropionic acid (OS **40**, 38; 84% yield).

$$C_6H_5CH_2CO_2H \longrightarrow C_6H_5\overset{|}{\underset{Na}{C}}HCO_2Na \xrightarrow[\;(2)\;\;HCl\;]{(1)\;C_6H_5CH_2Cl} C_6H_5\overset{|}{\underset{C_6H_5CH_2}{C}}HCO_2H$$

β-Chlorovinyl ketones are vinylogs (p. 308) of acid chlorides and resemble them in reactivity. An example is their use in the ketovinylation of β-keto esters; methyl β-chlorovinyl ketone reacts with the sodium derivative of ethyl ethylacetoacetate to give the ketovinylation product in 64.5% yield.[9]

$$[CH_3CO\overset{C_2H_5}{\underset{|}{C}}CO_2C_2H_5]Na + CH_3COCH{=}CHCl \;\rightarrow$$

$$CH_3CO\overset{C_2H_5}{\underset{CH=CHCOCH_3}{C}}CO_2C_2H_5 + NaCl$$

An alkylating agent of great interest is β-propiolactone (p. 440). With ethyl acetoacetate, for example, it yields a C-alkylation product, which when treated with acids is changed to 5-ketohexanoic acid.

$$\overset{CH_2CH_2}{\underset{O-C=O}{|\quad|}} + CH_3CO\overset{-}{C}HCO_2C_2H_5 \;\rightarrow$$

$$CH_3CO\overset{|}{\underset{CH_2CH_2CO_2^-}{C}}HCO_2C_2H_5 \;\rightarrow\; CH_3COCH_2CH_2CH_2CO_2H$$

[9] N. K. Kochetkov, L. J. Kudryashov, and B. P. Gottich, *Tetrahedron*, **12**, 63 (1961).

β-Propiolactone condenses with the enolates of acetylacetone, benzoyl-acetone, cyanoacetamide, and diethyl malonate in a similar way.

Active methylene compounds can also be condensed with a dihalide, one mole of which serves to alkylate two molecules of the active methylene compound. Diethyl malonate and ethylene bromide yield the ethyl ester of 1,1,4,4-butanetetracarboxylic acid.

$$\begin{array}{l} CH_2Br \\ | \\ CH_2Br \end{array} + 2\bar{C}H(CO_2C_2H_5)_2 \rightarrow \begin{array}{l} CH_2CH(CO_2C_2H_5)_2 \\ | \\ CH_2CH(CO_2C_2H_5)_2 \end{array} + 2Br^-$$

When the alkylating agent is chloroform, the product is an unsaturated ester, formed presumably by alkylation followed by dehydrochlorination.

$$2CH_2(CO_2C_2H_5)_2 \xrightarrow[C_2H_5ONa]{CHCl_3} \begin{array}{l} CH(CO_2C_2H_5)_2 \\ | \\ CHCl \\ | \\ CH(CO_2C_2H_5)_2 \end{array} \xrightarrow{-HCl} \begin{array}{l} C(CO_2C_2H_5)_2 \\ \| \\ CH \\ | \\ CH(CO_2C_2H_5)_2 \end{array}$$

Hydrolysis of the unsaturated ester from diethyl malonate and decarboxylation of the resulting acid yield glutaconic acid (p. 315).

A reaction of special utility takes place when the salt of ethyl aceto-acetate is treated with iodine; two molecules are coupled in the following manner.

$$2CH_3CO\bar{C}HCO_2C_2H_5 + I_2 \rightarrow \begin{array}{l} CH_3COCHCO_2C_2H_5 \\ | \\ CH_3COCHCO_2C_2H_5 \end{array} + 2I^-$$

This change probably involves an alkylation in which the alkylating agent is the iodo derivative of the ester. Diethyl malonate may be used to illustrate the mechanism.

$$\bar{C}H(CO_2C_2H_5)_2 + I_2 \rightarrow ICH(CO_2C_2H_5)_2 + I^-$$

$$\bar{C}H(CO_2C_2H_5)_2 + ICH(CO_2C_2H_5)_2 \rightarrow \begin{array}{l} CH(CO_2C_2H_5)_2 \\ | \\ CH(CO_2C_2H_5)_2 \end{array} + I^-$$

The coupling of two molecules of diethyl bromomalonate to produce the ethyl ester of ethylenetetracarboxylic acid (OS II, 273) appears to be a twofold alkylation; the yield is 57%.

$$2 \begin{array}{c} C_2H_5O_2C \\ \diagdown \\ C_2H_5O_2C \end{array} CHBr \xrightarrow{Na_2CO_3} \begin{array}{c} C_2H_5O_2C \\ \diagdown \\ C_2H_5O_2C \end{array} C\!\!=\!\!C \begin{array}{c} CO_2C_2H_5 \\ \diagup \\ CO_2C_2H_5 \end{array}$$

In this same category is the formation of 3,4-dinitro-3-hexene from 1-chloro-1-nitropropane by the action of potassium hydroxide (OS **37**, 23; yield 32%).

$$2CH_3CH_2\underset{\underset{Cl}{|}}{C}HNO_2 \rightarrow \underset{\underset{CH_3CH_2\overset{\|}{C}NO_2}{}}{CH_3CH_2\overset{\|}{\underset{O}{C}}NO_2} + 2HCl$$

A peculiar coupling occurs at the α-position of β-aroylacrylic acids when they are dehydrated; the products are bifunctional enol lactones, known as von Pechmann dyes (CR **54**, 59). The dye from β-mesitoylacrylic acid is obtained in especially high yields.

$$2Mes\underset{\underset{O}{\|}}{C}CH=CH\underset{\underset{OH}{|}}{C}=O \rightarrow Mes\overset{\overset{CO--O}{|\quad\ |}}{\underset{\underset{O----CO}{}}{C=CHC=CCH=C}}Mes + 2H_2O$$

Nitriles in general are less reactive than the compounds considered up to this point and are less easily alkylated. Sodium amide, however, serves to make alkylation a useful reaction with many nitriles. The NH_2^- ion is a much stronger base than $OC_2H_5^-$ and is used with compounds that do not enolize readily. Phenylacetonitrile, in which the methylene group is activated by the phenyl radical as well as the nitrile group, can be alkylated; α-cyclohexylphenylacetonitrile is made in 77% yield in this way (OS III, 219).

$$C_6H_5CH_2CN + C_6H_{11}Br \xrightarrow{\text{NaNH}_2} \overset{C_6H_5}{\underset{C_6H_{11}}{\diagdown\diagup}}CHCN + HBr$$

Acetonitrile reacts with sodium amide in liquid ammonia to form a salt that can be alkylated to mono-, di-, and trisubstituted acetonitriles by the action of an alkyl halide or an alkyl *p*-toluenesulfonate. It is remarkable that acetonitrile can be phenylated by treatment with chlorobenzene and potassium amide in liquid ammonia. Other phenylations of this type are known; benzyne (p. 388) has been postulated as an intermediate.

Certain α-amino nitriles can be alkylated by use of sodium amide in liquid ammonia. Methylation of α-dimethylaminophenylacetonitrile is an example.[10]

$$C_6H_5\underset{\underset{N(CH_3)_2}{|}}{C}HCN \rightarrow C_6H_5\overset{\overset{CH_3}{|}}{\underset{\underset{N(CH_3)_2}{|}}{C}}CN \rightarrow C_6H_5COCH_3$$

[10] H. M. Taylor and C. R. Hauser, *J. Am. Chem. Soc.*, **82**, 1960 (1960).

The methylation product is hydrolyzed by acids to acetophenone; since the original amino ketone is made from benzaldehyde, the over-all process is one for making ketones from aldehydes. The method has been extended to aliphatic aldehydes.[11]

Ketones also may be alkylated, sodium amide generally being used to form the enolate. From acetone, methyl ethyl ketone may be made.

$$CH_3COCH_3 \xrightarrow{NH_2^-} CH_3COCH_2^- \xrightarrow{CH_3I} CH_3COCH_2CH_3$$

This process may be continued until six methyl groups have been introduced, hexamethylacetone being formed.

The allylation of cyclohexanone is another example (OS III, 44; 62% yield).

The metal ion of an enolate may have a profound effect on the behavior of the carbanion. The alkylation of butyrophenone in ethereal solution, for example, is much faster when the cation is potassium than when it is lithium.[12]

Treatment of acetylacetone with two molecular equivalents of potassium amide in liquid ammonia generates a dicarbanion that reacts with benzyl chloride to undergo alkylation at a methyl group instead of the methylene group.

$$CH_3CO\overset{-}{C}HCOCH_2^- + C_6H_5CH_2Cl \rightarrow C_6H_5CH_2CH_2CO\overset{-}{C}HCOCH_3 + Cl^-$$

3-Phenylpentane-2,4-dione in a similar way is benzylated, benzoylated, and carbonated in a terminal position.[13]

Ring Closure. When diethyl malonate is treated with a suitably constituted dihalide, ring closure may occur. Ethylene bromide, for example, gives diethyl 1,1-cyclopropanedicarboxylate.

[11] Z. Welvart, *Bull. soc. chim. France*, 1653 (1961).
[12] H. D. Zook, and W. L. Gumby, *J. Am. Chem. Soc.*, **82**, 1386 (1960).
[13] W. M. I. O'Sullivan and C. R. Hauser, *J. Org. Chem.*, **25**, 1110 (1960).

This method of forming carbocycles, developed by Perkin, has been employed also to make the analogous four- , five- , six- , and seven-membered ring compounds. A convenient procedure for making cyclopropanecarboxylic acid involves a similar ring closure of γ-chlorobutyronitrile (OS III, 221) and hydrolysis of the resulting cyclopropyl cyanide; the over-all yield of acid by this method is 79%.

$$ClCH_2CH_2CH_2CN + NaOH \rightarrow \underset{CH_2}{\overset{CH_2}{|}}\!\!\diagdown CHCN + NaCl + H_2O$$

Methyl cyclopropyl ketone can be prepared from 5-chloro-2-pentanone (p. 165) in a similar way (OS **31**, 74; 83% yield).

$$ClCH_2CH_2CH_2COCH_3 + NaOH \rightarrow \overset{CH_2}{CH_2CHCOCH_3} + NaCl + H_2O$$

Cyclopropyl phenyl ketone has been made in four steps from γ-butyrolactone in a yield of 75%.[14]

$$\underset{L\!\!-\!\!O\!\!-\!\!\rfloor}{CH_2CH_2CH_2C\!\!=\!\!O} \xrightarrow[\text{(2) SOCl}_2]{\text{(1) HCl}} ClCH_2CH_2CH_2COCl \xrightarrow[AlCl_3]{C_6H_6}$$

$$ClCH_2CH_2CH_2COC_6H_5 \xrightarrow[CH_3OH]{KOH} \overset{CH_2}{CH_2\!\!-\!\!CHCOC_6H_5}$$

Dicyclopropyl ketone is formed from 1,7-dichloro-4-heptanone in an analogous way.[15]

$$ClCH_2CH_2CH_2COCH_2CH_2CH_2Cl \rightarrow \underset{CH_2}{\overset{CH_2}{|}}\!\!\diagdown \overset{O}{\underset{}{CHC\!\!-\!\!CH}}\diagup\!\!\underset{CH_2}{\overset{CH_2}{|}}$$

This type of ring closure occurs also in the cyclobutane series. When ω-halovaleronitriles are treated with sodium amide, cyanocyclobutane is produced in 30% yields.[16]

$$XCH_2CH_2CH_2CH_2CN \rightarrow \underset{CH_2\!\!-\!\!CH_2}{\overset{CH_2\!\!-\!\!CHCN}{|\qquad|}}$$

---

[14] W. J. Close, *J. Am. Chem. Soc.*, **79**, 1455 (1957).
[15] H. Hart and O. E. Curtis, Jr., *J. Am. Chem. Soc.*, **78**, 112 (1956).
[16] H. Normant and G. Voreux, *Compt. rend.*, **231**, 703 (1950).

Cyclobutanecarboxylic acid can be made also by the Perkin method, from diethyl malonate and trimethylene bromide (OS III, 213).

$$CH_2(CO_2C_2H_5)_2 + BrCH_2CH_2CH_2Br \xrightarrow{-2HBr}$$

Of particular interest is the resolvable spiroheptanedicarboxylic acid prepared from pentaerythrityl bromide by the following series of transformations.[17]

The condensation of enolates with dihalides to form rings is facilitated by the fact that the second step is intramolecular. A striking example is the behavior of bimalonic ester, which resists dialkylation with alkyl halides but with trimethylene bromide, for example, forms the corresponding cyclopentane derivative.[18]

[17] See L. M. Rice and C. H. Grogan, J. Org. Chem., 26, 54 (1961).
[18] See C. F. Koelsch and J. R. Sjolander, J. Org. Chem., 25, 1479 (1960).

The ethyl ester of 1,1,4,4-butanetetracarboxylic acid (p. 259) served as the starting point in Perkin's synthesis of 1,2-cyclobutanedicarboxylic acid. When its sodium derivative is treated with iodine or bromine, ring closure is effected.

$$CH_2\text{—}CH(CO_2C_2H_5)_2 \quad CH_2\text{—}C(CO_2C_2H_5)_2$$
$$| \qquad\qquad\qquad \rightarrow \quad | \qquad | \qquad\qquad \rightarrow$$
$$CH_2\text{—}CH(CO_2C_2H_5)_2 \quad CH_2\text{—}C(CO_2C_2H_5)_2$$

$$CH_2\text{—}C(CO_2H)_2 \qquad CH_2\text{—}CHCO_2H$$
$$| \qquad | \qquad\qquad \rightarrow \quad | \qquad |$$
$$CH_2\text{—}C(CO_2H)_2 \qquad CH_2\text{—}CHCO_2H$$

A ring closure that probably involves a mechanism similar to Perkin's occurs when diethyl α,α'-dibromoadipate is heated with sodium cyanide.

This method gives the four- , five- , and six-membered ring compounds in satisfactory yields.

The sodium derivatives of 1,1,4,4-butanetetracarboxylic esters and similar compounds have likewise been condensed with dihalides. This procedure is especially valuable because it makes possible the preparation of cyclic dicarboxylic acids in which the carboxyl groups are separated by three or more carbon atoms. The synthesis of 1,3-cyclobutanedicarboxylic acid and 1,4-cyclohexanedicarboxylic acid will suffice to indicate the broad scope of the method.

The Perkin ring closure, applied to ethyl acetoacetate, provides a route to ketones. Tetramethylene bromide gives as the principal product ethyl 1-aceto-1-cyclopentanecarboxylate, from which cyclopentyl methyl ketone is readily obtainable.

$$
\begin{array}{c}
CH_2CH_2Br \\
| \\
CH_2CH_2Br
\end{array}
+
\begin{array}{c}
CO_2C_2H_5 \\
\diagup \\
CH_2 \\
\diagdown \\
COCH_3
\end{array}
\xrightarrow[-2HBr]{NaOC_2H_5}
\begin{array}{c}
CH_2CH_2 \quad CO_2C_2H_5 \\
| \quad\quad \diagup \\
\quad\quad C \\
| \quad\quad \diagdown \\
CH_2CH_2 \quad COCH_3
\end{array}
\longrightarrow
$$

COCH₃

When *o*-xylylene bromide is condensed with ethyl cyanoacetate, 2-carbethoxy-2-cyanoindan is obtained in 95 % yield.[19]

A method of making β-lactams involves a ring closure that resembles the Perkin. Diethyl bromomalonate is allowed to react with aniline, for example, and the resulting amino ester is acylated with chloroacetic anhydride. The ring closure is effected with triethylamine.[20]

$$C_6H_5NH_2 + BrCH(CO_2C_2H_5)_2 \longrightarrow C_6H_5NHCH(CO_2C_2H_5)_2 \xrightarrow{(ClCH_2CO)_2O}$$

$$
\begin{array}{c}
C_6H_5NCH(CO_2C_2H_5)_2 \\
| \\
COCH_2Cl
\end{array}
\xrightarrow{HCl}
\begin{array}{c}
C_6H_5N\text{---}C(CO_2C_2H_5)_2 \\
| \qquad\qquad | \\
CO\text{---}CH_2
\end{array}
$$

In the presence of certain basic reagents α-halo ketones undergo a skeletal rearrangement, known as the Favorskii rearrangement (OR **11**, 261). 2-Chlorocyclohexanone, for example, is converted by alkali into cyclopentanecarboxylic acid.

---

[19] P. E. Gagnon and J. L. Boivin, *Can. J. Research*, **26B**, 503 (1948).
[20] J. C. Sheehan and A. K. Bose, *J. Am. Chem. Soc.*, **72**, 5158 (1950).

1,1,3-Tribromo-2-butanone, when heated with ethanolic potassium hydroxide, yields α-bromo-β-methylcrotonic acid.[21]

$$CH_3CHClCOCHBr_2 \rightarrow \underset{CH_3}{\overset{CH_3}{\diagup}} C{=}\underset{Br}{\overset{}{CCO_2H}}$$

A possible mechanism for this change involves the intermediate formation of a cyclopropanone ring by joining the two carbon atoms adjacent to the carbonyl group. Experiments with 2-chlorocyclohexanone, in which the carbon atom holding the chlorine atom is C^{14}, support this or some other mechanism in which carbon atoms 2 and 6 are at some time equivalent.[22]

A remarkable ring closure occurs when ethyl 3-bromocyclobutane-1-carboxylate is treated with triphenylmethylsodium; the product is ethyl bicyclo[1·1·0]butane-1-carboxylate.[23]

Many compounds such as the Mannich bases (p. 503) have amino groups that are sufficiently labile to permit their use as alkylating agents (OR 7, 99).

Phenolates

Phenolates, in contrast to enolates, generally give predominantly O-alkylation products, i.e., undergo the Williamson type of reaction. C-Alkylation occurs under favorable conditions, however; when the

[21] R. B. Wagner and J. A. Moore, *J. Am. Chem. Soc.*, **72**, 3655 (1950).
[22] R. B. Loftfield, *J. Am. Chem. Soc.*, **73**, 4707 (1951).
[23] K. B. Wiberg and R. P. Ciula, *J. Am. Chem. Soc.*, **81**, 5261 (1959).

lithium salt of 2,6-dimethylphenol is treated with methyl iodide, 2,6,6-trimethyl-3,5-cyclohexadienone is produced in 16% yield.[24]

Even the phenolic hydroxyl group may be replaced by a methyl group; when a mixture of phenol and methanol in large excess is heated at 378° in contact with activated alumina, hexamethylbenzene is formed in 60% yield (OS **35**, 73).

Procedures have been developed for the introduction of aminomethyl groups in a manner not unlike that employed in Mannich condensations (p. 503), the reactants being a phenol, formaldehyde, and an amine. With a secondary amine such as dimethylamine, phenol yields a trisubstituted derivative.

Another characteristic of this type of reaction that relates it to the Mannich reaction is that the o-position is generally involved in preference to the p-position. It provides a convenient method of preparing 2,6-xylenol from o-cresol; the over-all yield is 36%.[25]

[24] D. Y. Curtin and R. R. Fraser, *Chem. and Ind.*, 1358 (1957).
[25] R. B. Carlin and H. P. Landerl, *J. Am. Chem. Soc.*, **72**, 2762 (1950).

Olefins

Under sufficiently drastic treatment even olefins undergo alkylation in the presence of an alkyl halide and a base. 2-Methyl-2-butene, for example, yields a mixture of higher olefins when heated with methyl chloride and lime. About 15% of the original olefin is transformed into triptene.[26]

$$\underset{CH_3}{\overset{CH_3}{\diagdown}}C{=}CHCH_3 + CH_3Cl \xrightarrow{\text{lime}} CH_3\underset{\overset{|}{CH_3}}{\overset{\overset{|}{CH_3}\ \ \overset{|}{CH_3}}{C}}{-}C{=}CH_2 + HCl$$

One possibility is that the base converts the olefin into a carbanion, which displaces chloride ion from methyl chloride.

Chloroform

Chloroform gets its name from the fact that it undergoes hydrolysis to yield formic acid. The hydrolysis gives carbon monoxide also and has attracted attention because it proceeds more readily with chloroform than with methylene chloride or carbon tetrachloride. It has been concluded that dichlorocarbene is formed as an intermediate.[27]

$$CHCl_3 + OH^- \overset{\text{Fast}}{\rightleftharpoons} CCl_3^- + H_2O$$

$$CCl_3^- \xrightarrow{\text{Slow}} CCl_2 + Cl^-$$

$$CCl_2 \xrightarrow[\text{H}_2\text{O}]{\text{OH}^-,\ \text{Fast}} CO + HCO_2^-$$

Dichlorocarbene has been generated also by treating t-butyl dichloroacetate with potassium t-butoxide.[28]

It seems possible that the transformation of pyrrole into 3-chloropyridine by the action of chloroform and alkali may involve the intermediate formation of dichlorocarbene also.

A similar explanation has been put forward for the formation of chlorobenzene from cyclopentadiene.[29]

[26] V. A. Miller and W. G. Lovell, *Ind. Eng. Chem.*, **40**, 1138 (1948).

[27] J. Hine, *J. Am. Chem. Soc.*, **72**, 2438 (1950).

[28] W. E. Parham, F. C. Loew, and E. E. Schweizer, *J. Org. Chem.*, **24**, 1900 (1959).

[29] A. P. ter Borg and A. F. Bickel, *Proc. Chem. Soc.*, 283 (1958).

An important reaction involving chloroform, in which dichlorocarbene may possibly be an intermediate, is the Reimer-Tiemann reaction for the conversion of phenols into phenolic aldehydes (CR **60**, 169). Salicylaldehyde is formed, for example, from phenol and chloroform.

$$C_6H_5OH + CHCl_3 + 3KOH \rightarrow \text{[benzene ring]} \begin{array}{c} CHO \\ OH \end{array} + 3KCl + 2H_2O$$

Like the Hoesch, the Reimer-Tiemann reaction occurs only if the aromatic ring is very sensitive; nitro, carboxyl, and other *m*-directing groups inhibit the reaction. If an *o*-position is filled, the aldehyde group tends to go to the *p*-position; an example is the synthesis of vanillin from guaiacol.

Formylation of pyrimidines by the Reimer-Tiemann method has been accomplished also; 2,4,6-trihydroxypyrimidine gives 2,4,6-trihydroxypyrimidine-5-carboxaldehyde in 42 % yield.[30]

On the assumption that the reaction species is actually dichlorocarbene, the following mechanism can be written for the Reimer-Tiemann reaction.[31]

It is significant that in 2-naphthol the entering group takes the 1-position only; 2-hydroxy-1-naphthaldehyde can be made in 48 % yield by this method (OS III, 463).

On the other hand, in the 1,2,3,4-tetrahydro derivative the 7-position is favored, the aldehydic product being the 6,7-isomer; a dichloromethyl

[30] R. H. Wiley and Y. Yamamoto, *J. Org. Chem.*, **25**, 1906 (1960).
[31] H. Wynberg, *J. Am. Chem. Soc.*, **76**, 4998 (1954).

ketone is formed also. Reduction converts this derivative to a compound with an angular methyl group.

A similar dichloromethyl ketone has been made from 5-indanol.[32]

The low reactivity of the 3-position of naphthalene is illustrated further by the behavior of 1-methyl-2-hydroxynaphthalene, in which the 1-position is blocked; the dichloromethyl group nonetheless enters the 1- and not the 3-position.[33]

A method resembling that of Reimer and Tiemann, involving the use of hexamine, has been developed by Duff. The procedure is to heat the phenol at elevated temperatures with a mixture of hexamine, boric acid, and glycerol. Duff found that o-substitution and a small amount of o,p-disubstitution take place. The yields are only 15 to 20%, but the products are purer than those from the Reimer-Tiemann procedure, and the preparation requires less time (CR **38**, 230). An example is the conversion of pyrogallol-1,3-dimethyl ether into syringic aldehyde (OS **31**, 92; 32% yield).

Stevens rearrangement

Certain reactions that quaternary ammonium salts undergo in the presence of bases have been interpreted by reference to the substances,

[32] S. M. Bloom, *Tetrahedron Letters*, **21**, 7 (1959).
[33] F. Bell and W. H. Hunter, *J. Chem. Soc.*, 2903 (1950).

known as *ylid* compounds, that would be formed by the abstraction of a proton from a carbon atom that is attached to the quaternary nitrogen atom.

$$\underset{|}{\overset{\overset{\displaystyle H}{|}}{-C}}-\overset{+}{N}R_3 \;\rightarrow\; -\overset{\cdot\cdot}{\underset{|}{C}}-\overset{+}{N}R_3$$

In many instances one of the alkyl groups migrates from the nitrogen atom to the carbon atom represented as a carbanion. This type of rearrangement was discovered in 1928 by Stevens who observed the following transformation.

$$\underset{\underset{\displaystyle C_6H_5CH_2}{|}}{C_6H_5\overset{\overset{\displaystyle O}{\parallel}}{C}CH_2\overset{+}{N}(CH_3)_2} \xrightarrow{OH^-} \underset{\underset{\displaystyle C_6H_5CH_2}{|}}{C_6H_5\overset{\overset{\displaystyle O}{\parallel}}{C}\overset{\cdot\cdot}{C}H\overset{+}{N}(CH_3)_2} \longrightarrow \underset{\underset{\displaystyle C_6H_5CH_2}{|}}{C_6H_5\overset{\overset{\displaystyle O}{\parallel}}{C}CHN(CH_3)_2}$$

A rearrangement of this sort occurs when benzyl ether is treated with potassium amide; benzylphenylcarbinol is produced.[34] It has been postulated that the rearrangement involves a carbanion and takes the following course.

$$C_6H_5CH_2O\overset{\cdot\cdot}{C}HC_6H_5 \;\rightarrow\; \underset{\underset{\displaystyle C_6H_5CH_2}{|}}{C_6H_5CHO^-}$$

N-Alkylation

N-Alkylation occurs when ammonia or amines react with alkylating agents such as alkyl halides and sulfates. With cyanides N-alkylation leads to isonitriles and with nitrites to nitro compounds. The ease with which amino compounds undergo alkylation is related to their basicity, which is diminished by attachment of radicals such as acyl that are electron poor. Aryl radicals exert this effect also; aniline is far less basic than methylamine, for example. Aryl radicals holding *m*-directing groups in positions *ortho* or *para* to the amino group are particularly effective; in extreme cases amidelike properties are imparted to the amine. Picramide owes its name to this fact. It may be pointed out that *o*- and *p*-nitroanilines are vinylogs (p. 308) of nitramide, $H_2N\text{—}NO_2$.

As the amino group loses basicity, it acquires an increased facility in salt formation with metals. All amino compounds having a hydrogen atom on

---

[34] See C. R. Hauser and S. W. Kantor, *J. Am. Chem. Soc.*, **73**, 1437 (1951).

nitrogen decompose the Grignard reagent (p. 447), forming magnesium salts.

$$RMgX + R'NH_2 \rightarrow RH + R'NHMgX$$

Active metals such as sodium also displace the hydrogen atoms of amines. Aniline, for example, forms sodium anilide when treated with sodium metal. It is interesting, however, that the reaction must be catalyzed, copper being most effective.

Phthalimide reacts rapidly with potassium hydroxide in ethanolic solutions to yield potassium phthalimide (OS I, 119), which is employed in the Gabriel synthesis (p. 277). Succinimide forms salts in a similar manner. Pyrroles resemble imides in this respect; indole, for instance, may be methylated by treatment of its sodium salt, formed by the action of sodium amide, with methyl iodide (OS **40**, 68; yield 95%).

Primary and secondary sulfonamides are still more acidic. The various types of amino compounds arranged according to decreasing basicity fall in the following order.

$$R_2NH > RNH_2 > NH_3 > ArNH_2 >$$

$$RCONH_2 > (RCO)_2NH > RSO_2NH_2$$

Ammonolysis

Replacement of halogen atoms by the amino group, i.e., ammonolysis, can be effected with many types of halogen compounds. It has been especially useful in the preparation of α-amino acids, the corresponding halogen compounds being readily prepared by halogenation. An example is the synthesis of alanine (OS I, 23; 70% yield).

$$CH_3CHBrCO_2H + 2NH_3 \rightarrow CH_3CH(NH_2)CO_2H + NH_4Br$$

Glycine (OS I, 300; 65% yield), leucine (OS III, 523; 45% yield), and norleucine (OS I, 48; 67% yield) are made in a similar way. Other examples are isoleucine (OS III, 495; 49% yield), valine (OS III, 848; 48% yield), lysine (OS II, 374), threonine (OS III, 813), taurine (OS II, 563; 55% yield), serine (OS III, 774), and phenylalanine (OS III, 705). The α-halo acid usually is allowed to stand for several days with ammonia in great excess.

Replacement of halogen atoms by substituted amino groups usually is feasible and is employed extensively. β-Diethylaminoethyl alcohol, for example, is prepared in 70% yields by condensing diethylamine with ethylene chlorohydrin (OS II, 183).

$$(C_2H_5)_2NH + ClCH_2CH_2OH \xrightarrow{\text{NaOH}} (C_2H_5)_2NCH_2CH_2OH + HCl$$

β-Di-*n*-butylaminoethyl bromide is changed to β-di-*n*-butylaminoethyl-amine in a similar way (OS III, 254; yield 55%). N-Benzylaniline can be prepared in 87% yields by the interaction of benzyl chloride and aniline (OS I, 102).

$$C_6H_5CH_2Cl + C_6H_5NH_2 \rightarrow C_6H_5CH_2NHC_6H_5 + HCl$$

Sodium bicarbonate is used to neutralize the hydrogen chloride as it forms.

Another example of ammonolysis is the synthesis of aminoacetal from chloroacetal (OS III, 50; 39% yield).

$$ClCH_2CH(OC_2H_5)_2 + 2NH_3 \rightarrow H_2NCH_2CH(OC_2H_5)_2 + NH_4Cl$$

By use of two moles of chloroacetic acid to one mole of methylamine it is possible to make methyliminodiacetic acid in 71% yield (OS II, 397).

$$CH_3NH_2 + 2ClCH_2CO_2H \xrightarrow{\text{NaOH}} CH_3N(CH_2CO_2H)_2 + 2HCl$$

Primary and secondary amines react with methyl iodide to give quater-nary ammonium iodides, which can be reduced by lithium aluminum hydride to tertiary amines. Methane is formed, apparently by an S_N2 displacement reaction.[35]

$$R_3\overset{+}{N}\!\!-\!\!CH_3 \quad {}^{\curvearrowleft}H^- \rightarrow R_3N + CH_4$$

In a similar way lithium aluminum hydride debenzylates benzyl-containing phosphonium compounds to produce toluene and a phosphine; ethylmethylphenylphosphine is formed in this way, for example.[36]

Replacement of a hydroxyl group by an amino group may occur at the saturated carbon atom, but in all cases the process appears to be complex.

[35] A. C. Cope, E. Ciganek, L. J. Fleckenstein, and M. R. P. Meisinger, *J. Am. Chem. Soc.*, **82**, 4651 (1960).

[36] W. J. Bailey, S. A. Buckler, and F. Marktscheffel, *J. Org. Chem.*, **25**, 1996 (1960).

The synthesis of ethyleneurea from ethylene glycol and urea, for example, corresponds to the replacement of primary alcohol groups by amido groups.[37]

$$
\begin{array}{c}
CH_2OH \\
| \\
CH_2OH
\end{array}
+
\begin{array}{c}
H_2N \\
\diagdown \\
\diagup \\
H_2N
\end{array}
CO
\rightarrow
\begin{array}{c}
CH_2NH \\
| \qquad \diagdown \\
| \qquad \diagup \\
CH_2NH
\end{array}
CO + 2H_2O
$$

It seems probable, however, that ethylenediamine is formed first.

Cyanohydrins react with amino compounds to yield amino nitriles. The Strecker method for making amino acids depends on this reaction; an illustration is the preparation of alanine from acetaldehyde (OS I, 21; 60% yield).

$$
CH_3CHO \xrightarrow[NH_4Cl]{NaCN} \underset{\underset{NH_2}{|}}{CH_3CHCN} \rightarrow \underset{\underset{NH_2}{|}}{CH_3CHCO_2H}
$$

In a similar manner, α-aminodiethylacetic acid can be synthesized from diethyl ketone (OS III, 66; 43% yield).

$$
\begin{array}{c}
C_2H_5 \\
\diagdown \\
\diagup \\
C_2H_5
\end{array}
C{=}O \rightarrow
\begin{array}{c}
C_2H_5 \\
\diagdown \\
\diagup \quad | \\
C_2H_5 \quad OH
\end{array}
CCN \rightarrow
\begin{array}{c}
C_2H_5 \\
\diagdown \\
\diagup \quad | \\
C_2H_5 \quad NH_2
\end{array}
CCN \rightarrow
\begin{array}{c}
C_2H_5 \\
\diagdown \\
\diagup \quad | \\
C_2H_5 \quad NH_2
\end{array}
CCO_2H
$$

α-Aminophenylacetic acid has been prepared from benzaldehyde by the Strecker procedure (OS III, 84; 37% yield). An example of special interest is the synthesis of serine from ethoxyacetaldehyde.

$$
C_2H_5OCH_2CHO \xrightarrow{HCN} \underset{\underset{OH}{|}}{C_2H_5OCH_2CHCN} \xrightarrow{NH_3}
$$

$$
\underset{\underset{NH_2}{|}}{C_2H_5OCH_2CHCN} \xrightarrow{HBr} \underset{\underset{NH_2}{|}}{HOCH_2CHCO_2H}
$$

Use of an amine in place of ammonia is illustrated by the synthesis of α-(N,N-dimethylamino)phenylacetonitrile from benzaldehyde and dimethylamine.[38]

$$
C_6H_5CHO \xrightarrow{NaHSO_3} \underset{\underset{OH}{|}}{C_6H_5CHSO_3Na} \xrightarrow[NaCN]{(CH_3)_2NH} \underset{\underset{CN}{|}}{C_6H_5CHN(CH_3)_2}
$$

[37] C. E. Schweitzer, *J. Org. Chem.*, **15**, 475 (1950).
[38] C. R. Hauser, H. M. Taylor, and T. G. Ledford, *J. Am. Chem. Soc.*, **82**, 1960 (1960).

Hydrazine may serve in place of ammonia. When cyclohexanone, hydrazine hydrochloride, and sodium cyanide are mixed, 1,1'-hydrazodicyclohexanecarbonitrile is produced (OS **32**, 50; yield 70%).

$$2\left[\text{cyclohexanone} =O\right] + N_2H_4 \cdot HCl + 2NaCN \rightarrow$$

$$\underset{\text{CN}}{\text{cyclohexane}}-NHNH-\underset{\text{CN}}{\text{cyclohexane}} + 2NaCl + 2H_2O$$

Another example is the formation of diethylaminoacetonitrile from formaldehyde cyanohydrin. Actually it is more convenient to effect the *cyanomethylation* by heating a mixture of the amine, sodium cyanide, formaldehyde, and sodium bisulfite (OS III, 275; 90% yield).

$$(C_2H_5)_2NH + NaCN + CH_2O + NaHSO_3 \rightarrow$$

$$(C_2H_5)_2NCH_2CN + Na_2SO_3 + H_2O$$

Cyanomethylation of ethylenediamine is employed to make Sequestrene, which is valuable as a sequestering agent for metallic ions.

$$\begin{array}{ccc} CH_2NH_2 & CH_2N(CH_2CN)_2 & CH_2N(CH_2CO_2H)_2 \\ | & \rightarrow \quad | & \rightarrow \quad | \\ CH_2NH_2 & CH_2N(CH_2CN)_2 & CH_2N(CH_2CO_2H)_2 \end{array}$$

Chelate rings are formed in the complex by attachment of the metallic ion to the nitrogen atoms.

$$\begin{array}{c} NaO_2CCH_2 \qquad CH_2CH_2 \qquad CH_2CO_2Na \\ \diagdown \quad \diagup \qquad \diagdown \quad \diagup \\ N \qquad\qquad\quad N \\ \diagup \quad \diagdown \qquad\quad \diagup \quad \diagdown \\ CH_2 \qquad M \qquad CH_2 \\ | \qquad \diagup \quad \diagdown \qquad | \\ CO\text{—}O \qquad O\text{—}CO \end{array}$$

The carboxylic acid can be made in one step by slow addition of formaldehyde to an aqueous solution of ethylenediamine, sodium hydroxide, and sodium cyanide. This reaction has been called *carboxymethylation* and appears to be very different from that of Strecker.

Cyanomethylation of ammonia itself has been achieved by adding sodium cyanide slowly to an ice-cold mixture of formaldehyde and ammonium chloride (OS I, 355; 71% yield). The product is not cyanomethylamine but the trimeric form of the Schiff base, methyleneaminoacetonitrile, generated from it and formaldehyde.

$$2CH_2O + NH_4Cl + NaCN \rightarrow CH_2{=}NCH_2CN + NaCl + 2H_2O$$

A closely related reaction is the transformation of cyanohydrins to hydantoins. Acetone cyanohydrin reacts with ammonium carbonate, for example, to give 5,5-dimethylhydantoin in 56% yield (OS III, 323), the amino nitrile being a probable intermediate.

$$\text{(CH}_3)_2\text{C(OH)CN} + (NH_4)_2CO_3 \rightarrow \quad + 2H_2O + NH_3$$

Primary and secondary amides differ from amines in that they may undergo not only N-alkylation but O-alkylation as well. The course that the alkylation takes depends not only on the nature of the two reactants but also on the experimental conditions.

An example of N-alkylation is the methylation of N,N'-dibenzoyl-hydrazine by dimethyl sulfate (OS II, 208).

$$C_6H_5CONHNHCOC_6H_5 + 2(CH_3)_2SO_4 + 2NaOH \rightarrow$$

$$C_6H_5CON\underset{\underset{CH_3}{|}}{\quad}NCOC_6H_5 + 2CH_3SO_4Na + 2H_2O$$
$$\underset{CH_3\;\;CH_3}{}$$

On the other hand, when ε-caprolactam is heated with dimethyl sulfate in the absence of alkali, O-methylcaprolactim is obtained (OS **31**, 72; 68% yield).

$$\text{(CH}_2)_5\!\!\begin{array}{c}C=O\\|\\NH\end{array} \xrightarrow{(CH_3)_2SO_4} \text{(CH}_2)_5\!\!\begin{array}{c}COCH_3\\||\\N\end{array}$$

Diallylcyanamide is produced by the action of allyl bromide on sodium cyanamide (OS I, 203; 56% yield).

$$2CH_2\!\!=\!\!CHCH_2Br + Na_2NCN \rightarrow (CH_2\!\!=\!\!CHCH_2)_2NCN + 2NaBr$$

Alcohols and certain ethers have served as alkylating agents also. The use of ethylene oxide has already been cited (p. 257). An interesting reaction occurs when tetrahydropyran and aniline are heated in the presence of alumina, the product being N-phenylpiperidine (OS **34**, 79; 90% yield).

$$C_6H_5NH_2 + \text{O}\langle\text{THP}\rangle \rightarrow C_6H_5N\langle\text{piperidine}\rangle + H_2O$$

Gabriel synthesis

Amines are made from imides by alkylation followed by hydrolysis. This method, developed by Gabriel, normally involves potassium phthalimide and finds extensive use in synthesis. When the alkylating agent is γ-chlorobutyronitrile, for example, the final product is γ-aminobutyric acid (OS II, 25; 62% yield).

$$C_6H_4 \underset{CO}{\overset{CO}{\diagup\diagdown}} NK + ClCH_2CH_2CH_2CN \xrightarrow{-KCl}$$

$$C_6H_4 \underset{CO}{\overset{CO}{\diagup\diagdown}} NCH_2CH_2CH_2CN \xrightarrow[H_2SO_4]{H_2O} H_2NCH_2CH_2CH_2CO_2H$$

Other alkylating agents that have been employed are ethylene bromide (OS I, 119), diethyl bromomalonate (OS I, 271), and benzyl chloride (OS II, 83). When the solvent is dimethylformamide, in which potassium phthalimide is appreciably soluble, the alkylation is facilitated.[39]

A special case of the first step of the Gabriel synthesis involves carboxylate ion displacement by the interaction of potassium phthalimide and phthalide to give the potassium salt of α-phthalimido-o-toluic acid (OS **38**, 81; 67% yield).

Sommelet method

Hexamine, used in the Duff method for making phenolic aldehydes (p. 270), serves also in the transformation of chloromethyl compounds into aldehydes. When benzyl chloride is treated with hexamine, a quaternary ammonium salt is formed, which yields benzaldehyde when treated with water. The method, discovered by Sommelet, gives aromatic aldehydes in excellent yields accompanied by benzylamines and methylamine (OR **8**, 197). 1-Naphthaldehyde can be made in satisfactory yield from naphthalene by chloromethylation followed by the Sommelet treatment. One mechanism postulates that the benzylamine formed initially undergoes dehydrogenation to the imine, which is then hydrolyzed.

$$ArCH_2NH_2 \rightarrow ArCH{=}NH \rightarrow ArCHO$$

[39] J. C. Sheehan and W. A. Bolhofer, *J. Am. Chem. Soc.*, **72**, 2786 (1950).

In support of this assumption is the fact that benzylamines can be converted into the corresponding aldehydes by the use of hexamine. The oily product, obtained by treating benzylamine with formaldehyde, is dissolved in hydrochloric acid, and the solution is heated with an aqueous solution of hexamine. The aromatic aldehyde is formed in 60% yield. When α-phenylethylamine is used, acetophenone is produced.

A valuable example of this transformation is the production of 2-thiophenecarboxaldehyde from 2-chloromethylthiophene (OS III, 811; 53% yield). This type of procedure has proved to be successful in the synthesis of 3-thiophenecarboxaldehyde also. When heated with ammonia taken in excess, the hexamine-alkyl halides give amines in satisfactory yields. Benzylamine can be made from benzyl chloride, for example, by this method.

Another procedure for obtaining aldehydes from halomethyl compounds is illustrated by the preparation of o-tolualdehyde from o-xylyl bromide. The bromide is condensed with the sodium derivative of 2-nitropropane; the alkylation product decomposes to the aldehyde and the oxime of acetone.

Formation of nitro compounds

Nitrite ion being ambident reacts with alkyl halides or sulfonates to produce nitroalkanes as well as alkyl nitrites.

$$RX + NO_2^- \rightarrow RNO_2 \text{ (or } RONO) + X^-$$

1-Bromoöctane and silver nitrite react in dry ether to give 1-nitroöctane in 80% yield (OS 38, 75). The yield of n-octyl nitrite is 14%.

$$CH_3(CH_2)_7Br \xrightarrow{AgNO_2} CH_3(CH_2)_7NO_2 \quad \text{and} \quad CH_3(CH_2)_7ONO$$

A better method of making nitroalkanes, which serves for secondary as well as primary halides, is to treat the halide with sodium nitrite in a solvent such as dimethylformamide or dimethyl sulfoxide. With secondary bromides and iodides urea is added to the dimethylformamide along with the halide to promote solubility of the nitrite salt.

The method is useful in the synthesis of α-nitro esters also. Ethyl α-nitroisobutyrate is produced in 91% yield, for example, by treating ethyl α-bromoisobutyrate with sodium nitrite in dimethylformamide at room temperature.

$$
\begin{array}{c}
CH_3 \\
\diagdown \\
CCO_2C_2H_5 + NaNO_2 \rightarrow \\
\diagup \quad | \\
CH_3 \quad Br
\end{array}
\qquad
\begin{array}{c}
CH_3 \\
\diagdown \\
CCO_2C_2H_5 + NaBr \\
\diagup \quad | \\
CH_3 \quad NO_2
\end{array}
$$

α-Bromo esters having an α-hydrogen atom react also, but the nitro ester is rapidly converted by the joint action of the sodium nitrite and the alkyl nitrite into the corresponding oximino ester. The addition of phloroglucinol, which acts as a scavenger for nitrite esters, permits the isolation of the nitro ester in satisfactory yields. Ethyl α-nitrobutyrate can be made in this way in 75% yield.[40]

$$
\begin{array}{c}
CH_3CH_2CHCO_2C_2H_5 \\
| \\
Br
\end{array}
\xrightarrow{NaNO_2}
\begin{array}{c}
CH_3CH_2CHCO_2C_2H_5 \\
| \\
NO_2
\end{array}
$$

β-Nitro ketones can be prepared in a similar way. β-Bromoethyl phenyl ketone reacts with sodium nitrite in dimethylformamide at room temperature to give β-nitropropiophenone in 87% yield.[41]

$$C_6H_5COCH_2CH_2Br + NaNO_2 \rightarrow C_6H_5COCH_2CH_2NO_2 + NaBr$$

Carbylamine reaction

Primary amines are transformed into the corresponding isonitriles, or carbylamines, by heating with chloroform in the presence of alkalis.

$$RNH_2 + CHCl_3 + 3KOH \rightarrow RNC + 3KCl + 3H_2O$$

Because of the extraordinarily disagreeable odor of the isonitriles this reaction serves to detect even minute amounts of primary amines.

Isonitriles can be made by dehydration of the formamides of the appropriate primary amines with phosphorus oxychloride in the presence of a base. The preparation of cyclohexyl isonitrile is an example; when pyridine is used as the base, the yield is 85%.[42]

[40] N. Kornblum, R. K. Blackwood, and J. W. Powers, *J. Am. Chem. Soc.*, **79**, 2507 (1957).

[41] R. Fusco and S. Rossi, *Chem. and Ind.*, **51**, 1650 (1957).

[42] I. Ugi and R. Meyr, *Chem. Ber.*, **93**, 239 (1960).

O-Alkylation

Nucleophilic displacement at a saturated carbon atom by a hydroxyl or an alkoxyl ion brings about O-alkylation. Among the examples of this type of reaction are hydrolysis and alcoholysis of alkyl halides and similar alkylating agents.

Hydrolysis

Alkyl Halides. Hydrolysis of alkyl halides may be illustrated by the Sharples process for making amyl alcohols from chloropentanes (p. 605). Hydrolysis furnishes a mixture of alcohols, which is fractionated when the pure alcohols are desired. Among the alcohols so obtained are the following.[43]

2-Pentanol (25.1%)　　　　　　　$CH_3CH_2CH_2CHCH_3$
　　　　　　　　　　　　　　　　　　　　　　　　　$|$
　　　　　　　　　　　　　　　　　　　　　　　　　OH

1-Pentanol (25.5%)　　　　　　　$CH_3CH_2CH_2CH_2CH_2OH$

3-Methyl-1-butanol (11.9%)　　　$CH_3CHCH_2CH_2OH$
　　　　　　　　　　　　　　　　　　　　　　　$|$
　　　　　　　　　　　　　　　　　　　　　　　CH_3

2-Methyl-1-butanol (16.8%)　　　$CH_3CH_2CHCH_2OH$
　　　　　　　　　　　　　　　　　　　　　　　　$|$
　　　　　　　　　　　　　　　　　　　　　　　　CH_3

3-Pentanol (9.4%)　　　　　　　　$CH_3CH_2CHCH_2CH_3$
　　　　　　　　　　　　　　　　　　　　　　　　$|$
　　　　　　　　　　　　　　　　　　　　　　　　OH

　　Benzyl, allyl, and methallyl alcohols are produced on a large scale by hydrolysis of the corresponding chlorides. One method of making ethylene glycol consists in the alkali-catalyzed hydrolysis of ethylene chlorohydrin. The ethylene oxide that is produced undergoes hydrolysis at higher temperatures or in dilute acid. Propylene glycol is made from propylene by a similar series of reactions.

$$CH_3CH{=}CH_2 \rightarrow CH_3\overset{\displaystyle OH}{\underset{|}{C}}HCH_2Cl \rightarrow CH_3\overset{O}{\overbrace{CH{-}\!\!-\!\!CH_2}} \rightarrow CH_3\overset{\displaystyle OH\,OH}{\underset{|\ \ |}{C}}HCH_2$$

[43] R. L. Kenyon, G. C. Inskeep, L. Gillette, and J. F. Price, *Ind. Eng. Chem.*, **42**, 2388 (1950).

A method for synthetic glycerol involves the hydrolysis of glycerol α,γ-dichlorohydrin, obtained by the action of hypochlorous acid on allyl chloride (p. 139). β-Methylglycerol can be produced in a similar way from methallyl chloride.

$$CH_2{=}CCH_2Cl + HOCl \rightarrow \underset{\underset{CH_3}{|}}{CH_2{-}\underset{|}{C}{-}CH_2} \rightarrow \underset{\underset{CH_3}{|}}{CH_2{-}\underset{|}{C}{-}CH_2}$$

α-Halo ethers undergo rapid hydrolysis, of course. An example is the hydrolysis of 2,3-dichlorodioxane to ethylene glycol and glyoxal.

$$\begin{array}{c} \overset{O}{\overset{/ \backslash}{}} \\ \underset{CH_2}{CH_2} \ \ \underset{CHCl}{CHCl} \\ \underset{O}{\backslash /} \end{array} + 2H_2O \rightarrow \begin{array}{c} CH_2OH \\ | \\ CH_2OH \end{array} + \begin{array}{c} CHO \\ | \\ CHO \end{array} + 2HCl$$

2-Bromophthalide, produced by bromination of phthalide, illustrates the behavior of α-halo esters; it readily undergoes hydrolysis to phthal-aldehydic acid (OS III, 737); the over-all yield is 68%.

α-Halo Aldehydes and Ketones. The hydrolysis of α-halo aldehydes proceeds normally under carefully controlled conditions to yield the corresponding α-hydroxy aldehydes. When cyanide ion is present, an abnormal reaction occurs, the products being acids. The preparation of dichloroacetic acid from chloral depends on this behavior; the reaction is effected by heating chloral with sodium cyanide in the presence of calcium carbonate (OS II, 181; 92% yield). If ammonia and sodium cyanide are employed, the product is α,α-dichloroacetamide (OS III, 260, 78% yield).

$$CCl_3CHO + 2NH_3 \rightarrow CHCl_2CONH_2 + NH_4Cl$$

This type of behavior has been observed with other α-halo aldehydes also. A possible mechanism involves the formation of chloral cyanohydrin which then undergoes elimination of chloride ion to give the hydrolytically labile dichloroacetyl cyanide.[44]

$$Cl_3CC=O + CN^- + H_2O \xrightarrow{-OH^-} Cl-CCl_2-C-CN \longrightarrow CHCl_2CCN$$

$$CHCl_2CCN + H_2O \rightarrow CHCl_2COH + HCN$$

Dihalides. Compounds having two halogen atoms on the same carbon atom may be hydrolyzed to carbonyl compounds. The reaction is of little use for aldehydes in the aliphatic series because the dihalo compounds are hard to prepare, and their hydrolysis requires heating with alkali—a treatment that often causes the products to resinify. The method is excellent, however, for the preparation of aromatic aldehydes such as benzaldehyde, which is manufactured by hydrolysis of benzal chloride. *p*-Bromobenzaldehyde has been prepared in a similar way from *p*-bromobenzal bromide (OS II, 89).

$$p\text{-}BrC_6H_4CHBr_2 \rightarrow p\text{-}BrC_6H_4CHO$$

p-Chlorobenzaldehyde is made from *p*-chlorotoluene by way of the corresponding benzal chloride (OS II, 133). In a similar way terephthalaldehyde is obtained from *p*-xylene (OS III, 788), the over-all yield being 46%.

$$CH_3C_6H_4CH_3 \xrightarrow{4Br_2} Br_2CHC_6H_4CHBr_2 \xrightarrow[H_2SO_4]{H_2O} OHCC_6H_4CHO$$

Since aldehydes are sensitive to alkalis, hydrolysis of benzal halides is carried out with acids or with water in the presence of powdered calcium carbonate. A similar hydrolysis of a dichloromethyl group is believed to occur in the Reimer-Tiemann reaction (p. 269).

Benzophenone can be made satisfactorily from benzophenone dichloride (p. 74) (OS I, 95).

$$C_6H_5CCl_2C_6H_5 + H_2O \rightarrow C_6H_5COC_6H_5 + 2HCl$$

It is feasible to convert many suitably constituted ketones and acids into the corresponding α,α-dihalo derivatives, hydrolysis of which yields dicarbonyl compounds. Dichloroacetic acid, for example, gives glyoxylic acid.

$$CHCl_2CO_2H \rightarrow OHCCO_2H$$

[44] See C. Rosenblum, C. Taverna, and N. L. Wendler, *Chem. and Ind.*, 718 (1960).

Diphenyl triketone is produced by heating the dibromide from dibenzoylmethane with sodium acetate in glacial acetic acid. Addition of water precipitates the hydrate of the triketone (OS II, 244). The yield, based on dibenzoylmethane, is 59%.

$$\begin{array}{ccc}
C_6H_5CO & C_6H_5CO & C_6H_5CO \\
\diagdown & \diagdown & \diagdown \\
CH_2 \longrightarrow & CBr_2 \xrightarrow[CH_3CO_2H]{CH_3CO_2Na} & CO \\
\diagup & \diagup & \diagup \\
C_6H_5CO & C_6H_5CO & C_6H_5CO
\end{array}$$

Vinal chlorides yield acids when hydrolyzed. Di-(p-chlorophenyl)acetic acid, for example, is made from DDT, in this way (OS III, 270). The over-all yield of acid, based on DDT, is 73%.

$$(p\text{-ClC}_6H_4)_2\text{CHCCl}_3 \xrightarrow{\text{KOH}} (p\text{-ClC}_6H_4)_2\text{C}{=}\text{CCl}_2 \xrightarrow[(2)\ H^+]{(1)\ \text{KOH}}$$
$$(p\text{-ClC}_6H_4)_2\text{CHCO}_2H$$

The —CF_2— group undergoes hydrolysis in certain cases in which loss of fluoride ion would produce a relatively stable carbonium ion; such hydrolyses occur in strongly acidic media. 2-Chloro-1-ethoxy-1,1,2-trifluoroethane (p. 434), for example, reacts with sulfuric acid to give ethyl chlorofluoroacetate in 83% yield.[45]

$$\begin{array}{cc}
\text{FCHCFOCH}_2\text{CH}_3 + H_2O \xrightarrow{H_2SO_4} & \text{FCHCO}_2\text{CH}_2\text{CH}_3 + 2\text{HF} \\
\ |\ \ | & \ | \\
\text{Cl F} & \text{Cl}
\end{array}$$

Polyhalides. Compounds in which three halogen atoms are held by the same carbon atom can be hydrolyzed to acids. Trichloromethyl carbonyl compounds are, of course, exceptional and undergo chain cleavage. Chloral, for example, reacts with sodium hydroxide to yield chloroform and sodium formate. Trihalomethyl aldehydes and ketones are intermediates in the haloform reaction (p. 356).

Benzotrichloride is hydrolyzed rapidly and independently of the concentration of the hydroxide ion. Evidently, in the carbonium ion there is resonance interaction with the chlorine atoms as well as with the benzene ring.

$$\overset{+}{\text{Cl}}{=}\text{C}{-}\text{Cl} \qquad \text{Cl}{-}\overset{+}{\text{C}}{-}\text{Cl} \qquad \text{Cl}{-}\text{C}{=}\overset{+}{\text{Cl}}$$

[45] J. A. Young and P. Tarrant, *J. Am. Chem. Soc.*, **71**, 2432 (1949).

The trifluoromethyl group, normally refractory even when attached to an aryl radical, is sensitive to hydrolytic attack when situated o- or p- to a hydroxyl or amino substituent. The easy loss of fluorine from o-trifluoromethylphenol, for example, has been ascribed to contribution of resonance structures of the following type.[46]

The hydrolysis of carbon tetrachloride to phosgene is catalyzed by certain metal halides such as ferric chloride.[47]

$$CCl_4 + H_2O \xrightarrow{FeCl_3} COCl_2 + 2HCl$$

Williamson Ether Synthesis

The general method of forming an ether linkage, known as the Williamson synthesis, consists in treatment of an alkyl halide with a metal alkoxide or phenoxide. The syntheses of ethoxyacetic acid (OS II, 260; 74% yield) and l-menthoxyacetic acid (OS III, 544; 84% yield) are examples. 1,1-Dihalogen and 1,1,1-trihalogen compounds give acetals and ortho esters, respectively. Ethyl orthoformate is produced in 45% yield by heating chloroform with sodium ethoxide (OS I, 258).

$$CHCl_3 + 3C_2H_5ONa \rightarrow CH(OC_2H_5)_3 + 3NaCl$$

Ethyl orthocarbonate is not made from carbon tetrachloride but from chloropicrin (OS 32, 68; yield 49%).

$$Cl_3CNO_2 + 4CH_3CH_2ONa \rightarrow C(OCH_2CH_3)_4 + 3NaCl + NaNO_2$$

The transformation of chlorohydrins into the corresponding epoxides may be regarded as a special case of this type of reaction. Examples are the synthesis of cyclohexene oxide (OS I, 185; 73% yield) and of epihalohydrins (OS I, 233; II, 256). Dehydrochlorination of chlorohydrins may take place between two molecules, producing a cyclic diether. Ethylene chlorohydrin, for example, yields dioxane as a by-product when treated with alkali.

[46] J. D. Roberts, R. L. Webb, and E. A. McElhill, *J. Am. Chem. Soc.*, **72**, 408 (1950).
[47] M. E. Hill, *J. Org. Chem.*, **25**, 1115 (1960).

Alcoholysis of sulfates yields ethers rather than esters as is usual (p. 327) in the carboxylic acid series. When dimethyl sulfate and methanol are allowed to react in the presence of sodium hydroxide, methyl ether is obtained in nearly theoretical yield.

Enolates. Although enolates usually undergo C-alkylation, O-alkylation has been observed in several instances. Chloromethyl methyl ether, for example, is capable of producing enol ethers under ordinary conditions. Likewise many aliphatic nitro compounds undergo O-alkylation, regardless of the nature of the alkylating agent. O-Alkylation of hydroxymethylene compounds is effected by the method of Claisen, which consists of heating with an alkyl halide in the presence of potassium carbonate in acetone.[48] This method is not successful with β-keto esters or 1,3-diketones, the usual C-alkylation being observed.

O-Alkylation occurs with the enolates of certain β-bromoethyl esters, which yield ethylene acetals of the corresponding ketenes; the behavior of the enolate of β-bromoethyl cyanoacetate is illustrative.[49]

$$
\begin{array}{c}
\text{BrCH}_2 \quad \text{O}^- \\
\mid \qquad \mid \\
\text{CH}_2\text{OC}=\text{CHCN}
\end{array}
\rightarrow
\begin{array}{c}
\text{CH}_2\text{—O} \\
\mid \qquad\qquad \diagdown \\
\qquad\qquad\qquad \text{C}=\text{CHCN} + \text{Br}^- \\
\mid \qquad\qquad \diagup \\
\text{CH}_2\text{—O}
\end{array}
$$

Phenolates. C-Alkylation of phenolates occurs when they are treated with alkylating agents, but O-alkylation usually is the chief reaction. The synthesis of anisole is illustrative (OS I, 58; 75% yield). Another example is the conversion of *o*-nitrophenol into *o*-nitroanisole by the action of dimethyl sulfate.

$$o\text{-NO}_2\text{C}_6\text{H}_4\text{OH} + (\text{CH}_3)_2\text{SO}_4 \xrightarrow{\text{Na}_2\text{CO}_3} o\text{-NO}_2\text{C}_6\text{H}_4\text{OCH}_3 + \text{CH}_3\text{OSO}_3\text{H}$$

o-Nitrophenol and *n*-butyl bromide, when heated in the presence of potassium carbonate, afford *n*-butyl *o*-nitrophenyl ether in 80% yield (OS III, 140).

By condensation of sodium phenoxide with ethylene bromide in suitable proportions β-bromoethyl phenyl ether can be prepared (OS I, 436; 56% yield). γ-Bromopropyl phenyl ether is made in a similar way from trimethylene bromide (OS I, 435; 85% yield).

[48] K. von Auwers, *Ber.*, **71B**, 2082 (1938).
[49] C. O. Parker, *J. Am. Chem. Soc.*, **78**, 4944 (1956).

Aryloxyacetic acids, prepared from phenols and chloroacetic acid, are useful derivatives for purposes of identification. Of unusual interest is the formation of α-glyceryl phenyl ether by the interaction of sodium phenoxide and glycerol α-monochlorohydrin (OS I, 296; 64% yield).

Carbonates of 2,2-dialkyl-1,3-diols, when heated in the presence of a base, yield 3,3-dialkyloxetanes and carbon dioxide. An example is the formation of 3,3-diethyloxetane by heating the carbonate of 2,2-diethyl-1,3-propanediol with potassium cyanide; the yield is 65%. The mechanism suggested involves nucleophilic attack by the cyanide ion producing an ester-alkoxide ion, which then undergoes an internal Williamson reaction.[50]

Alkylation with esters of carboxylic acids

It will have been noticed that esters of sulfuric and sulfonic acids resemble alkyl halides in alkylation reactions. Esters of carboxylic acids normally behave in a different way; however, exceptions have been reported (QR **9**, 203). At 100° methyl benzoate reacts with sodium methoxide, for example, to give methyl ether in 74% yield.[51]

$$C_6H_5CO_2CH_3 + CH_3ONa \rightarrow C_6H_5CO_2Na + CH_3OCH_3$$

In a similar way dialkyl phthalates react with sodium phenoxides to produce alkyl ethers of the phenols. Guaiacol, for example, is converted into veratrole when its potassium salt is heated with dimethyl phthalate at 190 to 200° for 3 hours; the yield is 78%.[52]

In acidolysis of esters, one acid displaces another (p. 348); a change occurs with vinyl esters that is formally similar but can hardly involve the

[50] S. Searles, D. G. Hummel, S. Nukina, and P. E. Throckmorton, *J. Am. Chem. Soc.*, **82**, 2928 (1960).

[51] J. F. Bunnett, M. M. Robison, and F. C. Pennington, *J. Am. Chem. Soc.*, **72**, 2378 (1950).

[52] H. King and E. V. Wright, *J. Chem. Soc.*, **155**, 1168 (1939).

same type of mechanism. Vinyl oleate is produced in 60% yield by the interaction of oleic acid and vinyl acetate.

$$CH_3(CH_2)_7CH{=}CH(CH_2)_7CO_2H + CH_3CO_2CH{=}CH_2 \rightarrow$$
$$CH_3(CH_2)_7CH{=}CH(CH_2)_7CO_2CH{=}CH_2 + CH_3CO_2H$$

Vinyl laurate has been made in similar yields from vinyl acetate and lauric acid. It has been suggested that the vinyl ester dissociates in the presence of the catalyst (a mercuric compound) into the carboxylic acid and an acetylene-catalyst complex. The complex then reacts with the new acid, converting it into the vinyl ester.

A somewhat similar reaction occurs when vinyl acetate is treated with alcohols in the presence of mercury salts of strong acids at low temperatures. When pentamethylene glycol is used, for example, the yield of the divinyl ether is above 85%.[53]

$$HO(CH_2)_5OH + 2CH_2{=}CHOCOCH_3 \rightarrow$$
$$CH_2{=}CHO(CH_2)_5OCH{=}CH_2 + 2CH_3CO_2H$$

Esters from salts

Many esters are difficult to make by direct esterification, and other methods must be sought. Sometimes it is advisable to use a salt of the acid and an alkylating agent such as an alkyl halide or sulfate. p-Nitrobenzyl acetate can be prepared by the interaction of p-nitrobenzyl chloride and sodium acetate (OS III, 650; yield 82%).

$$p\text{-}O_2NC_6H_4CH_2Cl + CH_3CO_2Na \rightarrow p\text{-}O_2NC_6H_4CH_2OCOCH_3 + NaCl$$

Acetonyl formate is produced by the interaction of bromoacetone and potassium formate (OS II, 5).

$$CH_3COCH_2Br + HCO_2K \rightarrow CH_3COCH_2OCHO + KBr$$

Another procedure for the preparation of esters involves the pyrolysis of the tetramethylammonium salt; methyl mesitoate, for example, can be made in this way from tetramethylammonium mesitoate.

$$C_9H_{11}CO_2^-[N(CH_3)_4]^+ \rightarrow C_9H_{11}CO_2CH_3 \rightarrow (CH_3)_3N$$

Formation of peroxides

Displacement of the methanesulfonate group of alkyl methanesulfonates by the hydroperoxide group can be accomplished with 30% hydrogen peroxide. A remarkable example is the formation of allyl hydroperoxide.[54]

$$CH_3SO_3CH_2CH{=}CH_2 + H_2O_2 \xrightarrow[CH_3OH]{KOH} CH_3SO_3H + CH_2{=}CHCH_2OOH$$

[53] R. L. Adelman, *J. Am. Chem. Soc.*, **75**, 2678 (1953).
[54] S. Dykstra and H. S. Mosher, *J. Am. Chem. Soc.*, **79**, 3474 (1957).

Salts of hydrogen peroxide behave much like alkali disulfides toward alkyl and acyl halides, yielding alkyl and acyl peroxides, respectively. *p*-Nitrobenzoyl chloride, for example, reacts with sodium peroxide to yield di-*p*-nitrobenzoyl peroxide (OS III, 649; 89% yield).

$$2O_2N\langle\bigcirc\rangle COCl + Na_2O_2 \rightarrow \left[O_2N\langle\bigcirc\rangle CO_2 \right]_2 + 2NaCl$$

Alkylation of oximes

Oximes undergo alkylation to yield O-alkyl derivatives, or oxime ethers. The methyl ethers may be made by use of dimethyl sulfate.

$$\underset{\underset{NOH}{\|}}{R-C-R} \xrightarrow{(CH_3)_2SO_4} \underset{\underset{NOCH_3}{\|}}{R-C-R}$$

Generally an isomeric N-alkyl derivative is obtained also in which oxygen is joined to nitrogen by a coordinate covalent link. Compounds having this type of structure are called *nitrones*.

$$\underset{\underset{NOH}{\|}}{R-C-R} \xrightarrow{(CH_3)_2SO_4} \underset{\underset{CH_3N\rightarrow O}{\|}}{R-C-R}$$

Acetoxime is alkylated with bromoacetic acid to give acetone carboxymethoxime as the first step in the synthesis of carboxymethoxylamine (OS III, 172).

$$\underset{CH_3}{\overset{CH_3}{>}}C=NOH + BrCH_2CO_2H \xrightarrow{NaOH} \underset{CH_3}{\overset{CH_3}{>}}C=NOCH_2CO_2H + HBr$$

$$\underset{CH_3}{\overset{CH_3}{>}}C=NOCH_2CO_2H + H_2O \rightarrow \underset{CH_3}{\overset{CH_3}{>}}C=O + H_2NOCH_2CO_2H$$

S-Alkylation

Attachment of alkyl groups to sulfur in the preparation of mercaptans and thio ethers may be effected by methods that are analogous to those used to transform alkyl halides or sulfates into alcohols and ethers. S-Alkylation occurs also when alkali sulfites are treated with alkyl halides; the reaction of sodium sulfite with *bis*-4-chlorobutyl ether is illustrative (OS **37**, 55).

$$O\begin{matrix}(CH_2)_4Cl \\ \\ (CH_2)_4Cl\end{matrix} + 2Na_2SO_3 \rightarrow O\begin{matrix}(CH_2)_4SO_3Na \\ \\ (CH_2)_4SO_3Na\end{matrix} + 2NaCl$$

Mercaptan formation

Replacement of halogen by the sulfhydryl group to produce mercaptans can be accomplished by treating an alkyl halide with a hydrosulfide. Sodium hydrosulfide, made conveniently by saturating a solution of sodium ethoxide with hydrogen sulfide (OS II, 547), may be used.

$$C_2H_5ONa + H_2S \rightarrow C_2H_5OH + NaSH$$

$$RX + NaSH \rightarrow RSH + NaX$$

It is more usual, however, to effect this change indirectly. Thiourea and potassium ethyl xanthate can be alkylated to produce, respectively, S-alkylisothiouronium salts (OS II, 411) and S-alkyl ethyl xanthates. An example of the thiourea method is the preparation of benzyl mercaptan from benzyl chloride.

$$C_6H_5CH_2Cl + S=C\begin{matrix}NH_2 \\ \\ NH_2\end{matrix} \rightarrow \left[C_6H_5CH_2SC\begin{matrix}NH_2 \\ \\ NH_2\end{matrix}\right]^+ Cl^-$$

$$\left[C_6H_5CH_2SC\begin{matrix}NH_2 \\ \\ NH_2\end{matrix}\right]^+ Cl^- + NaOH \rightarrow$$

$$C_6H_5CH_2SH + NaCl + NH_2CN + H_2O$$

Dimethyl sulfate reacts with thiourea to yield S-methylisothiourea sulfate (OS II, 411), which gives methyl mercaptan when treated with sodium hydroxide (OS II, 345).

$$\underset{\substack{\| \\ S}}{H_2NCNH_2} + (CH_3)_2SO_4 \rightarrow (HN\!\!=\!\!\underset{\substack{| \\ SCH_3}}{C}NH_2)_2\cdot H_2SO_4 + 2NaOH \rightarrow$$

$$\underset{\substack{\| \\ NH}}{H_2NCNHCN} + 2CH_3SH + Na_2SO_4 + 2H_2O$$

S-Ethylthiourea hydrobromide, obtained from ethyl bromide and thiourea, yields ethyl mercaptan when hydrolyzed (OS III, 440). n-Dodecyl mercaptan is produced in a similar way (OS III, 363; 83% yield). The conversion of dihalides to dithiols can be effected also by way of the S-alkylisothiouronium salts.

Thiourea may be described as a resonance hybrid of the following structures.

$$S=C\begin{array}{c} NH_2 \\ \diagup \\ \diagdown \\ NH_2 \end{array} \quad \longleftrightarrow \quad {}^-S-C\begin{array}{c} NH_2{}^+ \\ \diagup\!\!\!/ \\ \diagdown \\ NH_2 \end{array}$$

Its reactions with alkylating agents correspond to the second (zwitterion) structure.

Preparation of thio ethers

Thio ethers may be produced by condensing alkyl halides with mercaptides. Obviously this synthesis may serve to give symmetrical or unsymmetrical thio ethers; it is analogous to the Williamson ether synthesis (p. 284) but occurs more rapidly. Polyhalogen compounds such as methylene chloride, chloroform, and ethylene bromide react normally, undergoing replacement of all the halogen atoms.

If the desired sulfide is symmetrical, the synthesis can be effected by treating the halide with sodium or potassium sulfide; an example is encountered in the synthesis of thiodiglycolic acid from chloroacetic acid, the reaction involving the sodium salts.

$$2ClCH_2CO_2Na + Na_2S \rightarrow S\begin{array}{c} CH_2CO_2Na \\ \diagup \\ \diagdown \\ CH_2CO_2Na \end{array} + 2NaCl$$

The preparation of n-propyl sulfide from n-propyl bromide is similar (OS II, 547; 85% yield). Suitably constituted dihalides provide a route to cyclic sulfides. Tetrahydrothiophene, for example, is prepared by the interaction of tetramethylene chloride and sodium sulfide (OS **36**, 89; 78% yield).

$$ClCH_2CH_2CH_2CH_2Cl + Na_2S \rightarrow \boxed{}_{S} + 2NaCl$$

Thiodiglycol is produced in 86% yield in this way from ethylene chlorohydrin (OS II, 576).

$$2HOCH_2CH_2Cl + Na_2S \rightarrow HOCH_2CH_2SCH_2CH_2OH + 2NaCl$$

14

Elimination reactions

The chief reason that nucleophilic substitution at the saturated carbon atom is less successful with secondary and tertiary alkylating agents than with primary is that elimination reactions intervene and unsaturated compounds are produced. Thus *t*-butyl chloride generally reacts with bases to give isobutylene as the principal product.

An elimination reaction may be defined as one in which two atoms or groups are removed from a molecule without being replaced by other atoms or groups. If the two groups are taken from the same atom, as in the formation of dichlorocarbene from chloroform (p. 268), the reaction is α-elimination; if from adjacent atoms, β-elimination. Most of the elimination reactions are of the β-type; two mechanisms have been suggested for them. One of these resembles the S_N1 type and is known as the E_1 mechanism (elimination, unimolecular). It involves as the initial step formation of a carbonium ion, which then releases a proton to a base and becomes an olefin or other molecule containing a multiple link.

The second mechanism, designated as E_2 (elimination, bimolecular), resembles the S_N2 mechanism for displacement reactions. In this type a β-hydrogen or other atom is removed by a base and simultaneously a base (B') is lost from the α-carbon atom. This mechanism is kinetically first order in RB and also in the base employed as reactant.

$$\text{B':}\ \text{H--C--C--B} \rightarrow \text{B'H} + \text{C=C} + \text{B:}$$

In general the E_1 and E_2 types of mechanism, like the S_N1 and S_N2 types, are not separated sharply but blend gradually into each other.

The atom that is lost as a positive entity must be loosely held if elimination is to occur readily. Many compounds having a hydrogen atom in the position *alpha* to a cyano, carbonyl, or similar function fall in this category; elimination reactions involving such α-hydrogen atoms are sometimes called α-hydrogen elimination reactions. An example is the formation of acrylonitrile by the action of lithium aluminum hydride on β-phenoxypropionitrile, which has been represented as follows.[1]

$$C_6H_5-O-CH_2CH_2CN \rightarrow C_6H_5O-CH_2CH-CN \rightarrow$$
$$C_6H_5O^- + CH_2=CHCN$$

A variant of the ether cleavage is the opening of certain epoxide rings. An example is the behavior of the chlorohydrin of allyl cyanide toward alkali.[2]

$$ClCH_2CHCH_2CN \xrightarrow{NaOH} CH_2-CHCH_2CN$$
$$\underset{OH}{} \qquad\qquad \underset{O}{}$$

$$CH_2-CH-\underset{CN}{C}-H \quad ^-OH \rightarrow {}^-OCH_2CH=CHCN$$

A similar example is the rearrangement of 1,2-epoxy-3-phenylpropane to cinnamyl alcohol under the influence of sodium amide in liquid ammonia; the yield is 80%.[3]

$$C_6H_5CH_2CH-CH_2 \rightarrow C_6H_5CH=CHCH_2OH$$
$$\underset{O}{}$$

The elimination of the elements of ethanol by slow distillation of diethyl ethoxymethylmalonate, formally similar, furnishes diethyl methylenemalonate (OS **38**, 22).

$$CH_3CH_2OCH_2CH(CO_2C_2H_5)_2 \rightarrow CH_2=C(CO_2C_2H_5)_2 + C_2H_5OH$$

When nitrosomethylurethan is treated with concentrated aqueous potassium hydroxide at 0°, a salt is formed having a composition corresponding to the formula $CH_3N=NOK \cdot H_2O$.

$$\underset{CH_3N-N=O}{\overset{CO_2C_2H_5}{|}} \xrightarrow{KOH} CH_3N=NOK \cdot H_2O$$

[1] L. M. Soffer and E. W. Parrotta, *J. Am. Chem. Soc.*, **76**, 3580 (1954).
[2] C. C. J. Culvenor, W. Davies, and F. G. Haley, *J. Chem. Soc.*, 3123 (1950).
[3] L. J. Haynes, I. Heilbron, E. R. H. Jones, and F. Sondheimer, *J. Chem. Soc.*, 1583 (1947).

The salt decomposes to give diazomethane.

$$\text{HO} \quad \text{H-CH}_2\text{-N=N-OH} \rightarrow \text{HOH} + \text{CH}_2\text{=}\overset{+}{\text{N}}\text{=N}:^- + \text{OH}^-$$

A number of other procedures for preparing diazomethane appear to involve this type of elimination reaction. One of the methods consists in the decomposition of nitrosomethylurea. Methylurea is prepared from methylamine hydrochloride and urea or from methylamine and potassium cyanate.

$$\text{H}_2\text{NCONH}_2 + \text{CH}_3\text{NH}_2\cdot\text{HCl} \rightarrow \text{CH}_3\text{NHCONH}_2 + \text{NH}_4\text{Cl}$$

$$\text{CH}_3\text{NH}_2\cdot\text{HCl} + \text{KCNO} \rightarrow \text{CH}_3\text{NHCONH}_2 + \text{KCl}$$

It is converted into the nitroso compound by the action of nitrous acid. Hydrolysis of the nitroso derivative with potassium hydroxide gives diazomethane (OS II, 165).

$$\text{CH}_3\text{NHCONH}_2 + \text{HONO} \rightarrow \text{CH}_3\text{N(NO)CONH}_2 + \text{H}_2\text{O}$$

$$\text{CH}_3\text{N(NO)CONH}_2 + \text{KOH} \rightarrow \text{CH}_2\text{N}_2 + \text{KCNO} + 2\text{H}_2\text{O}$$

Another method is to treat methyl N-nitroso-β-methylaminoisobutyl ketone with sodium isopropoxide (OS III, 244).

This scheme can be used to transform nearly any primary aliphatic amine into the corresponding diazo compound.

p-Toluenesulfonylmethylnitrosamide has the advantage of being easily prepared, non-toxic, and non-explosive (OS **36**, 16; 69% yield).

An example of β-elimination in which the proton is removed from oxygen is the alkali-catalyzed decomposition of acetone cyanohydrin.

$$\text{-OH} \quad \text{H-O-}\underset{\underset{\text{CH}_3}{|}}{\overset{\overset{\text{CH}_3}{|}}{\text{C}}}\text{-CN} \rightarrow \text{H}_2\text{O} + \text{O=}\underset{\underset{\text{CH}_3}{|}}{\overset{\overset{\text{CH}_3}{|}}{\text{C}}} + \text{CN}^-$$

Retrograde Aldol Condensation

An example of the retrograde aldol condensation is the formation of acetone from diacetone alcohol.

$$\text{OH}^- \quad \text{H-O-}\underset{\underset{\text{CH}_3}{|}}{\overset{\overset{\text{CH}_3}{|}}{\text{C}}}\text{-CH}_2\text{COCH}_3 \rightarrow \text{H}_2\text{O} + \text{O=}\underset{\underset{\text{CH}_3}{|}}{\overset{\overset{\text{CH}_3}{|}}{\text{C}}} + {}^-\text{CH}_2\text{COCH}_3$$

α,β-Unsaturated carbonyl compounds in general tend to undergo chain cleavage, particularly under the influence of alkalis. The alkoxide of the corresponding β-hydroxy compound is presumed to be an intermediate.

A synthesis of pimelic acid depends on the cleavage of cyclohexene-4-carboxylic acid (p. 684). The first step appears to be a shift of the double bond to the α,β-position.[4]

Dehydrohalogenation

Perhaps the most important type of β-elimination, as far as synthetic value is concerned, is the removal of the elements of a halogen acid, i.e., dehydro-halogenation. As an example may be taken the preparation of neurine (vinyltrimethylammonium hydroxide) from the corresponding β-bromo-ethyl compound. The ease with which this type of reaction occurs and the experimental conditions required vary widely with the structure of the halogen compound.[5]

$$\text{OH}^- \quad \text{H-}\underset{\underset{(\text{CH}_3)_3\overset{+}{\text{N}}}{|}}{\text{C}}\text{HCH}_2\text{-Br} \rightarrow \text{H}_2\text{O} + \underset{\underset{(\text{CH}_3)_3\overset{+}{\text{N}}}{|}}{\text{C}}\text{H=CH}_2 + \text{Br}^-$$

[4] F. X. Werber, J. E. Jansen, and T. L. Gresham, *J. Am. Chem. Soc.*, **74**, 532 (1952).
[5] See R. R. Renshaw and J. C. Ware, *J. Am. Chem. Soc.*, **47**, 2989 (1925).

Alkyl halides

The most common procedure for effecting such changes is to heat the alkyl halide with potassium hydroxide in ethanol. Under these conditions the elimination usually proceeds according to the Saytzeff rule, i.e., the hydrogen atom is removed from the β-carbon atom that has the fewest hydrogen atoms. The ethylene formed, therefore, is generally that which is most highly alkylated; an alkyl halide of the type $RCH_2C(CH_3)_2$ $\overset{|}{Cl}$ yields preferentially the olefin $RCH=C(CH_3)_2$ rather than the isomer $RCH_2C=CH_2$. It has been suggested that the stability of the olefin is the $\overset{|}{CH_3}$ determining factor in this type of elimination. From a practical point of view dehydrohalogenation is limited largely to halogen compounds that give rise to only one unsaturated product. An important example is the conversion of 1,1,2-trichloroethane into vinylidene chloride.

$$\begin{matrix} CHCl_2 \\ | \\ CH_2Cl \end{matrix} \rightarrow \begin{matrix} CCl_2 \\ \| \\ CH_2 \end{matrix} + HCl$$

2,3-Dibromopropene is made by heating 1,2,3-tribromopropane with a concentrated sodium hydroxide solution (OS I, 209; 84% yield).

$$\begin{matrix} CH_2Br \\ | \\ CHBr \\ | \\ CH_2Br \end{matrix} \xrightarrow{NaOH} CH_2=CBrCH_2Br$$

The product is distilled as fast as it is formed and is thus prevented from reacting further with the alkali. This example illustrates the rule that a vinyl bromide is relatively unreactive. The difference in reactivity of the two bromine atoms in the propene is predictable as an extension of Schmidt's rule (p. 581).

DDT readily loses one molecule of hydrogen chloride (OS III, 270).

$$(ClC_6H_4)_2CHCCl_3 \xrightarrow{-HCl} (ClC_6H_4)_2C=CCl_2$$

An extraordinary debromination occurs when hexa(α-bromoethyl)-benzene is treated with magnesium and methanol; then a hydrocarbon is formed that has been identified as hexaethylidenecyclohexane.[6]

$$
\begin{array}{ll}
\text{CH}_3\text{CHBr} & \overset{\text{CHBrCH}_3}{\underset{|}{\bigcirc}} \overset{\text{CHBrCH}_3}{} \\
\text{CH}_3\text{CHBr} & \overset{}{\underset{\text{CHBrCH}_3}{}} \overset{\text{CHBrCH}_3}{}
\end{array}
\quad\rightarrow\quad
\begin{array}{ll}
\text{CH}_3\text{CH} & \overset{\text{CHCH}_3}{} \overset{\text{CHCH}_3}{} \\
\text{CH}_3\text{CH} & \overset{}{} \overset{\text{CHCH}_3}{\underset{\text{CHCH}_3}{}}
\end{array}
$$

Halo ethers

Dehydrohalogenation of β-halo ethers furnishes vinyl ethers; allyl vinyl ether is produced when allyl β-bromoethyl ether is heated with potassium hydroxide.

$$\text{BrCH}_2\text{CH}_2\text{OCH}_2\text{CH=CH}_2 \rightarrow \text{CH}_2\text{=CHOCH}_2\text{CH=CH}_2$$

Dehydrochlorination of chloroethylene carbonate is similar; it is effected with triethylamine or, more simply, merely by heating.[7]

$$
\begin{array}{c}
\text{ClCH—O} \\
| \qquad \diagdown \\
| \qquad\; \text{CO} \\
| \qquad \diagup \\
\text{CH}_2\text{O}
\end{array}
\rightarrow
\begin{array}{c}
\text{CHO} \\
|| \qquad \diagdown \\
|| \qquad\; \text{CO} + \text{HCl} \\
|| \qquad \diagup \\
\text{CHO}
\end{array}
$$

Ketene diethylacetal is made in 75 % yield by treatment of the acetal of bromoacetaldehyde with potassium t-butoxide in t-butyl alcohol solution (OS III, 506).

$$
\text{BrCH}_2\text{CH}\overset{\displaystyle \diagup \text{OC}_2\text{H}_5}{\underset{\displaystyle \diagdown \text{OC}_2\text{H}_5}{}}
\rightarrow
\text{CH}_2\text{=C}\overset{\displaystyle \diagup \text{OC}_2\text{H}_5}{\underset{\displaystyle \diagdown \text{OC}_2\text{H}_5}{}}
+ \text{HBr}
$$

This method takes on greater significance in view of the development of a satisfactory route to the bromoacetal (p. 402).

An interesting elimination reaction occurs when the acetal of chloro-acetaldehyde is treated with sodium amide in liquid ammonia; the product is ethoxyacetylene (OS **34**, 46; yield 61 %). Presumably the ketene acetal formed initially loses the elements of ethanol.

$$\text{ClCH}_2\text{CH(OC}_2\text{H}_5)_2 + 3\text{NaNH}_2 \rightarrow$$

$$\text{NaCl} + \text{NaC} \equiv \text{COC}_2\text{H}_5 + \text{NaOC}_2\text{H}_5 + 3\text{NH}_3$$

$$\text{NaC} \equiv \text{COC}_2\text{H}_5 + \text{H}_2\text{O} \rightarrow \text{HC} \equiv \text{COC}_2\text{H}_5 + \text{NaOH}$$

[6] H. Hopff and A. K. Wick, *Helv. Chem. Acta,* **44**, 380 (1961).
[7] W. K. Johnson and T. L. Patton, *J. Org. Chem.,* **25**, 1042 (1960).

Carbonyl compounds

Dehydrohalogenation is favored in reactions that involve the development of olefinic and acetylenic compounds in which the newly created multiple linkage is part of a conjugated system. α-Halo carbonyl compounds readily yield the corresponding α,β-unsaturated compounds. An example is the preparation of 2-methyl-2-cyclohexenone by heating 2-chloro-2-methylcyclohexanone with collidine (OS **37**, 8; yield 96%).

When suitably constituted acid chlorides are allowed to stand 16 hours with triethylamine, the corresponding ketenes are produced (OR **3**, 108). An example is the dehydrochlorination of stearoyl chloride; as is usual, the ketene is isolated as the dimer.

$$2CH_3(CH_2)_{15}CH_2COCl \rightarrow [CH_3(CH_2)_{15}CH=C=O]_2 + 2HCl$$

The acid chloride of mesitylphenylacetic acid is converted into the corresponding ketene by heating with a mixture of benzene, thionyl chloride, and pyridine.

Nitrogen analogs of ketenes have been made in a similar way from imino chlorides. An example is dimethylketene *p*-tolylimine; the yield is 66%.[8]

Attempts to introduce a double bond at the bridgehead in carbonyl compounds of the camphane and pinane series are unsuccessful. In fact,

[8] C. L. Stevens and J. C. French, *J. Am. Chem. Soc.*, **76**, 4398 (1954).

no compound is known of the following types which has a double bond at A or B.

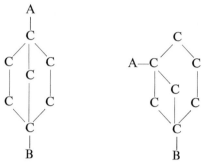

This generalization, known as Bredt's rule, finds support in attempts to dehydrohalogenate certain bicyclic compounds having a halogen atom at or near a bridgehead. In the course of time Bredt's rule has come to be applied more generally and has been stated in the following way (CR **47,** 219): *In polycyclic systems having atomic bridges, the existence of a compound having a carbon-carbon or carbon-nitrogen double bond at a bridgehead position is not possible, except when the ring is large, because of the strain that would be introduced in its formation by the distortion of bond angles and/or distances.*

Dehydrogenation of bromo esters is illustrated by the synthesis of muconic acid from diethyl α,α-dibromoadipate (OS III, 623; 43% yield).

$$
\begin{array}{c}
\overset{\displaystyle Br}{\underset{}{|}} \\
CH_2\overset{|}{C}HCO_2C_2H_5 \\
CH_2\overset{|}{C}HCO_2C_2H_5 \\
\overset{|}{Br}
\end{array}
\quad \xrightarrow[\text{(2) HCl}]{\text{(1) KOH}} \quad
\begin{array}{c}
CH{=}CHCO_2H \\
CH{=}CHCO_2H
\end{array}
$$

Pyridine, quinoline, and similar tertiary amines are good dehydrohalogenating agents for many compounds and are the reagents of choice when hydrolysis is to be avoided. The conversion of diethyl bromosuccinate into diethyl fumarate is an example of the use of pyridine.

$$
\begin{array}{c}
CO_2C_2H_5 \\
\overset{|}{C}HBr \\
\overset{|}{C}H_2 \\
\overset{|}{C}O_2C_2H_5
\end{array}
\;+\; C_5H_5N \;\rightarrow\;
\begin{array}{c}
CO_2C_2H_5 \\
\overset{|}{C}H \\
\overset{\|}{C}H \\
\overset{|}{C}O_2C_2H_5
\end{array}
\;+\; C_5H_5N{\cdot}HBr
$$

Methyl 2-bromo-2-methyldodecanoate, when heated with quinoline, yields *trans*-methyl 2-methyl-2-dodecenoate (OS **38**, 43).

$$CH_3(CH_2)_8CH_2\overset{\overset{\displaystyle CH_3}{|}}{\underset{\underset{\displaystyle Br}{|}}{C}}CO_2CH_3 \;\rightarrow\; CH_3(CH_2)_8CH=\overset{\overset{\displaystyle CH_3}{|}}{C}CO_2CH_3$$

Dehydrohalogenation of α-halo acids may lead to a mixture of the corresponding α,β- and β,γ-unsaturated acids. α-Bromododecanoic acid, for example, reacts with potassium *t*-butoxide to give the unsaturated acids corresponding to the two following structures of the enolate ion (OS **37**, 29).

$$n\text{-}C_8H_{17}\bar{C}HCH=CHCO_2^- \;\leftrightarrow\; n\text{-}C_8H_{17}CH=CH\bar{C}HCO_2^-$$

Dehydrohalogenation of coumarin dibromide is accompanied by diminution in the size of the heterocycle and the development of a carboxyl group, the final product being coumarilic acid (OS III, 209). It would appear that ring opening is followed by a ring closure that is an intramolecular alkylation. Dehydrobromination then takes place; the yield of coumarilic acid is 88%.

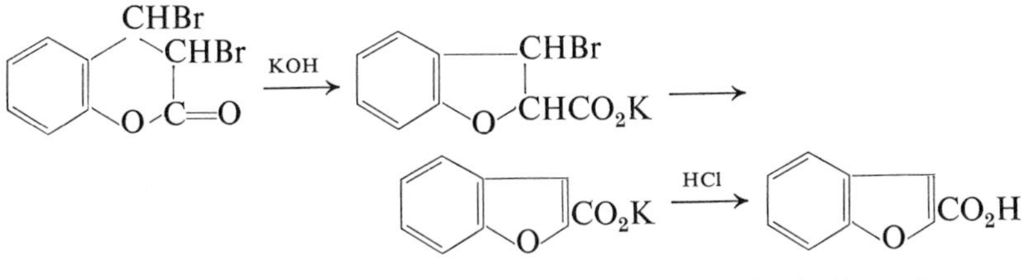

In α,β-dihalogen derivatives of carbonyl compounds, halogen is more readily removed from the β- than from the α-position. This difference is ascribed to the fact that the mobility of the α-hydrogen atom is greater than that of the β-hydrogen atom. When benzalacetone dibromide is treated with sodium acetate in ethanol, for example, α-bromobenzalacetone is produced in 73% yield (OS III, 125).

$$C_6H_5CHBrCHBrCOCH_3 + CH_3CO_2Na \rightarrow$$
$$C_6H_5CH=CBrCOCH_3 + CH_3CO_2H + NaBr$$

α-Bromocinnamaldehyde is formed in high yield by the action of potassium carbonate on the dibromide of cinnamaldehyde (OS III, 731).

$$C_6H_5\underset{\underset{\displaystyle Br}{|}}{C}H\underset{\underset{\displaystyle Br}{|}}{C}HCHO \xrightarrow{K_2CO_3} C_6H_5CH=\underset{\underset{\displaystyle Br}{|}}{C}CHO$$

Vinyl halides

Triple bonds are produced when vinyl halides are treated with very strong dehydrohalogenating agents such as sodium amide and molten alkali (OR **5**, 1). Phenylacetylene is made in 67% yield by dropping β-bromostyrene on molten potassium hydroxide at a temperature of 200 to 230° (OS I, 438). Since phenylacetylene boils at 143°, it distils from the unchanged bromostyrene (b.p. 220°).

$$C_6H_5CH{=}CHBr + KOH \rightarrow C_6H_5C{\equiv}CH + KBr + H_2O$$

Phenylacetylene can be obtained also by dehydrohalogenation of α-chlorostyrene, prepared by the action of phosphorus pentachloride on acetophenone (p. 150).

1-Decyne (OS I, 192; 68% yield) and 3-cyclohexylpropyne (OS I, 191; 66% yield) are made by the Lespieau-Bourguel method (p. 450).

$$CH_3(CH_2)_7CBr{=}CH_2 + NaNH_2 \rightarrow CH_3(CH_2)_7C{\equiv}CH + NaBr + NH_3$$

$$\left\langle \underset{}{\bigcirc} \right\rangle CH_2CBr{=}CH_2 + NaNH_2 \rightarrow \left\langle \underset{}{\bigcirc} \right\rangle CH_2C{\equiv}CH + NaBr + NH_3$$

In these reactions the dehydrohalogenating agent is powdered sodium amide suspended in mineral oil.

Many acetylenic acids can be made in satisfactory yields from dibromo acids by eliminating two molecules of hydrogen bromide. A salt of acetylenedicarboxylic acid is produced from α,β-dibromosuccinic acid by heating with methanolic potassium hydroxide (OS II, 10; 88% yield). Acetylenedicarboxylic acid is obtained by acidification of the reaction mixture.

$$\begin{array}{c} BrCHCO_2H \\ | \\ BrCHCO_2H \end{array} + 4KOH \rightarrow \begin{array}{c} CCO_2K \\ ||| \\ CCO_2K \end{array} + 2KBr + 4H_2O$$

Phenylpropiolic acid may be derived in a similar way from ethyl cinnamate (OS II, 515; yield 81%).

$$C_6H_5CH{=}CHCO_2C_2H_5 \rightarrow \underset{\underset{Br\ Br}{|\ \ |}}{C_6H_5CHCHCO_2C_2H_5} \rightarrow C_6H_5C{\equiv}CCO_2H$$

In a like fashion the dibromide of oleic acid, when allowed to react with sodium amide, furnishes stearolic acid (OS **37**, 77; 61% yield).

$$\underset{\underset{Br\ Br}{|\ \ |}}{CH_3(CH_2)_7CHCH(CH_2)_7CO_2H} \rightarrow CH_3(CH_2)_7C{\equiv}C(CH_2)_7CO_2H$$

1,4-Dichloro-2-butyne undergoes dehydrochlorination under the influence of sodium amide in liquid ammonia to yield diacetylene.[9]

$$ClCH_2C{\equiv}CCH_2Cl \rightarrow HC{\equiv}C{-}C{\equiv}CH$$

Propargyl alcohol is formed in yields as high as 69% by treating 3-chloro-2-propen-1-ol with sodium hydroxide solution.[10]

$$ClCH{=}CHCH_2OH \xrightarrow{-HCl} HC{\equiv}CCH_2OH$$

The chloropropenol is obtained readily by hydrolysis of 1,3-dichloropropene, a by-product in the preparation of allyl chloride from propylene.

$$ClCH{=}CHCH_2Cl \xrightarrow{NaOH} ClCH{=}CHCH_2OH$$

The hydrolysis of 1,3-dichloropropene to 3-chloro-2-propen-1-ol illustrates the great difference in the reactivity of allyl and vinyl chlorides.

2-Butyn-1-ol is made in a similar way from 1,3-dichloro-2-butene (OS 35, 20; 85% yield).

$$CH_3C{=}CHCH_2Cl \xrightarrow[H_2O]{Na_2CO_2} CH_3C{=}CHCH_2OH \xrightarrow[(2)\ NH_4Cl]{(1)\ NaNH_2} CH_3C{\equiv}CCH_2OH$$
$$\phantom{CH_3C{=}}| |$$
$$\phantom{CH_3C{=}}Cl Cl$$

Dehydrochlorination of 1,3-dichloro-2-butene gives vinylacetylene in yields of 60% (OS 38, 70).

Diphenylacetylene may be produced in 85% yield from stilbene bromide by dehydrobromination with ethanolic potassium hydroxide (OS III, 350).

$$C_6H_5CHCHC_6H_5 \xrightarrow{-2HBr} C_6H_5C{\equiv}CC_6H_5$$
$$|\ \ |$$
$$Br\ Br$$

Exhaustive Methylation

β-Elimination is postulated as the final step of the Hofmann *exhaustive methylation* (OR **11**, 317). This process, which serves to degrade an amine to the olefin or olefins corresponding to the alkyl radicals that are attached to the nitrogen atom, is very similar to dehydrohalogenation. By treatment with methyl iodide the amine is "exhaustively" methylated, the final product being a quarternary ammonium iodide. Moist silver oxide converts the salt into the corresponding base, which is then decomposed thermally.

[9] E. R. H. Jones, *Record Chem. Progress*, **14**, 1 (1953).
[10] L. F. Hatch and A. C. Moore, *J. Am. Chem. Soc.*, **66**, 285 (1944).

Tetramethylammonium hydroxide breaks down to give trimethylamine and methyl alcohol.

$$\begin{bmatrix} CH_3 & CH_3 \\ & N & \\ CH_3 & CH_3 \end{bmatrix}^+ OH^- \rightarrow \begin{array}{c} CH_3 \\ CH_3-N \\ CH_3 \end{array} + CH_3OH$$

Larger groups generally are eliminated as the corresponding olefins. It is a rule that, if one of the groups is ethyl, ethylene will be produced to the virtual exclusion of other olefins that are possible. The last step of the sequence, in the case of ethyltrimethylammonium hydroxide, has been formulated in the following way.

$$HO^- \ H-CH_2-CH_2-\overset{+}{N}(CH_3)_3 \rightarrow H_2O + CH_2{=}CH_2 + N(CH_3)_3$$

Exceptions that "prove the rule" are phenethyl compounds in which the hydrogen atom to be removed is attached to a benzyl position.

$$\begin{bmatrix} C_6H_5CH_2CH_2 & CH_3 \\ & N & \\ CH_3CH_2 & CH_3 \end{bmatrix}^+ OH^- \rightarrow$$

$$CH_3CH_2N(CH_3)_2 + H_2O + C_6H_5CH{=}CH_2$$

Decomposition of the p-nitrophenethyl base occurs spontaneously. In a similar way 2,4,6-trinitrostyrene is formed in preference to ethylene.[11]

$$\begin{bmatrix} O_2N\underset{NO_2}{\overset{NO_2}{\bigcirc}}CH_2CH_2\overset{C_2H_5}{\underset{C_2H_5}{N}}CH_3 \end{bmatrix}^+ OH^- \xrightarrow{-H_2O}$$

$$O_2N\underset{NO_2}{\overset{NO_2}{\bigcirc}}CH{=}CH_2 + (C_2H_5)_2NCH_3$$

If no ethyl group is present, larger groups can be eliminated. The rule, in contrast to that for Saytzeff elimination, is that the least alkylated ethylene predominates. Whereas Saytzeff elimination appears to be controlled by the relative stabilities of the olefins that are possible, Hofmann elimination has been interpreted as the result of steric control, the most accessible hydrogen atom being lost.

[11] R. H. Wiley and L. C. Behr, *J. Am. Chem. Soc.*, **72**, 1822 (1950).

When pyrrolidine, which has no ethyl group, is treated with methyl iodide it is converted into the corresponding quaternary ammonium iodide; the free base decomposes thermally to give a dimethylbutenylamine. Repetition of the process produces 1,3-butadiene.

$$\underset{\substack{\text{CH}_2 \\ | \\ \text{CH}_2 \\ \diagdown \\ \text{NH}}}{\text{CH}_2 - \text{CH}_2} \xrightarrow{\text{CH}_3\text{I}} \left[\underset{\substack{\text{CH}_2 \quad \text{CH}_2 \\ \diagdown \quad \diagup \\ \text{N} \\ \diagup \quad \diagdown \\ \text{CH}_3 \quad \text{CH}_3}}{\text{CH}_2 - \text{CH}_2}\right]^{+} \text{I}^{-} \xrightarrow{\text{Ag}_2\text{O}}$$

$$\left[\underset{\substack{\text{CH}_2 \quad \text{CH}_2 \\ \diagdown \quad \diagup \\ \text{N} \\ \diagup \quad \diagdown \\ \text{CH}_3 \quad \text{CH}_3}}{\text{CH}_2 - \text{CH}_2}\right]^{+} \text{OH}^- \xrightarrow[-\text{H}_2\text{O}]{\text{heat}} (\text{CH}_3)_2\text{NCH}_2 \underset{\text{CH}_2}{\overset{\text{CH}_2 - \text{CH}}{}}$$

In a similar way piperidine yields piperylene (p. 469).

$$\underset{\substack{\text{CH}_2 \\ \diagup \diagdown \\ \text{CH}_2 \quad \text{CH}_2 \\ | \qquad | \\ \text{CH}_2 \quad \text{CH}_2 \\ \diagdown \diagup \\ \text{N} \\ | \\ \text{H}}}{} \xrightarrow[\text{CH}_3\text{I}]{\text{excess}} \left[\underset{\substack{\text{CH}_2 \\ \diagup \diagdown \\ \text{CH}_2 \quad \text{CH}_2 \\ | \qquad | \\ \text{CH}_2 \quad \text{CH}_2 \\ \diagdown \diagup \\ \text{N} \\ \diagup \diagdown \\ \text{CH}_3 \quad \text{CH}_3}}{}\right]^{+} \text{I}^- \xrightarrow{\text{Ag}_2\text{O}} \left[\underset{\substack{\text{CH}_2 \\ \diagup \diagdown \\ \text{CH}_2 \quad \text{CH}_2 \\ | \qquad | \\ \text{CH}_2 \quad \text{CH}_2 \\ \diagdown \diagup \\ \text{N} \\ \diagup \diagdown \\ \text{CH}_3 \quad \text{CH}_3}}{}\right]^{+} \text{OH}^- \rightarrow$$

$$\underset{\substack{\text{CH}_2 \\ \diagup \diagdown \\ \text{CH} \quad \text{CH}_2 \\ \| \qquad | \\ \text{CH}_2 \quad \text{CH}_2\text{N(CH}_3)_2}}{} \rightarrow \text{CH}_2=\text{CHCH}_2\text{CH}=\text{CH}_2 \rightarrow \text{CH}_3\text{CH}=\text{CHCH}=\text{CH}_2$$

The final step is rearrangement of 1,4-pentadiene to piperylene, in which the double bonds are conjugated.

α-Coniine, which is optically active, is opened by exhaustive methylation in such a way as to preserve the optical activity.

$$\underset{\substack{\diagup \diagdown \\ | \qquad | \\ \diagdown \diagup \\ \text{N} \diagdown \text{CH}_2\text{CH}_2\text{CH}_3 \\ | \\ \text{H}}}{} \rightarrow \underset{\substack{\text{CH}_2 \\ \diagup \diagdown \\ \text{CH} \quad \text{CH}_2 \\ \| \qquad | \\ \text{CH}_2 \quad \text{CHCH}_2\text{CH}_2\text{CH}_3 \\ \qquad | \\ \qquad \text{N(CH}_3)_2}}{}$$

One of the most interesting olefins to be prepared by this method is cyclopropene. Trimethylcyclopropylammonium iodide is made from cyclopropylamine in 83% yield by treatment with methyl iodide. The free base is decomposed by heating at 320 to 330° on platinized asbestos. Cyclopropene is obtained in 45% yield along with dimethylcyclopropylamine in 30% yield.

$$
\begin{array}{c}
CH_2 \\
| \quad \diagdown \\
\quad \quad CHNH_2 \\
| \quad \diagup \\
CH_2
\end{array}
\xrightarrow{CH_3I}
\left[
\begin{array}{c}
CH_2 \\
| \quad \diagdown \\
\quad \quad CHN(CH_3)_3 \\
| \quad \diagup \\
CH_2
\end{array}
\right]^+
I^- \longrightarrow
$$

$$
\left[
\begin{array}{c}
CH_2 \\
| \quad \diagdown \\
\quad \quad CHN(CH_3)_3 \\
| \quad \diagup \\
CH_2
\end{array}
\right]^+
OH^- \longrightarrow
\begin{array}{c}
CH_2 \\
| \quad \diagdown \\
\quad \quad CH \\
\| \quad \diagup \\
CH
\end{array}
\quad and \quad
\begin{array}{c}
CH_2 \\
| \quad \diagdown \\
\quad \quad CHN(CH_3)_2 \\
| \quad \diagup \\
CH_2
\end{array}
$$

1,3,5-Hexatriene has been synthesized by this method from a 3-bromo-1,5-hexadiene.[12]

$$
CH_2{=}CHCH_2CHCH{=}CH_2 \rightarrow CH_2{=}CHCH{=}CHCH{=}CH_2
$$
$$
\overset{|}{Br}
$$

Examples are known in which the elimination yields, not an olefin but a cyclopropane derivative. 3-Phenylpropyltrimethylammonium iodide, for example, gives phenylcyclopropane in 80% yield when heated with sodium amide. It has been suggested that a benzyl type of anion forms and then displaces trimethylamine intramolecularly.[13]

$$
C_6H_5\overset{\frown}{\overset{|}{CH}} \quad CH_2{-}\overset{+}{N}(CH_3)_3 \rightarrow C_6H_5CH{-\!\!-\!\!-}CH_2 + (CH_3)_3N
$$
$$
\quad \diagdown CH_2 \quad \quad \quad \quad \quad \quad \quad \diagdown CH_2 \diagup
$$

It is interesting in this connection that hydrolysis of γ-halopropylboranes, made by adding diborane to the appropriate allyl halides, also leads to the formation of cyclopropanes. Thus 1-chloro-2-hexene gives n-propyl-cyclopropane in 61% yield.[14]

$$
C_3H_7CH{=}CHCH_2Cl \xrightarrow{B_2F_6} B\left(\begin{array}{c} CHCH_2CH_2Cl \\ | \\ C_3H_7 \end{array}\right)_3 \xrightarrow{OH^-} C_3H_7CH{-\!\!-\!\!-}CH_2
$$
$$
\quad \quad \quad \quad \quad \quad \quad \quad \quad \quad \quad \quad \quad \quad \quad \quad \quad \diagdown CH_2 \diagup
$$

[12] J. C. H. Hwa, P. L. de Benneville, and H. J. Sims, *J. Am. Chem. Soc.*, **82**, 2537 (1960).

[13] C. L. Bumgardner, *J. Am. Chem. Soc.*, **83**, 4420 (1961).

[14] M. F. Hawthorne, *J. Am. Chem. Soc.*, **82**, 1886 (1960).

In certain cases an α',β-elimination seems to occur; when dimethyl-iodomethylisopropylammonium iodide is treated with phenyllithium, the N-ylid is first formed. A hydride ion shift from a β- to an α'-position then occurs.[15]

$$(CH_3)_2\overset{+}{N}CH_2I \quad \rightarrow (CH_3)_2\overset{+}{N}-\overset{-}{C}H_2 \rightarrow (CH_3)_2NCH_3 + CH_3CH{=}CH_2$$

$$\underset{CH_3\overset{|}{C}H-CH_3}{} \qquad \underset{CH_3CH-CH_2}{\overset{H}{}}$$

Decomposition of Sulfonium Hydroxides

Changes analogous to exhaustive methylation lead to the production of olefins from thio ethers, which react with alkyl halides to give sulfonium halides. The sulfonium halides can be converted by treatment with moist silver oxide into sulfonium hydroxides, which when heated decompose to yield olefins and sulfides. Triethylsulfonium hydroxide, for example, is broken down to ethylene and diethyl sulfide.

$$[(C_2H_5)_3S]^+OH^- \rightarrow (C_2H_5)_2S + CH_2{=}CH_2 + H_2O$$

Triethylsulfonium bromide reacts readily with triphenylmethylsodium to give ethylene, diethyl sulfide, and triphenylmethane; α,β-elimination has been postulated here also.[16]

$$\underset{\underset{H}{\overset{|}{CH_3\overset{|}{C}H}}}{CH_3CH_2\overset{+}{S}}\!\!\!-\!\!\!\underset{\overset{|}{CH_2}}{CH_2} \rightarrow CH_3CH_2SCH_2CH_3 + CH_2{=}CH_2$$

Heat decomposes a sulfonium halide, regenerating the sulfide and the alkyl halide from which it was made. If the radicals are different, however, radical interchange may occur. Thus a symmetrical sulfide may be changed to an unsymmetrical one.

$$\underset{R}{\overset{R}{\diagdown}}S + R'X \rightarrow \underset{R}{\overset{R'}{\diagdown}}R{-}SX \rightarrow \underset{R}{\overset{R'}{\diagdown}}S + RX$$

Decarboxylation

When the dibromide of *trans*-cinnamic acid is heated with sodium acetate in acetone, carbon dioxide and bromide ion appear to separate from the

[15] G. Wittig and T. F. Burger, *Ann.*, **632**, 85 (1960).
[16] V. Franzen and C. Mertz, *Chem. Ber.*, **93**, 2819 (1960).

bromo carboxylate ion in a concerted manner to give *cis*-β-bromostyrene. This change is thus stereospecific and has been formulated as a 1,4-elimination reaction.[17]

$$Br\!-\!CH\!-\!\overset{\overset{\displaystyle Br}{|}}{CH}\!-\!C\!-\!O^- \;\rightarrow\; Br^- + C_6H_5CH\!=\!CHBr + CO_2$$
$$\underset{\displaystyle C_6H_5}{|}\qquad\quad\underset{\displaystyle O}{\|}$$

The decomposition of glycidic acids may be represented in a similar way. The acid obtained by hydrolysis of ethyl methylphenylglycidate (p. 495) breaks down to give hydratropaldehyde (OS III, 733; yield 70%).

$$C_6H_5\overset{\overset{\displaystyle CH_3}{|}}{C}\!-\!CH\!-\!C\!-\!O\!-\!H \xrightarrow[-CO_2]{-H^+} C_6H_5\overset{\overset{\displaystyle CH_3}{|}}{C}\!=\!CH \xrightarrow{H^+} C_6H_5\overset{\overset{\displaystyle CH_3}{|}}{C}HCHO$$

Dehalogenation

Compounds that contain halogen atoms on adjacent carbon atoms can be dehalogenated by the action of certain metals to yield the corresponding olefinic compounds (Angew., **72**, 391). Zinc, for example, converts ethylene bromide into ethylene. Similarly, from 1,1,1,2-tetrachloroethane vinylidene chloride can be made.

$$CH_2ClCCl_3 + Zn \;\rightarrow\; CH_2\!=\!CCl_2 + ZnCl_2$$

Hexachloroethane yields tetrachloroethylene.

$$CCl_3CCl_3 \;\rightarrow\; CCl_2\!=\!CCl_2$$

Tetrafluoroethylene has been prepared by dechlorination of *sym*-dichlorotetrafluoroethane.[18]

$$CF_2ClCF_2Cl + Zn \;\rightarrow\; CF_2\!=\!CF_2 + ZnCl_2$$

A better method, however, consists in non-catalytic pyrolysis of chloro-difluoromethane.[19]

$$2CF_2HCl \;\rightarrow\; CF_2\!=\!CF_2 + 2HCl$$

[17] S. J. Cristol and W. P. Norris, *J. Am. Chem. Soc.*, **75**, 2645 (1953).
[18] E. G. Locke, W. R. Brode, and A. L. Henne, *J. Am. Chem. Soc.*, **56**, 1726 (1934).
[19] J. D. Park, A. F. Benning, F. B. Downing, J. F. Laucius, and R. C. McHarness, *Ind. Eng. Chem.*, **39**, 354 (1947).

1,1,1,2-Tetrachloro-2,2-difluoroethane reacts with powdered zinc to give 1,1-dichloro-2,2-difluoroethylene (OS **36**, 19; 95% yield).

$$CCl_3\!-\!CClF_2 + Zn \rightarrow CCl_2\!=\!CF_2 + ZnCl_2$$

1,2-Diiodo compounds are unstable and dissociate into iodine and the corresponding unsaturated compound; ethylene iodide, for example, reverts to ethylene and iodine when heated. The decomposition is catalyzed by iodide ion.

A synthesis of dimethylketene involves debromination of α-bromo-isobutyryl bromide with zinc (OS **33**, 30; 54% yield).

The synthesis of allyl iodide from glycerol by the action of phosphorus and iodine may involve the following elimination reaction (Hine, 187).

Purification of α,β-unsaturated ketones sometimes gives trouble. Conversion into a solid dibromide is often helpful, since this derivative can be purified by recrystallization and from it the unsaturated ketone can be made in nearly pure condition. An interesting feature of this debromination is that the reagent is not a metal but potassium or sodium iodide.

$$RCH\!=\!CHCOR \xrightarrow{Br_2} \underset{\substack{|\ \ |\\ Br\ Br}}{RCHCHCOR} \xrightarrow{KI} RCH\!=\!CHCOR$$

Coupling has been observed also; the geminal dihalide, benzophenone dichloride, yields tetraphenylethylene.

This change may be accomplished more satisfactorily by treating benzophenone dichloride with powdered copper.

The production of cyclopropane derivatives by the action of metals on
1,3-dihalogen compounds and similar syntheses of higher cyclane derivatives will be discussed as examples of the Wurtz reaction (p. 623).
Mention may be made here, however, of the elimination of bromine from
certain 1,3-dibromides that is accompanied by rearrangement of the carbon
skeleton. An example is the conversion of 1,1-*bis*-(bromomethyl)cyclo-
propane into a mixture of methylenecyclobutane and 1-methylcyclobutene
by the action of sodium iodide.[20] The change to methylenecyclobutane
has been formulated in the following way.

$$ I^- \ Br{-}CH_2{-}C{-}CH_2{-}Br \ \rightarrow \ CH_2{=}C{-}\!\!\!-CH_2 \ + \ IBr \ + \ Br^- $$
$$ \underset{CH_2{-}CH_2}{} \qquad\qquad \underset{CH_2{-}CH_2}{} $$

Cumulenes

A compound that has a succession of ethylene linkages is known as a
cumulene. The chief method by which these substances have been synthesized is based on the dehalogenation, not of 1,2-dihalogen compounds,
but of their vinylogs. The term *vinylog* is used to describe compounds that
differ by one or more vinylene linkages. It is well known that vinylogs are
similar chemically (CR **16**, 1); vinylogs of 1,2-diiodo compounds, for
example, in which the iodine atoms are at the extremities of a conjugated
system also seem to lose iodine. When the glycols, obtained by condensing
the dibromomagnesium derivatives of acetylene and diacetylene with
benzophenone, are treated with phosphorus diiodide (P_2I_4) the expected
diiodo derivatives are not isolated; cumulenes are formed instead. An
example is the formation of tetraphenyl-1,2,3-butatriene.[21]

$$
\begin{array}{cccc}
C_6H_5COC_6H_5 & (C_6H_5)_2COH & (C_6H_5)_2CI & (C_6H_5)_2C \\
CMgBr & C & C & C \\
\;|||\quad \rightarrow & |||\quad \rightarrow & |||\quad \rightarrow & || \\
CMgBr & C & C & C \\
C_6H_5COC_6H_5 & (C_6H_5)_2COH & (C_6H_5)_2CI & (C_6H_5)_2C
\end{array}
$$

If the glycol from diacetylene and benzophenone is treated with hydrogen
chloride and chromous or vanadous chloride, tetraphenyl-1,2,3,4,5-
hexapentaene is formed in 93% yield. It is a dark-red, high-melting solid.

[20] W. M. Schubert and S. M. Leahy, Jr., *J. Am. Chem. Soc.*, **79**, 381 (1957).
[21] R. Kuhn and K. Wallenfels, *Ber.*, **71B**, 783, 1510 (1938).

$$C_6H_5COC_6H_5 \qquad (C_6H_5)_2COH \qquad (C_6H_5)_2C$$
$$CMgBr \qquad\qquad C \qquad\qquad\quad C$$
$$C \qquad\qquad\quad C \qquad\qquad\quad C$$
$$C \qquad\to\qquad C \qquad\to\qquad C$$
$$C \qquad\qquad\quad C \qquad\qquad\quad C$$
$$CMgBr \qquad\qquad C \qquad\qquad\quad C$$
$$C_6H_5COC_6H_5 \qquad (C_6H_5)_2COH \qquad (C_6H_5)_2C$$

The dechlorination step in the case of chromous chloride may be formulated as follows.

$$(C_6H_5)_2C\text{—}C\text{=}C\text{—}C\text{=}C\text{—}C(C_6H_5)_2 \xrightarrow[-CrCl_3]{-Cl^-}$$

with Cl, CrCl$_2$ substituents

$$(C_6H_5)_2C\text{=}C\text{=}C\text{=}C\text{=}C\text{=}C(C_6H_5)_2$$

The simplest cumulene, allene, has been made by the reaction of 2,3-dichloropropene with zinc.

$$CH_2\text{=}C\text{—}CH_2 + Zn \to CH_2\text{=}C\text{=}CH_2 + ZnCl_2$$
$$\quad\; Cl \;\; Cl$$

Butatriene is formed from 1,4-dibromobutyne in a similar way.[22]

$$BrCH_2C\text{≡}CCH_2Br + Zn \to CH_2\text{=}C\text{=}C\text{=}CH_2 + ZnBr_2$$

Dealkoxyhalogenation

β-Halo ethers in general react with metals to yield olefins and alcohols or phenols. An example is the conversion of β-bromophenetole into ethylene and phenol by treatment with magnesium. The formation of ethyl vinyl ether from β-chloroethyl acetal by the action of sodium is another example.

$$ClCH_2CH(OC_2H_5)_2 + 2Na \to CH_2\text{=}CHOC_2H_5 + C_2H_5ONa + NaCl$$

Applied to ortho esters of α-halogen acids, this procedure yields ketene acetals.

$$RCHC(OC_2H_5)_3 + 2Na \to RCH\text{=}C(OC_2H_5)_2 + NaBr + C_2H_5ONa$$
$$\,Br$$

[22] W. M. Schubert, J. H. Liddicoet, and W. A. Lanka, *J. Am. Chem. Soc.*, **74**, 569 (1952).

Tetrahydrofurfuryl bromide reacts with magnesium to give 4-penten-1-ol in 62% yield. This unsaturated alcohol is made in 83% yield by treating tetrahydrofurfuryl chloride with sodium (OS III, 698).

$$\underset{\overset{|}{O}}{\overset{}{\bigcirc}}\text{CH}_2\text{Cl} \xrightarrow[\text{(2) H}_2\text{O}]{\text{(1) Na}} \text{CH}_2\text{=CHCH}_2\text{CH}_2\text{CH}_2\text{OH}$$

A synthesis of olefins from α,β-dibromo ethers likewise consists in the removal of the elements of an alkyl hypobromite. The action of a Grignard reagent on an α,β-dibromo ether gives the bromo ether from which the olefin can be derived. The elimination is effected by the use of zinc. If allyl-magnesium bromide is used, the final product is a diene; the synthesis of 1,4-pentadiene is an example.

$$\underset{\overset{|}{\text{Br}}}{\text{BrCH}_2\text{CHOC}_2\text{H}_5} \xrightarrow{\text{CH}_2\text{=CHCH}_2\text{MgCl}} \underset{\overset{|}{\text{CH}_2\text{CH=CH}_2}}{\text{BrCH}_2\text{CHOC}_2\text{H}_5} \xrightarrow{\text{Zn}}$$
$$\text{CH}_2\text{=CHCH}_2\text{CH=CH}_2$$

The dibromo ether is formed by the action of bromine on α-chloroethyl ethyl ether, prepared from paraldehyde, ethanol, and hydrogen chloride (p. 402).

$$\text{CH}_3\text{CHO} + \text{CH}_3\text{CH}_2\text{OH} + \text{HCl} \rightarrow \underset{\overset{|}{\text{Cl}}}{\text{CH}_3\text{CHOCH}_2\text{CH}_3} + \text{H}_2\text{O}$$

$$\underset{\overset{|}{\text{Cl}}}{\text{CH}_3\text{CHOCH}_2\text{CH}_3} + \text{Br}_2 \rightarrow \underset{\overset{|}{\text{Br}}}{\text{BrCH}_2\text{CHOCH}_2\text{CH}_3} + \text{HCl}$$

The vinyl ethers available commercially may serve as a source of the corresponding dibromo ethers.[23]

Certain halo vinyl ethers yield acetylenic derivatives; β-bromovinyl phenyl ether gives the corresponding phenoxide and acetylene.

$$\text{C}_6\text{H}_5\text{OCH=CHBr} + 2\text{Na} \rightarrow \text{C}_6\text{H}_5\text{ONa} + \text{NaBr} + \text{C}_2\text{H}_2$$

An unusual example is the reaction of 2-(chloromethyl)benzofuran with magnesium; the product is o-allenylphenol.[24]

[23] D. C. Rowlands, K. W. Greenlee, J. M. Derfer, and C. E. Boord, *J. Org. Chem.*, **17**, 807 (1952).
[24] R. Gaertner, *J. Am. Chem. Soc.*, **73**, 4400 (1951).

Sodium amide in liquid ammonia converts tetrahydrofurfuryl chloride into an acetylenic compound, 4-pentyn-1-ol.[25]

$$\text{[structure]} \quad \rightarrow \quad HC{\equiv}CCH_2CH_2CH_2OH$$

Application of the method of dealkoxybromination to γ-bromo ethers provides a route to hydrocarbons of the cyclopropane series. The bromo ethers can be made conveniently from the hydroxy ethers produced by adding a Grignard to β-ethoxypropionaldehyde. The synthesis of ethyl-cyclopropane illustrates the method; the yield at the ring closure step is 51 %.[26]

$$C_2H_5OCH_2CH_2\overset{\overset{\displaystyle Br}{|}}{C}HCH_2CH_3 \xrightarrow[\text{ether}]{Mg} \quad \text{[cyclopropane structure]} \; CH_2{-}CHCH_2CH_3$$

1′-Chloro-2′-methoxy-o-xylene, a vinylog of a β-chloro ether, reacts with magnesium to produce a polymer presumably formed from the corresponding dimethylene compound, o-quinodimethane.[27]

$$\text{[structure with } CH_2{-}OCH_3 \text{ and } CH_2{-}MgCl \text{]} \rightarrow \text{[structure with } {=}CH_2 \text{ and } {=}CH_2 \text{]}$$

Dehydration

Olefins such as ethylene, propylene, and isobutylene can be made readily by treating the corresponding alcohols with dehydrating agents such as sulfuric acid. Elimination of water may also be accomplished by passing the alcohol over a hot catalyst such as aluminum oxide or clay. When cyclohexanol is distilled from a little sulfuric acid, cyclohexene is formed in 87 % yield (OS I, 183), the distillate being a mixture of cyclohexene and water. Silica gel or activated alumina may be used also as the catalyst.

$$\text{[cyclohexanol structure]} \xrightarrow{H_2SO_4} \text{[cyclohexene structure]} + H_2O$$

[25] G. Eglinton, E. R. H. Jones, and M. C. Whiting, *J. Chem. Soc.*, 2873 (1952).

[26] J. T. Gragson, K. W. Greenlee, J. M. Derfer, and C. E. Boord, *J. Org. Chem.*, **20**, 275 (1955).

[27] F. G. Mann and F. H. C. Stewart, *Chem. and Ind.*, 1153 (1953).

Catalytic dehydration of 1,3-butanediol produces butadiene as shown here.

$$\underset{\text{OH}}{\overset{|}{CH_3CHCH_2CH_2OH}} \xrightarrow{-2H_2O} CH_2\!=\!CHCH\!=\!CH_2$$

As would be expected, many types of oxygen derivatives of hydrocarbons have been found to yield butadiene by single-stage processes (CR **36,** 63).

A useful procedure for preparing vinylbenzenes consists in pyrolysis of the corresponding methylcarbinols, an example being the synthesis of *m*-chlorostyrene from *m*-chlorophenylmethylcarbinol (OS III, 204). The dehydration is effected in 82% yield by bringing the carbinol into contact with potassium hydrogen sulfate at 220 to 230°.

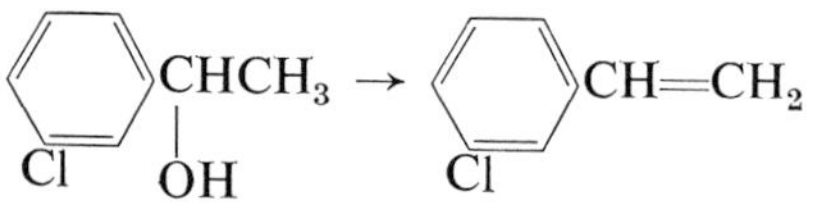

Dehydration occurs most readily if the alcohol is tertiary. Examples are the formation of 1,1-diphenylethylene (OS I, 226) and triphenylethylene (OS II, 606) from methyldiphenylcarbinol and benzyldiphenylcarbinol, respectively.

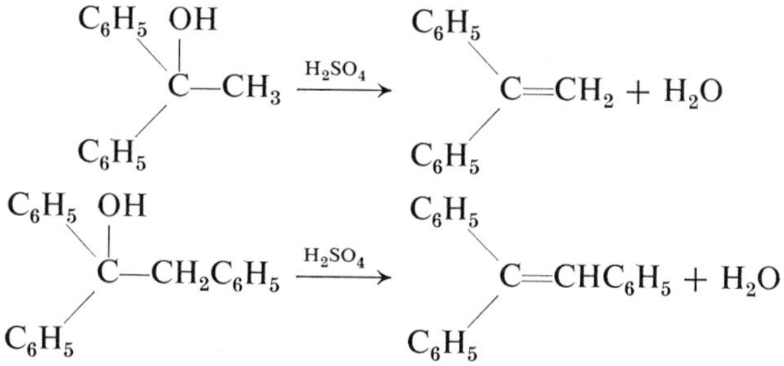

The usual method of effecting such dehydrations is to heat the carbinol with dilute sulfuric acid.

It is likely that, in the preparation of *trans*-stilbene by the action of zinc and hydrochloric acid on benzoin (OS III, 786), the final step is the dehydration of the alcohol, benzylphenylcarbinol. The first step will be recognized as a typical Clemmensen reduction (p. 560); the over-all yield is 57%.

$$C_6H_5COCHC_6H_5 \rightarrow \underset{\underset{OH}{|}}{C_6H_5CH_2CHC_6H_5} \rightarrow C_6H_5CH\!=\!CHC_6H_5$$
$$\underset{OH}{\underset{|}{}}$$

Isoprene has been prepared by dehydration of 3-methyl-1-buten-3-ol.

$$\underset{\underset{CH_3}{|}}{\overset{\overset{OH}{|}}{CH_3C}}-CH=CH_2 \rightarrow CH_2=\underset{\underset{CH_3}{|}}{C}-CH=CH_2 + H_2O$$

1-Phenyl-1,3-butadiene is formed by dehydration of the carbinol obtained from cinnamaldehyde and methylmagnesium iodide.

$$C_6H_5CH=CH\underset{\underset{OH}{|}}{CH}CH_3 \rightarrow C_6H_5CH=CHCH=CH_2 + H_2O$$

Dehydration of 2-pentanol by the sulfuric acid method is of special interest, since it illustrates the rule that β-olefins form more readily than α-olefins. The formation of 2-pentene occurs to the extent of 80% (OS I, 430).

$$CH_3CH_2CH_2\underset{\underset{OH}{|}}{CH}CH_3 \xrightarrow{H_2SO_4} CH_3CH_2CH=CHCH_3 + H_2O$$

Dehydration is facilitated if the hydroxyl group is adjacent to an active methylene group as in β-hydroxy carbonyl compounds, the mobility of the α-hydrogen atom being responsible for the ready loss of water. In fact this type of reaction is so easily brought about that in aldol-type condensations the aldol usually is isolated as its dehydration product, the corresponding α,β-unsaturated carbonyl compound.

Aldol, of course, readily yields crotonaldehyde. The method of Hibbert is particularly effective in such cases; the compound is simply distilled in the presence of a trace of iodine, which acts as a catalyst. Mesityl oxide is made in this way from diacetone alcohol (OS I, 345; 65% yield).

Many transformations of sugars and other polyhydroxy compounds involve dehydration of this general type. The synthesis of acrolein from glycerol by the dehydrating action of potassium acid sulfate is an example (OS I, 15; 48% yield).

$$\underset{\underset{H}{|}}{\overset{\overset{OH}{|}}{H-C}}-\underset{\underset{H}{|}}{\overset{\overset{OH}{|}}{C}}-\underset{\underset{H}{|}}{\overset{\overset{OH}{|}}{C}}-H \xrightarrow{-H_2O} \left[\underset{\underset{H}{|}}{\overset{\overset{OH}{|}}{H-C}}-\underset{\underset{H}{|}}{\overset{\overset{OH}{|}}{C}}=CH\right] \longrightarrow$$

$$\underset{\underset{H}{|}}{\overset{\overset{OH}{|}}{H-C}}-\underset{\underset{H}{|}}{\overset{\overset{H}{|}}{C}}-\overset{\overset{O}{\|}}{CH} \xrightarrow{-H_2O} CH_2=CHCHO$$

The first step is represented as dehydration of a secondary alcohol, the second as ketonization of the resulting enol, and the last as dehydration of β-hydroxypropionaldehyde.

The Reformatsky condensation (p. 523) generally produces β-hydroxy esters, which likewise are easily dehydrated. Dehydration may be carried out by heating the hydroxy compound with a variety of dehydrating agents such as sulfuric acid, fused potassium acid sulfate, acetic anhydride, and phosphorus pentoxide. The Hibbert method is also useful. Dehydration by passing dry hydrogen chloride through the hydroxy ester at 90 to 100°, followed by distillation, gives the unsaturated esters in high yields.

The first step in the synthesis of pyruvic acid by decomposition of tartaric acid (OS I, 475; 55% yield) illustrates the dehydration of a β-hydroxy acid.

$$\begin{array}{c} CO_2H \\ | \\ CHOH \\ | \\ CHOH \\ | \\ CO_2H \end{array} \xrightarrow{-H_2O} \left[\begin{array}{c} CO_2H \\ | \\ COH \\ \| \\ CH \\ | \\ CO_2H \end{array}\right] \longrightarrow \begin{array}{c} CO_2H \\ | \\ CO \\ | \\ CH_2 \\ | \\ CO_2H \end{array} \longrightarrow CH_3COCO_2H$$

Dehydration of a similar sort constitutes the initial step in the synthesis of itaconic, mesaconic, and citraconic acids from citric acid. When citric acid is destructively distilled, the chief product is itaconic anhydride (OS II, 368; 47% yield).

$$\begin{array}{c} CH_2CO_2H \\ | \\ HOCCO_2H \\ | \\ CH_2CO_2H \end{array} \rightarrow \begin{array}{c} CH_2CO \\ \diagdown \\ \qquad O \\ \diagup \\ CH_2{=}C{-}CO \end{array}$$

If aconitic acid is desired, citric acid is heated for several hours with dilute sulfuric acid (OS II, 12; 44% yield). Heat causes itaconic anhydride to rearrange to citraconic anhydride (OS II, 140; 66% yield).

$$\begin{array}{c} CH_2CO \\ | \qquad \diagdown \\ \qquad\quad O \rightarrow \\ | \qquad \diagup \\ CH_2{=}C{-}CO \end{array} \qquad \begin{array}{c} CHCO \\ \| \qquad \diagdown \\ \qquad\quad O \\ \| \qquad \diagup \\ CH_3C{-}CO \end{array}$$

Finally, heating citraconic acid with dilute nitric acid until nearly all the water has been driven off causes it to isomerize to mesaconic acid (OS II, 382; 52% yield).

$$\begin{array}{c} HCCO_2H \\ \| \\ CH_3CCO_2H \end{array} \rightarrow \begin{array}{c} HCCO_2H \\ \| \\ HO_2CCCH_3 \end{array}$$

By reducing acetonedicarboxylic acid and eliminating water from the resulting hydroxy acid, glutaconic acid is produced.

$$
\begin{array}{ccc}
\text{CH}_2\text{CO}_2\text{H} & \text{CH}_2\text{CO}_2\text{H} & \text{CH}_2\text{CO}_2\text{H} \\
| & | & | \\
\text{CO} & \rightarrow \quad \text{CHOH} & \rightarrow \quad \text{CH} \\
| & | & \| \\
\text{CH}_2\text{CO}_2\text{H} & \text{CH}_2\text{CO}_2\text{H} & \text{CHCO}_2\text{H}
\end{array}
$$

The manufacture of acrylonitrile from ethylene oxide and hydrogen cyanide illustrates the ease with which β-hydroxy nitriles lose water.

$$
\overset{\displaystyle O}{\underset{\displaystyle \text{CH}_2 - \text{CH}_2}{\diagup \diagdown}} \xrightarrow{\text{HCN}} \overset{\displaystyle OH}{\underset{\displaystyle \text{CH}_2\text{CH}_2\text{CN}}{|}} \xrightarrow{-\text{H}_2\text{O}} \text{CH}_2{=}\text{CHCN}
$$

α-Hydroxy carbonyl compounds lose water much less readily. If the hydroxyl group is on a tertiary carbon atom, however, the reaction is not difficult to bring about. Dehydration of methyl α-hydroxyisobutyrate to methyl methacrylate is an important example.

$$
\underset{\displaystyle \text{CH}_3 \;\; \text{OH}}{\overset{\displaystyle \text{CH}_3}{\diagdown}}\underset{}{\text{CCO}_2\text{CH}_3} \rightarrow \underset{\displaystyle \text{CH}_3}{\text{CH}_2{=}\text{CCO}_2\text{CH}_3} + \text{H}_2\text{O}
$$

Acetone cyanohydrin is dehydrated to methacrylonitrile by treatment with sulfuric acid.

$$
\underset{\displaystyle \text{CH}_3 \;\; \text{OH}}{\overset{\displaystyle \text{CH}_3}{\diagdown}}\underset{}{\text{CCN}} \xrightarrow{\text{H}_2\text{SO}_4} \underset{\displaystyle \text{CH}_3}{\text{CH}_2{=}\text{CCN}} + \text{H}_2\text{O}
$$

When α-hydroxy acids are treated with concentrated sulfuric acid, they lose not only water but carbon monoxide as well, the products being aldehydes or ketones.

Nitroethylene is made by dehydrating β-nitroethanol (p. 494).[28]

$$
\text{CH}_3\text{NO}_2 + \text{CH}_2\text{O} \rightarrow \text{HOCH}_2\text{CH}_2\text{NO}_2 \rightarrow \text{CH}_2{=}\text{CHNO}_2 + \text{H}_2\text{O}
$$

Ring Closure

If the two atoms or groups to be eliminated are separated by three or more atoms the normal product is a ring. The Perkin ring closure (p. 262) and other intramolecular alkylations on carbon are illustrative.

[28] See H. Hopff and M. Capaul, *Helv. Chim. Acta*, **43**, 1898 (1960).

15

Nucleophilic displacement at the aliphatic trigonal carbon atom

It is not easy to compare the various types of carbonyl compounds from the standpoint of reactivity of the carbonyl function itself. The primary difficulty arises from the fact that the acid derivatives undergo solvolytic cleavage (CR **60,** 53) whereas the aldehydes and ketones—often regarded as the true carbonyl compounds—generally do not. The most important solvolytic reactions, as the term is employed here, are hydrolysis, alcoholysis, ammonolysis, and acidolysis. These reactions may be generalized as follows.

$$\underset{\substack{\|\\ \text{RC}}}{\overset{\text{O}}{}}\!\!-\!\text{A} + \text{B}^- \rightarrow \underset{\substack{\|\\ \text{RC}}}{\overset{\text{O}}{}}\!\!-\!\text{B} + \text{A}^-$$

Since solvolytic reactions involve nucleophilic attack at the carbonyl carbon atom, it would be helpful to know the extent to which the electron deficit at that point is diminished by the attached function. Accession of electrons is greatest in salts and least in the acid chlorides and anhydrides; esters and amides are intermediate in this respect. The various classes of compounds fall in the following order of decreasing reactivity of the carbonyl function.

$$\underset{\substack{\|\\ \text{RCCl}}}{\overset{\text{O}}{}} > \underset{\substack{\|\\ \text{RCOR}}}{\overset{\text{O}}{}} > \underset{\substack{\|\\ \text{RCNH}_2}}{\overset{\text{O}}{}} > \underset{\substack{\|\\ \text{RCONa}}}{\overset{\text{O}}{}}$$

Nitriles are similar to amides in degree of reactivity, whereas anhydrides closely resemble acid chlorides. Variations within each class are great, and there are many exceptions to the foregoing order. As might be expected, reactions normally lead to products in which the carbonyl group is less reactive than in the original compounds.

In many of these reactions mineral acids are effective catalysts; they enhance the electron deficiency of the reactive carbon atom by coordination with the carbonyl oxygen atom or, in the case of nitriles, with the nitrogen atom. The catalyst reacts with esters, amides, and nitriles as follows.

$$R-\overset{\overset{\textstyle O}{\|}}{C}-OR + H^+ \rightarrow R-\overset{\overset{\textstyle OH}{|}}{\underset{+}{C}}-OR$$

$$R-\overset{\overset{\textstyle O}{\|}}{C}-NH_2 + H^+ \rightarrow R-\overset{\overset{\textstyle OH}{|}}{\underset{+}{C}}-NH_2$$

$$R-C{\equiv}N + H^+ \rightarrow R-\underset{+}{C}{=}NH$$

Hydrolysis

The rate at which hydrolysis takes place is most rapid with acid chlorides and anhydrides and slowest with nitriles and amides. It is related also to the strength of the acid involved, derivatives of strong acids being more susceptible to attack than those of weak acids.

The *hydrolysis of acid chlorides* occurs readily but is rarely useful. Trichloromethyl compounds, which may be regarded as acid chlorides of ortho acids, are exceptional. Chloroform and benzotrichloride are examples.

The *hydrolysis of anhydrides,* somewhat more sluggish than that of chlorides, is likewise generally to be avoided. Maleic and phthalic acids, however, are made from the corresponding anhydrides. When hydrogen sulfide is employed, thiol acids are generated. From acetic anhydride, for example, thiolacetic acid is formed (OS **31**, 105; 76% yield).

$$(CH_3CO_2)O + H_2S \rightarrow CH_3\overset{\overset{\textstyle O}{\|}}{C}SH + CH_3\overset{\overset{\textstyle O}{\|}}{C}OH$$

Mildly alkaline hydrogen peroxide, it may be mentioned, reacts with phthalic anhydride to give monoperphthalic acid.[1]

Hydrolysis of esters (Gould, 314) finds frequent use. The reaction between an acid and an alcohol is catalyzed by acids and is reversible (p. 330). In order to bring about complete hydrolysis, therefore, an alkali is introduced to neutralize the acids and render the process irreversible. When conducted in this way hydrolysis is termed *saponification.*

[1] G. B. Payne, *J. Org. Chem.*, **24**, 1354 (1959).

Many esters occur in nature or are more readily synthesized than the corresponding acids and thus are used in the production of acids. The most important group comprises the fats, oils, and waxes. An example of the synthesis of an acid from its ester is the saponification of myristin (OS I, 379). Myristic acid is produced in nearly theoretical yields.

$$\begin{array}{ll}
CH_2OCOC_{13}H_{27} & CH_2OH \\
| & | \\
CHOCOC_{13}H_{27} + 3NaOH \rightarrow 3C_{13}H_{27}CO_2Na + CHOH \\
| & | \\
CH_2OCOC_{13}H_{27} & CH_2OH
\end{array}$$

$$C_{13}H_{27}CO_2Na + HCl \rightarrow C_{13}H_{27}CO_2H + NaCl$$

Myristin can be obtained by extracting nutmegs with ether (OS I, 538). Erucic acid is made by the hydrolysis of rape seed oil (OS II, 258).

$$CH_3(CH_2)_7CH=CH(CH_2)_{11}CO_2H$$
$$\text{Erucic acid}$$

Oleic acid is obtained from various natural fats; both oleic and erucic acids have the *cis*-configuration.

Palmitic and stearic acid also come from fats. Bayberry wax, for example, is made up chiefly of myristin and palmitin. The problem of separating the acids has proved difficult; distillation and crystallization are ineffective because the acids are dimeric (p. 8) and mixed dimer is always present. The fats are converted into methyl esters, which are separated by fractionation (OS III, 605). The ethyl esters of lauric, caprylic, and myristic acids have been made in a similar way from coconut oil (OS III, 606). Linoleic (OS III, 526) and linolenic (OS III, 531) acids are produced by hydrolysis of their ethyl esters.

Synthesis of compounds by the acetoacetic and malonic ester methods generally involves hydrolysis. If decarboxylation (p. 664) is to be avoided, alkali must be employed. Examples are the syntheses of benzyl (OS III, 705), *sec*-butyl (OS III, 495), and *n*-heptyl (OS II, 474) derivatives of malonic acid.

In the preparation of methyl *n*-amyl ketone by the acetoacetic ester method it is recommended that hydrolysis and decarboxylation be carried out in separate steps (OS I, 351).

$$CH_3COCHCO_2C_2H_5 + NaOH \rightarrow CH_3COCHCO_2Na + C_2H_5OH$$
$$| |$$
$$C_4H_9 C_4H_9$$

$$CH_3COCHCO_2Na \xrightarrow{H_2SO_4} CH_3COC_5H_{11}$$
$$|$$
$$C_4H_9$$

A similar procedure for making cyclobutanecarboxylic acid has already been mentioned (p. 263). Hydrolysis and decarboxylation may be accomplished in one step, however, by the use of acid hydrolytic agents. The Michael condensation product between diethyl fumarate and diethyl malonate (p. 505), for example, is converted into tricarballylic acid in nearly quantitative yields by heating with hydrochloric acid (OS I, 523).

$$
\begin{array}{l}
CH(CO_2C_2H_5)_2 \\
| \\
CHCO_2C_2H_5 \\
| \\
CH_2CO_2C_2H_5
\end{array}
+ 4H_2O \rightarrow
\begin{array}{l}
CH_2CO_2H \\
| \\
CHCO_2H \\
| \\
CH_2CO_2H
\end{array}
+ 4C_2H_5OH + CO_2
$$

Glutaric acid is formed in 80% yield by submitting the ethyl ester of 1,1,3,3-propanetetracarboxylic acid to a similar treatment (OS I, 290).

$$
\begin{array}{l}
CH(CO_2C_2H_5)_2 \\
\diagup \\
CH_2 \\
\diagdown \\
CH(CO_2C_2H_5)_2
\end{array}
+ 4H_2O \xrightarrow{\text{HCl}}
\begin{array}{l}
CH_2CO_2H \\
\diagup \\
CH_2 \\
\diagdown \\
CH_2CO_2H
\end{array}
+ 4C_2H_5OH + 2CO_2
$$

α-Ketoglutaric may be produced in 93% yield by applying this method to the ethyl ester of oxalylsuccinic acid (OS III, 510).

$$
\begin{array}{l}
COCO_2C_2H_5 \\
| \\
CHCO_2C_2H_5 \\
| \\
CH_2CO_2C_2H_5
\end{array}
+ 3H_2O \xrightarrow{\text{HCl}}
\begin{array}{l}
COCO_2H \\
| \\
CH_2 \\
| \\
CH_2CO_2H
\end{array}
+ 3C_2H_5OH + CO_2
$$

The use of acids is to be preferred if the hydrolysis products are sensitive to alkalis. Acids are employed, for example, to convert o-nitrobenzaldiacetate into o-nitrobenzaldehyde (OS III, 641; 74% yield).

$$
\underset{\text{CH(OCOCH_3)_2}}{\bigcirc}\text{NO}_2 + H_2O \xrightarrow{\text{HCl}} \underset{\text{CHO}}{\bigcirc}\text{NO}_2 + 2CH_3CO_2H
$$

Other examples of esters that undergo saponification satisfactorily with alkalis are methyl m-nitrobenzoate (OS I, 391), 5-acetoxyacenaphthene (OS III, 3), p-nitrobenzyl acetate (OS III, 652), and ethyl 1,3-dihydroxy-2-naphthoate (OS III, 637).

Since the rate of hydrolysis of esters depends on the electron deficiency of the carbonyl carbon atom, aromatic esters that have electron-attracting nuclear substituents undergo hydrolysis more rapidly than those of benzoic acid itself. Increased carbonyl reactivity has been noted also when alkoxyl groups are replaced by aryloxyl radicals. Phenyl esters are saponified more readily than the corresponding methyl or ethyl esters. Esters that possess a high order of carbonyl activity include formates, chloroacetates, and pyruvates.

By employing only one equivalent of base it is possible to hydrolyze esters of dibasic acids to the corresponding "half esters." Diethyl malonate can be transformed into ethyl hydrogen malonate by treatment with potassium hydroxide (OS 37, 34). Barium hydroxide in methanol may be used to advantage with esters of dibasic acids above azelaic acid. The barium salt of the half ester is insoluble and can be removed as a solid. This device is illustrated by the preparation of methyl hydrogen undecanedioate (OS 38, 55; yield 64%).

$$(CH_2)_9 \Big\langle \begin{matrix} CO_2CH_3 \\ CO_2CH_3 \end{matrix} \quad \xrightarrow{\;Ba(OH)_2\;} \quad \xrightarrow{\;H^+\;} \quad (CH_2)_9 \Big\langle \begin{matrix} CO_2CH_3 \\ CO_2H \end{matrix}$$

This method is less tedious than the partial esterification procedure (p. 333) and is particularly advantageous for high-boiling half esters, which may undergo disproportionation when subjected to prolonged fractional distillation at high temperatures.

Hydrolysis of amides, which is the second step in the conversion of nitriles into acids (p. 322), may be effected with either acidic or basic catalysts. It is carried out frequently in connection with certain special types of syntheses, one of which is the Beckmann rearrangement of oximes (p. 197) followed by hydrolysis of the resulting amides. When applied to cyclohexanone oxime, this method gives ε-aminocaproic acid (OS II, 28; 60% yield; OS 32, 13).

$$\langle \hexagon \rangle{=}NOH \;\rightarrow\; CH_2 \Big\langle \begin{matrix} CH_2CH_2CO \\[4pt] CH_2CH_2NH \end{matrix} \Big| \;\rightarrow\; H_2N(CH)_{25}CO_2H$$

Sometimes amines are acylated in order to protect the amino group or change its influence during a reaction, after which the amides are deacylated. A well-known example is the acetylation of *p*-toluidine to permit controlled bromination. The final step is the hydrolysis of the bromo amide to produce 3-bromo-4-aminotoluene (OS I, 111).

In a somewhat similar way hydrazine is benzoylated (p. 338) in order to permit symmetrical methylation, the benzoyl groups being removed subsequently (OS II, 208).

$$C_6H_5CONHNHCOC_6H_5 \rightarrow C_6H_5CON\overset{|}{\underset{\underset{CH_3}{|}}{—}}NCOC_6H_5 \rightarrow CH_3NHNHCH_3$$

Hydrolysis to *sym*-dimethylhydrazine may be accomplished in 78% yield.

Another example of this type is the protection of the amino group in ϵ-aminocaproic acid during the introduction of an amino group in the α-position. Subsequent removal of the benzoyl group yields lysine (p. 198) (OS II, 374).

$$C_6H_5CONH(CH_2)_4CH_2CO_2H \rightarrow C_6H_5CONH(CH_2)_4\underset{\underset{NH_2}{|}}{C}HCO_2H \rightarrow$$

$$H_2N(CH_2)_4\underset{\underset{NH_2}{|}}{C}HCO_2H$$

Formylation serves a similar purpose in a threonine synthesis (OS III, 813), the last step of which is hydrolysis.

$$CH_3CH\overset{|}{\underset{\underset{OCH_3}{|}}{—}}\overset{|}{\underset{\underset{NHCHO}{|}}{C}}HCO_2H \rightarrow CH_3CH\overset{|}{\underset{\underset{OH}{|}}{—}}\overset{|}{\underset{\underset{NH_2}{|}}{C}}HCO_2H$$

Similarly deacetylation is the final step in a synthesis of β-phenylalanine (OS II, 491).

$$C_6H_5CH_2\underset{\underset{NHCOCH_3}{|}}{C}HCO_2H \rightarrow C_6H_5CH_2\underset{\underset{NH_2}{|}}{C}HCO_2H$$

N,N-Diacetylaniline is more readily hydrolyzed than acetanilide as would be expected because the nitrogen atom does not neutralize two carbonyl groups as effectively as one. One acetyl group may be removed with ammonia, aniline, hydrogen chloride, alcohol, or acetic acid.

$$C_6H_5N\overset{\nearrow COCH_3}{\underset{\searrow COCH_3}{}} + C_6H_5NH_2 \rightarrow 2C_6H_5NHCOCH_3$$

Imides, as would be expected, generally are more easily hydrolyzed than amides. Phthalimide and its derivatives are sometimes resistant to hydrolysis, however. Nevertheless, this step occurs in the Gabriel amine synthesis (p. 277). An example is the hydrolysis of 4-nitrophthalimide (OS II, 457; 99% yield).

The *hydrolysis of nitriles* is the final step in certain syntheses of acids from halides, aldehydes, or ketones with one less carbon atom. The usual procedure is to heat the nitrile with hydrochloric or sulfuric acid, although alkaline hydrolysis is used widely also. Amides are produced as intermediates but are rarely isolated; they can be prepared in various ways, one of which employs sulfuric acid. An example is the conversion of α,β-diphenylsuccinonitrile into α,β-diphenylsuccinamide. The nitrile is dissolved in 15 to 20 times its weight of 90% sulfuric acid, and the solution is allowed to stand for a few hours. Addition of water causes the amide to precipitate; the yield is 90%.

$$\begin{array}{c} C_6H_5CHCN \\ | \\ C_6H_5CHCN \end{array} + 2H_2O \rightarrow \begin{array}{c} C_6H_5CHCONH_2 \\ | \\ C_6H_5CHCONH_2 \end{array}$$

A general procedure for converting nitriles into the corresponding amides involves sulfuric acid monohydrate. Hydrogen peroxide is also utilized to accomplish this type of change. It serves, for example, to convert *o*-tolunitrile into *o*-toluamide (OS II, 586; yield 92%).

It has been assumed that the initial step in the process is attack of the carbon atom of the nitrile group by the peroxide anion; the resulting ion after being protonated reacts with hydrogen peroxide to give the amide. The hydration of benzonitrile would then proceed as follows.[2]

The use of sulfuric acid is further illustrated by the preparation of *o*-toluic acid (OS II, 588; 89% yield), mesitylacetic acid (OS III, 557; 87% yield), *p*-nitrophenylacetic acid (OS I, 406; 95% yield), homophthalic acid, (OS III, 451), and phenylacetic acid (OS I, 436; 77% yield) from the corresponding nitriles.

Hydrolysis of the nitrile and subsequent decarboxylation of the carboxylic acid may be accomplished in one step when mineral acids are employed as catalysts. A synthesis of phenylsuccinic acid involves this technique (OS I, 451; 95% yield).

[2] K. B. Wiberg, *J. Am. Chem. Soc.*, **75**, 3961 (1953).

$$\text{C}_6\text{H}_5\text{CHCN}$$
$$\underset{\underset{\text{CO}_2\text{C}_2\text{H}_5}{|}}{\overset{|}{\text{CHCN}}} \quad + 5\text{H}_2\text{O} + 2\text{HCl} \rightarrow$$

$$\underset{\overset{|}{\text{CH}_2\text{CO}_2\text{H}}}{\overset{\text{C}_6\text{H}_5\text{CHCO}_2\text{H}}{|}} + \text{C}_2\text{H}_5\text{OH} + \text{CO}_2 + 2\text{NH}_4\text{Cl}$$

Another example is the formation of benzyl methyl ketone from α-phenylacetoacetonitrile (OS II, 391; 86% yield).

$$\underset{\overset{|}{\text{CN}}}{\text{C}_6\text{H}_5\text{CHCOCH}_3} + 2\text{H}_2\text{O} \xrightarrow{\text{H}_2\text{SO}_4} \text{C}_6\text{H}_5\text{CH}_2\text{COCH}_3 + \text{CO}_2 + \text{NH}_3$$

Of unusual interest is the hydrolysis of diallylcyanamide to diallylamine, which must involve the intermediate formation of an unstable carbamic acid (OS I, 201; 88% yield).

$$(\text{CH}_2\text{=CHCH}_2)_2\text{NCN} \xrightarrow[\text{H}_2\text{SO}_4]{\text{H}_2\text{O}} (\text{CH}_2\text{=CHCH}_2)_2\text{NCO}_2\text{H} \xrightarrow{-\text{CO}_2}$$
$$(\text{CH}_2\text{=CHCH}_2)_2\text{NH}$$

Hydrochloric acid is especially valuable in the hydrolysis of nitriles because chloride ion has a catalytic effect on the reaction.[3] The use of this reagent has been described for the preparation of alanine (OS I, 21), benzoylformic acid (OS III, 114), and glutaric acid (OS I, 289; 85% yield) from the corresponding nitriles.

A superior procedure for transforming nitriles to amides consists in heating them for approximately an hour with polyphosphoric acid at 110°. The method, applicable to both aliphatic and aromatic nitriles, gives the amides in high yields.[4]

The use of alkalis is necessary, of course, if the resulting acid is readily decarboxylated or dehydrated. Malonic acid (OS II, 376; 80% yield) and β-hydroxypropionic (hydracrylic) acid (OS I, 321; 31% yield) are made in this way. Cyclopropanecarboxylic acid is prepared in this manner also; here mineral acids might cause ring opening (OS III, 221). The yield, based on γ-chlorobutyronitrile (p. 253), is 79%.

$$\underset{\text{CH}_2}{\overset{\text{CH}_2}{\diagdown}}\!\!\text{CHCN} \xrightarrow[\text{NaOH}]{\text{H}_2\text{O}} \underset{\text{CH}_2}{\overset{\text{CH}_2}{\diagdown}}\!\!\text{CHCO}_2\text{H}$$

[3] M. L. Kilpatrick, *J. Am. Chem. Soc.*, **69**, 40 (1947).
[4] H. R. Snyder and C. T. Elston, *J. Am. Chem. Soc.*, **76**, 3039 (1954).

Other acids prepared from nitriles by the use of alkali are *n*-tridecanoic acid (OS II, 292), methylsuccinic acid (OS II, 615), and β-alanine (OS III, 34; 90% yield). Alkalis cannot serve in the hydrolysis of allyl cyanide, since as was noted earlier (p. 254), they cause the olefinic bond to shift, yielding crotonic acid.

When cyanohydrins are subjected to hydrolysis, hydroxy acids are formed. An example is the production of α-hydroxyisobutyric acid from acetone cyanohydrin.

$$
\begin{array}{ccc}
CH_3 \quad OH & & CH_3 \quad OH \\
\diagdown \diagup & & \diagdown \diagup \\
C & \rightarrow & C \\
\diagup \diagdown & & \diagup \diagdown \\
CH_3 \quad CN & & CH_3 \quad CO_2H
\end{array}
$$

α-Hydroxy acids are also prepared from aldehydes by way of the corresponding cyanohydrins. Mandelic acid, for instance, is made from benzaldehyde in 52% yield by this method (OS I, 336).

$$
\underset{\underset{OH}{|}}{C_6H_5CHCN} + HCl + 2H_2O \rightarrow \underset{\underset{OH}{|}}{C_6H_5CHCO_2H} + NH_4Cl
$$

Atrolactic acid is obtained by hydrolysis of the cyanohydrin of acetophenone. It is convenient to carry the reaction to the amide stage with hydrochloric acid and to complete the hydrolysis with sodium hydroxide solution. The yield, based on the ketone, is 30% (OS **33**, 7).

$$
\underset{\underset{OH}{|}}{\overset{\overset{CH_3}{|}}{C_6H_5C}{-}CN} \rightarrow \underset{\underset{OH}{|}}{\overset{\overset{CH_3}{|}}{C_6H_5C}{-}CONH_2} \rightarrow \underset{\underset{OH}{|}}{\overset{\overset{CH_3}{|}}{C_6H_5C}{-}CO_2H}
$$

Ethylene cyanohydrin, as might be expected, reacts with hydrobromic acid to yield β-bromopropionic acid (OS I, 131; 83% yield).

$$
HOCH_2CH_2CN + 2HBr + H_2O \rightarrow BrCH_2CH_2CO_2H + NH_4Br
$$

Alcoholysis

A useful method of preparing esters consists in alcoholysis of acid chlorides or anhydrides. When an acid anhydride reacts with an alcohol in equimolecular proportions, equimolecular amounts of ester and acid are produced. When applied to cyclic anhydrides, this reaction leads to the formation of half esters; succinic anhydride and methanol yield methyl hydrogen succinate (OS III, 169).

$$\begin{array}{c}
\text{CH}_2\text{CO} \\
\;\;\;\;\;\;\;\;\;\;\text{O} + \text{CH}_3\text{OH} \rightarrow \\
\text{CH}_2\text{CO}
\end{array}
\qquad
\begin{array}{c}
\text{CH}_2\text{CO}_2\text{CH}_3 \\
\; \\
\text{CH}_2\text{CO}_2\text{H}
\end{array}$$

Acid chlorides, as mixed anhydrides, react to set free hydrogen chloride. Chlorides of aromatic acids, being less reactive than those of aliphatic acids, form esters less rapidly. One way of promoting reaction in such cases, known as the Schotten-Baumann method, is to treat the mixture of alcohol and acid chloride with alkali.

Carbonyl chloride or phosgene reacts with alcohols in the cold to produce alkyl chloroformates, which have the properties of acid chlorides. The chloroformates, also called chlorocarbonates, undergo alcoholysis and ammonolysis to yield carbonates and amides, respectively. One of the most interesting of the chloroformates is that formed from benzyl alcohol, benzyl chloroformate (OS III, 167).

$$\text{C}_6\text{H}_5\text{CH}_2\text{OH} + \text{COCl}_2 \rightarrow \text{C}_6\text{H}_5\text{CH}_2\text{OCOCl} + \text{HCl}$$

This compound, often called carbobenzoxy chloride, has proved useful in the preparation of the carbobenzoxy derivatives of amino acids (p. 649).

Tertiary alcohols react with acid chlorides to yield the corresponding tertiary alkyl chlorides. Triphenylcarbinol and acetyl chloride, for example, form triphenylmethyl chloride and acetic acid (OS III, 841; 95% yield). The reaction is believed to involve the intermediate formation of the acetate, which then undergoes cleavage by hydrogen chloride. In support of this hypothesis it has been found that normal acetylation occurs in the presence of amines, which combine with the hydrogen chloride as it forms. *t*-Butyl acetate can be obtained in 68% yield, for example, by treating *t*-butyl alcohol with acetyl chloride in the presence of dimethylaniline (OS III, 142). Similar results are obtained when *t*-butyl alcohol is treated with acetic anhydride in the presence of zinc chloride (OS III, 141).

$$(\text{CH}_3)_3\text{COH} + (\text{CH}_3\text{CO})_2\text{O} \xrightarrow{\text{ZnCl}_2} \text{CH}_3\text{CO}_2\text{C}(\text{CH}_3)_3 + \text{CH}_3\text{CO}_2\text{H}$$

Di-*t*-butyl malonate is formed in 84% yield by treating malonyl chloride with *t*-butyl alcohol in the presence of dimethylaniline (OS 33, 20).

$$\begin{array}{c}
\;\;\;\;\;\;\text{COCl} \\
\text{CH}_2 \\
\;\;\;\;\;\;\text{COCl}
\end{array}
+ 2(\text{CH}_3)_3\text{COH} \rightarrow
\begin{array}{c}
\;\;\;\;\;\;\text{CO}_2\text{C}(\text{CH}_3)_3 \\
\text{CH}_2 \\
\;\;\;\;\;\;\text{CO}_2\text{C}(\text{CH}_3)_3
\end{array}
+ 2\text{HCl}$$

Phenols also react with acid chlorides or anhydrides to form esters. Phenyl cinnamate, for example, is made in 75% yield by treating cinnamoyl chloride with phenol (OS III, 714).

$$C_6H_5CH=CHCOCl + C_6H_5OH \rightarrow C_6H_5CH=CHCO_2C_6H_5 + HCl$$

A superior route to phenyl esters of carboxylic acids consists in heating the free acids with phenol in the presence of polyphosphoric acid.[5] *p*-Chlorophenyl salicylate is made by heating a mixture of salicylic acid, *p*-chlorophenol, and phosphorus oxychloride (OS **32**, 25; yield 76%).

Diphenyl succinate is made by a similar procedure (OS **34**, 44; yield 67%).

Catechol, in the form of its sodium salt, reacts with phosgene to yield *o*-phenylene carbonate (OS **33**, 74; yield 86%).

Allophanates (CR **51**, 471) may be prepared by alcoholysis of carbamyl chloride or allophanyl chloride.

$$ROH + 2H_2NCOCl \rightarrow ROCONHCONH_2 + 2HCl$$

$$ROH + H_2NCONHCOCl \rightarrow ROCONHCONH_2 + HCl$$

Sulfonyl chlorides resemble the chlorides of carboxylic acids in many of their reactions. Hydrolysis, alcoholysis, and ammonolysis may be effected, although with greater difficulty than that encountered with chlorides of carboxylic acids. The reaction of sulfonyl chlorides with alcohols proceeds satisfactorily in the presence of a base such as sodium hydroxide, an example being the preparation of *n*-butyl *p*-toluenesulfonate by the interaction of *n*-butyl alcohol and *p*-toluenesulfonyl chloride (OS I, 145; 54% yield).

[5] A. R. Bader and A. D. Kontowicz, *J. Am. Chem. Soc.*, **75**, 5416 (1953).

$$p\text{-CH}_3\text{C}_6\text{H}_4\text{SO}_2\text{Cl} + \text{CH}_3(\text{CH}_2)_2\text{CH}_2\text{OH} \xrightarrow{\text{NaOH}}$$

$$p\text{-CH}_3\text{C}_6\text{H}_4\text{SO}_3\text{CH}_2(\text{CH}_2)_2\text{CH}_3 + \text{HCl}$$

Pyridine may serve also as the condensing agent, as is illustrated by the synthesis of *n*-dodecyl *p*-toluenesulfonate (OS III, 366; 90% yield).

Alcoholysis of esters is used to convert those of low-boiling alcohols into those of higher-boiling alcohols. *n*-Butyl acrylate can be made in 94% yield by heating methyl acrylate with *n*-butyl alcohol and removing the methanol as fast as it forms (OS II, 146).

$$\text{CH}_2\!\!=\!\!\text{CHCO}_2\text{CH}_3 + \text{C}_4\text{H}_9\text{OH} \rightarrow \text{CH}_2\!\!=\!\!\text{CHCO}_2\text{C}_4\text{H}_9 + \text{CH}_3\text{OH}$$

Since this process changes one ester to another, it is often called transesterification. Suitable catalysts for this type of reaction are aluminum alkoxides, sulfuric acid, and sulfonic acids.

Alcoholysis of β-keto esters takes place readily at steam bath temperatures and without a catalyst. Ethyl acetoacetate, for example, reacts with 1-octanol to give *n*-octyl acetoacetate.

$$\text{CH}_3\text{COCH}_2\text{CO}_2\text{C}_2\text{H}_5 + \text{CH}_2(\text{CH}_2)_6\text{CH}_2\text{OH} \rightarrow$$

$$\text{CH}_3\text{COCH}_2\text{CO}_2\text{CH}(\text{CH}_2)_6\text{CH}_3 + \text{C}_2\text{H}_5\text{OH}$$

It has been suggested that the acetoacetates, benzoylacetates, or acetonedicarboxylates of the higher alcohols may serve for purposes of identification.[6]

The last step in a synthesis of acetol from bromoacetone is methanolysis (OS II, 5).

$$\text{CH}_3\text{COCH}_2\text{OCHO} + \text{CH}_3\text{OH} \rightarrow \text{CH}_3\text{COCH}_2\text{OH} + \text{HCO}_2\text{CH}_3$$

The synthesis of lactic esters is best effected by converting lactic acid into the polymeric form and then subjecting the polymer to alcoholysis. The preparation of allyl lactate is illustrative (OS III, 46).

$$n\text{HOCHCO}_2\text{H} \rightarrow \text{HO}\!\!\begin{bmatrix}\text{CHCO}_2\\ \mid\\ \text{CH}_3\end{bmatrix}_n\!\!\text{H} + (n-1)\text{H}_2\text{O}$$
$$\quad\ \mid$$
$$\quad\ \text{CH}_3$$

$$\text{HO}\!\!\begin{bmatrix}\text{CHCO}_2\\ \mid\\ \text{CH}_3\end{bmatrix}_n\!\!\text{H} + n\text{CH}_2\!\!=\!\!\text{CHCH}_2\text{OH} \rightarrow$$

$$n\text{HOCHCO}_2\text{CH}_2\text{CH}\!\!=\!\!\text{CH}_2 + \text{H}_2\text{O}$$

[6] A. R. Bader, L. O. Cummings, and H. A. Vogel, *J. Am. Chem. Soc.*, **73**, 4195 (1951).

An unusual example of alcoholysis is the formation of ethylene carbonate by the interaction of diethyl carbonate and ethylene glycol.

$$
\begin{array}{c}
CH_2OH \\
| \\
CH_2OH
\end{array}
+ \;
\begin{array}{c}
OC_2H_5 \\
\diagup \\
C{=}O \\
\diagdown \\
OC_2H_5
\end{array}
\;\rightarrow\;
\begin{array}{c}
CH_2O \\
| \quad\diagdown \\
\quad\quad C{=}O \\
| \quad\diagup \\
CH_2O
\end{array}
+ \; 2C_2H_5OH
$$

Alcoholysis occurs in the synthesis of polyethylene terephthalate from ethylene glycol and methyl terephthalate.

$$
n CH_3OC\underset{O}{\overset{O}{\|}}\!\!\!\!\bigcirc\!\!\!\!\underset{O}{\overset{O}{\|}}COCH_3 + n HOCH_2CH_2OH \;\rightarrow
$$

$$
CH_3O\left[\; C\underset{O}{\overset{O}{\|}}\!\!\!\!\bigcirc\!\!\!\!\underset{O}{\overset{O}{\|}}COCH_2CH_2O\;\right]_n H + (n-1)CH_3OH
$$

Glycidic esters undergo alcoholysis under mild conditions without opening of the epoxide ring. Methyl 2,3-epoxybutyrate, for example, reacts with allyl alcohol in the presence of magnesium methoxide to give allyl 2,3-epoxybutyrate in 68% yield.[7]

$$
CH_3CH\!\!\underset{O}{\overset{\diagdown\,\diagup}{-\!\!-}}\!\!CHCO_2CH_3 + CH_2{=}CHCH_2OH \;\rightarrow
$$

$$
CH_3CH\!\!\underset{O}{\overset{\diagdown\,\diagup}{-\!\!-}}\!\!CHCO_2CH_2CH{=}CH_2 + CH_3OH
$$

Alcoholysis of amides produces the corresponding esters and, in the special case of urea, may be used to make alkyl carbamates. An example is the formation of benzyl carbamate.

$$
CO(NH_2)_2 + C_6H_5CH_2OH \;\rightarrow\; C_6H_5CH_2OCONH_2 + NH_3
$$

Nitriles can be converted into esters by treatment with aqueous alcohols —a transformation that combines hydrolysis and alcoholysis. An example of this type of reaction is the preparation of ethyl phenylacetate from phenylacetonitrile (OS I, 270; 87% yield).

$$
C_6H_5CH_2CN + C_2H_5OH + H_2SO_4 + H_2O \;\rightarrow
$$
$$
C_3H_5CH_2CO_2C_2H_5 + NH_4HSO_4
$$

A common procedure for this type of reaction is to dissolve the nitrile in the appropriate alcohol and saturate the solution with gaseous hydrogen chloride.

[7] P. S. Starcher, F. C. Frostick, Jr., and B. Phillips, *J. Org. Chem.*, **25**, 1420 (1960).

Imidate hydrochlorides may be caused to react with water to yield esters or with ammonia to produce amidines. These reactions are illustrated by acetonitrile (OS I, 5).

$$CH_3CN + C_2H_5OH + HCl \rightarrow CH_3C\overset{\displaystyle NH \cdot HCl}{\underset{\displaystyle OC_2H_5}{\big\langle}}$$

with H_2O giving $CH_3CO_2C_2H_5$

with NH_3 giving $CH_3C\overset{\displaystyle NH \cdot HCl}{\underset{\displaystyle NH_2}{\big\langle}}$

A more general method of converting nitriles into amidines involves treatment with an ammonium sulfonate.

$$RCN + R'SO_3NH_4 \rightarrow \left(RCH\overset{\displaystyle NH}{\underset{\displaystyle NH_2}{\big\langle}} \right) \cdot R'SO_3H$$

Conversion of phenylacetonitrile into esters can be carried out to advantage by way of the corresponding imidate hydrobromide.[8] When an imidate hydrochloride is treated with an alcohol, an ortho ester may be produced. Phenylacetonitrile, for example, is converted into ethyl ortho-phenylacetate by reaction with an ethanolic solution of hydrogen chloride, followed by ethanolysis of the resulting imidate hydrochloride.

$$C_6H_5CH_2CN \rightarrow C_6H_5CH_2\overset{\displaystyle OC_2H_5}{\underset{}{C}}=NH \cdot HCl \rightarrow C_6H_5CH_2C(OC_2H_5)_3$$

Base-catalyzed addition of alcohols to nitriles produces imidates; the formation of methyl m-nitrobenzimidate is an example.[9]

[8] D. J. Morgan, *Chem. and Ind.*, 854 (1959).
[9] F. C. Schaefer and G. A. Peters, *J. Org. Chem.*, **26**, 412 (1961).

Esterification

Acids also undergo alcoholysis, the hydroxyl group being replaced by an alkoxyl group. This type of reaction, generally known as *esterification*, is believed to proceed in the following way.

$$
\begin{array}{ccc}
\text{O} & & \overset{+}{\text{O}}\text{H} \\
\parallel & & \parallel \\
\text{R}-\text{C}-\text{OH} + \text{H}^+ & \rightleftharpoons & \text{R}\text{C}-\text{OH}
\end{array}
$$

$$
\begin{array}{ccc}
\overset{+}{\text{O}}\text{H} & \text{OH}\quad\text{R} & \text{OH} \\
\parallel & |\qquad\ | & | \\
\text{R}\text{C}-\text{OH} + \text{ROH} \rightleftharpoons \text{R}-\text{C}\!-\!-\!\text{O}^+ & \rightarrow & \text{R}\text{C}-\text{OR} + \text{H}^+ \\
& |\qquad\ | & | \\
& \text{OH}\quad\text{H} & \text{OH}
\end{array}
$$

The mono ester of the ortho acid is converted into the ester by loss of the elements of water.

The reverse reaction, hydrolysis, follows the same sequence of changes taken in the reverse order. Base-catalyzed hydrolysis, saponification, is believed to involve the addition of hydroxyl ion to the carbonyl carbon atom, followed by the release of the alkoxyl group. By use of the oxygen isotope of mass 18 it has been proved that the rupture occurs on the carbonyl rather than the alkyl side of the ether linkage.

In practice it is usual to employ one of the reactants, selected on the basis of availability and ease of recovery, in large excess in order to convert the other as completely as possible into the ester. In many cases the ester can be obtained in satisfactory yield by removal of one of the reactants during the process. Methyl pyruvate is made by heating a mixture of pyruvic acid, methanol, and benzene in the presence of p-toluenesulfonic acid. A methyl ester column is employed, which permits removal of the water as it forms (OS III, 610; 71% yield).

$$\text{CH}_3\text{COCO}_2\text{H} + \text{CH}_3\text{OH} \rightleftharpoons \text{CH}_3\text{COCO}_2\text{CH}_3 + \text{H}_2\text{O}$$

Esterification can be caused to proceed to virtual completion also by removal of the ester as it is produced. An example is the commercial preparation of ethyl acetate from aqueous solutions of ethanol, acetic acid, and sulfuric acid. It happens that the lowest-boiling liquid, that which is taken off by use of an efficient column, is a ternary mixture of ethyl acetate (83.2%), ethanol (9%), and water (7.8%). The ethanol is removed by washing with water. Many of the simpler esters can be made in this way.

Dimethyl acetylenedicarboxylate is produced in 88% yield by treating acetylenedicarboxylic acid with methanol in large excess in the presence of sulfuric acid (OS 32, 55).

$$\begin{array}{c} CCO_2H \\ \| \\ CCO_2H \end{array} + 2CH_3OH \rightarrow \begin{array}{c} CCO_2CH_3 \\ \| \\ CCO_2CH_3 \end{array} + 2H_2O$$

An ingenious device is to return the distillate to the reaction flask by way of a Soxhlet extractor containing calcium carbide, which removes the water. An example of the use of this procedure is the esterification of o-toluic acid with ethanol to produce ethyl o-toluate.

Diethyl adipate can be produced in nearly quantitative yields by heating a mixture of ethanol and adipic acid in the presence of sulfuric acid, the water being removed by adding toluene to the reaction mixture and conducting the reaction in such a way that distillation occurs; the distillate is an azeotropic mixture of toluene, ethanol, and water (OS II, 264; 97% yield).

Another procedure for removing water is to carry out the esterification in the presence of anhydrous calcium chloride; the preparation of ethyl n-tridecanoate is an example (OS II, 292). Dimethyl oxalate can be made satisfactorily by heating a mixture of anhydrous oxalic acid (OS I, 421) and methanol in the presence of concentrated sulfuric acid (OS II, 414; 76% yield).

Bromoacetic acid and ethanol afford ethyl bromoacetate in 70% yield when the esterification is carried out in a special apparatus permitting the removal of the water, which collects at the bottom of the reaction vessel (OS III, 381).

The necessity for continuous removal of water can be avoided by operating in a system composed of an aqueous and a non-aqueous layer. When a mixture of adipic acid, methanol, sulfuric acid, and ethylene chloride is heated, dimethyl adipate passes into the ethylene chloride layer; the upper layer contains the water.[10]

Acetone dimethyl acetal has been employed as a water scavenger.

$$\begin{array}{c} CH_3 \quad OCH_3 \\ \diagdown \diagup \\ C \\ \diagup \diagdown \\ CH_3 \quad OCH_3 \end{array} + H_2O \xrightarrow{H^+} \begin{array}{c} CH_3 \\ \diagdown \\ C{=}O + 2CH_3OH \\ \diagup \\ CH_3 \end{array}$$

It serves, for example, in the esterification of oxalic acid; in the presence of p-toluenesulfonic acid, one mole of oxalic acid dihydrate reacts with four

[10] R. O. Clinton and S. C. Laskowski, *J. Am. Chem. Soc.*, **70**, 3135 (1948).

moles of the acetal to give dimethyl oxalate. By distillation of methanol and acetone at the end of the reaction, the yield is raised to 91%.[11]

Esters can be produced in satisfactory yield by heating an alcohol with the ammonium salt of an acid under conditions permitting removal of both ammonia and water from the reaction mixture. The method is general and is especially to be recommended where acid conditions are deleterious to the reactants. An example is the preparation of 2-ethylhexyl glycolate; the yield is 68%.[12]

$$\text{HOCH}_2\text{CO}_2\text{NH}_4 + \begin{matrix} \text{C}_2\text{H}_5 \\ \diagdown \\ \text{CHCH}_2\text{OH} \\ \diagup \\ \text{C}_4\text{H}_9 \end{matrix} \rightarrow$$

$$\text{HOCH}_2\text{CO}_2\text{CH}_2\text{CH} \begin{matrix} \diagup \text{C}_2\text{H}_5 \\ \\ \diagdown \text{C}_4\text{H}_9 \end{matrix} + \text{NH}_3 + \text{H}_2\text{O}$$

A superior method for esterification of highly hindered acids consists in dissolving the acid in approximately 100% sulfuric acid and pouring the solution into an alcohol. The mechanism proposed for this reaction involves the removal of the hydroxyl group.

$$\overset{\text{O}}{\overset{\|}{\text{RC}}}\text{—OH} + \text{HA} \rightleftharpoons [\text{RC}{=}\text{O}]^+ + \text{H}_2\text{O} + \text{A}^-$$

$$[\text{RC}{=}\text{O}]^+ + \text{ROH} + \text{A}^- \rightleftharpoons \overset{\text{O}}{\overset{\|}{\text{RC}}}\text{—OR} + \text{HA}$$

Ethyl mesitoate is formed in this way, for example. Also, such esters are hydrolyzed by contact with sulfuric acid followed by treatment with water. Esters of benzoic acids are not produced, however, by this procedure, the acid being recovered. The explanation of the difference between the hindered and the unhindered acids is sought in the resonance stabilization of the protonated acid, possible only with the unhindered acid. The dissociation required is opposed by the resonance interaction with the ring.[13]

$$\overset{\overset{+}{\text{O}}\text{H}}{\overset{\|}{\text{RC}}}\text{—OH} \rightarrow \text{R}\overset{+}{\text{C}}{=}\text{O} + \text{H}_2\text{O}$$

[11] N. B. Lorette and J. H. Brown, Jr., *J. Org. Chem.*, **24**, 261 (1959).

[12] E. M. Filachione, E. J. Costello, and C. H. Fisher, *J. Am. Chem. Soc.*, **73**, 5265 (1951).

[13] P. D. Bartlett, *J. Chem. Education*, **30**, 22 (1953).

It is possible to effect half esterification of dicarboxylic acids by employing equimolecular amounts of the reactants. Ethyl hydrogen sebacate, for example, can be produced in yields of 70% or higher by this method. The reaction is conducted in the presence of diethyl sebacate to minimize the formation of this ester, which is the chief by-product (OS II, 276).

$$(CH_2)_8 \begin{array}{c} CO_2H \\ \\ CO_2H \end{array} + C_2H_5OH \xrightarrow{HCl} (CH_2)_8 \begin{array}{c} CO_2H \\ \\ CO_2C_2H_5 \end{array} + H_2O$$

Lactonization

Hydroxy acids may undergo esterification intramolecularly to yield lactones. Lactonization occurs readily with γ- and δ-hydroxy acids, since the resulting cycles are five- and six-membered, respectively. This type of behavior is encountered not only in hydroxy derivatives of aliphatic acids but in certain phenolic acids also.

γ-Keto acids, when distilled or heated with acetic anhydride, lose water to yield unsaturated lactones. Presumably, lactols (p. 396) are formed as intermediates. β-Benzoylpropionic acid, for example, yields a mixture of two isomeric lactones.

$$\underset{\underset{OH}{|}}{\overset{\overset{O}{\|}}{C_6H_5CCH_2CH_2C}}=O \rightarrow \underset{\underset{O}{\lfloor}}{\overset{\overset{OH}{|}}{C_6H_5CCH_2CH_2C}}=O \rightarrow$$

$$\underset{\lfloor O \rfloor}{C_6H_5CHCH=CHC}=O \quad \text{and} \quad \underset{\lfloor O \rfloor}{C_6H_5C=CHCH_2C}=O$$

Formation of the angelica lactones from levulinic acid appears to be similar. By use of 1% phosphoric acid it is possible to obtain the α-isomer in 95% yield.[14]

$$\underset{\underset{OH}{|}}{\overset{\overset{O}{\|}}{CH_3CCH_2CH_2C}}=O \rightarrow \underset{\lfloor O \rfloor}{\overset{\overset{OH}{|}}{CH_3CCH_2CH_2C}}=O \rightarrow \underset{\lfloor O \rfloor}{CH_3C=CHCH_2C}=O$$

Polyesterification

Hydroxy acids may form polyesters by intermolecular self-esterification. Similar results are obtained by condensing polyhydroxy compounds with

[14] J. H. Helberger, S. Ulubay, and H. Civelekoglu, *Ann.*, **561**, 215 (1949)

polybasic acids, for such compounds form esters that are at the same time hydroxy acids. An example is the reaction of ethylene glycol with oxalic acid, the first step of which is the following.

$$HOCH_2CH_2OH + HOC\overset{\overset{O}{\|}}{}-\overset{\overset{O}{\|}}{C}OH \rightarrow HOCH_2CH_2OC\overset{\overset{O}{\|}}{}-\overset{\overset{O}{\|}}{C}OH + H_2O$$

Polyesterification has furnished especially interesting results because it is a reversible process, permitting ready interconversion of products. Many six-membered lactones and cyclic esters change spontaneously into the corresponding polyesters. δ-Valerolactone, trimethylene carbonate, and ethylene oxalate are examples.

$$nCH_2CH_2CH_2CH_2C{=}O \xrightarrow{H_2O} HO[(CH_2)_4\overset{\overset{O}{\|}}{C}O]_nH$$
$$\underset{O}{\underline{\qquad\qquad}}$$

δ-Valerolactone

$$\begin{array}{c} CH_2\text{——}O \\ | \qquad\qquad \backslash \\ nCH_2 \qquad\quad C{=}O \xrightarrow{H_2O} HO[(CH_2)_3O\overset{\overset{O}{\|}}{C}O]_nH \\ | \qquad\qquad / \\ CH_2\text{——}O \end{array}$$

Trimethylene
carbonate

$$n \begin{array}{|cc|} CH_2OC{=}O \\ | \quad\quad | \\ CH_2OC{=}O \end{array} \xrightarrow{H_2O} HO[CH_2CH_2O\overset{\overset{O}{\|}}{C}{-}\overset{\overset{O}{\|}}{C}O]_nH$$

Ethylene
oxalate

By contrast, five-membered lactones and esters are stable. Examples are γ-butyrolactone and ethylene carbonate.

$$CH_2CH_2CH_2C{=}O$$
$$\underline{\qquad O \qquad}$$

γ-Butyrolactone

$$\begin{array}{c} CH_2\text{——}O \\ | \qquad\qquad \backslash \\ \qquad\qquad\qquad C{=}O \\ | \qquad\qquad / \\ CH_2\text{——}O \end{array}$$

Ethylene carbonate

As a rule lactones and cyclic esters having fewer than five members, or more than six readily form polyesters. Many linear polyesters, on the other hand, have been depolymerized under the influence of catalysts to yield monomeric and dimeric cyclic esters. An example is the conversion of the polyester from 14-hydroxymyristic acid into the corresponding monomer and dimer.

$$CH_2(CH_2)_{12}C{=}O$$

Monomer

$$CH_2(CH_2)_{12}{-}C{=}O$$
$$O{=}C{-}(CH_2)_{12}{-}CH_2$$

Dimer

If the polyester is heated at 270° under 1 millimeter of pressure, the yield of monomer is high, being fifteen times that of the dimer. The monomer is formed much less readily from the polyester of 10-hydroxy-capric acid. In this case the amount of dimer is about six times that of the monomer.

$$CH_2(CH_2)_8C{=}O$$

Monomer

$$CH_2(CH_2)_8C{=}O$$
$$O{=}C(CH_2)_8{-}CH_2$$

Dimer

This difference illustrates the well-established rule that very large rings are more easily formed than those of intermediate size.

If either the alcohol or the acid has more than two functional groups, *cross-linking* occurs, and the polyester is no longer linear but *three dimensional*. The polyester formed by treating glycerol with phthalic anhydride, for example, has a structure of the following type.

$$-O_2C\overbrace{\hspace{1cm}}-CO_2CH_2CHCH_2O_2C-\overbrace{\hspace{1cm}}-CO_2-$$

$$\overbrace{\hspace{1cm}}CO_2\atop CO_2$$

$$-O_2C\overbrace{\hspace{1cm}}-CO_2CH_2CHCH_2O_2C-\overbrace{\hspace{1cm}}-CO_2-$$

Three-dimensional polymers of this sort are known as *glyptals* or *alkyd resins* and are important industrially. Linear esters soften when heated and are said to be thermoplastic. Cross-linking, if it proceeds sufficiently far, deprives a polymer of its plasticity. In order to get a tractable product the reaction is modified by the use of glycol with glycerol or of a monobasic acid to replace part of the phthalic anhydride. By a proper balance of the reactive groups, flexible materials can be obtained with the correct degree of hardness and solubility for excellent surface coatings.

Polyethylene terephthalate (p. 328) is a linear, highly crystalline polyester that has achieved importance as a synthetic fiber (Terylene, Dacron) and as a synthetic film-forming material (Mylar). Most polyesters unless highly cross-linked to produce insolubility are hydrolyzed readily. But the highly crystalline polyethylene terephthalate is also extremely insoluble and does not undergo hydrolysis readily. Cold drawing of the material is necessary to give proper orientation for crystallization and increase in tensile strength.

The polycarbonate made by condensing *bis*phenol-A with phosgene forms extremely resistant materials which can be used in protective helmets.

$$-\overset{\overset{\textstyle O}{\|}}{OCO}\left[\underset{}{\bigcirc}-\underset{\underset{\textstyle CH_3}{|}}{\overset{\overset{\textstyle CH_3}{|}}{C}}-\bigcirc \overset{\overset{\textstyle O}{\|}}{OCO}\right]_n\bigcirc-$$

Ammonolysis

Ammonolysis of an acid chloride or anhydride with ammonia or a primary or secondary amine yields an amide. The formation of isobutyramide (OS III, 490) illustrates the method of making primary amides; the yield is 83%.

$$(CH_3)_2CHCOCl + 2NH_3 \rightarrow (CH_3)_2CHCONH_2 + NH_4Cl$$

Amino acids are often acylated for protective or other reasons. An example is the formation of hippuric acid (OS II, 328), the benzoyl derivative of glycine.

$$C_6H_5COCl + H_2NCH_2CO_2H \rightarrow C_6H_5CONHCH_2CO_2H + HCl$$

The fact that acid chlorides undergo ammonolysis faster than esters is illustrated by the preparation of methyl sebacamate (OS III, 613; 95% yield).

$$(CH_2)_8\overset{\textstyle COCl}{\underset{\textstyle CO_2CH_3}{<}} \xrightarrow{NH_3} (CH_2)_8\overset{\textstyle CONH_2}{\underset{\textstyle CO_2CH_3}{<}}$$

A similar behavior is exhibited by the chloroformates, which react with amines to generate urethans or carbamates. Ammonia and methylamine react with ethyl chloroformate to yield ethyl carbamate and ethyl N-methylcarbamate (OS II, 278; 90% yield), respectively. If sodium is added to the reaction mixture along with more ethyl chloroformate, ethyl carbamate can be doubly acylated to give triethyl N-tricarboxylate (OS III, 415; 57% yield).

$$\underset{\underset{\|}{H_2NCOC_2H_5}}{\overset{O}{}} + 2Cl\underset{\underset{\|}{COC_2H_5}}{\overset{O}{}} + 2Na \rightarrow N(\underset{\underset{\|}{COC_2H_5})_3}{\overset{O}{}} + 2NaCl + H_2$$

A similar reaction is involved in the preparation of the carbobenzoxy derivative of glycine (OS III, 168).

$$C_6H_5CH_2OCOCl + H_2NCH_2CO_2H \rightarrow$$
$$C_6H_5CH_2OCONHCH_2CO_2H + HCl$$

In these reactions alkali is added to neutralize the hydrochloric acid that is generated, according to the Schotten-Baumann method (p. 325).

An example of the formation of a tertiary amide is the benzoylation of piperidine (OS I, 99); the yield of N-benzoylpiperidine is 81%.

$$C_6H_5COCl + \underset{\substack{N \\ H}}{\bigcirc} \rightarrow \underset{\substack{N \\ COC_6H_5}}{\bigcirc} + HCl$$

N,N-Dimethylamides can be made conveniently by an exchange reaction brought about by treating an acid chloride or anhydride with dimethylformamide. When benzoyl chloride and dimethylformamide are heated together, for example, N,N-dimethylbenzamide is produced in 97% yield.[15]

Primary amines react with phosgene to give the corresponding carbamyl chlorides, which lose hydrogen chloride to yield isocyanates. Phenyl isocyanate is prepared from aniline in this way.

$$C_6H_5NH_2 \xrightarrow{COCl_2} C_6H_5NHCOCl \xrightarrow{-HCl} C_6H_5N{=}C{=}O$$

p-Chlorophenyl isocyanate (OS I, 165; 81% yield) and p-nitrophenyl isocyanate (OS II, 453; 95% yield) are made in a similar manner. This procedure has been applied successfully to diamines, which give diisocyanates. Hexamethylenediamine hydrochloride yields hexamethylene diisocyanate.

$$[H_3N(CH_2)_6NH_3]Cl_2 + 2COCl_2 \rightarrow OCN(CH_2)_6NCO + 6HCl$$

[15] G. M. Coppinger, *J. Am. Chem. Soc.*, **76**, 1372 (1954).

Isothiocyanates are produced by the interaction of primary amines and thiophosgene, as is illustrated by the synthesis of p-chlorophenyl isothiocyanate (OS I, 165; 81% yield).

$$Cl\langle\bigcirc\rangle NH_2 + CSCl_2 \rightarrow Cl\langle\bigcirc\rangle N{=}C{=}S + 2HCl$$

The use of acetic anhydride is illustrated by the acetylation of glycine (OS II, 11; 92% yield) and p-anisidine (OS III, 661).

$$(CH_3CO)_2O + H_2NCH_2CO_2H \rightarrow CH_3CONHCH_2CO_2H + CH_3CO_2H$$

$$(CH_3CO)_2O + p\text{-}H_2NC_6H_4OCH_3 \rightarrow p\text{-}CH_3CONHC_6H_4OCH_3 + CH_3CO_2H$$

When hydrazine is employed in place of ammonia, a hydrazide is produced. N,N′-Dibenzoylhydrazine is an example (OS II, 208).

$$2C_6H_5COCl + 2H_2NNH_2 \rightarrow C_6H_5CONHNHCOC_6H_5 + H_2NNH_2{\cdot}2HCl$$

Primary amines are capable of reacting with two moles of an acylating agent to yield an imide. When aniline is heated with acetic anhydride, for example, the diacetyl derivative is formed, acetanilide being an intermediate.

$$C_6H_5NH_2 + 2(CH_3CO)_2O \rightarrow C_6H_5N(COCH_3)_2 + 2CH_3CO_2H$$

The formation of phthalimide from phthalic anhydride and ammonia (OS I, 457) involves a similar reaction; the yield is nearly quantitative.

N-Phthalyl-β-phenylalanine is formed by interaction of the amino acid with phthalic anhydride (OS **40**, 82; yield 95%).

$$\bigcirc\begin{matrix}-CO\\ \\-CO\end{matrix}O + \begin{matrix}CH_2C_6H_5\\ | \\ CHCO_2H \\ | \\ NH_2\end{matrix} \xrightarrow{(C_2H_5)_3N} \bigcirc\begin{matrix}-CO\\ \\-CO\end{matrix}NCHCH_2C_6H_5 \atop CO_2H$$

The β-bromoethyl derivative of phthalimide may be made conveniently by condensing ethanolamine with phthalic anhydride and replacing the hydroxyl group by the action of phosphorus tribromide (OS **32**, 18).

The reaction of sulfonyl chlorides with amines is especially useful in characterizing primary and secondary amines. The sulfonamides not only are suitable derivatives for purposes of identification but also serve as intermediates in the Hinsberg method of separating amines. The usual procedure for the preparation of sulfonamides is to treat an amine with a sulfonyl chloride in the presence of sodium hydroxide.

Hydrazides are formed by reaction of sulfonyl chlorides with hydrazine; the preparation of p-toluenesulfonylhydrazide is an example (OS **40**, 93; 90% yield).

$$CH_3-\!\!\!\bigcirc\!\!\!-SO_2Cl + 2H_2NNH_2 \rightarrow$$

$$CH_3-\!\!\!\bigcirc\!\!\!-SO_2NHNH_2 + H_2NNH_2 \cdot HCl$$

Azide ion is capable of effecting nucleophilic displacement also. When acid chlorides are treated with sodium azide, for instance, the corresponding acyl azide is produced. The preparation of m-nitrobenzazide is an example (OS **33**, 53; yield 90%).

$$m\text{-}O_2NC_6H_4COCl + NaN_3 \rightarrow m\text{-}O_2NC_6H_4CON_3 + NaCl$$

Ammonolysis of esters provides an important route to amides, typical syntheses being those of chloroacetamide (OS I, 153) and cyanoacetamide (OS I, 179); the yields are 84 and 88%, respectively.

$$ClCH_2CO_2C_2H_5 + NH_3 \rightarrow ClCH_2CONH_2 + C_2H_5OH$$

$$NCCH_2CO_2C_2H_5 + NH_3 \rightarrow NCCH_2CONH_2 + C_2H_5OH$$

Ammonolysis is particularly useful in the synthesis of hydroxy amides, since the corresponding acids cannot form acid chlorides or anhydrides. Lactamide, for example, is obtained in 74% yield by ammonolysis of ethyl lactate (OS III, 516).

$$\underset{\overset{|}{OH}}{CH_3CHCO_2C_2H_5} + NH_3 \rightarrow \underset{\overset{|}{OH}}{CH_3CHCONH_2} + C_2H_5OH$$

When primary amines such as isobutyl- , allyl- , cyclohexyl- , and benzylamine are employed, the corresponding N-substituted amides form in yields, many of which are above 90%. Secondary amines can be used also; piperidine and methyl lactate give the piperidide in 84% yield.[16]

$$\underset{\overset{|}{OH}}{CH_3CHCO_2CH_3} + HN\!\!\bigcirc \rightarrow \underset{\overset{|}{OH}}{CH_3CHCON}\!\!\bigcirc + CH_3OH$$

Ammonolysis is important in the preparation of β-keto amides, which are obtained by way of the ester, the acids being unstable. Benzoylacetanilide is an example [OS III, 108 (76% yield); **37**, 2 (84% yield)].

$$C_6H_5COCH_2CO_2C_2H_5 + C_6H_5NH_2 \rightarrow$$

$$C_6H_5COCH_2CONHC_6H_5 + C_2H_5OH$$

[16] W. P. Ratchford and C. H. Fisher, *J. Org. Chem.*, **15**, 317 (1950).

Another example is the preparation of salicyl-*o*-toluide from phenyl salicylate and *o*-toluidine (OS III, 765; 77% yield).

Esters that react sluggishly with aromatic amines can be transformed into the corresponding anilides by the action of alkali metal derivatives of the amines. An example is the reaction of the sodium derivative of aniline with diethyl diethylmalonate; the *bis*-anilide is obtained in 75% yield.[17]

γ-Nitro esters undergo reduction to the corresponding amino esters, which form lactams. An illustration is the synthesis of 5,5-dimethyl-2-pyrrolidone (OS 32, 59; 96% yield).

The synthesis of parabanic acid from diethyl oxalate and urea is similar (OS **37**, 71; 76% yield).

Similarly diethyl malonate and urea form barbituric acid (OS II, 60; 78% yield).

[17] E. S. Stern, *Chem. and Ind.*, 277 (1956).

$$
\begin{array}{ccc}
\underset{|}{CO_2C_2H_5} & \underset{|}{NH_2} & \quad \overset{CO\text{——}NH}{\underset{|}{\quad\quad|}} \\
\underset{|}{CH_2} & + \underset{|}{C}{=}O & \xrightarrow{NaOC_2H_5} \quad \underset{|}{CH_2} \quad \underset{|}{CO} + 2C_2H_5OH \\
CO_2C_2H_5 & NH_2 & \quad CO\text{——}NH
\end{array}
$$

Ortho esters, being sensitive to acids, undergo ammonolysis in contact with amine salts. Ethyl orthoformate, for example, reacts with p-chloroaniline in the presence of hydrochloric acid to give ethyl N-p-chlorophenylformimidate.

$$p\text{-ClC}_6\text{H}_4\text{NH}_2 + (C_2H_5O)_3CH \rightarrow p\text{-ClC}_6\text{H}_4\text{N}{=}\text{CHOC}_2\text{H}_5 + 2C_2H_5OH$$

If sulfuric acid is used, the formimidate rearranges to N-ethyl-p-chloroformanilide.

$$p\text{-ClC}_6\text{H}_4\text{N}{=}\text{CHOC}_2\text{H}_5 \rightarrow p\text{-ClC}_6\text{H}_4\overset{\overset{\displaystyle C_2H_5}{|}}{N}\text{CHO}$$

Hydrolysis of the anilide gives N-ethyl-p-chloroaniline (OS **38**, 29). This synthesis has been found to be generally useful for making pure monoalkyl anilines.

Ammonolysis of the acetone derivative of mandelic acid, which may be classified as an ester, provides a convenient route to mandelamide (OS III, 536; yield 62%).

$$
\begin{array}{c}
\underset{|}{C_6H_5CH}\text{——}\underset{|}{CO} \\
\underset{\diagdown}{O} \quad \underset{\diagup}{O} \quad + NH_3 \rightarrow C_6H_5\underset{\underset{\displaystyle OH}{|}}{CH}CONH_2 + CH_3COCH_3 \\
C(CH_3)_2
\end{array}
$$

Esters react with hydroxylamine to yield hydroxamic acids; ethyl benzoate, for example, gives benzohydroxamic acid (OS II, 67; 46% yield).

$$C_6H_5CO_2C_2H_5 + H_2NOH \rightarrow C_6H_5CONHOH + C_2H_5OH$$

With ferric chloride solutions, hydroxamic acids give a deep magenta color, which forms the basis of a qualitative test for this type of compound. A test for carboxylic esters consists in treating the compound with hydroxylamine and noting the color produced by adding ferric chloride to the mixture.[18]

Ethyl carbamate reacts with hydroxylamine to give hydroxyurea (OS **40**, 60; 73% yield).

$$H_2NCO_2C_2H_5 + H_2NOH \rightarrow H_2NCONHOH + C_2H_5OH$$

[18] R. E. Buckles and C. J. Thelen, *Anal. Chem.*, **22**, 676 (1950).

Hydrazinolysis of esters produces hydrazides, an example being the production of formhydrazide from ethyl formate (OS III, 96).

$$HCO_2C_2H_5 + H_2NNH_2 \cdot H_2O \rightarrow HCONHNH_2 + C_2H_5OH + H_2O$$

One of the drawbacks of the Gabriel method (p. 277) is that the substituted phthalimides may be difficult to hydrolyze. Hydrazine attacks phthalimides readily and facilitates liberation of the amines.

A method of making solid derivatives, useful in the identification of esters, consists in treating the esters with phenylhydrazine in the presence of phosphoric acid; the products are phenylhydrazides.[19]

$$RCO_2R' + C_6H_5NHNH_2 \rightarrow RCONHNHC_6H_5 + R'OH$$

Ammonolysis of amides serves to produce one amide from another; it is a general reaction conveniently brought about by melting the hydrochloride of an amine with an amide. The amino group is acylated in a short time, and the new amide is obtained in superior yields. An example is the preparation of N-acetyl-1-naphthylamine; the yield is 80%.[20]

Urea is particularly well suited for this purpose. Phenylurea is prepared by heating urea with aniline hydrochloride (OS I, 453).

$$C_6H_5NH_2 \cdot HCl + CO(NH_2)_2 \rightarrow C_6H_5NHCONH_2 + NH_4Cl$$

sym-Diphenylurea can be produced from phenylurea in a similar way (OS I, 453).

$$C_6H_5NH_2 \cdot HCl + C_6H_5NHCONH_2 \rightarrow C_6H_5NHCONHC_6H_5 + NH_4Cl$$

When phenylurea is heated with hydrazine hydrate, phenylsemicarbazide is formed (OS I, 450; 40% yield).

$$C_6H_5NHCONH_2 + H_2NNH_2 \cdot H_2O \rightarrow C_6H_5NHCONHNH_2 + NH_3 + H_2O$$

The action of methylamine hydrochloride on nitroguanidine serves similarly to produce 1-methyl-3-nitroguanidine. The —NH₂ group is replaced preferentially.

---

[19] T. O. Jones, R. E. Halter, and W. L. Myers, *J. Am. Chem. Soc.*, **75**, 6055 (1953).
[20] A. Galat and G. Elion, *J. Am. Chem. Soc.*, **65**, 1566 (1943).

$$CH_3NH_2 \cdot HCl + H_2N\overset{\displaystyle NH}{\overset{\|}{C}}NHNO_2 + KOH \rightarrow$$

$$CH_3NH\overset{\displaystyle NH}{\overset{\|}{C}}NHNO_2 + NH_3 + KCl + H_2O$$

Nitrourea, on the other hand, suffers loss of the nitroamino group; with dimethylamine, for example, the product is *unsym*-dimethylurea (OS **32**, 61; yield 68%).

$$(CH_3)_2NH + H_2NCONHNO_2 \rightarrow (CH_3)_2NCONH_2 + N_2O + H_2O$$

This method is general for making ureas.

Amide interchange is reversible, of course. When a mixture of *p*-toluidine and acetanilide is heated on a steam bath in the presence of benzene and benzoic acid, for example, the following equilibrium is set up.[21]

$$C_6H_5NHCOCH_3 + CH_3C_6H_4NH_2 \rightleftharpoons C_6H_5NH_2 + CH_3CONHC_6H_4CH_3$$

Ammonolysis of acids may be effected simply by heating the ammonium salt of the acid; an example is the conversion of ammonium acetate to acetamide (OS I, 3; 90% yield). N-Methylformanilide is produced by heating methylaniline with formic acid in toluene, the water being removed by continuous distillation of the solvent (OS III, 590; 97% yield).

$$C_6H_5NHCH_3 + HCO_2H \rightarrow C_6H_5N\underset{CH_3}{\overset{CHO}{<}} + H_2O$$

Lactam formation occurs when suitably constituted amino acids are dehydrated; with nitro acids the first step is reduction of the nitro group. An example is the preparation of 6-carboxyindole from 2-nitro-4-carboxyphenylacetic acid.[22]

The formation of *cyclic imides* is illustrated by the preparation of glutarimide; the corresponding monoamide is heated at 220 to 225° (OS **37**, 47).

[21] R. Jaunin, *Helv. Chim. Acta*, **35**, 1414 (1952).
[22] E. Giovannini and P. Portmann, *Helv. Chim. Acta*, **31**, 1392 (1948).

Diketopiperazine formation takes place when α-amino acids are dehydrated. The simplest member of the class, diketopiperazine, is made by heating glycine in a sealed tube at 160°

$$2CH_2 \begin{array}{c} \diagup CO_2H \\ \\ \diagdown NH_2 \end{array} \rightarrow CH_2 \begin{array}{c} \diagup CONH \diagdown \\ \\ \diagdown NHCO \diagup \end{array} CH_2 + 2H_2O$$

At the same time a linear polypeptide is formed.

$$—NH[CH_2CONH]_nCH_2CO—$$

Diketopiperazine is produced also when esters of glycine are heated.

Polyamide formation

If the functional groups of the amino acids are sufficiently far apart, however, polyamides form the chief product. ε-Aminocaproic acid, for example, yields a polymer in equilibrium with a small amount of the seven-membered lactam.

$$—[NH(CH_2)_5CO]_n— \;\rightleftharpoons\; n\underset{\rule{2.5em}{0.4pt}}{HN(CH_2)_5CO}$$

Linear polyamides are produced also by the interaction of dibasic acids with diamines, an outstanding example being the reaction between adipic acid and hexamethylenediamine to give nylon, polyhexamethyleneadipamide.

$$HO_2C(CH_2)_4CO_2H + H_2N(CH_2)_6NH_2 \xrightarrow{-H_2O}$$

$$\cdots CO(CH_2)_4CONH(CH_2)_6NHCO(CH_2)_4CONH(CH_2)_6NH \cdots$$

Polyamides of this type that have sufficiently high molecular weights have the property of forming strong fibers.

A remarkable method of producing polyamides consists in heating the N-carboxyl anhydrides of α-amino acids. The reaction involves loss of carbon dioxide and takes the following course.

$$\begin{array}{c} HN—CO \\ | \qquad \diagdown \\ | \qquad \quad O \\ | \qquad \diagup \\ CHCO \\ | \\ R \end{array} \xrightarrow{-CO_2} \cdots \underset{R}{HNCHCO}\underset{R}{NHCHCO}\underset{R}{NHCHCO} \cdots$$

This type of polymer formation is involved in the preparation of polylysine; the ϵ-amino group is masked by conversion into the carbobenzoxy derivative, the actual monomer being ϵ-carbobenzoxy-α-carboxylysine anhydride (cb = $OCOCH_2C_6H_5$).[23]

$$
\begin{array}{c}
\text{HN——CO} \\
\quad\quad\quad \searrow \text{O} \xrightarrow{-CO_2} \cdots \text{HNCHCONHCHCONHCHCO} \cdots \\
\text{CH——CO} \\
\quad | \\
(\text{CH}_2)_4 \\
\quad | \\
\text{HNcb}
\end{array}
$$

$$
\cdots \text{HNCHCONHCHCONHCHCO} \cdots
$$

with $(\text{CH}_2)_4$ — $(\text{CH}_2)_4$ — $(\text{CH}_2)_4$ and HNcb   HNcb   HNcb

Treatment of the polymer with phosphonium iodide removes the carbobenzoxyl groups, producing the hydroiodide of polylysine.

$$
\cdots \text{HNCHCONHCHCONHCHCO} \cdots
$$

$(\text{CH}_2)_4$ $(\text{CH}_2)_4$ $(\text{CH}_2)_4$

NH_2 NH_2 NH_2

Polylysine

Cold drawing of polyamides is necessary to convert them into strong, tough fibers or films. In practice nylon is spun from a melt into fibers that are then stretched as much as 200 to 250% of their original length. This drawing or stretching seems to line up the linear polymers into an oriented state, which is made evident by the change in X-ray pattern as well as by a strong birefringence with parallel extinction and other properties not shown by undrawn material. Also there is a marked increase in elasticity and toughness, which seems to be due in part to hydrogen bonding between amide chains.

Dehydration of amides

When the dehydration of ammonium salts of carboxylic acids is carried out under sufficiently drastic conditions, nitriles are produced, presumably by way of the corresponding amides. Dehydration of amides provides, actually, an important synthetic route to nitriles; it usually is effected by heating with halides or anhydrides of organic or inorganic acids or by catalytic methods (CR **42**, 189). Perhaps the most useful chemical reagent for bringing about the change is phosphorus pentoxide, the usual procedure being to heat an intimate mixture of the reactants. A volatile nitrile such as isobutyronitrile may be distilled directly from the reaction mixture (OS III, 493; 86% yield).

[23] E. Katchalski, I. Grossfeld, and M. Frankel, *J. Am. Chem. Soc.*, **70**, 2094 (1948).

$$\begin{matrix} CH_3 \\ \diagdown \\ \quad CHCONH_2 \\ \diagup \\ CH_3 \end{matrix} \xrightarrow{P_2O_5} \begin{matrix} CH_3 \\ \diagdown \\ \quad CHCN + H_2O \\ \diagup \\ CH_3 \end{matrix}$$

Chloroacetonitrile can be produced in satisfactory yields by heating chloroacetamide with phosphorus pentoxide. Fumaronitrile is made in a similar way. This method has been applied successfully to nicotinamide also, nicotinonitrile being obtained in 84% yield (OS **33**, 52).

$$\text{[pyridine]}CONH_2 \rightarrow \text{[pyridine]}CN + H_2O$$

Methyl sebacamate is dehydrated with phosphorus pentoxide in tetrachloroethane, and the solution of the product, methyl ω-cyanopelargonate, in this solvent is removed by decantation (OS III, 584; 71% yield).

$$\begin{matrix} CONH_2 \\ \diagup \\ (CH_2)_8 \\ \diagdown \\ CO_2CH_3 \end{matrix} \xrightarrow{P_2O_5} \begin{matrix} CN \\ \diagup \\ (CH_2)_8 \\ \diagdown \\ CO_2CH_3 \end{matrix} + H_2O$$

Thionyl chloride is a popular reagent for dehydrating amides since the products, other than the nitriles, are gaseous. α-Ethylcapronitrile has been made by its use (OS **32**, 65; yield 94%).

$$\begin{matrix} CH_3CH_2CH_2CH_2 \\ \diagdown \\ \qquad CHCONH_2 + SOCl_2 \rightarrow \\ \diagup \\ CH_3CH_2 \end{matrix}$$

$$\begin{matrix} CH_3CH_2CH_2CH_2 \\ \diagdown \\ \qquad CHCN + SO_2 + 2HCl \\ \diagup \\ CH_3CH_2 \end{matrix}$$

Phosphorus pentachloride is another valuable reagent for converting amides into nitriles; an example is the dehydration of cyanoacetamide (OS II, 379; 80% yield).

$$NCCH_2CONH_2 + PCl_5 \rightarrow CH_2(CN)_2 + POCl_3 + 2HCl$$

The phosphorus oxychloride that is formed in this reaction is an effective dehydrating agent also.

$$2NCCH_2CONH_2 + POCl_3 \rightarrow 2CH_2(CN)_2 + HPO_3 + 3HCl$$

The combined effect is represented by the following equation, the final product being malononitrile.

$$3NCCH_2CONH_2 + PCl_5 \rightarrow 3CH_2(CN)_2 + HPO_3 + 5HCl$$

When heated alone, amides yield nitriles along with ammonia and free acid. Sebacamide, for example, gives sebaconitrile (49%) and ω-cyano-pelargonic acid (34%) (OS III, 768).

$$(CH_2)_8 \overset{CONH_2}{\underset{CONH_2}{}} \rightarrow (CH_2)_8 \overset{CN}{\underset{CN}{}} \quad \text{and} \quad (CH_2)_8 \overset{CN}{\underset{CO_2H}{}}$$

In several industrial processes the dehydration of amides is carried out in the vapor phase over a catalyst such as pumice. Hydrogen cyanide, acrylonitrile, and methacrylonitrile can be produced in this manner.

Another method is to pass a mixture of the acid and ammonia in the vapor phase over a catalyst. A modification of this procedure is illustrated by the synthesis of azelanitrile, which is produced by dropping molten azelaic acid on hot (500°) silica gel in a stream of ammonia (OS **34**, 4; 68% yield).

$$(CH_2)_7 \overset{CO_2H}{\underset{CO_2H}{}} + 2NH_3 \rightarrow (CH_2)_7 \overset{CN}{\underset{CN}{}} + 4H_2O$$

Also, nitriles are produced by blowing ammonia into molten acid at elevated temperatures. This technique is employed in making nitriles of long-chain fatty acids such as lauric acid. It serves, also, in the manufacture of adiponitrile. These reactions involve the dehydration of ammonium salts of acids, a method that has long been used to produce acetamide (p. 343). The synthesis of succinimide from ammonium succinate is similar (OS II, 562; 83% yield).

An analogous change is involved in the conversion of acids into benzimidazoles by heating with o-phenylenediamine. When formic acid is used, the product is benzimidazole (OS II, 65; 85% yield).

$$\underset{NH_2}{\overset{NH_2}{\bigcirc}} + HCO_2H \rightarrow \underset{N}{\overset{NH}{\bigcirc}} CH + 2H_2O$$

Dehydration of aldoximes has much in common with that of amides beside the fact that nitriles are produced. An example of this type of behavior is the conversion of the oxime of veratraldehyde into veratronitrile (OS II, 622; 76% yield).

Aldehydes can be converted into the corresponding nitriles simply by heating under reflux a mixture of the aldehyde, hydroxylamine hydrochloride, and sodium acetate in acetic acid.[24]

Dehydration of dimethylglyoxime, which can be effected by heating with succinic anhydride, brings about ring closure to give 3,4-dimethylfurazan (OS **34**, 40; yield 64%).

Acidolysis

Acidolysis of esters is illustrated by the interaction of ethyl α-chlorophenylacetate and acetic acid in the presence of hydrochloric acid to give α-chlorophenylacetic acid (OS **36**, 3; 82% yield).

$$C_6H_5CHCO_2C_2H_5 + CH_3CO_2H \xrightarrow{HCl} C_6H_5CHCO_2H + CH_3CO_2C_2H_5$$
$$\quad\; \underset{Cl}{|} \qquad\qquad\qquad\qquad\qquad\qquad \underset{Cl}{|}$$

Another example is the production of acrylic acid by heating methyl acrylate with formic acid in the presence of a little sulfuric acid. Hydroquinone is employed to prevent polymerization. Continuous removal of methyl formate makes possible yields as high as 78%.

$$CH_2{=}CHCO_2CH_3 + HCO_2H \xrightarrow{H_2SO_4} CH_2{=}CHCO_2H + HCO_2CH_3$$

An interesting synthesis of ketones involves acidolysis of acylmalonic esters. When diethyl lauroylmalonate is treated with boiling propionic

[24] J. H. Hunt, *Chem. and Ind.*, 1873 (1961).

acid containing a small amount of sulfuric acid, methyl n-undecyl ketone is produced in 97% yield.

$$\begin{array}{c} CO_2C_2H_5 \\ | \\ CH_3(CH_2)_{10}COCH + 2C_2H_5CO_2H \rightarrow \\ | \\ CO_2C_2H_5 \end{array}$$

$$CH_3(CH_2)_{10}COCH_3 + 2CO_2 + 2C_2H_5CO_2C_2H_5$$

The acyl malonates are made from malonic ester and acid chlorides; the over-all transformation is the conversion of a carboxylic acid into a methyl ketone containing one additional carbon atom.

When ethyl acetoacetate is heated with acetic acid at 130°, acidolysis occurs; acetone, carbon dioxide, and ethyl acetate are formed.[25]

$$CH_3COCH_2CO_2C_2H_5 + CH_3CO_2H \rightarrow$$
$$CH_3CO_2C_2H_5 + CH_3COCH_3 + CO_2$$

Acidolysis of acid chlorides and anhydrides takes place reversibly. When acetic anhydride and benzoic acid are brought together in the presence of a little phosphoric acid, the following equilibrium is set up (OS I, 91).

$$(CH_3CO)_2O + 2C_6H_5CO_2H \rightleftharpoons (C_6H_5CO)_2O + 2CH_3CO_2H$$

Undoubtedly the mixed anhydride, C_6H_5CO—O—$COCH_3$, is formed also. If acetic anhydride is used in excess, benzoic anhydride can be obtained in 74% yield. The anhydrides of higher acids in general can be made by treating the acids with acetic anhydride in excess and distilling the acetic acid that is formed. This method is particularly useful with succinic and glutaric acids; β-methylglutaric anhydride is an example (OS **38**, 52). Succinic anhydride is made in 95% yield by treatment of the acid with acetyl chloride (OS II, 560).

When d-tartaric acid is treated with acetic anhydride and a small amount of sulfuric acid, acetylation and ring closure occur to give diacetyl-d-tartaric anhydride (OS **35**, 49; 77% yield).

$$\begin{array}{c} HOCHCO_2H \\ | \\ HOCHCO_2H \end{array} \xrightarrow[H_2SO_4]{(CH_3CO)_2O} \begin{array}{c} CH_3CO_2CHCO \\ | \qquad\qquad\quad\searrow \\ \qquad\qquad\qquad O \\ | \qquad\qquad\quad\nearrow \\ CH_3CO_2CHCO \end{array}$$

---

[25] E. Cherbuliez and M. Fuld, *Helv. Chim. Acta*, **35**, 1280 (1952).

n-Heptanoic anhydride is produced in 83% yield by mixing equimolecular amounts of the acid, the acid chloride, and pyridine. The base serves to remove the hydrogen chloride (OS III, 28).

$$CH_3(CH_2)_5CO_2H + CH_3(CH_2)_5COCl + C_5H_5N \rightarrow$$

$$[CH_3(CH_2)_5CO]_2O + C_5H_5N \cdot HCl$$

This procedure is applicable to aromatic acids also, as is illustrated by the preparation of *p*-chlorobenzoic anhydride (OS III, 29; 98% yield).

The formation of anhydrides by the interaction of phosgene and an amino acid, involving a similar change, is illustrated by the behavior of glycine.

$$H_2NCH_2CO_2H \rightarrow \underset{\overset{|}{COCl}}{HNCH_2CO_2H} \rightarrow \underset{\overset{|}{CO-O}}{HNCH_2CO}$$

Acidolysis of acid chlorides may serve to convert them into more volatile ones; acetyl chloride is made conveniently by distilling an equimolecular mixture of acetic acid and benzoyl chloride.

$$C_6H_5COCl + CH_3CO_2H \rightleftharpoons C_6H_5CO_2H + CH_3COCl$$

Benzotrichloride can be used in this way also; when it is heated with acetic acid, a mixture of acetyl and benzoyl chlorides is formed. The two acid chlorides are separated easily by distillation.

$$C_6H_5CCl_3 + CH_3CO_2H \rightleftharpoons C_6H_5COCl + CH_3COCl + HCl$$

Oxalyl chloride is an excellent reagent for conversion of acids into acid chlorides and is especially valuable if a salt of the acid is employed.

$$RCO_2Na + \underset{\overset{|}{COCl}}{COCl} \rightarrow RCOCl + CO + CO_2 + NaCl$$

This reagent has proved to be useful with keto acids and unsaturated acids.[26]

Although formyl chloride and formic anhydride are unstable, formylation may nevertheless be accomplished by use of a mixture of formic acid and acetic anhydride.[27] An example is the formylation of α-amino-β-methoxybutyric acid (OS III, 813).

$$\underset{\overset{|}{OCH_3}\ \overset{|}{NH_2}}{CH_3CH-CHCO_2H} \xrightarrow[\text{HCO}_2\text{H}]{(CH_3CO)_2O} \underset{\overset{|}{OCH_3}\ \overset{|}{NHCHO}}{CH_3CH-CHCO_2H}$$

[26] A. L. Wilds and C. H. Shunk, *J. Am. Chem. Soc.*, **70**, 2427 (1948).
[27] C. W. Huffman, *J. Org. Chem.*, **23**, 727 (1958).

It is presumed that a mixed anhydride of acetic and formic acids is the reactant and that it reacts as rapidly as it is produced.

$$(CH_3CO)_2O + HCO_2H \rightleftharpoons CH_3\overset{\displaystyle O}{\overset{\|}{C}}-O-\overset{\displaystyle O}{\overset{\|}{C}}H + CH_3CO_2H$$

An acyl trifluoroacetate is formed when a carboxylic acid is mixed with trifluoroacetic anhydride. Benzoyl trifluoroacetate, for instance, is produced in this way in 55% yield.[28]

$$C_6H_5CO_2H + (CF_3CO)_2O \rightarrow C_6H_5CO-O-COCF_3 + CF_3CO_2H$$

The suggestion has been made that such mixed anhydrides dissociate so as to give predominantly the acylium ion (RCO^+) corresponding to the weaker acid.[29]

$$CF_3CO-O-COR \rightleftharpoons CF_3CO_2^- + RCO^+$$

When an alcohol or phenol is added to the resulting mixture, the corresponding halogen-free ester is the principal product. 2-Naphthol can be acetylated in satisfactory yields by this procedure.

Mixed anhydrides involving carbonic acid are also known. An example is the mixed benzoic carbonic anhydride, which is made by the interaction of benzoic acid and ethyl chlorocarbonate in the presence of triethylamine (OS **37**, 21).

$$C_6H_5CO_2H + C_2H_5OCOCl \xrightarrow{(C_2H_5)_3N} C_6H_5CO-O-CO_2C_2H_5 + HCl$$

Acidolysis of amides has been realized also; an example is the preparation of *n*-heptamide by heating *n*-heptoic acid with urea (OS **37**, 50; 74% yield).

$$2C_6H_{13}CO_2H + CO(NH_2)_2 \rightarrow C_6H_{13}CONH_2 + CO_2 + H_2O$$

One route to β-lactams (OR **9**, 388) involves intramolecular acidolysis of an amide group; an example is the following.

$$\begin{array}{l} (CH_3)_2C\!-\!\!-\!CO_2H \\ \;\;\;\;| \\ C_6H_5CH\!-\!NCOCH(CH_3)_2 \\ \;\;\;\;\;\;\;\;\;\;\;| \\ \;\;\;\;\;\;\;\;\;\;\;CH_2C_6H_5 \end{array} \rightarrow \begin{array}{l} (CH_3)_2C\!-\!\!-\!CO \\ \;\;\;\;|\;\;\;\;\;\;\;| \\ C_6H_5CH\!-\!NCH_2C_6H_5 \end{array} + (CH_3)_2CHCO_2H$$

[28] W. D. Emmons, K. S. McCallum, and A. F. Ferris, *J. Am. Chem. Soc.*, **75**, 6047 (1953).

[29] E. J. Bourne, J. E. B. Randles, J. C. Tatlow, and J. M. Tedder, *Nature*, **168**, 942 (1951).

Solvolytic Chain Cleavage

Solvolytic reactions of derivatives of acids are possible because of the presence of a leaving group such as NH_2^-, OR^-, and Cl^-. For aldehydes and ketones to undergo reactions of this type it would be necessary for a hydride or an alkide ion to function as the leaving group. Since these ions are very strong bases, solvolytic cleavage ordinarily does not occur. There are alkide ions, however, that are feebly basic and therefore lend themselves to chain fission. Examples are the enolate ions formed by cleavage of β-dicarbonyl compounds. The hydrolysis of acetylacetone may be taken as an example.

$$CH_3\overset{O}{\overset{\|}{C}}CH_2\overset{O}{\overset{\|}{C}}CH_3 \xrightarrow{OH^-} CH_3\overset{O^-}{\underset{O-H}{\overset{|}{C}}}CH_2\overset{O}{\overset{\|}{C}}CH_3 \rightarrow CH_3\overset{O}{\overset{\|}{C}} + {}^-CH_2\overset{O}{\overset{\|}{C}}CH_3$$

Ethanolysis of acetylacetone has been shown to be a reaction of the first order, a fact that has been interpreted to mean that the decomposition of the adduct formed by the diketone and an ethoxide ion is rate controlling (Hine, 293).[30]

$$CH_3\overset{O^-}{\underset{OC_2H_5}{\overset{|}{C}}}CH_2COCH_3 \rightarrow CH_3\overset{O}{\underset{OC_2H_5}{\overset{\|}{C}}} + {}^-CH_2COCH_3$$

In unsymmetrical 1,3-dicarbonyl compounds the break occurs at the more reactive of the two carbonyl groups. In benzoylacetone and ethyl acetoacetate, which illustrate this point, cleavage of the chain occurs preferentially at the acetyl group (indicated by a broken line).

$$C_6H_5\overset{O}{\overset{\|}{C}}CH_2 - \overset{O}{\overset{\|}{C}}CH_3 \qquad CH_3\overset{O}{\overset{\|}{C}} - CH_2\overset{O}{\overset{\|}{C}}OC_2H_5$$

The acetoacetic ester method of converting acetic acid into its mono- and dialkyl derivatives depends on the introduction of the labilizing acetyl group (to facilitate alkylation) and its subsequent removal by alkaline cleavage. In practice this procedure is generally less satisfactory than the malonic ester method.

Hydrolytic cleavage of the cyclohexanone ring is involved in certain syntheses of pimelic acid. One of these involves treatment of salicylic acid with sodium and isoamyl alcohol. A better method is to hydrolyze the

[30] R. G. Pearson and A. C. Sandy, *J. Am. Chem. Soc.*, **73**, 931 (1951).

keto ester obtained by pyrolysis of the ethoxalyl derivative of cyclohexanone (OS II, 531); the yield, based on cyclohexanone, is 54%.

The hydroxymethylene group has been introduced for the purpose of protecting a methylene group; it is possible to methylate 2-methylcyclohexanone in the 2-position by first condensing it with ethyl formate and converting the hydroxymethylene derivative into the isopropyl ether. After the methyl group has been introduced, the hydroxymethylene group can be removed by hydrolysis.[31]

The last step in this synthesis corresponds to the hydrolytic cleavage of a β-keto aldehyde.

Solvolytic chain cleavage occurs readily with compounds having three carbonyl groups joined to the same carbon atom. A particularly interesting example is encountered in a synthesis of ethyl benzoylacetate; hydrolysis of α-benzoylacetoacetic ester with a dilute solution of ammonia removes the acetyl group and provides a preparative method (OS II, 266; 78% yield).

$$C_6H_5COCH_2CO_2C_2H_5 + CH_3CO_2NH_4$$

[31] W. S. Johnson and H. Posvic, *J. Am. Chem. Soc.*, **69**, 1361 (1947).

The cleavage may be accomplished also by treating the sodium enolate of the diketo ester with aqueous ammonium chloride (OS **37,** 32).

This example illustrates a general method of preparing higher β-keto esters from acetoacetic esters. When nonanoyl chloride and methyl acetoacetate are employed, the product is methyl 3-oxoundecanoate. The deacetylation is effected by treatment of the diketo ester with sodium methoxide.

$$CH_3CO \diagdown \\ \diagup CHCO_2CH_3 + CH_3OH \rightarrow \\ CH_3(CH_2)_7CO$$

$$CH_3(CH_2)_7COCH_2CO_2CH_3 + CH_3CO_2CH_3$$

Ethyl γ-phenylacetoacetate may be made from ethyl acetoacetate and phenylacetyl chloride in a similar way.[32]

The readiness with which acylation can be reversed makes possible acyl interchange, which has been accomplished by treating the sodium enolate of a 1,3-diketone or a β-keto ester with a simple ester. Ethyl acetoacetate, for example, has been transformed to ethyl benzoylacetate in 55% yield by treatment of its sodium enolate with ethyl benzoate (OS III, 379).

$$CH_3COCH_2CO_2C_2H_5 + C_6H_5CO_2C_2H_5 \overset{NaOC_2H_5}{\underset{}{\rightleftharpoons}}$$

$$C_6H_5COCH_2CO_2C_2H_5 + CH_3CO_2C_2H_5$$

The condensation is carried out under conditions that permit the removal of ethyl acetate as it forms. Presumably the process involves the following steps.

$$CH_3CO\overset{-}{C}HCO_2C_2H_5 + C_6H_5CO_2C_2H_5 \rightleftharpoons$$

$$CH_3CO \diagdown \\ \diagup \overset{-}{C}CO_2C_2H_5 + C_2H_5OH \\ C_6H_5CO$$

$$CH_3CO \diagdown \\ \diagup \overset{-}{C}CO_2C_2H_5 + C_2H_5OH \rightleftharpoons \\ C_6H_5CO$$

$$C_6H_5CO\overset{-}{C}HCO_2C_2H_5 + CH_3CO_2C_2H_5$$

[32] D. Libermann, J. Himbert, L. Hengl, and G. Kirchhoffer, *Compt. rend.*, **229,** 765 (1949).

One of the few methods that are valuable in closing large rings involves ω-bromoacylacetic esters, made from acetoacetic ester by acylation followed by deacetylation. For example, methyl 15-bromo-3-ketopentadecanoate is made as follows.

$$CH_3CO\overset{-}{C}HCO_2CH_3 + Br(CH_2)_{12}COCl \xrightarrow{-Cl^-}$$

$$\begin{array}{c} CH_3CO \\ \diagdown \\ \qquad CHCO_2CH_3 \xrightarrow{CH_3ONa} Br(CH_2)_{12}COCH_2CO_2CH_3 \\ \diagup \\ Br(CH_2)_{12}CO \end{array}$$

When the corresponding iodo ester, made by reaction of the bromo ester with sodium iodide in acetone (p. 249), is treated with potassium carbonate, cyclization occurs, yielding methyl 2-cyclotetradecanone-1-carboxylate. Hydrolysis and decarboxylation are effected by allowing the keto ester to stand a few days in 80% sulfuric acid.

$$\begin{array}{c} CH_2I \\ | \\ CH_2(CH_2)_{10}COCH_2CO_2CH_3 \end{array} \xrightarrow{K_2CO_3} \begin{array}{c} CH_2 \\ \diagup \quad \diagdown \\ (CH_2)_{11} \quad CHCO_2CH_3 \\ \diagdown \quad \diagup \\ CO \end{array} \longrightarrow$$

$$\begin{array}{c} CH_2 \\ \diagup \quad \diagdown \\ (CH_2)_{11} \quad CH_2 \\ \diagdown \quad \diagup \\ CO \end{array}$$

β-Keto esters are made conveniently by acylation of malonic ester followed by removal of one of the carbethoxyl groups by heating with a sulfonic acid. Diethyl β-ketoadipate, for example, is prepared as follows.

$$\begin{array}{c} CH_2CH_2COCl \\ | \\ CO_2C_2H_5 \end{array} \xrightarrow{\overset{-}{C}H(CO_2C_2H_5)_2} \begin{array}{c} CH_2CH_2COCH(CO_2C_2H_5)_2 \\ | \\ CO_2C_2H_5 \end{array} \xrightarrow{2-C_{10}H_7SO_3H}$$

$$\begin{array}{c} CH_2CH_2COCH_2CO_2C_2H_5 \\ | \\ CO_2C_2H_5 \end{array}$$

If a monoalkyl derivative of ethyl acetoacetate is acylated, a diacyl derivative is obtained that in many cases can be hydrolyzed in such a way as to eliminate both the acetyl and carbethoxyl groups. This ketone synthesis has been adapted to the preparation of keto acids as is illustrated by the production of 4-ketomyristic acid from diethyl acetosuccinate.

$$\underset{\underset{\displaystyle CH_2CO_2C_2H_5}{|}}{\overset{\overset{\displaystyle CO_2C_2H_5}{|}}{CH_3COCH}} \quad \rightarrow \quad \underset{\underset{\displaystyle CH_2CO_2C_2H_5}{|}}{\overset{\overset{\displaystyle CO_2C_2H_5}{|}}{CH_3COCCO(CH_2)_9CH_3}} \quad \rightarrow$$

$$CH_3(CH_2)_9COCH_2CH_2CO_2H$$

Loss of carbon dioxide from β-keto acids and many similarly constituted acids (p. 664) and of carbon monoxide from oxalyl esters (p. 662) is likewise to be ascribed to the weak bonding power of the active methylene carbon atom.

Many monocarbonyl compounds undergo cleavage of the carbon chain when treated with alkaline reagents. Although the reaction appears to be characteristic of carbonyl compounds in general, simple aldehydes, ketones, and esters rarely react in this way. Cleavage of such compounds, when it does occur, requires relatively drastic treatment and is useful only with ketones that are non-enolizable (OR 9, 1). The cleavage of β-benzo-pinacolone to potassium benzoate and triphenylmethane is an example.

$$(C_6H_5)_3CCOC_6H_5 + KOH \rightarrow (C_6H_5)_3CH + C_6H_5CO_2K$$

Other examples are the scission of 10,10-diaryl-9-phenanthrones and 2,2-diaryl-1-acenaphthenones.

Perhaps the most striking illustration of this type of cleavage occurs in the haloform reaction, in which trihalomethyl ketones are formed as intermediates (CR 15, 275). Examples of acids made by this method are trimethylacetic acid (OS I, 526; 74% yield) and 2-naphthoic acid (OS II, 428; 88% yield).

The trihalomethide ion is fairly stable because of extensive inductive withdrawal of electrons from the carbon atom by the halogen atoms; the alkide ion is therefore a good leaving group.

$$R-\overset{\overset{\displaystyle O}{\|}}{C}-CX_3 + OH^- \rightarrow R-\overset{\overset{\displaystyle O^-}{|}}{\underset{\underset{\displaystyle OH}{|}}{C}}-CX_3 \rightarrow R-\overset{\overset{\displaystyle O}{\|}}{\underset{\underset{\displaystyle OH}{|}}{C}} + \bar{C}X_3$$

The haloform procedure has an advantage in that the reagent does not attack ethylene linkages; it is effective in the oxidation of benzalacetone to cinnamic acid and of mesityl oxide to β-methylcrotonic acid (OS III, 302; 53% yield).

$$C_6H_5CH{=}CHCOCH_3 \rightarrow C_6H_5CH{=}CHCO_2H$$

$$(CH_3)_2C{=}CHCOCH_3 \rightarrow (CH_3)_2C{=}CHCO_2H$$

Hypohalites oxidize ethanol to acetaldehyde and alcohols of the type $RCH(OH)CH_3$ to methyl ketones; hence such alcohols give positive iodoform tests. Addition of cyanide ion to the hypoiodite solution reduces its oxidizing power and makes the test more selective; methyl ketones react much more rapidly than the corresponding alcohols.[33]

This type of reaction serves also in the commercial production of chloroform, bromoform, and iodoform, the raw material being ethanol or acetone. When ethanol is employed the intermediate formation of chloral, bromal, or iodal is assumed. Chloral and bromal are known to undergo cleavage with alkali. Iodal, however, has not yet been prepared. When chloral is heated with morpholine in isopropyl alcohol, N-formylmorpholine is produced in 92% yield; the reaction is an ammonolysis.[34]

$$CCl_3CHO + O{\bigcirc}NH \rightarrow CHCl_3 + O{\bigcirc}NCHO$$

A similar ammonolysis occurs when hexachloroacetone is allowed to react with aniline; α,α,α-trichloroacetanilide is produced in 91% yield (OS **40**, 103).

The haloform reaction occurs also with compounds that readily undergo alkaline hydrolysis to yield ketones or alcohols of the types specified. Such

---

[33] R. N. Seelye and T. A. Turney, *J. Chem. Education*, **36**, 572 (1959).
[34] G. B. L. Smith, M. Silver, and E. I. Becker, *J. Am. Chem. Soc.*, **70**, 4254 (1948).

hydrolytic cleavages would be promoted, of course, by preliminary introduction of halogen in place of active hydrogen atoms. An example is the degradation of methone to the sodium salt of β,β-dimethylglutaric acid with sodium hypochlorite (OS **31**, 40; 91% yield).

$$
\begin{array}{c}
CH_3 \qquad CH_2CO \\
\diagdown \qquad \diagup \\
C \qquad\qquad CH_2 + 3NaOCl \rightarrow \\
\diagup \qquad \diagdown \\
CH_3 \qquad CH_2CO
\end{array}
$$

$$
\begin{array}{c}
CH_3 \qquad CH_2CO_2Na \\
\diagdown \qquad \diagup \\
C \qquad\qquad\qquad + CHCl_3 + NaOH \\
\diagup \qquad \diagdown \\
CH_3 \qquad CH_2CO_2Na
\end{array}
$$

Hypohalite cleavage has been effected also with higher ketones; propiophenone, for example, affords benzoic acid in 64% yield. In a similar way the succinoyl group has been degraded to a carboxyl group by the action of hypochlorite. An illustration is the conversion of β-(4-methoxy-1-naphthoyl)propionic acid into 4-methoxy-1-naphthoic acid; the yield is 21%.[35]

$$
\begin{array}{ccc}
COCH_2CH_2CO_2H & & CO_2H \\
\text{(naphthalene ring)} & \rightarrow & \text{(naphthalene ring)} \\
OCH_3 & & OCH_3
\end{array}
$$

Ethyl ketones react with hypoiodite to give mixtures of products; diethyl ketone, for example, yields acetic and propionic acids along with iodoform. The following course of reaction has been suggested for the formation of the iodoform.[36]

$$C_2H_5COCH_2CH_3 \rightarrow C_2H_5COCl_2CH_3 \rightarrow C_2H_5COCOCH_3 \rightarrow CHI_3$$

Methyl and methylene groups attached to the ring in methyl aryl ketones are also oxidized by hypohalites; p-ethyl- and p-methylacetophenone give terephthalic acid.[37] It appears that degradation of the ketone group occurs first since under the same conditions p-toluic acid also gives terephthalic acid.[38]

[35] L. E. Miller, A. S. Neave, Jr., G. E. Szosz, and L. H. Wiedermann, *J. Am. Chem. Soc.*, **71**, 2120 (1949).
[36] C. F. Cullis and M. H. Hashmi, *J. Chem. Soc.*, 1548 (1957).
[37] D. D. Neiswender, Jr., W. B. Moniz, and J. A. Dixon, *J. Am. Chem. Soc.*, **82**, 2876 (1960).
[38] J. P. Feifer and W. J. Welstead, Jr., *J. Org. Chem.*, **26**, 2567 (1961).

A reaction that is analogous to the haloform cleavage occurs when certain arylcyanopyruvic esters are treated with solutions of sodium hypobromite. Ethyl phenylcyanopyruvate, for example, yields α-bromophenylacetonitrile.[39]

$$
\underset{\overset{|}{CN}}{C_6H_5CHCOCO_2C_2H_5} \rightarrow \underset{\overset{|}{CN}\ \ \overset{\|}{O}}{C_3H_5\overset{\overset{Br}{|}}{C}\text{---}C\text{---}CO_2C_2H_5} \rightarrow \underset{\overset{|}{Br}}{C_6H_5CHCN}
$$

The bromine atom and the phenyl and cyano groups combine to impart considerable stability to the anion $\underset{\overset{|}{Br}}{C_6H_5\overset{-}{C}\text{---}CN}$.

Halodecarboxylation of cyanoacetic acid, if assumed to proceed by way of the dihalo derivative, represents a similar change. Dibromoacetonitrile can be made in this way; the brominating agent is N-bromosuccinimide (OS **38**, 16; yield 87%).

$$NCCH_2CO_2H \rightarrow NCCBr_2CO_2H \rightarrow NCCHBr_2$$

Formation of Acid Chlorides

Acidolysis of acid halides resembles the reaction that occurs when acids are allowed to react with certain inorganic halides, notably those of sulfur and phosphorus. In this category is the conversion of acids into acid chlorides by the action of phosphorus pentachloride, phosphorus trichloride, thionyl chloride, or similar inorganic "acid chlorides."

The use of phosphorus pentachloride is illustrated by the preparation of *p*-nitrobenzoyl chloride (OS I, 394; 96% yield).

$$O_2N\langle\bigcirc\rangle CO_2H + PCl_5 \rightarrow O_2N\langle\bigcirc\rangle COCl + POCl_3 + HCl$$

If the acid chloride to be made boils near 107°, the boiling point of phosphorus oxychloride, phosphorus trichloride may be chosen. Removal of phosphorus oxychloride presents difficulty, and the method has largely been abandoned in favor of that involving thionyl chloride. An example of the use of thionyl chloride is the preparation of the acid chloride from methyl hydrogen succinate (OS III, 169; 93% yield).

$$
\underset{\overset{|}{CH_2CO_2H}}{CH_2CO_2CH_3} \rightarrow \underset{\overset{|}{CH_2COCl}}{CH_2CO_2CH_3}
$$

[39] S. Wideqvist, *J. Am. Chem. Soc.*, **71**, 4152 (1949).

Thionyl chloride is a superior reagent because it gives only gaseous by-products; by its use acid chlorides may be obtained directly in a fairly pure state. It has been employed in the preparation of chlorides of *n*-butyric (OS I, 147; 85% yield), isobutyric (OS III, 490; 90% yield), mesitoic (OS III, 555; 97% yield), cinnamic (OS III, 714), adipic (OS III, 623), and oleic acids (OS 37, 66). A somewhat unusual application is the conversion of *p*-phenylazobenzoic acid into the corresponding acid chloride (OS III, 712; 89% yield).

$$C_6H_5N{=}NC_6H_4CO_2H + SOCl_2 \rightarrow C_6H_5N{=}NC_6H_4COCl + HCl + SO_2$$

Methacrylic acid reacts with thionyl chloride to give methacrylyl chloride.

$$CH_2{=}\underset{\underset{CH_3}{|}}{C}{-}CO_2H + SOCl_2 \rightarrow CH_2{=}\underset{\underset{CH_3}{|}}{C}{-}COCl + HCl + SO_2$$

Thionyl chloride alone is not effective, however, with all acids; it converts succinic, glutaric, and phthalic acids into the corresponding anhydrides and fails to attack oxalic, tartaric, fumaric, and terephthalic acids. Addition of small amounts of zinc chloride and use of higher temperatures, however, bring satisfactory results with fumaric, succinic, and phthalic acids. The preparation of phthalyl chloride is effected in 86% yield by treating the anhydride with thionyl chloride at 220° in the presence of a trace of zinc chloride.

Sulfonic acids differ in many ways from carboxylic acids, but resemble them in their behavior toward the halides of phosphorus. Sulfonic acids, generally encountered in the form of salts, serve in synthetic work as sources of sulfonyl chlorides, which can be made from them by the action of phosphorus oxychloride or phosphorus pentachloride. Benzenesulfonyl chloride may be made in high yields by use of either of the phosphorus compounds (OS I, 84).

$$3C_6H_5SO_3Na + PCl_5 \rightarrow 3C_6H_5SO_2Cl + 2NaCl + NaPO_3$$
$$2C_6H_5SO_3Na + POCl_3 \rightarrow 2C_6H_5SO_2Cl + NaCl + NaPO_3$$

α-Keto acids cannot be converted directly into acid chlorides; with thionyl chloride, for example, they lose carbon monoxide and yield the acid chloride with one less carbon atom. The enol acetates and methyl ethers, however, give acid chlorides. An example is the formation of the acid chloride of the enol acetate of α-ketobutyric acid.[40]

$$CH_3CH_2COCO_2H \xrightarrow{(CH_3CO)_2O} CH_3CH{=}\underset{\underset{OCOCH_3}{|}}{C}CO_2H \xrightarrow{SOCl_2} CH_3CH{=}\underset{\underset{OCOCH_3}{|}}{C}COCl$$

[40] P. Seifert, E. Vogel, A. Rossi, and H. Schinz, *Helv. Chim. Acta*, **33**, 725 (1950).

When sulfonic acids are heated with phosphoric anhydride, they are converted into the corresponding anhydrides; an example is the formation of benzenesulfonic anhydride.[41]

$$2C_6H_5SO_3H \rightarrow (C_6H_5SO_2)_2O + H_2O$$

Interconversion

If two esters are brought together in the presence of sodium alkoxides or sulfonic acids, *ester interchange* occurs; ethyl acetate and methyl propionate form an equilibrium mixture containing not only the original esters but ethyl propionate and methyl acetate as well.

$$CH_3CO_2C_2H_5 + CH_3CH_2CO_2CH_3 \rightleftharpoons CH_3CO_2CH_3 + CH_3CH_2CO_2C_2H_5$$

A similar equilibrium is set up when two different acid halides or anhydrides are mixed. An example is the conversion of maleic anhydride into fumaryl chloride by treatment with phthalyl chloride in the presence of zinc chloride (OS III, 422; 95% yield).

Amide interchange is possible also; it occurs extensively, for example, in the manufacture of nylon. Sebacamide and the diacetyl derivative of hexamethylenediamine yield acetamide and polyhexamethylenesebacamide.[42]

$$H_2NOC(CH_2)_8CONH_2 + CH_3CONH(CH_2)_6NHCOCH_3 \rightarrow$$
$$2CH_3CONH_2 + \cdots (CH_2)_6NHCO(CH_2)_8CONH \cdots$$

[41] L. Field, *J. Am. Chem. Soc.*, **74**, 394 (1952).
[42] L. F. Beste and R. C. Houtz, *J. Polymer Sci.*, **8**, 395 (1952).

16

Nucleophilic displacement
in the aromatic series

Nucleophilic substitution in the aromatic series, i.e., displacement of hydrogen as hydride ion, is difficult to effect and appears to require the assistance of a reducible substance to destroy the hydride ion. An example is the classical synthesis of picric acid by heating 1,3,5-trinitrobenzene with potassium ferricyanide in water made alkaline with sodium carbonate.

Hydroxylamine is peculiarly suited to serve as an aminating agent; the hydroxyl group combines with the hydrogen atom being displaced to form water. The amination of 1-nitronaphthalene is an example (OS III, 664; 60% yield).

1,3,5-Trinitrobenzene reacts with this reagent in cold alcohol solution to produce picramide.

The behavior of the pyridine ring in substitution reactions has been compared to that of nitrobenzene (p. 59). That the nitro group is more

362

effective than the nitrogen atom of the pyridine ring in creating an electron deficit is indicated by the action of hydroxylamine on 5- and 7-nitro-quinolines. In each the amino group enters a position *ortho* or *para* to the nitro group.[1]

Pyridine undergoes certain substitution reactions that are not successful with nitrobenzene, however. Amination, for example, can be effected by treatment with sodium amide; 2-aminopyridine is made in this way.

Hydride ion, the leaving group in this reaction (Hine, 371), attacks the aminopyridine to form a relatively stable anion.

4-Aminopyridine is produced also. Amination of quinoline with potassium amide in liquid ammonia gives 2- and 4-aminoquinoline in a ratio of 5 to 1, respectively.

Sodium amides made from primary amines aminate pyridine and similar compounds when the reaction is carried out in boiling toluene. The formation of 2-*n*-butylaminopyridine is an example.[2]

Although nucleophilic substitution proper, i.e., displacement of hydrogen, is of limited value, the displacement of substituents such as halogen, amino, and alkoxyl—which might be termed indirect substitution —is widely used in synthesis (CR **49**, 273; QR **12**, 1). This type of reaction

[1] M. Colonna and F. Montanari, *Gazz. chim. ital.*, **81**, 744 (1951).
[2] T. Vajda and K. Kovács, *Rec. trav. chim.*, **80**, 47 (1961).

is facilitated, of course, by the presence on the ring of electron-withdrawing groups such as nitro. The resultant depletion, which makes hydroxyl groups more acidic and amino groups less basic, also renders the ring more vulnerable to nucleophilic attack. Aryl halides, amines, and ethers tend to become like acyl halides, amides and esters, respectively. As a consequence such compounds may undergo hydrolysis, alcoholysis, ammonolysis, and other solvolytic reactions. Aromatic diazonium salts are exceptional in that they readily undergo nucleophilic displacement of the diazonium function, regardless of the nature of the substituents that the ring may hold.

Displacement of the Diazonium Group

The remarkable ease with which displacement of the diazonium group takes place suggests that the stability of molecular nitrogen contributes greatly to the driving force of the reaction. The diazonium function can be displaced by hydrogen and halogens as well as by many groups such as hydroxyl, nitro, and cyano. Aryl radicals can be introduced also.

Displacement by hydrogen

Diazotization and reduction constitute a standard procedure for deamination of primary aromatic amines, useful in syntheses in which the amino group is needed to guide an entering substituent to the desired position. The formation of m-nitrotoluene from p-toluidine is an example. Nitration of p-acetotoluide followed by hydrolysis of the acetamido group gives 4-amino-3-nitrotoluene, which can then be deaminated by treating the diazotized amine with ethanol (OS I, 415). The yield of m-nitrotoluene, based on the nitro amine, is 72%.

The use of ethanol as the reducing agent is to be recommended only with compounds that contain electron-withdrawing groups or atoms, preferably *ortho* to the diazonium group. 1,3,5-Tribromobenzene, for example, is formed in 71% yield when tribromoaniline sulfate is diazotized in hot ethanolic solution (OS II, 592).

A similar procedure converts *m*-aminobenzoic acid into 2,4,6-tribromo-benzoic acid (OS **36**, 94; 80% yield).

In some cases replacement is facilitated if copper or copper bronze is added to catalyze decomposition of the diazonium salt. An example is the last step in the classical synthesis of *m*-bromotoluene from *p*-toluidine (OS I, 133).

$$
\underset{\substack{\text{N}_2\text{OSO}_3\text{H}}}{\overset{\text{CH}_3}{\bigcirc}}\text{Br} + \text{C}_2\text{H}_5\text{OH} \xrightarrow{\text{Cu}} \overset{\text{CH}_3}{\bigcirc}\text{Br} + \text{N}_2 + \text{CH}_3\text{CHO} + \text{H}_2\text{SO}_4
$$

Copper salts are effective also. *m*-Iodobenzoic acid, for example, is obtained in high yield by decomposition of diazotized 5-iodoanthranilic acid in the presence of ethanol and a small amount of copper sulfate (OS II, 353).

$$
\underset{\text{I}}{\overset{\text{CO}_2\text{H}}{\bigcirc}}\text{N}_2\text{Cl} \rightarrow \underset{\text{I}}{\overset{\text{CO}_2\text{H}}{\bigcirc}}
$$

In general, alcohols are not satisfactory reducing agents because of ether formation. Indeed, introduction of alkoxyl groups in this manner can be effected in some instances on a preparative scale. Fortunately, a number of other methods are available for the replacement of a diazonium group by hydrogen (OR **2**, 262). A superior reducing agent, hypophosphorous acid, has been employed successfully with a wide variety of amines and is convenient to use. The preparation of 3,3'-dimethoxybiphenyl from *o*-dianisidine is an example (OS III, 295; 78% yield).

$$
\text{ClN}_2\underset{\text{CH}_3\text{O}}{\bigcirc}\underset{\text{OCH}_3}{\bigcirc}\text{N}_2\text{Cl} \xrightarrow{\text{H}_3\text{PO}_2} \underset{\text{CH}_3\text{O}}{\bigcirc}\underset{\text{OCH}_3}{\bigcirc}
$$

This type of reduction can be accomplished also with formaldehyde in alkaline solution, a procedure that is particularly useful for those compounds with which ethanol leads primarily to ether formation.

Displacement by hydroxyl

When an aqueous diazonium salt solution is allowed to decompose, the corresponding phenol is formed. This is the classical method of making phenol from diazotized aniline. The decomposition must be carried out in a strongly acid solution, however, to prevent coupling of the phenol with the diazonium compound. The rate of decomposition varies greatly with the structure of the compound, being especially sluggish when nitro, chloro, or alkoxyl substituents are present. Perhaps the most satisfactory procedure is to isolate the diazonium salt and add it, while still damp, to boiling water or sulfuric acid. *m*-Hydroxybenzaldehyde is produced in 64% yields, for example, when the complex salt of the corresponding diazonium chloride and stannic chloride is added portion-wise to boiling water (OS III, 453).

$$\text{(ring)} N_2Cl + H_2O \rightarrow \text{(ring)} OH + N_2 + HCl$$
$$\quad CHO \qquad\qquad\qquad CHO$$

In a similar way diazotized *m*-nitroaniline yields *m*-nitrophenol, the corresponding diazonium sulfate being added to a boiling (160°) sulfuric acid solution (OS I, 404).

$$\text{(ring)} N_2OSO_3H + H_2O \rightarrow \text{(ring)} OH + N_2 + H_2SO_4$$
$$\quad NO_2 \qquad\qquad\qquad NO_2$$

Diazotized 3-bromo-*p*-toluidine is changed to 3-bromo-4-hydroxytoluene in a similar manner (OS III, 130).

Displacement by iodide ion

Displacement of the diazonium group by iodide ion is easier than displacement by chloride or bromide ions. The displacing species in the case of iodide, at least in certain reactions, is the triiodide ion.[3] When a solution of a diazonium chloride or sulfate is mixed with one of potassium iodide, nitrogen is evolved and the aryl iodide is formed. The simplest example is the preparation of iodobenzene from aniline; the yield is 76%, based on the amine (OS II, 351). In a similar way *p*-aminophenol gives *p*-iodophenol (OS II, 355). Another example is the transformation of 2,6-diiodo-4-nitroaniline to 1,2,3-triiodo-5-nitrobenzene (OS II, 604); the yield is very high.

$$\begin{array}{ccc} & NO_2 & NO_2 \\ I\text{(ring)}I & \rightarrow & I\text{(ring)}I \\ & NH_2 & I \end{array}$$

o-Bromoaniline gives *o*-bromoiodobenzene in 83% yield (OS **40**, 105).

[3] J. G. Carey and I. T. Millar, *Chem. and Ind.*, 97 (1960).

Displacement by fluoride ion

If fluoboric acid is added to a solution of a diazonium salt, the corresponding diazonium fluoborate forms a precipitate that can be washed and dried. Heat decomposes the salt to an aryl fluoride and fluoboric acid. This method of replacing a diazonium group by fluoride ion, credited to Schiemann (OR **5**, 193), is satisfactory because the diazonium fluoborates are stable and can be manipulated with safety. An illustration of the Schiemann method is the preparation of fluorobenzene from benzene-diazonium chloride (OS II, 295).

$$C_6H_5N_2Cl \xrightarrow{\text{HBF}_4} C_6H_5N_2BF_4 \longrightarrow C_6H_5F$$

The yield, based on aniline, is 57%.

Another example, is the conversion of benzidine into 4,4'-difluoro-biphenyl (OS II, 188).

The yield, based on the fluoborate, is 81%.

A similar series of changes occurs in the preparation of ethyl *p*-fluoro-benzoate from ethyl *p*-aminobenzoate (OS II, 299; 89% yield). An example of interest is the synthesis of 5-fluoro-3-methylpyridine from 5-amino-3-methylpyridine.

The three pyridinediazonium fluoborates and the 2- and 4-quinoline-diazonium fluoborates decompose at room temperature or below. 3-Quinolinediazonium fluoborate, on the other hand, melts at 95°.[4]

The Schiemann procedure gives better results if tetrahydrofuran is used as solvent.[5]

Displacement by nitro

Treatment of a diazonium fluoborate with sodium nitrite in the presence of copper brings about replacement of the diazonium group by a nitro group. This method is illustrated by the synthesis of *o*-dinitrobenzene from *o*-nitroaniline (OS II, 226; 38% yield).

[4] A. Roe and C. E. Teague, Jr., *J. Am. Chem. Soc.*, **73**, 687 (1951).
[5] T. L. Fletcher and M. J. Namkung, *Chem. and Ind.*, 179 (1961).

$$\text{[benzene ring]}\underset{NO_2}{\overset{NH_2}{<}} + HONO + HBF_4 \longrightarrow \text{[benzene ring]}\underset{NO_2}{\overset{N_2BF_4}{<}} + 2H_2O$$

$$\text{[benzene ring]}\underset{NO_2}{\overset{N_2BF_4}{<}} + NaNO_2 \overset{Cu}{\longrightarrow} \text{[benzene ring]}\underset{NO_2}{\overset{NO_2}{<}} + N_2 + NaBF_4$$

The procedure is employed also in the preparation of p-dinitrobenzene from p-nitroaniline (OS II, 225; 82% yield). The same transformation has been effected by treating p-nitrobenzenediazonium sulfate with sodium nitrite. This method is strange in that it entails preparation of a nitro compound from an amine, whereas amines are normally made from nitro compounds.

Another compound for which replacement of an amino group provides a good preparative method is 2-nitronapthalene. This compound is produced only in low yield by nitration of naphthalene (p. 36) but can be made readily from 2-naphthylamine. In this category also is 1,4-dinitronaphthalene, which can be produced in fairly satisfactory yields (60%) from 4-nitro-1-naphthylamine (OS III, 341). The replacement is effected by adding a solution of the diazonium sulfate to a solution of sodium nitrite. The reaction is catalyzed by a cupro-cupric sulfite prepared by the interaction of copper sulfate and sodium sulfite. 3-Bromo-4-nitrotoluene has been prepared in this way also; the yield, based on the amine, is 37%.[6]

$$\underset{NH_2}{\overset{CH_3}{\text{[benzene ring]}}}Br \rightarrow \underset{NO_2}{\overset{CH_3}{\text{[benzene ring]}}}Br$$

Replacement of the diazonium group by the nitro group occurs only in neutral or alkaline media. A superior procedure is to add the solution of the diazonium salt to a sodium nitrite solution containing an excess of sodium bicarbonate.[7]

Bart reaction

The most useful method of preparing aromatic arsonic acids consists in treatment of diazonium salts with sodium arsenite (OR 2, 415). The procedure, originated by Bart, has been improved by various modifications, one of the most satisfactory of which is illustrated by the synthesis of p-nitrophenylarsonic acid. The sodium salt of this acid is formed by allowing p-nitrobenzenediazonium fluoroborate to react with sodium

[6] M. Rieger and F. H. Westheimer, J. Am. Chem. Soc., 72, 28 (1950).
[7] E. R. Ward, C. D. Johnson, and J. G. Hawkins, J. Chem. Soc., 894 (1960).

metaarsenite in the presence of sodium hydroxide and cuprous chloride (OS III, 665).

$$\underset{NO_2}{\underset{|}{C_6H_4}}N_2BF_4 + NaAsO_2 + 2NaOH \xrightarrow{CuCl} \underset{NO_2}{\underset{|}{C_6H_4}}AsO_3Na_2 + N_2 + H_2O + NaBF_4$$

The acid may be obtained in 79% yield.

Diazotized aniline reacts with sodium arsenite in the presence of copper sulfate to produce sodium phenylarsonate (OS II, 494; 45% yield).

$$C_6H_5N_2Cl + Na_3AsO_3 \xrightarrow{CuSO_4} C_6H_5AsO_3Na_2 + N_2 + NaCl$$

Formation of Thiophenols, Aryl Sulfides, and Sulfinic Acids

Diazonium salts react with potassium ethyl xanthate to form diazo xanthates, which lose nitrogen when warmed. From the S-aryl ethyl xanthates that are produced thiophenols are made by alkaline hydrolysis. The synthesis of m-thiocresol is an example (OS III, 809).

$$\underset{CH_3}{\underset{|}{C_6H_4}}N_2Cl \xrightarrow{KS\overset{S}{\overset{||}{C}}OC_2H_5} \underset{CH_3}{\underset{|}{C_6H_4}}S\overset{S}{\overset{||}{C}}OC_2H_5 \xrightarrow[\text{(2) } H_2SO_4]{\text{(1) KOH}} \underset{CH_3}{\underset{|}{C_6H_4}}SH$$

Thiophenols are made also from diazonium salts by way of the S-arylisothiouronium salts that form when thiourea is introduced into solutions of diazotized amines. S-Arylisothiouronium salts are converted into thiophenols by alkaline hydrolysis (p. 289). Another indirect method for preparing thiophenols from diazonium compounds calls for the intermediate formation of the corresponding disulfides, which can be achieved by treating solutions of diazotized amines with sodium disulfide. An example is the conversion of anthranilic acid into thiosalicylic acid (OS II, 580).

$$\underset{NH_2}{\underset{|}{\overset{CO_2H}{C_6H_4}}} \rightarrow \underset{N_2Cl}{\underset{|}{\overset{CO_2H}{C_6H_4}}} \rightarrow \underset{S-S}{\underset{|}{\overset{CO_2H}{C_6H_4}}}\underset{}{\overset{CO_2H}{C_6H_4}} \rightarrow \underset{SH}{\underset{|}{\overset{CO_2H}{C_6H_4}}}$$

The last step is accomplished by reduction with zinc and acetic acid.

Aryl sulfides may be produced by treating diazonium salts with sodium sulfide.

$$2ArN_2X + Na_2S \rightarrow Ar_2S + 2NaX + 2N_2$$

Unsymmetrical sulfides are obtained by employing sodium salts of mercaptans or thiophenols (p. 373).

$$ArN_2X + RSNa \rightarrow ArSR + NaX + N_2$$

When sulfur dioxide is passed into a solution of a diazotized amine in the presence of copper powder, a sulfinic acid is formed.

$$ArN_2OSO_3H + 2SO_2 + 2H_2O \xrightarrow{Cu} ArSO_2H + N_2 + 2H_2SO_4$$

Displacement in Halonium Salts

Halonium compounds resemble the diazonium salts in having salt-like properties; also, they undergo nucleophilic displacement reactions. Diphenyliodonium iodide, for example, decomposes thermally to give two molecules of iodobenzene. Similarly, diphenyliodonium bromide yields one mole each of iodobenzene and bromobenzene.

$$\begin{array}{c} C_6H_5 \\ \diagdown \\ \quad I^+Br^- \rightarrow C_6H_5I + C_6H_5Br \\ \diagup \\ C_6H_5 \end{array}$$

Many bases, both organic and inorganic, have been arylated by interaction with aryl iodonium compounds. In addition to amines and mercaptans the list includes such relatively weak nucleophilic agents as cyanide, nitrite, sulfite, and sulfinates. Nitrobenzene, for example, is obtained in 66% yield by the action of sodium nitrite on diphenyliodonium bromide.

$$(C_6H_5)_2I^+Br^- + NaNO_2 \rightarrow C_6H_5I + C_6H_5NO_2 + NaBr$$

Biphenyleneiodonium salts behave in a similar way. The sulfate, for example, reacts with sodium acetate in the presence of cupric sulfate to give 2-acetoxy-2'-iodobiphenyl in nearly theoretical yields.[8]

[8] R. C. Fuson and R. L. Albright, *J. Am. Chem. Soc.*, **81**, 487 (1959).

Displacement may take place also on iodine; triphenyliodine is formed at $-80°$ by the interaction of diphenyliodonium iodide and phenyllithium.[9]

$$(C_6H_5)I^+I^- + C_6H_5Li \rightarrow (C_6H_5)_3I + LiI$$

Phenylbiphenyleneiodine, prepared in an analogous fashion, is so stable that it can be heated without immediate decomposition; it decomposes at 105 to $115°$.[10]

$$I^+I^- + C_6H_5Li \rightarrow IC_6H_5 + LiI$$

Aromatic bromonium and chloronium salts likewise have been used to effect arylation. Diphenylbromonium fluoborate is produced by heating benzenediazonium fluoborate with bromobenzene.

$$C_6H_5N_2BF_4 + C_6H_5Br \rightarrow (C_6H_5)_2BrBF_4 + N_2$$

The iodide, made by treating the fluoborate with sodium iodide, reacts with sodium nitrite to give nitrobenzene.

Displacement of the Sulfo Group

Another substituent that can be displaced readily without the aid of activators on the ring is the sulfo group. In fact, aromatic sulfonic acids derive much of their importance from the ability of the sulfo group to undergo replacement by hydrogen or by groups such as hydroxyl and nitro. When a sulfonic acid is cleaved in an acid medium, the electron pair joining the sulfur atom to carbon is retained by the carbon atom, sulfuric acid being produced. Fusion with alkali, on the other hand, converts the sulfonic acid into a phenoxide and sulfite, the bonding pair being retained by the sulfur atom. Phenol may be obtained in nearly quantitative yields by heating sodium benzenesulfonate with sodium hydroxide in 50% excess for 30 minutes at $300°$.

$$C_6H_5SO_3Na + NaOH \rightarrow C_6H_5OH + Na_2SO_3$$

Similarly, p-cresol is produced from sodium p-toluenesulfonate by heating with potassium hydroxide (OS I, 175).

Benzoic acid is changed to its 3,5-dihydroxy derivative by twofold sulfonation followed by alkali fusion at 250 to $260°$ (OS III, 288); the yield is 65%.

[9] G. Wittig and M. Rieber, *Ann.*, **562**, 187 (1949).
[10] K. Klauss, *Chem. Ber.*, **88**, 268 (1955).

The formation of 2-naphthol from 2-naphthalenesulfonic acid is an especially important example, since the sulfo group is one of the few that can be introduced directly into the 2-position of naphthalene (p. 48).

Fusion of sulfonates with alkalis sometimes gives isomers of the expected phenolic compounds, the best-known example being the conversion of benzenedisulfonic acids into resorcinol. Not only the *m*- but also the *o*- and *p*-disulfonic acids yield resorcinol.

Oxidation may accompany the replacement reaction, as in the classic conversion of 2-anthraquinonesulfonic acid into alizarin.

The sulfo group is replaced also be heating sulfonates with sodium cyanide or potassium ferricyanide, the product being a nitrile.

Sodium β-naphthalenesulfonate, when heated with the sodium derivative of piperidine, gives N-β-naphthylpiperidine (OS **40**, 74; yield 71%).

Sommelet Rearrangement

When the methiodide of benzyldimethylamine is treated with sodium amide in liquid ammonia it gives 2-methylbenzyldimethylamine. The methiodide of the product, under similar treatment, yields 2,3-dimethylbenzyldimethylamine. This progressive introduction of vicinal methyl groups may be continued until the ring is completely substituted.

The rearrangement occurs with 2- and 4-substituted benzyltrimethyl-ammonium ions also when the substituent is ethyl, methoxyl, or chloro.[11]

The Sommelet rearrangement has been interpreted as a nucleophilic substitution reaction of a carbanion made possible by elimination of the ammonium group as a tertiary amine.[12]

The Diazonium Group as an Activator

The most powerful activator is the diazonium group (Angew., **72**, 294), a circumstance that sometimes causes trouble in diazotization work. Thus, when conversion of 1-nitro-2-naphthylamine into the corresponding nitrosulfinic acid is attempted in hydrochloric acid, chloride ion tends to displace the nitro group.

This synthesis of sulfinic acids, when carried out in sulfuric acid, is valuable in preparative work. In this reaction, discovered by Gattermann, the catalyst is copper or a cuprous salt.

An interesting example from the quinoline series is the preparation of 5-iodo-6-nitroquinoline from 5-amino-6-nitroquinoline. If carried out in the presence of hydrochloric acid the process gives 5-iodo-6-chloro-quinoline in a yield of 28%.[13]

It is to be noted that the nitro group is detached as nitrite, thus providing the conditions for chain diazotization.

[11] W. Q. Beard and C. R. Hauser, *J. Org. Chem.*, **25**, 334 (1960).
[12] F. N. Jones and C. R. Hauser, *J. Org. Chem.*, **26**, 2979 (1961).
[13] R. Huisgen, *Ann.*, **559**, 143 (1948).

The Nitroso Group as an Activator

The nitroso group, as an activator, seems to be at least twice as effective as the nitro group. p-Nitrosodimethylaniline, for example, is hydrolyzed readily and completely by boiling sodium hydroxide solution, whereas 2,4-dinitrodimethylaniline, under identical conditions, is barely attacked.[14]

Hydrolysis of p-nitrosodialkylanilines is a time-honored method of preparing pure secondary amines, especially unsymmetrical amines. An example is 3-diethylamino-1-methylaminopropane.[15]

Another example is the synthesis of piperazine from ethylene bromide and aniline by way of N,N'-diphenylpiperazine.

The Nitro Group as an Activator

Displacement of nitro groups

The nitro group is the most powerful activator that is stable under ordinary conditions of nucleophilic displacement. It is also readily displaced. An example is the methanolysis of o-dinitrobenzene to give o-nitroanisole.

[14] R. J. W. Le Fèvre, *J. Chem. Soc.*, 810 (1931).

[15] R. Munch, G. T. Thannhauser, and D. L. Cottle, *J. Am. Chem. Soc.*, **68**, 1297 (1946).

$$\text{(benzene)}NO_2 + CH_3ONa \rightarrow \text{(benzene)}OCH_3 + NaNO_2$$

In p-dinitrobenzenes, in which one nitro group is flanked by other substituents, the flanked nitro group is displaced preferentially. Ammonolysis of 2,5-dinitro-m-xylene, for example, gives 2,6-dimethyl-4-nitroaniline.

$$\underset{NO_2}{\overset{NO_2}{CH_3\text{(benzene)}CH_3}} \xrightarrow{NH_3} \underset{NO_2}{\overset{NH_2}{CH_3\text{(benzene)}CH_3}}$$

The unhindered nitro group exerts the greater activating power because it can react by way of a transition state similar to a. The corresponding transition state (b) for displacement of the unhindered nitro group in less favored because it requires the hindered nitro group to be coplanar with the benzene ring.

$$a$$

$$b$$

The entering —NH_2 group and the leaving —NO_2 group, of course, lie out of (one above and the other below) the plane of the ring. In o-dinitrobenzene a substituent at position 3, for a similar reason, causes the nitro group at position 2 to be the more labile of the two.

The electron deficiency is localized at positions that are *ortho* or *para* to electron-attracting substituents, but operates to some extent at other positions as is illustrated by the methanolysis of 1,3,5-trinitrobenzene in the synthesis of 3,5-dinitroanisole (OS I, 219; 77% yield).

$$\underset{O_2N \quad NO_2}{\overset{NO_2}{\text{(benzene)}}} + CH_3ONa \rightarrow \underset{O_2N \quad NO_2}{\overset{OCH_3}{\text{(benzene)}}} + NaNO_2$$

The isomeric trinitrobenzenes react more rapidly, of course.

A practical application of this type of displacement is found in the manufacture of TNT. Isomeric trinitrotoluenes are removed by treatment with sodium sulfite as is illustrated by β-TNT.

$$\underset{\substack{NO_2}}{\underset{NO_2}{\overset{CH_3}{\bigcirc}}}\!NO_2 + Na_2SO_3 \rightarrow \underset{\substack{NO_2}}{\underset{SO_3Na}{\overset{CH_3}{\bigcirc}}}\!NO_2 + NaNO_2$$

Displacement of halides and sulfonates

Hydrolysis of aryl halides is possible without the assistance of electron-withdrawing functions. A familiar example is found in the manufacture of phenol from chlorobenzene.[16]

$$C_6H_5Cl + OH^- \rightarrow C_6H_5OH + Cl^-$$

In this process chlorobenzene is treated with sodium hydroxide at 350 to 400° under a pressure of 5000 pounds per square inch. The chief by-product is phenyl ether, the formation of which is suppressed by adding the ether to the original charge. These facts suggest that the chloride ion is displaced reversibly by phenoxide ion.

$$C_6H_5Cl + C_6H_5O^- \rightleftharpoons C_6H_5OC_6H_5 + Cl^-$$

The comparison holds also for the formation of the other principal by-products, o- and p-phenylphenol. For phenols, as mentioned earlier, yield both O- and C-alkylation products; the phenylated phenols are C-phenylation products.

Similar treatment of chlorotoluenes gives cresols. Since the chlorination of toluene yields almost exclusively the o- and p-isomers, it would appear that this method would be useful only for producing o- and p-cresol. This is not the case, however. Rearrangement occurs by which o- and p-chlorotoluenes are converted in considerable part into m-cresol (p. 372).

The manufacture of catechol by hydrolysis of o-dichlorobenzene is remarkable in that two adjacent halogen atoms are displaced. If the reaction is assumed to proceed in a stepwise fashion, the displacement of the second halogen atom must occur on a chlorophenoxide ion. In such electron-rich nuclei nucleophilic displacement should be extremely difficult. Moreover, the reaction brings together two ions of like charge.

$$\underset{Cl}{\overset{Cl}{\bigcirc}} \xrightarrow{OH^-} \underset{Cl}{\overset{O^-}{\bigcirc}} \xrightarrow{OH^-} \underset{O^-}{\overset{O^-}{\bigcirc}} \xrightarrow{H_2O} \underset{OH}{\overset{OH}{\bigcirc}}$$

A possibility is that the chlorophenoxide ion loses chloride ion and forms a keto carbene that reacts with hydroxide ion.

[16] W. J. Hale and E. C. Britton, *Ind. Eng. Chem.*, **20**, 114 (1928).

In the presence of copper powder and at 200° bromobenzene reacts with the potassium salt of guaiacol to produce o-methoxyphenyl phenyl ether (OS III, 566).

The enolate formed by treating o-acetoacetochloroanilide with potassium amide in liquid ammonia undergoes cyclization to 3-acetyloxindole (OS **40**, 1; 67% yield).

Drastic conditions are not necessary, of course, with electron-deficient nuclei such as those of o- and p-chloronitrobenzene, which yield the corresponding nitrophenols.

2,4-Dinitrofluorobenzene, widely used to protect amino groups, is also an excellent reagent for preparing derivatives to serve in the identification of alcohols.[17]

The most satisfactory procedure for making o- and p-nitroaniline is by ammonolysis of the corresponding chlorides. From 2,4-dinitrochlorobenzene 2,4-dinitrophenol is obtained in 76% yield (OS II, 221).

If sodium iodide is the reagent, 2,4-dinitrochlorobenzene yields 2,4-dinitroiodobenzene (OS **40**, 34; 71% yield).[18]

[17] W. B. Whalley, *J. Chem. Soc.*, 2241 (1950).
[18] J. F. Bunnett and R. M. Conner, *J. Org. Chem.*, **23**, 305 (1958).

p-Nitrophenyl phenyl ether is made by heating *p*-chloronitrobenzene with phenol and potassium hydroxide. The reaction is carried out without solvent and in the presence of copper as a catalyst (OS II, 445; 82% yield).

$$O_2N\text{—}C_6H_4\text{—}Cl + C_6H_5OH + KOH \rightarrow O_2N\text{—}C_6H_4\text{—}OC_6H_5 + KCl + H_2O$$

Ammonolysis has been realized also without the aid of electron-withdrawing groups. 4-Bromo-*o*-xylene gives 3,4-dimethylaniline when treated with ammonia at 195° under a pressure of 700 to 1000 pounds per square inch, the reaction being catalyzed by cuprous chloride (OS III, 307; 66% yield).

Chlorobenzene itself has been ammonolyzed to produce aniline on a commercial scale.

Iodides are, of course, more reactive than chlorides or bromides; it is not surprising then that iodobenzene reacts with diphenylamine at relatively high temperatures to produce triphenylamine in 85% yield (OS I, 544). Nitrobenzene is employed as solvent with copper powder as a catalyst, potassium carbonate being added to neutralize the acid that is liberated. N-Phenylanthranilic acid is synthesized in a similar way from aniline and *o*-chlorobenzoic acid (OS II, 15; 93% yield).

Use of the sulfo group as a blocking agent is illustrated by the preparation of 2,6-dinitroaniline from chlorobenzene (OS **31**, 45; 36% yield).

If but one nitro group is introduced, the product is *o*-nitroaniline (OS I, 388).

1,3-Dichloro-4,6-dinitrobenzene is ammonolyzed to 1,3-diamino-4,6-dinitrobenzene (OS **40**, 96; yield 96%).

2-Chloro-5-nitropyridine undergoes ammonolysis more readily than 2,4-dinitrochlorobenzene, which may be regarded as its benzene analog.[19]

$$O_2N \overset{\displaystyle \bigcirc}{\underset{N}{}} Cl \quad > \quad O_2N \overset{\displaystyle \bigcirc}{\underset{NO_2}{}} Cl$$

Hydrazinolysis serves to produce arylhydrazines, an example being the synthesis of 2,4-dinitrophenylhydrazine from 2,4-dinitrochlorobenzene (OS II, 228; 85% yield).

$$\underset{NO_2}{\overset{Cl}{\bigcirc}} NO_2 \rightarrow \underset{NO_2}{\overset{NHNH_2}{\bigcirc}} NO_2$$

Di-*p*-nitrophenyl sulfide is made by treating *p*-chloronitrobenzene with potassium ethyl xanthate (OS III, 667; 82% yield).

$$2 O_2N \bigcirc Cl \xrightarrow{\text{KSCSOC}_2\text{H}_5} O_2N \bigcirc S \bigcirc NO_2$$

Sulfonate groups, like halides, are replaced readily; when the tosyl ester of 2,4-dinitrophenol is treated with aniline, ammonolysis occurs, the product being 2,4-dinitrodiphenylamine.

$$O_2N \underset{NO_2}{\overset{OSO_2 \bigcirc CH_3}{\bigcirc}} + C_6H_5NH_2 \rightarrow O_2N \underset{NO_2}{\overset{NHC_6H_5}{\bigcirc}} + CH_3 \bigcirc SO_3H$$

Replacement of fluorine in *p*-fluoronitrobenzene by azide ion is believed to proceed by way of the following intermediate.[20]

$$\underset{O}{\overset{-O}{}} \overset{+}{N} = \bigcirc \overset{F}{\underset{N_3}{}}$$

[19] A. Mangini and B. Frenguelli, *Gazz. chim. ital.*, **69**, 86, 97 (1939).
[20] R. Bolton, J. Miller, and A. J. Parker, *Chem. and Ind.*, 1026 (1960).

Displacement of alkoxyl and aroxyl groups

Ethers of phenols are cleaved by alkalis, the ease of cleavage increasing with the acid strength of the phenol from which the ether is derived. Ethers of strongly acidic phenols, in fact, may be compared to esters with respect to many of their reactions. These two classes of compounds differ from ordinary ethers in that one of the groups attached to the ether oxygen atom is electron poor and therefore vulnerable to attack by nucleophilic agents. Anisole reacts very sluggishly with alkalis, undergoing partial hydrolysis at 180 to 200°. 2,4-Dinitroanisole, on the other hand, gives 2,4-dinitrophenol when boiled for one hour with one equivalent of potassium hydroxide in ethanol.

The phenyl ether of 2,4-dinitrophenol reacts with hydroxylamine to yield 2,4-dinitrophenylhydroxylamine. The action of potassium ethoxide on 2,4,6-trinitroanisole produces the corresponding phenetole. This reaction has been carried out in such a way as to permit the isolation of the potassium salt containing both ether functions; the following is one of its principal resonance structures.

Convincing evidence for this structure is the fact that the compound may be prepared also from potassium methoxide and 2,4,6-trinitrophenetole. Similar intermediates have been isolated; indeed they may be formed in all types of aromatic nucleophilic displacement reactions. It seems probable that the transition states are very close to these intermediates and that the resonance stabilization of such intermediates gives a fairly accurate measure of the driving force of the displacements (Hine, 366).

Displacement of phenolic hydroxyl groups

Displacement of phenolic hydroxyl groups is usually difficult to effect. The preparation of aryl halides from phenols, for example, even with the phosphorus halides, is seldom achieved in satisfactory yields. The reaction is favored, as might be expected, by groups such as nitro. An example is the synthesis of picryl chloride from picric acid.

2-Naphthol is exceptional, affording 2-chloronaphthalene and 2-bromo-naphthalene in yields of 55 and 38%, respectively. The reaction is carried out by treating sodium 2-naphthoxide with the appropriate phosphorus trihalide. The unusual nature of 2-naphthol shows up also in ether formation. This phenol yields ethers when treated with alcohols in the presence of an acid catalyst.

The etherification is stopped almost completely by a bromine atom or a nitro or alkyl group in position 1.

Etherification with methanol occurs also with resorcinol but not with phenol, catechol, or hydroquinone and produces the mono- but not the dimethyl ether. Similarly phloroglucinol readily yields a dimethyl but not a trimethyl ether. By use of β-naphthol as an example the mechanism can be formulated in the following way.

This mechanism is supported by the fact that when oxygen-18-labeled methanol is used, nearly quantitative transfer of the heavy oxygen to the ether is observed.[21]

Certain enols can be etherified in a similar way; dihydroresorcinol reacts with ethanol in the presence of p-toluenesulfonic acid to give the ethyl ether, 3-ethoxy-2-cyclohexenone (OS **40**, 41; yield 75%).

[21] K. B. Wiberg and K. A. Saegebarth, *J. Org. Chem.*, **25**, 832 (1960).

Similar results have been presented by Bucherer, who isolated an addition compound from 2-naphthol and sodium bisulfite.

Bucherer Reaction. Replacement of phenolic hydroxyl groups by amino groups, rarely possible by direct means, can be accomplished with ease in the naphthalene series. Naphthols when treated with ammonia and sodium bisulfite give the corresponding naphthylamines. This transformation, known as the Bucherer reaction, is reversible and can be employed to convert naphthylamines into the corresponding naphthols (OR **1**, 105). 1-Naphthol reacts with sodium bisulfite to form an addition compound, which is believed to be the corresponding *m*-tetralonesulfonate.[22]

The only benzene derivative that undergoes this type of reaction at all satisfactorily is resorcinol; *m*-phenylenediamine is formed in 80% yields. Another example outside the naphthalene group is 8-hydroxyquinoline, which gives the corresponding amine in nearly quantitative yields.

In some instances replacement can be effected by heating with ammonia under pressure or in the presence of a catalyst such as zinc chloride. The conversion of 3-hydroxy-2-naphthoic acid into 3-amino-2-naphthoic acid illustrates the use of zinc chloride (OS III, 78; 70% yield).

Displacement of amino groups

Displacement of amino groups, which occurs readily with *p*-nitrosoanilines (p. 374), is facilitated also by other electron-withdrawing groups. 2,4-Dinitroaniline, for example, can be changed to the corresponding phenol by hydrolysis and to 2,4-dinitrophenyl ethers by alcoholysis.

Industrial production of phloroglucinol involves hydrolysis of 1,3,5-triaminobenzene by heating with hydrochloric acid for 20 hours.[23]

[22] A. Rieche and H. Seeboth, *Ann.*, **638**, 66 (1960).
[23] M. L. Kastens and J. F. Kaplan, *Ind. Eng. Chem.*, **42**, 402 (1950).

The Carbonyl Group as an Activator

The carbonyl group falls rather far down in the list of activators, but has the same type of influence as other m-directing groups. When 2,4-dichloroacetophenone is treated with ammonium hydroxide, for example, both halogen atoms are replaced by amino groups; the yield of 2,4-diaminoacetophenone is low, however.[24]

Bromide ion displacement

Although displacement of halogen atoms *ortho* or *para* to a nitro group has often been observed, a similar transformation of o- or p-halobenzophenone has not been reported. This is presumably because the carbonyl group becomes involved. In the hindered ketone series such involvement is unlikely; duryl o-bromophenyl ketone undergoes methanolysis in the presence of 4.7N potassium methoxide to give the corresponding methoxy compound in 95% yield.

p-Bromophenyl mesityl ketone behaves in a similar way, but the m-isomer reacts sluggishly and in a different manner; by 48 hours of heating 78% of the bromine is replaced, the product being phenyl mesityl ketone.

Displacements with Grignard reagents

The ethers of o- and p-hydroxyaryl ketones would be expected to behave as esters. With Grignard reagents, for example, they might be expected to suffer displacement of the alkoxyl group by the hydrocarbon radical of the Grignard reagent. By blocking the approach to the carbonyl group it has been possible to realize changes of this character. Mesityl o-methoxyphenyl ketone reacts with phenylmagnesium bromide at 30° to produce 2-biphenylyl mesityl ketone in 35% yield.

This type of reaction appears to be general for hindered o-methoxy ketones and for both aliphatic and aromatic Grignard reagents. A

[24] N. J. Leonard and S. N. Boyd, Jr., *J. Org. Chem.*, **11**, 405 (1946).

particularly impressive example is the conversion of duryl 2,6-dimethoxy-phenyl ketone into duryl 2,6-xylyl ketone in 47% yield.

$$\text{DurC=O} \qquad\qquad \text{DurC=O}$$

CH$_3$O⟨⟩OCH$_3$ $\xrightarrow{\text{CH}_3\text{MgI}}$ CH$_3$⟨⟩CH$_3$

Very odd is the displacement of the methoxyl group in the 2-position of 2,3-dimethoxybenzonitrile; the isopropyl reagent, for example, gives an 83% conversion. The most curious feature of this displacement is that the reaction does not occur without the flanking methoxyl group in position 3; and a second methoxyl group elsewhere on the ring does not have this effect.[25]

Rosemund–von Braun Reaction

Aromatic halides give the corresponding nitriles when treated with cuprous cyanide. 1-Naphthonitrile, for example, is formed in 90% yield from either the chloride or bromide in the presence of pyridine (OS III, 631). Another example is the conversion of 9-bromophenanthrene into 9-cyanophenanthrene (OS III, 212; 87% yield). This reaction, discovered long ago, has come to be known as the Rosenmund-von Braun reaction (CR **42**, 189). It proceeds satisfactorily only at relatively high temperatures and is autocatalytic. The reaction is not limited to simple aryl halides, as is shown by the preparation of *p*-cyanobenzoic acid from *p*-bromobenzoic acid. Likewise, 3-bromopyridine is converted into nicotinonitrile by this procedure.

⟨⟩Br → ⟨⟩CN

Excellent results have been obtained by use of quinoline in place of pyridine. Tri(*p*-bromophenyl)ethylene, for instance, affords the corresponding tricyano compound in 97% yield.[26]

Br⟨⟩CH=C⟨⟩Br → NC⟨⟩CH=C⟨⟩CN

Superior solvents for the reaction are dimethylformamide[27] and N-methylpyrrolidone.[28]

[25] R. Richtzenhain, *Ber.*, **77B**, 1 (1944).

[26] R. E. Allen, E. L. Schumann, W. C. Day, and M. G. Van Campen, Jr., *J. Am. Chem. Soc.*, **80**, 591 (1958).

[27] L. Friedman and H. Shechter, *J. Org. Chem.*, **26**, 2522 (1961).

[28] M. S. Newman and H. Boden, *J. Org. Chem.*, **26**, 2525 (1961).

Arylation of Active Methylene Compounds

Active methylene compounds also can be condensed with aryl halides in which the halogen atom is activated. An example is the synthesis of α-(4-cinnolyl)phenylacetonitrile from 4-chlorocinnoline and phenylacetonitrile; the yield is 94%.[29]

Another example is the arylation of ethyl cyanoacetate by treatment with 2,4-dinitrochlorobenzene. The yield of ethyl 2,4-dinitrophenylcyanoacetate is 90%.[30]

Smiles Rearrangement

Certain intramolecular nucleophilic displacements are known collectively as the Smiles rearrangement. An example is the conversion of 2-hydroxy-5-methyl-2'-nitrodiphenyl sulfone into 4-methyl-2'-nitro-2-sulfinodiphenyl ether in the presence of alkali.[31]

The essential feature is the displacement of the $-SO_2^-$ group by $-O^-$.

Another illustration is the formation of 2-carboxy-4'-nitrodiphenyl ether from 4-nitrophenyl salicylate.[32]

[29] R. N. Castle and F. H. Kruse, *J. Org. Chem.*, **17**, 1571 (1952).
[30] A. Fairbourne and H. R. Fawson, *J. Chem. Soc.*, 46, (1927).
[31] A. A. Levy, H. C. Rains, and S. Smiles, *J. Chem. Soc.*, 3264 (1931).
[32] B. T. Tozer and S. Smiles, *J. Chem. Soc.*, 1897 (1938).

Displacements in Nitrogen Heterocycles

The azomethine group shown by the Kekulé structures of pyridine and similar aromatic rings may be compared to a carbonyl group, and on this basis the electron deficit at the α- and γ-positions is predictable. Furthermore, substituents in these positions might be expected to imitate the behavior of those in the analogous carbonyl derivatives. Amino groups, for example, can be replaced by the attack of various nucleophiles. Thus 2-hydroxyquinoline can be made from 2-aminoquinoline by hydrolysis.

Replacement of hydroxyl groups by chlorine occurs readily in α- and γ-hydroxy derivatives of pyridine and quinoline, but not with the β-isomers. An example is the preparation of 2-chlorolepidine by the action of phosphorus oxychloride on 4-methylcarbostyril (OS III, 194; 89% yield).

Pyridine N-oxides react to give 2- and 4-chloropyridines. An example is the conversion of the N-oxide of nicotinamide (p. 241) into 2-chloro-nicotinonitrile by treatment with phosphorus pentachloride. Dehydration of the amide group accompanies the introduction of chlorine (OS **37**, 12; 38% yield).

An example of ammonolysis from the pyrimidine series is the preparation of 2-(dimethylamino)pyrimidine from the corresponding chloro compound (OS **35**, 58; 86% yield).

Cine-Substitution

A number of nucleophilic displacements are known in which the position taken by the entering group is not the same as that vacated by the leaving group. The phenomenon is known as cine-substitution (CR **49**, 273). The *von Richter reaction*, for instance, transforms aromatic nitro compounds into aromatic acids in which the carboxyl group is in a position *ortho* to that originally occupied by the nitro group. Examples are the conversion of *p*-bromonitrobenzene into *m*-bromobenzoic acid and of *m*-bromonitrobenzene into a mixture of *o*- and *p*-bromobenzoic acids.

2-Bromo-4-nitrotoluene gives 2-bromo-3-methylbenzoic acid in low yield (OS **38**, 12).

It seems likely that conjugate addition is the first step of the process. The evidence supports the following mechanism.[33]

[33] M. Rosenblum, *J. Am. Chem. Soc.*, **82**, 3796 (1960).

It has been suggested that the nitroso amide could be formed in the following way.[34]

The first step in the conversion of *m*-dinitrobenzene into 2,6-dimethoxy-benzonitrile is similar. This change is effected by heating with a methanolic solution of potassium cyanide (OS III, 293).

The formation of *m*-cresol as a by-product in the hydrolysis of *o*- or *p*-chlorotoluene (p. 372) is another example of cine-substitution. In an effort to explain such rearrangements an elimination-addition mechanism was suggested that postulates the transitory existence of an electrically neutral intermediate known as *benzyne* (*Angew.* **72**, 91). Evidence in support of this mechanism is that chlorobenzene-1-C[14] in the reaction with ammonia gives almost exactly equal amounts of aniline-1-C[14] and aniline-2-C[14].[35]

Moreover, benzyne has been captured by dienic molecules (p. 689); when *o*-bromofluorobenzene is treated with magnesium in the presence of anthracene, triptycen is obtained.[36]

---

[34] E. Cullen and P. L'Écuyer, *Can. J. Chem.*, **39**, 862 (1961).
[35] See M. Panar and J. D. Roberts, *J. Am. Chem. Soc.*, **82**, 3629 (1960).
[36] G. Wittig and E. Benz, *Tetrahedron*, **10**, 37 (1960).

o-Bromoiodobenzene reacts with metallic lithium to give triphenylene, a trimer of benzyne; it is obtained in 83% yield (OS **40**, 105).

Similar evidence has been presented for the intervention of cyclohexyne and cyclopentyne in nucleophilic substitution reactions of cyclohexenyl and cyclopentenyl halides, respectively.[37]

A general method for making N,N-dialkylanilines is to heat an aryl bromide with sodium amide in a refluxing solution of a secondary amine. Thus piperidine and bromobenzene afford N-phenylpiperidine in 99% yield. It is presumed that benzyne is an intermediate; bromomesitylene and 1-bromo-2-methylnaphthalene, which are unable to form a benzyne derivative, do not react in this way.[38]

A method of ring closure has been developed that depends on the production of a benzyne with a side chain bearing a nucleophile. An example is the formation of phenothiazene by treating 2-amino-2′-bromo-diphenyl sulfide with potassium amide.[39]

Phenylation of enolates of ketones has been accomplished also; diethyl ketone, for example, yields 2-phenyl-3-pentanone when treated with bromobenzene and sodium amide in liquid ammonia.[40]

$$CH_3CH_2COCH_2CH_3 \rightarrow CH_3CH_2COCHCH_3$$
$$\overset{|}{C_6H_5}$$

[37] L. K. Montgomery and J. D. Roberts, *J. Am. Chem Soc.*, **82**, 4750 (1960).
[38] J. F. Bunnett and T. K. Brotherton, *J. Org. Chem.*, **22**, 832 (1957).
[39] J. F. Bunnett and B. F. Hrutfiord, *J. Am. Chem. Soc.*, **83**, 1691 (1961).
[40] W. W. Leake and R. Levine, *J. Am. Chem. Soc.*, **81**, 1169 (1959).

When benzenediazonium-2-carboxylate is decomposed by flash photolysis, biphenylene is formed; in the interval between its formation and its
dimerization benzyne has been detected by measurement of its infrared
spectrum.[41]

$$\text{(structure with } CO_2^- \text{ and } N_2^+) \rightarrow \text{(benzyne structure)} + N_2 + CO_2$$

[41] M. Stiles and R. G. Miller, *J. Am. Chem. Soc.*, **82**, 3802 (1960).

17

Nucleophilic addition reactions of unsaturated compounds

The salient feature of the carbonyl group is that the carbon atom is electron deficient, i.e., carries a partial positive charge.

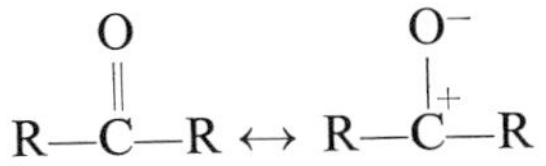

$$
\begin{array}{ccc}
\text{O} & & \text{O}^- \\
\parallel & & | \\
\text{R—C—R} & \leftrightarrow & \text{R—C}^+\text{—R}
\end{array}
$$

This atom is therefore the site of attack of nucleophilic agents.[1] The driving force of such attack depends in part on the availability of the electron pair (the basicity of the attacking agent) and in part on the degree of electron deficiency of the carbonyl carbon atom. Attachment of electron-donating groups to the carbonyl group diminishes the electron deficit, which accounts for the observation that carbonyl characteristics are low in acids, amides, and esters.

The electron shortage at the carbonyl carbon atom in a carboxylate ion is practically nullified by the accession of electrons from the oxygen atoms.

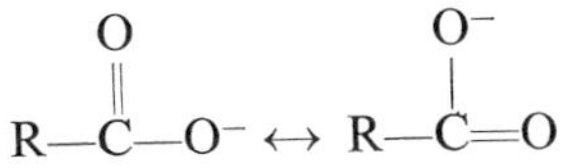

$$
\begin{array}{ccc}
\text{O} & & \text{O}^- \\
\parallel & & | \\
\text{R—C—O}^- & \leftrightarrow & \text{R—C=O}
\end{array}
$$

The carbonate ion represents the extreme case.

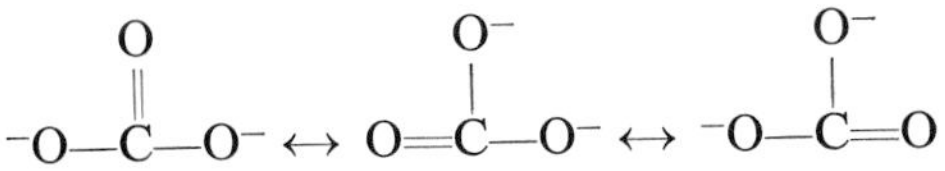

$$
\begin{array}{ccccc}
\text{O} & & \text{O}^- & & \text{O}^- \\
\parallel & & | & & | \\
^-\text{O—C—O}^- & \leftrightarrow & \text{O=C—O}^- & \leftrightarrow & ^-\text{O—C=O}
\end{array}
$$

Halogen atoms, particularly in α-positions, would be expected to enhance the reactivity of carbonyl compounds, since they withdraw electrons, thus

[1] A. Gero, *J. Chem. Education*, **31**, 136 (1954).

increasing the electron shortage at the carbonyl carbon atom. Such compounds as chloral and bromal in fact do possess unusually reactive carbonyl groups. The aldehyde function in glyoxals ranks as one of the most reactive types, the extreme example being glyoxal itself.

$$\underset{\text{Glyoxal}}{H-\underset{\underset{\displaystyle O}{\|}}{C}-\underset{\underset{\displaystyle O}{\|}}{C}-H}$$

The steric factor is also of great importance; reactivity falls off with increasing size and bulkiness of the attached radicals. When these are sufficiently large and complex, the carbonyl group may become almost inert. In dimesityl ketone, for example, the carbonyl group is practically immune to nucleophilic attack.

Dimesityl ketone

That methyl ketones are more reactive than their higher homologs would be predicted from a consideration of the steric factors involved. In general, reactivity falls off with increasing space-filling capacity of the radicals.

As might have been expected on steric grounds, the lower members of the cyclic ketone series are more reactive than the corresponding open chain ketones. This difference is illustrated by the behavior toward sodium bisulfite (p. 422). The cyclanones, however, show unexpected differences among themselves. Cyclohexanone, for example, is highly reactive toward cyanide ion and semicarbazide whereas cyclopentanone and cycloheptanone are surprisingly resistant to attack by these reagents.[2]

[2] V. Prelog and M. Kobelt, *Helv. Chem. Acta*, **32**, 1187 (1949).

These three ketones exhibit the same difference of reactivity toward per-benzoic acid.[3] These and other peculiar changes in reactivity with ring size have been ascribed to internal strain.[4] The cyclohexane ring with six tetrahedral carbon atoms is highly symmetrical and stable, with hydrogen-hydrogen repulsions at a minimum in the chair form, which permits the fully staggered conformation (Gould, 240). Reactions of cyclohexanone in which the trigonal carbonyl carbon atom goes to a tetrahedral configuration should then be specially favored.

For purposes of discussion alicyclic compounds have been divided into classical (three- to seven-membered) and many-membered (eight-membered and larger) ring compounds. The classical group is subdivided into small (three- and four-membered) and common (five-, six-, and seven-membered) ring compounds. Many-membered ring compounds comprise medium (eight- to twelve-membered) and large (thirteen-membered and higher) ring compounds.[4]

As would be expected, conjugation of the carbonyl group with an olefinic linkage or an aryl radical diminishes its reactivity. This resonance effect is pronounced in the aromatic aldehydes and ketones.

Another way in which one might hope to increase the reactivity of a carbonyl group is to introduce a metal such as silver or nickel, which can coordinate with the carbonyl oxygen atom to effect electron withdrawal. Actually such metals are effective catalysts in the Cannizzaro reaction, for example (p. 552).

Self-condensation

The extensive polarization of the carbonyl group makes it bifunctional, with an electrophilic as well as a nucleophilic center. As a consequence the lower aldehydes show a marked tendency to undergo self-condensation. Formaldehyde, for example, yields a cyclic trimer, s-trioxane.

$$3CH_2O \xrightarrow{\;H_2SO_4\;}$$

Paraldehyde, formed from acetaldehyde, seems to have an analogous structure.

[3] S. L. Friess, *J. Am. Chem. Soc.*, **71**, 2571 (1949).

[4] H. C. Brown, R. S. Fletcher, and R. B. Johannesen, *J. Am. Chem. Soc.*, **73**, 212 (1951).

Alternatively, formaldehyde undergoes polymerization to paraformaldehyde.

$$HOCH_2(OCH_2)_n OCH_2OH$$

Polymers having very long chains, known as polyoxymethylenes (Angew. **73**, 177), are obtained from liquid formaldehyde at low temperatures. Delrin is a commercially important polyoxymethylene with the ends capped; one type has acetoxyl end groups.

$$CH_3CO_2CH_2(OCH_2)_n OCH_2OCOCH_3$$
Delrin

The tendency of the simpler aldehydes to form cyclic trimers is much more marked in the thiocarbonyl compounds; the simple monomeric sulfur compounds, in fact, are difficult to isolate. When formaldehyde reacts with hydrogen sulfide in the presence of hydrochloric acid, the product is not thioformaldehyde but its cyclic trimer, s-trithiane (OS II, 610; 94% yield).

$$3CH_2O + 3H_2S \xrightarrow{HCl} \begin{matrix} S \\ CH_2 \quad CH_2 \\ | \qquad | \\ S \qquad S \\ CH_2 \end{matrix} + 3H_2O$$

Acetophenone and certain of its derivatives behave in a similar way.[5]

Nitriles exhibit this type of bifunctionality also, being able to trimerize to triazines in the presence of acidic catalysts. Benzonitrile, for example, forms 2,4,6-triphenyl-s-triazine.

$$3C_6H_5CN \rightarrow \begin{matrix} N \\ C_6H_5C \quad CC_6H_5 \\ | \qquad || \\ N \qquad N \\ CC_6H_5 \end{matrix}$$

The same product can be obtained by treating benzonitrile with sodium, but the reaction in this case proceeds in a more complex manner.[6]

Hydration

Highly reactive aldehydes such as chloral form hydrates, the corresponding 1,1-dihydroxy compounds. Perfluoroaldehydes, made by reduction of the

[5] E. Campaigne, W. B. Reid, Jr., and J. D. Pera, *J. Org. Chem.*, **24**, 1229 (1959).
[6] J. J. Ritter and R. D. Anderson, *J. Org. Chem.*, **24**, 208 (1959).

corresponding acids with lithium aluminum hydride, form hydrates that are relatively stable; perfluorobutyraldehyde is an example.

$$CF_3CF_2CF_2CHO + H_2O \rightarrow CF_3CF_2CF_2CH(OH)_2$$

Glyoxals of the formula RCOCHO are hydrated readily; glyoxal itself holds water so tenaciously as to be difficult to obtain in pure form. Diketo-succinic acid exists as the dihydrate, dihydroxytartaric acid. The hydrate of glyoxylic acid is known as dihydroxyacetic acid. Solutions of form-aldehyde in water have properties which indicate that it is hydrated to a large degree. From these observations it seems very likely that the tendency of carbonyl compounds to become hydrated is general, the hydrates usually being too unstable to be isolated. The cleavage of certain keto alcohols and acids by periodic acid or lead tetraacetate has been explained on this assumption (p. 225).

Certain aldehydes react with hydrogen sulfide under high pressure to give the corresponding 1,1-dithiols; propionaldehyde, for example, yields 1,1-propanedithiol, which is stable enough to be distilled without decomposition.[7]

$$CH_3CH_2CHO + 2H_2S \rightarrow CH_3CH_2CH\begin{smallmatrix} SH \\ \\ SH \end{smallmatrix} + H_2O$$

Analogous olthiols have been prepared by treating certain halo aldehydes and ketones with hydrogen sulfides under pressure. s-Dichlorotetrafluoro-acetone, for example, gives the corresponding olthiol in 91 % yield.[8]

$$\begin{smallmatrix} ClCF_2 \\ \\ ClCF_2 \end{smallmatrix}C{=}O + H_2S \rightarrow \begin{smallmatrix} ClCF_2 \\ \\ ClCF_2 \end{smallmatrix}C\begin{smallmatrix} OH \\ \\ SH \end{smallmatrix}$$

Still more remarkable is the isolation of distillable 1,1-halohydrins by the addition of hydrogen halides to hexafluorocyclobutanone.[9]

$$\begin{matrix} F_2C{-}C{=}O \\ | \quad | \\ F_2C{-}CF_2 \end{matrix} + HX \rightarrow \begin{matrix} & X & \\ & | & \\ F_2C{-}C{-}OH \\ | \quad | \\ F_2C{-}CF_2 \end{matrix}$$

[7] T. L. Cairns, G. L. Evans, A. W. Larchar, and B. C. McKusick, *J. Am. Chem. Soc.*, **74**, 3982 (1952).

[8] J. F. Harris, Jr., *J. Org. Chem.*, **25**, 2259 (1960).

[9] S. Andreades and D. C. England, *J. Am. Chem. Soc.*, **83**, 4670 (1961).

Aldehydes and a wide variety of ketones react with hydrogen sulfide in the presence of hydrochloric acid or zinc chloride to yield the corresponding thio compounds. Thiobenzophenone, for example, is made from benzophenone by the action of hydrogen sulfide in the presence of hydrogen chloride (OS **35**, 97; 77% yield).

$$(C_6H_5)_2CO + H_2S \xrightarrow{HCl} (C_6H_5)_2CS + H_2O$$

Reaction with Alcohols

Hemiacetals

Hydroxy compounds other than water may combine additively with carbonyl compounds also; such addition compounds with alcohols are known as *hemiacetals*.

$$RCHO + R'OH \rightleftharpoons RCH \Big\langle {\overset{\displaystyle OH}{\underset{\displaystyle OR'}{}}}$$

Like hydrates, the hemiacetals are formed reversibly and are rarely stable enough to be isolated. Hydroxy aldehydes and ketones in which the two groups are not too far apart show a tendency to form cyclic hemiacetals. Glycolaldehyde and acetol are examples.

$$\begin{array}{ccc} CH_2CHO & \rightleftharpoons & CH_2 \!\!-\!\! CH \\ | & & \diagdown\!\diagup \; | \\ OH & & O \;\; OH \end{array}$$

Glycolaldehyde

$$\begin{array}{ccc} CH_3COCH_2OH & \rightleftharpoons & CH_3C\!\!-\!\!-\!\!-\!\!CH_2 \\ & & | \diagdown\!\diagup \\ & & HO \;\; O \end{array}$$

Acetol

This behavior is of course more marked in γ- and δ-hydroxy aldehydes and ketones, which form rings of five and six members, respectively. In aqueous dioxane 4-hydroxybutanal and 5-hydroxypentanal, for instance, exist predominantly as cyclic hemiacetals, containing an estimated 11.4 and 6.1%, respectively, of free aldehyde at 25°.[10] These reactions are especially important in sugar chemistry, the ring forms of monosaccharides being hemi-acetals.

Many keto acids behave as though the hydroxyl group had added to the carbonyl group to produce cyclic derivative analogous to hemiacetals. These compounds, known as hydroxy lactones or lactols, are exemplified by the cyclic form of o-benzoylbenzoic acid.

[10] C. D. Hurd and W. H. Saunders, Jr., *J. Am. Chem. Soc.*, **74**, 5324 (1952).

o-Benzoylbenzoic acid

Levulinic acid, formed by heating sucrose or starch with concentrated hydrochloric acid (OS I, 335), likewise yields a lactol.

Such keto acids exhibit a tendency to form *pseudo esters*, i.e., esters which correspond to the lactol forms.

The formation of furans by dehydration of 1,4-diketones presumably involves the hemiacetal as an intermediate. The preparation of 2,5-dimethylfuran by heating acetonylacetone with zinc chloride is an example.

When the diketone is heated with phosphorus trisulfide or pentasulfide, 2,5-dimethylthiophane is produced (OR **6**, 410).

Acetalization. When an aldehyde is treated with an alcohol in the presence of an acidic catalyst, the hemiacetal formed initially may react with a second molecule of the alcohol to yield an acetal. Calcium, boron, and ammonium chlorides are useful catalysts for this type of reaction. An example of acetalization is the preparation of acetal from ethanol and acetaldehyde (OS I, 1).

In this synthesis acetaldehyde, calcium chloride, and 95% ethanol are put together in such proportions as to to cause the mixture to separate into two layers during the course of the reaction. The acetal goes into the upper, ethanolic layer where it is out of contact with the catalyst, causing the equilibrium to be shifted in the desired direction. Under these conditions the yield is 64%.

β-Ketoacetals are made conveniently from the corresponding hydroxymethylene compounds. In the actual procedure the sodium salt of the hydroxymethylene compound, made by condensing a ketone with methyl formate in the presence of sodium methoxide, is subjected directly to acetalization. An example is the preparation of the dimethylacetal of acetoacetaldehyde from acetone; the yield is 65%.[11]

$$CH_3COCH_3 \rightarrow CH_3COCH{=}CHONa \rightarrow CH_3COCH_2CH(OCH_3)_2$$

Cyclic acetals or *dioxolanes* are formed by 1,2-glycols, such as glycerol, which reacts with acetone to yield the dioxolane usually called isopropylideneglycerol. A suitable catalyst is *p*-toluenesulfonic acid (OS III, 502; 90% yield). Part of the success of this method is undoubtedly due to the fact that the second step is intramolecular. It appears to take place in the following way.

Acetaldehyde and ethylene glycol react in a similar manner.

Most ketones form cyclic acetals when heated with suitably constituted glycols in the presence of benzene- or *p*-toluenesulfonic acid. The reaction is conducted in such a way that the water produced is removed by distillation as the reaction proceeds. 1,3-Glycols, as indicated earlier (p. 158),

[11] E. E. Royals and K. C. Brannock, *J. Am. Chem. Soc.*, **75**, 2050 (1953).

react in a similar way to give 1,3-dioxanes, the parent compound being produced when trimethylene glycol is treated with formaldehyde or polyoxymethylene in the presence of phosphoric acid.

$$\begin{array}{c} CH_2OH \\ \diagup \\ CH_2 \\ \diagdown \\ CH_2OH \end{array} + CH_2O \rightarrow \begin{array}{c} CH_2\!\!-\!\!O \\ \diagup \qquad \diagdown \\ CH_2 \qquad\quad CH_2 \\ \diagdown \qquad \diagup \\ CH_2\!\!-\!\!O \end{array} + H_2O$$

Pentaerythritol reacts readily with aldehydes and ketones, preferably in the presence of a small amount of anhydrous zinc chloride, to yield spirans. The reaction with cyclopentanone is an example.

$$2\ \square\!\!=\!\!O + C(CH_2OH)_4 \rightarrow$$

$$+ 2H_2O$$

The monobenzal derivative can be made in 77% yield by using benzaldehyde and pentaerythritol in equimolecular proportions (OS **38**, 65).

α-Hydroxy acids are 1,2-dihydroxy compounds and are capable of forming dioxolones. Mandelic acid, for example, combines with acetone under the influence of sulfuric acid as shown in the following equation.

$$\begin{array}{c} C_6H_5CH\!\!-\!\!C\!\!=\!\!O \\ \quad| \qquad\quad | \\ OH \quad\ \ OH \end{array} + CH_3COCH_3 \rightarrow \begin{array}{c} C_6H_5CH\!\!-\!\!\!-\!\!CO \\ \quad| \qquad\qquad | \\ O \qquad\quad O \\ \diagdown \quad\ \diagup \\ C \\ \diagup \quad \diagdown \\ CH_3 \quad CH_3 \end{array} + H_2O$$

With the exception of the derivatives of 1,2- and 1,3-glycols already noted, acetals of ketones do not form readily and are generally made by treating the ketone with an orthoformic ester. The ketal from acetone and ethanol, for example, can be made satisfactorily in this way.

$$\begin{array}{c} CH_3 \\ \diagdown \\ C\!\!=\!\!O \\ \diagup \\ CH_3 \end{array} + HC(OC_2H_5)_3 \ \overset{HCl}{\rightleftharpoons}\ \begin{array}{c} CH_3 \quad\ OC_2H_5 \\ \diagdown \quad\ \diagup \\ C \\ \diagup \quad \diagdown \\ CH_3 \quad\ OC_2H_5 \end{array} + HCO_2C_2H_5$$

In this type of reaction the alcohol corresponding to the ortho ester is chosen as the solvent. The ortho ester method can be employed with aldehydes also.

Cyclohexanone is exceptional in that its dimethyl ketal is formed by direct reaction with methanol.[12] With ethanol the reaction proceeds also, but the equilibrium is unfavorable. In the presence of the dimethyl ketal of acetone, however, even isopropyl alcohol reacts to form ketals. A mixture of cyclohexanone, isopropyl alcohol, and 2,2-dimethoxypropane gives cyclohexanone diisopropyl ketal and also the mixed ketal, cyclohexanone isopropyl methyl ketal. It seems likely that acetalization occurs between the ketone and the alcohol but that the equilibrium is not favorable.

$$
\underset{\substack{\text{O}}}{\bigcirc} + 2 \underset{\substack{CH_3 \\ CH_3}}{CHOH} \overset{H^+}{\rightleftharpoons} \underset{\substack{(CH_3)_2CHO \quad OCH(CH_3)_2}}{\bigcirc} + H_2O
$$

The reaction may proceed, however, if the water is removed by the dimethyl ketal of acetone (p. 331).[13]

$$
\underset{\substack{CH_3 \\ CH_3}}{\overset{OCH_3}{C}}\overset{OCH_3}{\underset{OCH_3}{}} + H_2O \overset{H^+}{\longrightarrow} \underset{\substack{CH_3 \\ CH_3}}{CO} + 2CH_3OH
$$

The dimethyl acetal of acetone reacts with alcohols to form higher ketals in which one or both of the methoxy groups have been replaced by higher alkoxyl groups. Transketalization thus serves for the synthesis of both symmetrical and mixed ketals. In the presence of *p*-toluenesulfonic acid butyl alcohol leads to the formation of the following equilibria.[14]

$$
(CH_3)_2C(OCH_3)_2 + C_4H_9OH \rightleftharpoons (CH_3)_2C\underset{OC_4H_9}{\overset{OCH_3}{}} + CH_3OH
$$

$$
(CH_3)_2C\underset{OC_4H_9}{\overset{OCH_3}{}} + C_4H_9OH \rightleftharpoons (CH_3)_2C\underset{OC_4H_9}{\overset{OC_4H_9}{}} + CH_3OH
$$

Also, the mixed ketal undergoes disproportionation reversibly to yield the two symmetrical ketals.

[12] R. E. McCoy, A. W. Baker, and R. S. Gohlke, *J. Org. Chem.*, **22**, 1175 (1957).
[13] W. L. Howard and N. B. Lorette, *J. Org. Chem.*, **25**, 525 (1960).
[14] N. B. Lorette and W. L. Howard, *J. Org. Chem.*, **25**, 521 (1960).

$$2(CH_3)_2C\!\!\begin{array}{c} \diagup OCH_3 \\ \diagdown OC_4H_9 \end{array} \rightleftharpoons (CH_3)_2C(OCH_3)_2 + (CH_3)_2C(OC_4H_9)_2$$

Transketalization is similar to the formation of ortho esters by the alcoholysis of lower ortho esters (p. 164).

Acetals, being sensitive to acids but stable to alkalis, serve to protect aldehyde groups in the presence of alkalis, as was illustrated in the preparation of glyceraldehyde from acrolein (p. 122). Propiolaldehyde (propargylaldehyde) is made in this manner also.

$$CH_2{=}CHCH(OC_2H_5)_2 + Br_2 \rightarrow BrCH_2\overset{\overset{\displaystyle Br}{|}}{C}HCH(OC_2H_5)_2$$

$$BrCH_2\overset{\overset{\displaystyle Br}{|}}{C}HCH(OC_2H_5)_2 + 2NaOH \rightarrow$$

$$HC{\equiv}C{-}CH(OC_2H_5)_2 + 2NaBr + 2H_2O$$

$$HC{\equiv}C{-}CH(OC_2H_5)_2 + H_2O \rightarrow HC{\equiv}C{-}CHO + 2C_2H_5OH$$

Phenylpropiolaldehyde is derived from cinnamaldehyde by a similar series of reactions (OS III, 731).

$$C_6H_5CH{=}CHCHO \xrightarrow{Br_2} C_6H_5\underset{\underset{\displaystyle Br}{|}}{C}H\underset{\underset{\displaystyle Br}{|}}{C}HCHO \xrightarrow{K_2CO_3}$$

$$C_6H_5CH{=}CBrCHO \xrightarrow{HC(OC_2H_5)_3} C_6H_5CH{=}CBrCH(OC_2H_5)_2 \xrightarrow{KOH}$$

$$C_6H_5C{\equiv}CCH(OC_2H_5)_2 \xrightarrow[H_2SO_4]{H_2O} C_6H_5C{\equiv}CCHO$$

Acetalization has been employed to achieve reduction of the ester groups of the aldehyde-ester $OCHCH_2CH_2CH(CO_2C_2H_5)_2$ without attack of the aldehyde function. With lithium aluminum hydride the reduction of the acetal-ester to the acetal-glycol occurs in 33% yield.[15]

$$(C_2H_5O)_2CHCH_2CH_2CH(CO_2C_2H_5)_2 \rightarrow$$

$$(C_2H_5O)_2CHCH_2CH_2CH(CH_2OH)_2$$

The formation of an α-chloro ether from an aldehyde, an alcohol, and hydrochloric acid appears to resemble acetalization, a hemiacetal probably being formed as an intermediate. The preparation of chloromethyl methyl

[15] C. S. Marvel and H. W. Hill, Jr., *J. Am. Chem. Soc.*, **73**, 481 (1951).

ether, the simplest example, is carried out by passing hydrogen chloride into a mixture of methanol and formalin (OS I, 377).

$$CH_2O + CH_3OH + HCl \rightarrow CH_3OCH_2Cl + H_2O$$

α-Chloroethyl ethyl ether is made in an analogous fashion (OS **36**, 60; 92% yield).

Chloromethyl ether is formed from concentrated hydrochloric acid and paraformaldehyde (OS **36**, 1).

$$2CH_2O + 2HCl \rightarrow ClCH_2OCH_2Cl + H_2O$$

Addition of chlorosulfonic acid improves the procedure (OS **36**, 1; 76% yield).

A method of preparing bromoacetal involves acetalization of bromoacetaldehyde, formed by ethanolysis of α,β-dibromoethyl acetate (OS III, 123; 64% yield).

$$CH_3CO_2CH{=}CH_2 \xrightarrow{Br_2} CH_3CO_2CHBrCH_2Br \xrightarrow{C_2H_5OH}$$

$$BrCH_2CHO \xrightarrow[HBr]{C_2H_5OH} BrCH_2CH(OC_2H_5)_2$$

Acyl halides combine with aldehydes to produce esters holding a halogen atom in the α-position of the alkyl group. An example is the reaction of acetyl bromide with polyoxymethylene to produce bromomethyl acetate.

$$CH_3COBr + CH_2O \rightarrow CH_3CO_2CH_2Br$$

The reaction occurs in the aromatic series also and affords esters in high yields. For example, benzoyl bromide combines with p-bromobenzaldehyde to give the corresponding ester in 80% yield.

Pyranylation with 2,3-dihydropyran has the advantage that the hydroxyl group can be regenerated merely by heating. It serves, for example, to protect the hydroxyl group of phenols during halogen-lithium exchange. 2,6-Dihydroxybenzoic acid may be made from resorcinol by the following sequence of changes.

Carboxyl groups can be protected in a similar way.

Although thiophenol is pyranylated less rapidly than phenol, the reaction of the thio compound is catalyzed by phenol; consequently, thiophenol is pyranylated preferentially in competition with phenol.[16]

The addition of certain tertiary acetylenic alcohols to 2,3-dihydropyran has also been realized.[17]

$$
\text{(ring)}_O + R_2CC{\equiv}CH \rightarrow \text{(ring)}_O{-}OCR_2
$$
$$
\underset{OH}{\big|} \qquad \underset{C{\equiv}CH}{\big|}
$$

t-Butyl hydroperoxide combines with aldehydes and ketones to give peroxy compounds analogous to acetals. With acetone 2,2-*bis*(*t*-butyl-peroxy)propane is formed in 80% yield.[18]

$$
\begin{array}{c} CH_3 \\ \diagdown \\ \diagup \\ CH_3 \end{array}\!\!C{=}O + 2(CH_3)_3COOH \xrightarrow{HCl} \begin{array}{c} CH_3 \quad OOC(CH_3)_3 \\ \diagdown \diagup \\ C \\ \diagup \diagdown \\ CH_3 \quad OOC(CH_3)_3 \end{array} + H_2O
$$

Conjugate addition

Alcohols may be added to α,β-unsaturated carbonyl compounds by use of an alkaline or acid catalyst. Ethyl β-ethoxypropionate is formed from ethyl acrylate and ethanol in the presence of sodium ethoxide.

$$
CH_2{=}CHCO_2C_2H_5 + C_2H_5OH \rightarrow C_2H_5OCH_2CH_2CO_2C_2H_5
$$

Acetalization of α,β-unsaturated aldehydes leads to complications, one product being the β-alkoxy acetal formed by addition of a molecule of alcohol to the aldehyde and subsequent transformation to the acetal. When acrolein is treated with ethanol in the presence of hydrogen chloride, for example, the product consists of a mixture of acrolein acetal and β-ethoxy-propionaldehyde acetal (OS III, 371). By use of ammonium nitrate and ethyl orthoformate, however, the acetal can be prepared in 80% yield (OS **32**, 5). Crotonaldehyde with ethyl alcohol gives the ethyl acetal of β-ethoxybutyraldehyde.

$$
CH_3CH{=}CHCHO \xrightarrow{3C_2H_5OH} CH_3\underset{\underset{OC_2H_5}{\big|}}{C}HCH_2CH(OC_2H_5)_2
$$

One way around the difficulty is illustrated in the synthesis of glycer-aldehyde (p. 222).

[16] W. E. Parham and D. M. DeLaitsch, *J. Am. Chem. Soc.*, **76**, 4962 (1954).

[17] D. N. Robertson, *J. Org. Chem.*, **25**, 931 (1960).

[18] F. H. Dickey, F. F. Rust, and W. E. Vaughan, *J. Am. Chem. Soc.*, **71**, 1432 (1949).

β-Chlorovinyl ketones yield the corresponding keto acetals. An example is β-ketoisoöctaldehyde dimethyl acetal (OS **32**, 79; yield 90%).

$$(CH_3)_2CH(CH_2)_2COCH{=}CHCl + 2CH_3OH + NaOH \rightarrow$$
$$(CH_3)_2CH(CH_2)_2COCH_2CH(OCH_3)_2 + NaCl + H_2O$$

Reaction with Mercaptans

Aldehydes and ketones react with sulfhydryl compounds to yield derivatives that are analogous to acetals and hemiacetals, the reactivity of the sulfhydryl compounds being much greater than that of alcohols. Aldehydes yield hemimercaptals, which may react with another molecule of mercaptan to produce mercaptals.

$$RCHO + R'SH \rightarrow RC\overset{\displaystyle OH}{\underset{\displaystyle SR'}{H}} \quad \xrightarrow{\ R'SH\ } \quad RC\overset{\displaystyle SR'}{\underset{\displaystyle SR'}{H}}$$

The hemimercaptals derived from aldehydes, for example, are stable compounds having sharp melting points. Illustrative are those produced when phenylglyoxal and furfural are mixed with n-propyl mercaptan.[19]

$$C_6H_5CO C\overset{\displaystyle OH}{\underset{\displaystyle SC_3H_7}{H}}$$
(m.p. 84°)

$$\underset{O}{\text{furyl}}{-}C\overset{\displaystyle OH}{\underset{\displaystyle SC_3H_7}{H}}$$
(m.p. 105–106°)

Similarly, ketones give hemimercaptols and mercaptols. Acetone, for example, reacts with ethyl mercaptan as follows.

$$\overset{\displaystyle CH_3}{\underset{\displaystyle CH_3}{C}}{=}O + C_2H_5SH \rightarrow \overset{\displaystyle CH_3}{\underset{\displaystyle CH_3}{C}}\overset{\displaystyle OH}{\underset{\displaystyle SC_2H_5}{}} \quad \xrightarrow{\ C_2H_5SH\ } \quad \overset{\displaystyle CH_3}{\underset{\displaystyle CH_3}{C}}\overset{\displaystyle SC_2H_5}{\underset{\displaystyle SC_2H_5}{}}$$

Conjugate addition

Sulfhydryl compounds are more effective nucleophilic agents than hydroxyl compounds. β-Ketomercaptans are produced by the addition of hydrogen sulfide to α,β-unsaturated ketones. Benzalacetophenone reacts with hydrogen sulfide according to the following equation.

$$C_6H_5CH{=}CHCOC_6H_5 + H_2S \rightarrow C_6H_5\underset{\displaystyle SH}{\overset{\displaystyle |}{C}}HCH_2COC_6H_5$$

[19] F. Kipnis and J. Ornfelt, *J. Am. Chem. Soc.*, **74**, 1068 (1952).

In the presence of sodium, hydrogen sulfide unites with two moles of methyl acrylate, the second phase of the reaction involving the addition of a mercaptan.

$$H_2S + CH_2{=}CHCO_2CH_3 \rightarrow HSCH_2CH_2CO_2CH_3 \xrightarrow{CH_2=CHCO_2CH_3}$$

$$\begin{array}{c} CH_2CH_2CO_2CH_3 \\ / \\ S \\ \backslash \\ CH_2CH_2CO_2CH_3 \end{array}$$

Mercaptans in general react readily with α,β-unsaturated carbonyl compounds and nitriles. 2-Mercaptoethanol, for example, undergoes cyanoethylation (p. 509) without a catalyst (OS III, 458; 94% yield).

$$HOCH_2CH_2SH + CH_2{=}CHCN \rightarrow HOCH_2CH_2SCH_2CH_2CN$$

In fact, catalysts are to be avoided in this particular reaction, since they lead to the dicyanoethylated product ($NCCH_2CH_2OCH_2CH_2SCH_2{-}CH_2CN$).

Reactions with Ammonia and Amino Compounds

Preparation of Schiff bases is most satisfactorily accomplished with aromatic amines and aromatic aldehydes. An example is the formation of benzalaniline from aniline and benzaldehyde (OS I, 80; yield 87%).

$$C_6H_5CH{=}O + C_6H_5NH_2 \rightleftharpoons C_6H_5\overset{\overset{\displaystyle OH}{|}}{C}HNHC_6H_5 \rightleftharpoons$$

$$C_6H_5CH{=}NC_6H_5 + H_2O$$

The benzal derivative of m-toluidine is produced in a similar way (OS III, 827). Reactions of this type probably proceed by way of aldehyde-ammonias and are reversible; no catalyst is needed.

The reaction between aldehydes and ammonia, however, often yields complex products. Four molecules of ammonia, for example, condense with six of formaldehyde to produce hexamine (hexamethylenetetramine).

$$6CH_2O + 4NH_3 \rightarrow \quad \begin{array}{c} N \\ /|\backslash \\ | \; CH_2 \\ / \; | \; \backslash \\ H_2C \;\; N \;\; CH_2 \\ / \backslash \; / \backslash \\ CH_2 \;\; CH_2 \\ / \quad\quad \backslash \\ N{-}{-}{-}CH_2{-}N \end{array} \quad + 6H_2O$$

Benzaldehyde condenses with ammonia to yield hydrobenzamide, a complex molecule formed from three molecules of aldehyde and two of ammonia.

$$3C_6H_5CHO + 2NH_3 \rightarrow C_6H_5CH \underset{N=CHC_6H_5}{\overset{N=CHC_6H_5}{\big<}} + 3H_2O$$

Polymer formation occurs when formaldehyde is allowed to combine with compounds having more than one amino or amido function. Urea and formaldehyde, for example, condense under alkaline or acid conditions to give methylol and dimethylol ureas that can be isolated as crystalline materials. The reaction is reversible; formaldehyde can be lost from a methylol or dimethylol urea to regenerate the —NH_2 group.

$$NH_2CONH_2 \rightleftharpoons NH_2CONHCH_2OH \rightleftharpoons HOCH_2NHCONHCH_2OH$$

Further heating of these intermediates with formaldehyde leads to the formation of urea-formaldehyde resins, which soon become insoluble and infusible. In practice a relatively low-molecular-weight polymer is made and heated in a mold under pressure to produce the commercial articles.

A close relative of the urea-formaldehyde type of polymer is the melamine resin produced from melamine and formaldehyde.

$$
\begin{array}{c}
NH_2 \\
| \\
C \\
\diagup \diagdown \\
N \qquad N \\
| \qquad\quad || \\
H_2N-C \qquad C-NH_2 \\
\diagdown \diagup \\
N
\end{array}
$$

Melamine

Melamine is trimerized cyanamide. The formaldehyde condensation is believed to give triple Schiff bases, which in turn trimerize to provide the complex cyclic derivative. The low-molecular-weight, methylol-rich intermediates are soluble enough for use in textile applications.

Aldehydes combine with two molecules of a secondary amine to give nitrogen analogs of acetals. The simplest example is the condensation of formaldehyde with dimethylamine to give *bis*(dimethylamino)methane (b.p. 85°).

$$2(CH_3)_2NH + CH_2O \rightarrow (CH_3)_2NCH_2N(CH_3)_2 + H_2O$$

1,2-*bis*(*p*-Chlorobenzylamino)ethane yields cyclic derivatives of this type with almost all common aldehydes.[20]

$$Cl\text{---}C_6H_4\text{---}CH_2NHCH_2CH_2NHCH_2\text{---}C_6H_4\text{---}Cl \xrightarrow{\text{RCHO}}$$

$$
\begin{array}{c}
CH_2\text{---}CH_2 \\
| \qquad | \\
Cl\text{---}C_6H_4\text{---}CH_2N \qquad NCH_2\text{---}C_6H_4\text{---}Cl \\
\diagdown \qquad \diagup \\
CHR
\end{array}
$$

1,2-Dianilino-1,2-diphenylethane reacts with aliphatic aldehydes but not ketones; the products, 1,3,4,5-tetraphenylimidazolidines, have sharp melting points and are useful in the identification of aldehydes.[21]

$$
\begin{array}{c}
\qquad NHC_6H_5 \\
\diagup \\
C_6H_5CH \\
| \\
C_6H_5CH \\
\diagdown \\
\qquad NHC_6H_5
\end{array}
+ RCHO \rightarrow
\begin{array}{c}
\qquad NC_6H_5 \\
\diagup \qquad \diagdown \\
C_6H_5CH \qquad \\
| \qquad CHR + H_2O \\
C_6H_5CH \qquad \\
\diagdown \qquad \diagup \\
\qquad NC_6H_5
\end{array}
$$

Tertiary amines also are capable of reacting with carbonyl compounds as is shown by the behavior of certain cyclic amino ketones. One of the most interesting of these is the following eight-membered ring compound. With perchloric acid it forms a salt that has no carbonyl group but instead a hydroxyl group.[22]

$$
\begin{array}{c}
O \\
\| \\
C \\
\ddot{N} \\
| \\
CH_3
\end{array}
+ H^+ \rightarrow
\begin{array}{c}
OH \\
| \\
C \\
N^+ \\
| \\
CH_3
\end{array}
$$

The condensation of aniline with benzonitrile to form N-phenylbenz-amidine illustrates the addition of an amine to a nitrile; the reaction is catalyzed by aluminum chloride (OS **36**, 64; 66% yield).

$$C_6H_5CN + C_3H_5NH_2 \rightarrow C_6H_5\underset{\underset{NH}{\|}}{C}NHC_6H_5$$

[20] J. H. Billman, J.-Y. Chen Ho, and L. R. Caswell, *J. Org. Chem.*, **22**, 538 (1957).

[21] R. Jaunin and J.-P. Godat, *Helv. Chim. Acta*, **44**, 95 (1961).

[22] N. J. Leonard, R. C. Fox, M. Ōki, and S. Chiavarelli, *J. Am. Chem. Soc.*, **76**, 630 (1954).

Reaction of ammonia and primary amines with β-keto esters may form enamines instead of Schiff bases. Ethyl acetoacetate, for example, reacts with ammonia to yield ethyl β-aminocrotonate.

$$CH_3\overset{\overset{\displaystyle O}{\|}}{C}CH_2CO_2C_2H_5 + NH_3 \rightarrow [CH_3\overset{\overset{\displaystyle OH}{|}}{\underset{\underset{\displaystyle NH_2}{|}}{C}}{-}CH_2CO_2C_2H_5] \rightarrow$$

$$CH_3\overset{\overset{\displaystyle NH_2}{|}}{C}{=}CHCO_2C_2H_5 + H_2O$$

Ethyl β-anilinocrotonate is produced in a similar way (OS III, 374; 80% yield). Replacement of this type may involve addition of ammonia or an amine followed by elimination of water.

When ethyl acetoacetate is treated with formaldehyde and ammonia, a dihydropyridine compound is produced. Presumably a twofold replacement of enolic hydroxyl by amino occurs, the second being intramolecular.

Dehydrogenation followed by removal of the carbethoxyl groups yields 2,6-dimethylpyridine (OS II, 214).

Urea, which is basic, can serve also to replace an enolic hydroxyl group, as is exemplified by the first step in the preparation of 6-methyluracil from urea and ethyl acetoacetate (OS II, 422; 77% yield).

$$CH_3COCH_2CO_2C_2H_5 + H_2NCONH_2 \rightarrow CH_3\overset{\overset{\displaystyle NHCONH_2}{|}}{C}{=}CHCO_2C_2H_5 + H_2O$$

The free β-uraminocrotonic acid, obtained by saponification of the ester, undergoes ring closure immediately.

$$\overset{\displaystyle \text{NHCONH}_2}{\underset{\displaystyle \vert}{\text{CH}_3\text{C}}}\!=\!\text{CHCO}_2\text{H} \;\rightarrow\; \overset{\displaystyle \text{NHCONH}}{\underset{\displaystyle \vert}{\text{CH}_3\text{C}}}\!=\!\text{CHCO} + \text{H}_2\text{O}$$

Urea formation occurs when ammonia or an amine is added to the carbonyl group of cyanic acid. The classical experiment of Wöhler may be cited.

$$\text{NH}_3 + \text{HNCO} \;\rightarrow\; \text{NH}_4\text{CNO} \;\rightarrow\; \text{CO(NH}_2)_2$$

This type of reaction is general; the first step in the conversion of anthranilic acid into benzoyleneurea is an interesting example (OS II, 79).

This transformation is of special value with α-amino acids, since the initial products readily form lactams, known as hydantoins. With glycine the transformation takes the following path, the final product being hydantoin.

Thioureas are produced in an analogous fashion by use of thiocyanates, ammonium thiocyanate yielding thiourea itself.

$$\text{NH}_4\text{SCN} \;\rightarrow\; \text{C}\!=\!\text{S}\overset{\displaystyle \diagup\text{NH}_2}{\underset{\displaystyle \diagdown\text{NH}_2}{}}$$

p-Toluidine reacts with thiocyanic acid to yield *p*-tolylthiourea (OS III, 76).

When *o*-chloroaniline hydrochloride is heated with ammonium thiocyanate, *o*-chlorophenylthiourea is produced in 63% yield (OS **31**, 21).

This method is generally applicable to the preparation of aromatic thioureas.

Isocyanates react with amino compounds to give ureas.

$$RN{=}C{=}O + R'NH_2 \rightarrow RNHCONHR'$$

In a similar manner isothiocyanates yield thioureas when treated with ammonia or primary or secondary amines. An example is the formation of methylthiourea from methyl isothiocyanate (OS III, 617; 81% yield).

$$CH_3N{=}C{=}S + NH_3 \rightarrow CH_3NHCSNH_2$$

This procedure provides a useful method of detecting primary and secondary amines, 2-naphthyl isothiocyanate being especially valuable because of the relatively high melting points of the derivatives. Cyclohexylamine, for example, yields N-2-naphthyl-N'-cyclohexylurea, melting at 141 to 142°.

$$+ C_6H_{11}NH_2 \rightarrow$$

Reductive alkylation of amines by carbonyl compounds (OR **4**, 174), when formic acid is the reducing agent, has been called the Wallach reaction. When the carbonyl compound is formaldehyde the term Clarke-Eschweiler is employed. The Leuckart reaction (OR **5**, 301) comprises the more drastic procedures involving formamides or formates of ammonia or amines in the absence of appreciable amounts of free acid. An example is the preparation of α-phenethylamine (OS II, 503; 66% yield), which requires an extended period of heating of acetophenone with ammonium formate at temperatures up to 185°. There is evidence that ammonium formate rather than formamide is the reducing reagent.

$$C_6H_5COCH_3 + 2HCO_2NH_4 \rightarrow$$

$$\underset{\underset{CH_3}{|}}{C_6H_5CHNHCHO} + 2H_2O + CO_2 + NH_3$$

$$\underset{\underset{CH_3}{|}}{C_6H_5CHNHCHO} + H_2O \rightarrow \underset{\underset{CH_3}{|}}{C_6H_5CHNH_2} + HCO_2H$$

The essential step is probably the transfer of a hydride ion from the formate ion to the imonium ion (Hine, 265).

$$\overset{+}{C}{=}\overset{+}{N}H_2 \leftrightarrow \overset{+}{C}{-}NH_2 + HCO_2^- \rightarrow \underset{\underset{H}{|}}{\overset{|}{C}}{-}NH_2 + CO_2$$

α-Phenethylamine can be made also by heating acetophenone with ammonia and hydrogen in the presence of Raney nickel (OS III, 717; 52% yield). In this process the first step probably is the addition of ammonia to the carbonyl group. The methylation of amines by treatment with a mixture of formaldehyde and formic acid is an example of reductive alkylation. The preparation of phenethyldimethylamine is illustrative (OS III, 723; 83% yield).

Reductive alkylation can be realized also with primary amines in place of ammonia. For example, when a mixture of methylamine and levulinic acid is hydrogenated, γ-N-methylaminovaleric acid is produced. However, it readily undergoes cyclization to yield 1,5-dimethyl-2-pyrrolidone (OS III, 328; 77% yield).

$$CH_3COCH_2CH_2CO_2H \xrightarrow[H_2]{CH_3NH_2} CH_3\underset{\underset{CH_3\overset{|}{N}H}{|}}{C}HCH_2CH_2CO_2H \xrightarrow{-H_2O}$$

$$\begin{array}{ccc} CH_2 & \!\!-\!\! & CH_2 \\ | & & | \\ CH_3CH & & CO \\ & \searrow \underset{\underset{CH_3}{|}}{N} \swarrow & \end{array}$$

Although this type of reaction generally is carried out under high pressure, satisfactory low-pressure procedures are available. 2-Isopropylaminoethanol can be prepared at low pressure from acetone and ethanolamine (OS III, 501; 95% yield).

$$\begin{array}{c} CH_3 \\ \diagdown \\ C{=}O + H_2NCH_2CH_2OH + H_2 \xrightarrow{Pt} \\ \diagup \\ CH_3 \end{array}$$

$$\begin{array}{c} CH_3 \\ \diagdown \\ CHNHCH_2CH_2OH + H_2O \\ \diagup \\ CH_3 \end{array}$$

Conjugate addition

Although 1,2-addition of ammonia and primary and secondary amines to carbonyl compounds must be supposed to be general, only a few of the most reactive carbonyl compounds yield stable addition products. Conjugate addition, on the other hand, has been realized with a wide variety of carbonyl compounds as well as with nitriles.

Addition of ammonia and primary and secondary amines to α,β-unsaturated ketones and esters gives β-amino compounds (CR 38, 83). Mesityl oxide, for example, combines with methylamine (OS III, 244) as follows.

$$\underset{CH_3}{\overset{CH_3}{>}}C\!\!=\!\!CHCOCH_3 + CH_3NH_2 \rightarrow \underset{CH_3\ \ NHCH_3}{\overset{CH_3}{>}}CCH_2COCH_3$$

When an alcohol solution of ethyl acrylate and methylamine is allowed to stand for 6 days, di-β-carbethoxyethylmethylamine is produced in 86% yield (OS III, 258).

$$CH_3NH_2 + 2CH_2\!\!=\!\!CHCO_2C_2H_5 \rightarrow CH_3N\!\!\underset{CH_2CH_2CO_2C_2H_5}{\overset{CH_2CH_2CO_2C_2H_5}{<}}$$

Conjugate addition of α,β-unsaturated nitriles with ammonia is illustrated by the first step in a synthesis of β-alanine, which consists of the addition of ammonia to acrylonitrile (OS III, 93); if two moles of nitrile are employed, the chief product (57% yield) is *bis*(β-cyanoethyl)amine.

$$CH_2\!\!=\!\!CHCN + NH_3 \rightarrow H_2NCH_2CH_2CN$$

$$H_2NCH_2CH_2CN + CH_2\!\!=\!\!CHCN \rightarrow HN(CH_2CH_2CN)_2$$

Cyanoethylation of anilines is catalyzed by cupric acetate; 3-(*o*-chloro-anilino)propionitrile, for example, is made from *o*-chloroaniline and acrylonitrile by use of cupric acetate monohydrate (OS 38, 14).

N-2-Cyanoethylaniline can be made by heating a mixture of acrylonitrile, aniline hydrochloride, and diethylamine (OS **36**, 6; 78% yield).

2,4,6-Trinitrostyrene reacts with ammonia in the conjugate manner; the yield of amine is 70%.[23]

α,β-Unsaturated sulfones undergo many reactions that can be classified as conjugate addition. Divinyl sulfone, for example, reacts with methylamine to yield a cyclic amino sulfone.[24]

[23] C. F. Bjork, W. A. Gey, J. H. Robson, and R. W. Van Dolah, *J. Am. Chem. Soc.*, **75**, 1988 (1953).

[24] A. H. Ford-More, *J. Chem. Soc.*, 2433 (1949).

$$\underset{\displaystyle\underset{CH=CH_2}{\big|}}{\overset{\displaystyle\overset{CH=CH_2}{\big|}}{SO_2}} + CH_3NH_2 \xrightarrow{Na_2CO_3} \underset{\displaystyle\underset{CH_2CH_2}{\diagdown}}{\overset{\displaystyle\overset{CH_2CH_2}{\diagup}}{SO_2}}\underset{\diagup}{\overset{\diagdown}{}}NCH_3$$

The reaction between aldehydes and hydrazine normally leads to the formation of azines (p. 418). However, hydrazones of unsaturated aldehydes may undergo ring closure to yield pyrazolines. Cinnamaldehyde reacts in this manner when heated with hydrazine, the product being 5-phenylpyrazoline.

$$C_6H_5CH=CHCHO + H_2NNH_2 \xrightarrow{-H_2O} C_6H_5CH=CHCH=NNH_2 \rightarrow$$

$$\underset{\displaystyle NH-N}{\overset{\displaystyle C_6H_5CH-CH_2}{\underset{\big|}{}\diagdown\underset{\displaystyle CH}{\diagup\!\!\diagup}}}$$

Phenylhydrazine reacts similarly to produce 1,5-diphenylpyrazoline.

$$C_6H_5CH=CHCHO + C_6H_5NHNH_2 \xrightarrow{-H_2O}$$

$$C_6H_5CH=CHCH=NNHC_6H_5 \rightarrow \underset{\displaystyle C_6H_5N-N}{\overset{\displaystyle C_6H_5CHCH_2}{\underset{\big|}{}\diagdown\underset{\displaystyle CH}{\diagup\!\!\diagup}}}$$

The ring closure in these examples is due to an addition of the conjugate type.

Ring closure

A synthesis of pyrimidine derivatives is illustrated by the interaction of ethyl acetoacetate and acetamidine to give 2,6-dimethyl-4-hydroxypyrimidine.

$$\underset{\displaystyle \underset{O}{\overset{\big\|}{}}\quad\underset{O}{\overset{\big\|}{}}}{CH_3C\diagup\overset{\displaystyle CH_2}{}\diagdown COC_2H_5} \rightarrow \underset{\displaystyle N\diagdown\!\diagup N}{\overset{\displaystyle CH_3}{}}\overset{\displaystyle OH}{} + H_2O + C_2H_5OH$$
$$\underset{CH_3}{}$$

$$\underset{\displaystyle \underset{\displaystyle \underset{CH_3}{\big|}}{C}}{\overset{\displaystyle NH_2 \quad NH}{\diagdown\quad\diagup}}$$

Intramolecular reaction of amino and carbonyl groups is involved in the *Friedlander quinoline synthesis*; quinoline itself is produced from *o*-amino-cinnamaldehyde.

This method is capable of extension to a wide variety of types of substituted quinolines, being particularly useful for quinolines substituted in the pyridine ring.

o-Aminobenzaldehyde or an *o*-aminophenyl ketone and any compound containing the structure —$COCH_2$— give the same result, the amino-cinnamaldehyde type of structure being involved in each case as an intermediate. Ethyl acetoacetate and *o*-aminobenzaldehyde yield ethyl 2-methyl-3-quinolinecarboxylate.

Pfitzinger Modification. Pfitzinger found that isatin, which is more readily available than *o*-aminobenzaldehyde, could serve also; the product is a cinchoninic acid. The isatin ring is opened by the alkaline catalyst, whereupon the condensation proceeds in the Friedlander manner. An example is the formation of 2-methylcinchoninic acid from isatin and acetone.

When pyruvic acid is employed, the product is 2,4-quinolinedicarboxylic acid.

Chloropyruvic acid gives 3-hydroxycinchoninic acid (OS **40**, 54; 71% yield).

Keto ethers are useful in preparing aryloxy or alkoxy derivatives of cinchoninic acid. An example is the synthesis of 2-phenyl-3-propoxy-cinchoninic acid from phenyl *n*-propoxymethyl ketone.

$$\text{[structure: anthranilic-type ketone]} + \text{H}_2\text{COC}_3\text{H}_7 \text{ / O=CC}_6\text{H}_5 \rightarrow \text{[cinchoninic acid derivative with OC}_3\text{H}_7\text{, C}_6\text{H}_5\text{]}$$

Knorr Methods. Knorr discovered that γ-diketones react with ammonia and primary amines to give pyrrole derivatives. For example, acetonyl-acetone and ammonia yield 2,5-dimethylpyrrole (OS II, 219; 86 % yield).

$$\begin{matrix} \text{CH}_2\text{COCH}_3 \\ | \\ \text{CH}_2\text{COCH}_3 \end{matrix} + \text{NH}_3 \rightarrow \begin{matrix} \text{CH}=\text{CCH}_3 \\ \diagdown \\ \quad\quad \text{NH} \\ \diagup \\ \text{CH}=\text{CCH}_3 \end{matrix} + 2\text{H}_2\text{O}$$

The reaction occurs with both aliphatic and aromatic amines as well as with hydroxylamine and hydrazine.

Another route to pyrroles, also discovered by Knorr, consists of the condensation of a ketone with an α-amino ketone. The amino ketone is prepared most conveniently from the ketone by way of the oxime and usually is allowed to condense with the ketone without being isolated. With acetone the product is 2,4-dimethylpyrrole, formed in the following way.

$$\text{CH}_3\text{COCH}_3 \xrightarrow{\text{HONO}} \text{CH}_3\text{COCH}=\text{NOH} \xrightarrow{\text{H}_2} \begin{matrix} \text{CH}_3\text{CO} \quad\quad \text{CH}_3 \\ | \quad\quad\quad | \\ \text{CH}_2\text{NH}_2 + \text{COCH}_3 \end{matrix} \xrightarrow{-\text{H}_2\text{O}}$$

$$\begin{matrix} \text{CH}_3\text{CO} \quad\quad \text{CH}_3 \\ | \quad\quad\quad | \\ \text{CH}_2\text{N}=\text{CCH}_3 \end{matrix} \xrightarrow{-\text{H}_2\text{O}} \begin{matrix} \text{CH}_3\text{C}\text{------}\text{CH} \\ || \quad\quad\quad || \\ \text{HC} \quad\quad \text{CCH}_3 \\ \diagdown \quad \diagup \\ \text{NH} \end{matrix}$$

The synthesis of 3-acetyl-5-carbethoxy-2,4-dimethylpyrrole from ethyl acetoacetate and acetylacetone is another example of this method (OS III, 513).

$$\begin{matrix} \text{CH}_3\text{CO} \\ | \\ \text{CHNH}_2 \\ | \\ \text{CO}_2\text{C}_2\text{H}_5 \end{matrix} + \begin{matrix} \text{CH}_2\text{COCH}_3 \\ | \\ \text{OCCH}_3 \end{matrix} \xrightarrow{-2\text{H}_2\text{O}} \begin{matrix} \text{CH}_3\text{COC}\text{------}\text{CCH}_3 \\ || \quad\quad\quad || \\ \text{CH}_3\text{C} \quad\quad \text{CCO}_2\text{C}_2\text{H}_5 \\ \diagdown \quad \diagup \\ \text{NH} \end{matrix}$$

γ-Amino ketones yield dihydropyrroles or pyrrolines; an interesting example is the conversion of β-benzoyl-α-phenylpropionitrile into

2,4-diphenyl-2-pyrroline by catalytic hydrogenation of the cyano group (OS III, 358).

$$\underset{\underset{\text{CN}}{|}}{C_6H_5CHCH_2COC_6H_5} \rightarrow \underset{\underset{\text{CH}_2\text{NH}_2}{|}}{C_6H_5CHCH_2COC_6H_5} \rightarrow$$

From ethyl acetoacetate, formaldehyde, and ammonia it is possible to prepare 3,5-dicarbethoxy-1,4-dihydro-2,6-dimethylpyridine (OS II, 214).

Hantzsch Pyridine Synthesis. The Hantzsch synthesis involves condensation of two molecules of a β-keto ester or β-diketone with one of an aldehyde and one of ammonia. An example is the condensation of ethyl acetoacetate with acetaldehyde and ammonia. The intermediates in this reaction are undoubtedly the β-ethylideneacetoacetic ester and the β-aminocrotonic ester. If it is imagined that the imino tautomer of the latter condenses with the ethylidene compound in the Michael manner (p. 504) with subsequent ring closure, the cyclization is seen to be similar to the early Knorr closure.

Thiazole formation

α-Halo carbonyl compounds react with thioamides to form thiazoles (OR **6**, 367). If chloroacetone and thioacetamide are used, the product is 2,4-dimethylthiazole (OS III, 332).

$$\underset{\underset{\text{NH}}{\|}}{\overset{\text{SH}}{\underset{\text{CH}_3\text{C}}{|}}} + \underset{\underset{\text{O}}{\|}}{\overset{\text{ClCH}_2}{\underset{\text{CCH}_3}{|}}} \rightarrow \text{CH}_3\text{C} \overset{\text{S}---\text{CH}}{\underset{\text{N}}{\diagdown \diagup}} \text{CCH}_3 + \text{H}_2\text{O}$$

Oximation

Hydroxylamine probably behaves in the same way as ammonia, but in this reaction water is eliminated from the initial product and *oximes* result. The preparation of benzophenone oxime is an example (OS II, 70).

$$\underset{\text{C}_6\text{H}_5}{\overset{\text{C}_6\text{H}_5}{\diagdown}}\text{C}{=}\text{O} + \text{NH}_2\text{OH} \rightleftharpoons \underset{\text{C}_6\text{H}_5}{\overset{\text{C}_6\text{H}_5}{\diagdown}}\text{C}{-}\text{NHOH} \rightleftharpoons \underset{\text{C}_6\text{H}_5}{\overset{\text{C}_6\text{H}_5}{\diagdown}}\text{C}{=}\text{NOH} + \text{H}_2\text{O}$$

Oxime formation is general for aldehydes and ketones and is reversible in acid media. The formation of aldoximes is illustrated by the synthesis of *n*-heptaldoxime (OS II, 313; 93% yield).

It is to be noted that oximate ions are resonance hybrids, which accounts for the acidic character of oximes.

$$\underset{\text{R}}{\overset{\text{R}}{\diagdown}}\text{C}{=}\text{N}{-}\text{O}^- \leftrightarrow \underset{\text{R}}{\overset{\text{R}}{\diagdown}}\overset{-}{\text{C}}{-}\text{N}{=}\text{O}$$

Advantage is taken of the reversibility in converting oximes into the corresponding ketones. An example is the hydrolysis of the oxime of methyl phenyl diketone (p. 536) by heating with 10% sulfuric acid; the diketone is obtained in a yield of 70% (OS III, 20).

$$\underset{\|}{\overset{\text{NOH}}{\text{C}_6\text{H}_5\text{COCCH}_3}} + \text{H}_2\text{O} \xrightarrow{\text{H}_2\text{SO}_4} \text{C}_6\text{H}_5\text{COCOCH}_3 + \text{H}_2\text{NOH}$$

It is advantageous to hydrolyze oximes in the presence of a hydroxylamine acceptor such as formaldehyde, pyruvic acid, or levulinic acid.[25]

As would be expected, dicarbonyl compounds react with hydroxylamine to form dioximes; dimethylglyoxime, for example, can be made from biacetyl in this way. Actually this dioxime is prepared more conveniently from methyl ethyl ketone (p. 537).

[25] C. H. DePuy and B. W. Ponder, *J. Am. Chem. Soc.*, **81**, 4629 (1959).

Oximation has been achieved with acetomesitylene, in which steric hindrance is so great as to prevent attack by most nucleophiles. The oxime has been produced in 40% yield by treating the ketone with hydroxylamine in dry pyridine for one month at room temperature.[26]

$$CH_3CO \underset{CH_3}{\overset{CH_3}{\bigcirc}} CH_3 + H_2NOH \rightarrow CH_3 C{=}NOH \underset{CH_3}{\overset{CH_3}{\bigcirc}} CH_3 + H_2O$$

Oxime formation has also been realized with hindered ketones by use of high pressure. Hexamethylacetone, unreactive under ordinary conditions, forms an oxime in 70% yield at a pressure of about 9500 atmospheres.[27]

$$(CH_3)_3C\overset{O}{\overset{\|}{C}}C(CH_3)_3 + H_2NOH \rightarrow (CH_3)_3C\overset{NOH}{\overset{\|}{C}}C(CH_3)_3 + H_2O$$

Hydrazone formation

Hydrazine reacts with aldehydes and ketones to give hydrazones, which in turn may react with a second molecule of the carbonyl compound to yield *azines*.

$$R_2CO + H_2NNH_2 \rightarrow R_2C{=}N{-}NH_2 + H_2O$$

$$R_2C{=}N{-}NH_2 + OCR_2 \rightarrow R_2C{=}N{-}N{=}CR_2 + H_2O$$

Hydrazone formation is useful in the aromatic series, benzophenone hydrazone being formed in 87% yield, for example (OS III, 352).

Azines are produced generally when two moles of aldehydes are employed, as is illustrated by the preparation of benzalazine (OS II, 395; 94% yield).

$$2C_6H_5CHO + H_2NNH_2 \rightarrow C_6H_5CH{=}NN{=}CHC_6H_5 + 2H_2O$$

Aliphatic aldehydes react so rapidly that the intermediate hydrazones cannot be isolated; even when an excess of hydrazine is employed, the azine is practically the only product. Hydrazones of ketones tend to undergo disproportionation to form the azine and free hydrazine.

Suitably constituted dicarbonyl compounds may yield cyclic compounds. Thus the *cis*-forms of 1,2-diaroylethylenes readily give the corresponding 1,2-pyridazines whereas the *trans*-forms do not.[28]

[26] F. Greer and D. E. Pearson, *J. Am. Chem. Soc.*, **77**, 6649 (1955).

[27] W. H. Jones, E. W. Tristram, and W. F. Benning, *J. Am. Chem. Soc.*, **81**, 2151 (1959).

[28] R. E. Lutz and S. M. King, *J. Org. Chem.*, **17**, 1519 (1952).

$$
\begin{array}{ccc}
\text{R—C}{=}\text{O} & & \text{R—C} \\
\quad\diagdown & & \quad\diagdown\quad\diagup \\
\text{HC} & & \text{HC} \quad\quad \text{N} \\
\;\| & \rightarrow & \;\| \quad\quad\;\;| \\
\text{HC} & & \text{HC} \quad\quad \text{N} \\
\quad\diagdown & & \quad\diagdown\quad\diagup \\
\text{R—C}{=}\text{O} & & \text{R—C}
\end{array}
$$

Benzil gives a monohydrazone as well as a dihydrazone. The dihydrazone reacts with benzil to give an eight-membered heterocyclic compound.[29]

$$
\begin{array}{ccc}
\text{N—NH}_2 & & \text{N—N} \\
\diagup & & \diagup\quad\diagdown \\
\text{C}_6\text{H}_5\text{C} & \quad\text{O}{=}\text{CC}_6\text{H}_5 & \text{C}_6\text{H}_5\text{C} \quad\quad \text{CC}_6\text{H}_5 \\
| & + \quad | & | \quad\quad | \quad\quad + 2\text{H}_2\text{O} \\
\text{C}_6\text{H}_5\text{C} & \quad\text{O}{=}\text{CC}_6\text{H}_5 & \text{C}_6\text{H}_5\text{C} \quad\quad \text{CC}_6\text{H}_5 \\
\diagdown & & \diagdown\quad\diagup \\
\text{N—NH}_2 & & \text{N—N}
\end{array}
$$

One of the classical procedures for characterizing aldehydes and ketones is treatment with phenylhydrazine, which converts them reversibly into phenylhydrazones.

$$
\begin{array}{l}
\text{R} \\
\;\diagdown \\
\quad\text{C}{=}\text{O} + \text{H}_2\text{NNHC}_6\text{H}_5 \rightleftharpoons \\
\;\diagup \\
\text{R}
\end{array}
\quad
\begin{array}{l}
\text{R} \quad\text{OH} \quad\text{H} \\
\;\diagdown \;\;|\quad\quad| \\
\quad\text{C——N—NHC}_6\text{H}_5 \rightleftharpoons \\
\;\diagup \\
\text{R}
\end{array}
$$

$$
\begin{array}{l}
\text{R} \\
\;\diagdown \\
\quad\text{C}{=}\text{NNHC}_6\text{H}_5 + \text{H}_2\text{O} \\
\;\diagup \\
\text{R}
\end{array}
$$

The reversibility is illustrated by one of the methods of recovering the carbonyl compounds, which consists in heating the phenylhydrazone with a highly reactive carbonyl compound (p. 417). β-Diketones or β-keto esters yield phenylhydrazones that undergo ring formation. Acetylacetone, for example, yields 3,5-dimethyl-1-phenylpyrazole.

$$
\text{CH}_3\text{COCH}_2\text{COCH}_3 \xrightarrow{\text{C}_6\text{H}_5\text{NHNH}_2} \text{CH}_3\text{CCH}_2\text{COCH}_3 \rightarrow
\begin{array}{l}
\text{CH}_3\text{C——CH} \\
\;\;\|\quad\quad\|\\
\;\;\text{N}\quad\;\text{CCH}_3 \\
\;\;\diagdown\quad\diagup \\
\;\;\;\text{C}_6\text{H}_5\text{N}
\end{array}
$$

$$
\begin{array}{c}
\quad\quad\quad\quad\quad\quad \| \\
\quad\quad\quad\quad\quad\quad \text{NNHC}_6\text{H}_5
\end{array}
$$

[29] See H. Schlesinger, *Angew. Chem.*, **72**, 563 (1960).

In a similar way 3,5-dimethylpyrazole is formed by the interaction of acetylacetone and hydrazine (OS **31**, 43; 81% yield).

$$CH_3COCH_2COCH_3 + H_2NNH_2 \rightarrow \underset{\underset{NH}{\diagdown \diagup}}{\overset{\overset{HC\text{------}CCH_3}{\underset{CH_3C \qquad N}{\| \qquad \|}}}{}} + 2H_2O$$

Ethyl acetoacetate reacts similarly to produce 3-methyl-1-phenyl-5-pyrazolone.

$$\underset{\overset{\|}{N\text{---}NHC_6H_5}}{\overset{CH_3C\text{---}CH_2CO_2C_2H_5}{}} \rightarrow \underset{\underset{C_6H_5N}{\diagdown \diagup}}{\overset{CH_3C\text{------}CH_2}{\underset{N \qquad CO}{\| \qquad \|}}} + C_2H_5OH$$

Ketohydrazones react with lead tetraacetate to produce azoacetates; the behavior of acetone phenylhydrazone is an example.[30]

$$\underset{\overset{|}{CH_3}}{\overset{\overset{|}{CH_3}}{C_6H_5NHN{=}C}} \xrightarrow{Pb(OCOCH_3)_4} \underset{\overset{|}{CH_3}}{\overset{\overset{|}{CH_3}}{C_6H_5N{=}NCOCOCH_3}}$$

2,4-Dinitrophenylhydrazine offers special advantages in identification work, chiefly because the 2,4-dinitrophenylhydrazones generally possess relatively high melting points. The reagent is not very soluble in ordinary solvents; the dimethyl ether of diethylene glycol (diglyme) has been recommended.[31] This reagent is useful also with dicarbonyl compounds.[32] 2,4-Dinitrophenylhydrazine is one of the few reagents that can overcome the steric hindrance that exists in ketones such as acetomesitylene (p. 418); 2,4-dinitrophenylhydrazones have been made from this ketone and also from 4-*t*-butyl-2,6-dimethylacetophenone and 2,6-dimethylacetophenone.[33]

Semicarbazide gives hydrazone derivatives known as semicarbazones; the reaction is reversible.

$$\underset{R}{\overset{R}{\diagdown}}C{=}O + H_2NNHCONH_2 \rightleftharpoons \underset{R}{\overset{R}{\diagdown}}C{=}NNHCONH_2 + H_2O$$

[30] D. C. Iffland, L. Salisbury, and W. R. Schafer, *J. Am. Chem. Soc.*, **83**, 747 (1961).
[31] H. J. Shine, *J. Org. Chem.*, **24**, 252 (1959).
[32] L. A. Jones, C. K. Hancock, and R. B. Seligman, *J. Org. Chem.*, **26**, 228 (1961).
[33] D. E. Pearson and F. Greer, *J. Am. Chem. Soc.*, **77**, 1294 (1955).

Whereas hydrolysis of oximes and phenylhydrazones presents difficulties, regeneration of aldehydes and ketones from their semicarbazones is eminently feasible.

Girard's reagent T, useful in the isolation of carbonyl compounds, is a hydrazine derivative containing a quaternary ammonium group. It is made by condensing trimethylamine, ethyl chloroacetate, and hydrazine (OS II, 85; 89% yield).

$$(CH_3)_3N + ClCH_2CO_2C_2H_5 + NH_2NH_2 \rightarrow$$
$$[(CH_3)_3NCH_2CONHNH_2]Cl + C_2H_5OH$$

It yields derivatives that are highly polar and consequently soluble in water. With ketones, for example, it reacts to give the following type of salt.

$$\left[(CH_3)_3NCH_2CONHN{=}C\underset{R}{\overset{R}{\diagup}} \right] Cl$$

Girard's reagent P is made by using pyridine in place of trimethylamine.

$$[C_5H_5NCH_2CONHNH_2]Cl$$

Recovery of the carbonyl compound may be realized by hydrolysis with dilute hydrochloric acid.

Twinned carbonyl groups

α-Keto aldehydes and α-diketones, as would be expected, react with phenylhydrazine to give diphenylhydrazones known as *phenylosazones.* These compounds are formed by α-hydroxy aldehydes and ketones, also.

$$\begin{array}{l} CHO \\ | \\ CHOH \\ | \end{array} + 3C_6H_5NHNH_2 \rightarrow$$

$$\begin{array}{l} CH{=}NNHC_6H_5 \\ | \\ C{=}NNHC_3H_5 \\ | \end{array} + C_3H_5NH_2 + NH_3 + 2H_2O$$

The osazones are yellow solids that crystallize well and are of great value in the purification and characterization of sugars.

o-Phenylenediamine reacts with 1,2-dicarbonyl compounds to produce quinoxalines. Glyoxal, for example, gives quinoxaline in 94% yield.

$$\begin{array}{l} CHO \\ | \\ CHO \end{array} + \begin{array}{l} H_2N \\ H_2N \end{array} \!\! \bigcirc \rightarrow \begin{array}{l} HC \\ HC \end{array} \!\! \underset{N}{\overset{N}{\diagup}} \!\! \bigcirc + 2H_2O$$

Similarly, biacetyl is transformed into 2,3-dimethylquinoxaline. The method of formation indicates that the quinoxalines are Schiff bases; however, the new rings are aromatic in character and belong to the category of pyrazines.

Benzils react readily to yield the corresponding 2,3-diarylquinoxalines, an illustration being the preparation of 2,3-diphenylquinoxaline from benzil itself.

$$C_6H_5C=O \atop C_6H_5C=O \quad + \quad {H_2N \atop H_2N} \bigcirc \quad \rightarrow \quad {C_6H_5 \atop C_6H_5} \diagdown \bigcirc \diagdown \bigcirc \quad + \quad 2H_2O$$

When an *o*-quinone is employed, the product is a phenazine. α-Methoxyphenazine can be made, for example, from pyrogallol monomethyl ether by the following sequence of changes (OS III, 753; 33% yield).

This type of reaction serves not only as a test for the 1,2-dicarbonyl structure but likewise for *o*-diaminobenzenes. For the latter purpose phenanthrenequinone is to be recommended.

Formation of Sodium Bisulfite Addition Compounds

Aldehydes, aliphatic methyl ketones, and alicyclic ketones up to cyclo-öctanone yield sodium bisulfite addition compounds.

Aliphatic methyl ketones become progressively less reactive toward this reagent as the size and complexity of the second alkyl radical are increased. Diethyl ketone forms a bisulfite addition compound very slowly.

Many keto esters, such as ethyl pyruvate, ethyl acetoacetate, and ethyl levulinate, form bisulfite addition compounds. A number of aliphatic dike-tones yield derivatives containing two moles of bisulfite for each mole of diketone. Acetylacetone and biacetyl show this behavior. As would be expected, aromatic ketones, including acetophenone, fail to form bisulfite addition compounds. In the quantitative estimation of aldehydes sodium bisulfite is taken in excess, and the excess is titrated with alkali.

Conjugate addition

An interesting example of conjugate addition is observed when cinnam-aldehyde is treated with sodium bisulfite. The primary addition product, if allowed to stand in solution, gradually changes to the dibisulfite with the liberation of an equivalent amount of aldehyde. Evidently conjugate ad-dition, although slower than 1,2-addition, is favored by the equilibria in-volved. It is not surprising that the product of conjugate addition, being saturated, is more reactive than the unsaturated aldehyde and is able to compete successfully for the second mole of bisulfite.

$$C_6H_5CH{=}CHCH{=}O + NaHSO_3$$

$$C_6H_5CH{=}CHCHOH$$
$$\overset{|}{SO_3Na}$$

$$C_6H_5CHCH_2CH{=}O \xrightarrow{NaHSO_3}$$
$$\overset{|}{SO_3Na}$$

$$C_6H_5CHCH_2CHOH$$
with SO_3Na on both carbons
$$\overset{|}{SO_3Na}$$

Acrolein combines with two moles of sodium bisulfite in a similar way. Crotonaldehyde appears to behave in this fashion also. Numerous exam-ples of conjugate addition of bisulfite are known with compounds that fail to yield products of 1,2-addition. Sodium bisulfite reacts with many un-saturated ketones, acids, and esters to yield β-sulfonates. An example is benzalacetophenone.

$$C_6H_5CH{=}CHCOC_6H_5 + NaHSO_3 \rightarrow C_6H_5CHCH_2COC_6H_5$$
$$\overset{|}{SO_3Na}$$

Formation of Cyanohydrins

Bisulfite addition compounds react with sodium or potassium cyanide to give cyanohydrins. Examples are the formation of the cyanohydrins of acetone and benzaldehyde (OS I, 336).

$$\begin{matrix} CH_3 & OH \\ & \diagdown \diagup \\ & C \\ & \diagup \diagdown \\ CH_3 & SO_3Na \end{matrix} + NaCN \rightarrow \begin{matrix} CH_3 & OH \\ & \diagdown \diagup \\ & C \\ & \diagup \diagdown \\ CH_3 & CN \end{matrix} + Na_2SO_3$$

$$\begin{matrix} & OH \\ & \diagup \\ C_6H_5CH \\ & \diagdown \\ & SO_3Na \end{matrix} + NaCN \rightarrow \begin{matrix} & OH \\ & \diagup \\ C_6H_5CH \\ & \diagdown \\ & CN \end{matrix} + Na_2SO_3$$

By the interchange method acetoacetic ester gives the cyanohydrin in 85% yield.

$$\underset{\underset{SO_3Na}{|}}{\overset{\overset{OH}{|}}{CH_3C}}CH_2CO_2C_2H_5 + NaCN \rightarrow \underset{\underset{CN}{|}}{\overset{\overset{OH}{|}}{CH_3C}}CH_2CO_2C_2H_5 + Na_2SO_3$$

The replacement of the —SO$_3$Na group by the cyano group appears to be similar to the reaction of bisulfite addition compounds with sodium acetylide. The bisulfite addition compound of acetone reacts with sodium acetylide to give 2-methyl-3-butyn-2-ol in 46% yield.[34]

$$\begin{matrix} CH_3 & OH \\ & \diagdown \diagup \\ & C \\ & \diagup \diagdown \\ CH_3 & SO_3Na \end{matrix} + NaC\equiv CH \rightarrow \begin{matrix} CH_3 & OH \\ & \diagdown \diagup \\ & C \\ & \diagup \diagdown \\ CH_3 & C\equiv CH \end{matrix} + Na_2SO_3$$

The similarity of the cyanide and acetylide ions has been mentioned elsewhere (p. 56).

All aldehydes and many of the more reactive ketones undergo nucleophilic attack by cyanide ion, and in the presence of hydrogen cyanide yield the corresponding cyanohydrins. Hydrogen cyanide does not unite with the carbonyl compound to produce a cyanohydrin; if a small amount of cyanide ion is present, however, reaction occurs.

The reaction may proceed by way of attack of cyanide ion on a complex formed by the carbonyl compound and a proton donor such as hydrogen cyanide.[35]

$$\begin{matrix} R \\ \diagdown \\ C=O\cdots HCN + CN^- \rightarrow \\ \diagup \\ R \end{matrix} \quad \begin{matrix} R & OH \\ \diagdown \diagup \\ C \\ \diagup \diagdown \\ R & CN \end{matrix} + CN^-$$

[34] J. Cymerman and K. J. Wilks, *J. Chem. Soc.*, 1208 (1950).
[35] H.-H. Hustedt and E. Pfeil, *Ann.*, **640**, 15 (1961).

The cyanohydrin of formaldehyde, or glycolonitrile, is made in 80% yield by this method (OS III, 436).

$$CH_2O + HCN \xrightarrow{CN^-} HOCH_2CN$$

If methyl sulfate is added to the reaction mixture containing the glycolonitrile, the product is methoxyacetonitrile (OS II, 387; 77% yield).

The limitation of this type of reaction in the aliphatic ketone series is indicated roughly by the fact that acetone, methyl ethyl ketone, diethyl ketone, and pinacolone form cyanohydrins, whereas diisopropyl ketone does not. Probably the most important example is acetone, which affords acetone cyanohydrin in 78% yield (OS II, 7).

$$(CH_3)_2CO + HCN \xrightarrow{CN^-} (CH_3)_2C \begin{matrix} OH \\ \diagup \\ \diagdown \\ CN \end{matrix}$$

That cyanide ion is more effective than bisulfite ion is demonstrated also by the fact that cyanohydrin formation occurs with aromatic methyl ketones. Acetophenone cyanohydrin, for example, can be made by treating the ketone with cyanide and hydrogen cyanide. Gulonic-γ-lactone is produced in 33% yield by treating D-xylose with a mixture of sodium cyanide and ammonium chloride (OS **36**, 38). Presumably the cyanohydrin undergoes hydrolysis to the hydroxy acid, which then forms the lactone.

$$
\begin{array}{ccc}
\text{CHO} & & \text{┌──CO} \\
| & & | \\
\text{HCOH} & & \text{HCOH} \\
| & & | \\
\text{HOCH} & \rightarrow & \text{HCOH} \\
| & & | \\
\text{HCOH} & & \text{└──OCH} \\
| & & | \\
\text{CH}_2\text{OH} & & \text{HCOH} \\
& & | \\
& & \text{CH}_2\text{OH}
\end{array}
$$

Conjugate addition

Whereas the formation of cyanohydrins by the addition of hydrogen cyanide is limited to aldehydes and the more reactive ketones, conjugate addition occurs with many ketones and esters. Ethyl crotonate, for example, yields the sodium salt of β-cyanobutyric acid (OS III, 615).

$$CH_3CH{=}CHCO_2C_2H_5 \rightarrow CH_3\underset{\underset{\text{CN}}{|}}{C}HCH_2CO_2Na$$

Benzalacetophenone undergoes this type of reaction also (OS II, 498); the yield of α-phenyl-β-benzoylpropionitrile is 96%.

$$C_6H_5CH{=}CHCOC_6H_5 + HCN \xrightarrow{CN^-} C_6H_5\underset{\underset{CN}{|}}{C}HCH_2COC_6H_5$$

Conjugate addition does occur, however, with ketones that are capable of forming cyanohydrins. For example, levulinonitrile has been produced from methyl vinyl ketone by the addition of hydrogen cyanide.

$$CH_3COCH{=}CH_2 + HCN \xrightarrow{CN^-} CH_3COCH_2CH_2CN$$

This reaction is interesting because its course depends on the temperature. The formation of the keto nitrile is observed at 15–80° whereas at lower temperatures the cyanohydrin is produced.

The addition of cyanide to ethyl cinnamate, followed by hydrolysis furnishes a route to phenylsuccinic acid, but the yield is low. Much better results are obtained from benzal and substituted benzal derivatives of malonic and cyanoacetic esters. The preparation of *m*-nitrophenylsuccinic acid is an illustration.

These results accord with the expectation that conjugation of the olefinic linkage with a second carbonyl group intensifies the electron shortage at position 4. A similar example is the combination of cyanide with ethyl α-cyanocinnamate to produce ethyl α,β-dicyano-β-phenylpropionate (OS I, 451).

$$C_6H_5CH{=}\underset{\underset{CN}{|}}{C}CO_2C_2H_5 + HCN \xrightarrow{CN^-} C_6H_5\underset{\underset{CN}{|}}{C}H\underset{\underset{CN}{|}}{C}HCO_2C_2H_5$$

Succinonitrile may be prepared by the addition of hydrogen cyanide to acrylonitrile.

$$CH_2{=}CHCN + HCN \xrightarrow{CN^-} \underset{\underset{CH_2CN}{|}}{C}H_2CN$$

α,α-Diphenylsuccinonitrile is produced in high yield by the addition of cyanide to α-phenylcinnamonitrile (OS **32**, 63).

$$C_6H_5CH{=}\underset{\underset{CN}{|}}{C}C_6H_5 + HCN \xrightarrow{CN^-} C_6H_5\underset{\underset{CN}{|}}{C}H{-}\underset{\underset{CN}{|}}{C}HC_6H_5$$

This compound can be made more conveniently in a single procedure from benzaldehyde, phenylacetonitrile, and sodium cyanide.[36]

Conjugate addition has been realized also with nitro compounds, an example being 1-nitro-1-pentene.[37]

$$C_3H_7CH{=}CHNO_2 \rightarrow C_3H_7\underset{\underset{CN}{|}}{C}HCH_2NO_2$$

Ethyl vinyl sulfone behaves in a similar way.

$$C_2H_5SO_2CH{=}CH_2 \rightarrow C_2H_5SO_2CH_2CH_2CN$$

Cyanide also combines with quinone in the conjugate manner. The second cyano group, however, appears in the 3- rather than the 5-position, the product being 2,3-dicyanohydroquinone. The preference for the 3-position is evidently due to the influence of the cyano group already present; addition occurs more readily to the crossed conjugated system

than to the simpler systems present in the molecule.[38]

[36] R. B. Davis, *J. Am. Chem. Soc.*, **80**, 1752 (1958).
[37] P. Kurtz, *Ann.*, **572**, 23 (1951).
[38] C. F. H. Allen and C. V. Wilson, *J. Am. Chem. Soc.*, **63**, 1756 (1941).

This synthesis appears to be anomalous in one respect; the monocyano hydroquinone, presumed to be an intermediate, cannot be isolated as would be expected if the cyano group stabilizes the hydroquinone toward oxidation.

Benzoin Condensation

In an alkaline medium the condensation product of an aldehyde and cyanide ion may combine with another molecule of aldehyde in the aldol manner to produce an α-hydroxy ketone, or acyloin. In the aromatic series, where the reaction is of greatest importance, the products are benzoins (OR **4**, 269). Benzoin, the simplest acyloin in the aromatic series, is formed in 92% yield (OS I, 94).

$$2C_6H_5CHO \xrightarrow{\text{KCN}} C_6H_5CO\overset{\overset{\displaystyle OH}{|}}{C}HC_6H_5$$

Furfural behaves much like benzaldehyde, giving furoin; the yield, however, is only 38%.

It is possible in certain instances to obtain mixed benzoins in satisfactory yields by heating a mixture of two different aldehydes in the presence of a cyanide. Thus p-dimethylaminobenzaldehyde and m-bromobenzaldehyde form 3′-bromo-4-dimethylaminobenzoin in 50% yield.

Similarly anisaldehyde and benzaldehyde form 4-methoxybenzoin in 70% yield.

These results are explained by reference to the tendency of an aldehyde to condense as a carbonyl compound on the one hand or as an active hydrogen compound on the other hand. In the above examples, m-bromobenzaldehyde and benzaldehyde fall in the first category, p-dimethylaminobenzaldehyde and anisaldehyde in the second. It is not surprising, then, that many aromatic aldehydes fail to yield symmetrical benzoins; among these are the nitro- and hydroxybenzaldehydes. The chloro-, bromo-, and p-dimethylaminobenzaldehydes afford benzoins in low yields.

When benzoin is treated with certain substituted benzaldehydes in the presence of potassium cyanide, mixed benzoins may be formed. With anisaldehyde 4-methoxybenzoin forms in 79% yield.

$$C_6H_5\underset{\underset{OH}{|}}{CH}COC_6H_5 + 2CH_3O\!\!\left\langle\bigcirc\right\rangle\!\!CHO \rightarrow 2CH_3O\!\!\left\langle\bigcirc\right\rangle\!\!\overset{\overset{O}{\|}}{C}\!\!-\!\!\underset{\underset{|}{C_6H_5}}{\overset{|}{C}}HC_6H_5$$

This reaction demonstrates the reversibility of the benzoin condensation.

Also, from two symmetrical benzoins it is possible to make a mixed benzoin. Benzoin and furoin, for example, interact in the presence of aqueous ethanolic cyanide to yield benzfuroin.

$$\left[\bigcirc\!\!\right]_{O}\!\!-\!\!\overset{\overset{O}{\|}}{C}\!\!-\!\!\underset{\underset{OH}{|}}{CH}\!\!-\!\!\left[\bigcirc\!\!\right]_{O} + C_6H_5CO\underset{\underset{OH}{|}}{CH}C_6H_5 \rightarrow 2\left[\bigcirc\!\!\right]_{O}\!\!-\!\!\overset{\overset{O}{\|}}{C}\!\!-\!\!\underset{\underset{OH}{|}}{CH}C_6H_5$$

Pivalaldehyde, which fails to form pivaloin, reacts with benzaldehyde to give a mixture of phenylpivalylcarbinol and benzoyl-t-butylcarbinol.[39]

$$\left.\begin{array}{l}C_6H_5CHO\\(CH_3)_3CCHO\end{array}\right\} \rightarrow C_6H_5\overset{\overset{O}{\|}}{C}\!\!-\!\!\underset{\underset{OH}{|}}{CH}C(CH_3)_3 \text{ and } (CH_3)_3C\overset{\overset{O}{\|}}{C}\overset{\overset{OH}{|}}{C}HC_6H_5$$

In all the mixed benzoins that have been prepared by the benzoin condensation, the carbonyl group is attached to the aryl ring that is richer in electrons and that, accordingly, has the greater power to "neutralize" the electron deficiency of the carbonyl carbon atom.

The following mechanism has been proposed for the benzoin condensation.

$$C_6H_5\overset{\overset{O}{\|}}{C}\!\!-\!\!H + CN^- \rightleftharpoons C_6H_5\underset{\underset{CN}{|}}{\overset{\overset{O^-}{|}}{C}}\!\!-\!\!H \rightleftharpoons C_6H_5\underset{\underset{CN}{|}}{\overset{\overset{OH}{|}}{C}}{}^-$$

$$C_6H_5\underset{\underset{CN}{|}}{\overset{\overset{OH}{|}}{C}}{}^- + \overset{\overset{O}{\|}}{C}C_6H_5 \rightleftharpoons C_6H_5\underset{\underset{CN}{|}}{\overset{\overset{OH}{|}}{C}}\!\!-\!\!\!-\!\!\underset{\underset{H}{|}}{\overset{\overset{O^-}{|}}{C}}C_6H_5$$

$$C_6H_5\underset{\underset{CN}{|}}{\overset{\overset{OH}{|}}{C}}\!\!-\!\!\!-\!\!\underset{\underset{H}{|}}{\overset{\overset{O^-}{|}}{C}}C_6H_5 \rightleftharpoons C_6H_5\underset{\underset{CN}{|}}{\overset{\overset{O^-}{|}}{C}}\!\!-\!\!\!-\!\!\underset{\underset{H}{|}}{\overset{\overset{OH}{|}}{C}}C_6H_5 \overset{-CN^-}{\rightleftharpoons} C_6H_5\overset{\overset{O}{\|}}{C}\!\!-\!\!\underset{\underset{H}{|}}{\overset{\overset{OH}{|}}{C}}C_6H_5$$

[39] T. G. Roberts and P. C. Teague, *J. Am. Chem. Soc.*, **77**, 6258 (1955).

It would appear that migration of hydrogen from carbon to oxygen is the crucial phase of the reaction. The hydrogen atom is mobile because it is *alpha* to the cyano group and at the same time is in a benzyl position. These considerations afford an explanation of the fact that cyanide ion can serve as the catalyst and that the reaction is chiefly limited to aromatic aldehydes. In glyoxals the hydrogen atom is *alpha* to a carbonyl group as well as a cyano group. The formation of acyloins in the aliphatic series is illustrated by the conversion of phenylglyoxal to dibenzoylformoin.

$$2C_6H_5COCHO \xrightarrow{\text{KCN}} C_6H_5COCOCHCOC_6H_5$$
$$\underset{\text{OH}}{|}$$

Methylglyoxal forms the corresponding acyloin rapidly in the presence of catalytic amounts of cyanide ion.[40]

$$2CH_3COCHO \xrightarrow{\text{CN}^-} CH_3COCHCOCOCH_3$$
$$\underset{\text{OH}}{|}$$

2-Pyridinecarboxaldehyde, which is formally similar to a dicarbonyl compound, has been found to undergo the benzoin condensation with acid catalysts. When boron fluoride, for example, is passed into the cold aldehyde, 2-pyridoin is formed in 34% yield.[41]

Glyoxal, in the presence of oxygen and sodium bisulfite, yields tetrahydroxyquinone, which corresponds to an oxidation product of the cyclic acyloin that can be imagined.[42]

In the fermentation of sugars acetoin is formed, presumably from two

[40] B. Görlich, *Chem. Ber.*, **89**, 2145 (1956).
[41] C. S. Marvel and J. K. Stille, *J. Org. Chem.*, **21**, 1313 (1956).
[42] B. Eistert and G. Bock, *Angew. Chem.*, **70**, 595 (1958).

molecules of acetaldehyde. Another example of this type of condensation is the formation of glycolaldehyde from formaldehyde.

$$2CH_2O \rightarrow HOCH_2CHO$$

Diazo Compounds

Aliphatic diazo compounds such as diazomethane appear to attack carbonyl compounds in the nucleophilic manner (OR **8**, 364). Diazomethane, taken as an example, may be represented by the following three structures, the first of which seems to be the most important.

$$^-\overset{..}{C}H_2{-}\overset{+}{N}{\equiv}N: \leftrightarrow CH_2{=}\overset{+}{N}{=}\overset{-}{\underset{..}{N}}: \leftrightarrow \overset{..}{C}H_2{-}\overset{+}{N}{=}\overset{-}{\underset{..}{N}}:$$

The reaction of diazomethane with acetone, for example, may be formulated as follows.

It is postulated that, by loss of molecular nitrogen, a labile intermediate is produced that can form either an epoxide or a ketone in which the chain has been extended by one methylene group. In the example given the two products are formed in approximately equal amounts. This type of homologation has been observed with other ketones; acetophenone, for example, yields benzyl methyl ketone.

$$C_6H_5COCH_3 \rightarrow C_6H_5CH_2COCH_3$$

As in other similar rearrangements, the phenyl group migrates in preference to the alkyl group.

Aldehydes react with diazomethane to give methyl ketones (CR **23**, 193); *m*-nitrobenzaldehyde, for example, yields *m*-nitroacetophenone.

$$\text{CHO} \qquad\qquad \text{COCH}_3$$

In this transformation hydrogen migrates in preference to the aryl group. The reaction is not of general utility, however, because of the formation of olefin oxides.

The diazomethane method is of especial importance in the alicyclic series because it brings about ring enlargement. Cyclohexanone, for example, gives a mixture of cycloheptanone and cycloöctanone, the seven-membered ketone being the chief product. The principal product from cyclopentanone is cycloheptanone also. One procedure for expanding the cyclohexanone ring involves treatment with *p*-tolylsulfonylmethylnitros-amide; the yield of cycloheptanone is 36% (OS **34**, 24).

$$p\text{-CH}_3\text{C}_6\text{H}_4\text{SO}_2\text{NNO} + \text{C}_2\text{H}_5\text{OH} \xrightarrow[\text{H}_2\text{O}]{\text{KOH}}$$
$$\underset{\text{CH}_3}{\big|}$$

$$p\text{-CH}_3\text{C}_6\text{H}_4\text{SO}_2\text{OC}_2\text{H}_5 + \text{CH}_2\text{N}_2 + \text{H}_2\text{O}$$

The process of ring enlargement does not stop, of course, when one methylene group has been introduced and therefore yields a mixture of ketones. Ketene reacts with diazomethane to give chiefly cyclobutanone; presumably cyclopropanone is an intermediate. By use of an excess of ketene with diazomethane it is possible to isolate the hydrate and hemiacetal of cyclopropanone.

By the use of phenyldiazomethane it is possible to introduce a phenyl-methinyl group into a ring. The synthesis of 2-phenylcycloheptanone from cyclohexanone is an example. The reaction is carried out by treating cyclohexanone with ethyl N-nitroso-N-benzylcarbamate in the presence of methanol and powdered potassium carbonate (OS **35**, 91; yield 96%).

Arndt-Eistert reaction

One of the most useful methods of homologation is based on the Arndt-Eistert reaction (OR **1**, 38), the first step of which consists in treatment of an acid chloride with diazomethane in excess; the corresponding diazo-ketone is formed.

$$\underset{RC-Cl}{\overset{O}{\parallel}} + CH_2N_2 \rightarrow \underset{RC-CHN_2}{\overset{O}{\parallel}} + HCl$$

Unless the diazomethane is in excess, a halomethyl ketone is produced by the action of hydrogen chloride on the diazo ketone.

$$\underset{RC-CHN_2}{\overset{O}{\parallel}} + HCl \rightarrow \underset{RC-CH_2Cl}{\overset{O}{\parallel}} + N_2$$

Benzyl chloromethyl ketone can be made in 85% yield from phenylacetyl chloride (OS III, 119).

In the presence of metallic silver and water the Wolff rearrangement (p. 190) occurs, and the diazoketone is converted into an acid that is the next higher homolog of the parent acid.

$$RCOCHN_2 + H_2O \xrightarrow{Ag} RCH_2CO_2H + N_2$$

If the decomposition is carried out in the presence of an alcohol or ammonia, the product is the corresponding ester or amide, respectively.

$$RCOCHN_2 + R'OH \xrightarrow{Ag} RCH_2CO_2R' + N_2$$

$$RCOCHN_2 + NH_3 \xrightarrow{Ag} RCH_2CONH_2 + N_2$$

The synthesis of diethyl cyclopropylmalonate from cyclopropane-carboxylic acid by way of the acid bromide is an illustration of the use of ethyl diazoacetate.[43]

$$\underset{\underset{CH_2}{\diagdown\diagup}}{CH_2-CHCOBr} + N_2CHCO_2C_2H_5 \xrightarrow{-HBr}$$

$$\underset{\underset{CH_2}{\diagdown\diagup}}{CH_2-CHCOCN_2CO_2C_2H_5} \xrightarrow[-N_2]{Ag_2O}$$

$$\underset{\underset{CH_2 \quad CO_2C_2H_5}{\diagdown\diagup}}{CH_2-CHC=C=O} \xrightarrow{C_2H_5OH} \underset{\underset{CH_2}{\diagdown\diagup}}{CH_2-CHCH(CO_2C_2H_5)_2}$$

[43] L. I. Smith and S. MacKenzie, Jr., *J. Org. Chem.*, **15**, 74 (1950).

The Arndt-Eistert method has the advantage that the product, being an acid, may serve as starting material for making still higher homologs. The yields are 50 to 80% of the theoretical amount. It is the method of choice when only a small amount of material is required.

The most useful methods of homologation of aliphatic acids are summarized in the following diagram.

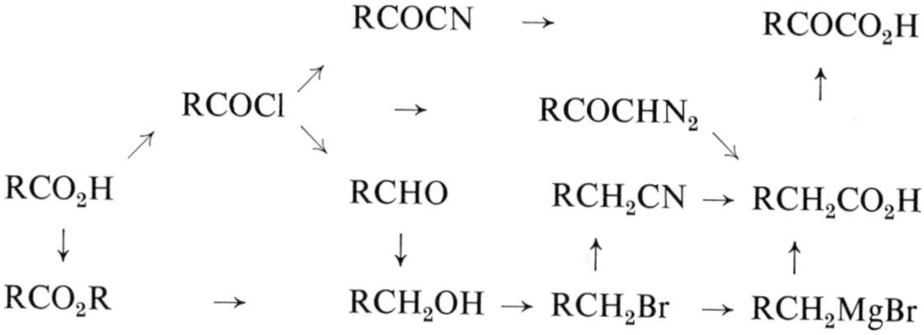

$$
\begin{array}{ccc}
& RCOCN & \rightarrow & RCOCO_2H \\
& \nearrow & & \uparrow \\
RCOCl & \rightarrow & RCOCHN_2 & \\
\nearrow & \searrow & & \searrow \\
RCO_2H & RCHO & RCH_2CN \rightarrow RCH_2CO_2H \\
\downarrow & \downarrow & \uparrow & \uparrow \\
RCO_2R & \rightarrow RCH_2OH \rightarrow RCH_2Br \rightarrow RCH_2MgBr
\end{array}
$$

Of all these methods, the Arndt-Eistert is the only one that does not require reduction. For this reason it is extremely useful for compounds that contain nitro, quinone, keto, lactone, ester, or other groups that might be attacked by reducing agents. An example is the conversion of *o*-nitrobenzoic acid into *o*-nitrophenylacetic acid.

Addition to Olefins and Acetylenes

It has been seen that the ease of addition of an electrophile is greater if the intermediate carbonium ion has a high order of stability. In a similar way nucleophilic attack of a carbon-carbon multiple linkage is possible if the intermediate carbanion is sufficiently stable.

Olefins

Nucleophilic attack of an olefin may be formulated as follows.

$$ A^- + \overset{|}{\underset{|}{C}} = \overset{|}{\underset{|}{C}} \rightarrow A - \overset{|}{\underset{|}{C}} - \overset{|}{\underset{|}{C}}{}^- $$

Chlorotrifluoroethylene, for example, combines with ethanol in the presence of sodium ethoxide to give 2-chloro-1,1,2-trifluoroethyl ethyl ether (OS **34**, 16; 92% yield).

$$ CF_2{=}CFCl + C_2H_5OH \rightarrow C_2H_5OCF_2CHFCl $$

Alcohols combine with octafluoroisobutylene in neutral or slightly acidic media; methanol is an example.[44]

$$CF_3\overset{\overset{\displaystyle CF_3}{|}}{C}{=}CF_2 + CH_3OH \rightarrow CF_3\overset{\overset{\displaystyle CF_3}{|}}{C}HCF_2OCH_3$$

Polyfluoroölefins react with cyanide ion also; when chlorotrifluoro-ethylene is treated with a mixture of sodium cyanide, water, and aceto-nitrile at 75 to 80° and under 2.7 atmospheres of pressure, and the reaction mixture is treated with sulfuric acid, 3-chloro-2,2,3-trifluoropropionic acid is produced in 79% yield (OS **40**, 11).

$$CFCl{=}CF_2 \xrightarrow[H_2O]{NaCN} ClCHFCF_2CO_2Na \xrightarrow{H^+} ClCHFCF_2CO_2H$$

As the examples show, highly fluorinated olefins characteristically react with nucleophiles; they resist attack by cations. Effective reagents include such relatively weak nucleophiles as the halide ions, of which the most reactive is fluoride ion.[45]

Familiar examples are found in the addition of alcohols to α,β-unsaturated compounds in the presence of a sodium alkoxide catalyst (Hine, 221).

$$RO^- + CH_2{=}CHCOR' \rightarrow ROCH_2\overset{\overset{\displaystyle O}{\|}}{C}HCR' \leftrightarrow ROCH_2CH{=}\overset{\overset{\displaystyle O^-}{|}}{C}R'$$

Acetylenes

Acetylene has a marked capacity for combining with alcohols as is illus-trated by the Reppe process for making vinyl ethers. It consists in the condensation of alcohols with acetylene at 150 to 160° in the presence of a small amount of sodium or potassium hydroxide. Primary and secondary alcohols undergo vinylation readily.[46]

$$ROH + C_2H_2 \rightarrow ROCH{=}CH_2$$

Since vinyl ethers are hydrolyzed easily, this type of reaction makes possible the conversion of acetylene into acetaldehyde.

$$CH_2{=}CHOR + H_2O \xrightarrow{H^+} CH_3CHO + ROH$$

Mercaptans are vinylated in a similar way.

$$RSH + HC{\equiv}CH \rightarrow RSCH{=}CH_2$$

[44] R. J. Koshar, T. C. Simmons, and F. W. Hoffmann, *J. Am. Chem. Soc.*, **79**, 1741 (1957).
[45] W. J. Miller, Jr., J. H. Fried, and H. Goldwhite, *J. Am. Chem. Soc.*, **82**, 3091 (1960).
[46] C. E. Schildknecht, A. O. Zoss, and C. McKinley, *Ind. Eng. Chem.*, **39**, 180 (1947).

Vinyl ethers may combine with alcohols to yield acetals, which occur as by-products in the vinylation of alcohols. This type of reaction may be made to predominate under properly chosen conditions. From ethylene glycol, by suitable control of the reaction conditions, may be prepared not only the normal divinylation product but also the monovinyl ether and the isomeric cyclic acetal.

$$\begin{array}{c} CH_2OCH{=}CH_2 \\ | \\ CH_2OCH{=}CH_2 \end{array}$$

$$\begin{array}{c} CH_2OH \\ | \\ CH_2OH \end{array} \nearrow$$

$$\searrow$$

$$\begin{array}{c} CH_2OH \\ | \\ CH_2OCH{=}CH_2 \end{array} \rightarrow \quad \begin{array}{c} CH_2{-}O \\ | \qquad\qquad \diagdown \\ \qquad\qquad\qquad CHCH_3 \\ | \qquad\qquad \diagup \\ CH_2{-}O \end{array}$$

Phenols are vinylated more rapidly than alcohols. In fact, methanol and ethanol can serve as media for the reaction. Phenol and 2-naphthol condense with acetylene at 180 to 200° and an acetylene-nitrogen pressure of 100 to 500 pounds per square inch in the presence of sodium phenoxide or potassium hydroxide to give the corresponding vinyl ethers in yields of 80 to 90%.

$$C_6H_5OH + HC{\equiv}CH \rightarrow C_6H_5OCH{=}CH_2$$

$$C_{10}H_7OH + HC{\equiv}CH \rightarrow C_{10}H_7OCH{=}CH_2$$

Secondary amines, such as carbazole are vinylated also. Succinimide readily yields vinylsuccinimide in the presence of a zinc catalyst; the yield is about 85%.

$$\begin{array}{c} CH_2{-}CO \\ | \qquad\qquad \diagdown \\ \qquad\qquad\qquad NH \\ | \qquad\qquad \diagup \\ CH_2{-}CO \end{array} \rightarrow \quad \begin{array}{c} CH_2{-}CO \\ | \qquad\qquad \diagdown \\ \qquad\qquad\qquad NCH{=}CH_2 \\ | \qquad\qquad \diagup \\ CH_2{-}CO \end{array}$$

The conditions for the vinylation of carbazole and succinimide are a temperature of approximately 180° and a pressure of 200 pounds per square inch.

A remarkable reaction is the vinylation of hydrogen cyanide to produce acrylonitrile.

$$C_2H_2 + HCN \rightarrow CH_2{=}CHCN$$

This reaction is carried out in the presence of a catalyst made by adding an alkali chloride to copper acetylide.

Acetylene reacts additively with nitromethane to yield 1-nitropropene. The initial condensation product is presumed to be 3-nitropropene, which would undergo rearrangement to bring the double bond into conjugation with the nitro group.

$$HC\equiv CH + CH_3NO_2 \rightarrow CH_2=CHCH_2NO_2 \rightarrow CH_3CH=CHNO_2$$

Nitriles from hydrocarbons

Ammonia attacks olefins under drastic conditions, but the nitrogenous products are nitriles rather than amines. Propylene, for example, yields a mixture of acetonitrile and propionitrile; under suitable conditions acrylonitrile is formed. This method of producing nitriles obviously involves complex chemical changes since it is applicable also to paraffins and methylbenzenes. Benzonitrile, for example, can be manufactured by treating toluene with ammonia at temperatures near 1000° F. in the presence of catalysts containing oxides of phosphorus, molybdenum, or tungsten supported on alumina.

$$C_6H_5CH_3 + NH_3 \rightarrow C_6H_5CN + 3H_2$$

Ethylene reacts with ammonia under similar conditions to give acetonitrile. It has been suggested that amines are intermediates; ethylamine and *n*-propylamine can be dehydrogenated to give nitriles.

$$CH_3CH_2NH_2 \rightarrow CH_3CN + 2H_2$$

$$CH_3CH_2CH_2NH_2 \rightarrow CH_3CH_2CN + 2H_2$$

Ketenes

The electron deficit is extreme in carbon dioxide, ketenes, isocyanates, and other molecules of the cumulene type. As would be expected, these substances combine readily with water, alcohols, amines, and other donor molecules. The behavior of ketenes is illustrative; with water, ammonia or amines, and halogen acids they yield acids, amides, and acid chlorides, respectively. These reactions are formulated as involving 1,2-addition to the carbonyl group followed by ketonization of the unstable enol.

$$R_2C=C=O + H_2O \rightarrow [R_2C=\overset{\displaystyle OH}{\overset{\displaystyle |}{C}}OH] \rightarrow R_2CHCO_2H$$

$$R_2C=C=O + RNH_2 \rightarrow [R_2C=\overset{\displaystyle OH}{\overset{\displaystyle |}{C}}NHR] \rightarrow R_2CHCONHR$$

$$R_2C=C=O + HX \rightarrow [R_2C=\overset{\displaystyle OH}{\overset{\displaystyle |}{C}}X] \rightarrow R_2CHCOX$$

Both aliphatic and aromatic acids react with ketene to give anhydrides.[47] An important example is acetic acid, with which ketene forms acetic anhydride.

$$CH_2{=}C{=}O + CH_3CO_2H \rightarrow (CH_3CO)_2O$$

Ketene is used as an acetylating agent for phenols, mercaptans, and alcohols, the reaction being carried out in the presence of a small amount of sulfuric acid.

Aldehydes and ketones may yield acetates when treated with ketene in the presence of sulfuric acid or p-toluenesulfonic acid. Acetylsulfoacetic acid, formed from sulfuric acid and acetic anhydride, is particularly effective.

$$H_2SO_4 + 2(CH_3CO)_2O \rightarrow CH_3CO_2SO_2CH_2CO_2H + 2CH_3CO_2H$$

By this method enol acetates are made readily from such compounds as acetaldehyde, acetone, and methyl ethyl ketone. An interesting example is crotonaldehyde, which yields 1-acetoxy-1,3-butadiene.

$$CH_3CH{=}CHCH{=}O + CH_2{=}C{=}O \rightarrow CH_3CO_2CH{=}CH{-}CH{=}CH_2$$

The preparation of enol acetates can be carried out more conveniently by treatment of enolizable carbonyl compounds with isopropenyl acetate, which is formed reversibly from ketene and acetone.

$$CH_3COCH_3 + CH_2{=}C{=}O \rightleftharpoons \underset{\underset{CH_3}{|}}{CH_2{=}COCOCH_3}$$

Acetylation is brought about by heating the reaction mixture under conditions that permit continuous distillation of the acetone that is generated.[48]

$$R_2CHCOR + \underset{\underset{CH_3}{|}}{CH_2{=}COCOCH_3} \rightarrow \underset{\underset{CH_3}{|}}{R\overset{\overset{OCOCH_3}{|}}{C}{=}CR_2} + CH_3COCH_3$$

Although the acetylating agent is probably ketene, formed by dissociation of isopropenyl acetate, the net change is the transformation of one acetate into another.

Ketene readily forms a dimer, known as diketene. Infrared studies indicate that diketene is a mixture of two or more forms, the most likely being vinylaceto-β-lactone and β-crotonalactone.

[47] See R. N. Lacey, *Advances in Organic Chemistry*, Interscience Publishers, Inc., New York, Vol. II, p. 213, 1960.

[48] H. J. Hagemeyer and D. C. Hull, *Ind. Eng. Chem.*, **41**, 2920 (1949).

$$CH_2=C-CH_2$$
$$O-C=O$$

Vinylaceto-β-lactone

$$CH_3C=CH$$
$$O-C=O$$

β-Crotonolactone

$$O=C-CH_2$$
$$CH_2-C=O$$

1,3-Cyclobutanedione

Tracer work involving C^{14} has confirmed this opinion and established that 1,3-cyclobutanedione is not an important component of the mixture.

Diketene has found use in the preparation of acetoacetanilide (OS III, 10; 74% yield).

$$(CH_2=C=O)_2 + C_6H_5NH_2 \rightarrow CH_3COCH_2CONHC_6H_5$$

Methyl and ethyl acetoacetate are formed by combining the correspond-ing alcohols with diketene. This is a general method for the preparation of such esters; from *t*-butyl alcohol *t*-butyl acetoacetate can be made in high yields.[49]

A convenient synthesis of β-keto esters consists in converting an acid chloride into the corresponding ketene dimer and subsequent treatment of the dimer with an alcohol (OR **3**, 108). The dimer is produced by allowing the acid chloride to stand 16 hours with triethylamine. An example is the synthesis of ethyl α-stearoylstearate.

$$2CH_3(CH_2)_{15}CH_2COCl \xrightarrow{(C_2H_5)_3N} [CH_3(CH_2)_{15}CH=C=O]_2 \xrightarrow{C_2H_5OH}$$
$$CH_3(CH_2)_{15}CHCO_2C_2H_5$$
$$CH_3(CH_2)_{16}C=O$$

The reactions of ketene dimers are those to be expected of acyl ketenes, $RCOC=C=O$. Water converts them into β-keto acids, which are readily
$$\quad\ \ |$$
$$\quad\ \ R$$
transformed into ketones by decarboxylation. An example is the prepa-ration of laurone from lauroyl chloride (OS **31**, 68; 55% yield).

$$2C_{11}H_{23}COCl + 2(C_2H_5)_3N \rightarrow C_{11}H_{23}COC=C=O + 2(C_2H_5)_3N\cdot HCl$$
$$C_{10}H_{21}$$

$$C_{11}H_{23}COC=C=O + H_2O \rightarrow C_{11}H_{23}COC_{11}H_{23} + CO_2$$
$$C_{10}H_{21}$$

6-Oxohendecanoic acid has been made in a similar way from the acid chloride of methyl hydrogen adipate (OS **38**, 38).

[49] A. Treibs and K. Hintermeier, *Ber.*, **87**, 1163 (1954).

Carbocycles can be formed from bifunctional ketenes, the procedure being to dehydrochlorinate the acid chloride of a dibasic acid and subject the resulting ketene dimer to hydrolysis or alcoholysis. From adipyl chloride, for example, 2-carbethoxycyclopentanone is obtained in 40% yield.

$$
\begin{array}{ccc}
\text{COCl} & \text{C}{=}\text{O} & \text{CO} \\
\diagup & \diagup\!\diagup & \diagup\;\diagdown \\
\text{CH}_2\;\;\text{COCl} & \text{CH}\;\;\;\text{C}{=}\text{O} & \text{CH}_2\;\;\;\text{CHCO}_2\text{C}_2\text{H}_5 \\
| \qquad | & | \qquad \| & | \qquad\quad | \\
\text{CH}_2\;\;\;\text{CH}_2 & \text{CH}_2\;\;\;\text{CH} & \text{CH}_2{-}\text{CH}_2 \\
\diagdown\;\;\diagup & \diagdown\;\;\diagup & \\
\text{CH}_2 & \text{CH}_2 &
\end{array}
$$

with "internal 'dimer'" and C_2H_5OH shown over the arrows.

Applied to the chlorides of higher dibasic acids, this procedure affords a method of making large carbocyclic rings.

In the presence of suitable catalysts, ketenes combine with many carbonyl compounds to produce four-membered or β-lactones (OR **8**, 305); an example is the formation of β-propiolactone from ketene and formaldehyde in the presence of zinc chloride.

$$
\text{CH}_2{=}\text{C}{=}\text{O} + \text{CH}_2{=}\text{O} \xrightarrow{\text{ZnCl}_2}
\begin{array}{c}
\text{CH}_2{-}\text{C}{=}\text{O} \\
| \qquad\quad | \\
\text{CH}_2{-}\text{O}
\end{array}
$$

Acetone yields a similar product.

$$
\text{CH}_2{=}\text{C}{=}\text{O} + (\text{CH}_3)_2\text{C}{=}\text{O} \rightarrow
\begin{array}{c}
\text{CH}_2{-}\text{C}{=}\text{O} \\
| \qquad\quad | \\
(\text{CH}_3)_2\text{C}{-\!-\!-}\text{O}
\end{array}
$$

The β-lactones are decarboxylated by heat to give unsaturated compounds; benzaldehyde, for example, affords styrene in high yields.

$$
\text{CH}_2{=}\text{C}{=}\text{O} + \text{C}_6\text{H}_5\text{CH}{=}\text{O} \rightarrow
\begin{array}{c}
\text{CH}_2{-}\text{C}{=}\text{O} \\
| \qquad\quad | \\
\text{C}_6\text{H}_5\text{CH}{-}\text{O}
\end{array}
\xrightarrow{-\text{CO}_2} \text{C}_6\text{H}_5\text{CH}{=}\text{CH}_2
$$

In a similar way, biacetyl combines with ketene in the presence of a boron trifluoride etherate to form a di-β-lactone, which is pyrolyzed to 2,3-dimethyl-1,3-butadiene.

$$
2\text{CH}_2{=}\text{C}{=}\text{O} +
\begin{array}{c}
\text{CH}_3\text{C}{=}\text{O} \\
| \\
\text{CH}_3\text{C}{=}\text{O}
\end{array}
\rightarrow
\begin{array}{c}
\text{CH}_2{-}\text{C}{=}\text{O} \\
| \qquad\quad | \\
\text{CH}_3\text{C}{-\!-\!-}\text{O} \\
| \\
\text{CH}_3\text{C}{-\!-\!-}\text{O} \\
| \qquad\quad | \\
\text{CH}_2{-}\text{C}{=}\text{O}
\end{array}
\xrightarrow{-2\text{CO}_2}
\begin{array}{c}
\text{CH}_2{=}\text{C}{-}\text{C}{=}\text{CH}_2 \\
| \qquad | \\
\text{CH}_3\;\;\text{CH}_3
\end{array}
$$

The reaction between phosphorus pentachloride and ketene yields chloroacetyl chloride.

$$
\text{CH}_2{=}\text{C}{=}\text{O} \xrightarrow{\text{PCl}_5} \text{ClCH}_2\text{COCl}
$$

This and a good many other reactions appear to involve only the carbon-carbon double bond.

Carbon suboxide, produced by treating malonic acid with phosphorus pentoxide, behaves much like other ketenes. It combines with water to regenerate malonic acid and with alcohols to yield malonic esters.

$$O{=}C{=}C{=}C{=}O + 2ROH \rightarrow \underset{\underset{OR}{|}}{O{=}C}{-}CH_2{-}\underset{\underset{OR}{|}}{C{=}O}$$

Isocyanates combine with alcohols to give urethans; presumably the initial product is a hemiacetal that rearranges. The formation of *p*-nitrophenylurethans is illustrative.

$$O_2NC_6H_4N{=}C{=}O + ROH \rightarrow [O_2NC_6H_4N{=}\overset{\overset{OH}{|}}{C}{-}OR] \rightarrow$$
$$O_2NC_6H_4NHCO_2R$$

Combination of diisocyanates with glycols produces polyurethans, a number of which have achieved practical importance. One of the first of these was the polymer prepared from hexamethylene diisocyanate (p. 337) and tetramethylene glycol.

$$O{=}C{=}N(CH_2)_6N{=}C{=}O + HO(CH_2)_4OH \rightarrow$$
$$O{=}C{=}N(CH_2)_6NHCO_2(CH_2)_4OH \rightarrow polymer$$

Carbon disulfide and primary amines may be used to make isothiocyanates, dithiocarbamates being intermediates. A more convenient method, however, involves the condensation of the amine and carbon disulfide in the presence of ammonium hydroxide, which yields the ammonium salt of the dithiocarbamic acid. This salt is readily converted into the isothiocyanate by oxidation with lead nitrate. An example is the synthesis of phenyl isothiocyanate (OS I, 447; the yield is 78%).

$$C_6H_5NH_2 + CS_2 + NH_4OH \rightarrow C_6H_5NHCS_2NH_4 + H_2O$$

$$C_6H_5NHCS_2NH_4 + Pb(NO_3)_2 \rightarrow$$
$$C_6H_5N{=}C{=}S + NH_4NO_3 + PbS + HNO_3$$

Another method is illustrated by the synthesis of methyl isothiocyanate (OS III, 599; 76% yield). The initial condensation is carried out in the presence of sodium hydroxide, and the sodium salt thus obtained is treated with ethyl chloroformate.

$$CH_3NH_2 + CS_2 + NaOH \rightarrow CH_3NHCS_2Na + H_2O$$

$$CH_3NHCS_2Na + ClCO_2C_2H_5 \rightarrow CH_3NHCS_2CO_2C_2H_5 + NaCl$$

$$CH_3NHCS_2CO_2C_2H_5 \rightarrow CH_3N{=}C{=}S + COS + C_2H_5OH$$

Ethylenediamine reacts with carbon disulfide to yield ethylenethiourea, the thiocarbamic acid being an intermediate (OS III, 394; 89% yield).

$$
\begin{array}{c}
CH_2NH_2 \\
| \\
CH_2NH_2
\end{array}
+ CS_2 \rightarrow
\begin{array}{c}
\overset{\displaystyle S}{\overset{\|}{CH_2NHC S^-}} \\
| \\
CH_2NH_3^+
\end{array}
\xrightarrow{HCl}
\begin{array}{c}
CH_2NH \\
\diagdown \\
\diagup \quad C{=}S + H_2S \\
CH_2NH
\end{array}
$$

Wittig Reaction

An unusual process for converting carbonyl derivatives into the corresponding olefinic compounds consists in the interaction of the carbonyl compound with triphenylphosphinealkylidenes.[50] An example is the conversion of benzophenone into 1,1-diphenylethylene by treatment with the triphenylphosphinemethylene. A betaine is postulated as an intermediate.

$$
\begin{array}{c}
C_6H_5 \\
\diagdown \\
\diagup \quad C{=}O + (C_6H_5)_3P{=}CH_2 \rightarrow (C_6H_5)_3\overset{+}{P}\!-\!CH_2 \rightarrow \\
C_6H_5 \qquad\qquad\qquad\qquad\qquad\quad {}^-O\!-\!C(C_6H_5)_2
\end{array}
$$

$$(C_6H_5)_3PO + (C_6H_5)_2C{=}CH_2$$

Similar treatment converts cyclohexanone into methylenecyclohexane (OS **40**, 66; yield 40%).

The phosphorus ylenes are made by the action of organolithium compounds on appropriately constituted phosphonium salts. Triphenylmethylphosphonium bromide and phenyllithium yield the simplest triphenylphosphorus ylene, triphenylphosphinemethylene.

$$[(C_6H_5)_3PCH_3]Br + C_6H_5Li \rightarrow (C_6H_5)_3P{=}CH_2 + LiBr + C_6H_6$$

1,4-Diphenylbutadiene is prepared from triphenylcinnamylphosphonium chloride and benzaldehyde (OS **40**, 36; 67% yield).

$$C_6H_5CH{=}CHCH_2\overset{+}{P}(C_6H_5)_3Cl^- + C_6H_5CHO + LiOC_2H_5 \rightarrow$$
$$C_6H_5CH{=}CHCH{=}CHC_6H_5 + (C_6H_5)_3PO + C_2H_5OH + LiCl$$

If the alkyl halide is α,α'-dichloro-p-xylene and the carbonyl compound is cinnamaldehyde, the product is 1,4-bis(4-phenylbutadienyl)benzene (OS **40**, 85).

$$C_6H_5CH{=}CHCH{=}CH\!\!\left\langle\!\!\bigcirc\!\!\right\rangle\!\!CH{=}CHCH{=}CHC_6H_5$$

[50] S. Trippett, *Advances in Organic Chemistry*, Interscience Publishers, Inc., New York, Vol. I, p. 83, 1960.

When a solution of benzaldehyde and the bisphosphonium salt from α,α'-dichloro-p-xylene and triphenylphosphine is treated with a solution of lithium ethoxide in ethanol, 1,4-distyrylbenzene is formed.[51]

$$\left[(C_6H_5)_3\overset{+}{P}CH_2\left\langle\underset{=}{\bigcirc}\right\rangle CH_2\overset{+}{P}(C_3H_5)_3\right]Cl_2 \xrightarrow[C_6H_5CHO]{CH_3CH_2OLi}$$

$$C_6H_5CH{=}CH\left\langle\underset{=}{\bigcirc}\right\rangle CH{=}CHC_6H_5$$

Other examples of the Wittig transformation are the following.[52]

$$(C_6H_5)_3P{=}CH_2 + O_2N\left\langle\underset{=}{\bigcirc}\right\rangle COC_6H_5 \rightarrow O_2N\left\langle\underset{=}{\bigcirc}\right\rangle \underset{\underset{C_6H_5}{|}}{C}{=}CH_2 \ (70\%)$$

$$(C_6H_5)_3P{=}CHCO_2C_2H_5 + C_6H_5CHO \rightarrow C_6H_5CH{=}CHCO_2C_2H_5 \ (77\%)$$

$$(C_6H_5)_3P{=}CHC_6H_5 + C_6H_5CHO \rightarrow C_6H_5CH{=}CHC_6H_5 \ (82\%)$$

[51] T. W. Campbell and R. N. McDonald, *J. Org. Chem.*, **24**, 1246 (1959).
[52] G. Wittig, *Angew. Chem.*, **68**, 505 (1956).

18

Reactions of organomagnesium compounds and similar reagents

Organometallic compounds include those substances in which carbon is joined directly to a metal. Among the most useful are those derived from magnesium, zinc, cadmium, lithium, aluminum, and sodium. By far the most important organometallic compounds are the Grignard reagents. An insight into the behavior of Grignard reagents may be gained by regarding them as sources of carbanions corresponding to the hydrocarbon radicals involved. Since such carbanions are very strong bases, it is to be foreseen that they will attack centers of low electron density such as the carbon atom of a carbonyl or nitrile group. The reactions that occur are of the *addition* type.

Moreover, these highly basic carbanions may be expected to displace weaker bases such as OH^-, OR^-, and NR_2^-. Reactions of this category occur, for example, with hydroxy compounds, halogen compounds, ortho esters, sulfhydryl compounds, certain active methylene compounds, primary and secondary amino compounds, and 1-alkynes.

Discussion of Grignard reagents in this way is obviously an over-simplification since the apparent nucleophilicity of a given alkyl or aryl group varies greatly with the nature of the metal with which it is associated. Methylmagnesium iodide is used to determine active hydrogen in the Zerewitinov procedure in which the reagent reacts with the active hydrogen compound in pyridine. Under these conditions water is reported to give only 1 mole of methane.[1]

$$CH_3MgI + H_2O \rightarrow CH_4 + Mg(OH)I$$

Halogens

Halogens cleave Grignard reagents as follows

$$RMgX + X_2 \rightarrow RX + MgX_2$$

[1] D. L. Klass and W. N. Jensen, *J. Org. Chem.*, **26**, 2110 (1961).

This reaction gives iodo compounds in excellent yields and provides a method of getting them from the corresponding chloro or bromo compounds. *n*-Propyl bromide, isoamyl chloride, bromobenzene, and *p*-bromotoluene afford the corresponding iodo derivatives in yields of 80 %.

Oxygen

When a Grignard reagent is exposed to air or oxygen, oxygen is absorbed and chemiluminescence is observed; the oxidation of *p*-chlorophenylmagnesium bromide is accompanied by a particularly intense glow. The reaction, like other autoxidation reactions, may be regarded as radical in type; it is complex and seems to consist of the following steps.

$$RMgX + O_2 \rightarrow RO_2MgX$$

$$RO_2MgX + RMgX \rightarrow 2ROMgX$$

From the alkoxide so formed the alcohol is obtained by treatment with dilute acids.

$$ROMgX + HX \rightarrow ROH + MgX_2$$

Absorption of oxygen is very rapid; and when oxidation is not desired, care must be taken to exclude air from the apparatus containing the reagent. This is generally done by using ether as solvent; the blanket of ether vapor prevents the oxygen from entering.

Aliphatic and alicyclic reagents lead to the corresponding alcohols in 60 to 80 % yields, but this transformation has little synthetic value, since the halides used in preparing the reagents themselves are generally made from the alcohols. Cyclopropylmagnesium bromide reacts with oxygen to give cyclopropanol in 9 % yield.[2]

In the aromatic series where the reaction might be useful it is much more complex, phenols being obtained only in unsatisfactory yields. The reaction is most satisfactory with Grignard reagents that are able to act as reducing agents, the aryl Grignard reagents being very poor in this respect. If a mixture of an aryl Grignard reagent and a suitable alkyl Grignard reagent is oxidized, however, the peroxide from the aromatic compound is reduced by the alkyl Grignard reagent, and phenols may be obtained in satisfactory yields. Oxidation of 1-naphthylmagnesium bromide, for example, in the presence of isopropylmagnesium bromide (maintained in excess) affords 1-naphthol in 70 % yield; the yield with the aryl Grignard reagent alone is only 25 %.

$$C_{10}H_7MgBr + O_2 \rightarrow C_{10}H_7O_2MgBr$$

$$C_{10}H_7O_2MgBr + (CH_3)_2CHMgBr \rightarrow C_{10}H_7OMgBr + (CH_3)_2CHOMgBr$$

[2] J. D. Roberts and V. C. Chambers, *J. Am. Chem. Soc.*, **73**, 3176 (1951).

Further evidence for this theory is the observation that organic hydroperoxides can be formed by the slow addition of Grignard reagents to oxygen-saturated solvents at about $-70°$.[3]

t-Butyl hydroperoxide reacts with alkyl- and arylmagnesium halides to give the corresponding alcohols and phenols, respectively.[4]

Sulfur, like oxygen, reacts additively with the Grignard reagent, the products being mercaptans or thiophenols. The synthesis of methyl 2-thienyl sulfide from 2-iodothiophene depends on this reaction (OS **35**, 84).

$$\underset{S}{\boxed{}}\text{MgI} \xrightarrow{\ S\ } \underset{S}{\boxed{}}\text{SMgI} \xrightarrow{\ CH_3I\ } \underset{S}{\boxed{}}\text{SCH}_3$$

Selenium behaves in a similar way; selenophenol can be made in 71 % yield, for example, by allowing dry, powdered, black selenium to react with phenylmagnesium bromide (OS III, 771).

$$C_6H_5MgBr + Se \longrightarrow C_6H_5SeMgBr \xrightarrow{HCl} C_6H_5SeH$$

Coupling

Certain inorganic halides are able to couple the alkyl groups of the reagent. Since the metallic ion involved is reduced, the coupling may be classed as an oxidation reaction. Thus cupric chloride converts benzylmagnesium chloride largely into bibenzyl.

$$2C_6H_5CH_2MgCl + 2CuCl_2 \rightarrow C_6H_5CH_2CH_2C_6H_5 + 2CuCl + 2MgCl_2$$

Silver bromide is particularly effective; by its use coupling products such as biphenyl, bianisyl, n-octane, and bicyclohexyl have been obtained in high yields.

$$2RMgX + 2AgBr \rightarrow R\!-\!R + 2Ag + 2MgXBr$$

Other metal salts have been used also; in all cases the salt acts as an oxidizing agent. When phenylmagnesium bromide is treated with ferric chloride, biphenyl is obtained in high yields.

Very reactive organic halides may bring about coupling also. Benzyl chloride, for example, reacts with methylmagnesium iodide under favorable conditions to give bibenzyl in yields of about 75 %.

$$2C_6H_5CH_2Cl + 2CH_3MgI \rightarrow C_6H_5CH_2CH_2C_6H_5 + C_2H_6 + 2MgICl$$

A certain amount of alkylation is observed also.

$$C_6H_5CH_2Cl + CH_3MgI \rightarrow C_6H_5C_2H_5 + MgICl$$

[3] C. Walling and S. A. Buckler, *J. Am. Chem. Soc.*, **77**, 6032 (1955).
[4] S.-O. Lawesson and N. C. Yang, *J. Am. Chem. Soc.*, **81**, 4230 (1959).

Most of the coupling reactions of this type involve benzyl halides or their derivatives. Such reactions are promoted by the presence of certain halides such as cobaltous chloride. An interesting example is the formation of the dimethyl ether of hexestrol by the action of Grignard reagents in the presence of a halide of cobalt, nickel, or iron on the bromide obtained by adding hydrogen bromide to anethole.

$$CH_3CH_2CHBr \qquad CH_3CH_2CH\text{———}CHCH_2CH_3$$

$$2\underset{OCH_3}{\bigcirc} \rightarrow \underset{OCH_3}{\bigcirc}\underset{OCH_3}{\bigcirc}$$

Hindered benzoyl chlorides undergo coupling also; from mesitoyl chloride and methylmagnesium iodide, mesitil is obtained. This type of coupling has been interpreted by reference to the formation of radicals as intermediates. The addition of catalytic amounts of cobaltous chloride favors diketone formation. The following reaction scheme has been suggested.[5]

$$CH_3MgBr + CoCl_2 \rightarrow CH_3CoCl + MgBrCl$$
$$CH_3CoCl \rightarrow CH_3\cdot + CoCl\cdot$$
$$MesCOCl + CoCl\cdot \rightarrow MesCO\cdot + CoCl_2$$
$$2MesCO\cdot \rightarrow MesCOCOMes$$

Displacement Reactions

Grignard reagents and other organometallic compounds, acting as the corresponding carbanions, displace other bases from such atoms as hydrogen, halogen, and carbon.

Displacement on hydrogen

Displacements on hydrogen, for example, occur when Grignard reagents are treated with water, alcohols, acids, and other compounds having hydrogen on a highly electronegative element. The driving force in these reactions is the production of a new base such as OH^-, OR^-, or NR_2^- that is weaker than the alkide or aride ion of the reagent.

$$R^- + HOH \rightarrow RH + OH^-$$
$$R^- + CH_3OH \rightarrow RH + CH_3O^-$$
$$R^- + (CH_3)_2NH \rightarrow RH + (CH_3)_2N^-$$

A few weakly basic carbanions can be displaced from hydrogen. The acetylide ion is an example; by suitable procedures either the mono- or

---

[5] M. S. Kharasch, R. Morrison, and W. H. Urry, *J. Am. Chem. Soc.*, **66**, 368 (1944).

the bifunctional derivative can be made. It is of particular interest that propargylmagnesium bromide, which contains an acetylenic hydrogen atom, is nevertheless capable of existence.

$$HC{\equiv}CCH_2MgBr$$

The activation of methylene groups by adjacent unsaturation may be sufficient to enable them to react with Grignard reagents. For example, cyclopentadiene decomposes methylmagnesium iodide.

The preparation of 9-fluorenylmagnesium bromide by the action of ethylmagnesium bromide on fluorene proceeds with difficulty. Indeed it is actually possible to prepare 2-fluorenylmagnesium bromide in the usual way and to convert it into 2-fluorenecarboxylic acid.[6]

Fluoradene, a fluorene derivative, is a very acidic hydrocarbon.[7]

Fluoradene

Carbonyl compounds that have α-hydrogen atoms form weakly basic enolate ions and hence may decompose Grignard reagents; ethyl acetoacetate reacts in this way, for example.

$$CH_3COCH_2CO_2C_2H_5 + CH_3MgI \rightarrow [CH_3COCHCO_2C_2H_5]MgI + CH_4$$

The reaction of active hydrogen compounds with RMgX compounds is employed occasionally to make hydrocarbons. The preparation of n-pentane from 2-bromopentane by way of the corresponding Grignard reagent is an example (OS II, 478; 53% yield). The common use of this type of reaction is in analytical work, forming the basis of the Chugaev-Zerevitinov method of determining active hydrogen atoms. The method consists

[6] D. C. Morrison, *J. Am. Chem. Soc.*, **74**, 3430 (1952).
[7] H. Rapoport and G. Smolinsky, *J. Am. Chem. Soc.*, **82**, 934 (1960).

in treating a weighed amount of the compound to be tested with an excess of a methylmagnesium halide and measuring the methane evolved. One mole of resorcinol, for example, gives two moles of methane. Lithium aluminum hydride (p. 572) has been found to be superior to methylmagnesium iodide, in many instances, for active hydrogen determination.

Hindered ketones such as acetomesitylene and 2,6-dimethylacetophenone, which are completely enolized by methylmagnesium iodide, are reduced by lithium aluminum hydride, no hydrogen being formed. This observation demonstrates the absence of the enol forms in solutions of these ketones.[8]

A method of determining active hydrogen in the presence of ester groups involves titration with triphenylmethylsodium. This reagent has an intense red color; when a standard solution is used in titration, the color of the reagent serves as the end point. The method has an advantage over that involving Grignard reagents in permitting recovery of the original ester.

Decomposition of the Grignard reagent by active hydrogen compounds is to be avoided, of course, in synthetic work. The solvent and reactants should be free from water, alcohols, and all other compounds that have active hydrogen atoms. It is to be emphasized that this type of reaction is faster than those generally sought in synthetic work. When salicylaldehyde, for instance, is treated with a Grignard reagent, the hydroxyl group decomposes the reagent before the aldehyde group is attacked. If the halomagnesium derivative formed in such cases is soluble, further action of the reagent is possible, and useful condensation reactions can be realized in spite of the active hydrogen. Its presence, however, requires the use of an additional mole of reagent.

Attention may be directed to the pyrroles, which decompose Grignard reagents to yield magnesium derivatives capable of undergoing reactions characteristic of Grignard reagents. 5-Carbethoxy-2,4-dimethylpyrrole is produced in 58% yield by treating 2,4-dimethylpyrrole with ethylmagnesium bromide and then adding ethyl chloroformate to the reaction mixture (OS II, 198).

[8] L. H. Schwartzman and B. B. Corson, *J. Am. Chem. Soc.*, **76**, 781 (1954).

This reaction illustrates the fact that halomagnesium derivatives of pyrroles behave toward many types of compounds as though the magnesium were attached to a carbon atom in the 2-position.

Displacement on halogen

Enolization by displacement on halogen is known also and may be formulated in much the same way as enolizations on hydrogen. This type of reaction occurs with the hindered trihalomethyl ketones, which react with Grignard reagents to give the corresponding dihalogen compounds. The dihalo ketones, in which hydrogen and halogen are in competition, are likewise dehalogenated. Mesityl tribromomethyl ketone is an example.

$$MesCOCBr_3 \rightarrow MesCOCHBr_2 \rightarrow MesCOCH_2Br \rightarrow MesCOCH_3$$

In the monohalogen derivatives, however, the competition is apparently less one-sided. Whereas α-bromoacetomesitylene yields acetomesitylene, the corresponding chloro ketone is recovered.

Displacement on carbon

Alkyl Halides. Alkyl halides such as allyl bromide and benzyl chloride, which contain very reactive halogen atoms, may be alkylated or arylated by reaction with Grignard reagents. An example is the preparation of allylbenzene from allyl bromide and phenylmagnesium bromide.

$$C_6H_5MgBr + CH_2{=}CHCH_2Br \rightarrow C_6H_5CH_2CH{=}CH_2 + MgBr_2$$

The method of Lespieau and Bourguel (OR **5**, 22) is based on this reaction. 2,3-Dibromopropene (p. 295) reacts with *n*-butylmagnesium bromide, for example, to give a bromoheptene, which is converted into 1-heptyne by the action of alkali.

$$C_4H_9MgX + BrCH_2\overset{\overset{\displaystyle Br}{|}}{C}{=}CH_2 \rightarrow C_4H_9CH_2\overset{\overset{\displaystyle Br}{|}}{C}{=}CH_2 \rightarrow C_5H_{11}C{\equiv}CH$$

2,3-Dibromopropene has been alkylated similarly by cyclohexyl, benzyl, and *n*-heptyl Grignard reagents (OS I, 186).

α-Halo ethers are alkylated readily; a synthesis of olefins from α,β-dibromo ethers (p. 300) depends on this type of reaction.

Sulfates and Sulfonates. The similarity in behavior of the esters of sulfuric acid and sulfonic acids to that of the corresponding halides extends to the reaction with Grignard reagents. *n*-Propylbenzene, for example, is made in 75% yield by the interaction of benzylmagnesium chloride and diethyl sulfate (OS I, 471).

$$C_6H_5CH_2MgCl + (C_2H_5)_2SO_4 \rightarrow$$
$$C_6H_5CH_2CH_2CH_3 + C_2H_5Cl + (C_2H_5SO_4)MgCl$$

Similarly, isodurene is formed in 60 % yield by treating mesitylmagnesium bromide with dimethyl sulfate (OS II, 360). Also, *n*-amylbenzene is made in 59 % yield from benzylmagnesium chloride and *n*-butyl *p*-toluenesulfonate (OS II, 47).

Ethers. The use of ethers as solvents for Grignard reagents is possible because ordinary ethers are resistant to attack by such reagents. Ethers of the allyl type, however, are cleaved readily. The interaction of allyl phenyl ether and phenylmagnesium bromide, for example, gives allylbenzene.

$$C_6H_5MgBr + C_6H_5OCH_2CH{=}CH_2 \rightarrow$$
$$C_6H_5OMgBr + C_6H_5CH_2CH{=}CH_2$$

Of especial interest is the cleavage of certain α,β-unsaturated ethers; α-ethoxystyrene, for example, reacts with phenylmagnesium bromide to yield 1,1-diphenylethylene.[9]

$$C_6H_5C{=}CH_2 + C_6H_5MgBr \rightarrow (C_6H_5)_2C{=}CH_2 + C_2H_5OMgBr$$
$$\underset{OC_2H_5}{|}$$

Ortho Esters. The ease of displacement of an alkoxide group from an ether depends in large part on the electron deficiency of the carbon atom that is the site of the reaction. Orthocarbonic esters react more readily than other esters. The reaction with orthoformic esters is the critical step in the Bodroux-Chichibabin method for making aldehydes. An example of this procedure is the preparation of caproaldehyde from *n*-amylmagnesium bromide and ethyl orthoformate (OS II, 323; 50 % yield).

$$C_5H_{11}MgBr + CH(OC_2H_5)_3 \rightarrow C_5H_{11}CH(OC_2H_5)_2 + C_2H_5OMgBr$$
$$C_5H_{11}CH(OC_2H_5)_2 + H_2O \xrightarrow{H_2SO_4} C_5H_{11}CHO + 2C_2H_5OH$$

9-Phenanthrenecarboxaldehyde can be made from the corresponding bromo compound in a similar way (OS III, 701; 42 % yield).

Esters of Carboxylic Acids. Esters of highly hindered carboxylic acids may be cleaved by Grignard reagents. The change, a displacement of carboxylate ion, can be effected if the alkyl group of the ester is of a type that can form a relatively stable carbonium ion. Allyl mesitoate, for example, is cleaved by phenylmagnesium bromide to give allylbenzene in 70 % yield along with mesitoic acid.

$$MesCO_2CH_2CH{=}CH_2 + C_6H_5MgBr \rightarrow$$
$$C_6H_5CH_2CH{=}CH_2 + MesCO_2MgBr$$

[9] C. M. Hill, R. A. Walker, and M. E. Hill, *J. Am. Chem. Soc.*, **73**, 1663 (1951).

An S_N2' displacement (Gould, 291) occurs between the acetate of di-methylvinylcarbinol and mesitylmagnesium bromide; 1-mesityl-3-methyl-2-butene is produced.

$$CH_2=CH-\underset{\underset{CH_3}{|}}{\overset{\overset{CH_3}{|}}{C}}-O-\overset{\overset{O}{||}}{C}CH_3 \xrightarrow[\text{30 hr.}]{\text{MesMgBr}} MesCH_2CH=C(CH_3)_2$$

$$25\text{--}30\%$$

The cleavage of certain allyl ethers also appears to take place by an S_N2' mechanism. For example, when n-butyl γ-phenylallyl ether is treated with n-heptylmagnesium bromide the products are 3-phenyl-1-decene (52%) and n-butyl alcohol (76%).[10]

$$C_6H_5CH=CH-CH_2O-C_4H_9 \rightarrow \underset{\underset{C_7H_{15}}{|}}{C_6H_5CHCH}=CH_2 + C_4H_9OH$$

Displacement of carboxylate ion has been observed in a number of other cases; esters of duryl p-hydroxyphenyl ketone, for example, are cleaved by t-butylmagnesium chloride; the benzoate may be cited.

Epoxides. The epoxides, because of the strain in the three-membered ring, are opened by the action of Grignard reagents to give alcohols. An alkoxide group is displaced, the reaction being actually one of addition. It appears to involve the intermediate formation of a complex between ethylene oxide and a magnesium halide. The reaction with ethylene oxide provides a way of lengthening the carbon chain by two carbon atoms.

$$RMgX + \overset{\overset{O}{\diagup\diagdown}}{CH_2-CH_2} \longrightarrow RCH_2CH_2OMgX \xrightarrow{H_2O} RCH_2CH_2OH$$

A specific example is the preparation of 1-hexanol (OS I, 306; 62% yield).

2-(1-Naphthyl)ethanol can be made from 1-bromonaphthalene in 68% yield by this method.

[10] C. M. Hill, D. E. Simmons, and M. E. Hill, J. Am. Chem. Soc., 77, 3889 (1955).

Propylene oxide reacts with Grignard reagents in a manner similar to that indicated for ethylene oxide; the products, however, are secondary alcohols. It is a rule, first recognized by Krassusky, that monosubstituted ethylene oxides react with Grignard reagents so as to leave the oxygen atom on the more highly substituted carbon atom of the original oxide. An example is the reaction between 3,4-epoxy-1-butene and 1-naphthyl-magnesium bromide; the secondary alcohol is obtained in 58% yield.[11]

$$CH_2{=}CHCH{-}{-}CH_2 \rightarrow CH_2{=}CHCHCH_2C_{10}H_7$$
$$OH$$

Oxetane (OS III, 835) reacts with certain Grignard reagents to give the expected 3-substituted propanols in yields of 60 to 85%. Phenylmagnesium bromide, for example, affords 3-phenyl-1-propanol in 84% yield.[12]

$$C_6H_5MgBr + CH_2CH_2CH_2O \rightarrow C_6H_5CH_2CH_2CH_2OMgBr \rightarrow$$
$$C_6H_5CH_2CH_2CH_2OH$$

Displacement on other elements

Many organometallic compounds may be made by the reaction of Grignard reagents with the appropriate metal halides. Diphenylzinc, for example, may be obtained from zinc chloride and phenylmagnesium bromide.

$$2C_6H_5MgBr + ZnCl_2 \rightarrow (C_6H_5)_2Zn + MgBr_2 + MgCl_2$$

Phenylzinc chloride is the principal product when the reactants are taken in equimolecular amounts.

$$C_6H_5MgBr + ZnCl_2 \rightarrow C_6H_5ZnCl + MgBrCl$$

Organocadmium compounds (p. 471) are made simply by adding cadmium chloride to a solution of an organomagnesium bromide. Yields of the cadmium compound are lower when an organomagnesium iodide is employed.

A reaction of extreme interest has been reported to occur when Grignard reagents are treated with boron hydride. Displacement on boron leads to the formation of trialkylboron and HMgX, which may be regarded as the first member of the Grignard reagent series. An example is the formation of etherated HMgCl from ethylmagnesium chloride.[13]

$$3C_2H_5MgCl + BH_3 \rightarrow (C_2H_5)_3B + 3HMgCl$$

[11] N. G. Gaylord and E. I. Becker, *J. Org. Chem.*, **15**, 305 (1950).
[12] S. Searles, *J. Am. Chem. Soc.*, **73**, 124 (1951).
[13] E. Wiberg and P. Strebel, *Ann.*, **607**, 9 (1957).

Addition Reactions

1,2-Addition

The addition of a Grignard reagent to a carbonyl compound is similar in principle to that with cyclic ethers; in either case the new alkoxide function merely remains in the molecule.

$$R^- + \overset{|}{\underset{|}{C}}{=}O \rightarrow R{-}\overset{|}{\underset{|}{C}}{-}O^-$$

It is predictable that multiple linkages joining carbon to other more electronegative atoms will react also. In this category are such compounds as the anils and the nitriles; the guiding principle is that, for reaction to occur, the anion generated must be weaker than the attacking carbanion. Indeed it seems certain that the failure of olefins to react additively with Grignard reagents is to be ascribed to the fact that the resulting carbanion would be of the same order of basicity as that of the reagent.

$$R^- + \overset{|}{\underset{|}{C}}{=}\overset{|}{\underset{|}{C}} \rightarrow R{-}\overset{|}{\underset{|}{C}}{-}\overset{|}{\underset{|}{C}}{}^-$$

The fulvenes are highly exceptional in this respect since attack of the carbanion releases to the ring an electron pair of the exocyclic double bond. The cyclopentadienyl carbanion, as has been mentioned (p. 15), is actually aromatic, the negative charge being distributed throughout the ring. An example is the addition of *t*-butylmagnesium chloride to 1,2,3,4-tetraphenylfulvene.

Grignard reagents react with various fluoroölefins. An example is the condensation of phenylmagnesium bromide with dichlorodifluoroethylene to give α-fluoro-β-dichlorostyrene in 64% yield.[14]

$$C_6H_5MgBr + F_2C{=}CCl_2 \rightarrow [C_6H_5CF_2CCl_2MgBr] \rightarrow$$
$$C_6H_5CF{=}CCl_2 + MgBrF$$

Aldehydes. The Grignard reagent serves to great advantage in building up carbon chains. When formaldehyde, for example, is employed, the next higher alcohol is formed. *n*-Octyl and undecyl alcohols may be made from their next lower homologs in this way. Cyclohexylcarbinol is obtained from cyclohexyl chloride in 69% yield (OS I, 188).

[14] P. Tarrant and D. A. Warner, *J. Am. Chem. Soc.*, **76**, 1624 (1954).

Aldehydes, other than formaldehyde, combine readily with Grignard reagents to give alkoxides from which secondary alcohols are obtained by hydrolysis. The reaction is used primarily to produce alcohols in which the two radicals are different. An example is methylisopropylcarbinol, one of the few low-molecular-weight alcohols not available in quantity; it is made in 54% yield from acetaldehyde and isopropylmagnesium bromide (OS II, 406).

$$CH_3CHO + (CH_3)_2CHMgBr \rightarrow CH_3\overset{\overset{\displaystyle OMgBr}{|}}{C}HCH(CH_3)_2 \rightarrow CH_3\overset{\overset{\displaystyle OH}{|}}{C}HCH(CH_3)_2$$

The preparation of *m*-chlorophenylmethylcarbinol from acetaldehyde and *m*-bromochlorobenzene can be accomplished in 88% yield (OS III, 200). In a similar way, 3-penten-2-ol is produced in 86% yield from croton-aldehyde and methylmagnesium chloride (OS III, 696).

$$CH_3CH=CHCHO + CH_3MgCl$$

$$\longrightarrow CH_3CH=CH\overset{\overset{\displaystyle}{|}}{C}HCH_3 \overset{H_2O}{\longrightarrow} CH_3CH=CH\overset{\overset{\displaystyle}{|}}{C}HCH_3$$
$$\qquad\qquad\quad OMgCl \qquad\qquad\qquad OH$$

Bromomagnesium derivatives of sulfones likewise behave as true Grignard reagents. *p*-Tolylsulfonylmethylmagnesium bromide, for example, condenses with acetaldehyde to give the expected carbinol in very high yield.[15]

$$p\text{-}CH_3C_6H_4SO_2CH_2MgBr \xrightarrow[\text{(2) } H_2O]{\text{(1) } CH_3CHO} p\text{-}CH_3C_6H_4SO_2CH_2\overset{\overset{\displaystyle}{|}}{C}HOH$$
$$\qquad\qquad\qquad\qquad\qquad\qquad\qquad\qquad\qquad CH_3$$

With aldehydes an excess of the reagent is used to obtain good results. If excess aldehyde is present, the alkoxide may undergo oxidation. Further-more, the halomagnesium alkoxides catalyze condensation reactions of the aldol type. In practice an excess of the reagent is prepared, and the alde-hyde is added to it gradually.

Nitro aldehydes ordinarily cannot serve since the nitro group reacts readily with the Grignard reagent. At −70°, however, *m*-nitrobenz-aldehyde reacts with the phenyl reagent to give *m*-nitrophenylphenyl-carbinol in 77% yield.

[15] L. Field and J. W. McFarland, *J. Am. Chem. Soc.*, **75**, 5582 (1953).

Ketones.   Ketones are converted to tertiary alcohols by the Grignard method. The tertiary alcohols obtained from aryl Grignard reagents and cyclohexanone and its derivatives are of particular interest because, by successive dehydration and dehydrogenation, they furnish biaryls. The method is especially valuable for the preparation of unsymmetrical biaryls such as 1-phenylnaphthalene (OS III, 729), which may be produced in an over-all yield of 45 %.

If benzylmagnesium chloride is used, the final product is 1-benzylnaphthalene.[16]

Bifunctional reagents have been employed to make glycols; 1,4-butylenedimagnesium bromide reacts with acetone, for example, to give 2,7-dihydroxy-2,7-dimethyloctane in 46 % yield.[17]

Formates.   Esters of formic acid can be compared to aldehydes; they react with the Grignard reagent to yield secondary alcohols. An example is the synthesis of di-*n*-butylcarbinol from *n*-butylmagnesium bromide and ethyl formate (OS II, 179); the yield is 85 %. Formates are useful therefore in producing symmetrical secondary alcohols.

Higher Esters.   Esters generally lead to the formation of tertiary alcohols, in which at least two of the radicals are alike. The method is of great synthetic value; from ethyl acetate and phenylmagnesium bromide it is possible to obtain methyldiphenylcarbinol in 75 % yield (OS I, 226). Triphenylcarbinol is made in a similar way from ethyl benzoate and phenylmagnesium bromide (OS III, 839; 93 % yield).

By the use of bifunctional Grignard reagents cyclanols may be obtained. An example is the formation of 1-*n*-propyl-1-cyclopentanol; the yield is 65 %.

[16] H. A. Fahim, A. M. Fleifel, and F. Fahim, *J. Org. Chem.*, **25**, 1040 (1960).
[17] E. Buchta and E. Weidinger, *Ann.*, **580**, 109 (1953).

Acetals are relatively unreactive toward Grignard reagents as is illustrated by the condensation of ethyl β,β-diethoxypropionate with methylmagnesium iodide. β-Methylcrotonaldehyde is formed in 60% yield by this reaction followed by treatment of the carbinol with acid.[18]

$$(C_2H_5O)_2CHCH_2CO_2C_2H_5 \rightarrow (C_2H_5O)_2CHCH_2\overset{\overset{\displaystyle OH}{\displaystyle |}}{C}(CH_3)_2 \rightarrow$$
$$(CH_3)_2C{=}CHCHO$$

Esters of Peracids. Grignard reagents react with *t*-butyl perbenzoate to give the corresponding *t*-butyl ethers and benzoic acid. Phenylmagnesium bromide, for example, furnishes *t*-butyl phenyl ether. The reaction has been represented as follows.[19]

$$\rightarrow C_6H_5CO_2MgBr + C_6H_5OC(CH_3)_3$$

Lactones. Lactones combine with Grignard reagents after the manner of esters; the products, however, are glycols. An example is the conversion of γ-pelargonolactone into 2-methyl-2,5-decanediol (OS **38**, 41; yield 57%).

$$CH_3(CH_2)_4CHCH_2CH_2CO \xrightarrow[(2)\ H_2O]{(1)\ CH_3MgBr} CH_3(CH_2)_4\overset{\overset{\displaystyle OH}{\displaystyle |}}{C}HCH_2CH_2\overset{\overset{\displaystyle OH}{\displaystyle |}}{C}(CH_3)_2$$

Carbonates. Diethyl carbonate affords tertiary alcohols in which all three radicals are alike. Triethylcarbinol is produced in 88% yield from ethylmagnesium bromide and diethyl carbonate (OS II, 602).

Occasionally esters are made directly by use of the Grignard reagent; 1-naphthylmagnesium bromide can be caused to react with diethyl carbonate to give ethyl 1-naphthoate in 73% yield (OS II, 282). This is an example of the so-called *inverse Grignard reaction*, in which the Grignard reagent is added to the other reactant, to keep the latter in excess at all times.

[18] N. L. Wendler and H. L. Slates, *J. Am. Chem. Soc.*, **72**, 5341 (1950).
[19] S. -O. Lawesson and N. C. Yang, *J. Am. Chem. Soc.*, **81**, 4230 (1959).

Although esters yield ketones these are rarely isolated inasmuch as they react more rapidly than esters. The preparation of carbonyl compounds from acids or their derivatives may be accomplished by way of acid chlorides and anhydrides, but amides and nitriles are more useful.

Anhydrides. When a Grignard reagent is allowed to react with acetic anhydride at $-70°$, the corresponding methyl ketone is formed in excellent yields. There is convincing evidence that the success of this method is due to the stability at low temperature of the addition complex.[20]

Inverse Grignard condensations with cyclic anhydrides often furnish keto acids in satisfactory yields. An example is the formation of β-(6-methoxy-1-naphthoyl)propionic acid from 6-methoxy-1-naphthylmagnesium bromide and succinic anhydride; the yield is 41%.[21]

Ketenes. The ketenes react as anhydrides also; ketene condenses with phenylmagnesium bromide to yield acetophenone.

$$CH_2{=}C{=}O + C_6H_5MgBr \rightarrow CH_2{=}\overset{\overset{\displaystyle OMgBr}{|}}{C}C_6H_5 \rightarrow$$

$$\left[CH_2{=}\overset{\overset{\displaystyle OH}{|}}{C}C_6H_5 \right] \rightarrow CH_3\overset{\overset{\displaystyle O}{\|}}{C}C_6H_5$$

The yield, however, is not high. Moreover, attempts to extend the reaction to aliphatic Grignard reagents give unsatisfactory results.

That vinyl alcohols are formed as intermediates in these condensations is established by the fact that the highly hindered ones can be isolated; dimesitylketene, for example, reacts with the phenyl reagent to give a stable vinyl alcohol.

Acid Chlorides. Since acid chlorides are mixed anhydrides (p. 52), their reactions are naturally similar to those of anhydrides proper. With Grignard reagents they yield carbinols or, if the reaction is

[20] M. S. Newman and A. S. Smith, *J. Org. Chem.*, **13**, 592 (1948).
[21] W. G. Dauben and K. A. Saegebarth, *J. Am. Chem. Soc.*, **73**, 1853 (1951).

carried out in the inverse manner, ketones. Such reactions are promoted by the presence of ferric chloride, which may be taken to mean that the reaction proceeds by an ionic mechanism. By this method, for example, *t*-butylmagnesium chloride combines with pivalyl chloride to give hexamethylacetone in 84% yield.[22]

$$(CH_3)_3CMgCl + (CH_3)_3CCOCl \rightarrow (CH_3)_3CCOC(CH_3)_3 + MgCl_2$$

When phthalyl chloride is treated with phenylmagnesium bromide at $-55°$, *o*-dibenzoylbenzene is produced in 32% yield.[23]

No ketone forms when triphenylmethylacetyl chloride is treated with Grignard reagents. Methylmagnesium iodide does not produce methyl trityl ketone (p. 183) but instead ethyl triphenylacetate; the ethyl group comes from the ethyl ether used as solvent.[24]

$$(C_6H_5)_3CCOCl \xrightarrow[\text{(C}_2\text{H}_5)_2\text{O}]{\text{CH}_3\text{MgI}} (C_6H_5)_3CCO_2C_2H_5$$

Carbon Dioxide. Carbon dioxide condenses with Grignard reagents to give salts of the corresponding acids.

$$RMgX + CO_2 \rightarrow RCO_2MgX$$

The reaction is carried out by adding gaseous or solid carbon dioxide to the solution of Grignard reagent. Low temperature is necessary to prevent transformation of the salt into a tertiary alcohol. Solid carbon dioxide not only serves as reactant but acts as a refrigerant as well. A convenient technique involves the addition of the Grignard reagent to a well-stirred slurry of solid carbon dioxide and dry ether.[25]

The Grignard synthesis thus provides a general method of obtaining acids from the corresponding alkyl and aryl halides. Its utility can best be appreciated by reference to the limitations of the nitrile method (p. 322), which is to be preferred for most primary alkyl halides. Secondary and tertiary alkyl halides do not give nitriles in satisfactory yields when treated with alkali cyanides. However, the Rosenmund–von Braun nitrile synthesis (p. 384) makes possible the conversion of aryl halides into carboxylic acids.

Among the acids that are made conveniently by the Grignard method are trimethylacetic (OS I, 524; 70% yield), methylethylacetic (OS I, 361;

[22] W. C. Percival, R. B. Wagner, and N. C. Cook, *J. Am. Chem. Soc.*, **75**, 3731 (1953).

[23] F. E. Jensen, *J. Org. Chem.*, **25**, 269 (1960).

[24] J. L. Greene, D. Abraham, and H. D. Zook, *J. Org. Chem.*, **24**, 132 (1959).

[25] A. S. Hussey, *J. Am. Chem. Soc.*, **73**, 1364 (1951).

86% yield), 1-naphthoic (OS II, 425; 70% yield), and mesitoic acids (OS III, 553, 86% yield).

The reaction of sulfur dioxide, the anhydride of sulfurous acid, with Grignard reagents is analogous to that of carbon dioxide, sulfinic acids being produced.

$$RMgX + SO_2 \rightarrow RSO_2MgX \xrightarrow{H_2O} RSO_2H$$

Isocyanates. Similar in structure to carbon dioxide are the alkyl and aryl isocyanates, which readily react with Grignard reagents to yield the corresponding amides. Thus *t*-butylmagnesium chloride and phenyl isocyanate give trimethylacetanilide.

$$(CH_3)_3CMgCl + C_6H_5N=C=O \rightarrow C_6H_5N=C\overset{\displaystyle OMgCl}{\underset{\displaystyle C(CH_3)_3}{\diagup\diagdown}} \rightarrow$$

$$C_6H_5NHCOC(CH_3)_3$$

Anilides and α-naphthalides made in this way are useful as derivatives of alkyl halides, particularly the secondary and tertiary types.

Amides. Primary and secondary amides have active hydrogen and decompose the reagent. Ketones may be obtained from them in satisfactory yields, however, by use of three or four equivalents of reagent and long periods of heating. Benzamide, for example, reacts with benzylmagnesium chloride to give desoxybenzoin in 77% yield. 3,5-Dimethoxyphenyl propyl ketone is formed in 88% yield from 3,5-dimethoxybenzamide and propylmagnesium bromide.

Ketones can be made also from tertiary amides. In all these cases the intermediate addition products are stable and can be isolated, which makes possible interruption of the reaction at the ketone stage.

$$RCONR_2 + R'MgX \rightarrow RR'C\overset{\displaystyle OMgX}{\underset{\displaystyle NR_2}{\diagup\diagdown}} \rightarrow RCOR' + MgXNR_2$$

Formamides of the type $HCONR_2$ lead to the production of aldehydes. Because of the formation of by-products this method, developed by Bouveault, gives aldehydes in yields not above 50%. An example is the preparation of *o*-phenylbenzaldehyde from 2-biphenylylmagnesium iodide and N-formylmethylaniline.

Nitriles. Grignard reagents react with nitriles to produce imino derivatives, from which ketones are formed by hydrolysis. An example is the preparation of ω-methoxyacetophenone from methoxyacetonitrile and phenylmagnesium bromide (OS III, 562; 78% yield).

$$C_6H_5MgBr + CH_3OCH_2CN \rightarrow C_6H_5\overset{\overset{\textstyle NMgBr}{\|}}{C}CH_2OCH_3 \xrightarrow{H_2O} C_6H_5COCH_2OCH_3$$

Aromatic nitriles also undergo the reaction, including those that have two *o*-substituents.

Replacement of the cyano group by hydrogen has been effected by treating certain nitriles with Grignard reagents. Diphenylacetonitrile, for example, reacts with ethylmagnesium bromide to give not only 1,1-diphenyl-2-butanone but also diphenylmethane.[26]

$$\underset{C_6H_5}{\overset{C_6H_5}{>}}CHCN \rightarrow \underset{C_6H_5}{\overset{C_6H_5}{>}}CHCOCH_2CH_3 \quad \text{and} \quad C_6H_5CH_2C_6H_5$$

It is especially interesting that propionitrile is also produced in this reaction. The following mechanism has been suggested to account for this anomalous behavior.

[26] F. F. Blicke and E. -P. Tsao, *J. Am. Chem. Soc.*, **75**, 5587 (1953).

Conjugate Addition.   The addition of Grignard reagents to conjugated systems may be illustrated by the condensation of benzalacetophenone with phenylmagnesium bromide.

$$C_6H_5CH{=}CHCOC_6H_5 + C_6H_5MgBr \rightarrow (C_6H_5)_2CHCH{=}C \begin{matrix} OMgBr \\ \diagup \\ \diagdown \\ C_6H_5 \end{matrix} \xrightarrow{H_2O}$$

$$(C_6H_5)_2CHCH{=}C \begin{matrix} OH \\ \diagup \\ \diagdown \\ C_6H_5 \end{matrix} \rightarrow (C_6H_5)_2CHCH_2COC_6H_5$$

Stable enols have likewise been prepared in this way; 1,2-dimesitylbuten-1-ol is an example.

$$\underset{MesC}{\overset{CH_2}{\|}}\!\!-\!\!\underset{CMes}{\overset{O}{\|}} + CH_3MgI \longrightarrow \underset{MesC}{\overset{CH_3CH_2}{|}}\!\!=\!\!\underset{CMes}{\overset{OMgI}{|}} \xrightarrow{H_2O} \underset{MesC}{\overset{CH_3CH_2}{|}}\!\!=\!\!\underset{CMes}{\overset{OH}{|}}$$

Whether addition occurs in the 1,2- or the conjugate fashion is determined by the substituents. α,β-Unsaturated aldehydes nearly always react in the 1,2-manner; exceptional is the conjugate addition of certain Grignard reagents, among them the *t*-butyl, to crotonaldehyde. The yields of such conjugate addition compounds are as high as 20%. This result is particularly surprising in view of the fact that acrolein, which has no substituent in the 4-position fails to yield any conjugate addition product.

A greater tendency to undergo conjugate addition has been observed in salts. Cinnamic acid, for example, condenses with certain Grignard reagents to give the corresponding β-substituted hydrocinnamic acids. The reaction with *t*-butylmagnesium chloride is an example; the yield is 45%.[27]

$$C_6H_5CH{=}CHCO_2H \rightarrow \underset{\underset{C(CH_3)_3}{|}}{C_6H_5CHCH_2CO_2H}$$

Similarly, isopropylmagnesium chloride reacts with crotonic and atropic acids in the 1,4-manner.[28]

$$CH_3CH{=}CHCO_2H \rightarrow \underset{\underset{CH_3}{|}}{(CH_3)_2CHCHCH_2CO_2H}$$

$$\underset{\underset{C_6H_5}{|}}{CH_2{=}CCO_2H} \rightarrow \underset{\underset{C_6H_5}{|}}{(CH_3)_2CHCH_2CHCO_2H}$$

[27] J. H. Wotiz, J. S. Matthews, and H. Greenfield, *J. Am. Chem. Soc.*, **75**, 6342 (1953).
[28] F. F. Blicke and H. Zinnes, *J. Am. Chem. Soc.*, **77**, 5399, 6051 (1955).

The tendency toward conjugate addition is enhanced by the presence of small amounts of cuprous chloride. An example is the addition of *n*-butyl-magnesium bromide to *sec*-butyl crotonate; the presence of cuprous chloride increases the amount of 1,4-addition product from 25 to 60%.[29]

The influence of substituents is shown by the data in the accompanying table, which gives the amount of conjugate addition for a number of reactions; the remainder of the product in each case is that produced by 1,2-addition. A primary factor in determining whether the hydrocarbon radical will attack position 2 or position 4 is the size and complexity of the group attached to the carbonyl carbon atom. When a hydrogen atom is attached at this point, as has been seen, the 4-position is almost never occupied. If methyl, ethyl, isopropyl, and *t*-butyl radicals are successively introduced, the amount of 1,2-addition decreases, presumably because the carbonyl carbon atom is increasingly screened from attack. Addition is also predominantly conjugate when a phenyl group is inserted as in benzal-acetophenone.

One generalization that emerges from these data is that, in most condensations in which both 1,2- and conjugate addition occur, the relative quantity of conjugate addition product is larger with alkyl than with aryl Grignard reagents.

Methylmagnesium iodide combines with ethyl cinnamate to yield the 1,2-addition product. As might be expected, however, this reagent does give a conjugate addition product with diethyl benzalmalonate.

$$C_6H_5CH{=}C(CO_2C_2H_5)_2 \;\rightarrow\; C_6H_5\underset{\underset{\displaystyle CH_3}{|}}{C}HCH(CO_2C_2H_5)_2$$

Methyl cinnamate and phenylmagnesium bromide yield methyl β,β-diphenylpropionate and a small amount of benzohydrylacetophenone. The formation of the ketone can be explained by assuming that 1,2-addition occurs and is followed by conjugate addition. A mesityl group in the 2-position inhibits 1,2-addition with nearly all reagents. Methylmagnesium iodide does attack the 2-position, however, in certain aryl mesityl ketones. More remarkable is the 1,2-addition to acetomesitylene of benzylmagnesium chloride and butenylmagnesium bromide.

The ease of this type of addition has been interpreted by reference to a *quasi* six-membered ring that permits the reaction to proceed with inversion in an intramolecular fashion.[30]

[29] J. Munch-Petersen, *J. Org. Chem.*, **22**, 170 (1957).
[30] W. G. Young and J. D. Roberts, *J. Am. Chem. Soc.*, **68**, 1472 (1946).

Reaction of Grignard Reagents with α,β-Unsaturated Carbonyl Compounds

Carbonyl Compounds	Conjugate Addition (%)	
	C_6H_5MgBr	C_2H_5MgBr
$C_6H_5CH=CHCH=O$	0	0
$C_6H_5CH=CHCCH_3$ (O)	12	60
$C_6H_5CH=CHCCH_2CH_3$ (O)	40	71
$C_6H_5CH=CHCCH(CH_3)_2$ (O)	88	100
$C_6H_5CH=CHCC(CH_3)_3$ (O)	100	100
$C_6H_5CH=CHCC_6H_5$ (O)	94	99
$(C_6H_5)_2C=CHCC_6H_5$ (O)	0	18
$C_6H_5CH=CCC_6H_5$ (O), C_6H_5	100	100
$C_6H_5C=CHCC_6H_5$ (O), CH_3	44	41

$$MesC \overset{O \cdots MgBr}{\underset{CH_3}{\diagdown}} \quad \underset{CH=CH}{\overset{CH_2}{\bigg)}} \quad \rightarrow \quad MesC \overset{O-MgBr}{\underset{CH_3}{\diagup}} \quad \overset{CH_2}{\underset{CH-CH}{\diagdown}}$$
$$\underset{CH_3}{|} \qquad\qquad \underset{CH_3}{|}$$

The carbinol undergoes pyrolysis to regenerate the original ketone as well as to form water and a mixture of the 2-butenes.

$$\overset{OH}{\underset{CH_3CHCH=CH_2}{MesCCH_3}} \qquad \rightarrow \quad MesCOCH_3 + CH_3CH=CHCH_3 + H_2O$$

A route to ethyl *t*-alkylcyanoacetates involves the condensation of Grignard reagents with ethyl alkylidenecyanoacetates or diethyl alkylidenemalonates. With the *n*-butyl reagent and *sec*-butylidenecyanoacetate, the product is ethyl α-cyano-β-ethyl-β-methylheptanoate; the yield is 51 %.[31]

$$\underset{CH_3}{\overset{CH_3CH_2}{\diagdown}} C=C \underset{CO_2C_2H_5}{\overset{CN}{\diagup}} \quad \rightarrow \quad CH_3(CH_2)_3 \underset{CH_3}{\overset{CH_3CH_2}{-}} C-CH \underset{CO_2C_2H_5}{\overset{CN}{\diagup}}$$

One reason for the low yields generally realized is that conjugate reduction also takes place especially with the isobutyl, *sec*-butyl, and *t*-butyl reagents. The reduction products are of the type $R_2CHCH \overset{CN}{\underset{CO_2C_2H_5}{\diagdown}}$

Conjugate addition reactions are especially valuable because the products are converted into acetic acid derivatives holding a tertiary radical. An example is the synthesis of 3-benzyl-3-methylpentanoic acid (OS **35,** 6).

$$\underset{C_2H_5}{\overset{CH_3}{|}} \overset{CN}{\underset{|}{|}} \\ C_2H_5-C=CCO_2C_2H_5 \rightarrow C_6H_5CH_2C \underset{C_2H_5}{\overset{CH_3}{\underset{|}{|}}} CHCO_2C_2H_5 \rightarrow$$

$$C_6H_5CH_2C\underset{C_2H_5}{\overset{CH_3}{\underset{|}{\overset{|}{}}}}CH_2CO_2H$$

[31] F. S. Prout, *J. Am. Chem. Soc.*, **74**, 5915 (1952)

Conjugate addition has been noted with certain α,β-unsaturated nitro compounds. Nitrostilbene, for example, yields a conjugate addition product with phenylmagnesium bromide.

$$C_6H_5CH{=}CNO_2 \underset{(2)\ H_2O}{\overset{(1)\ C_6H_5MgBr}{\xrightarrow{\hspace{1cm}}}} \overset{C_6H_5}{\underset{C_6H_5}{\diagdown}} CHCHNO_2$$

Similar results have been obtained with nitroölefins. For example, when a solution of ethylmagnesium bromide is added slowly, with stirring, to a solution of 1-nitro-2-methyl-1-propene, 1-nitro-2,2-dimethylbutane is produced in 60% yield.[32]

$$(CH_3)_2C{=}CHNO_2 \rightarrow (CH_3)_2\underset{CH_2CH_3}{\overset{|}{C}}CH_2NO_2$$

An interesting theory, put forward to account for the relative ease with which Grignard reagents lend themselves to conjugate addition, postulates the formation of a *quasi* six-membered ring by coordination of the magnesium atom with the carbonyl carbon atom.

$$RCH{=}CH{-}\overset{\overset{\textstyle O}{\|}}{C}R + RMgX \rightarrow$$

It is known however that 2-cyclohexenone, in which positions 1 and 4 would appear to be too far apart to permit the formation of such a ring, reacts with Grignard reagents in much the same way as do its open chain analogs such as 3-hexen-2-one.[33]

Moreover, attack of the Grignard reagent at the 6-position has been observed; fuchsone, naphthofuchsone, and methyleneanthrone are known to undergo this type of addition. Also, hindered ketones such as duryl

[32] G. D. Buckley and E. Ellery, *J. Chem. Soc.*, 1497 (1947).
[33] E. R. Alexander and G. R. Coraor, *J. Am. Chem. Soc.*, **73**, 2721 (1951).

phenyl ketone are alkylated at the *p*-position of the phenyl ring by reagents such as *sec*-butylmagnesium bromide.

CH₃, CH₃, CH₃, CH₃, CO → CH₃, CH₃, CH₃, CH₃, CO, CH₃CHCH₂CH₃

1,8-Addition of methylmagnesium iodide to tropone has been realized.[34]

O → O CH₃

Reducing Action of the Grignard Reagent

In certain instances Grignard reagents react with carbonyl compounds as reducing agents. This type of behavior usually occurs with carbonyl compounds in which the functional group is highly hindered. The complexity of the radical of the reagent is also a contributing factor. An example is the reduction of diisopropyl ketone by isopropylmagnesium bromide.

$$\text{CH}_3\text{CHCOCH}\text{CH}_3 \quad + (\text{CH}_3)_2\text{CHMgBr} \rightarrow$$

$$\text{CH}_3\text{CHCHCH}\text{CH}_3 \quad + \text{CH}_3\text{CH}=\text{CH}_2$$

Isopropylmagnesium bromide reduces cyclohexanone to cyclohexanol in 75% yield. Benzyl alcohol is obtained in 56% yield by the action of isobutylmagnesium bromide on benzaldehyde. Pivalaldehyde is reduced extensively by *t*-butylmagnesium bromide. Chloral gives trichloroethyl alcohol in 53% yield when treated with cyclohexylmagnesium bromide.

[34] O. L. Chapman and D. J. Pasto, *Chem. and Ind.*, 54 (1961).

Fluoral is converted by isopropylmagnesium bromide into trifluoroethyl alcohol in 87% yield. Pentafluoropropionaldehyde, heptafluorobutyraldehyde, 1,1,1-trifluoroacetone, and similar compounds likewise show a remarkable tendency to undergo reduction rather than addition.

Esters of perfluorinated acids are reduced readily by Grignard reagents such as isopropylmagnesium bromide. A method of preparing secondary alcohols has been developed that depends on the use of a mixture of two Grignard reagents, only one of which has reducing power. An example is the reaction of methyl perfluorobutyrate with a mixture of the phenyl and isopropyl reagents. The secondary alcohol is produced in yields of 49%.[35]

$$CF_3CF_2CF_2CO_2CH_3 \rightarrow \underset{\underset{OH}{|}}{CF_3CF_2CF_2CHC_6H_5}$$

An insight into the mechanism of the reduction is furnished by the observation that pinacolone undergoes partial asymmetric reduction when treated with (+)2-methylbutylmagnesium chloride. On the basis of this fact it has been postulated that the reduction involves a six-membered cyclic transition state.[36]

Rearrangements

A number of rearrangements produced by alkaline reagents are explained by reference to the carbanion that would be generated by removal of a proton. Abstraction of a proton from an allyl or benzyl position gives an anion of unusual stability; the effect is more marked of course if the position is "doubly" allylic.

Acetylenic hydrocarbons sometimes undergo a shift of the triple bond, in the presence of alkaline reagents, from a terminal to a nonterminal position (OR **5**, 13). 1-Butyne, for example, rearranges to 2-butyne when heated at 170° for 16 hours in the presence of alcoholic potash. Acetylenic hydrocarbons may give allenes also. 1-Pentyne, when heated at 175° in the

[35] O. R. Pierce, J. C. Siegle, and E. T. McBee, *J. Am. Chem. Soc.*, **75**, 6324 (1953).
[36] H. S. Mosher and E. La Combe, *J. Am. Chem. Soc.*, **72**, 4991 (1950).

presence of potassium hydroxide, yields an equilibrium mixture containing
1-pentyne (1.3%), 2-pentyne (95.2%), and 1,2-pentadiene (3.5%).[37]

$$CH_3CH_2CH_2C\equiv CH \rightleftharpoons CH_3CH_2C=C=CH_2 \rightleftharpoons CH_3CH_2C\equiv CCH_3$$

Allylbenzene rearranges readily to propenylbenzene in the presence of
alkali.

The isomerization of safrole and eugenol (p. 230) by alkali further illustrates this type of rearrangement. 1,4-Dihydronaphthalene likewise rearranges to the 1,2-isomer. The conditions that serve to bring about this
kind of isomerization are illustrated by the procedure for converting
2-allyphenol into 2-propenylphenol. The allyl compound is dissolved in
three times its volume of a saturated solution of potassium hydroxide in
methanol. The solution is heated until distillation of solvent brings the
temperature of the reaction mixture to 110°. The rearrangement is completed by heating the mixture for 6 hours under reflux (OR **2**, 27).

1,4-Pentadiene likewise has an active methylene group and, as stated
earlier (p. 303), rearranges, under the influence of alkalis, to the conjugated
diene, piperylene.

$$CH_2=CHCH_2CH=CH_2 \rightarrow CH_3CH=CHCH=CH_2$$

In a number of condensations with Grignard reagents of the allyl type,
rearrangement leading to isomers of the expected products has been
observed (Gould, 286).[38] Benzylmagnesium chloride condenses with formaldehyde to yield *o*-tolylcarbinol instead of the normal product, phenethyl
alcohol. By repetition of the process it has been possible to make a series
of methylated benzyl alcohols.

[37] T. L. Jacobs, R. Akawie, and R. G. Cooper, *J. Am. Chem. Soc.*, **73**, 1273 (1951).
[38] W. G. Young, *Record of Chem. Progress*, **11**, 129 (1950).

When *m*-methylbenzylmagnesium bromide is treated with carbon dioxide, the normal product, *m*-tolylacetic acid, is obtained only in low yield; the chief product is 2,4-dimethylbenzoic acid.[39]

Carbonation of the Grignard reagent prepared from 3-furylmethyl chloride leads to a mixture consisting of approximately 90% of 3-methyl-2-furoic acid and 10% of 3-furylacetic acid. With formaldehyde this Grignard reagent yields only the "abnormal" product, 3-methyl-2-furfuryl alcohol.[40]

Both 1,3- and 1,5-shifts have been observed in the condensation of benzyl reagents with ethylene oxide. *p*-Methylbenzylmagnesium bromide gives a mixture 20% of which is 2,5-dimethylphenethyl alcohol.

Carbonation of benzylmagnesium chloride, however, gives the normal product, phenylacetic acid. Cinnamylmagnesium chloride, on the other hand, yields the rearrangement product, 2-phenyl-3-butenoic acid.

$$C_6H_5CH{=}CHCH_2MgCl \rightarrow C_6H_5\underset{\underset{CO_2H}{|}}{C}HCH{=}CH_2$$

Similarly, the Grignard reagent prepared from crotyl bromide, when treated with carbon dioxide, gives only 2-methyl-3-butenoic acid.

$$CH_3CH{=}CHCH_2Br \xrightarrow[\text{(2) } CO_2]{\text{(1) Mg}} CH_3\underset{\underset{CO_2H}{|}}{C}HCH{=}CH_2$$

[39] C. M. Moser and H. W. Sause, *J. Org. Chem.*, **15**, 631 (1950).
[40] E. Sherman and E. D. Amstutz, *J. Am. Chem. Soc.*, **72**, 2195 (1950).

The product corresponds to the secondary structure of the carbanion.

$$CH_3CH{=}CH\bar{C}H_2 \leftrightarrow CH_3\bar{C}HCH{=}CH_2$$

One of the most remarkable members of this family of anomalous reactions is that which occurs between benzyl type Grignard reagents and cyanogen; a cyano group enters an *o*-position. Benzylmagnesium chloride, for example, gives *o*-tolunitrile.[41]

$$C_6H_5CH_2MgCl \xrightarrow[(2)\ H_2O]{(1)\ (CN)_2}$$

Organozinc Compounds

Reaction of an alkylzinc iodide with an acid chloride produces a ketone.

$$RCOCl + R'ZnI \rightarrow RCOR' + ZnICl$$

This method, developed by Blaise, serves to transform acid chlorides of the higher dibasic acids in the aliphatic series into diketones. Alkylzinc iodides do not react with esters, however. The acid chlorides of half esters of dibasic aliphatic acids above adipic afford the corresponding keto esters.[42]

By the use of tetrahydrofuran or a mixture of tetrahydrofuran and ether as solvent it is possible to prepare mixed organozinc compounds from very reactive bromides such as propargyl, allyl, and benzyl. The reagents obtained in this way are capable of undergoing hydrolysis and carbonation and can be condensed with carbonyl compounds.[43]

The rule that organozinc compounds are less reactive than the corresponding magnesium compounds is illustrated by the fact that dialkylzinc derivatives can be handled in an atmosphere of carbon dioxide. The zinc compounds, widely used before 1900, generally have been replaced in synthetic work by magnesium compounds.

Organocadmium Compounds

Organocadmium compounds are somewhat less reactive than organozinc compounds and have proved to be more useful in the synthesis of ketones

---

[41] See J. F. Eastham and D. Y. Cannon, *J. Org. Chem.*, **25**, 1504 (1960).

[42] H. Klein and H. Neff, *Angew. Chem.*, **68**, 681 (1956).

[43] M. Gaudemar, *Compt. rend.*, **246**, 1229 (1958).

(CR **40**, 15; OR **8**, 28). Their use is illustrated by the synthesis of methyl 4-keto-7-methyloctanoate from β-carbomethoxypropionyl chloride and diisoamylcadmium (OS III, 601).

$$[(CH_3)_2CHCH_2CH_2]_2Cd + 2ClCOCH_2CH_2CO_2CH_3 \rightarrow$$
$$2(CH_3)_2CHCH_2CH_2COCH_2CH_2CO_2CH_3 + CdCl_2$$

The yield, based on the acid chloride, is 75%.

Anhydrides have been used also. Phthalic and succinic anhydrides yield keto acids.

Since organocadmium reagents normally do not react with the ester function, it is possible to protect hydroxyl groups by esterification. 3,5-Dihydroxyacylophenones, for example, may be prepared in good yields by the action of alkylcadmium reagents on the diacetate of 3,5-dihydroxybenzoyl chloride followed by hydrolysis of the ester groups. An example is the synthesis of ethyl 3,5-dihydroxyphenyl ketone.[44]

Whereas Grignard reagents react additively with the carbonyl group of acid chlorides, organocadmium compounds react by first removing the chlorine atom; as a consequence of this difference in mode of attack, the respective products may have very different structures.[45]

Organolithium Compounds

Organolithium compounds (p. 634) can often be used to advantage in place of Grignard reagents. Special mention should be made of the fact that 2- and 4-picoline and similar compounds having active methyl groups can be employed in synthesis by virtue of their capacity of yielding lithium derivatives when treated with organolithium compounds such as phenyllithium. 2-Picoline, for example, can be condensed with acetaldehyde to yield 1-(2-pyridyl)-2-propanol (OS III, 757; 50% yield).

[44] R. Huls and A. Hubert, *Bull. soc. chim. Belges*, **65**, 596 (1956).
[45] M. Renson and F. Schoofs, *Bull. soc. chim. Belges*, **69**, 236 (1960).

Lithium derivatives are useful also for introducing carboxyl groups into heterocyclic compounds such as 2- and 4-picoline, the lutidines, quinaldine, and 2-methylthiazole. Ethyl 2-pyridylacetate is made by the following procedure.

In order to stop the reaction at the acid stage it is necessary to pour the solution of the organolithium compound on solid carbon dioxide. If the carbon dioxide is not present in excess the reaction proceeds to the ketone stage.

Alkenyllithium compounds, prepared by the action of lithium on alkenyl bromides or chlorides, react with aldehydes, ketones, and esters in the normal way. An example is the condensation of cyclohexenyllithium with crotonaldehyde.[46]

In connection with the theory that a *quasi* six-membered ring may be formed in the transition state of 1,4-addition (p. 466) it is interesting that organolithium compounds seldom react in the 1,4-manner. Phenyllithium combines with *trans*-benzalacetophenone (*trans*-chalcone) to give diphenyl-styrylcarbinol.

$$C_6H_5CH{=}CHCOC_6H_5 \rightarrow C_6H_5CH{=}CHC(C_6H_5)_2 \overset{OH}{}$$

It must be added that phenyllithium combines with *cis*-chalcone chiefly in the 1,4-manner.[47] Also, *p*-butylation of duryl *o*-tolyl ketone corresponding to 1,6-addition of butyllithium has been accomplished.[48]

[46] E. A. Braude and J. A. Coles, *J. Chem. Soc.*, 2014 (1950).
[47] R. E. Lutz and J. O. Weiss, *J. Am. Chem. Soc.*, **77**, 1814 (1955).
[48] R. C. Fuson and J. R. Larson, *J. Am. Chem. Soc.*, **81**, 2149 (1959).

Organoaluminum Compounds

Alkylaluminum chlorides serve also in the preparation of ketones. An example is the formation of ethyl 6-ketoheptanoate by the interaction of methylaluminum dichloride with δ-carbethoxyvaleryl chloride; the yield of the keto ester is 95 %[49]

$$(CH_2)_4 \begin{matrix} COCl \\ \\ CO_2C_2H_5 \end{matrix} + CH_3AlCl_2 \rightarrow (CH_2)_4 \begin{matrix} COCH_3 \\ \\ CO_2C_2H_5 \end{matrix} + AlCl_3$$

Polymerization of Olefins by Complex Metal Catalysts

The importance of organoaluminum compounds was enhanced spectacularly by Ziegler's discovery that aluminum alkyls may serve as catalysts in the polymerization of α-olefins. For good results a cocatalyst is needed; the most generally used combination is triethylaluminum with titanium tetrachloride or trichloride (CR **58**, 541). Diethylaluminum chloride and many other organometallic compounds may serve also. The Ziegler polymerization, first described for ethylene, takes place at room temperature and pressure. In one procedure the catalyst is formed by adding titanium tetrachloride under nitrogen to a Fischer-Tropsch diesel oil (p. 646) that contains diethylaluminum chloride. When ethylene is bubbled through this mixture, polyethylene is produced. Other processes involve metals such as chromium, nickel, zirconium, and molybdenum.

Many α-olefins have been polymerized by such processes. The polyethylene differs from that made in other ways in having relatively little chain branching. Also, it is highly crystalline and has other physical properties that distinguish it sharply from the high-pressure polyethylene. Monomers of the type $RCH{=}CH_2$ yield polymers having asymmetric centers along the chain at the tertiary carbon atoms. The process is such that the monomer takes a steric configuration that corresponds to a determined order of attachment to the catalyst and makes the polymerization stereospecific. If the tertiary carbon atoms have the same configuration, the polymer is said to be *isotactic*. If, however, the asymmetric center alternate as to configuration, the polymer is *syndiotactic*. A structure in which the two types of asymmetric centers are arranged at random is *atactic*. All three types of polymers have been encountered.

[49] H. Adkins and C. Scanley, *J. Am. Chem. Soc.*, **73**, 2854 (1951).

It is by use of such catalysts that isoprene has been converted into the so-called synthetic natural rubber. Another accomplishment is the production of Cis-4, an all-*cis*, all-1,4 polymer of butadiene and of Trans-4.

It seems probable that this type of polymerization is fundamentally the addition of an organometallic compound to the olefin. Diethylaluminum chloride, for example, might absorb ethylene in the following manner.

$$
\underset{\underset{Cl}{|}}{\overset{\overset{C_2H_5}{|}}{CH_3CH_2Al}} \;+\; CH_2{=}CH_2 \;\rightarrow\; \underset{\underset{Cl}{|}}{\overset{\overset{C_2H_5}{|}}{CH_3CH_2-CH_2CH_2Al}}
$$

The newly added ethane link at each step is the one attached to the metal. This process is comparable to the addition of *t*-butylmagnesium to a fulvene (p. 454) and may be classified as anionic.

Organosodium and Organopotassium Compounds

Alkyl and aryl sodium compounds combine with carbon dioxide to yield sodium salts of acids. For example, carbon dioxide converts methylsodium into sodium acetate.

$$CH_3Na + CO_2 \rightarrow CH_3CO_2Na$$

The potassium derivative of diphenylmethane, obtained by the action of potassium amide on the hydrocarbon, reacts with carbon dioxide to give diphenylacetic acid in a yield of 90%.

$$(C_6H_5)_2CHK \rightarrow (C_6H_5)_2CHCO_2H$$

Certain olefins, such as *trans*-stilbene, are capable of combining with metallic sodium and can be converted into the corresponding sodium succinates by subsequent treatment of the disodium derivative with carbon dioxide.

$$
C_6H_5CH{=}CHC_6H_5 \xrightarrow{2Na} \underset{\underset{C_6H_5CHNa}{|}}{\overset{C_6H_5CHNa}{}} \xrightarrow{2CO_2} \underset{\underset{C_6H_5CHCO_2Na}{|}}{\overset{C_6H_5CHCO_2Na}{}}
$$

1,3-Butadiene reacts with sodium under suitable condition to yield a disodium derivative of the dimeric octadiene; the organosodium compound reacts with carbon dioxide to produce unsaturated ten-carbon dicarboxylic acids. Hydrogenation gives the corresponding saturated acids chief of which are sebacic, 2-ethylsuberic, and 2,5-diethyladipic acids.[50]

$$2CH_2=CHCH=CH_2 + 2Na \longrightarrow$$

$$NaCH_2CH=CHCH_2CH_2CH=CHCH_2Na \xrightarrow{2CO_2} \text{unsaturated acids} \xrightarrow{H_2}$$

$$(CH_2)_8 \underset{CO_2H}{\overset{CO_2H}{<}} \quad , \quad CH_3CH_2\underset{(CH_2)_5CO_2H}{\overset{|}{C}HCO_2H} , \quad CH_3CH_2\underset{(CH_2)_2}{\overset{|}{C}HCO_2H}$$

$$CH_3CH_2\overset{|}{C}HCO_2H$$

The three acids correspond to the following resonance structures of the divalent octadiene anion.

$$^-CH_2CH=CHCH_2CH_2CH=CHCH_2^-$$

$$CH_2=CH\overset{-}{C}HCH_2CH_2CH=CHCH_2^-$$

$$CH_2=CH\overset{-}{C}HCH_2CH_2\overset{-}{C}HCH=CH_2$$

Alkylsodium and alkylpotassium compounds are able to combine with ordinary olefins. The alkylation of olefins by arylalkanes in the presence of metallic sodium or potassium falls in this category. The formation of *n*-propylbenzene from ethylene and toluene in the presence of potassium, for example, may take the following course.[51]

$$C_6H_5CH_3 \xrightarrow{K} C_6H_5CH_2^-$$

$$C_6H_5CH_2^- + CH_2=CH_2 \rightarrow C_6H_5CH_2CH_2CH_2^-$$

$$C_6H_5CH_2CH_2CH_2^- + C_6H_5CH_3 \rightarrow C_6H_5CH_2CH_2CH_3 + C_6H_5CH_2^-$$

Metal Acetylides

The condensation of acetylene with carbonyl compounds can be effected with the alkali metal derivatives. Cyclohexanone, for example, combines with acetylene to give 1,5-ethynylene-*bis*-cyclohexanol; the reaction is carried out by adding the ketone to a mixture of calcium carbide, potassium hydroxide, and benzene (OS **32**, 70; yield 52%).

[50] C. E. Frank and W. E. Foster, *J. Org. Chem.*, **26**, 303 (1961).
[51] L. Schaap and H. Pines *J. Am. Chem. Soc.*, **79**, 4967 (1957).

Acetone reacts in a similar way to give 2,5-dimethyl-3-hexyne-2,5-diol.

$$2CH_3COCH_3 + HC\equiv CH \rightarrow$$

$$\begin{array}{c} OH \quad\quad OH \\ CH_3 \mid \quad\quad \mid CH_3 \\ CC\equiv CC \\ CH_3 \quad\quad CH_3 \end{array}$$

If the condensation is carried out at 5° in methylal in the presence of potassium hydroxide, the yield of the diol is 95%.[52]

Condensation of acetone with acetylene in equimolecular proportions is effected by adding acetylene to the sodium enolate of the ketone (OS III, 320; 46% yield).

$$CH_3COCH_3 \xrightarrow{NaNH_2} CH_3COCH_2Na \xrightarrow{C_2H_2}$$

$$\begin{array}{c} ONa \quad\quad\quad\quad OH \\ \mid \quad\quad\quad\quad\quad\quad \mid \\ (CH_3)_2CC\equiv CH \xrightarrow{H_2SO_4} (CH_3)_2CC\equiv CH \end{array}$$

Such reactions, often called ethynylation, occur also with copper acetylide as the catalyst; formaldehyde, for example, yields propargyl alcohol and 2-butyne-1,4-diol.

$$C_2H_2 + CH_2O \rightarrow HC\equiv CCH_2OH$$

$$C_2H_2 + 2CH_2O \rightarrow HOCH_2C\equiv CCH_2OH$$

From the acetylenic diol 1,4-butanediol can be made by hydrogenation. The butanediol can be dehydrated to 1,3-butadiene or to tetrahydrofuran, a compound which serves as a raw material in the synthesis of many substances, including 4-chloro-1-butanol, 1,4-dichlorobutane, adiponitrile, and hexamethylenediamine.

$$HOCH_2CH_2CH_2CH_2OH \xrightarrow{-2H_2O} CH_2=CH-CH=CH_2$$

$$\begin{array}{c} CH_2\!-\!\!-CH_2 \\ \mid \quad\quad \mid \\ CH_2 \quad CH_2 \xrightarrow{HCl} ClCH_2CH_2CH_2CH_2Cl \longrightarrow \\ \diagdown \diagup \\ O \end{array}$$

$$NCCH_2CH_2CH_2CH_2CN \longrightarrow H_2NCH_2CH_2CH_2CH_2CH_2CH_2NH_2$$

Sodium acetylide reacts with alkyl halides in liquid ammonia to yield acetylenic hydrocarbons, as is illustrated by the synthesis of 1-hexyne.

$$CH_3CH_2CH_2CH_2Br + NaC\equiv CH \rightarrow CH_3CH_2CH_2CH_2C\equiv CH + NaBr$$

[52] H. Richet, *Ann. chim.* [12] **3**, 317 (1948).

19

Reactions of carbonyl compounds
with enolates and phenolates

Numerous types of condensation reactions of carbonyl compounds are considered to involve nucleophilic attack by enolates or phenolates. A few of these, such as the aldol and acetoacetic ester condensations, have chemical names; but most of them are associated with names of chemists such as Claisen, Perkin, Dieckmann, Mannich, Michael, and Knoevenagel. These condensations fall into three categories: acylation, aldol-type condensations, and the Michael reaction.[1] When the carbonyl compound involved is an acid derivative, the attack of the enolate is followed by elimination of a base, and thus acylation occurs. With aldehydes and ketones, however, the addition compound, the aldol, often can be isolated, especially when mild experimental conditions are chosen. More drastic treatment generally brings about dehydration of the aldol, when this is possible, and leads to the formation of α,β-unsaturated carbonyl compounds. These have the possibility of reacting with enolates in the conjugate manner, which is known as the Michael reaction.

Acylation

Acylation reactions of the category under discussion usually are carried out by condensing an enolate with an ester. The ensuing elimination of an alkoxide ion gives an over-all change very similar to those that have been classified as solvolyses.

$$
\underset{\substack{\|\\ \text{O}}}{\text{R}\overset{\text{O}}{\text{C}}\text{OR}'} + {}^-\text{CH}_2\text{CO} \rightarrow \text{R}-\underset{\substack{|\\ \text{CH}_2\text{CO}\\ |}}{\overset{\substack{\text{O}^-\\ |}}{\text{C}}}-\text{OR}' \rightarrow \underset{\substack{\|\\ \text{O}}}{\text{R}\overset{\text{O}}{\text{C}}\text{CH}_2\text{CO}} + {}^-\text{OR}'
$$

---

[1] C. R. Hauser and D. S. Breslow, *J. Am. Chem. Soc.*, **62**, 2389 (1940).

Acetoacetic ester condensation

If the enolate is derived from an ester, the acylation takes the form known as the *acetoacetic ester condensation* (OR **1**, 266). It may be illustrated by the formation of ethyl acetoacetate from ethyl acetate. The change probably is made up of the following three steps.

(1) $CH_3CO_2C_2H_5 + \bar{O}C_2H_5 \rightleftharpoons \bar{C}H_2CO_2C_2H_5 + C_2H_5OH$

(2)
$$CH_3\overset{O}{\overset{\|}{C}}OC_2H_5 + \bar{C}H_2CO_2C_2H_5 \rightleftharpoons CH_3\overset{O^-}{\overset{|}{\underset{\underset{OC_2H_5}{|}}{C}}}-CH_2CO_2C_2H_5 \xrightleftharpoons{-^-OC_2H_5}$$

$$CH_3COCH_2CO_2C_2H_5$$

(3) $CH_3COCH_2CO_2C_2H_5 + \bar{O}C_2H_5 \rightleftharpoons CH_3CO\bar{C}HCO_2C_2H_5 + C_2H_5OH$

The equilibrium of the acid-base reaction between most esters and ethoxide ion is probably on the side of unchanged ester and ethoxide ion. In order for this base to effect the condensation of an ester it would appear that the β-keto ester formed must be converted largely into its anion; that is, the third step of the reaction must take place. In general, the acetoacetic ester condensation occurs if a base is formed that is weaker than that which serves as the condensing agent. Ethyl acetoacetate is formed from ethyl acetate and sodium ethoxide because the enolate anion,

$CH_3CO\bar{C}HCO_2C_2H_5$, is a weaker base than the ethoxide ion.

Esters that have but one α-hydrogen atom cannot give an enolate of this type and hence cannot be made to condense by ethoxide ion. They do react, however, in the presence of a stronger base such as the triphenylmethyl anion. Conversion of the β-keto ester into its anion (the third step above) may occur but is not required for condensations with the triphenylmethyl anion. Ethyl benzoyldimethylacetate can be made by condensing ethyl isobutyrate with ethyl benzoate in the presence of triphenylmethylsodium.

$$C_6H_5CO_2C_2H_5 + \overset{CH_3}{\overset{|}{\underset{\underset{CH_3}{|}}{C}H}}CO_2C_2H_5 \xrightarrow{(C_6H_5)_3CNa} C_6H_5CO\overset{CH_3}{\overset{|}{\underset{\underset{CH_3}{|}}{C}}}CO_2C_2H_5 + C_2H_5OH$$

The acetoacetic ester condensation is therefore general for esters that have hydrogen on the α-carbon atom. It has been used successfully also with many of the higher esters. β-Keto esters from esters of valeric, caproic, heptanoic, caprylic, pelargonic, capric, lauric, and myristic acids form in high yields (77 to 84%).

Lactones, which are cyclic esters, may undergo a similar change. In the presence of alkoxides, for example, γ-butyrolactone forms dibutyrolactone (OS **38**, 19).

$$2 \; \begin{array}{c} CH_2-CO \\ | \qquad \backslash \\ \qquad \quad O \; \rightarrow \\ | \qquad / \\ CH_2-CH_2 \end{array} \quad \begin{array}{c} CH_2-C=\!\!=\!\!=C-CO \\ | \qquad\qquad\qquad | \qquad \backslash \\ \qquad O \qquad\qquad\qquad O + H_2O \\ | \qquad\qquad\qquad | \qquad / \\ CH_2-CH_2 \quad CH_2-CH_2 \end{array}$$

Reversibility

Since the methylene group in ethyl acetoacetate is more reactive than the methyl group of ethyl acetate, it is pertinent to inquire why the acetylation process does not continue until all three hydrogen atoms of the original methyl group are replaced. The answer is that these condensation reactions are reversible and are equilibrium-controlled. If an acyl chloride is employed in place of an ester, the acylation is irreversible and provides a route to diacylated acetic esters. Ethyl acetoacetate with benzoyl chloride gives ethyl benzoylacetoacetate in 75% yield (OS II, 266).

$$CH_3CO\bar{C}HCO_2C_2H_5 + C_6H_5COCl \rightarrow \begin{array}{c} CH_3CO \\ \backslash \\ \quad CHCO_2C_2H_5 + Cl^- \\ / \\ C_6H_5CO \end{array}$$

If acetoacetic ester and acetyl chloride are heated with magnesium, acetylation occurs (OS III, 390); ethyl diacetylacetate is produced in 52% yield.

$$2CH_3COCH_2CO_2C_2H_5 + 2CH_3COCl + Mg \rightarrow$$

$$2 \; \begin{array}{c} CH_3CO \\ \backslash \\ \quad CHCO_2C_2H_5 + H_2 + MgCl_2 \\ / \\ CH_3CO \end{array}$$

Magnesium derivatives of diethyl malonate react in a similar way; with phenylacetyl chloride this ester gives diethyl phenylacetylmalonate in satisfactory yields (OS III, 637). Benzoylation proceeds under mild conditions when the mixed anhydride of benzoic and carbonic acids is used (OS **37**, 20).

$$\begin{array}{ccc} O & O & CO_2C_2H_5 \\ \| & \| & / \\ C_6H_5C-O-COC_2H_5 + CHMgOC_2H_5 \rightarrow \\ & & \backslash \\ & & CO_2C_2H_5 \end{array}$$

$$C_6H_5COCH(CO_2C_2H_5)_2 + CO_2 + Mg(OC_2H_5)_2$$

A method of converting acid chlorides into the corresponding methyl ketones consists in acylating diethyl malonate and subsequently removing the ester groups. An example is the preparation of *o*-nitroacetophenone from *o*-nitrobenzoyl chloride (OS **30**, 70; yield 83%).

$$CH_2(CO_2C_2H_5)_2 \xrightarrow[C_2H_5OH]{Mg} C_2H_5OMgCH(CO_2C_2H_5)_2 \xrightarrow{o\text{-}O_2NC_6H_4COCl}$$

Ethyl benzoyldimethylacetate is made by use of benzoyl chloride (OS II, 268; yield 55%).

O-Acylation

Acid chlorides and anhydrides normally give C-acyl products, although under certain special conditions O-acyl derivatives or enol esters may be produced. O-Acylation is the result of the action of acetyl chloride on the sodium derivative of ethyl acetoacetate in the presence of pyridine.

O-Acylation is observed also when ethyl acetoacetate is heated for several hours in the presence of sodium bicarbonate; alcohol is given off and dehydroacetic acid is formed in 53% yield (OS III, 231). Acylation is followed by cyclization of the condensation product in the form of its enolate.

Diethyl Oxalate. Condensation of different esters is also possible but generally leads to mixtures. It is most useful when the more reactive of the two esters has no α-hydrogen atom. Diethyl oxalate, because of the great reactivity of its carbonyl groups, can be condensed with ethyl propionate to give ethyl ethoxalylpropionate in 70% yield (OS II, 272).

$$\begin{array}{l} CO_2C_2H_5 \\ | \\ CO_2C_2H_5 \end{array} + CH_3CH_2CO_2C_2H_5 \xrightarrow{NaOC_2H_5} \begin{array}{l} CH_3CHCO_2C_2H_5 \\ | \\ COCO_2C_2H_5 \end{array} + C_2H_5OH$$

Ethyl ethoxalylacetate is made by a similar method.

Diethyl succinate condenses with diethyl oxalate to give diethyl ethoxalylsuccinate (OS III, 510; 83% yield).

$$\begin{array}{l} CH_2CO_2C_2H_5 \\ | \\ CH_2CO_2C_2H_5 \end{array} + (CO_2C_2H_5)_2 \xrightarrow{NaOC_2H_5} \begin{array}{l} CH_2CO_2C_2H_5 \\ | \\ CHCO_2C_2H_5 \\ | \\ COCO_2C_2H_5 \end{array} + C_2H_5OH$$

Diethyl Carbonate. Diethyl carbonate, as would be expected, is not highly reactive, and special conditions are necessary in order to effect carbethoxylation in high yields. Removal of the ethanol by distillation during the reaction serves to displace the equilibrium in the desired direction. The synthesis of diethyl phenylmalonate can be accomplished directly from diethyl carbonate and ethyl phenylacetate. Equimolecular proportions of the ester and sodium ethoxide are heated with the carbonate in excess, and the alcohol is removed continuously. This is a general method for making malonic esters from simple esters.

$$C_6H_5CH_2CO_2C_2H_5 + CO \begin{array}{l} ^{OC_2H_5} \\ \\ _{OC_2H_5} \end{array} \xrightarrow{NaOC_2H_5} C_6H_5CH(CO_2C_2H_5)_2 + C_2H_5OH$$

The conversion of ketones into the corresponding β-keto acids may be accomplished by the use of magnesium methyl carbonate, the magnesium chelate being an intermediate. Benzoylacetic acid, for example, is made from acetophenone in 68% yield.[2]

$$2C_6H_5COCH_3 + \left[CO \begin{array}{l} ^{O^-} \\ \\ _{OCH_3} \end{array} \right]_2 Mg \rightarrow 2C_6H_5C \underset{CH}{\overset{Mg}{\underset{\diagdown \diagup}{\overset{\diagup \diagdown}{O \qquad O}}}} CO + 2CH_3OH$$

$$C_6H_5C \underset{CH}{\overset{Mg}{\underset{\diagdown \diagup}{\overset{\diagup \diagdown}{O \qquad O}}}} CO \xrightarrow{H^+} C_6H_5COCH_2CO_2H$$

[2] M. Stiles, *J. Am. Chem. Soc.*, **81**, 2598 (1959).

If the enolate is treated with an alkylating agent and the product decomposed with loss of carbon dioxide, alkylation of the ketone may be accomplished.

Ethyl Formate. Ethyl formate has a very reactive carbonyl group and can be condensed with other esters; ethyl formate and ethyl acetate, for instance, yield ethyl formylacetate, which exists chiefly in the enol modification.

$$CH_3CO_2C_2H_5 + HCO_2C_2H_5 \rightarrow$$

$$C_2H_5OH + \left[\begin{matrix} CHO \\ / \\ CH_2 \\ \backslash \\ CO_2C_2H_5 \end{matrix} \rightleftharpoons \begin{matrix} CHOH \\ \nearrow \\ CH \\ \backslash \\ CO_2C_2H_5 \end{matrix} \right]$$

Ethyl Benzoate. Ethyl benzoate, another ester without α-hydrogen atoms, is less reactive than aliphatic esters. It has been condensed with other esters, but generally the yields are unsatisfactory. It would appear that benzoylation by this method would be at its best with esters that are least reactive as active methylene components. Indeed, condensation of ethyl benzoate and ethyl isobutyrate affords ethyl benzoyldimethylacetate in moderate yields (p. 479).

Ring closure

Application of the acetoacetic ester type of condensation to the closure of rings was discovered by Dieckmann. The method may be illustrated by the closure of diethyl adipate to 2-carbethoxycyclopentanone, which occurs in 81 % yield (OS II, 116).

$$\begin{matrix} & CH_2 & \\ / & & \backslash \\ CH_2 & & CO_2C_2H_5 \\ | & & | \\ CH_2 & & CO_2C_2H_5 \\ \backslash & & / \\ & CH_2 & \end{matrix} \quad \xrightarrow{NaOC_2H_5} \quad \begin{matrix} CH_2CH_2 \\ | \quad\quad \backslash \\ \quad\quad CHCO_2C_2H_5 \\ | \quad\quad / \\ CH_2—CO \end{matrix} + C_2H_5OH$$

Diethyl succinate may be caused to condense with itself in a manner that involves two acylations, the second of which is of the Dieckmann type. The product is known as diethyl succinylsuccinate.

$$2 \begin{matrix} CH_2CO_2C_2H_5 \\ | \\ CH_2CO_2C_2H_5 \end{matrix} \xrightarrow{-C_2H_5OH} \begin{matrix} CH_2CO_2C_2H_5 \\ / \\ CH_2 \quad\quad CO_2C_2H_5 \\ | \quad\quad\quad | \\ CO \quad\quad CH_2 \\ \backslash \quad\quad / \\ CHCO_2C_2H_5 \end{matrix} \xrightarrow{-C_2H_5OH} \begin{matrix} CHCO_2C_2H_5 \\ / \quad\quad \backslash \\ CH_2 \quad\quad CO \\ | \quad\quad\quad | \\ CO \quad\quad CH_2 \\ \backslash \quad\quad / \\ CHCO_2C_2H_5 \end{matrix}$$

A useful variant of Dieckmann's method involves the condensation of oxalic ester with esters of other dibasic acids. Diethyl glutarate yields a derivative of 1,2-cyclopentanedione.

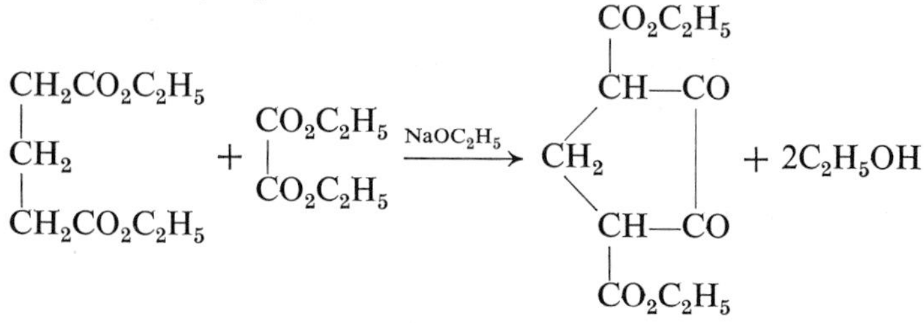

$$
\begin{array}{c}
CH_2CO_2C_2H_5 \\
| \\
CH_2 \\
| \\
CH_2CO_2C_2H_5
\end{array}
\quad + \quad
\begin{array}{c}
CO_2C_2H_5 \\
| \\
CO_2C_2H_5
\end{array}
\quad \xrightarrow{NaOC_2H_5} \quad
\begin{array}{c}
CO_2C_2H_5 \\
| \\
CH-CO \\
CH_2 \qquad | \\
CH-CO \\
| \\
CO_2C_2H_5
\end{array}
\quad + 2C_2H_5OH
$$

The oxalic ester is added in small amounts to sodium ethoxide in ether, then the glutarate is introduced; the yield of diketo ester is 65%.

The Dieckmann method serves also to close heterocycles, as is exemplified by the synthesis of 1-ethyl-4-piperidone from the condensation product of ethylamine and ethyl acrylate.

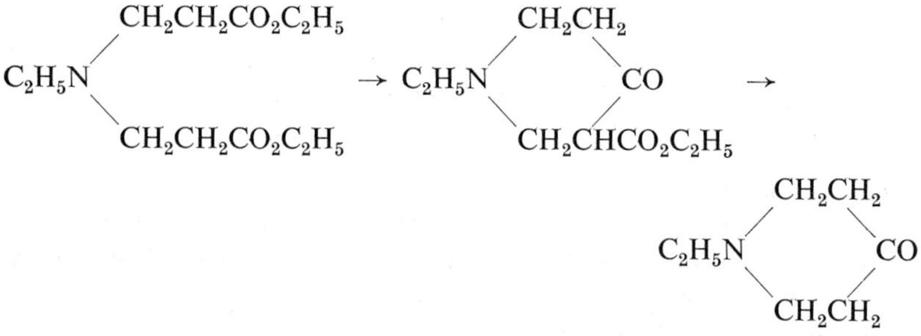

$$
C_2H_5N
\begin{array}{c}
CH_2CH_2CO_2C_2H_5 \\
\\
CH_2CH_2CO_2C_2H_5
\end{array}
\quad \rightarrow \quad
C_2H_5N
\begin{array}{c}
CH_2CH_2 \\
\quad CO \\
CH_2CHCO_2C_2H_5
\end{array}
\quad \rightarrow
$$

$$
C_2H_5N
\begin{array}{c}
CH_2CH_2 \\
\quad CO \\
CH_2CH_2
\end{array}
$$

By use of high dilution technique the Dieckmann method has been adapted to the closure of larger rings; an example is found in the synthesis of 1,2-dimethyl-1-azacycloöctan-3-one. The catalyst for the ring closure is potassium t-butoxide.[3]

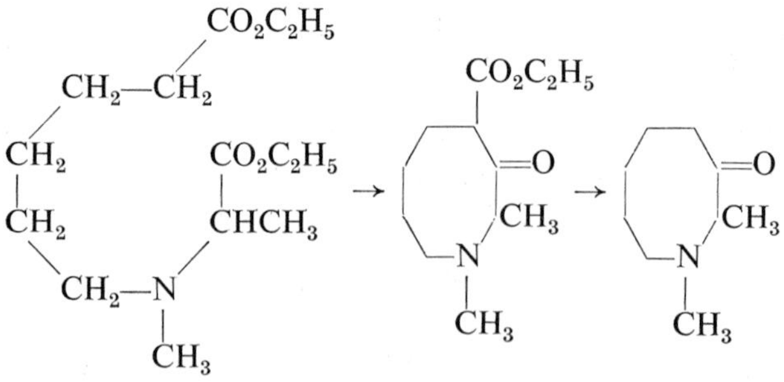

[3] N. J. Leonard and R. C. Sentz, *J. Am. Chem. Soc.*, **74**, 1704 (1952).

When dimethyl azelate is used and the catalyst is sodium hydride, 2-carbomethoxycycloöctanone is obtained in 48% yield.[4]

$$
\begin{array}{c}
\quad\quad CH_2CO_2CH_3 \\
(CH_2)_5 \\
\quad\quad CH_2CO_2CH_3
\end{array}
\quad\rightarrow\quad
\begin{array}{c}
\quad\quad CHCO_2CH_3 \\
(CH_2)_5 \quad\quad C{=}O \\
\quad\quad CH_2
\end{array}
$$

Acylation of nitriles

Products that are difficult to prepare by condensing two different esters, each of which possesses an α-hydrogen atom, may be arrived at in certain cases by replacing one of the esters by the corresponding nitrile. An example is the condensation of ethyl acetate with phenylacetonitrile to give α-phenylacetoacetonitrile.

$$
C_6H_5CH_2CN + CH_3CO_2C_2H_5 \rightarrow \underset{\underset{CN}{|}}{C_6H_5CHCOCH_3} + C_2H_5OH
$$

The cyano ketone can be converted into ethyl α-phenylacetoacetate by treatment with ethanolic hydrogen chloride or into benzyl methyl ketone by hydrolysis with aqueous sulfuric acid (OS II, 284, 391).

$$
C_6H_5CH_2COCH_3 \leftarrow \underset{\underset{CN}{|}}{C_6H_5CHCOCH_3} \rightarrow \underset{\underset{CO_2C_2H_5}{|}}{C_6H_5CHCOCH_3}
$$

This route to keto nitriles is improved if sodium amide is used as the catalyst.

Condensation of phenylacetonitrile with diethyl oxalate gives ethyl phenylcyanopyruvate (OS II, 287; 75% yield).

$$
C_6H_5CH_2CN + \underset{\underset{CO_2C_2H_5}{|}}{CO_2C_2H_5} \xrightarrow{NaOC_2H_5} \underset{\underset{COCO_2C_2H_5}{|}}{C_6H_5CHCN} + C_2H_5OH
$$

Condensation of nitriles

Nitriles undergo reactions that are analogous to the acetoacetic ester condensation. Ethyl cyanoacetate, in the presence of sodium ethoxide, for example, combines with itself to give an imino compound.

$$
2\underset{\underset{CO_2C_2H_5}{|}}{\overset{CN}{CH_2}} \rightarrow \underset{\underset{CO_2C_2H_5}{|}}{\overset{\overset{NH}{||}}{CH_2C}}{-}\underset{\underset{CO_2C_2H_5}{|}}{\overset{CN}{CH}}
$$

Applied to appropriate dinitriles, this method leads to the formation of cycloalkanone derivatives. Ethyl α,ε-dicyanovalerate, for example, may be

[4] F. F. Blicke, J. Azuara, N. J. Doorenbos, and E. B. Hotelling, *J. Am. Chem. Soc.*, **75**, 5418 (1953).

converted into α,α'-cyclopentanonedicarboxylic acid. This acid loses carbon dioxide to give cyclopentanone.

$$
\begin{array}{llll}
CH_2CH_2CN & CH_2CHCN & CH_2CHCO_2H & CH_2CH_2 \\
| & \diagdown & | & | \\
CN & C{=}NH \rightarrow & CO \rightarrow & CO \\
| & \diagup & | & \diagup \\
CH_2CHCO_2C_2H_5 & CH_2CHCO_2C_2H_5 & CH_2CHCO_2H & CH_2CH_2
\end{array}
$$

In a similar way 4-piperidone has been made from bis(β-cyanoethyl)-amine. The cyclization is catalyzed by sodium, sodium amide, or sodium alkoxides. When sodium is employed, it is desirable that the solvent be an ether and that a metal carrier such as naphthalene be present; the yield is 70%.

$$
\begin{array}{lll}
\quad CH_2CH_2CN & \quad CH_2CHCN & \quad CH_2CH_2 \\
\diagup & \diagup \qquad \diagdown & \diagup \qquad \diagdown \\
HN & \rightarrow HN \qquad C{=}NH \rightarrow HN \qquad CO \\
\diagdown & \diagdown \qquad \diagup & \diagdown \qquad \diagup \\
\quad CH_2CH_2CN & \quad CH_2CH_2 & \quad CH_2CH_2
\end{array}
$$

By the use of lithium amides as catalysts it has been possible to obtain large rings. The remarkable feature of this process is that even in this range it affords the ketones in yields as high as 40% of the theoretical amount. This procedure is therefore one of the best available for synthesizing large rings.

$$
\begin{array}{ll}
\quad CH_2CN & \quad CH_2 \\
\diagup & \diagup \qquad \diagdown \\
(CH_2)n \xrightarrow{\text{LiNR}_2} (CH_2)n \qquad C{=}NH \\
\diagdown & \diagdown \qquad \diagup \\
\quad CH_2CN & \quad CH \\
& \qquad | \\
& \qquad CN
\end{array}
$$

It is essential that these reactions be carried out at high dilution, which favors the desired intramolecular condensation as opposed to intermolecular combination.

Acylation of aldehydes and ketones

If the enolate that reacts with an ester is derived from an aldehyde or ketone, the product is an aldehydic or ketonic ester, and the process is known as the Claisen acylation (OR **8**, 59). Nitriles and certain other classes of compounds may be acylated in this way also. The original procedure involved a sodium alkoxide, but other catalysts may be employed. Acetylacetone, for example, can be made by the condensation of acetone with ethyl acetate in the presence of sodium ethoxide (OS III, 17).

$$
CH_3COCH_3 + CH_3CO_2C_2H_5 \xrightarrow{\text{NaOC}_2H_5} CH_3COCH_2COCH_3 + C_2H_5OH
$$

This transformation, as was mentioned earlier (p. 159), can be brought about also with acidic catalysts. Such catalysts are effective in many of the types of reactions under discussion.

Dibenzoylmethane is produced in 71% yield by the interaction of acetophenone and ethyl benzoate in the presence of sodium ethoxide (OS III, 251).

β-Keto esters can be made by condensing ketones with diethyl carbonate, the ethyl alcohol being distilled as fast as it forms. An example is the preparation of ethyl β-oxocaprylate from methyl n-amyl ketone.

$$CH_3(CH_2)_3CH_2COCH_3 + (C_2H_5)_2CO_3 \rightarrow$$
$$CH_3(CH_2)_3CH_2COCH_2CO_2C_2H_5 + C_2H_5OH$$

The catalyst is sodium ethoxide. It is to be noted that the condensation involves the methyl rather than the methylene group; the yield of keto ester is 65%.

This type of behavior is characteristic of methyl ketones in general as is illustrated by the synthesis of diisovalerylmethane from methyl isobutyl ketone and ethyl isovalerate in the presence of sodium amide (OS III, 291; 76% yield).

$$(CH_3)_2CHCH_2CO_2C_2H_5 + CH_3COCH_2CH(CH_3)_2 \xrightarrow{-C_2H_5OH}$$
$$(CH_3)_2CHCH_2COCH_2COCH_2CH(CH_3)_2$$

Diethyl oxalate, widely used in Claisen acylations, condenses with acetone to give ethyl acetopyruvate in 66% yield (OS I, 238).

$$CH_3COCH_3 + \begin{matrix} CO_2C_2H_5 \\ | \\ CO_2C_2H_5 \end{matrix} \xrightarrow{\text{NaOC}_2\text{H}_5} CH_3COCH_2COCO_2C_2H_5 + C_2H_5OH$$

Two moles of the ester are employed in the synthesis of chelidonic acid (OS II, 126).

Diethyl oxalate has been condensed also with toluene derivatives in which the methyl group is activated by nitro groups. An example is 2-nitro-*p*-xylene.[5]

$$CH_3 \underset{NO_2}{\langle \bigcirc \rangle} CH_3 + \begin{array}{l} CO_2C_2H_5 \\ | \\ CO_2C_2H_5 \end{array} \rightarrow CH_3 \underset{NO_2}{\langle \bigcirc \rangle} CH_2COCO_2C_2H_5 + C_2H_5OH$$

Cyclopentadiene, like other active methylene compounds, reacts with ethyl oxalate in the presence of sodium ethoxide to yield the ethoxalyl derivative.

$$\begin{array}{c} CH=CH \\ | \qquad\qquad \diagdown \\ \qquad\qquad CH_2 + \begin{array}{l} CO_2C_2H_5 \\ | \\ CO_2C_2H_5 \end{array} \xrightarrow{NaOC_2H_5} \\ | \qquad\qquad \diagup \\ CH=CH \end{array}$$

$$\begin{array}{c} CH=CH \\ | \qquad\qquad \diagdown \\ \qquad\qquad CHCOCO_2C_2H_5 + C_2H_5OH \\ | \qquad\qquad \diagup \\ CH=CH \end{array}$$

Diethyl carbonate may serve to prepare carbethoxy derivatives of nitriles. The method, similar to that described for esters (p. 482), consists in heating the nitrile with a metal alkoxide and the carbonate in large excess. The alcohol is removed by distillation. By this method stearonitrile, for example, gives ethyl α-cyanostearate in 75% yield.

In many reactions sodium hydride is as good as or superior to sodium or sodium alkoxides; it is comparable to sodium amide as a catalyst for this type of reaction.

The dicarbanions formed from certain β-diketones and potassium amide (p. 261) undergo acylation in a terminal methyl group rather than at the usual site, the methylene group. An example is the formation of 1,5-diphenyl-1,3,5-pentanetrione from benzoylacetone and methyl benzoate.[6]

$$C_6H_5COCH_2COCH_3 + C_6H_5CO_2CH_3 \xrightarrow{KNH_2}$$

$$C_6H_5COCH_2COCH_2COC_6H_5 + CH_3OH$$

Acylation of nitroparaffins

Enolates derived from nitroparaffins generally undergo O- rather than C-acylation. When the acylating agent is an α-keto nitrile, however,

[5] H. R. Snyder and F. J. Pilgrim, *J. Am. Chem. Soc.*, **70**, 3787 (1948).
[6] R. J. Light and C. R. Hauser, *J. Org. Chem.*, **25**, 538 (1960).

C-acylation can be accomplished. α-Nitropropiophenone, for example, can be made by condensing the lithium derivative of nitroethane with benzoyl cyanide (p. 254).[7]

$$\underset{\underset{NO_2}{|}}{CH_3CHLi} + C_6H_5COCN \rightarrow \underset{\underset{NO_2}{|}}{CH_3CHCOC_6H_5} + LiCN$$

Condensations of the Aldol Type

Enolates combine with aldehydes and ketones in the same way that Grignard reagents do, but the two types of reaction show certain important differences. First, the addition reaction with enolates is reversible whereas that with organometallic reagents is not. The difference is easily appreciated when it is recalled that the enolate ion is much more stable than an alkyl or aryl carbanion. The reversal of the condensation is, then, but another example of the rule that the ease of breaking a bond is related to the stability of the radicals or ions that are generated.

A second important difference is that condensation reactions of enolates give rise to β-hydroxy carbonyl compounds, which readily lose the elements of water to give α,β-unsaturated carbonyl compounds. In fact, the usual products of this type of condensation are the unsaturated compounds, since reaction conditions are generally too drastic to permit isolation of the hydroxy derivatives.

Aldol condensation

The term aldol condensation (Gould, 389) is generally applied to those reactions that proceed readily and under conditions that permit isolation of the hydroxy carbonyl compound. The classic example is the transformation of acetaldehyde to aldol.

$$CH_3CHO + CH_3CHO \rightleftharpoons \underset{\overset{|}{OH}}{CH_3CHCH_2CHO}$$

The condensation is reversible.

The formation of aldols is general for low-molecular-weight aldehydes and ketones. The use of two different carbonyl compounds normally leads to the formation of mixtures and is accordingly of little value in synthesis. If only one of them has α-hydrogen atoms, however, satisfactory results can often be obtained.

Aldolization does not, of course, stop at the dimeric stage but produces a complex mixture of aldehydes of higher molecular weight. Crotonization

---

[7] G. B. Bachman and T. Hokama, *J. Am. Chem. Soc.*, **81**, 4882 (1959).

following aldolization produces unsaturated aldehydes. Cinnamaldehyde, for example, reacts with acetaldehyde to yield higher vinylogs.

$$C_6H_5CH{=}CHCHO \rightarrow C_6H_5CH{=}CHCH{=}CHCHO \rightarrow$$

$$C_6H_5CH{=}CHCH{=}CHCH{=}CHCHO$$

The various products may be changed by hydrogenation to saturated aldehydes or alcohols. From acetaldehyde may be obtained *n*-butyraldehyde, caproaldehyde, α-ethyl-*n*-butyraldehyde, and α-ethylcaproaldehyde, as well as 1-butanol, 1-hexanol, 2-ethyl-1-butanol, and 2-ethyl-1-hexanol.

$$CH_3CH_2CH_2CHO$$
Butyraldehyde

$$CH_3CH_2CH_2CH_2OH$$
1-Butanol

$$CH_3CH_2\underset{\underset{\displaystyle C_2H_5}{|}}{C}HCHO$$
α-Ethylbutyraldehyde

$$CH_3CH_2\underset{\underset{\displaystyle C_2H_5}{|}}{C}HCH_2OH$$
2-Ethyl-1-butanol

$$CH_3CH_2CH_2CH_2\underset{\underset{\displaystyle C_2H_5}{|}}{C}HCHO$$
α-Ethylcaproaldehyde

$$CH_3CH_2CH_2CH_2\underset{\underset{\displaystyle C_2H_5}{|}}{C}HCH_2OH$$
2-Ethyl-1-hexanol

$$CH_3CH_2CH_2CH_2CH_2CHO$$
Caproaldehyde

$$CH_3CH_2CH_2CH_2CH_2CH_2OH$$
1-Hexanol

1-Butanol is available also, along with acetone, from the Weizmann fermentation of glucose.

A method of avoiding the retrograde aldol reaction is illustrated by the procedure employed in dimerizing acetone. In the presence of barium hydroxide, acetone is converted reversibly into diacetone alcohol (OS I, 199).

$$2CH_3COCH_3 \rightleftharpoons CH_3\underset{\underset{\displaystyle CH_3}{|}}{\overset{\overset{\displaystyle OH}{|}}{C}}CH_2COCH_3$$

The equilibrium lies so far to the left, however, that little product is obtained under ordinary conditions. The condensation can be made useful (71% yields), nevertheless, by placing the catalyst in a Soxhlet extractor and allowing acetone to flow over it. The diacetone alcohol that is formed, because of its higher boiling point, accumulates in the flask. Out of contact with the catalyst, it is stable.

The simplest aldol condensation occurs between formaldehyde and acetaldehyde; acrolein is made commercially by a catalytic condensation of the two aldehydes.

Aqueous sodium hydroxide method

The procedure involving aqueous sodium hydroxide solution as catalyst, generally known as the Claisen-Schmidt method, is especially valuable for the preparation of α,β-unsaturated ketones. Benzaldehyde is caused to react with acetophenone, for example, to give benzalacetophenone or chalcone (OS I, 78; 85% yield).

$$C_6H_5CHO + CH_3COC_6H_5 \xrightarrow{\text{NaOH}} C_6H_5CH{=}CHCOC_6H_5 + H_2O$$

From benzaldehyde and acetone are obtained benzalacetone (OS I, 77; 78% yield) and dibenzalacetone (OS II, 167; 94% yield).

$$C_6H_5CHO + CH_3COCH_3 \xrightarrow{\text{NaOH}} C_6H_5CH{=}CHCOCH_3 + H_2O$$

$$C_6H_5CHO + CH_3COCH{=}CHC_6H_5 \xrightarrow{\text{NaOH}}$$
$$C_6H_5CH{=}CHCOCH{=}CHC_6H_5 + H_2O$$

Benzalpinacolone (OS I, 81; 93% yield), 2-furfuralacetone (OS I, 283; 66% yield), and difurfuralacetone are made in this way also.

Similarly, β-nitrostyrene can be synthesized in 83% yield by stirring a mixture of benzaldehyde, nitromethane, methanol, water, and sodium hydroxide (OS I, 413).

$$C_6H_5CHO + CH_3NO_2 + NaOH \xrightarrow{-H_2O}$$
$$\underset{\overset{|}{OH}}{C_6H_5CHCH}{=}NO_2Na \xrightarrow{\text{HCl}} C_6H_5CH{=}CHNO_2$$

Chloroform and bromoform are capable of entering into condensations of the aldol type. Chloroform reacts with p-chlorobenzaldehyde, for example, to yield p-chlorophenyltrichloromethylcarbinol.[8]

When the reaction is carried out in methanol the carbinol is transformed, perhaps by way of an epoxide, into methyl α-methoxyphenylacetate.[9]

[8] J. W. Howard, *J. Am. Chem. Soc.*, **57**, 2317 (1935).
[9] W. Reeve and E. L. Compere, Jr., *J. Am. Chem. Soc.*, **83**, 2755 (1961).

The product obtained from chloroform and acetone is known as acetonechloroform or chloretone.

$$\underset{CH_3}{\overset{CH_3}{\diagup}}C{=}O + CHCl_3 \xrightarrow{\text{KOH}} \underset{CH_3}{\overset{CH_3}{\diagup}}C\underset{CCl_3}{\overset{OH}{\diagup}}$$

The preparation of fulvenes from cyclopentadiene corresponds to an aldol condensation followed by loss of water; acetone, for example, gives 6,6-dimethylfulvene.[10]

Condensation with formaldehyde

Condensation of formaldehyde with aldehydes and ketones is accomplished by the use of calcium hydroxide or an alkali carbonate as catalyst. This method, developed by Tollens, requires long treatment and yields methylol derivatives. An example is the conversion of isobutyraldehyde into 2,2-dimethyl-1,3-propanediol. The first reaction, an aldol condensation, is followed by a crossed Cannizzaro reaction (p. 554), which changes the carbonyl group to a carbinol group. By limiting the amount of formaldehyde, the condensation may be halted at the first stage, yielding the methylol derivative of the aldehyde.

Another example is the conversion of isovaleraldehyde into a trihydroxyheptane.

[10] G. Crane, C. E. Boord, and A. L. Henne, *J. Am. Chem. Soc.*, **67**, 1237 (1945).

Cyclohexanone is transformed into the tetramethylol derivative of cyclohexanol (OS **31**, 101; 85% yield).

$$\text{(cyclohexanone)} + 5CH_2O + H_2O \xrightarrow{\text{CaO}} (HOCH_2)_2\text{(cyclohexanol-OH)}(CH_2OH)_2 + HCO_2H$$

Perhaps the most important example of the Tollens reaction is the conversion of acetaldehyde into pentaerythritol (OS I, 425; 57% yield).

$$CH_3CHO + 4CH_2O + H_2O \rightarrow C(CH_2OH)_4 + HCO_2H$$

The crossed Cannizzaro reaction is evidently much less rapid than the aldol condensation; however, it is irreversible. Pentaerythritol is always accompanied by dipentaerythritol, the formation of which appears to be due to the intermediate production of acrolein. It would be expected to react additively with β-hydroxypropionaldehyde to yield the dialdehyde, from which the dipentaerythrityl ether would be formed in the normal way.

$$CH_3CHO + CH_2O \rightarrow \underset{\underset{OH}{|}}{CH_2}CH_2CHO \rightarrow CH_2{=}CHCHO$$

$$CH_2{=}CHCHO + \underset{\underset{OH}{|}}{CH_2}CH_2CHO \rightarrow O(CH_2CH_2CHO)_2$$

Cyclic ethers are produced also; glutaraldehyde gives a pyran derivative, for example.[11]

$$\text{(glutaraldehyde structure)} \rightarrow (HOCH_2)_2\text{(pyran)}(CH_2OH)_2$$

Pentaerythritol has been prepared, curiously, by the action of formaldehyde on unsaturated aldehydes such as crotonaldehyde and cinnamaldehyde. The explanation is to be found in the reversibility of the aldol condensation (p. 294); in alkaline media these aldehydes may yield acetaldehyde.

Nitroparaffins condense with formaldehyde to give the corresponding methylol compounds; nitromethane, nitroethane, and 2-nitropropane

[11] T. J. Prosser, *J. Org. Chem.*, **26**, 242 (1961).

yield the corresponding tri-, di-, and monomethylol derivatives (CR **32,** 373), respectively.

$$CH_3NO_2 + 3CH_2O \rightarrow (HOCH_2)_3CNO_2$$

$$CH_3CH_2NO_2 + 2CH_2O \rightarrow CH_3\overset{\overset{\displaystyle CH_2OH}{|}}{\underset{\underset{\displaystyle CH_2OH}{|}}{C}}NO_2$$

$$(CH_3)_2CHNO_2 + CH_2O \rightarrow (CH_3)_2C\overset{\nearrow CH_2OH}{\searrow_{NO_2}}$$

It is possible to introduce the methylol groups one at a time by choosing suitable amounts of the reactants. Paraformaldehyde and nitromethane, taken in excess, react in the presence of potassium carbonate to produce β-nitroethanol in good yields. Use of two moles of the aldehydes permits the synthesis of the nitroglycol.

$$CH_3NO_2 + CH_2O \xrightarrow{K_2CO_3} HOCH_2CH_2NO_2 \longrightarrow (HOCH_2)_2CHNO_2$$

Nitroform (p. 148) reacts with paraformaldehyde to give 2,2,2-trinitroethanol in 75 % yield.[12]

$$(NO_2)_3CH + CH_2O \rightarrow (NO_2)_3CCH_2OH$$

Use of alkoxides

Aldol condensations that involve an ester usually are carried out with an alkoxide as catalyst, since esters are hydrolyzed by aqueous alkalis. The classical example is the *Claisen cinnamic ester synthesis*, which is accomplished by treating an aliphatic ester with an aromatic aldehyde in the presence of sodium ethoxide. The preparation of ethyl cinnamate from ethyl acetate and benzaldehyde is illustrative (OS I, 252; 74 % yield).

$$C_6H_5CHO + CH_3CO_2C_2H_5 \xrightarrow{NaOC_2H_5} C_6H_5CH{=}CHCO_2C_2H_5 + H_2O$$

Another example of the use of benzaldehyde is the formation of α-phenylcinnamonitrile from phenylacetonitrile (OS III, 715; 91 % yield).

$$C_6H_5CHO + C_6H_5CH_2CN \xrightarrow{NaOC_2H_5} C_6H_5CH{=}\overset{\overset{\displaystyle }{}}{\underset{\underset{\displaystyle C_6H_5}{|}}{C}}CN + H_2O$$

[12] N. S. Marans and R. P. Zelinski, *J. Am. Chem. Soc.*, **72,** 5329 (1950).

Condensation with benzaldehyde often serves as a test for the presence of an active methylene group. *p*-Chlorobenzaldehyde and *p*-nitrobenzaldehyde are superior to benzaldehyde for this purpose, since they react much more rapidly.

Acetophenone is less reactive than aliphatic methyl ketones but, under the influence of aluminum *t*-butoxide (OS III, 367), reacts with itself to yield dypnone.

$$2C_6H_5COCH_3 \xrightarrow{Al[OC(CH_3)_3]_3} \overset{\displaystyle CH_3}{\underset{\displaystyle |}{C_6H_5C}}{=}CHCOC_6H_5 + H_2O$$

The catalyst is decomposed, of course, by the water that is formed, yielding aluminum hydroxide and *t*-butyl alcohol. The condensation is carried out at 133 to 137°, the alcohol being removed by distillation as fast as it is produced. The reaction, completed in about 2 hours, gives the unsaturated ketone in 82% yield.

Use of lithium amide

Ethyl acetate condenses with aldehydes and ketones in the presence of lithium amide in liquid ammonia to yield the corresponding β-hydroxy esters. With benzophenone, for example, it gives ethyl β-hydroxy-β,β-diphenylpropionate in 84% yield.[13]

$$(C_6H_5)_2CO + CH_3CO_2C_2H_5 \rightarrow \overset{\displaystyle OH}{\underset{\displaystyle |}{(C_6H_5)_2CCH_2CO_2C_2H_5}}$$

The procedure has been used with other esters and seems to be more convenient than that of Reformatsky (p. 523).

Glycidic ester condensation

When the aldol type of condensation is caused to take place between an aldehyde or ketone and an α-halo ester, a glycidic ester is produced (CR **55**, 283). An example is the preparation of ethyl methylphenylglycidate by condensing acetophenone with ethyl chloroacetate in the presence of sodium amide (OS III, 727; 64% yield).

$$C_6H_5COCH_3 + ClCH_2CO_2C_2H_5 + NaNH_2 \rightarrow$$

$$\overset{\displaystyle CH_3}{\underset{\displaystyle \underset{\displaystyle O}{\diagdown\diagup}}{C_6H_5C\text{————}CHCO_2C_2H_5}} + NaCl + NH_3$$

[13] C. R. Hauser and W. R. Dunnavant, *J. Org. Chem.*, **25**, 1206 (1960).

This type of condensation, developed by Darzens (OR **5,** 413), is of interest chiefly because the glycidic esters provide a route to aldehydes and ketones having more carbon atoms than those employed as starting materials.

Potassium *t*-butoxide is especially effective as is illustrated by the condensation of cyclohexanone with ethyl chloroacetate (OS **34,** 54; yield 95%).

The Darzens reaction has been used with chloroacetone also, which condenses with benzaldehyde to give only the *trans*-form of benzalacetone oxide.[14]

$$C_6H_5CHO + ClCH_2COCH_3 \xrightarrow{NaOCH_3} C_6H_5CH\overset{O}{\triangle}CHCOCH_3 + HCl$$

Succinic ester condensation

The alkoxide-catalyzed aldol type of condensation of succinic esters with an aldehyde or ketone, often called the Stobbe condensation (OR **6,** 1), makes it possible to introduce a propionic acid residue at the site of the carbonyl group. The general scheme is illustrated by the conversion of 2-acetylnaphthalene into γ-(2-naphthyl)valeric acid.

[14] H. Kwart and L. G. Kirk, *J. Org. Chem.,* **22,** 116 (1957).

The most satisfactory condensing agents are potassium t-butoxide and sodium hydride. The product of the condensation is a half ester, which yields a saturated lactone when heated with a mixture of 48 % hydrobromic acid and glacial acetic acid. The synthesis is completed by hydrolysis of the lactone and hydrogenolysis of the hydroxy acid over copper-chromium oxide.

When the synthesis is carried to the unsaturated half-ester stage with 2-phenylcycloheptanone the olefinic bond is found to be in the ring.[15]

Perkin cinnamic acid synthesis

Anhydrides, as active methylene compounds are relatively unreactive and, even with aldehydes, require long treatment at elevated temperatures. These are the conditions that characterize the cinnamic acid synthesis, generally known as the Perkin reaction (OR **1**, 210). Benzaldehyde, when heated with a mixture of potassium acetate and acetic anhydride, gives rise to cinnamic acid.

$$C_6H_5CHO + (CH_3CO)_2O \xrightarrow{CH_3CO_2K} C_6H_5CH{=}CHCO_2H + CH_3CO_2H$$

The condensation is clearly of the aldol type, the salt of a hydroxy acid being an intermediate. Potassium acetate is superior to sodium acetate because it causes the reaction to proceed more rapidly; with it cinnamic acid may be obtained in 60 % yield by 5 hours of heating at 170 to 175°. An air-cooled condenser permits the acetic acid to escape, which favors the formation of cinnamic acid by shifting the equilibrium. Furylacrylic acid is prepared from furfural by this procedure (OS III, 425, 92 % yield). Another example is the synthesis of m-nitrocinnamic acid from m-nitrobenzaldehyde (OS I, 398; 77 % yield).

It is generally accepted that the condensation takes place between the aldehyde and the anhydride, the salt merely acting as a catalyst. Condensation always occurs at the α-carbon atom; from propionic anhydride and sodium propionate, α-methylcinnamic acid is produced.

$$C_6H_5CHO + (CH_3CH_2CO)_2O \xrightarrow{CH_3CH_2CO_2Na}$$

$$C_6H_5CH{=}\underset{\underset{CH_3}{|}}{C}CO_2H + CH_3CH_2CO_2H$$

[15] S. Yaroslavsky and E. D. Bergmann, *Tetrahedron*, **11**, 158 (1960).

This method, though limited to the aromatic series, is capable of considerable extension. From salicylaldehyde *trans-o*-hydroxycinnamic acid or coumaric acid is formed. Vigorous dehydration converts this acid to coumarin, which is the lactone derived from the unstable *cis*-hydroxy acid.

Coumaric acid   Coumarin

The Perkin method has been employed also with anhydrides in place of the aldehyde. When a mixture of phthalic anhydride, acetic anhydride, and potassium acetate is heated for 10 minutes at 150 to 160°, phthalylacetic acid is obtained in 50% yield.

When this acid is treated with sodium methoxide and the reaction mixture is subsequently warmed with hydrochloric acid, 1,3-indandione is produced.

Cold aqueous alkalis open the lactone ring to form 2-carboxybenzoyl-acetic acid, which loses carbon dioxide to yield *o*-acetylbenzoic acid.

When phthalic anhydride and malonic acid are heated in the presence of pyridine, *o*-acetylbenzoic acid is obtained in 48% yield. A mixture of phthalic anhydride, phenylacetic acid, and sodium acetate, when heated for 3 hours at 230 to 240°, gives benzalphthalide (OS II, 61; 74% yield).

Benzalphthalide is converted by sodium methoxide into 2-phenyl-1,3-indandione and by concentrated alkalis into o-phenylacetylbenzoic acid (OR **1**, 223). The indandione formation can be explained plausibly by assuming methanolysis followed by intramolecular Claisen acylation.

A particularly valuable modification of the Perkin reaction is illustrated by the condensation of benzaldehyde, succinic anhydride, and sodium acetate. The aldol undergoes intramolecular acylation, and the final product is the lactonic acid, phenylparaconic acid.

$$
C_6H_5CHO + \begin{matrix} CH_2-CO \\ | \quad\quad\quad \diagdown \\ | \quad\quad\quad\quad O \\ | \quad\quad\quad \diagup \\ CH_2-CO \end{matrix} \xrightarrow{CH_3CO_2Na} \begin{matrix} C_6H_5CH-CH-CO \\ | \quad\quad | \quad\quad \diagdown \\ | \quad\quad | \quad\quad\quad O \\ | \quad\quad | \quad\quad \diagup \\ OH \quad CH_2CO \end{matrix} \longrightarrow
$$

$$
\begin{matrix} C_6H_5CH\text{———}CHCO_2H \\ | \quad\quad\quad\quad\quad | \\ O \quad\quad\quad\quad CH_2 \\ \diagdown \quad\quad \diagup \\ CO \end{matrix}
$$

By a similar method unsaturated aldehydes are condensed with succinic acid in the presence of acetic anhydride and lead oxide (PbO) to yield polyenes (CR **34**, 435). The synthesis of the diphenylhexadecaoctaene may be taken as an illustration. The octaene has a copper-red color and melts at 285°.

$$
2C_6H_5(CH{=}CH)_3CHO + \begin{matrix} CH_2\text{——}CH_2 \\ | \quad\quad\quad | \\ CO_2H \quad CO_2H \end{matrix} \rightarrow
$$

$$
C_6H_5(CH{=}CH)_8C_6H_5 + 2H_2O + 2CO_2
$$

1,4-Diphenyl-1,3-butadiene is prepared by condensing cinnamaldehyde with phenylacetic acid (OS II, 229; 25% yield).

$$
C_6H_5CH_2CO_2H + C_6H_5CH{=}CHCHO \xrightarrow[\text{(CH}_3\text{CO)}_2\text{O}]{\text{PbO}}
$$

$$
C_6H_5CH{=}CHCH{=}CHC_6H_5 + CO_2 + H_2O
$$

Although the Perkin reaction is believed to involve the anhydride, there are instances in which the resulting α,β-unsaturated acid corresponds to that derived from the salt rather than to the anhydride that is used. For example, potassium phenylacetate, benzaldehyde, and acetic anhydride afford α-phenylcinnamic acid in 55% yield (OR **1**, 252). Such reactions are explained by reference to the exchange reaction between the salt and the anhydride.

$$
2C_6H_5CH_2CO_2Na + (CH_3CO)_2O \rightarrow 2CH_3CO_2Na + (C_6H_5CH_2CO)_2O
$$

A valuable application of the Perkin method was developed by Erlenmeyer in the synthesis of unsaturated azlactones. These important substances are formed by condensation of aromatic aldehydes with acyl derivatives of glycine (OR **3**, 198).

$$ArCHO + \begin{array}{c} CH_2CO_2H \\ | \\ NHCOR \end{array} \xrightarrow[CH_3CO_2Na]{(CH_3CO)_2O} \begin{array}{c} ArCH{=}C{-\!\!-}C{=}O \\ | \qquad | \\ N \qquad O \\ \diagdown \diagup \\ CR \end{array} + 2H_2O$$

The first step in the process probably is the conversion of the acylamino acid into an azlactone, which then undergoes the Perkin reaction with the aldehyde.

$$\begin{array}{c} CH_2CO_2H \\ | \\ NHCOR \end{array} \rightarrow \begin{array}{c} CH_2{-\!\!-}CO \\ | \qquad | \\ N \qquad O \\ \diagdown \diagup \\ CR \end{array} \rightarrow \begin{array}{c} ArCH{=}C{-\!\!-}C{=}O \\ | \qquad | \\ N \qquad O \\ \diagdown \diagup \\ CR \end{array}$$

The Erlenmeyer azlactone synthesis is illustrated by the condensation of benzaldehyde with N-benzoylglycine (OS II, 1).

$$C_6H_5CHO + \begin{array}{c} CH_2CO_2H \\ | \\ NHCOC_6H_5 \end{array} \rightarrow \begin{array}{c} C_6H_5CH{=}C{-\!\!-}C{=}O \\ | \qquad | \\ N \qquad O \\ \diagdown \diagup \\ CC_6H_5 \end{array} + 2H_2O$$

Hydrolysis of the azlactone gives α-acetamidocinnamic acid in an over-all yield of 65%.

$$\begin{array}{c} C_6H_5CH{=}C{-\!\!-}C{=}O \\ | \qquad | \\ N \qquad O \\ \diagdown \diagup \\ C \\ | \\ CH_3 \end{array} + H_2O \xrightarrow{heat} \begin{array}{c} C_6H_5CH{=}CCO_2H \\ | \\ NHCOCH_3 \end{array}$$

Many condensation reactions of the aldol type require strong bases; an example is the synthesis of α,β-diphenylcinnamonitrile from phenylacetonitrile and benzophenone, which is carried out with sodium amide (OS **31**, 52; 66% yield).

$$C_6H_5CH_2CN + (C_6H_5)_2CO \xrightarrow{NaNH_2} \begin{array}{c} (C_6H_5)_2C{=}CCN \\ | \\ C_6H_5 \end{array} + H_2O$$

Use of ammonia and amines

Two large groups of reactions of active methylene compounds—the Knoevenagel and the Mannich types—are so similar to the ones just discussed that it seems best to deal with them here The Knoevenagel procedure is illustrated by the formation of diethyl benzalmalonate by the condensation of benzaldehyde with diethyl malonate in the presence of piperidine (OS III, 377; 91% yield).

The condensation product that is formed when diethyl malonate and salicylaldehyde are brought together in the presence of piperidine, undergoes ring closure to yield 3-carbethoxycoumarin (OS III, 165; 83% yield).

$$\text{(salicylaldehyde) } + CH_2(CO_2C_2H_5)_2 \rightarrow \text{(coumarin) } CO_2C_2H_5 + C_2H_5OH + H_2O$$

Malonic acid condenses with furfural, in the presence of piperidine, to give furylacrylic acid in 92% yield (OS III, 425). 2,3-Dimethoxycinnamic acid can be made in a similar way from 2,3-dimethoxybenzaldehyde (OS **31**, 35; 98% yield).

$$\text{CHO} + CH_2(CO_2H)_2 \xrightarrow[\text{piperidine}]{\text{pyridine}}$$

$$\text{CH}=\text{CHCO}_2\text{H} + H_2O + CO_2$$

With acetoacetic ester the product, after hydrogenation, is ethyl α-acetyl-β-(2,3-dimethoxyphenyl)propionate (OS **31**, 56).

Crotonaldehyde and malonic acid give sorbic acid in 32 % yield (OS III, 783).

$$CH_3CH{=}CHCHO + CH_2(CO_2H)_2 \xrightarrow{\text{pyridine}}$$

$$CH_3CH{=}CHCH{=}CHCO_2H + CO_2 + H_2O$$

m-Nitrocinnamic acid can be made by heating a mixture of *m*-nitrobenzaldehyde and malonic acid in the presence of pyridine (OS **33**, 62; yield 80 %).

Furfural and cyanoacetic acid, in the presence of ammonium acetate and pyridine, give β-(2-furyl)acrylonitrile in 78 % yield (OS **40**, 46).

The methylene group of phenylacetic acid is sufficiently reactive to enter into condensation reactions of the Knoevenagel type. This acid, for example, reacts with benzaldehyde in the presence of triethylamine to give α-phenylcinnamic acid (OS **33**, 70; yield 59 %).

α-Phenyl-*p*-nitrocinnamic acid can be made in 61 % yield by condensing *p*-nitrobenzaldehyde with phenylacetic acid in the presence of triethylamine and acetic anhydride. When *o*-nitrobenzaldehyde is used, the product is *trans*-α-phenyl-*o*-nitrocinnamic acid (OS **35**, 89; 72 % yield).

This synthesis is superior to the Perkin (p. 497) in that it does not require the anhydrous salt of the acid and that it is conducted at a lower temperature. Acetic anhydride converts phenylacetic acid into phenylacetic anhydride, which is the actual reactant. The condensation may, therefore, be classified as a modified Perkin reaction.

Although glyoxals undergo rearrangement when treated with strong alkalis (p. 554), they can be condensed with malonic acid in the presence of pyridine. From 2-naphthylglyoxal, for instance, it is possible to prepare β-(2-naphthoyl)acrylic acid in 12 % yield.[16]

[16] M. Goldman and E. I. Becker, *Nature*, **170**, 35 (1952).

$$\text{(naphthalene)}-COCHO \;\rightarrow\; \text{(naphthalene)}-COCH{=}CHCO_2H$$

It has been shown that the catalyst in the Knoevenagel reaction is really the ammonium (piperidinium, diethylammonium, etc.) salt. Ordinarily the ion is formed by an acid reactant or by traces of acid present in the aldehyde. If the aldehyde is freed from acid, the reaction does not take place. Unless one of the reactants is an acid, it is best to use a salt such as piperidinium acetate.

An interesting example of reductive alkylation is the formation of ethyl *n*-butylcyanoacetate by hydrogenation of a mixture of *n*-butyraldehyde, ethyl cyanoacetate, and pyridinium acetate (OS III, 385). The yield is nearly quantitative.

$$C_3H_7CHO + \underset{CO_2C_2H_5}{\overset{CN}{CH_2}} + H_2 \xrightarrow{\text{Pd}} \underset{CO_2C_2H_5}{\overset{CN}{C_4H_9CH}} + H_2O$$

Aminomethylation

In the Mannich type of reaction the amine is incorporated in the product and the change is one of aminomethylation. The interaction of formaldehyde, acetophenone, and dimethylamine is an example (OS III, 305). In practice the base usually is isolated as the hydrochloride.

$$C_6H_5COCH_3 + CH_2O + (CH_3)_2NH{\cdot}HCl \rightarrow$$
$$C_6H_5COCH_2CH_2N(CH_3)_2{\cdot}HCl + H_2O$$

This type of condensation has been employed with a wide variety of amines and is successful not only with ketones but also with aldehydes, esters, phenols, acetylenes, and certain other compounds containing reactive hydrogen atoms (OR **1**, 303). Acetone and diethylamine yield 1-diethylamino-3-butanone (OS **37**, 18; 70% yield).

$$CH_3COCH_3 + CH_2O + (C_2H_5)_2NH{\cdot}HCl \rightarrow$$
$$CH_3COCH_2CH_2N(C_2H_5)_2{\cdot}HCl + H_2O$$

An unusual example is involved in the preparation of 5-methylfurfuryl-dimethylamine; the yield is 86%.[17]

$$CH_3{-}\text{(furan)} \;\rightarrow\; CH_3{-}\text{(furan)}{-}CH_2N(CH_3)_2$$

[17] E. L. Eliel and P. E. Peckham, *J. Am. Chem. Soc.*, **72**, 1209 (1950).

Since a β-amino ketone is decomposed by heat to give an amine and an α,β-unsaturated ketone, the Mannich reaction affords an indirect route to unsaturated ketones. Acetophenone, for instance, yields phenyl vinyl ketone.

$$C_6H_5COCH_3 \rightarrow C_6H_5COCH_2CH_2NH_2 \rightarrow C_6H_5COCH{=}CH_2$$

If the Mannich base contains reactive hydrogen atoms, a second basic group may be introduced.

$$RCOCH_2CH_2N(CH_3)_2{\cdot}HCl \xrightarrow[\text{(CH}_3)_2\text{NH}\cdot\text{HCl}]{\text{CH}_2\text{O}} RCOCH \begin{smallmatrix} CH_2N(CH_3)_2{\cdot}HCl \\ \\ CH_2N(CH_3)_2{\cdot}HCl \end{smallmatrix}$$

On the other hand, Mannich bases that are themselves secondary amines may react further to yield tertiary amines.

$$RCOCH_3 + CH_2O + RCOCH_2CH_2NHR'{\cdot}HCl \rightarrow$$

$$\begin{matrix} RCOCH_2CH_2 \\ \diagdown \\ NR'{\cdot}HCl + H_2O \\ \diagup \\ RCOCH_2CH_2 \end{matrix}$$

From these considerations it is evident that this method is widely applicable to synthetic problems. The condensation can be effected with basic or acidic catalysts, and the mechanism seems to depend on the pH value.[18]

Conjugate Addition

Enolates, like other so-called carbonyl reagents, may combine with α,β-unsaturated carbonyl compounds in the conjugate manner. An example is the addition of diethyl malonate to benzalacetophenone.

$$C_6H_5CH{=}CHCOC_6H_5 + CH_2(CO_2C_2H_5)_2 \rightarrow C_6H_5\underset{\underset{CH(CO_2C_2H_5)_2}{|}}{C}HCH_2COC_6H_5$$

This type of reaction was discovered by Claisen and later studied extensively by Michael. Many unsaturated ketones, esters, nitriles, and similar substances have been condensed in the 1,4-manner with a wide variety of active hydrogen compounds. In this type of condensation, generally called the Michael reaction (OR **10**, 178), the unsaturated

[18] T. F. Cummings and J. R. Shelton, *J. Org. Chem.*, **25**, 419 (1960).

compound is known as the *acceptor*, the active hydrogen compound as the *addendum*, and the product as the *adduct*. In the example given diethyl malonate is the addendum and benzalacetophenone the acceptor.

Among the most useful catalysts for the condensation are amines such as piperidine. Undesired reactions leading to ring closure, rearrangement, or the formation of trimolecular products generally can be avoided by recourse to such catalysts. Catalysts of this type, unfortunately, often fail to bring about reaction, and even in favorable cases reaction is slow. It is then necessary to use a sodium alkoxide; one-sixth to one-third of an equivalent of sodium ethoxide is generally employed. Condensations of this type, like the aldol condensation, are reversible.

Unsaturated esters are particularly useful in Michael condensations; an example is the addition of diethyl malonate to diethyl fumarate (OS I, 272).

$$C_2H_5O_2CCH{=}CHCO_2C_2H_5 \xrightarrow[CH_2(CO_2C_2H_5)_2]{NaOC_2H_5} \begin{array}{l} CH(CO_2C_2H_5)_2 \\ | \\ CHCO_2C_2H_5 \\ | \\ CH_2CO_2C_2H_5 \end{array}$$

Acetylenic esters enter into the Michael condensation readily. Of especial interest are the esters of propiolic acid, which offer the possibility of producing β-substituted acrylic esters. An example is the condensation of methyl propiolate with 1-tetralone.[19]

Diethyl methylmalonate, although it has but one active hydrogen atom, may nevertheless act as the addendum with acetylenic as well as ethylenic acceptors.

$$CH_3CH{=}CHCO_2C_2H_5 + CH_3CH(CO_2C_2H_5)_2 \rightarrow \begin{array}{l} CH_3CHCH_2CO_2C_2H_5 \\ | \\ CH_3C(CO_2C_2H_5)_2 \end{array}$$

$$CH_3C{\equiv}CCO_2C_2H_5 + CH_3CH(CO_2C_2H_5)_2 \rightarrow \begin{array}{l} CH_3C{=}CHCO_2C_2H_5 \\ | \\ CH_3C(CO_2C_2H_5)_2 \end{array}$$

Primary and secondary nitro compounds also function as addenda; triethylamine is a suitable catalyst. An example is the reaction between methyl acrylate and nitroethane.

[19] W. E. Bachmann, G. I. Fujimoto, and E. K. Raunio, *J. Am. Chem. Soc.*, **72**, 2533 (1950).

$$CH_2\!=\!CHCO_2CH_3 + C_2H_5NO_2 \rightarrow CH_3\underset{\underset{NO_2}{|}}{C}HCH_2CH_2CO_2CH_3$$

Another example is the condensation of 1,4-dinitrobutane with two equivalents of methyl vinyl ketone in the presence of a small amount of sodium hydroxide.[20]

$$\underset{\underset{CH_2}{|}}{\overset{NO_2}{|}} \underset{\underset{CH_2CH_2CH_2CH_2}{}}{\overset{NO_2}{|}} + 2CH_3COCH\!=\!CH_2 \rightarrow$$

$$CH_3COCH_2CH_2\underset{\underset{NO_2}{|}}{C}HCH_2CH_2\underset{\underset{NO_2}{|}}{C}HCH_2CH_2COCH_3$$

o-Nitrostyrene combines readily with ethyl cyanoacetate to give a condensation product into which two molecules of the styrene are incorporated.[21]

When benzalacetone is treated with 1-nitropropane in the presence of diethylamine, 5-nitro-4-phenyl-2-heptanone is produced in 90% yield.

$$C_6H_5CH\!=\!CHCOCH_3 + CH_3CH_2CH_2NO_2 \rightarrow \quad C_6H_5\underset{\underset{CH_3CH_2CHNO_2}{|}}{C}HCH_2COCH_3$$

The condensation of ethyl α,β-dibromopropionate with diethyl malonate to yield the ethyl ester of 1,1,2-cyclopropanetricarboxylic acid might be supposed to comprise dehydrobromination followed by conjugate condensation and, finally, ring closure.

Michael found support for this hypothesis by making the cyclopropane derivative from diethyl malonate and ethyl α-bromoacrylate. Also in the condensation of ethyl β-bromopropionate with ethyl acetoacetate to give

[20] H. Feuer and R. Harmetz, *J. Org. Chem.*, **26**, 1061 (1961).
[21] W. J. Dale and C. W. Strobel, *J. Am. Chem. Soc.*, **76**, 6172 (1954).

diethyl α-acetoglutarate (OS II, 263), it is possible that Michael condensation is involved.

$$CH_3COC\overline{H}CO_2C_2H_5 + BrCH_2CH_2CO_2C_2H_5 \rightarrow$$

$$CH_3COCHCO_2C_2H_5 + Br^-$$
$$\underset{CH_2CH_2CO_2C_2H_5}{|}$$

The bromo compound might yield ethyl acrylate by loss of hydrogen bromide, and the unsaturated ester might then condense with ethyl acetoacetate in the conjugate manner.

$$CH_3COCH_2CO_2C_2H_5 + CH_2{=}CHCO_2C_2H_5 \rightarrow CH_3COCHCO_2C_2H_5$$
$$\underset{CH_2CH_2CO_2C_2H_5}{|}$$

In the formation of α,β-unsaturated carbonyl compounds by the aldol type of condensation, it has been noted (p. 478) that the Michael reaction may follow. Usually, it can be avoided except with aldehydes. The condensation of diethyl malonate with formaldehyde, for example, does not stop at the first or aldol stage (OS I, 290). It appears to involve 1,2-addition, loss of water, and finally conjugate addition; the product is the ethyl ester of 1,1,3,3-propanetetracarboxylic acid.

$$H_2C{=}O + \underset{CO_2C_2H_5}{\overset{CO_2C_2H_5}{CH_2}} \longrightarrow H_2C{-}\underset{CO_2C_2H_5}{\overset{OH \quad CO_2C_2H_5}{CH}} \overset{-H_2O}{\longrightarrow}$$

$$\underset{CO_2C_2H_5}{\overset{CO_2C_2H_5}{CH_2{=}C}} + CH_2(CO_2C_2H_5)_2 \longrightarrow \underset{CH(CO_2C_2H_5)_2}{\overset{CH(CO_2C_2H_5)_2}{CH_2}}$$

Acetaldehyde combines with ethyl acetoacetate in a similar way (OS III, 317).

$$CH_3CHO + 2CH_3COCH_2CO_2C_2H_5 \xrightarrow{\text{piperidine}} CH_3COCHCO_2C_2H_5$$
$$\underset{CH_3COCHCO_2C_2H_5}{\overset{CH_3CH}{|}}$$

Condensation of malononitrile with formaldehyde would be expected to provide a route to vinylidene cyanide. Conjugate addition occurs so readily, however, that the product is the tetracyanopropane.

$$\text{CH}_2\!\!=\!\!\underset{\text{CN}}{\overset{\text{CN}}{\text{C}}} + \underset{\text{CN}}{\overset{\text{CN}}{\text{CH}_2}} \rightarrow \underset{\text{CN}}{\overset{\text{CN}}{\text{CHCH}_2}}\underset{\text{CN}}{\overset{\text{CN}}{\text{CH}}}$$

This condensation is reversed by heat, yielding vinylidene cyanide.[22]

If one mole of diethyl malonate is added dropwise to a solution containing two moles of formaldehyde in the presence of potassium bicarbonate, diethyl *bis*(hydroxymethyl)malonate is formed (OS **40**, 27; 75% yield).

$$\text{CH}_2(\text{CO}_2\text{C}_2\text{H}_5)_2 + 2\text{CH}_2\text{O} \rightarrow \underset{\text{HOCH}_2}{\overset{\text{HOCH}_2}{\text{C}}}\underset{\text{CO}_2\text{C}_2\text{H}_5}{\overset{\text{CO}_2\text{C}_2\text{H}_5}{}}$$

The use of methone in the characterization of aldehydes depends on a condensation of the Michael type.

$$(\text{CH}_3)_2\text{C}\underset{\text{CH}_2\text{CO}}{\overset{\text{CH}_2\text{CO}}{}}\text{CH}_2 \xrightarrow{\text{RCHO}} (\text{CH}_3)_2\text{C}\underset{\text{CH}_2\text{CO}}{\overset{\text{CH}_2\text{CO}}{}}\text{C}\!\!=\!\!\text{CHR} \xrightarrow{\text{methone}}$$

$$\left[(\text{CH}_3)_2\text{C}\underset{\text{CH}_2\text{CO}}{\overset{\text{CH}_2\text{CO}}{}}\text{CH} \right]_2 \text{CHR}$$

When acetone is condensed with two molecules of ethyl cyanoacetate in the presence of ammonia, β,β-dimethyl-α,α'-dicyanoglutarimide—known as Guareschi's imide—is produced.

$$\underset{\text{CH}_3}{\overset{\text{CH}_3}{\text{C}}}\!\!=\!\!\text{O} + 2\underset{}{\overset{\text{CN}}{\text{CH}_2\text{CO}_2\text{C}_2\text{H}_5}} + \text{NH}_3 \rightarrow$$

$$\underset{\text{CH}_3}{\overset{\text{CH}_3}{\text{C}}}\underset{\overset{\text{CHCO}}{\underset{\text{CN}}{}}}{\overset{\overset{\text{CN}}{}}{\overset{\text{CHCO}}{}}}\text{NH} + 2\text{C}_2\text{H}_5\text{OH} + \text{H}_2\text{O}$$

[22] A. E. Ardis, S. J. Averill, H. Gilbert, F. F. Miller, R. F. Schmidt, F. D. Stewart, and H. L. Trumbull, *J. Am. Chem. Soc.*, **72**, 1305 (1950).

Hydrolysis of Guareschi's imide yields β,β-dimethylglutaric acid. Other β,β-dialkylglutaric acids may be made in a similar way; if methyl ethyl ketone is employed, the product is β-ethyl-β-methylglutaric acid (OS **36**, 28).

A Michael condensation occurs as a side reaction in the preparation of benzalacetophenone from benzaldehyde and acetophenone. At temperatures below 30° benzalacetophenone—the result of 1,2-addition—is the principal product. At higher temperature conjugate addition of acetophenone to benzalacetophenone occurs.

$$C_6H_5CH{=}CHCOC_6H_5 + C_6H_5COCH_3 \rightarrow \begin{array}{c} C_6H_5COCH_2 \\ {\diagdown} \\ CHC_6H_5 \\ {\diagup} \\ C_6H_5COCH_2 \end{array}$$

It is to be noted that in this example the addendum is a simple ketone.

Another example of a Michael condensation with an unsaturated ketone is found in the synthesis of methone from malonic ester and mesityl oxide, which involves also subsequent ring closure, hydrolysis, and decarboxylation (OS II, 200).

$$\begin{array}{c} CH_3 \\ {\diagdown} \\ C{=}CHCOCH_3 + CH_2(CO_2C_2H_5)_2 \rightarrow \\ {\diagup} \\ CH_3 \end{array} \quad \begin{array}{c} CH_3 \\ {\diagdown} \\ CCH_2COCH_3 \\ {\diagup}\ | \\ CH_3\ CHCO_2C_2H_5 \\ | \\ CO_2C_2H_5 \end{array} \rightarrow$$

$$\begin{array}{c} CH_3 \quad CH_2 \\ {\diagdown}\ C\ {\diagup}\ CO \\ {\diagup}\quad|\qquad| \\ CH_3\ | \\ C_2H_5O_2CCH\quad CH_2 \\ {\diagdown}\ CO\ {\diagup} \end{array} \rightarrow CH_3 \begin{array}{c} CH_3 \quad CH_2 \\ {\diagdown}\ C\ {\diagup}\ CO \\ {\diagup}\quad|\qquad| \\ CH_2 \quad CH_2 \\ {\diagdown}\ CO\ {\diagup} \end{array}$$

Cyanoethylation

Active methylene compounds undergo cyanoethylation (OR **5**, 79) when treated with acrylonitrile in the presence of a strong base, notably aqueous trimethylbenzylammonium hydroxide ("Triton B"). Fluorene, for example, readily yields a dicyanoethyl derivative.

$$\text{(fluorene)} + 2CH_2{=}CHCN \rightarrow \text{(product)}$$
$$NCCH_2CH_2 \quad CH_2CH_2CN$$

1-Tetralone behaves similarly.

Nitromethane, having three active hydrogen atoms, gives rise to a tricyanoethyl derivative.

$$CH_3NO_2 + 3CH_2=CHCN \rightarrow (NCCH_2CH_2)_3CNO_2$$

As these examples show, the reaction generally produces polycyano-ethylation products when these are possible. Monocyanoethylation of 2-phenylcyclohexanone has been effected, however, in 70% yield.[23]

It might be expected that monocyanoethylation could be achieved by using a large excess of the carbonyl component. This procedure does not afford the desired compounds in high yield, however. Cyclohexanone gives the monocyanoethylation product in 47% yield when treated with acrylonitrile in the ratio of five moles of ketone to one mole of nitrile.[24]

Active hydrogen compounds of all types undergo cyanoethylation; indeed this reaction is one of the most searching tests for active hydrogen on carbon. An extreme example is chloroform, which is very different from the usual active hydrogen compounds. It is capable of under-going aldol condensation (p. 489), however, and can be cyanoethylated.

$$HCCl_3 + CH_2=CHCN \rightarrow Cl_3CCH_2CH_2CN$$

Diethyl acetosuccinate (p. 257) undergoes cyanoethylation, thus affording a convenient route to 1,2,4-butanetricarboxylic acid.

[23] W. E. Bachmann and L. B. Wick, *J. Am. Chem. Soc.*, **72**, 3388 (1950).
[24] H. E. Baumgarten and R. L. Eifert, *J. Am. Chem. Soc.*, **75**, 3015 (1953).

Crossed conjugated systems

Three or more conjugated multiple linkages that are not arranged in a linear manner form what is known as a *crossed conjugated system*. Important examples are diethyl benzalmalonate and ethyl α-cyanocinnamate.

$$
\begin{array}{cc}
\underset{\displaystyle |}{OC_2H_5} & \underset{\displaystyle |}{OC_2H_5} \\
C{=}O & C{=}O \\
C_6H_5CH{=}C & C_6H_5CH{=}C \\
C{=}O & C{\equiv}N \\
\underset{\displaystyle}{OC_2H_5} &
\end{array}
$$

A group of compounds containing a crossed conjugated system of a different type is formed by the divinyl ketones, of which dibenzalacetone is an example.

$$
\begin{array}{c}
C_6H_5CH{=}CH \\
\diagdown \\
C{=}O \\
\diagup \\
C_6H_5CH{=}CH
\end{array}
$$

The Michael condensation takes place with dibenzalacetone and similar pentadienones and active methylene compounds; in the presence of piperidine, dimethyl malonate for example combines with dibenzalacetone to yield each of the three possible products.

$$
\begin{array}{ccc}
CH(CO_2CH_3)_2 & CH(CO_2CH_3)_2 & \\
| & | & C_6H_5CHCH_2 \\
C_6H_5CHCH_2 & C_6H_5CH{-}CH_2 & (CH_3O_2C)_2C \quad\quad CO \\
\diagdown & \diagdown & C_6H_5CHCH_2 \\
CO & CO & \\
\diagup & & \\
C_6H_5CHCH_2 & C_6H_5CH{=}CH & \\
| & & \\
CH(CO_2CH_3)_2 & &
\end{array}
$$

Long conjugated systems

Long conjugated systems terminated by a carbonyl or similar group may undergo reaction at points farther away than the 4-position. Dimethyl malonate attacks a more distant position in certain cases; an example is its reaction with methyl sorbate.

$$
CH_3CH{=}CH{-}CH{=}CHCO_2CH_3 \rightarrow CH_3\underset{\displaystyle \underset{|}{CH(CO_2CH_3)_2}}{CH}CH{=}CHCH_2CO_2CH_3 \quad (72\%)
$$

Methyl 2,4,6-heptatrienoate reacts with diethyl malonate chiefly at the 7-position.[25]

$$CH_2{=}CHCH{=}CHCH{=}CHCO_2CH_3 + CH_2(CO_2C_2H_5)_2 \xrightarrow{\text{NaOCH}_3}$$

$$CH_2CH{=}CHCH{=}CHCH_2CO_2CH_3$$
$$|$$
$$CH(CO_2C_2H_5)_2$$

Similarly condensation with formaldehyde in the presence of sulfuric acid proceeds in the Prins manner (p. 157) and involves the terminal position also.

$$CH_2{=}CHCH{=}CHCH{=}CHCO_2CH_3 \xrightarrow{CH_2O}$$

Reactions entirely analogous to cyanoethylation are observed with 1-cyano-1,3-butadiene, a vinylog of acrylonitrile; 2-nitropropane reacts with one mole of the diene.

Diethyl malonate in a similar way combines with two moles of the diene.

Nitromethane, malonic ester, and similar compounds also combine with quinones, but the product usually is a complex mixture. 2,5-Dihydroxy-*p*-benzenediacetic acid can be made from benzoquinone and ethyl cyanoacetate, however, in 35% yields (OS III, 286).

[25] D. S. Acker and B. C. Anderson, *J. Org. Chem.*, **24**, 1162 (1959).

Conjugate Activation

Among the most remarkable of the peculiarities of unsaturated carbonyl compounds and similarly constituted substances is the activation of hydrogen atoms in positions remote from the activating group. This phenomenon is illustrated by the condensation of crotonaldehyde with benzaldehyde.

$$C_6H_5CHO + CH_3CH\!\!=\!\!CHCHO \rightarrow C_6H_5CH\!\!=\!\!CHCH\!\!=\!\!CHCHO + H_2O$$

Such effects are correlated by the *principle of vinylogy*, which refers to the observation that one functional group may influence another to which it is joined directly or through a chain of one or more vinylene links. In crotonaldehyde the methyl group is activated by the aldehyde group much as in acetaldehyde, of which it is a vinylog (p. 308). Reactions of this sort are ascribed to the intermediate formation of conjugated enolates produced by removal of an active hydrogen atom as a proton.

The transmission of activating influences through a conjugated chain, formulated empirically by the principle of vinylogy, is a necessary consequence of the factors promoting conjugate addition. The activation of the methyl group in acetaldehyde, for example, is associated with the electron deficit of the carbon atom to which it is attached. The methyl groups in crotonaldehyde and sorbaldehyde show a similar activity, since the carbon atoms to which they are joined are likewise electron-poor.

Esters exhibit the same phenomenon. Ethyl crotonate and ethyl sorbate, for example, undergo condensation with diethyl oxalate to give ethoxalyl derivatives.

$$\overset{\displaystyle CO_2C_2H_5}{\underset{\displaystyle CO_2C_2H_5}{|}} + \bar{C}H_2\!\!-\!\!CH\!\!=\!\!CH\!\!-\!\!CO_2C_2H_5 \rightarrow$$

$$\underset{\displaystyle COCO_2C_2H_5}{\overset{\displaystyle CH_2\!\!-\!\!CH\!\!=\!\!CH\!\!-\!\!CO_2C_2H_5}{|}} + C_2H_5O^-$$

$$\overset{\displaystyle CO_2C_2H_5}{\underset{\displaystyle CO_2C_2H_5}{|}} + \bar{C}H_2\!\!-\!\!CH\!\!=\!\!CH\!\!-\!\!CH\!\!=\!\!CH\!\!-\!\!CO_2C_2H_5 \rightarrow$$

$$\underset{\displaystyle COCO_2C_2H_5}{\overset{\displaystyle CH_2\!\!-\!\!CH\!\!=\!\!CH\!\!-\!\!CH\!\!=\!\!CH\!\!-\!\!CO_2C_2H_5}{|}} + C_2H_5O^-$$

These reactions further illustrate the principle of vinylogy; ethyl crotonate and ethyl sorbate are vinylogs of ethyl acetate.

Another interesting illustration is found in the glutaconic esters, which are to be regarded as vinylogous with malonic esters. The methylene group in diethyl glutaconate is similar to that in diethyl malonate. For example, sodium ethoxide and methyl iodide bring about methylation.

$$\begin{array}{c} \bar{C}HCO_2C_2H_5 \\ | \\ CH \\ \| \\ CHCO_2C_2H_5 \end{array} + CH_3I \rightarrow \begin{array}{c} CH_3CHCO_2C_2H_5 \\ | \\ CH \\ \| \\ CHCO_2C_2H_5 \end{array} + I^-$$

A second methyl group can also be introduced, but becomes attached to a different carbon atom. The enolate is a resonance hybrid of the two structures *a* and *b*; the methylation corresponds to structure *b*.

$$\begin{array}{c} CH_3\bar{C}CO_2C_2H_5 \\ | \\ CH \\ \| \\ CHCO_2C_2H_5 \\ a \end{array} \leftrightarrow \begin{array}{c} CH_3CCO_2C_2H_5 \\ \| \\ CH \\ | \\ H\bar{C}CO_2C_2H_5 \\ b \end{array} \xrightarrow{CH_3I} \begin{array}{c} CH_3CCO_2C_2H_5 \\ \| \\ CH \\ | \\ CH_3CHCO_2C_2H_5 \end{array} + I^-$$

The condensation of TNT, a vinylog of nitromethane, with benzaldehyde to give 2,4,6-trinitrostilbene illustrates the fact that aromatic rings likewise are capable of relaying activating influences.

$$O_2N \underset{NO_2}{\overset{NO_2}{\bigcirc}} CH_3 + C_6H_5CHO \xrightarrow[\substack{\text{alcohol or} \\ \text{benzene}}]{\text{piperidine}} O_2N \underset{NO_2}{\overset{NO_2}{\bigcirc}} CH=CHC_6H_5 + H_2O$$

Anthrone is a typical active methylene compound, being capable of giving the reactions of both the keto and enol forms. The enol, anthranol, can be obtained from anthrone by the action of alkali followed by precipitation with acid. In solution these forms appear to be in tautomeric equilibrium.

Anthrone ⇌ Anthranol

Ring closures are known that consist of conjugate addition of an active methylene component to an α,β-unsaturated carbonyl compound or its equivalent, i.e., a Michael reaction; the formation of isophorone from phorone is an example.

Phorone　　　　　　　　　　　　　　Isophorone

Elbs reaction

The Elbs reaction, useful in the preparation of certain polynuclear aromatic hydrocarbons, is exemplified by cyclization of o-methylbenzophenone to anthracene (OR **1,** 129).

This reaction, a cyclodehydration, occurs with diaryl ketones having a methyl or methylene group *ortho* to the ketone group. In other words, the methyl or methylene group that takes part in the intramolecular condensation derives its activity from a distant carbonyl group. Since the reaction is a high-temperature pyrolysis (400 to 450°) it usually gives the products in low yields—frequently only a few per cent. It has played an important role, however, in connection with the synthesis of certain of the more complex aromatic hydrocarbons such as 1,2,5,6-dibenzanthracene, which is made rather easily from 2-naphthoyl chloride and 2-methylnaphthalene. The ketone produced by the Friedel-Crafts condensation is pyrolyzed to the desired hydrocarbon in yields as high as 32%.

The Elbs reaction has a formal resemblance to the Michael reaction. It involves no catalyst, however, and occurs only at high temperatures.

Ring Closures of the Aldol Type

Intramolecular aldol condensation may be effected with suitably constituted compounds such as 1,5-diketones to yield cyclohexene derivatives.

The condensation product of ethyl acetoacetate with acetaldehyde (p. 507), for example, undergoes ring closure when treated with sulfuric acid in glacial acetic acid; one of the ester groups is removed at the same time (OS III, 317; 50% yield).

$$CH_3CO \diagdown CHCO_2C_2H_5$$

$$CH_3C \overset{O}{\underset{\parallel}{C}} \quad CHCH_3$$

$$CHCO_2C_2H_5 \quad \rightarrow$$

$$CO \diagdown$$

$$CH \quad CH_2$$

$$CH_3C \quad CHCH_3$$

$$CHCO_2C_2H_5$$

If the keto ester is saponified and the resulting acid heated with sulfuric acid, 3,5-dimethyl-2-cyclohexen-1-one is produced (OS III, 317; 55% yield).

$$CH_3 \quad CH_3 \quad \rightarrow \quad CH_3 \quad CH_3$$

$$CO_2H$$

In the preparation of 2-carbethoxy-Δ^2-cyclohexenone, ethyl 3-keto-7,7-diethoxyheptanoate is heated in acetone in the presence of p-toluene-sulfonic acid monohydrate.[26]

$$H_2C \diagup \overset{O}{\underset{\parallel}{C}} \diagdown CH_2CO_2C_2H_5$$

$$H_2C \quad CH(OC_2H_5)_2$$

$$CH_2 \quad \rightarrow$$

$$H_2C \diagup \overset{O}{\underset{\parallel}{C}} \diagdown CH_2CO_2C_2H_5$$

$$H_2C \quad CHO$$

$$CH_2 \quad \rightarrow$$

$$CO_2C_2H_5$$

Condensation of cyclohexanone with benzalacetophenone involves a ring closure of the aldol type.[27]

$$\text{cyclohexanone} =O + C_6H_5CH=CHCOC_6H_5 \rightarrow$$

$$OCC_6H_5 \diagdown$$

$$=O \quad CH_2 \rightarrow$$

$$CHC_6H_5$$

$$CO \diagup C_6H_5 \diagdown C_6H_5$$

[26] J. E. Brenner, *J. Org. Chem.*, **26**, 22 (1961).
[27] A. C. Cope, F. S. Fawcett, and G. Munn, *J. Am. Chem. Soc.*, **72**, 3399 (1950).

When benzalphthalide is condensed with phenylmagnesium bromide and the mixture is decomposed with sulfuric acid, 2,3-diphenylindone is produced. This compound is the aldol condensation product of the diketone presumably formed as an intermediate (OS III, 353; 71% yield).

An example of the use of the Mannich reaction to form rings is the preparation of 3,5-dimethyl-2,6-diphenyl-4-piperidone (75% yield) from diethyl ketone, benzaldehyde, and ammonia.

The formation of 2-methylindole from o-acetotoluide is formally similar to the aldol type of reaction. The nuclear methyl group would hardly be expected to be reactive, however. Actually the cyclization requires heating with sodium amide at 240 to 260° (OS III, 597); the yield is 83%.

The formation of indole by heating the formyl derivative of o-toluidine (OS III, 479; 79% yield) is similar.

A characteristic reaction of α-diketones having the group $-CH_2COCO-$ is quinone formation by a twofold aldol condensation. Methyl phenyl diketone, for example, condenses (under the influence of alkaline catalysts) to 2,5-diphenylquinone.

$$2C_6H_5COCOCH_3 \rightarrow C_6H_5C \begin{array}{c} O \\ \| \\ C \\ \diagup \quad \diagdown \\ CH \\ \| \qquad \| \\ CH \quad CC_6H_5 \\ \diagdown \quad \diagup \\ C \\ \| \\ O \end{array} CH \quad + 2H_2O$$

A similar condensation is involved in the preparation of tetraphenyl-cyclopentadienone from benzil and dibenzyl ketone (OS III, 806; 96% yield).

$$C_6H_5COCOC_6H_5 + C_6H_5CH_2COCH_2C_6H_5 \xrightarrow{KOH} \begin{array}{c} C_6H_5 \qquad C_6H_5 \\ C_6H_5 \diagdown \quad \diagup C_6H_5 \\ C \\ \| \\ O \end{array} + 2H_2O$$

A methyl or methylene ketone should be capable of forming a benzene ring by three successive aldol condensations, the last of which is intramolecular. The preparation of mesitylene from acetone is well known (OS I, 341). The ring closure takes place under the influence of sulfuric acid and appears to depend on the activation of a methyl group by a distant carbonyl group (p. 513). A large amount of tar is formed, presumably by linear aldol condensation; the yield of mesitylene seldom exceeds 15%.

$$2 \begin{array}{c} CH_3 \\ | \\ CH_3C{=}O \end{array} \rightarrow \begin{array}{c} CH_3 \quad CH_3 \\ | \qquad | \\ CH_3C{=}CHCO \end{array} \xrightarrow{CH_3COCH_3}$$

$$\begin{array}{c} CH \\ \diagup \quad \diagdown \\ CH_3C \qquad CCH_3 \\ | \qquad \| \\ HCH_2 \quad CH \\ \diagdown \quad \diagup \\ O{=}CCH_3 \end{array} \rightarrow \begin{array}{c} CH_3 \qquad CH_3 \\ \hexagon \\ CH_3 \end{array}$$

The closure step presumably would involve a protonated enol.

$$
\begin{array}{c}
\text{CH} \\
\text{CH}_3\text{C} \quad\quad \text{CCH}_3 \\
\text{CH}_2 \quad \text{CH}_2 \\
\text{HOC}^+ \\
\text{CH}_3
\end{array}
\xrightarrow[-\text{H}^+]{-\text{H}_2\text{O}}
\begin{array}{c}
\text{CH} \\
\text{CH}_3\text{C} \quad\quad \text{CCH}_3 \\
\text{HC} \quad\quad \text{CH} \\
\text{C} \\
\text{CH}_3
\end{array}
$$

The production of 1,3,5-triarylbenzenes is general for methyl aryl ketones; acetophenone, for example, yields 1,3,5-triphenylbenzene.

$$3\text{CH}_3\text{COC}_6\text{H}_5 \rightarrow \text{C}_6\text{H}_5\underset{\text{C}_6\text{H}_5}{\bigcirc}\text{C}_6\text{H}_5 + 3\text{H}_2\text{O}$$

As in the acetoacetic ester condensation (p. 483), ethyl formate leads to unstable hydroxymethylene compounds. For example, the derivative obtained from acetone condenses with itself to give 1,3,5-triacetylbenzene (OS III, 829; 38% yield); presumably the following steps are involved.

$$
2\text{CH}_3\text{COCH}_2\text{CHO} \xrightarrow{-\text{H}_2\text{O}}
\begin{array}{c}
\text{CHO} \\
\text{CH}_3\text{COC}{=}\text{CHCH}_2\text{COCH}_3
\end{array}
\xrightarrow{\text{CH}_3\text{COCH}_2\text{CHO}}
$$

$$
\begin{array}{c}
\text{CH}_2\text{COCH}_3 \\
\text{CH} \quad\quad \text{CHO} \\
\text{CH}_3\text{COC} \quad\quad \text{CCOCH}_3 \\
\text{CH}
\end{array}
\xrightarrow{-\text{H}_2\text{O}}
\text{CH}_3\text{CO}\underset{}{\overset{\text{COCH}_3}{\bigcirc}}\text{COCH}_3
$$

In the presence of sulfuric acid and various other catalysts (CR **60**, 313) cyclohexanone condenses with itself to yield dodecahydrotriphenylene.

$$3\,\bigcirc\!\!=\!\!O \rightarrow \text{(dodecahydrotriphenylene)} + 3\text{H}_2\text{O}$$

An unusual reaction occurs when acetone is treated with the sodium derivative of nitromalonaldehyde (OS **32**, 95); p-nitrophenol is the product.

$$O=C\begin{array}{c} CH_3 \\ \diagdown \\ \diagup \\ CH_3 \end{array} + \left[\begin{array}{c} OCH \\ \diagdown \\ CNO_2 \\ \diagup \\ OCH \end{array} \right]^{-} Na^{+} \xrightarrow{2H_2O}$$

$$\left[\begin{array}{c} CH=CH \\ O=C \diagup \quad \diagdown CNO_2 \\ \diagdown \quad \diagup \\ CH=CH \end{array} \right]^{-} Na^{+} \xrightarrow{H_2O} HO\text{—}\bigcirc\text{—}NO_2$$

When cyclanones are employed, *m*-bridged nitrophenols are produced.

$$(CH_2)n \begin{array}{c} CH_2CH_2 \\ \diagup \quad \diagdown \\ \quad \quad CO \\ \diagdown \quad \diagup \\ CH_2CH_2 \end{array} \rightarrow (CH_2)n \begin{array}{c} CH_2 \\ \diagup \\ \\ \diagdown \\ CH_2 \end{array} HO\text{—}\bigcirc\text{—}NO_2$$

The sodium derivative of nitromalonaldehyde (CR **60**, 261) is prepared from mucobromic (p. 65).

$$\begin{array}{c} BrCCO_2H \\ \| \\ BrCCHO \end{array} \xrightarrow{NaNO_2} \left[\begin{array}{c} OCH \\ \diagdown \\ CNO_2 \\ \diagup \\ OCH \end{array} \right]^{-} Na^{+}$$

Hooker oxidation

One of the most interesting transformations in the field of quinone chemistry was discovered by Hooker (QR **10**, 261) in a study of the oxidation of lapachol and related derivatives of 2-hydroxy-1,4-naphthoquinone. The over-all change is the elimination of a methylene group and interchange of the positions of the hydroxyl and alkyl groups.

$$\bigcirc\hspace{-1em}\bigcirc \begin{array}{c} O \\ \| \\ OH \\ CH_2R \\ \| \\ O \end{array} \rightarrow \bigcirc\hspace{-1em}\bigcirc \begin{array}{c} O \\ \| \\ R \\ OH \\ \| \\ O \end{array}$$

This remarkable transformation has been shown to involve a series of reactions including ring opening and reclosure, the closure being of the aldol type.[28]

[28] L. F. Fieser and M. Fieser, *J. Am. Chem. Soc.*, **70**, 3215 (1948).

Not the least remarkable feature of the Hooker oxidation is that it can be repeated as long as there is a methylene group at position 3. By a sevenfold performance of the operation the 3-*n*-heptyl derivative is converted into 2-hydroxy-1,4-naphthoquinone.

Magnesium and Zinc Enolates

As was mentioned earlier, certain highly hindered ketones react with Grignard reagents to form magnesium enolates. Enolates of this type may be produced also by the action of magnesium or Grignard reagents on α-halo ketones (p. 450). The magnesium enolate of acetomesitylene may be made from acetomesitylene or from α-bromoacetomesitylene.

Enolates of this type behave in many reactions as though they were true Grignard reagents. The acetomesitylene reagent, for example, reacts with aldehydes and ketones to yield keto carbinols and with carbon dioxide to give mesitoylacetic acid.

With nitriles that possess α-hydrogen atoms the primary side reaction is replacement of an active hydrogen atom. The resulting salt, by combining with a molecule of nitrile, leads to the formation of a β-ketonitrile. When phenylacetonitrile is treated with methylmagnesium iodide, for example, α-phenylacetylphenylacetonitrile is the chief (71 %) product, benzyl methyl ketone being formed in low (8 %) yield.[29]

$$C_6H_5CH_2CN + CH_3MgI \rightarrow C_6H_5\underset{\underset{MgI}{|}}{C}HCN + CH_4$$

$$C_6H_5\underset{\underset{MgI}{|}}{C}HCN + C_6H_5CH_2CN \rightarrow C_6H_5CH_2\overset{\overset{NMgI}{||}}{C}\underset{\underset{C_6H_5}{|}}{C}HCN \xrightarrow{H_2O} C_6H_5CH_2\overset{\overset{O}{||}}{C}\underset{\underset{C_6H_5}{|}}{C}HCN$$

Ivanov reagent

A similar type of reagent was developed by Ivanov, who found that phenylacetic acid decomposes two moles of a Grignard reagent to generate a magnesium enolate of the halomagnesium salt of phenylacetic acid.

$$C_6H_5CH_2CO_2H + 2RMgX \rightarrow C_6H_5\underset{\underset{MgX}{|}}{C}HCO_2MgX + 2RH$$

This substance as well as the sodium salt behaves as a Grignard reagent. Its reaction with aldehydes and ketones furnishes a route to α-aryl-β-hydroxypropionic acids. For example, it reacts with 2,5-dimethoxy-benzophenone to give β-(2,5-dimethoxyphenyl)-α,β-diphenylhydracrylic acid.[30]

[29] C. R. Hauser and W. J. Humphlett, *J. Org. Chem.*, **15**, 359 (1950).
[30] C. F. Koelsch and E. J. Prill, *J. Am. Chem. Soc.*, **67**, 1296, 1299 (1945).

In such situations, in which two diastereoisomers are possible, the reaction is stereoselective; usually only one isomer is isolated.[31]

Like other enolates the Ivanov reagents undergo coupling with iodine. The reagent from phenylacetic acid, for example, gives α,β-diphenyl-succinic acid.[32]

$$2C_6H_5CHCO_2MgCl \rightarrow C_6H_5CHCO_2H$$
$$\underset{MgCl}{|} \qquad\qquad \underset{C_6H_5CHCO_2H}{|}$$

Reformatsky Reaction

Zinc enolates, made by treating α-halo esters with zinc, have found extensive use in synthesis. The method of Reformatsky (OR **1**, 1) involves the preparation of the enolate in the presence of the aldehyde or ketone with which it is to react. An example is the formation of ethyl β-hydroxy-β-phenylpropionate from benzaldehyde and ethyl bromoacetate (OS III, 408); the yield is 64%.

$$C_6H_5CHO + BrCH_2CO_2C_2H_5 + Zn \longrightarrow$$

$$\underset{C_6H_5CHCH_2CO_2C_2H_5}{\overset{OZnBr}{|}} \xrightarrow{H_2O} \underset{C_6H_5CHCH_2CO_2C_2H_5}{\overset{OH}{|}}$$

Although ethyl bromoacetate is the usual reagent, other α-halogen esters, particularly the bromo esters, can serve also. Frequently the hydroxy ester is not isolated, the product being the corresponding unsaturated ester. Condensation of 2-thiophenecarboxaldehyde with ethyl bromoacetate yields ethyl β-(2-thienyl)acrylate (55%).[33]

From 2-ethylhexanal and ethyl α-bromopropionate it is possible to prepare ethyl 4-ethyl-2-methyl-2-octenoate (OS **37**, 37).

[31] H. E. Zimmerman and M. D. Traxler, *J. Am. Chem. Soc.*, **79**, 1920 (1957).
[32] F. F. Blicke, P. E. Wright, and W. A. Gould, *J. Org. Chem.*, **26**, 2114 (1961).
[33] R. E. Miller and F. F. Nord, *J. Org. Chem.*, **15**, 89 (1950).

$$CH_3(CH_2)_3CHCHO + BrCHCO_2C_2H_5 \xrightarrow[\text{(2) } H_2O]{\text{(1) Zn}}$$
$$\qquad\qquad |\qquad\qquad\qquad\quad |$$
$$\qquad CH_3CH_2\qquad\qquad CH_3$$

$$\qquad\qquad\quad OH$$
$$\qquad\qquad\quad |$$
$$CH_3(CH_2)_3CHCHCHCO_2C_2H_5 \xrightarrow{-H_2O} CH_3(CH_2)_3CHCH{=}CCO_2C_2H_5$$
$$\qquad\qquad\; |\quad\; |\qquad\qquad\qquad\qquad\qquad |\qquad\quad |$$
$$\qquad\quad CH_3CH_2\;\; CH_3\qquad\qquad\qquad\qquad CH_3CH_2\quad CH_3$$

Application of the Reformatsky method to ketones is illustrated by the preparation of ethyl β-hydroxy-β-phenylbutyrate from zinc, acetophenone, and ethyl bromoacetate.

$$\qquad\qquad\qquad\qquad\qquad\qquad\qquad\quad OZnBr$$
$$\qquad\qquad\qquad\qquad\qquad\qquad\qquad\quad |$$
$$C_6H_5COCH_3 + BrCH_2CO_2C_2H_5 \xrightarrow{Zn} C_6H_5C{-}CH_2CO_2C_2H_5 \longrightarrow$$
$$\qquad\qquad\qquad\qquad\qquad\qquad\qquad\quad |$$
$$\qquad\qquad\qquad\qquad\qquad\qquad\qquad\quad CH_3$$

$$\qquad\qquad\qquad\qquad\qquad\qquad\qquad OH$$
$$\qquad\qquad\qquad\qquad\qquad\qquad\qquad |$$
$$\qquad\qquad\qquad\qquad\qquad\qquad C_6H_5C{-}CH_2CO_2C_2H_5$$
$$\qquad\qquad\qquad\qquad\qquad\qquad\qquad |$$
$$\qquad\qquad\qquad\qquad\qquad\qquad\qquad CH_3$$

The use of zinc in the Reformatsky method has the advantage that the organozinc intermediate has little tendency to attack ordinary esters. This fact makes the method possible; otherwise, the organozinc compound would be unstable, since it contains groups that would interact.

Ester groups having branched radicals are less sensitive and may permit successful operation even with nitriles. An example is the condensation of sec-butyl α-bromopropionate with n-capronitrile (OS **35**, 15; 58% yield).

$$\qquad\qquad\qquad\qquad\quad CH_3$$
$$\qquad\qquad\qquad\qquad\quad |$$
$$CH_3(CH_2)_4CN + BrCHCO_2CHC_2H_5 + Zn \longrightarrow$$
$$\qquad\qquad\qquad\qquad\quad |$$
$$\qquad\qquad\qquad\qquad\quad CH_3$$

$$\qquad\qquad NZnBr$$
$$\qquad\qquad \|$$
$$CH_3(CH_2)_4CCHCO_2CHC_2H_5 \xrightarrow{H_2O} CH_3(CH_2)_4COCHCO_2CHC_2H_5$$
$$\qquad\qquad\quad |\qquad |\qquad\qquad\qquad\qquad\qquad\quad |\qquad\; |$$
$$\qquad\qquad\; CH_3\;\; CH_3\qquad\qquad\qquad\qquad\quad CH_3\;\; CH_3$$

It is true that a few esters can be used instead of aldehydes or ketones, but these are formates, oxalates, or α-alkoxy esters—compounds in which the ester carbonyl group possesses usually high activity. An extremely interesting example is the condensation of ethyl bromoacetate with ethyl formate. The expected aldehyde ester is not obtained; under the conditions of the experiment it undergoes ring closure to give the ethyl ester of trimesic acid.

$$\text{C}_2\text{H}_5\text{OCHO} + \text{BrCH}_2\text{CO}_2\text{C}_2\text{H}_5 \xrightarrow{\text{Zn}} \overset{\overset{\textstyle\text{OZnBr}}{\textstyle|}}{\text{C}_2\text{H}_5\text{OCHCH}_2\text{CO}_2\text{C}_2\text{H}_5}$$

$$\Big\downarrow \text{H}_2\text{O}$$

OCHCH$_2$CO$_2$C$_2$H$_5$

γ-Halocrotonic esters, being vinylogs of haloacetic esters, might be expected to serve in Reformatsky reactions likewise. Reactions of this type are known, one of which involves the condensation of methyl γ-bromocrotonate with 2-tetralone; the expected hydroxy acid is produced in 34% yield.[34]

Ethyl γ-bromo-β-methylcrotonate combines with isovaleraldehyde in a similar way.[35]

$$\underset{\underset{\textstyle\text{CH}_3}{\textstyle|}}{\text{CH}_3\text{CHCH}_2\text{CHO}} \quad \text{and} \quad \underset{\underset{\textstyle\text{CH}_3}{\textstyle|}}{\text{BrCH}_2\text{C}=\text{CHCO}_2\text{C}_2\text{H}_5} \xrightarrow[\text{(2) H}_2\text{O}]{\text{(1) Zn}}$$

$$\underset{\underset{\textstyle\text{CH}_3}{\textstyle|}\underset{\textstyle\text{OH}}{\textstyle|}\underset{\textstyle\text{CH}_3}{\textstyle|}}{\text{CH}_3\text{CHCH}_2\text{CHCH}_2\text{C}=\text{CHCO}_2\text{C}_2\text{H}_5}$$

Tertiary amides of bromoacetic acid have given satisfactory results in the Reformatsky reaction; an example is the condensation of cyclohexanone with N,N-diethylbromoacetamide.[36]

$$\text{and} \quad \text{BrCH}_2\text{CON(C}_2\text{H}_5)_2 \xrightarrow[\text{(2) H}_2\text{O}]{\text{(1) Zn}}$$

[34] W. G. Dauben and R. Teranishi, *J. Org. Chem.*, **16**, 550 (1951).

[35] L. Canonica and M. Martinolli, *Gazz. chim. ital.*, **83**, 431 (1953).

[36] N. L. Drake, C. M. Eaker, and W. Shenk, *J. Am. Chem. Soc.*, **70**, 677 (1948).

It is noteworthy that few Reformatsky reactions of the conjugate type have been observed. The following results with benzalacetophenone are illustrative.

α-Halo Ester	% 1,2-Addition	% 1,4-Addition
$BrCH_2CO_2CH_3$	100	0
$CH_3CHBrCO_2CH_3$	55	45
$CH_3CH_2CHBrCO_2CH_3$	50	50
$(CH_3)_2CBrCO_2CH_3$	0	100
$BrCH(CO_2CH_3)_2$	0	100

These findings may be accounted for on the assumption that the organo-zinc compounds in the enolate form are coordinated with the carbonyl compound of the ketone. It is postulated that 1,2-addition proceeds by way of a *quasi* six-membered ring. It is clear that substituents on the carbon atom of the ester would oppose such a ring closure.

Reactions of Phenolates

Just as phenols can be compared to enols so may the phenolates be expected to react in ways similar to those outlined for enolates. Among the important condensation reactions of phenolates is that with formaldehyde. If carefully controlled, it may serve to produce relatively simple alkylation products. This reaction, known as the Lederer-Manasse reaction, is brought about by alkaline catalysts and affords many methylol derivatives in satisfactory yields. An example is the conversion of *o*-ethylphenol into a dimethylol derivative.[37]

[37] I. W. Ruderman, *J. Am. Chem. Soc.*, **70**, 1662 (1948).

The monomethyl ether of hydroquinone gives the dimethylol derivative in 79% yield.[38]

$$\text{OH} \qquad \text{OH}$$

$$\underset{\text{OCH}_3}{\bigcirc} \rightarrow \text{HOCH}_2\underset{\text{OCH}_3}{\bigcirc}\text{CH}_2\text{OH}$$

Phenol-aldehyde resins

The condensation of phenols with aldehydes to produce polymers may be catalyzed by either bases or acids. In the case of formaldehyde and phenol, for example, it is believed that the methylol compounds (p. 526) undergo further condensation in such a way as to join phenol nuclei by methylene links. The first important industrial synthetic polymers, the Bakelite polymers, were of this type. Since the nuclei are trifunctional and the aldehyde is bifunctional, cross-linked polymers are produced. In condensations that are catalyzed by bases the low-molecular-weight polymers are soluble in alkali and are thought to be of the following type.

In the presence of acidic catalysts condensation involves ether formation.[39]

Carboxylation

Certain hydroxybenzoic acids can be made by the introduction of a carboxyl group into a phenol, as illustrated by the use of carbon tetrachloride in the Reimer-Tiemann method (p. 269). A much better procedure for this purpose is Schmitt's modification of the Kolbe synthesis (CR **57**, 583). In the preparation of salicylic acid by Kolbe's original procedure sodium phenoxide was treated with carbon dioxide under pressure at 180 to 200°. The method had the disadvantage that it yielded only one-half mole of acid for each mole of phenol.

$$\text{ONa}$$

$$2\text{C}_6\text{H}_5\text{ONa} + \text{CO}_2 \rightarrow \underset{}{\bigcirc}\text{CO}_2\text{Na} + \text{C}_6\text{H}_5\text{OH}$$

[38] W. J. Moran, E. C. Schreiber, E. Engel, D. C. Behn, and J. L. Yamins, *J. Am. Chem. Soc.*, **74**, 127 (1952).

[39] J. S. Rodia and J. H. Freeman, *J. Org. Chem.*, **24**, 21 (1959).

The Schmitt modification avoids this loss of phenol by use of a lower temperature and a longer time of reaction. Schmitt had the idea that the first stage of the process involved the formation of phenyl sodium carbonate $C_6H_5OCO_2Na$, which then rearranged, and that by use of a low temperature at the outset the formation of the carbonate could be completed before rearrangement began.

The conversion of two moles of sodium phenoxide into phenol by one mole of salicylic acid shows that the phenolic hydroxyl group in the latter is more acidic than that in phenol, which would be expected on the basis of vinylogy (p. 513).

The Kolbe-Schmitt reaction proceeds somewhat differently if the potassium salt is used; at temperatures above 100° isomerization to p-hydroxybenzoic acid occurs. The latter is made in 80% yield by heating potassium salicylate at 230° (OS II, 341).

p-Hydroxybenzoic acid can be obtained in nearly quantitative yield by heating the dry dipotassium salt of salicylic acid with carbon dioxide.

p-Cresol in which the p-position is blocked gives 2-hydroxy-5-methylbenzoic acid in yields as high as 87% when a mixture of the cresol and potassium carbonate is heated for 8 hours at 175° under a carbon dioxide pressure of 250 pounds per square inch.[40]

The migration of carboxylate groups is not limited to phenolic compounds.[41] Potassium terephthalate, for instance, can be made by heating potassium phthalate.[42]

[40] D. Cameron, H. Jeskey, and O. Baine, *J. Org. Chem.*, **15**, 233 (1950).
[41] B. Raecke, *Angew. Chem.*, **70**, 1 (1958).
[42] See Y. Ogata, M. Hojo, and M. Morikawa, *J. Org. Chem.*, **25**, 2082 (1960).

When the isomerization is conducted in an atmosphere of $^{14}CO_2$, the product is radioactive; it is concluded that the reaction is intermolecular.[43]

Potassium 1,8-naphthalenedicarboxylate yields the 2,6-dicarboxylate (OS 40, 71).

Potassium diphenate isomerizes to the 4,4'-isomer.

The Kolbe-Schmitt reaction occurs with remarkable ease with o- or p-dihydroxybenzenes. Catechol, for example, is converted into protocatechuic acid merely by heating with aqueous ammonium carbonate at 140°.

Similarly, pyrogallol yields pyrogallolcarboxylic acid.

β-Resorcylic acid is obtained in 60% yield (OS II, 557) by passing a stream of carbon dioxide through a boiling aqueous solution of the sodium salt of resorcinol; the reaction is complete in 30 minutes.

[43] O. Riedel and H. Kienitz, *Angew. Chem.*, **72**, 738 (1960).

A remarkable example of the Kolbe-Schmitt synthesis is the carbonation of 2-naphthol. At 120 to 145° under pressure the product is 2-hydroxy-1-naphthoic acid; at 280 to 290° 3-hydroxy-2-naphthoic acid is produced.

The formation of the 2,3-derivative is notable because substitution in the 3-position of 2-naphthol is exceedingly rare. The result suggests that the Kolbe reaction is reversible, that the carboxyl group enters the 1-position readily but reversibly, whereas its introduction into the 3-position, though difficult, is essentially irreversible. A similar explanation may be advanced for the isomerization of potassium salicylate to potassium p-hydroxybenzoate.

A reaction that is similar to the Kolbe-Schmitt process occurs when a mixture of sodium ethyl carbonate and phenol is heated at 175°; salicylic acid is produced in 95%.[44]

[44] J. I. Jones, *Chem. and Ind.*, 228 (1958).

20

Nitrogen analogs of carbonyl compounds

Compounds containing the N=O group may be regarded as nitrogen analogs of carbonyl compounds. Many of the reactions of nitrites, nitrous acid, and nitroso compounds are indeed similar to those observed with carbonyl compounds.

Nitroso Compounds

Nitroso compounds react with hydroxylamine in a manner similar to that observed with carbonyl compounds. This reagent, for example, converts nitrosobenzene into benzenediazoic acid, formally similar to an oxime.

$$C_6H_5N\!=\!O + H_2NOH \rightarrow C_6H_5N\!=\!NOH + H_2O$$

Similarly, aniline and nitrosobenzene yield azobenzene.

$$C_6H_5N\!=\!O + H_2NC_6H_5 \rightarrow C_6H_5N\!=\!NC_6H_5 + H_2O$$

p-Aminobenzoic acid behaves in an analogous fashion to give p-phenyl-azobenzoic acid in 61 % yield (OS III, 711).

$$C_6H_5N\!=\!O + H_2N\!\!\left\langle\!\!\bigcirc\!\!\right\rangle\!\!CO_2H \rightarrow C_6H_5N\!=\!N\!\!\left\langle\!\!\bigcirc\!\!\right\rangle\!\!CO_2H + H_2O$$

The formation of azoxybenzene from nitrosobenzene and β-phenyl-hydroxylamine is similar.

$$C_6H_5N\!=\!O + C_6H_5NHOH \rightarrow C_6H_5N\!=\!NC_6H_5 + H_2O$$
$$\downarrow$$
$$O$$

Certain nitroso compounds simulate the behavior of carbonyl compounds with enolates; an example is the condensation of p-nitrosodimethylaniline with TNT. The reaction provides an indirect method of oxidizing an active methyl group to an aldehyde group, since the Schiff base formed initially is hydrolyzed readily to the corresponding aldehyde.

$$(CH_3)_2NC_6H_4N=O + CH_3\text{—}\underset{O_2N}{\overset{O_2N}{\bigcirc}}\text{—}NO_2 \xrightarrow{-H_2O}$$

$$(CH_3)_2NC_6H_4N=CH\text{—}\underset{O_2N}{\overset{O_2N}{\bigcirc}}\text{—}NO_2$$

2,4-Dinitrobenzaldehyde (OS II, 223) is made by a similar method. The Schiff base is produced by condensing 2,4-dinitrotoluene with p-nitroso-dimethylaniline in the presence of sodium carbonate. Hydrolysis of the base in the presence of hydrochloric acid furnishes the aldehyde in 32% yield.

$$(CH_3)_2NC_6H_4NO + CH_3\text{—}\underset{NO_2}{\overset{}{\bigcirc}}\text{—}NO_2 \xrightarrow{Na_2CO_3}$$

$$(CH_3)_2NC_6H_4N=CH\text{—}\underset{NO_2}{\overset{}{\bigcirc}}\text{—}NO_2$$

Nitrosobenzene combines with malonic ester in much the same way.

$$C_6H_5N=O + CH_2(CO_2C_2H_5)_2 \rightarrow C_6H_5N=C(CO_2C_2H_5)_2 + H_2O$$

The use of aromatic nitroso compounds in this fashion is peculiarly suitable for the synthesis of vicinal triketones. It serves, for example, to produce 2,3,4-pentanetrione.

$$\underset{CH_3CO}{\overset{CH_3CO}{>}}CH_2 + ONC_6H_4N(CH_3)_2 \xrightarrow{-H_2O}$$

$$\underset{CH_3CO}{\overset{CH_3CO}{>}}C=NC_6H_4N(CH_3)_2 \xrightarrow[HCl]{H_2O} \underset{CH_3CO}{\overset{CH_3CO}{>}}CO$$

Since the nitro group is a modified nitroso group, it is not surprising that nitro compounds react with active methylene compounds. This reaction has been realized intramolecularly. For example, 2-phenacyl-2′-nitro-biphenyl reacts in the presence of a base to give phenanthridine-5-oxide and sodium benzoate. Apparently 6-benzoylphenanthridine-5-oxide is formed as an intermediate.[1]

Another ring closure that may be in this class occurs when a solution of diazotized 2-amino-5-nitrotoluene is allowed to stand for 3 days at room temperature; 5-nitroindazole is formed in 80% yield (OS III, 660).

Nitrobenzene reacts with phenylacetonitrile also but in a very unexpected manner; the product, 4-(phenylcyanomethylene)cyclohexa-2,5-dien-1-one oxime, corresponds rather to a 1,6-addition involving the *p*-position of the nitrobenzene ring.[2]

[1] C. W. Muth, N. Abraham, M. L. Linfield, R. B. Wotring, and E. A. Pacofsky, *J. Org. Chem.*, **25**, 736 (1960).

[2] R. B. Davis, L. C. Pizzini, and J. D. Benigni, *J. Am. Chem. Soc.*, **82**, 2913 (1960).

Nitroso compounds react with Grignard reagents to give hydroxylamine derivatives. The preparation of diphenylhydroxylamine from nitrosobenzene and phenylmagnesium bromide is an example.

$$C_6H_5N{=}O + C_6H_5MgBr \longrightarrow (C_6H_5)_2NOMgBr \xrightarrow{H_2O} (C_6H_5)_2NOH$$

Schiff bases resemble carbonyl compounds in their behavior toward Grignard reagents. The anil of benzophenone, however, fails to undergo 1,2-addition with phenylmagnesium bromide. Allylmagnesium bromide, on the other hand, attacks this and similar anils readily to give 1,2-addition products.[3]

The electron shortage at positions 2 and 4 of the pyridine ring makes the system vulnerable to attack by Grignard reagents and by other organometallic compounds. The allyl Grignard reagents react readily with azaaromatic heterocycles such as those of pyridine, quinoline, and isoquinoline.[4]

The nitro group is attacked by Grignard reagents, but the reaction gives rise to a mixture of products and is not of preparative value. At $-70°$ methyl p-nitrobenzoate reacts with the phenyl reagent to give p-carbomethoxydiphenylamine in 45% yield (based on the Grignard reagent).[5]

The electron deficit at the 2- and 4-positions of pyridine reveals itself also in the behavior of substituents at those sites. A methyl group in one of these positions, for example, exhibits an activity reminiscent of that of methyl ketones. Both 2- and 4-picoline are capable of undergoing aldol condensation with benzaldehyde. The 3-isomer fails to react.

---

[3] H. Gilman and J. Eisch, *J. Am. Chem. Soc.*, **79**, 2150 (1957).
[4] H. Gilman, J. Eisch, and T. Soddy, *J. Am. Chem. Soc.*, **79**, 1245 (1957).
[5] D. Y. Curtin and J. C. Kauer, *J. Am. Chem. Soc.*, **75**, 6041 (1953).

The reactivity of these methyl groups is, of course, of a much lower order than that observed in methyl ketones. The usual conditions for bringing about the condensations cited are rather drastic, involving zinc chloride as a catalyst and temperatures from 180 to 230°. The corresponding methiodides, however, react readily, for in them the polarization of the —N=CH— linkage is more extensive. For example, when a mixture of the methiodide of 2-picoline, benzaldehyde, a small amount of ethanol, and a few drops of piperidine is allowed to stand at room temperature, the condensation product separates in crystalline form.[6]

$$\left[\underset{\underset{CH_3}{N^{\diagup}CH_3}}{\bigodot}\right]^+ I^- + C_6H_5CHO \rightarrow \left[\underset{CH_3}{\underset{N^{\diagup}CH=CHC_6H_5}{\bigodot}}\right]^+ I^- + H_2O$$

The methiodide of 3-picoline, as was to be expected, fails to react.

Condensation of 2-picoline with formaldehyde leads to the formation of 2-vinylpyridine.

$$\underset{N^{\diagup}CH_3}{\bigodot} + CH_2O \rightarrow \underset{N^{\diagup}CH=CH_2}{\bigodot} + H_2O$$

The methyl group in 4-methylcinnoline is reactive also; with benzaldehyde in the presence of anhydrous zinc chloride it yields 4-styrylcinnoline.[7]

$$\underset{\underset{N^{\diagdown}N}{\bigodot}}{\overset{CH_3}{\bigodot}} \rightarrow \underset{\underset{N^{\diagdown}N}{\bigodot}}{\overset{CH=CHC_6H_5}{\bigodot}}$$

Acylation occurs also with such compounds; the synthesis of 2-phenacylpyridine, for instance, is achieved by adding 2-picoline and ethyl benzoate to a solution of potassium amide in liquid ammonia. The product, isolated as the hydrobromide, is obtained in 44% yield.[8]

$$\underset{N^{\diagup}CH_3}{\bigodot} + C_6H_5CO_2C_2H_5 \rightarrow \underset{N^{\diagup}CH_2COC_6H_5}{\bigodot} + C_2H_5OH$$

Nitrites and Nitrous Acid

Attack of enolates on alkyl nitrites produces nitroso compounds (OR 7, 327). The condensation, which usually is effected with an ester of nitrous acid, can be formulated in the following way.

[6] C. F. Koelsch, *J. Am. Chem. Soc.*, **66**, 2126 (1944).

[7] R. N. Castle and D. B. Cox, *J. Org. Chem.*, **18**, 1706 (1953).

[8] D. R. Howton and D. R. V. Golding, *J. Org. Chem.*, **15**, 1 (1950).

$$-\overset{\overset{\displaystyle |}{C}=O}{\underset{\overset{\displaystyle |}{C}=O}{\overset{\displaystyle |}{\underset{|}{C^-}}}} + \overset{O}{\overset{\|}{N}}-OR \rightarrow -\overset{\overset{\displaystyle |}{C}=O}{\underset{\overset{\displaystyle |}{C}=O}{\overset{\displaystyle |}{\underset{|}{C}}}}-N\overset{O^-}{\underset{}{}}OR \rightarrow -\overset{\overset{\displaystyle |}{C}=O}{\underset{\overset{\displaystyle |}{C}=O}{\overset{\displaystyle |}{\underset{|}{C}}}}-N=O + \bar{O}R$$

Nitrosation of alkylated malonic, acetoacetic, and benzoylacetic esters provides a way of preparing oximino esters, which are formed when the nitroso esters are treated with sodium ethoxide. As in the Japp-Klingemann reaction (p. 160), one of the acyl groups is removed. The reaction of ethyl nitrite with ethyl α-benzoylvalerate is illustrative. The yields of ethyl α-oximinovalerate and ethyl benzoate are 75 and 70%, respectively.[9]

$$\overset{CH_2CH_2CH_3}{\underset{}{C_6H_5COCHCO_2C_2H_5}} \xrightarrow[NaOC_2H_5]{C_2H_5ONO} \overset{CH_2CH_2CH_3}{\underset{N=O}{C_6H_5COCCO_2C_2H_5}} \xrightarrow{NaOC_2H_5}$$

$$\underset{NOH}{CH_3CH_2CH_2CCO_2C_2H_5} + C_6H_5CO_2C_2H_5$$

One step in a synthesis of lysine from ε-aminocaproic acid involves a similar change.[10]

$$C_6H_5CONH(CH_2)_4CH(CO_2C_2H_5)_2 \xrightarrow{C_4H_9ONO} \underset{NOH}{C_6H_5CONH(CH_2)_4CCO_2C_2H_5}$$

Oximes are, of course, obtained from active methylene compounds since the nitroso derivatives are able to undergo enolization (p. 168). The synthesis of methyl phenyl diketone from propiophenone (OS III, 20) involves oximation as the first step (OS II, 363; 68% yield).

$$C_6H_5COCH_2CH_3 + CH_3ONO \xrightarrow{HCl} \underset{NOH}{C_6H_5COCCH_3} + CH_3OH$$

In a similar way diethyl malonate yields the oxime of diethyl mesoxalate.

$$\overset{CO_2C_2H_5}{\underset{CO_2C_2H_5}{CH_2}} + HONO \rightarrow \overset{CO_2C_2H_5}{\underset{CO_2C_2H_5}{C=NOH}} + H_2O$$

[9] C. R. Hauser and G. A. Reynolds, *J. Am. Chem. Soc.*, **70**, 4250 (1948).
[10] D. E. Floyd and S. E. Miller, *J. Org. Chem.*, **16**, 1764 (1951).

When the nitrosation product from dimethyl malonate is reduced with zinc and formic acid, dimethyl formylaminomalonate is formed. Alkylation of this ester followed by acid hydrolysis provides a route to α-amino acids.[11]

$$\underset{\substack{\\ \text{HCNHCH}}}{\overset{\substack{O \\ \parallel}}{}}\overset{CO_2CH_3}{\diagup}\underset{CO_2CH_3}{\diagdown} \rightarrow \underset{\substack{\\ \text{HCNHC—R}}}{\overset{\substack{O \\ \parallel}}{}}\overset{CO_2CH_3}{\diagup}\underset{CO_2CH_3}{\diagdown} \rightarrow \underset{\substack{\\ NH_2}}{\overset{\substack{\\ }}{\text{RCHCO}_2\text{H}}}$$

Cyclohexanone gives a dioxime in 76 % yield (p. 198).[12]

The oxime obtained from ethyl acetoacetate has been employed to make α-amino-β-hydroxybutyric acid.

$$CH_3COCH_2CO_2C_2H_5 + HONO \rightarrow \underset{\substack{\parallel \\ NOH}}{CH_3COCCO_2C_2H_5} + H_2O$$

The preparation of dimethylglyoxime from methyl ethyl ketone likewise depends on this type of transformation (OS II, 204).

$$CH_3COCH_2CH_3 + C_2H_5ONO \rightarrow \underset{CH_3C=NOH}{CH_3C=O} + C_2H_5OH$$

Primary nitro compounds react with nitrous acid to yield nitro oximes, known as nitrolic acids, distinguished by the fact that they form bright-red salts.

$$RCH_2NO_2 + HONO \rightarrow \underset{\substack{\parallel \\ RCNO_2}}{\overset{NOH}{}} + H_2O$$

Secondary nitro compounds form nitroso derivatives, known as *pseudonitroles*, which are blue in solution and generally colorless in the solid state.

$$R_2CHNO_2 + HONO \rightarrow \underset{\substack{| \\ R_2CNO_2}}{\overset{NO}{}} + H_2O$$

[11] See J. S. Meek, S. Minkowitz, and M. M. Miller, *J. Org. Chem.*, **24**, 1397 (1959).
[12] A. F. Ferris, G. S. Johnson, F. E. Gould, and H. K. Latourette, *J. Org. Chem.*, **25**, 492 (1960).

Cyclic ketones undergo nitrosation preferentially at a tertiary carbon atom; an example is the nitrosation of menthone.

$$CH_3\langle\ \rangle CH(CH_3)_2\ \rightarrow\ CH_3\langle\ \rangle \overset{CH(CH_3)_2}{\underset{NO}{}}$$

Use of the name isonitroso compounds for oximes accords with the fact that certain oximes are formed by isomerization of the corresponding nitroso compounds (p. 168) and that oximes may react as the nitroso compound would be expected to do; with bromine they may form the corresponding bromo nitroso compounds (p. 549) and with lead tetra-acetate yield nitrosoacetates.[13]

Reaction of Nitrous Acid with Amino Compounds

Nitrosation

Secondary amines react with nitrous acid to yield nitroso derivatives, the usual procedure being to add sodium nitrite to a solution of the amine in a mineral acid (CR **59**, 497). An example is the formation of nitroso-dimethylamine from dimethylamine in hydrochloric acid (OS II, 211).

$$(CH_3)_2NH \cdot HCl + HONO \rightarrow (CH_3)_2NNO + H_2O + HCl$$

Methyl N-nitroso-β-methylaminoisobutyl ketone, an intermediate in one method of making diazomethane (p. 293), is formed in an analogous fashion (OS III, 244).

$$\underset{CH_3NH}{(CH_3)_2CCH_2COCH_3} \rightarrow \underset{CH_3NNO}{(CH_3)_2CCH_2COCH_3}$$

Aromatic secondary amines react in a similar manner, as is illustrated by the formation of N-nitrosomethylaniline (OS II, 460).

$$\underset{CH_3}{\overset{C_6H_5}{}}NH + HCl + NaNO_2 \rightarrow \underset{CH_3}{\overset{C_6H_5}{}}NNO + H_2O + NaCl$$

Even diarylamines yield nitrosamines, as is exemplified by the behavior of diphenylamine.

$$(C_6H_5)_2NH \rightarrow (C_6H_5)_2NNO$$

[13] D. C. Iffland and G. X. Criner, *Chem. and Ind.*, 176 (1956).

Secondary amides likewise yield nitroso derivatives, called nitrosamides, those from anilides being best known. The nitrosamide from acetanilide is an example.

$$C_6H_5NHCOCH_3 \rightarrow C_6H_5N \begin{smallmatrix} NO \\ \\ COCH_3 \end{smallmatrix}$$

Ethyl N-methylcarbamate (p. 336) forms nitrosomethylurethan (OS II, 464; 75% yield), another intermediate in the synthesis of diazomethane (p. 292).

$$CH_3NHCO_2C_2H_5 \rightarrow CH_3\underset{\underset{NO}{|}}{N}CO_2C_2H_5$$

Still another nitroso compound that has served in the preparation of diazomethane (p. 293) is nitrosomethylurea, produced by the action of nitrous acid on methylurea (OS II, 461).

$$CH_3NHCONH_2 + HONO \rightarrow CH_3\underset{\underset{NO}{|}}{N}CONH_2 + H_2O$$

This reaction is especially interesting, since it illustrates the rule that the attack of nitrous acid occurs preferentially at the more basic of the two amido groups. Similar results have been obtained with alkylhydrazines, which suffer nitrosation at the more basic amino group.

$$RNHNH_2 + HONO \rightarrow RN\underset{\underset{NO}{|}}{N}NH_2 + H_2O$$

The readiness with which secondary amines form nitrosamines affords a convenient means of separating amines of this class from mixtures with primary and tertiary amines. The primary amines are decomposed by nitrous acid, and the tertiary amines do not react. Moreover, nitrosamines are but feebly basic and can be separated from the tertiary amines. The nitrosamines are reconverted to the original amines by reduction or by hydrolysis. An example of the use of this method is the purification of N-ethyl-*m*-toluidine, prepared from *m*-toluidine and ethyl bromide (OS II, 290). The reducing agent is stannous chloride.

β-Arylhydroxylamines react with nitrous acid to yield nitroso derivatives, the best known of which is nitrosophenylhydroxylamine (OS I, 177). The ammonium salt of this compound, known as *cupferron*, is employed in analytical chemistry to precipitate certain metal ions in acid media. As its name implies, it was used first for copper and iron. The metal complexes have been assigned the following structure.

$$C_6H_5-N\underline{\qquad}N$$
$$| \qquad\qquad \|$$
$$O \qquad\quad O$$
$$\diagdown\quad \diagup$$
$$M$$

Diazotization

The formation of diazonium salts from primary aromatic amines by reaction with nitrous acid in the presence of mineral acids usually is rapid and quantitative. Aniline, of course, is the outstanding example (OS I, 442).

$$C_6H_5NH_2 \cdot HCl + NaNO_2 + HCl \rightarrow C_6H_5N_2Cl + NaCl + 2H_2O$$

Satisfactory procedures are available for a large number of other amines, including *o*-toluidine (OS I, 514), *p*-toluidine (OS I, 136, 515), and 2-naphthylamine (OS II, 432).

It is possible also to carry out the reaction with compounds having more than one amino group. Benzidine is an important example in this category.

$$HCl \cdot H_2N\!\!\diagdown\!\!\bigcirc\!\!\diagup\!\!-\!\!\diagdown\!\!\bigcirc\!\!\diagup\!\!NH_2 \cdot HCl + 2HNO_2 \rightarrow$$

$$ClN_2\!\!\diagdown\!\!\bigcirc\!\!\diagup\!\!-\!\!\diagdown\!\!\bigcirc\!\!\diagup\!\!N_2Cl + 4H_2O$$

o-Dianisidine undergoes tetrazotization in a similar way (OS III, 295).

m-Directing groups and halogen substituents, when situated in positions *ortho* or *para* to the amino group, make diazotization more difficult. A single halogen atom offers no problem, however, as illustrated by the readiness with which *o*-chloroaniline (OS III, 185) and 4-amino-3-bromo-toluene (OS III, 130) undergo diazotization.

A single nitro group causes no trouble, as is shown by the diazotization of *p*-nitroaniline (OS II, 225), *m*-nitroaniline (OS I, 404), 4-amino-3-nitrotoluene (OS I, 415), and 2-amino-5-nitrotoluene (OS III, 660).

Aldehyde groups do not interfere, as is illustrated by the successful diazotization of *m*-aminobenzaldehyde (OS III, 453). Ester groups likewise can be tolerated; ethyl *p*-aminobenzoate undergoes diazotization satisfactorily in hydrochloric acid (OS II, 299). Even aminophenols give no trouble; p-aminophenol, for example, is diazotized readily in dilute sulfuric acid (OS II, 355). Examples of amino acids are anthranilic acid (OS II, 580) and its 5-iodo derivative (OS II, 353).

A number of m-directing groups or halogen substituents may, however, lower the basicity of the amine to a point where it cannot be diazotized in the usual way. 2,4,6-Tribromoaniline and 2,4-dinitroaniline, for example, can be diazotized only in high concentration of acids. Moreover, sulfuric acid combines with nitrous acid to form nitrosylsulfuric acid, which is a weak diazotizing agent. If, however, phosphoric acid is added to the mixture, the nitrous acid is freed, and diazotization occurs with weakly basic amines. An example is the diazotization of 2,6-diiodo-4-nitroaniline (OS II, 604).

$$
\underset{\underset{NH_2}{\overset{I \quad \quad I}{\bigcirc}}}{\overset{NO_2}{}} \xrightarrow[\text{H}_2\text{SO}_4]{\text{NaNO}_2} \underset{\underset{N_2HSO_4}{\overset{I \quad \quad I}{\bigcirc}}}{\overset{NO_2}{}}
$$

Another procedure that is effective with weakly basic amines is to dissolve the amine in glacial acetic acid and then add nitrosylsulfuric acid diluted with sulfuric acid.

3-Aminopyridine forms diazonium salts in much the same fashion as do amino derivatives of other fully aromatic rings. The 2- and 4-isomers, however, can be diazotized only with difficulty, a fact that can be correlated with their structures. 2-Aminopyridine is analogous to an amide, and the 4-isomer is its next higher vinylog. Satisfactory results with such amines have been obtained, however, by resorting to special procedures.[14]

In many diazotization reactions it is important to avoid an excess of nitrous acid. Sulfamic acid has long been used to destroy excess nitrous acid in diazotization reactions. It reacts with a number of diazo compounds, however.[15]

Aliphatic primary amines do not react with nitrous acid at a pH below about 3, whereas aromatic primary amines are diazotized readily at a pH below 1. In a diamine that contains both types of amino groups it is possible to diazotize and replace the aromatic amino group without disturbing the aliphatic amino group. An example is the conversion of p-aminobenzylamine to benzylamine by diazotization and subsequent replacement of the diazonium group by means of hypophosphorous acid; the yield is 84%.[16]

[14] L. C. Craig, *J. Am. Chem. Soc.*, **56**, 231 (1934).
[15] H. W. Grimmel and J. F. Morgan, *J. Am. Chem. Soc.*, **70**, 1750 (1948).
[16] N. Kornblum and D. C. Iffland, *J. Am. Chem. Soc.*, **71**, 2137 (1949).

The aliphatic amino group is much more basic than the aromatic amino group and hence is transformed preferentially to the salt. The fact that the more weakly basic group is diazotized means that it is the free amino group, not the salt, that undergoes diazotization.[17]

The stability of the diazonium ion is to be explained on the basis of resonance (Angew. **67**, 439).

It would be expected that electron-donating substituents would favor the delocalization of the positive charge to the ring. The extreme example is the phenoxide oxygen atom, which inparts a high order of stability to the diazonium function. This molecule is seen to represent a transition from the aromatic to the aliphatic series.

Amides

Primary amides react with nitrous acid to generate the corresponding acids, a reaction that has proved to be valuable with amides so highly hindered as to resist hydrolysis. An example is the conversion of 2,4,6-trichlorobenzamide into the corresponding acid.

Aliphatic diazo compounds

Primary aliphatic amines, as has been seen (p. 187), react with nitrous acid to give alcohols and olefins. This reaction has been particularly valuable with amino acids since the amount of nitrogen evolved makes it possible to determine the number of amino groups that are present. The Van Slyke method of determining amino groups in amino acids, peptides, and proteins is based on this reaction.

[17] R. G. Gillis, *J. Chem. Education*, **31**, 344 (1954).

If the amino group is *alpha* to a carbethoxyl, cyano, or ketone group, however, a diazo compound may be formed. Glycine ester hydrochloride, for example, yields diazoacetic ester (OS III, 392; 85% yield).

$$HCl \cdot H_2NCH_2CO_2C_2H_5 + HNO_2 \rightarrow N_2CHCO_2C_2H_5 + 2H_2O + NaCl$$

It will be observed than an α-hydrogen atom is a prerequisite for this type of transformation (CR **23**, 193).

Hydrazines react with nitrous acid to yield the corresponding azides. Phenylhydrazine, for example, combines with nitrous acid in the presence of hydrochloric acid to produce phenyl azide (OS III, 710; 68% yield).

$$C_6H_5NHNH_2 + HCl + NaNO_2 \rightarrow C_6H_5N_3 + NaCl + 2H_2O$$

Phenyl azide has been represented by the following structures, of which *a* appears to be more important.

$$C_6H_5-\overset{+}{N}=\overset{-}{N}=\overset{..}{\overset{|}{N}}: \qquad C_6H_5-\overset{-}{\overset{..}{N}}-\overset{+}{N}\equiv N:$$

$$a \qquad\qquad\qquad b$$

The degree of stability of a given diazo compound appears to be determined by the resonance interaction that is possible (Angew. **67**, 439). The alkyl diazonium ions, since there can be no delocalization of the positive charge to the alkyl radical, are unstable. Stabilization can be achieved, however, by removal of a proton from the carbon atom that holds the diazonium group. Diazomethane, which is stable, can be represented as follows (p. 431).

$$H_2\overset{-}{\overset{..}{C}}-\overset{+}{N}\equiv N: \leftrightarrow H_2C=\overset{+}{N}=\overset{-}{\overset{..}{N}}:$$

Still greater stabilization occurs in the diazo esters.

$$RO-\overset{\overset{\displaystyle O}{\|}}{C}-\overset{-}{\overset{..}{\underset{H}{C}}}-\overset{+}{N}\equiv N: \leftrightarrow RO-\overset{\overset{\displaystyle O^-}{|}}{C}=\overset{+}{\underset{H}{C}}-\overset{}{N}\equiv N: \leftrightarrow RO-\overset{\overset{\displaystyle O}{\|}}{C}-\overset{+}{\underset{H}{C}}=\overset{-}{\overset{..}{N}}:$$

The speeds with which the various aliphatic diazo compounds react with acids, which may be taken as an index of their relative basicities, place them in the following order.

$$H_2\overset{..}{C}-N_2 \; > \; \underset{C_6H_5}{\overset{C_6H_5}{\diagdown}}\overset{..}{C}-N_2 \; > \qquad \overset{..}{-}N_2 \; >$$

$$\underset{\underset{O}{\overset{\|}{C}}}{\overset{H}{RO-C}}\overset{H}{\diagup}\overset{..}{C}-N_2 \qquad > \qquad \underset{\underset{O}{\overset{\|}{C_6H_5C}}}{\overset{\overset{O}{\overset{\|}{C_6H_5C}}}{\diagdown}}\overset{..}{C}-N_2$$

Of especial interest is diazocyclopentadiene, which represents a stable *quasi*-aromatic system.[18]

$$\overset{+}{-N}=N: \quad \leftrightarrow \quad =\overset{+}{N}=\overset{-}{\underset{..}{N}}:$$

[18] W. von E. Doering and C. H. DePuy, *J. Am. Chem. Soc.*, **75**, 5955 (1953).

21

Reduction

In most of the reactions classified as reduction the over-all change is the addition of hydrogen to a multiple linkage. Addition to simple olefins and acetylenes on the surface of a transition metal has the characteristics of radical reactions; this type of reduction is discussed in Chapter 26. Reduction by dissolving metals, such as sodium, may be classified as nucleophilic addition; as would be expected on this basis, it is observed with carbonyl groups, certain conjugated olefinic and aromatic systems, and with many nitrogen-containing compounds, such as nitro, nitroso, and azo compounds. It is with this second type of reduction that the present chapter is primarily concerned. Certain reductions by electrolytic methods and by metals or metallic ions, which may proceed by the formation of radicals, have been included also.

Olefins and Acetylenes

Olefinic double bonds can be reduced by sodium metal only when they form part of a highly conjugated system. The reduction of tetraphenylethylene to the corresponding ethane is an example. Diphenylpolyenes, when reduced with sodium amalgam, take up hydrogen atoms at the positions adjacent to the rings, and the reaction stops at this point. 1,4-Diphenyl-1,3-butadiene, for example, yields 1,4-diphenyl-2-butene.

$$C_6H_5CH{=}CH{-}CH{=}CHC_6H_5 \rightarrow C_6H_5CH_2CH{=}CHCH_2C_6H_5$$

In contrast to simple olefins, acetylenic hydrocarbons can be reduced by chemical means. When treated with sodium in liquid ammonia they take up two atoms of the metal and give the corresponding *trans*-olefins in satisfactory yields. Olefins made by catalytic hydrogenation of acetylenes over Raney nickel, as might be expected, possess *cis*-configurations. The *cis*- and *trans*-forms of all straight-chain hexenes and octenes, for example, have been made by these methods. The sodium reduction method is superior, since it yields no paraffins.

Chemical reduction by means of such agents as alkali metal-ammonia and chromous ion solutions generally yield *trans*-olefins. Various zinc-acid reducing agents, on the contrary, give *cis*-olefins.[1]

It is interesting in this connection that hydrogenation of olefinic compounds can be accomplished with hydrazine provided that oxygen is present. Under these conditions oleic acid, for instance, is changed to stearic acid.[2]

Aromatic Systems

Naphthalene, which presents a formal structural analogy to the polyenes, reacts with sodium to form a disodium derivative.

Treatment of the disodium derivative with water produces 1,4-dihydronaphthalene.

Reduction of aromatic system to dihydroaromatic derivatives can be effected by sodium and alcohols in liquid ammonia (QR **12**, 17). An example is the reduction of *m*-xylene to the corresponding 1,4-cyclohexadiene; the method is known as the Birch reduction.

When 2-naphthol is reduced with sodium and *t*-amyl alcohol in liquid ammonia 2-tetralone is formed in 61% yield.[3]

Another synthesis of 2-tetralone involves reduction of ethyl 2-naphthyl ether with sodium and ethanol followed by hydrolysis of the resulting dihydro compound (OS **32**, 97; yield 70%).

[1] B. S. Rabinovitch and F. S. Looney, *J. Am. Chem. Soc.*, **75**, 2652 (1953).
[2] F. Aylward and M. Sawistowska, *Chem. and Ind.*, 433 (1961).
[3] W. G. Dauben and R. Teranishi, *J. Org. Chem.*, **16**, 550 (1951).

The hydrolysis takes place readily because the ether is of the vinyl type (p. 435).

If lithium is used in place of sodium and the alcohol is added last, the reduction products generally are obtained in higher yields. An example is the conversion of 1-naphthol to 5,8-dihydro-1-naphthol (OS **37**, 80).

The reaction provides a route to 1-hydroxy-5,6,7,8-tetrahydronaphthalene (OS **37**, 80; yield 88%).

These reductions effect the addition of hydrogen at positions that are α, δ to each other. Attack is avoided at positions holding dimethylamino, alkoxyl, or alkyl group. A carboxyl group on the other hand strongly favors attack. Benzoic acid, when treated with sodium and ethanol in liquid ammonia, gives 1,4-dihydrobenzoic acid.[4]

Carbonyl Compounds

All aldehydes and ketones can be reduced but differ widely in the conditions necessary to bring about the reaction. Typical procedures for the reduction involve tin and hydrochloric acid, sodium amalgam, iron and acetic acid, aluminum amalgam, sodium and moist ether, and electrolytic methods. Under suitable conditions catalytic hydrogenation gives the corresponding alcohols. This method is very general, the usual catalysts being platinum and nickel. It is important, however, only in the event that the alcohol is less readily obtainable than the carbonyl compound.

[4] See M. E. Kuehne and B. F. Lambert, *J. Am. Chem. Soc.*, **81**, 4278 (1959).

Aromatic ketones, available from the various acylation procedures, are often employed as sources of the corresponding alcohols. Zinc in aqueous sodium hydroxide, for example, reduces benzophenone to benzohydrol (OS I, 90; 97% yield).

$$(C_6H_5)_2CO + H_2(Zn + NaOH) \rightarrow (C_6H_5)_2CHOH$$

Alkaline reagents are to be recommended for reducing ketones to secondary alcohols, since pinacol formation is favored by acid media.

When sodium amalgam (OS I, 554) is added gradually to an aqueous solution of ethyl acetoacetate, reduction of the ketone group occurs; β-hydroxybutyric acid is obtained in 90% yield.

$$CH_3COCH_2CO_2C_2H_5 \rightarrow CH_3\underset{\underset{OH}{|}}{C}HCH_2CO_2H$$

2-Heptanol may be prepared from methyl n-amyl ketone by reduction with sodium and ethanol (OS II, 317; 65% yield). n-Heptaldehyde is reduced to 1-heptanol by certain metals in acetic acid; with iron filings, for example, the alcohol is produced in 81% yield (OS I, 304). Strong reducing agents such as sodium in alcohol may carry the reduction to the hydrocarbon stage; an example is the conversion of acridone into acridan by treatment with sodium in amyl alcohol.

In reduction by metals it seems probable that the metal gives up electrons to the carbonyl compound directly; the carbanion so generated acquires a hydride ion from water.

α,β-Unsaturated carbonyl compounds may behave similarly, i.e., undergo 1,2-reduction, or they may react in such a way as to bring about saturation of the olefinic bond.

$$RCH{=}CH\overset{\overset{\displaystyle OH}{|}}{C}{}^{+} + 2e \longrightarrow RCH{=}CH\overset{\overset{\displaystyle OH}{|}}{\underset{\underset{\displaystyle R}{|}}{C}}{}^{\displaystyle\bar{\;}} \leftrightarrow R\overset{\displaystyle\cdot\cdot}{C}HCH{=}\overset{\overset{\displaystyle OH}{|}}{\underset{\underset{\displaystyle R}{|}}{C}} \overset{H_2O}{\longrightarrow}$$

$$RCH_2CH{=}\overset{\overset{\displaystyle OH}{|}}{\underset{\underset{\displaystyle R}{|}}{C}} \longrightarrow RCH_2CH_2\overset{\overset{\displaystyle O}{\|}}{C}R$$

Aluminum alkoxides

Aluminum alkoxides are effective reducing agents and seem to be specific for conversion of a carbonyl function into the corresponding carbinol group (OR **2**, 178). Benzophenone can be reduced to benzohydrol in nearly quantitative yields by the action of isopropyl alcohol in the presence of aluminum isopropoxide (OR **2**, 203). The reaction is reversible and is brought to completion by distillation of the acetone; the reduction is complete when the distillate no longer gives a precipitate with 2,4-dinitrophenyl-hydrazine (p. 420). Another test for acetone is carried out by adding hydroxylamine hydrochloride and alkali followed by bromine water. The oxime, which forms initially, is transformed into 2-bromo-2-nitrosopropane, readily detected by its blue color.

$$\begin{array}{c}CH_3\\[-2pt]\diagdown\\[-2pt]CO\\[-2pt]\diagup\\[-2pt]CH_3\end{array}\rightarrow\;\begin{array}{c}CH_3\\[-2pt]\diagdown\\[-2pt]C{=}NOH\\[-2pt]\diagup\\[-2pt]CH_3\end{array}\rightarrow\;\begin{array}{c}CH_3\quad NO\\[-2pt]\diagdown\;\diagup\\[-2pt]C\\[-2pt]\diagup\;\diagdown\\[-2pt]CH_3\quad Br\end{array}$$

Chloral is reduced to trichloroethyl alcohol by aluminum ethoxide in ethanol (OS II, 598; 84% yield). This method, often called the Meerwein-Ponndorf-Verley reduction, is especially valuable with compounds that contain ethylenic linkages, nitro groups, and other unsaturated functions, since they are unaffected. The reduction of crotonaldehyde by the use of aluminum isopropoxide for example, produces crotyl alcohol in practically quantitative yields (OR **2**, 200).

$$3CH_3CH{=}CHCHO + Al[OCH(CH_3)_2]_3 \rightarrow$$

$$(CH_3CH{=}CHCH_2O)_3Al + 3CH_3COCH_3$$

$$(CH_3CH{=}CHCH_2O)_3Al \overset{H_2O}{\longrightarrow} CH_3CH{=}CHCH_2OH$$

Under similar conditions *o*-nitrobenzaldehyde gives *o*-nitrobenzyl alcohol in 92% yield (OR **2**, 207).

$$O_2NC_6H_4CHO \overset{Al[OCH(CH_3)_2]_3}{\longrightarrow} O_2NC_6H_4CH_2OH$$

The reduction of acetylenic compounds is illustrated by the conversion of phenylpropiolaldehyde into 3-phenyl-2-propyn-1-ol; the yield is 65%.[5]

$$C_6H_5C{\equiv}CCHO \rightarrow C_6H_5C{\equiv}CCH_2OH$$

Selective reduction of certain compounds has been accomplished by resort to protective devices. Phenylglyoxal, for example, can be converted into the dimethyl acetal, reduction of which gives the corresponding hydroxyl acetal in 55% (OR **2**, 183).

$$C_6H_5COCH(OCH_3)_2 \rightarrow C_6H_5\underset{\underset{\displaystyle OH}{|}}{C}HCH(OCH_3)_2$$

Use of this reaction for the purpose of oxidation (Oppenauer oxidation) has already been mentioned (p. 214). Transfer of the hydride ion from the alkoxide to the ketone has been pictured as follows (Hine, 263).

Rate measurements suggest that part of the reduction proceeds by way of a noncyclic transition state.[6]

A transformation that seems to resemble the Meerwein-Pondorf-Verley reduction occurs when fulvenes are treated with alcohols in the presence of alkalis. Benzalfluorene is rapidly reduced by benzyl alcohol in the presence of potassium hydroxide.[7]

[5] J. J. Dudkowski and E. I. Becker, *J. Org. Chem.*, **17**, 201 (1952).
[6] W. N. Moulton, R. E. Van Atta, and R. R. Ruch, *J. Org. Chem.*, **26**, 290 (1961).
[7] Y. Sprinzak, *J. Am. Chem. Soc.*, **78**, 466 (1956).

This type of reduction has been proposed to explain the base-catalyzed alkylation of fluorene with alcohols.[8] Benzyl alcohol in the presence of strong bases is particularly effective. When a mixture of 2-aminopyridine and benzyl alcohol is heated in the presence of potassium hydroxide, 2-benzylaminopyridine is obtained (OS **38**, 3; yield 99%). Presumably benzaldehyde reacts to form the Schiff base, which is then reduced by the alcohol.

$$\underset{N \diagdown N=CHC_6H_5}{\bigcirc} + C_6H_5CH_2OH \rightarrow \underset{N \diagdown NHCH_2C_6H_5}{\bigcirc} + C_6H_5CHO$$

N-Benzylaniline is made in 99% yield by a similar procedure (OS **38**, 3). With two moles of benzyl alcohol p-phenylenediamine forms N,N'-dibenzyl-p-phenylenediamine (OS **38**, 4; 92% yield).

In a similar way β-phenylpropiophenones can be made by the interaction of appropriate acetophenones and benzyl alcohols in the presence of catalytic amounts of lithium benzylate. The preparation of β-phenylpropiophenone is an example; the reaction appears to take the following course.[9]

$$C_6H_5CH_2OH + CH_3COC_6H_5 \rightleftharpoons C_6H_5CHO + CH_3\overset{\overset{\displaystyle OH}{|}}{C}HC_6H_5$$

$$C_6H_5CHO + CH_3COC_6H_5 \rightarrow C_6H_5CH=CHCOC_6H_5 + H_2O$$

$$C_6H_5CH=CHCOC_6H_5 + C_6H_5CH_2OH \rightarrow$$
$$C_6H_5CH_2CH_2COC_6H_5 + C_6H_5CHO$$

As would be expected on the basis of this mechanism, β-phenylpropiophenone is formed also from benzaldehyde and methylphenylcarbinol.

Potassium benzylate reduces certain acrylonitriles to the corresponding propionitriles. α-Phenylcinnamonitrile, when heated with benzyl alcoholic potassium hydroxide from which the water has been distilled, gives α,β-diphenylpropionitrile in 62% yield.[10]

$$C_6H_5CH=\underset{\underset{\displaystyle C_6H_5}{|}}{C}CN \rightarrow C_6H_5CH_2\underset{\underset{\displaystyle C_6H_5}{|}}{C}HCN$$

If water is present the cyano group undergoes hydrolysis and the corresponding propionic acid is produced.

Benzylation by use of benzyl alcohol is analogous to the Guerbet reaction (p. 655).

[8] E. I. Becker, *J. Chem. Education*, **36**, 119 (1959).

[9] E. F. Pratt and A. P. Evans, *J. Am. Chem. Soc.*, **78**, 4950 (1956).

[10] M. Avramoff and Y. Sprinzak, *J. Am. Chem. Soc.*, **80**, 493 (1958).

Electrolytic reduction may be employed to convert α,β-unsaturated acids to the corresponding saturated acids and is especially successful with β-aryl acrylic acids. Examples are the preparation of hydrocinnamic acid (OS I, 311; 90% yield) and β-furylpropionic acid (OS I, 313; 70% yield) from the corresponding α,β-unsaturated acids.

$$C_6H_5CH{=}CHCO_2Na \rightarrow C_6H_5CH_2CH_2CO_2Na \xrightarrow{H^+} C_6H_5CH_2CH_2CO_2H$$

Cannizzaro reaction

In the presence of aqueous or alcoholic alkali (50%) an aldehyde may undergo dismutation to yield the corresponding alcohol and the salt of the corresponding acid. This transformation, known as the Cannizzaro reaction, is observed with nearly all aromatic aldehydes and with a number of aldehydes of the aliphatic series (OR 2, 94). An example is the conversion of o-methoxybenzaldehyde into a mixture of the potassium salt of o-methoxybenzoic acid and o-methoxybenzyl alcohol.

The Cannizzaro reaction occurs also with aromatic aldehydes of the heterocyclic series. Furfural in the presence of sodium hydroxide readily yields sodium 2-furoate and furfuryl alcohol (OS I, 276). Both the alcohol and the acid are obtained in 63% yield.

The chief limitations of the Cannizzaro reaction in the aromatic series are due to steric hindrance. Di-o-substituted benzaldehydes fail to react normally. When both o-positions are filled by halogen or nitro substituents, the formyl group is removed as formic acid.

One mechanism proposed for the Cannizzaro reaction is the following.[11]

$$
\underset{\substack{\|\\ O}}{R-C-H} + OH^- \rightleftharpoons \underset{\substack{|\\ OH}}{R-\overset{O^-}{\underset{|}{C}}-H}
$$

$$
\underset{\substack{|\\ OH}}{R-\overset{O^-}{\underset{|}{C}}-H} \quad \underset{\substack{|\\ H}}{\overset{O}{\underset{|}{C}}-R} \;\rightarrow\; \underset{\substack{|\\ OH}}{R-\overset{O}{\underset{\|}{C}}} + H-\underset{\substack{|\\ H}}{\overset{O^-}{\underset{|}{C}}-R}
$$

The essential feature of the change is the transfer of a hydride ion (CR **60**, 7). This mechanism relates the reaction to the ability of the aldehyde group to react with nucleophilic agents and is in accord with the observation that aromatic aldehydes holding amino or hydroxyl groups in *o*- or *p*-positions fail to undergo the Cannizzaro reaction as it is ordinarily carried out. Apparently increase in the electron density of the ring because of the amino or the —O⁻ substituent (the reaction occurs in alkaline media) diminishes the electron deficit of the carbonyl carbon atom to such a degree that attack of hydroxyl ion is ineffective.

Transfer of hydride ion occurs directly and not through the reaction medium; when benzaldehyde undergoes the Cannizzaro reaction in the presence of heavy water, the benzyl alcohol produced is deuterium free.[12] The presence of peroxides seems to be necessary for the Cannizzaro reaction, for when peroxide-free aldehydes are employed no dismutation occurs.

As might be expected, aliphatic aldehydes with no α-hydrogen atoms behave much like their aromatic analogs, undergoing dismutation only. Examples are formaldehyde, pivalaldehyde, and α-hydroxyisobutyraldehyde.

$$2CH_2O + NaOH \rightarrow CH_3OH + HCO_2Na$$

$$2(CH_3)_3CCHO + KOH \rightarrow (CH_3)_3CCH_2OH + (CH_3)_3CCO_2K$$

$$
2 \;\; \underset{\substack{\diagup\\ CH_3}}{\overset{CH_3}{\diagdown}}C-CHO + KOH \rightarrow \underset{\substack{\diagup\\ CH_3}}{\overset{CH_3\;\; OH}{\diagdown}}CCH_2OH + \underset{\substack{\diagup\\ CH_3}}{\overset{CH_3\;\; OH}{\diagdown}}CCO_2K
$$

The more active aldehydes reduce the less active ones, and in particular many aromatic aldehydes have been reduced to the corresponding alcohols

[11] M. S. Kharasch and R. H. Snyder, *J. Org. Chem.*, **14**, 819 (1949).
[12] C. R. Hauser, P. J. Hamrick, Jr., and A. T. Stewart, *J. Org. Chem.*, **21**, 260 (1956).

by formaldehyde. The list includes veratraldehyde, piperonal, anisaldehyde, opianic acid, furfural, and phthalaldehydic acid; the yields are in the range of 70 to 90%. This reaction, used also to prepare p-tolylcarbinol (OS II, 590; 90% yield), is known as the *crossed Cannizzaro reaction*. It is valuable because formaldehyde is cheap.

Aldehydes of the type RCH_2CHO undergo the aldol condensation so rapidly that the Cannizzaro reaction does not occur to any great extent except under the influence of enzymes. With Raney nickel and alkali, however, many aliphatic aldehydes undergo the Cannizzaro reaction.

Valuable syntheses are known that involve both the Cannizzaro and the aldol reactions. Examples are given in connection with the discussion of the Tollens condensation (p. 492).

A reaction not unlike that of Cannizzaro occurs when formaldehyde is treated with nitrogen bases. An illustration is the conversion of formaldehyde into methylamine and formic acid by heating with ammonium chloride (OS I, 347; 51% yield).

$$2CH_2O + NH_4Cl \rightarrow CH_3NH_2 \cdot HCl + HCO_2H$$

The process is actually reductive alkylation (p. 410).

Reactions analogous to that of Cannizzaro take place when glyoxals are treated with aqueous alkalis, transformations that may be regarded as intramolecular Cannizzaro reactions. α-Keto aldehydes are converted to salts of α-hydroxy acids; glyoxal yields a salt of glycolic acid.

$$\begin{array}{l} CHO \\ | \\ CHO \end{array} + NaOH \rightarrow \begin{array}{l} CH_2CO_2Na \\ | \\ OH \end{array}$$

Phenylglyoxal is changed to salts of mandelic acid.

$$C_6H_5COCHO + NaOH \rightarrow \begin{array}{l} C_6H_5CHCO_2Na \\ | \\ OH \end{array}$$

Migration of hydride ion occurs intramolecularly; rearrangement of phenylglyoxal having deuterium in the aldehyde group proceeds without loss of deuterium.[13]

$$\begin{array}{l} \\ C_6H_5COC{=}O \\ | \\ D \end{array} \rightarrow \begin{array}{l} D \\ | \\ C_6H_5CCO_2H \\ | \\ OH \end{array}$$

[13] K. Heyns, W. Walter, and H. Scharmann, *Chem. Ber.*, **93**, 2057 (1960).

Hydrolysis of dihalides of the type $ArCOCHX_2$ does not yield the glyoxal to be expected but the corresponding mandelic acid. An example is the formation of sodium mandelate from dichloroacetophenone (OS III, 538).

$$C_6H_5COCHCl_2 + 3NaOH \rightarrow C_6H_5\underset{\underset{OH}{|}}{C}HCO_2Na + 2NaCl + H_2O$$

The over-all yield of mandelic acid, based on acetophenone, is 87%. p-Bromomandelic acid can be made from p-bromoacetophenone by way of its dibromo derivative (OS 35, 11; yield 63%).

$$p\text{-}BrC_6H_4COCH_3 \rightarrow p\text{-}BrC_6H_4COCHBr_2 \rightarrow p\text{-}BrC_6H_4\underset{\underset{OH}{|}}{C}HCO_2H$$

Ketones also have been reduced by formaldehyde. Benzophenone, for example, forms benzohydrol in 80% yield when treated with formaldehyde in boiling methanol.[14]

This type of interaction of carbonyl groups has been observed also with γ-keto aldehydes; β-desylbutyraldehyde, prepared from desoxybenzoin and crotonaldehyde, is transformed by the action of aqueous methanolic potassium hydroxide to β-methyl-γ,δ-diphenylvalerolactone. The yield, based on desoxybenzoin, is 47%.

$$C_6H_5COCH_2C_6H_5 + CH_3CH{=}CHCHO \rightarrow \underset{CH_3CHCH_2CHO}{\overset{C_6H_5CHCOC_6H_5}{|}} \rightarrow$$

$$\underset{\underset{\underset{CH_2}{\diagdown\diagup}}{CH_3CH \quad CO}}{\overset{\overset{CHC_6H_5}{\diagup\diagdown}}{C_6H_5CH \quad O}}$$

In a similar way β,γ-diphenylvalerolactone is formed from phenylacetaldehyde and cinnamaldehyde.

$$C_6H_5CH_2CHO + C_6H_5CH{=}CHCHO \rightarrow$$

$$\underset{C_6H_5CHCH_2CHO}{\overset{C_6H_5CHCHO}{|}} \rightarrow \underset{\underset{\underset{CH_2}{\diagdown\diagup}}{C_6H_5CH \quad CO}}{\overset{\overset{CH_2}{\diagup\diagdown}}{C_6H_5CH \quad O}}$$

[14] T. Mole, *J. Chem. Soc.*, 2132 (1960).

Tischenko reaction

If an alkoxide is employed in the Cannizzaro procedure, the product is an ester; an example is the formation of benzyl benzoate from benzaldehyde in the presence of sodium benzylate (OS I, 104; 93% yield).

$$2C_6H_5CHO \xrightarrow{C_6H_5CH_2ONa} C_6H_5CO_2CH_2C_6H_5$$

This conversion of aldehydes to esters, known as the Tischenko reaction, succeeds with aliphatic aldehydes also; acetaldehyde in the presence of aluminum ethoxide gives ethyl acetate.

$$2CH_3CHO \xrightarrow{Al(OC_2H_5)_3} CH_3\overset{\overset{\displaystyle O}{\|}}{C}OCH_2CH_3$$

The rate of ester formation varies greatly with different aldehydes; by slow addition of a fast-reacting aldehyde to a slow-reacting one, it is possible to prepare a mixed ester in high yield.[15] The product is the ester of the acid corresponding to the fast-reacting aldehyde and of the alcohol corresponding to the slow-reacting aldehyde.

Benzilic acid rearrangement

In the reactions just considered the hydrogen atom of the aldehyde group moves to the adjacent carbon atom. A similar change occurs when α-diketones are treated with alkali; benzil, for example, forms a salt of benzilic acid.

$$C_6H_5COCOC_6H_5 + NaOH \rightarrow (C_6H_5)_2\underset{\underset{\displaystyle OH}{|}}{C}CO_2Na$$

This reaction, which involves migration of an aryl radical rather than hydrogen, is general for benzils and is known as the benzilic acid rearrangement (QR **14**, 221). By treatment with a mixture of sodium bromate and sodium hydroxide, benzoin can be converted into sodium benzilate in one step (OS I, 89; 90% yield).

$$3C_6H_5\underset{\underset{\displaystyle OH}{|}}{C}HCOC_6H_5 + NaBrO_3 + 3NaOH \rightarrow$$

$$3(C_6H_5)_2\underset{\underset{\displaystyle OH}{|}}{C}CO_2Na + NaBr + 3H_2O$$

Phenanthrenequinone, which may be classed as a benzil, also undergoes the benzilic acid rearrangement.

---

[15] I. Lin and A. R. Day, *J. Am. Chem. Soc.*, **74**, 5133 (1952).

A few aliphatic diketones behave in this way also. When 1,2-cyclo-hexanedione is treated with alkali, 1-hydroxy-1-cyclopentanecarboxylic acid is formed.[16]

α,α-Dibromopropiophenone reacts with 20% sodium hydroxide to yield the sodium salt of atrolactic acid, presumably by rearrangement of methyl phenyl diketone.[17]

By use of labeling techniques it has been demonstrated that the benzilic acid rearrangement is irreversible.[18]

Reduction of esters to alcohols

Esters may be converted into alcohols by catalytic hydrogenation (p. 641). This change can be realized also by treating the ester with sodium and an alcohol. The method, known as the Bouveault-Blanc reduction, serves in the preparation of lauryl alcohol from ethyl laurate (OS II, 372; 75% yield), for example.

$$CH_3(CH_2)_{10}CO_2C_2H_5 \xrightarrow{\text{Na} + C_2H_5OH} CH_3(CH_2)_{10}CH_2OH$$

It is useful also in the conversion of esters of dibasic acids into glycols; the synthesis of decamethylene glycol from diethyl sebacate is an example (OS II, 154; 75% yield).

[16] G. Schwarzenbach and C. Wittwer, *Helv. Chim. Acta*, **30**, 663 (1947).
[17] R. Levine and J. R. Stephens, *J. Am. Chem. Soc.*, **72**, 1642 (1950).
[18] J. F. Eastham and S. Selman, *J. Org. Chem.*, **26**, 293 (1961).

Reduction of simple unsaturated esters is illustrated by the conversion of ethyl oleate into oleyl alcohol (OS III, 671; 51 % yield).

In the Bouveault-Blanc reduction the disodium derivative of the ester is postulated to react with alcohol to give the aldehyde and sodium ethoxide.

$$
\begin{array}{ccc}
\overset{\displaystyle ONa}{|} & & \overset{\displaystyle ONa}{|} \\
R\overset{|}{\underset{|}{C}}OC_2H_5 + C_2H_5OH & \rightarrow & R\overset{|}{\underset{|}{C}}OC_2H_5 + C_2H_5ONa \\
\underset{\displaystyle Na}{|} & & \underset{\displaystyle H}{|}
\end{array}
$$

The aldehyde is attacked immediately by sodium, yielding a second disodium derivative, which goes to the sodium alkoxide.

$$
\overset{ONa}{\underset{H}{\overset{|}{\underset{|}{R\overset{}{C}OC_2H_5}}}} \xrightarrow{-C_2H_5ONa} \overset{O}{\overset{\|}{RCH}} \xrightarrow{2Na} \overset{ONa}{\underset{Na}{\overset{|}{\underset{|}{RCH}}}} \xrightarrow{C_2H_5OH} RCH_2ONa + C_2H_5ONa
$$

These assumptions require that, in the Bouveault-Blanc reduction, alcoholysis of the first sodium derivative occurs before it has time to condense with the ester as in the acyloin synthesis. Experiments based on this concept have led to the development of a procedure that gives alcohols in practically quantitative yields. It provides for the rapid introduction of a mixture of the ester and alcohol to a vessel containing molten sodium with little or no solvent. This modified Bouveault-Blanc method involves only enough alcohol to alcoholyze the sodium derivatives. The formation of hydrogen by the interaction of sodium and alcohol serves no useful purpose and is largely avoided. Reactions of this type give alcohols in greatly improved yields when the sodium is employed in highly dispersed form.[19]

The availability of metal hydrides (p. 572) has diminished the importance of indirect methods of reducing carboxylic acids. A number of substituted benzoic acids have been reduced electrolytically to the corresponding benzyl alcohols. Anthranilic acid is converted in this way into *o*-aminobenzyl alcohol (OS III, 60; yield 78 %).

α-Diketones

Since twinned carbonyl groups form a conjugated system, it might be expected that most of the addition reactions of the group —COCO— would involve the extremities of the system. This is true, however, to a limited degree only. Hydrogen and metals are added in this manner, the products being enediols and enediolates, respectively.

$$
\overset{O\ \ O}{\overset{\|\ \ \|}{RC-CR}} + H_2 \rightarrow [\overset{OH\ \ OH}{\overset{|\ \ \ \ |}{RC=CR}}] \rightarrow \overset{O\ \ OH}{\overset{\|\ \ \ |}{RC-CHR}}
$$

[19] V. L. Hansley, *Ind. Eng. Chem.*, **43**, 1759 (1951).

The enediols usually rearrange at once to the corresponding acyloins. Stable enediols have been produced, however, from certain highly hindered benzils; if each of the aryl radicals bears two *o*-alkyl groups, the enediols are stable under nitrogen. They are very sensitive to oxidizing agents, being rapidly oxidized to benzils on exposure to air or oxygen.

The preparation of acyloins from esters is thought to involve the reduction of a diketone (OR **4**, 256). The reaction, known as the acyloin condensation—in contrast to the Bouveault-Blanc reduction—, is carried out in the absence of alcohols. One possibility is the formation of a disodium derivative, which combines with a molecule of unchanged ester to yield a diketone. The diketone is then transformed to the acyloin. The various steps may be illustrated by the synthesis of butyroin, which can be produced in 70% yield by this method (OS II, 114).

$$
\underset{\text{O}}{\overset{\text{O}}{\text{C}_3\text{H}_7\overset{\|}{\text{C}}\text{OC}_2\text{H}_5}} \xrightarrow{\text{2Na}} \text{C}_3\text{H}_7\overset{\overset{\text{ONa}}{|}}{\underset{\underset{\text{Na}}{|}}{\text{C}}}\text{OC}_2\text{H}_5
$$

$$
\text{C}_3\text{H}_7\overset{\overset{\text{ONa}}{|}}{\underset{\underset{\text{Na}}{|}}{\text{C}}}\text{OC}_2\text{H}_5 + \text{C}_3\text{H}_7\overset{\|}{\underset{\underset{\text{O}}{}}{\text{C}}}\text{OC}_2\text{H}_5 \longrightarrow \begin{array}{c} \overset{\text{ONa}}{|} \\ \text{C}_3\text{H}_7\text{C}-\text{OC}_2\text{H}_5 \\ | \\ \text{C}_3\text{H}_7\text{C}-\text{OC}_2\text{H}_5 \\ \underset{\text{ONa}}{|} \end{array} \xrightarrow{-2\text{C}_2\text{H}_5\text{ONa}}
$$

$$
\begin{array}{c} \text{C}_3\text{H}_7\text{CO} \\ | \\ \text{C}_3\text{H}_7\text{CO} \end{array} \xrightarrow{\text{2Na}} \begin{array}{c} \text{C}_3\text{H}_7\text{CONa} \\ \| \\ \text{C}_3\text{H}_7\text{CONa} \end{array} \xrightarrow{\text{H}_2\text{O}} \begin{array}{c} \text{C}_3\text{H}_7\text{COH} \\ \| \\ \text{C}_3\text{H}_7\text{COH} \end{array} \longrightarrow \begin{array}{c} \text{C}_3\text{H}_7\text{CHOH} \\ | \\ \text{C}_3\text{H}_7\text{CO} \end{array}
$$

The method is general for esters; propionoin, isobutyroin, and pivaloin can be made in yields of 55, 75, and 60%, respectively. Xylene or toluene as the solvent makes possible higher reaction temperatures and consequently greater solubility of the sodium derivatives and permits extension of the method to the synthesis of acyloins containing 12 to 36 carbon atoms. The yields are high. Five- and six-membered rings have been made also by this method. An example is the preparation of adipoin from dimethyl adipate; the yield is 57%.

$$
\begin{array}{c} \text{CH}_2\text{CH}_2\text{CO}_2\text{CH}_3 \\ | \\ \text{CH}_2\text{CH}_2\text{CO}_2\text{CH}_3 \end{array} \rightarrow \begin{array}{c} \text{CH}_2\text{CH}_2\text{CO} \\ | \quad\quad | \\ \text{CH}_2\text{CH}_2\text{CHOH} \end{array}
$$

A remarkable ring formation occurs when *cis*-diethyl hexahydrophthalate is treated with sodium under conditions of high dilution; the four-membered cyclic acyloin is produced in 12% yield.[20]

[20] A. C. Cope and E. C. Herrick, *J. Am. Chem. Soc.*, **72**, 983 (1950).

$$\text{[cyclohexane ring]}\begin{matrix}-CO_2C_2H_5\\-CO_2C_2H_5\end{matrix} \rightarrow \text{[bicyclic ring]}\begin{matrix}=O\\-OH\end{matrix}$$

The procedure has been employed with great success in the synthesis of large rings from esters of α,ω-dicarboxylic acids, yields of cyclic acyloins being from 29 to 96%. An example is the formation of sebacoin from dimethyl sebacate (OS **36**, 79; 66% yield).

$$(CH_2)_8 \begin{matrix}CO_2CH_3\\ \\CO_2CH_3\end{matrix} \rightarrow (CH_2)_8 \begin{matrix}CO\\ |\\CHOH\end{matrix}$$

An unusually interesting example of the acyloin condensation is the formation of 2-hydroxy-6,6-diphenylcyclononanone from diethyl δ,δ-diphenylazelate; the yield is 35%.[21]

$$\begin{matrix}C_6H_5\\ \\C_6H_5\end{matrix}C\begin{matrix}(CH_2)_3CO_2C_2H_5\\ \\(CH_2)_3CO_2C_2H_5\end{matrix} \rightarrow \begin{matrix}C_6H_5\\ \\C_6H_5\end{matrix}C\begin{matrix}(CH_2)_3CO\\ |\\(CH_2)_3CHOH\end{matrix}$$

The acyloin condensation is superior to all other methods of preparing macrocyclic compounds.[22]

Clemmensen reduction

Treatment of an aldehyde or ketone with amalgamated zinc and hydrochloric acid transforms the functional group to a methylene group. The procedure, known as the Clemmensen reduction (OR **1**, 155), is successful with both aliphatic and aromatic ketones and with a few aldehydes. It is especially to be recommended for the introduction of saturated side chains into aromatic compounds.[23] Acetophenone, for example, is converted into ethylbenzene. Reduction of o-heptanoylphenol gives o-n-heptylphenol (OS III, 444; yield 86%).

$$\text{[benzene ring]}\begin{matrix}OH\\CO(CH_2)_5CH_3\end{matrix} \rightarrow \text{[benzene ring]}\begin{matrix}OH\\CH_2(CH_2(_5CH_3\end{matrix}$$

n-Hexylresorcinol and γ-phenylbutyric acid (OS II, 499; 89% yield) are prepared in a similar way. The Clemmensen method is superior to the Wurtz-Fittig procedure (p. 626) for making n-alkylbenzenes.[24]

The procedure makes possible the conversion of vanillin into creosol in 67% yield (OS 33, 17).

[21] A. T. Blomquist and C. J. Buck, *J. Am. Chem. Soc.*, **81**, 672 (1959).
[22] V. Prelog, *J. Chem. Soc.*, 420 (1950).
[23] M. Poutsma and E. Wolthius, *J. Org. Chem.*, **24**, 875 (1959).
[24] H. A. Fahim and A. Mustafa, *J. Chem. Soc.*, 519 (1949).

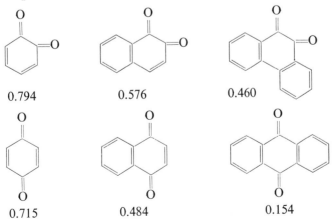

This method has been modified so as to convert acyloins into ketones. An example is the preparation of cyclodecanone from sebacoin (OS **36**, 14; 78% yield).

In the Clemmensen reduction pinacol formation is often observed, especially in the aromatic series. Amino ketones may undergo rearrangement. The results are similar to those obtained by electrochemical reduction.[25]

Quinones

Quinones are cyclic unsaturated diketones so constituted that addition of hydrogen to the terminal oxygen atoms produces dihydroxy derivatives, hydroquinones, that are fully aromatized. This process is reversible, permitting measurement of the reduction potential, which is an index of the tendency of the quinone to revert to an aromatic molecule. The aromatization process liberates less energy if one or both of the ethylenic bonds are already part of an aromatic nucleus. In other words, the stability of a quinone is increased (potential decreased) when the unsaturation is decreased. The following quinones illustrate this effect; the numbers are the reduction potentials measured at 25°.

0.794   0.576   0.460

0.715   0.484   0.154

[25] T. Nakabayashi, *J. Am. Chem. Soc.*, **82**, 3909 (1960).

The influence of a substituent on the reduction potential of a quinone may be predicted qualitatively by consideration of its electron-attracting power. Substituents that donate electrons, i.e., *o,p*-directing groups (excepting the halogens), lessen the receptivity of the quinone to external electrons, making the formation of the hydroquinone less easy.

$$\text{quinone} + 2e \rightarrow \text{quinone dianion} + 2H^+ \rightleftharpoons \text{hydroquinone (OH, OH)}$$

The hydroquinone itself is produced by a secondary reaction between the hydroquinone ion and hydrogen ion, a process that is affected by the pH of the medium.

As would be expected, *m*-directing substituents such as CN, CO_2H, NO_2, and COR have the opposite effect, making the corresponding hydroquinone less easy to oxidize. The halogen atoms, since they tend to withdraw electrons, fall in this category also. When quinone is treated with hydrochloric acid, the product is the corresponding chloro hydroquinone.

$$\text{quinone} + HCl \rightarrow \text{(OH, H, Cl, O adduct)} \rightarrow \text{chlorohydroquinone (OH, OH, Cl)}$$

Quinone, on the other hand, reacts with aniline to yield 2,5-dianilino-quinone. The initial addition product rearranges to the corresponding hydroquinone, which in turn is oxidized by unchanged quinone.

$$\text{quinone} \rightarrow \text{(O, OH, H, NHC}_6\text{H}_5\text{)} \rightarrow \text{(OH, OH, NHC}_6\text{H}_5\text{)} \rightarrow \text{(O, O, NHC}_6\text{H}_5\text{)}$$

A repetition of this series of reactions yields the dianilino derivative, the over-all change being represented by the following equation.

$$3 \text{ (quinone)} + 2C_6H_5NH_2 \rightarrow C_6H_5NH \text{ (quinone with } NHC_6H_5) + 2 \text{ (hydroquinone, OH/OH)}$$

It is possible to reduce certain quinones to ketones. Anthraquinone, for example, is transformed to anthrone by the action of tin and hydrochloric acid (OS I, 60; yield 83%).

Nitrogen Compounds

A variety of chemical procedures has been used to reduce *nitro compounds*. Reduction of primary and secondary nitroparaffins with stannous chloride produces oximes, as is illustrated by the behavior of 1-nitropropane.

$$CH_3CH_2CH_2NO_2 \rightarrow CH_3CH_2CH{=}NOH$$

Aromatic nitro compounds yield primary amines when reduced catalytically or by procedures involving acid media. Iron and hydrochloric acid, for example, serve to reduce 2,4-dinitrotoluene to 2,4-diaminotoluene (OS II, 160; 74% yield). The reduction of *m*-nitrobenzaldehyde is accomplished by the action of stannous chloride in hydrochloric acid (OS III, 453).

Sulfides in alkaline media likewise are capable of reducing nitro compounds to amines. An example is the reduction of *p*-nitrophenylacetic acid (OS I, 52). The amino acid is obtained in 84% yield.

Partial reduction of dinitro compounds can be accomplished by this procedure also; 2,4-dinitrophenol is reduced to 2-amino-4-nitrophenol by treatment with a mixture of sodium sulfide and ammonium chloride (OS III, 82; 61% yield).

$$\text{2,4-dinitrophenol} + 3Na_2S + 6NH_4Cl \rightarrow$$

$$\text{2-amino-4-nitrophenol} + 2H_2O + 6NH_3 + 6NaCl + 3S$$

In a similar way, 2,4-dinitroaniline may be reduced to 1,2-diamino-4-nitrobenzene (OS III, 242; 58% yield).

$$\text{2,4-dinitroaniline} + 3H_2S \xrightarrow{NH_4OH} \text{1,2-diamino-4-nitrobenzene} + 2H_2O + 3S$$

Another example is the reduction of 1,3-diamino-4,6-dinitrobenzene to 2,4,5-triaminonitrobenzene (OS **40**, 96; yield 52%).

$$\text{1,3-diamino-4,6-dinitrobenzene} \rightarrow \text{2,4,5-triaminonitrobenzene}$$

o-Aminobenzaldehyde is prepared in 75% yield by reducing o-nitrobenzaldehyde with ferrous sulfate and ammonia (OS III, 56).

$$\text{o-nitrobenzaldehyde (CHO, NO}_2) \xrightarrow[NH_4OH]{FeSO_4} \text{o-aminobenzaldehyde (CHO, NH}_2)$$

Zinc dust in sodium hydroxide serves to convert o-nitroaniline into o-phenylenediamine in 85% yield (OS II, 501).

$$\text{o-nitroaniline (NO}_2\text{, NH}_2) \rightarrow \text{o-phenylenediamine (NH}_2\text{, NH}_2)$$

Hydrazine in the presence of palladium-on-charcoal reduces many aromatic nitro compounds to the corresponding amines; the conversion of 2-nitrofluorene into 2-aminofluorene is an example (OS **40**, 5; 96% yield).

$$2\ \text{(fluorene)}NO_2 + 3N_2H_4 \rightarrow$$

$$2\ \text{(fluorene)}NH_2 + 3N_2 + 4H_2O$$

Zinc and ammonium chloride reduce nitro compounds to the corresponding β-arylhydroxylamines. β-Phenylhydroxylamine can be made by this procedure in yields of 68% (OS I, 445; III, 668).

$$C_6H_5NO_2 \xrightarrow[NH_4Cl]{Zn} C_6H_5NHOH$$

Reduction of a nitro compound produces the nitroso compound, which in acid media is rapidly reduced to the amine; the hydroxylamine is an intermediate. If the reduction is effected in an alkaline medium, however, the nitroso compound reacts with the hydroxylamine to yield the azoxy derivative (p. 531). Arsenious oxide and sodium hydroxide convert nitrobenzene to azoxybenzene (OS II, 57; 85% yield).

$$4C_6H_5NO_2 + 3As_2O_3 + 18NaOH \rightarrow$$

$$2C_6H_5N\!\!=\!\!\overset{\displaystyle\downarrow}{\underset{\displaystyle O}{N}}C_6H_5 + 6Na_3AsO_4 + 9H_2O$$

Reaction with zinc in sodium hydroxide reduces nitrobenzene to azobenzene (OS III, 103; 86% yield).

$$2C_6H_5NO_2 + 4Zn + 8NaOH \rightarrow C_6H_5N\!\!=\!\!NC_6H_5 + 4Na_2ZnO_2 + 4H_2O$$

Reduction of the azoxy compound yields the hydrazo derivative, which may be oxidized by the nitro compound to the azo compound.

Reduction of *nitroamides* serves to produce hydrazides; nitrourea, for example, can be reduced by zinc in acid solution to semicarbazide.

$$\underset{\displaystyle NHNO_2}{\overset{\displaystyle NH_2}{C\!\!=\!\!O}} + 6(H) \rightarrow \underset{\displaystyle NHNH_2}{\overset{\displaystyle NH_2}{C\!\!=\!\!O}} + 2H_2O$$

The same change may be effected electrolytically (OS I, 485).

Nitroguanidine has been reduced to aminoguanidine in various ways (CR **25**, 213). The product may be obtained in 64% yield by treatment of the nitro compound with zinc dust and glacial acetic acid; the amine is isolated as the bicarbonate (OS III, 73).

Nitroso compounds may be reduced to primary amines or oxidized to nitro compounds. An example of reduction is encountered in the preparation of *unsym*-dimethylhydrazine by treating nitrosodimethylamine with zinc and acetic acid (OS II, 211; 73% yield).

$$(CH_3)_2NNO + 4(H) \rightarrow (CH_3)_2NNH_2 + H_2O$$

Similarly α-methyl-α-phenylhydrazine can be produced from N-nitrosomethylaniline (OS II, 418; 56% yield).

$$\begin{array}{c} C_6H_5 \\ \diagdown \\ \diagup \quad NNO \rightarrow \\ CH_3 \end{array} \qquad \begin{array}{c} C_6H_5 \\ \diagdown \\ \diagup \quad NNH_2 \\ CH_3 \end{array}$$

Diazonium compounds may be reduced with sodium sulfite to the corresponding arylhydrazines. Diazotized aniline, for example, yields phenylhydrazine as the sodium salt of the hydrazinesulfonic acid, which gives phenylhydrazine when boiled with hydrochloric acid (OS I, 442). The yield, based on aniline, is 84%.

$$C_6H_5N_2Cl \rightarrow C_6H_5NHNHSO_3Na \rightarrow C_6H_5NHNH_2$$

If no other easily reducible groups are present, stannous chloride in acid solution may serve as the reducing agent.

Acetamidomalonic ester is made by reduction of the isonitroso derivative of malonic ester with zinc in a mixture of acetic acid and acetic anhydride (OS **40**, 21; the yield, based on malonic ester, is 78%).

$$\begin{array}{c} CO_2C_2H_5 \\ \diagup \\ CH_2 \\ \diagdown \\ CO_2C_2H_5 \end{array} \rightarrow \begin{array}{c} CO_2C_2H_5 \\ \diagup \\ CHNO \\ \diagdown \\ CO_2C_2H_5 \end{array} \rightarrow \begin{array}{c} CO_2C_2H_5 \\ \diagup \\ CHNHCOCH_3 \\ \diagdown \\ CO_2C_2H_5 \end{array}$$

Oximes may be reduced to amines by metal combinations also, as is illustrated by the conversion of *n*-heptaldoxime into *n*-heptylamine by the action of sodium and ethanol (OS II, 318; 73% yield).

Azo compounds undergo reductive cleavage with reducing agents such as sodium hydrosulfite to yield the corresponding aniline derivatives. This reaction has been made the basis of a procedure for introducing amino groups into phenols. An example is the synthesis of 1,4-aminonaphthol by reduction of Orange I (OS II, 39).

1-Amino-2-naphthol is produced from 2-naphthol in a similar way (OS II, 35).

A remarkable example of this method of indirect amination is the synthesis of *p*-phenetidine. Diazotized *p*-phenetidine is coupled with phenol, and the azo compound is ethylated. Reduction of the azophenetole yields two moles of the amine employed as a raw material.

$$C_2H_5O\langle\ \rangle N_2Cl + \langle\ \rangle OH \rightarrow C_2H_5O\langle\ \rangle N{=}N\langle\ \rangle OH \rightarrow$$

$$C_2H_5O\langle\ \rangle N{=}N\langle\ \rangle OC_2H_5 \rightarrow 2C_2H_5O\langle\ \rangle NH_2$$

The preparation of 2-amino-4-methoxyphenol from the monomethyl ether of hydroquinone, effected in a yield of 89%, illustrates the rule that the hydroxyl group is a more powerful director than the methoxyl group (p. 12).[26]

Acid Chlorides

Sulfonyl chlorides

Sulfonyl chlorides may be converted into sulfinic acids or their salts by a number of reducing agents, among the best of which is zinc dust. This reagent is employed, for example, in the preparation of sodium *p*-toluenesulfinate (OS I, 492).

$$2p\text{-}CH_3C_6H_4SO_2Cl \xrightarrow{\text{Zn}} (p\text{-}CH_3C_6H_4SO_2)_2Zn \xrightarrow{\text{Na}_2CO_3} 2p\text{-}CH_3C_6H_4SO_2Na$$

Sodium sulfite has been used also; an example is the conversion of *p*-acetamidobenzenesulfonyl chloride into *p*-acetamidobenzenesulfinic acid (OS I, 7; 47% yield).

$$p\text{-}CH_3CONHC_6H_4SO_2Cl + Na_2SO_3 + H_2O \rightarrow$$
$$p\text{-}CH_3CONHC_6H_4SO_2H + NaCl + NaHSO_4$$

[26] W. J. Close, B. D. Tiffany, and M. A. Spielman, *J. Am. Chem. Soc.*, **71**, 1265 (1949).

Sulfinates react with alkyl or aryl halides to give sulfones; sodium *p*-toluenesulfinate and dimethyl sulfate, for example, yield methyl *p*-tolyl sulfone (OS **38**, 62; yield 73%).

$$2p\text{-}C_6H_4SO_2Na + (CH_3)_2SO_4 \rightarrow 2p\text{-}C_6H_4SO_2CH_3 + Na_2SO_4$$

In a similar way, *p*-acetamidophenyl *p*-nitrophenyl sulfone is obtained from sodium *p*-acetamidobenzenesulfinate and *p*-chloronitrobenzene (OS III, 239).

$$p\text{-}CH_3CONHC_6H_4SO_2Na + p\text{-}O_2NC_6H_4Cl \rightarrow$$

$$\begin{array}{c} p\text{-}CH_3CONHC_6H_4 \\ \diagdown \\ SO_2 + NaCl \\ \diagup \\ p\text{-}O_2NC_6H_4 \end{array}$$

Stronger reducing agents convert sulfonyl chlorides into thiophenols and provide the most satisfactory method of obtaining thiophenols that do not have reducible substituents. Thiophenol itself is made in 91% yield by treating benzenesulfonyl chloride with zinc dust and sulfuric acid at -5 to $0°$ (OS I, 504).

$$C_6H_5SO_2Cl \xrightarrow[H_2SO_4]{Zn} C_6H_5SH$$

In a similar way 1,5-naphthalenedithiol is prepared from the chloride of the corresponding disulfonic acid (OS **33**, 47; yield 76%).

Many aromatic sulfonyl chlorides can be reduced by hydrogen iodide to the corresponding disulfides; *m*-nitrobenzenesulfonyl chloride, for example, gives di-*m*-nitrophenyl disulfide in 91% yield (OS **40**, 80).

$$2m\text{-}O_2NC_6H_4SO_2Cl \rightarrow (m\text{-}O_2NC_6H_4)_2S_2$$

Reissert reduction

A method that has a great degree of selectivity was developed by Reissert (OR **8**, 220), who treated acid chlorides with hydrogen cyanide in the presence of quinoline. The reaction is conducted in benzene or other inert solvent, and the condensation product is decomposed with sulfuric acid. Both aliphatic and aromatic aldehydes can be made satisfactorily by this method; an example is the synthesis of *p*-nitrobenzaldehyde.

$$p\text{-}O_2NC_6H_4COCl \xrightarrow[\text{quinoline}]{\text{HCN}}$$

$$\xrightarrow[\text{H}_2\text{SO}_4]{\text{H}_2\text{O}}$$

$$p\text{-}O_2NC_6H_4CHO +$$

The Reissert adducts also serve in the preparation of compounds other than aldehydes. They may be alkylated, for example, by use of certain Mannich bases and by successive hydrolysis and decarboxylation yield alkyl quinolines or isoquinolines. 1-Methylisoquinoline, for example, can be made by the following sequence of changes (OS **38**, 58).

$$C_6H_5COCl \xrightarrow[\text{isoquinoline}]{\text{KCN}}$$

Nitriles

Stephen method

Several procedures are available for dechlorinating imide chlorides to produce aldimines, which in turn furnish aldehydes. In one of these, developed by Stephen (OR **8**, 246), the imide chloride is obtained from a nitrile and reduced by stannous chloride. Anhydrous stannous chloride is suspended in dry ether, and dry hydrogen chloride is passed in until the mixture separates into two layers. The nitrile is added, and the treatment is continued for 2 hours. The double salt of stannic chloride and imine hydrochloride that separates is removed and hydrolyzed with boiling water. The conversion of 2-naphthonitrile into 2-naphthaldehyde is an example (OS III, 626). The over-all yield is 80%.

$$C_{10}H_7CN + HCl \longrightarrow C_{10}H_7CCl{=}NH$$

$$C_{10}H_7CCl{=}NH \xrightarrow[\text{SnCl}_2]{\text{HCl}} C_{10}H_7CH{=}NH$$

$$C_{10}H_7CH{=}NH \xrightarrow{\text{H}_2\text{O}} C_{10}H_7CHO$$

The method of Stephen has been used to make aliphatic as well as aromatic aldehydes, and in many cases the yields are excellent. The aldimine hydrochloride-stannic chloride complexes formed from the higher aliphatic nitriles do not precipitate at ordinary temperatures; if the reaction mixture is kept for 2 days at 0°, however, separation occurs. By this procedure lauraldehyde, for example, can be obtained from lauronitrile in nearly quantitative yields. The procedure is not always successful, however; *o*-tolualdehyde and 1-naphthaldehyde, for example, cannot be prepared satisfactorily in this way.

An interesting application of this method is the synthesis of indole by the reduction of *o*-nitrophenylacetonitrile. Both the imide chloride and nitro groups are reduced when enough reagent is employed.

A modification of the Stephen method, developed by Sonn and Müller (OR **8**, 240), involves the production of an imide chloride made by mixing an anilide with phosphorus pentachloride in benzene, toluene, or tetrachloroethane and heating until solution takes place. The solvent and phosphorus oxychloride are distilled under diminished pressure, and the imide chloride is reduced with stannous chloride as in the method of Stephen. The aldehyde is obtained by steam distillation of the whole reaction mixture or by isolating the complex salt, boiling it with acid, and distilling with steam or extracting with a suitable solvent. The yields amount to about 85%. The method may be illustrated by the synthesis of *o*-tolualdehyde from *o*-toluanilide (OS III, 818); the over-all yield is 70%.

$$CH_3C_6H_4CONHC_6H_5 \xrightarrow{PCl_5} CH_3C_6H_4CCl{=}NC_6H_5$$

$$CH_3C_6H_4CCl{=}NC_6H_5 \xrightarrow{SnCl_2} CH_3C_6H_4CH{=}NC_6H_5$$

$$CH_3C_6H_4CH{=}NC_6H_5 \xrightarrow{H_2O} CH_3C_6H_4CHO$$

The method is not useful for aliphatic aldehydes unless they contain α,β-unsaturation. The imide chlorides of saturated aliphatic aldehydes are unstable presumably because of ready migration of a hydrogen atom, a change that cannot occur with α,β-unsaturated compounds. With α,β-unsaturated anilides, however, stannous chloride must be replaced by a stronger reducing agent; chromous chloride is used.

A method for converting oximes into aldehydes depends on the intermediate formation of an imide chloride, which is then reduced with stannous chloride. An example is the preparation of p-chlorobenzaldehyde from the *syn*-oxime of p-chlorobenzophenone.

$$ClC_6H_4$$
$$\diagdown$$
$$C{=}NOH \xrightarrow{PCl_5} ClC_6H_4CCl{=}NC_6H_5$$
$$\diagup \qquad\qquad\qquad\qquad \downarrow SnCl_2$$
$$C_6H_5$$
$$ClC_6H_4CH{=}NC_6H_5 \xrightarrow{H_2O} ClC_6H_4CHO$$

Wolff-Kishner method

The Wolff-Kishner method (OR **4**, 378) of reducing aldehydes and ketones to the corresponding hydrocarbons involves formation of the hydrazone, which is decomposed catalytically by heating with a base.

$$R_2CO \xrightarrow{N_2H_4} R_2C{=}NHNH_2 \longrightarrow RCH_2R + N_2$$

If the hydrazone is represented by the tautomeric structure ($R_2CHN{=}NH$), a form that would be favored by alkaline media, the parallel between this reaction and the decomposition of azo compounds as a class becomes apparent.

In an improved procedure a mixture of sodium or potassium hydroxide, 85% hydrazine hydrate, triethylene glycol, and the ketone is heated for an hour under reflux and then for 3 hours after the temperature has been brought to 195 to 200° by distilling volatile constituents. An example is the conversion of propiophenone into n-propylbenzene.[27]

Dimethylketene dimer, produced in high yield by the action of triethylamine on isobutyryl chloride, undergoes reduction by this method to yield 2,2,4,4-tetramethylcyclobutanone and 1,1,3,3-tetramethylcyclobutane.[28]

Another example is the conversion of 6-ketohendecanedioic acid into hendecanedioic acid (OS **38**, 34; yield 93%).

[27] Huang-Minlon, *J. Am. Chem. Soc.*, **68**, 2487 (1946).
[28] H. L. Herzog and E. R. Buchman, *J. Org. Chem.*, **16**, 99 (1951).

MacFadyen-Stevens method

This scheme for preparing aldehydes depends on the alkali-catalyzed decomposition of acylsulfonylhydrazides (OR **8**, 232). Benzaldehyde is formed, for example, when benzoylbenzenesulfonehydrazide is heated with sodium carbonate.

$$C_6H_5CONHNHSO_2C_6H_5 + OH^- \rightarrow C_6H_5CHO + C_6H_5SO_2^- + N_2 + H_2O$$

The method appears to be fairly general for the preparation of aromatic aldehydes but is nearly useless in the aliphatic series. An unusual example is the conversion of cyclopropanecarboxylic acid into cyclopropane-carboxyaldehyde; the yield is only 16%, however.[29]

$$
\begin{array}{ccc}
CH_2 & & CH_2 \\
| \diagdown & & | \diagdown \\
| CHCONHNHSO_2C_6H_5 \rightarrow & & | CHCHO \\
| \diagup & & | \diagup \\
CH_2 & & CH_2
\end{array}
$$

Powdered solids catalyze the reaction; an improved procedure involves the use of powdered glass.[30]

Metal Hydrides

The most important metal hydride, lithium aluminum hydride, is very powerful and is of exceptional value in the reduction of various polar functional groups (OR **6**, 469). Normally used in ether solution, it reduces aldehydes, ketones, esters, carboxylic acids, acid anhydrides, acid chlorides, and epoxides to the corresponding alcohols. Amides, nitriles, aliphatic nitro compounds, and anils are converted to the expected amines.[31]

The reagent is remarkable because of its selectivity; at -30 to $-60°$, for example, it serves to reduce the ester group of nitro esters without altering the nitro group.[32] An example is the reduction of methyl 4-methyl-4-nitropentanoate to 4-methyl-4-nitropentanol; the yield is 76%.

$$
\begin{array}{ccc}
NO_2 & & NO_2 \\
| & & | \\
(CH_3)_2CCH_2CH_2CO_2CH_3 & \rightarrow & (CH_3)_2CCH_2CH_2CH_2OH
\end{array}
$$

Taken in limited amounts, this reagent serves to transform amides into the corresponding amines; N-methyllauramide, for example, yields laurylmethylamine (OS **36**, 48).

[29] J. D. Roberts, *J. Am. Chem. Soc.*, **73**, 2959 (1951).
[30] M. S. Newman and E. G. Caflisch, Jr., *J. Am. Chem. Soc.*, **80**, 862 (1958).
[31] N. G. Gaylord, *J. Chem. Education*, **34**, 367 (1957).
[32] H. Feuer and T. J. Kucera, *J. Am. Chem. Soc.*, **77**, 5740 (1955).

$$CH_3(CH_2)_{10}CONHCH_3 \xrightarrow{\text{LiAlH}_4} CH_3(CH_2)_{10}CH_2NHCH_3$$

Another example is the preparation of 2,2-dimethylpyrrolidine from 5,5-dimethyl-2-pyrrolidone (OS **33**, 32; yield 79%).

If the amount of reducing agent is limited and the temperature is kept low, the reaction with nitriles can be interrupted at the end of the first step and furnishes a preparative method for aldehydes (OR **8**, 252). An extremely interesting example is the synthesis of fluoral from trifluoroacetonitrile.[33]

In a similar way aldehydes may be made from carboxylic acids and their derivatives (OR **8**, 254).

The reduction of acid chlorides to alcohols is illustrated by the preparation of 2,2-dichloroethanol from dichloroacetyl chloride (OS **32**, 46; 65% yield).

$$CHCl_2COCl \xrightarrow{\text{LiAlH}_4} CHCl_2CH_2OH$$

When ortho esters are treated with lithium aluminum hydride, hydrogenolysis occurs, and the corresponding acetals are obtained in high yields. Since ortho esters can be made readily from nitriles, this cleavage offers a route to aldehydes.[34]

The reduction of esters to alcohols is further illustrated by the preparation of 2-(1-pyrrolidyl)propanol (OS **33**, 82).

Lithium aluminum hydride is superior for reducing the chloromethyl group to a methyl group; the preparation of isodurene from mesitylene illustrates this method.[35]

[33] A. L. Henne, R. L. Pelley, and R. M. Alm, *J. Am. Chem. Soc.*, **72**, 3370 (1950).
[34] C. J. Claus and J. L. Morgenthau, Jr., *J. Am. Chem. Soc.*, **73**, 5005 (1951).
[35] C. S. Shacklett and H. A. Smith, *J. Am. Chem. Soc.*, **73**, 766 (1951).

The hydrogenolysis reaction is retarded by a catalyst made of lithium aluminum hydride and aluminum chloride, which is excellent for converting β-bromo acids, esters, and acid chlorides into the corresponding bromohydrins.[36]

Sodium borohydride ($NaBH_4$) is an especially versatile reducing agent because it can be employed with such polar solvents as water, methanol, and pyridine.[37] Lithium tributoxyaluminohydride [$Li(OC_4H_9)_3AlH$] is capable of reducing acid chlorides to aldehydes (*Angew.*, **73**, 81). *p*-Nitrobenzaldehyde, for example, is produced in 80% yield.[38]

$$p\text{-}O_2NC_6H_4COCl \rightarrow p\text{-}O_2NC_6H_4CHO$$

[36] R. F. Nystrom, *J. Am. Chem. Soc.*, **81**, 610 (1959).
[37] H. C. Brown, *J. Chem. Education*, **38**, 173 (1961).
[38] H. C. Brown and R. F. McFarlin, *J. Am. Chem. Soc.*, **78**, 252 (1956).

22

Reactions of radicals

Nearly all the reactions discussed in the preceding chapters, ascribed to the intermediate formation of ions, are normally carried out in solution under conditions favorable to ionization. The high dielectric constants of the solvents most frequently used greatly decrease the electrostatic work necessary for ion separation. Homolytic fission, on the other hand, is the rule in reactions that take place in the gas phase; for this type of bond cleavage involves much less energy, of course, than that requiring charge separation. Radical reactions are further differentiated from ionic reactions in that they usually are brought about simply by the input of energy, i.e., by heat or light. Ionic reactions, as has been seen, are catalyzed by acids or bases.

Formation

The existence of free radicals was demonstrated by Gomberg in 1900, his work with triarylmethyls being done in solution. The first convincing evidence that simple alkyl radicals are capable of existence was furnished in 1929–1931 by Paneth and his co-workers. To prepare free methyl they passed tetramethyllead vapors at low pressure through a tube at 600 to 800°. The lead compound decomposed into methyl and lead, which was deposited as a mirror.

$$Pb(CH_3)_4 \rightarrow Pb + 4CH_3 \cdot$$

The half-life period of methyl was found to be about 0.006 second at a pressure of 2 millimeters, which is even less than that of atomic hydrogen. Free ethyl is produced from tetraethyllead in a similar manner.

Methyl is formed also by pyrolysis of azomethane; at 200° the gas decomposes by a unimolecular reaction into nitrogen and methyl.

$$CH_3-N{=}N-CH_3 \rightarrow 2CH_3 \cdot + N_2$$

Most of the studies involving the deliberate formation and use of free radicals have been carried out in the liquid phase, however. For example, 2,2′-azo-*bis*-isobutyronitrile decomposes in toluene according to the following equation.[1]

$$\underset{\underset{CH_3}{|}}{\overset{\overset{CN}{|}}{CH_3-C}}-N{=}N-\underset{\underset{CH_3}{|}}{\overset{\overset{CN}{|}}{C}}-CH_3 \; \rightarrow \; 2 \quad \underset{CH_3}{\overset{CH_3}{\diagdown}}\dot{C}CN + N_2$$

Acetyl peroxide dissociates to yield neutral acetate radicals, which in turn form free methyl radicals and carbon dioxide. Similarly, benzoyl peroxide decomposes slowly to produce carbon dioxide and phenyl radicals (CR **21**, 169).

$$(C_6H_5CO)_2O_2 \; \rightarrow \; 2C_6H_5COO\cdot \; \rightarrow \; 2C_6H_5\cdot + 2CO_2$$

Benzenediazoacetate breaks down spontaneously at room temperature to yield phenyl and methyl radicals.

$$C_6H_5N{=}NOCOCH_3 \; \rightarrow \; C_6H_5\cdot + CH_3\cdot + N_2 + CO_2$$

The formation of free radicals from acyl peroxides may have its counterpart in the Kolbe electrolysis (p. 592) in which it is presumed that the carboxylate ion loses an electron at the anode, and becomes a free radical. Loss of carbon dioxide would form a hydrocarbon radical, which would undergo coupling to yield the hydrocarbon.

$$\underset{\underset{O^-}{|}}{R-C{=}O} \; \overset{-e}{\longrightarrow} \; \underset{\underset{O\cdot}{|}}{R-C{=}O} \; \overset{-CO_2}{\longrightarrow} \; R\cdot$$

$$2R\cdot \; \rightarrow \; R-R$$

Stability

Organic radicals have an incomplete octet and owe their reactivity to the tendency to acquire the electron that is needed to complete the shell of eight. The electron deficiency, like that in carbonium ions, may be delocalized by resonance interaction. The high order of stability of the allyl radical, for example, is ascribed to this phenomenon.

$$CH_2{=}CHCH_2\cdot \; \leftrightarrow \; \cdot CH_2CH{=}CH_2$$

[1] C. G. Overberger, M. T. O'Shaughnessy, and H. Shalit, *J. Am. Chem. Soc.*, **71**, 2661 (1949).

The effect of aryl groups on the stability of the methyl radical is remarkable. Free benzyl, which has been shown to have a transitory existence, can be represented by five different structures; like the allyl radical, it is a resonance hybrid.

As in the carbonium ion series, the effect is still greater in the benzohydryl radical; cleavage of tetraphenylethane by potassium shows that the central carbon-carbon bond is not strong. In the hexaarylethanes this weakening process has increased to a point at which dissociation occurs at ordinary temperatures. The energy necessary for the cleavage of the carbon-carbon bond in hexaphenylethane is only 19 kilocalories whereas for that in ethane itself it is 80 kilocalories. An inspection of the following formulas suggests that triphenylmethyl, for example, may be a hybrid of many different resonance structures.

The triarylmethyls are, in fact, very reactive and highly colored. The dissociation has been demonstrated by determination of molecular weight and magnetic susceptibility as well as spectral data in conjunction with photochemical instability and rapid reaction with oxygen.[2] It is probable, however, that steric factors prevent coplanarity of the three rings and that, in the resonance hybrid, the electron deficit is delocalized over only one or possibly two of the rings.[3]

As might be expected, a biradical such as I does not exist; the compound behaves as though it had the corresponding quinoid structure (II).

[2] H. P. Leftin and N. N. Lichtin, *J. Am. Chem. Soc.*, **79**, 2475 (1957).
[3] See N. C. Deno, J. J. Jaruzelski, and A. Schriesheim, *J. Org. Chem.*, **19**, 155 (1954).

On the other hand, the following biradicals have been prepared.

The stabilities of alkyl radicals fall in the same order as those of the corresponding carbonium ions.

Reactivity

The reactions of a free radical depend greatly on its stability; the more stable it is, the more specific are its reactions. Methyl radicals react immediately with all organic solvents whereas, as has been noted, stable solutions of triphenylmethyl can be made. The chief reaction of methyl and of ethyl radicals in the gas phase is recombination on the walls to give ethane and n-butane, respectively. The wall or some other agency is necessary to take up the energy given off by the coupling reaction. At higher temperatures the ethyl radical also disproportionates to ethane and ethylene. The change involves the passage of a hydrogen atom from one ethyl radical to another.

$$2CH_3CH_2\cdot \rightarrow CH_2{=}CH_2 + CH_3CH_3$$

Isopropyl and t-butyl radicals decompose in a similar way, but n-propyl and higher radicals undergo fission of a C—C rather than a C—H linkage. This difference is related to the lower energy of the C—C bond (58.6 kilocalories/mole) as compared with that of the C—H bond (87.3 kilocalories/mole).

In the reaction of a free radical with an alkane molecule, hydrogen is abstracted in preference to an alkyl group, presumably because the peripheral hydrogen atoms are more accessible than the C—C bond. Ethane yields an ethyl rather than a methyl radical.

$$R\cdot + CH_3\text{—}CH_3 \rightarrow RH + \cdot CH_2CH_3$$

This reaction illustrates the usual mode of attack by a free radical, which is known as radical transfer (CR **57**, 123). Methyl radicals have been employed to dehydrogenate a variety of compounds; the conversion of acetic acid into succinic acid is an example. The $\cdot CH_2CO_2H$ radicals are relatively stable and survive long enough to couple.

$$CH_3\cdot + CH_3CO_2H \rightarrow CH_4 + \cdot CH_2CO_2H$$

$$2\cdot CH_2CO_2H \rightarrow \begin{array}{c} CH_2CO_2H \\ | \\ CH_2CO_2H \end{array}$$

Nitriles and ketones have been coupled in a like manner; alkylbenzenes yield bibenzyls. An example is the synthesis of 2,3-dimethyl-2,3-diphenylbutane from cumene.[4]

$$\begin{array}{ccccc} CH_3 & & CH_3 & & CH_3 \quad CH_3 \\ | & & | & & | \qquad | \\ C_6H_5CH & \rightarrow & C_6H_5C\cdot & \rightarrow & C_6H_5C\text{——}CC_6H_5 \\ | & & | & & | \qquad | \\ CH_3 & & CH_3 & & CH_3 \quad CH_3 \end{array}$$

Decomposition of acetyl peroxide in alcohols produces aldehydes and ketones; isopropyl and *sec*-butyl alcohols yield, respectively, acetone and methyl ethyl ketone. By tracer techniques it has been established that the hydrogen atom removed first from the alcohol is not that attached to oxygen but one joined to carbon. The methyl radical may remove a halogen atom instead of a hydrogen atom. This type of reaction occurs readily with α-bromo esters, the methyl radical forming methyl bromide. When such a reaction takes place in an olefin as solvent, the olefin combines with the free radical, to give a γ-bromo acid; ethyl bromoacetate and 1-octene yield ethyl γ-bromocaprate.[5] It will be noted that the reaction is of the chain type; a single methyl radical may serve to bring about the condensation of many molecules of the bromo ester with the olefin, since the ethyl acetate radical ($\cdot CH_2CO_2C_2H_5$) is continuously regenerated.

[4] M. S. Kharasch, H. C. McBay, and W. H. Urry, *J. Org. Chem.*, **10**, 401 (1945).

[5] M. S. Kharasch, P. S. Skell, and P. Fisher, *J. Am. Chem. Soc.*, **70**, 1055 (1948).

$$CH_3\cdot + BrCH_2CO_2C_2H_5 \rightarrow CH_3Br + \cdot CH_2CO_2C_2H_5$$

$$\cdot CH_2CO_2C_2H_5 + C_6H_{13}CH{=}CH_2 \rightarrow C_6H_{13}\overset{.}{C}HCH_2CH_2CO_2C_2H_5$$

$$C_6H_{13}\overset{.}{C}HCH_2CH_2CO_2C_2H_5 + BrCH_2CO_2C_2H_5 \rightarrow$$

$$C_6H_{13}\underset{\overset{|}{Br}}{C}HCH_2CH_2CO_2C_2H_5 + \cdot CH_2CO_2C_2H_5$$

Hydroxyl radicals, generated by reaction of hydrogen peroxide with ferrous sulfate, have been used also to effect coupling; *t*-butyl alcohol, for example, is converted into α,α,α′,α′-tetramethyltetramethylene glycol in 46% yield (OS **40**, 90).

$$2CH_3\underset{\overset{|}{CH_3}}{\overset{\overset{CH_3}{|}}{C}}OH \xrightarrow{2\cdot OH} 2\cdot CH_2\underset{\overset{|}{CH_3}}{\overset{\overset{CH_3}{|}}{C}}OH \longrightarrow HO\underset{\overset{|}{CH_3}}{\overset{\overset{CH_3}{|}}{C}}CH_2CH_2\underset{\overset{|}{CH_3}}{\overset{\overset{CH_3}{|}}{C}}OH$$

t-Butyl perbenzoate in the presence of a catalyst such as cuprous bromide reacts with olefins to produce allylic benzoates. Cyclohexene, for instance, gives the corresponding cyclohexenyl benzoate.[6]

$$\bigcirc + C_6H_5CO_3C(CH_3)_3 \xrightarrow{CuBr} C_6H_5CO_2\text{—}\bigcirc + (CH_3)_3COH$$

Radicals generated by the decomposition of certain azo compounds may couple. When 1,1′-azo-*bis*-cyclohexane, for example, is heated in boiling toluene, nitrogen is evolved and 1,1′-dicyano-1,1′-bicyclohexyl is produced (OS **32**, 48; 69% yield).

$$\bigcirc\text{—}N{=}N\text{—}\bigcirc \rightarrow \bigcirc\text{—}\bigcirc + N_2$$

Coupling occurs also when the silver salts of perfluoro acids are decomposed thermally; fluorocarbons corresponding to the coupling products of the perfluoro radicals are formed. Thus perfluorobutyric acid gives perfluorohexane.[7]

$$2CF_3CF_2CF_2CO_2Ag \rightarrow C_6F_{14} + 2CO_2 + 2Ag$$

[6] M. S. Kharasch and G. Sosnovsky, *J. Am. Chem. Soc.*, **80**, 756 (1958).

[7] A. D. Kirshenbaum, A. G. Streng, and M. Hauptschein, *J. Am. Chem. Soc.*, **75**, 3141 (1953).

Pyrolysis

It is a rule that olefinic compounds are more readily cleaved by heat than the corresponding saturated hydrocarbons. An examination of the structures of olefins and their pyrolysis products reveals that cleavage occurs most readily at an *allyl position*, i.e., at a point that will give rise to a radical stabilized by resonance. This generalization is related to the Schmidt double bond rule, which states that a double bond strengthens the adjacent single bond and weakens the next following.

The pyrolysis of cyclohexene to butadiene (p. 694) and ethylene and of myrcene and limonene to isoprene illustrates the rule.

$$CH_3C=CHCH_2-CH_2CCH=CH_2$$

Myrcene   Limonene

The occurrence of dehydrogenation in the cracking process makes it seem likely that cleavage of the resulting olefins at an allyl position is important in the pyrolysis of paraffins.

1,5-Hexadienes when pyrolyzed appear to break down homolytically to form two radicals of the allyl type; the simplest example, 1,5-hexadiene or biallyl (p. 632), gives two allyl radicals.[8]

$$CH_2=CHCH_2CH_2CH=CH_2 \rightarrow 2CH_2=CHCH_2\cdot$$

Thermal decomposition of organic compounds other than hydrocarbons frequently is of synthetic value. Examples are reversal of the Diels-Alder reaction (p. 694), decarboxylation (p. 664), and decarbonylation (p. 662). A specific example is the formation of ketene by dehydration of acetic acid.

$$CH_3CO_2H \rightarrow CH_2=C=O + H_2O$$

Another process for forming ketene is pyrolysis of acetone.

$$CH_3COCH_3 \rightarrow CH_2=C=O + CH_4$$

Fission of olefinic compounds other than ketene has been attempted. In the following case there is evidence that an equilibrium exists between the carbene and its dimer.[9]

[8] W. D. Huntsman, *J. Am. Chem. Soc.*, **82**, 6389 (1960).
[9] H.-W. Wanzlick and E. Schinkora, *Angew. Chem.*, **72**, 494 (1960).

When tetra-α-naphthylethylene is heated at 250°, products are obtained that suggest the intermediate formation of di-α-naphthylcarbene.[10]

Pyrazolines are thermally unstable and, when heated with potassium hydroxide in the presence of platinum, yield cyclopropane derivatives. α,β-Unsaturated ketones and aldehydes can be converted by this method into the corresponding cyclopropane derivatives; cinnamaldehyde, for example, gives phenylcyclopropane.

Similarly, mesityl oxide yields 1,1,2-trimethylcyclopropane.

[10] V. Franzen and H.-I. Joschek, *Ann.*, **633**, 7 (1960).

The similarity between this type of decomposition and that of azo compounds is apparent if the pyrazoline is written in the azo form.

$$RCH \underset{CH_2CH_2}{\overset{N=N}{\diagup \diagdown \vert}}$$

Styrene reacts with ethyl diazoacetate to give ethyl 2-phenylcyclopropane-carboxylate in 85% yield.

$$C_6H_5CH{=}CH_2 + N_2CHCO_2C_2H_5 \rightarrow C_6H_5CH\underset{CH_2}{\diagdown \diagup}CHCO_2C_2H_5 + N_2$$

The reaction is effected in one step by dropping an equimolecular mixture of styrene and the diazo ester into an excess of styrene at 125°.

This remarkable reaction has been extended to aromatic hydrocarbons such as *p*-xylene, naphthalene, and phenanthrene; the products are, respectively, I, II, and III.

| I | II | III |

It seems probable that carbethoxycarbene, $CHCO_2C_2H_5$, is an intermediate in these condensations.

Benzalazine undergoes pyrolysis to lose nitrogen and form stilbene.[11] The decomposition proceeds by an ionic chain mechanism rather than by way of a carbene.

Peroxide Effect

One of the early triumphs of the radical theory was the elucidation of the process by which olefinic compounds undergo hydrobromination. Such addition reactions usually take place according to Markownikoff's rule; i.e., the bromine atom is attached to the carbon atom having the fewer hydrogen atoms. Allyl bromide gives propylene bromide, for example.

$$CH_2{=}CHCH_2Br + HBr \rightarrow CH_3CHBrCH_2Br$$

[11] H. E. Zimmerman and S. Somasekhara, *J. Am. Chem. Soc.*, **82**, 5865 (1960).

In the presence of small quantities of oxygen or peroxides, however, the reaction takes a different course; trimethylene bromide is almost the only product.

$$CH_2{=}CHCH_2Br + HBr \rightarrow BrCH_2CH_2CH_2Br$$

In many similar reactions the direction of addition is reversed by the presence of peroxides. This phenomenon was discovered by Kharasch and Mayo and is known as the *peroxide effect* (CR **27**, 351).

The peroxide effect has been observed also with acetylenic hydrocarbons; 1-hexyne, for example, in the presence of peroxides combines with hydrogen bromide to yield 1-bromo-1-hexene, whereas in the presence of antioxidants the product is 2-bromo-1-hexene. In these reactions, as in others mentioned elsewhere, the catalytic activity of the peroxide is ascribed to the production of free radicals. The free radical is postulated to react with hydrogen bromide to liberate a bromine atom that, having an odd number of electrons, is itself a free radical. The odd or unpaired electron forms a pair with one of the electrons of the olefinic bond, adding in such a way as to give the most stable radical possible.

$$Catalyst \rightarrow R\cdot$$

$$R\cdot + HBr \rightarrow RH + Br\cdot$$

$$RCH{=}CH_2 + Br\cdot \rightarrow R\dot{C}HCH_2Br$$

$$R\dot{C}HCH_2Br + HBr \rightarrow RCH_2CH_2Br + Br\cdot$$

The effect has been noted with compounds other than hydrocarbons. Diethyl allylmalonate takes up hydrogen bromide in the presence of dibenzoyl peroxide to give diethyl γ-bromopropylmalonate in 79 % yield.[12]

$$CH_2{=}CHCH_2CH(CO_2C_2H_5)_2 + HBr \rightarrow BrCH_2CH_2CH_2CH(CO_2C_2H_5)_2$$

3,3,3-Trifluoropropene, $CF_3CH{=}CH_2$, behaves in an interesting way; because of the great electron attracting power of the trifluoromethyl group, hydrogen bromide reacts under polar conditions to give the primary bromide exclusively. As was to be expected on theoretical grounds, the addition yields the same compound under free radical conditions.[13]

Addition of certain sulfur-containing compounds, such as mercaptans and thiophenols (p. 169), to unsaturated hydrocarbons is influenced by peroxides in a similar manner. Ethyl mercaptan combines with propylene, for example, in accord with Markownikoff's rule; in the presence of peroxides, however, the sense of the addition is reversed.

[12] H. M. Walborsky, *J. Am. Chem. Soc.*, **71**, 2941 (1949).
[13] A. L. Henne and M. Nager, *J. Am. Chem. Soc.*, **73**, 5527 (1951).

$$CH_3CH{=}CH_2 + C_2H_5SH \nearrow \quad \underset{\overset{|}{CH_3}}{CH_3CHSC_2H_5} \qquad \begin{array}{c}\text{peroxides} \\ \text{absent}\end{array}$$

$$\searrow \quad CH_3CH_2CH_2SC_2H_5 \qquad \begin{array}{c}\text{peroxides} \\ \text{present}\end{array}$$

Advantage has been taken of this reaction in the preparation of polyalkylene sulfides from dimercaptans and nonconjugated diolefins.[14]

Even bisulfite can be induced to undergo anti-Markownikoff addition. Bisulfites are typical carbonyl reagents and do not react with unconjugated olefinic linkages unless an oxidizing agent is present. Propylene, allyl alcohol, cyclohexene, and similar compounds take up bisulfite in the presence of oxygen; during the reaction the oxygen reacts slowly. If it is removed, the reaction stops.

In the addition of mercaptans and bisulfite the free radicals involved are $RS\cdot$ and $\cdot SO_3^-$, respectively. The mechanism proposed for the addition of bisulfite is the following.

$$HSO_3^- \xrightarrow{\text{Oxidant}} \cdot SO_3^-$$

$$\cdot SO_3^- + RCH{=}CH_2 \rightarrow R\underset{\cdot}{C}HCH_2SO_3^-$$

$$R\underset{\cdot}{C}HCH_2SO_3^- + HSO_3^- \rightarrow RCH_2CH_2SO_3^- + \cdot SO_3^-$$

Although hydrogen bromide is the only hydrogen halide with which the peroxide effect is readily observed, hydrogen chloride combines with ethylene and propylene in the vapor phase by a free radical mechanism.

Bimolecular Reduction of Carbonyl Compounds

Another reaction that appears to proceed by the intermediate formation of radicals is the bimolecular reduction of aldehydes and ketones. This type of change may be accomplished by a variety of reagents, the most useful of which are metals, metal amalgams, and the binary mixture, $Mg + MgI_2$. Electrolytic and photochemical methods are also valuable. The first step postulated in the process involving metals is the attachment of the metal in question to the oxygen atom, the resulting compound being a free radical known as a *ketyl*. Association of two molecules of the ketyl produces the pinacolate. In the reduction of dry acetone with magnesium amalgam, for example, the reaction may take the following course. The yield of pinacol is 50% (OS I, 459).

[14] C. S. Marvel, *Record of Chem. Progress*, **12**, 185 (1951).

$$2 \quad \underset{CH_3}{\overset{CH_3}{>}} CO + Mg(Hg) \longrightarrow \underset{CH_3}{\overset{CH_3}{>}} \overset{\cdot}{C}-O-Mg-O-\overset{\cdot}{C} \overset{CH_3}{\underset{CH_3}{<}} \longrightarrow$$

$$\underset{CH_3}{\overset{CH_3}{>}} C-O \diagdown \underset{\substack{CH_3 \\ \\ CH_3}}{\big|} Mg \xrightarrow{H_2O} \underset{CH_3}{\overset{CH_3}{>}} COH \overset{CH_3}{\underset{CH_3}{\big|}} COH$$

Pinacol can be isolated conveniently as the hexahydrate. A modification of the procedure has been developed in which ordinary acetone instead of the dried compound is employed.[15] Other aliphatic ketones give pinacols also, but not ordinarily in satisfactory yields.

Pinacol formation is much more easily effected in the aromatic series, and several methods are available for bringing it about. The most satisfactory of these is treatment with the binary mixture, Mg + MgI_2, a reagent that acts as though it were magnesious iodide, MgI. The preparation of benzopinacol is an example.

$$2 \quad \underset{C_6H_5}{\overset{C_6H_5}{>}} C{=}O + Mg + MgI_2 \longrightarrow \underset{C_6H_5}{\overset{C_6H_5}{>}} \overset{\overset{C_6H_5}{\diagup}}{\underset{\diagdown}{C}}OMgI \overset{COMgI}{\underset{C_6H_5}{\big|}} \xrightarrow{H_2O} \underset{(C_6H_5)_2COH}{(C_6H_5)_2COH}$$

The formation of biradicals in the ketyl series has been demonstrated.[16]

Many aryl ketones have been reduced to the corresponding pinacols by isopropyl alcohol; the reaction is carried out by exposing a solution of the ketone and alcohol to sunlight.[17] Benzopinacol can be made in 95% yield by this method (OS II, 71).

[15] J. E. Weber and A. D. Boggs, *J. Chem. Education*, **29**, 363 (1952).
[16] N. Hirota and S. I. Wiessman, *J. Am. Chem. Soc.*, **83**, 3533 (1961).
[17] V. Franzen, *Ann.*, **633**, 1 (1960).

$$2C_6H_5COC_6H_5 + CH_3CHCH_3 \rightarrow (C_6H_5)_2C\text{---}C(C_6H_5)_2 + CH_3COCH_3$$
$$\underset{OH}{|} \qquad\qquad \underset{OH}{|}\ \underset{OH}{|}$$

For alkyl aryl ketones the electrolytic method appears to be the most satisfactory. It has been employed successfully with acetophenone, propiophenone, aceto-*m*-xylene, *p*-phenylacetophenone, and surprisingly also with acetomesitylene, acetoisodurene, and 2,4,6-triethylacetophenone. The yields are seldom above 50%, however. An example is the formation of acetophenone pinacol, which can be made in this way in 40% yield.

$$2C_6H_5COCH_3 \rightarrow C_6H_5\overset{OH}{\underset{CH_3}{\overset{|}{\underset{|}{C}}}}\text{---}\overset{OH}{\underset{CH_3}{\overset{|}{\underset{|}{C}}}}C_6H_5$$

Acetophenone pinacol is produced also by use of amalgamated aluminum as the reducing agent.[18]

Suitably constituted diketones yield cyclic pinacols; an example is the reduction of 1,3-dibenzoyl-1,3-diphenylpropane by zinc in acetic acid.[19]

$$\begin{array}{ccc}
C_6H_5COCHC_6H_5 & & C_6H_5\overset{OH}{\overset{|}{C}}\text{-----}CHC_6H_5 \\
\diagdown & & | \qquad\qquad \diagdown \\
\quad CH_2 \rightarrow & & \qquad CH_2 \\
\diagup & & | \qquad\qquad \diagup \\
C_6H_5COCHC_6H_5 & & C_6H_5\overset{|}{\underset{OH}{C}}\text{-----}CHC_6H_5
\end{array}$$

α,β-Unsaturated ketones and esters when subjected to electrolytic reduction or when treated with a metal often undergo bimolecular reduction in which the two simple molecules are joined at position 4. An example of bimolecular reaction of this type is the reduction of methyl cinnamate to dimethyl β,γ-diphenyladipate.

$$2C_6H_5CH{=}CHCO_2CH_3 \xrightarrow{\text{Al(Hg)}} \begin{array}{c} C_6H_5CHCH_2CO_2CH_3 \\ | \\ C_6H_5CHCH_2CO_2CH_3 \end{array}$$

Bimolecular reduction of diethyl propylidenemalonate with aluminum amalgam, followed by hydrolysis and decarboxylation, yields β,γ-diethyladipic acid.

[18] K. Sisido and H. Nozaki, *J. Am. Chem. Soc.*, **70**, 776 (1948).

[19] N. O. V. Sonntag, S. Linder, E. I. Becker, and P. E. Spoerri, *J. Am. Chem. Soc.*, **75**, 2283 (1953).

$$2C_2H_5CH{=}C(CO_2C_2H_5)_2 \rightarrow \begin{array}{c} C_2H_5CHCH(CO_2C_2H_5)_2 \\ | \\ C_2H_5CHCH(CO_2C_2H_5)_2 \end{array} \rightarrow$$

$$\begin{array}{c} C_2H_5CHCH_2CO_2H \\ | \\ C_2H_5CHCH_2CO_2H \end{array}$$

Hunsdiecker Reaction

When silver salts of carboxylic acids are treated with bromine, carbon dioxide is lost and an alkyl or aryl bromide is formed (CR **40**, 381; **56**, 219; OR **9**, 332). The procedure is of special value with the silver salts of the half esters of dibasic acids since it offers a route to ω-bromo esters; an example is the synthesis of methyl δ-bromovalerate (OS III, 578; 54% yield).

$$\begin{array}{c} CH_2CO_2CH_3 \\ | \\ CH_2CH_2CH_2CO_2Ag \end{array} + Br_2 \rightarrow \begin{array}{c} CH_2CO_2CH_3 \\ | \\ CH_2CH_2CH_2Br \end{array} + CO_2 + AgBr$$

The method has served also for the preparation of long-chain bromo esters; methyl ω-bromolaurate, for example, can be produced in 78% yield.

$$(CH_2)_9\begin{array}{c} {}^{\diagup CH_2CO_2CH_3} \\ {}_{\diagdown CH_2CO_2Ag} \end{array} \rightarrow (CH_2)_9\begin{array}{c} {}^{\diagup CH_2CO_2CH_3} \\ {}_{\diagdown CH_2Br} \end{array}$$

Another example is the preparation of cyclobutyl bromide from cyclobutanecarboxylic acid.

$$\boxed{}{-}CO_2H \rightarrow \boxed{}{-}Br$$

A free radical mechanism has been proposed for the pyrolysis of acyl hypohalites, known as the Hunsdiecker reaction.[20]

Initiation: $RCO_2Br \rightarrow RCO_2{\cdot} + Br{\cdot}$

Propagation: $RCO_2{\cdot} \rightarrow R{\cdot} + CO_2$

$R{\cdot} + RCO_2Br \rightarrow RBr + RCO_2{\cdot}$

Termination: $2R{\cdot} \rightarrow R{-}R$ or $RH +$ olefin

and/or $R{\cdot} + RCO_2{\cdot} \rightarrow RCO_2R$

Not all the evidence, however, is consistent with this mechanism.[21]

[20] See E. L. Eliel and R. V. Acharya, *J. Org. Chem.*, **24**, 151 (1959).
[21] S. J. Cristol, J. R. Douglass, W. C. Firth, Jr., and R. E. Krall, *J. Am. Chem. Soc.*, **82**, 1829 (1960).

Sandmeyer Reaction

When diazonium salts are decomposed in the presence of halogen acids, the diazonium group is replaced by halogen (p. 366). It was discovered by Sandmeyer in 1884 that cuprous chloride and cuprous bromide are effective catalysts and that cuprous cyanide plays a similar role in the replacement of a diazonium group by the cyano group. This type of replacement, called the Sandmeyer reaction, is known to occur with other catalysts, but only rarely are the yields as high as those obtained by use of the cuprous salts (CR **40**, 251; QR **6**, 358). The reaction may proceed by way of an aryl radical.[22]

For the preparation of aryl halides it is usual to allow the freshly prepared diazonium halide to flow into a boiling 10% solution of the cuprous halide in the appropriate halogen acid, the aryl halide being removed by steam distillation. By this method, for example, *o*- and *p*-chlorotoluene can be prepared in 79% yields (OS I, 170).

$$CH_3C_6H_4N_2Cl \xrightarrow{\text{CuCl}} CH_3C_6H_4Cl + N_2$$

m-Chloronitrobenzene (OS I, 162) and *m*-chlorobenzaldehyde (OS II, 130) are made in a similar way.

A similar procedure serves to convert 2,6-dinitroaniline into 1-chloro-2,6-dinitrobenzene (OS **32**, 23).

A double salt is formed by combination of equimolecular amounts of the diazonium halide and the cuprous halide. For this reason it is necessary to employ a mole of the catalyst for each mole of the diazonium salt. The

[22] J. K. Kochi, *J. Am. Chem. Soc.*, **79**, 2942 (1957).

procedure for bromides is illustrated by the preparation of o-bromochloro-benzene from o-chlorobenzenediazonium bromide (OS III, 185).

o-Bromotoluene forms when the corresponding diazonium bromide is treated with copper powder (OS I, 135). Diazonium sulfates can be employed also; when p-toluenediazonium sulfate is added to a solution of cuprous bromide in hydrobromic acid, p-bromotoluene is produced in 73% yield (OS I, 136).

Diazotization of 2-amino-1-naphthalenesulfonic acid gives an insoluble zwitterion, which can be isolated by filtration. It reacts in the usual way to yield 2-bromo-1-naphthalenesulfonic acid. This transformation is of especial interest because it provides a route to the difficultly accessible 2-bromonaphthalene. The final step is removal of the sulfo group; the over-all yield is 64%. This method affords 2-bromonaphthalene in lower yields when 2-naphthylamine is the starting material.[23]

Replacement by a cyano group is effected by adding a neutral solution of a diazonium salt to a cuprous cyanide solution. For example, o- and p-tolunitrile are made from the corresponding diazotized toluidines (OS I, 514).

$$CH_3C_6H_4N_2Cl + CuCN \rightarrow CH_3C_6H_4CN + N_2 + CuCl$$

Meerwein Reaction

α,β-Unsaturated carbonyl compounds are capable of displacing the diazonium group; the product usually is a mixture of addition and substitution

[23] H. Wahl and H. Basilios, *Bull. soc. chim. France*, 482 (1947).

compounds (OR **11**, 189). An example is the synthesis of dimethyl α-chloro-β-(p-chlorophenyl)succinate from dimethyl maleate by treatment with diazotized p-chloroaniline.

$$\begin{array}{l} \text{CHCO}_2\text{CH}_3 \\ \| \\ \text{CHCO}_2\text{CH}_3 \end{array} + \text{ClC}_6\text{H}_4\text{N}_2\text{Cl} \rightarrow \begin{array}{l} \text{ClC}_6\text{H}_4\text{CHCO}_2\text{CH}_3 \\ | \\ \text{ClCHCO}_2\text{CH}_3 \end{array} + \text{N}_2$$

Usually, however, the chlorine is lost also, and the product is unsaturated. Cinnamaldehyde reacts with p-chlorobenzenediazonium chloride, for example, to yield α-(p-chlorophenyl)cinnamaldehyde. This type of reaction is carried out in weakly acidic media.[24]

$$\text{C}_6\text{H}_5\text{CH}{=}\text{CHCHO} + \text{ClC}_6\text{H}_4\text{N}_2\text{Cl} \rightarrow \underset{\underset{\text{C}_6\text{H}_4\text{Cl}}{|}}{\text{C}_6\text{H}_5\text{CH}{=}\text{CCHO}} + \text{N}_2 + \text{HCl}$$

Butadiene reacts in a similar way with p-nitrobenzenediazonium chloride to yield 1-chloro-4-(p-nitrophenyl)-2-butene.

$$\text{O}_2\text{NC}_6\text{H}_4\text{N}_2\text{Cl} + \text{CH}_2{=}\text{CH}{-}\text{CH}{=}\text{CH}_2 \rightarrow$$
$$\text{O}_2\text{NC}_6\text{H}_4\text{CH}_2\text{CH}{=}\text{CHCH}_2\text{Cl} + \text{N}_2$$

Quinones may be arylated, often in high yields, by treatment with diazonium salts. Benzoquinone, for example, may be phenylated by the action of benzenediazonium salts to give phenylquinone in 85% yield.

Another example is the formation of 2-p-acetylphenylquinone from quinone and diazotized p-aminoacetophenone (OS **34**, 1).

[24] H. Meerwein, E. Buchner, and K. van Emster, *J. prakt. Chem.*, **152**, 237 (1939).

Kolbe Electrolysis

Kolbe's electrolytic method,[25] as has been indicated (p. 576), can be interpreted by the assumption of radicals as intermediates. An example of this procedure is the preparation of tetratriacontane from stearic acid; the yield of the hydrocarbon is 95%.

$$2CH_3(CH_2)_{16}CO_2H \rightarrow CH_3(CH_2)_{32}CH_3$$

As in the action of halogens on the silver salt of a carboxylic acid, it seems probable that a free acyloxy radical is formed, which subsequently loses carbon dioxide to yield a hydrocarbon radical.[26]

$$\underset{\displaystyle RC\!-\!O^-}{\overset{\displaystyle O}{\|}} \xrightarrow{-e} \underset{\displaystyle RC\!-\!O\cdot}{\overset{\displaystyle O}{\|}} \longrightarrow R\cdot + CO_2$$

The Kolbe method is most useful with dibasic acids; diethyl suberate, for example, can be made by the electrolysis of potassium ethyl glutarate.

$$2KO_2C(CH_2)_3CO_2C_2H_5 \rightarrow \begin{matrix}(CH_2)_3CO_2C_2H_5 \\ | \\ (CH_2)_3CO_2C_2H_5\end{matrix}$$

Diethyl 1,16-hexadecanedicarboxylate is made in 55% yield by electrolysis of potassium ethyl sebacate (OS III, 401).

$$2C_2H_5O_2C(CH_2)_8CO_2K \xrightarrow{\text{Electrolysis}} C_2H_5O_2C(CH_2)_{16}CO_2C_2H_5$$

Kolbe's method is general for making esters of dibasic acids having an even number of carbon atoms.

A mixture of the salt of a monobasic acid with that of an acid ester gives long-chain esters. Of particular interest are those made from optically active dibasic acids; the use of β-methylglutaric acid is illustrative.

$$\begin{matrix}CO_2CH_3 \\ | \\ CH_2 \\ | \\ CH_3CH \\ | \\ CH_2 \\ | \\ CO_2^-\end{matrix} \quad + CH_3(CH_2)_nCO_2^- \xrightarrow{-2e} \begin{matrix}CO_2CH_3 \\ | \\ CH_2 \\ | \\ CH_3CH \\ | \\ CH_2 \\ | \\ (CH_2)_n \\ | \\ CH_3\end{matrix} \quad + 2CO_2$$

[25] B. C. L. Weedon, *Advances in Organic Chemistry*, Interscience Publishers, Inc., New York, Vol. I, p. 1, 1960.

[26] W. B. Smith and H, G. Gilde, *J. Am. Chem. Soc.*, **83**, 1355 (1961).

Dimethylformamide is a good solvent in which to perform Kolbe electrolyses.[27]

Homolytic Aromatic Substitution

Arylation and alkylation of aromatic rings have been effected with a number of compounds known to decompose to give hydrocarbon free radicals (CR 57, 77, 123). In all such reactions the o- and p-isomers are produced preferentially. For example, when nitrobenzene is treated with p-tolyl and p-bromophenyl reagents, the yield of m-isomer is 9% for p-tolyl and 12% for p-bromophenyl.[28] The reagents may be the aroyl peroxides, sodium benzenediazotate, acylarylnitrosamines, or 1-aryl-3,3-dimethyltriazenes. All four reagents give the isomers in the same proportions. When benzoyl peroxide is decomposed in benzene, pyridine, benzonitrile, methyl benzenesulfonate, or chlorobenzene, biaryls are produced.[29]

The rate-determining step of the phenylation of an aromatic nucleus by a phenyl radical is the addition of the radical to the nucleus of the substrate molecule to give an arylcyclohexadienyl radical; loss of a hydrogen radical to another radical such as the benzoyloxyl radical converts the complex into the biaryl.[30]

$$ArH + C_6H_5\cdot \rightarrow \left[Ar \begin{array}{c} C_6H_5 \\ \diagup \\ \diagdown \\ H \end{array} \right] \cdot + C_6H_5COO\cdot \rightarrow ArC_6H_5 + C_6H_5CO_2H$$

Another way of producing biaryls involves irradiation of aryl iodides in aromatic solvents; o-iodophenol in benzene gives 2-hydroxybiphenyl in 60 to 70% yield.[31]

The three phenylpyridines form when bromobenzene is electrolyzed in pyridine with magnesium electrodes.[32]

Decomposition of diazonium salts in alkaline media in the presence of the aromatic compound to be arylated produces biaryls by what is known as the Gomberg reaction.[33] It is illustrated by the synthesis of 4-bromobiphenyl by treatment of benzene with p-bromobenzenediazonium chloride in the presence of sodium hydroxide (OS I, 113; 35% yield).

$$BrC_6H_4N_2Cl + C_6H_6 + NaOH \rightarrow BrC_6H_4C_6H_5 + N_2 + NaCl + H_2O$$

[27] M. Finkelstein and R. C. Petersen, *J. Org. Chem.*, **25**, 136 (1960).

[28] D. H. Hey, A. Nechvatal, and T. S. Robinson, *J. Chem. Soc.*, 2892 (1951).

[29] R. L. Dannley and E. C. Gregg, Jr., *J. Am. Chem. Soc.*, **76**, 2997 (1954).

[30] D. H. Hey, S. Orman, and G. H. Williams, *J. Chem. Soc.*, 565 (1961).

[31] W. Wolf and N. Kharasch, *J. Org. Chem.*, **26**, 283 (1961).

[32] T. T. Tsai, W. E. McEwen, and J. Kleinberg, *J. Org. Chem.*, **26**, 318 (1961).

[33] H. Weingarten, *J. Org. Chem.*, **26**, 730 (1961).

Diazonium compounds can be reduced by finely divided metals such as copper and zinc in acid solution or by cuprous salts in alkaline solution, to effect loss of nitrogen and coupling of two aryl radicals. The use of copper is the Gattermann method. Substituents have a profound influence; nitro groups in the o-position exert the most favorable effect. An example is the preparation of 2,2'-dinitrobiphenyl from diazotized o-nitroaniline.

$$\left[\cdot\underset{NO_2}{\bigcirc}N_2\right]_2^{++} SO_4^= + 2Cu \rightarrow \underset{NO_2\ \ NO_2}{\bigcirc-\bigcirc} + 2Cu^+ + 2N_2 + SO_4^=$$

Diphenic acid is made in high yields from diazotized anthranilic acid by treatment with ammoniacal cuprous salts (OS I, 222).

$$2\underset{}{\overset{CO_2H}{\bigcirc}}N_2^+ + 2Cu^+ \xrightarrow{NH_4OH} \underset{}{\bigcirc}CO_2H + 2N_2 + 2Cu^{++}$$
$$\underset{}{\bigcirc}CO_2H$$

An important technical procedure is based on this type of reaction. 8-Amino-1-naphthoic acid, by diazotization and treatment with ammoniacal cuprous oxide, yields 1,1'-binaphthyl-8,8'-dicarboxylic acid, an intermediate in the preparation of anthanthrone.

$$\underset{NH_2}{\overset{CO_2H}{\bigcirc}} \rightarrow \underset{HO_2C}{\overset{CO_2H}{\bigcirc}} \rightarrow \underset{OC-}{\overset{-CO}{\bigcirc}}$$

Anthanthrone

Another example of this method is the formation of 5,5'-dimethoxydiphenic acid from 2-amino-4-methoxybenzoic acid.

$$2\underset{OCH_3}{\overset{CO_2H}{\bigcirc}}N_2Cl \xrightarrow{CuOH} \underset{OCH_3\ \ OCH_3}{\overset{CO_2H\ \ CO_2H}{\bigcirc-\bigcirc}}$$

The Pschorr ring closure (OR 9, 409) seems to be similar to the intermolecular arylations. The synthesis of 1,4-dimethylphenanthrene is an example.

Carbazole may be formed in a like manner from *o*-aminodiphenylamine.

This method is particularly valuable for substituted carbazoles; an example is the synthesis of 3-benzoylcarbazole.

The formation of fluorenones from *o*-aminobenzophenones has proved to be valuable; the preparation of 3-methylfluorenone is an example.[34]

N-Alkylphenanthridones can be made also by the Pschorr procedure; N-methylphenanthridone, for example, is formed when diazotized *o*-amino-N-methylbenzanilide is decomposed thermally or in the presence of copper.[35]

[34] See D. F DeTar and T. E. Whiteley, *J. Am. Chem. Soc.*, **79**, 2498 (1957).
[35] See T. Cohen, R. M. Moran, Jr., and G. Sowinski, *J. Org. Chem.*, **26**, 1 (1961).

Persulfate Oxidation of Phenols

Another reaction for which a free radical mechanism has been suggested is the persulfate oxidation of phenols, which serves to introduce a hydroxyl group, usually in the position *para* to a hydroxyl group already present. A hydroxyphenyl alkali sulfate is formed as an intermediate. Phenol gives hydroquinone, for example (CR **49**, 91).

This procedure, known as the Elbs method, serves also to prepare gentisic acid from salicylic acid.[36]

Persulfate oxidation of *o*-coumaric acid followed by decarboxylation affords a route to vinylhydroquinone.[37]

Vinyl Polymerization

Many olefinic compounds undergo polymerization when treated with substances that generate free radicals. The polymerization of styrene under the influence of benzoyl peroxide is illustrative. The peroxide decomposes to yield free radicals, which then initiate the polymerization. As would be expected, the attack of the olefin is always such as to give the free radical with the least possible free energy.

$$C_6H_5\cdot + CH_2{=}CH \underset{\underset{\displaystyle C_6H_5}{|}}{} \rightarrow C_6H_5CH_2\overset{\displaystyle \cdot}{C}H \underset{\underset{\displaystyle C_6H_5}{|}}{} \quad (\text{not } C_6H_5\overset{\displaystyle}{C}HCH_2\cdot) \underset{\underset{\displaystyle C_6H_5}{|}}{}$$

The propagation consists of a continuation of this process.

[36] R. U. Schock, Jr. and D. L. Tabern, *J. Org. Chem.*, **16**, 1772 (1951).
[37] I. H. Updegraff and H. G. Cassidy, *J. Am. Chem. Soc.*, **71**, 407 (1949).

$$C_6H_5CH_2CH\cdot + xCH_2{=}CH \rightarrow C_6H_5CH_2CH{-}\left[CH_2CH{-}\right]CH_2{-}CH\cdot$$
$$\underset{C_6H_5}{|} \qquad \underset{C_6H_5}{|} \qquad\qquad \underset{C_6H_5}{|} \quad \underset{C_6H_5}{|}_{x-1} \quad \underset{C_6H_5}{|}$$

Growth of the polymer chain may be interrupted in several ways. The growing free radical chain may combine with one of the free radicals from the peroxide ($C_6H_5\cdot$ or $C_6H_5\overset{\displaystyle O}{\overset{\|}{C}}\!\text{O}\cdot$), it may couple with itself, or it may undergo disproportionation. The latter process occurs when one free radical abstracts a hydrogen atom (with one electron) from another free radical at a point near the unpaired electron it already possesses. The resulting diradical rearranges to an olefin. If the two unpaired electrons are sufficiently far apart, chain propagation may occur at each of them. This is one of the ways in which branched polymers may form.

With the passage of the hydrogen atom from one radical or molecule to another, the point of propagation is transferred. Chain transfer can be accomplished deliberately by addition of chain transfer agents such as mercaptans. The mercaptan reacts with the growing radical by supplying a hydrogen atom, being itself transformed to a radical.

$$R\cdot + RSH \rightarrow RS\cdot + RH$$

The newly formed radical can initiate the formation of a new chain; chain transfer agents operate to reduce the molecular weight of the polymer that is being formed.

Olefinic compounds that undergo free radical polymerization are usually of the type $CH_2{=}CHA$, in which A is a negative atom or group such as $-CO_2CH_3$, $-CN$, $-Cl$, or $-C_6H_5$. Of the simple olefins only ethylene forms a polymer in this way and then only at very high pressures. Electron-attracting functions when attached to the olefinic group usually facilitate polymerization. Remarkable examples are the esters of acrylic and methacrylic acids. The polymerization of methyl methacrylate will serve to illustrate this type of polymerization; long chains are formed in which the vinyl groups are linked end to end.

$$\cdots CH_2\underset{\underset{CH_3}{|}}{\overset{\overset{CO_2CH_3}{|}}{C}}\!{-}CH_2\underset{\underset{CH_3}{|}}{\overset{\overset{CO_2CH_3}{|}}{C}}\!{-}CH_2\underset{\underset{CH_3}{|}}{\overset{\overset{CO_2CH_3}{|}}{C}}\!{-}CH_2\underset{\underset{CH_3}{|}}{\overset{\overset{CO_2CH_3}{|}}{C}}\cdots$$

The product, polymethyl methacrylate, is a thermoplastic polymer that has the appearance of glass and is sold under the trade names Plexiglas and Lucite.

Many other vinyl monomers have become important industrially; the following are examples.

Styrene	$CH_2\!=\!CHC_6H_5$
Acrylates	$CH_2\!=\!CHCO_2R$
Vinyl chloride	$CH_2\!=\!CHCl$
Vinylidene chloride	$CH_2\!=\!CCl_2$
Vinyl acetate	$CH_2\!=\!CHOCOCH_3$
Vinyl ketones	$CH_2\!=\!CHCOR$
Vinyl ethers	$CH_2\!=\!CHOR$
Divinyl ether	$CH_2\!=\!CHOCH\!=\!CH_2$
Acrylonitrile	$CH_2\!=\!CHCN$
Methacrylonitrile	$CH_2\!=\!\underset{\underset{CH_3}{\mid}}{C}CN$
1,3-Butadiene	$CH_2\!=\!CHCH\!=\!CH_2$
Isoprene	$CH_2\!=\!\underset{\underset{CH_3}{\mid}}{C}CH\!=\!CH_2$
Chloroprene	$CH_2\!=\!\underset{\underset{Cl}{\mid}}{C}CH\!=\!CH_2$
2,3-Dimethyl-1,3-butadiene	$CH_2\!=\!\underset{\underset{CH_3}{\mid}}{C}\!\!-\!\!-\!\!\underset{\underset{CH_3}{\mid}}{C}\!=\!CH_2$

The failure of propylene, 1-butene, isobutylene, and other simple olefins to polymerize under these conditions has been ascribed to the presence in such olefins of allylic hydrogen atoms, which enable them to serve as radical transfer agents.

$$R\cdot + RCH_2CH\!=\!CH_2 \rightarrow RH + R\dot{C}HCH\!=\!CH_2$$

Apparently conjugated olefinic bonds are so reactive that allylic hydrogen atoms do not interfere; isoprene polymerizes more readily than methyl acrylate. α-Methylstyrene, however, cannot be polymerized satisfactorily by the radical method.

Hydrogen peroxide, acetyl peroxide, benzoyl peroxide, and sodium persulfate are among the catalysts most frequently employed. Heat and irradiation likewise may serve to start the polymerization. The hypothesis that these reactions are initiated by radicals is supported by the fact that diazo compounds, metal alkyls, and other substances that decompose by way of free radicals may serve as catalysts. In a peroxide-catalyzed polymerization that is interrupted before it is complete, one never finds polymers of intermediate weight, but only monomers and polymers having very high molecular weights. Since traces of peroxides commonly are present in organic compounds of many types, it often happens that polymerization occurs prematurely by adventitious contact of the monomer with a catalyst. For this reason antioxidants are commonly added to the monomers to preserve them. Among the most useful of these are phenolic, amino, and nitro compounds. Hydroquinone is an important example. This preservative is effective only in the presence of oxygen and is believed to function as a source of quinone, which is the real stabilizer.

The inhibitory effects of quinones and aromatic polynitro compounds appear to be due to their reaction with the free radicals to form new free radicals that are resonance stabilized to such a high degree that they are not effective in promoting polymerization.

Modifiers, such as dodecyl mercaptan, used in the manufacture of GR-S rubbers (p. 600), are believed to act as chain-transfer agents. It has been mentioned (p. 153) that vinyl polymerization can be brought about by electrophiles, such as boron fluoride and aluminum chloride, as well as by peroxides.

Polymerization systems

Polymerization of vinyl compounds by free radical initiation may be carried out in bulk, in solution, in suspension, or in emulsion. In bulk polymerization the initiator is usually a compound that decomposes to give radicals at a fairly rapid rate at relatively low temperatures. Bulk polymerization is used mainly to cast objects in a particular shape where molding at elevated temperatures is not feasible; it serves, for example, in casting a methyl methacrylate polymer over a flower, insect, or other object that would be destroyed by heat. When large amounts of monomer are polymerized in bulk, the heat transfer problem becomes serious, and local overheating in the reacting mass causes decomposition and side reactions.

Solution polymerization, for the same reason, is not entirely satisfactory. As the polymer grows the viscosity of the solution becomes very great, and stirring to facilitate heat transfer becomes difficult. In some procedures the polymer, at a certain stage of growth, becomes insoluble and separates as a bead. This method gives satisfactory results with methyl methacrylate in methanol and with acrylonitrile in water. The initiator must be soluble in the solvent and must produce radicals at the temperature desired.

Emulsion polymerization is widely used in commercial work. The monomer is emulsified in water with an acidic, basic, or neutral emulsifier. The chief advantage of emulsion systems is their fluidity, which permits adequate heat transfer and takes care of the problems of local overheating. There is no chain transfer with water, so high-molecular weight material can be formed and transferred in emulsion without viscosity effects interfering. The emulsion system cannot be used with water-sensitive monomers. Soaps and synthetic detergents are widely used as emulsifiers. Even polymeric materials such as polyvinyl alcohol and proteins are satisfactory.

Copolymerization

When a mixture of different vinyl compounds undergoes polymerization, chains may be formed that contain more than one type of structural unit. Vinylite polymers, for example, are made by polymerizing a mixture of vinyl chloride and vinyl acetate. The product, a *copolymer*, is made up of chains that probably are unlike, since the two monomers do not react at the same rate and the relative concentrations of reactants do not remain constant. Although copolymerization does not occur with every pair of polymerizable vinyl compounds, many copolymers have been made.

The best-known copolymers are a group of synthetic rubbers produced by the so-called GR-S recipe. It involves polymerizing a mixture of styrene and butadiene in the ratio of about 1 to 3, dodecyl mercaptan being employed as a modifier. The diene enters the polymer chain by 1,4- as well as 1,2-addition, thus giving rise to the following types of structural units in the polymer.

$$-CH-CH_2- \qquad -CH_2CH=CHCH_2- \qquad -CH_2CH-$$
$$\underset{C_6H_5}{\big|} \qquad\qquad\qquad\qquad\qquad\qquad \underset{\underset{CH_2}{\overset{\|}{CH}}}{\big|}$$

The structure of the polymer is not known, but there is evidence that chains of the following type may be present.

$$-CH_2CH=CHCH_2CH_2CH\text{---------}(CH_2CH)_x-CH_2CH=CHCH_2-$$
$$\underset{CH=CH_2}{\big|}\underset{C_6H_5}{\big|}$$

The so-called *cold rubber* differs from the GR-S types in that it is produced at much lower temperatures (5°) and in the mode of initiation of the copolymerization.[38]

Heteropolymerization

It is extremely interesting that certain unsaturated substances that do not polymerize readily alone may be caused to enter polymer chains by the copolymerization technique. An example is the copolymerization of styrene and maleic anhydride. Maleic anhydride does not polymerize readily alone but combines with styrene to produce polymers. Presumably

[38] W. B. Reynolds, *J. Chem. Education*, **27**, 494 (1950).

the radicals formed by the maleic anhydride unit are too stable to attack maleic anhydride but can react with styrene. The product is a *heteropolymer*.

Another example of heteropolymerization is the copolymerization of olefinic compounds with sulfur dioxide, which does not polymerize alone; the products are polysulfones.

$$-[\overset{\overset{\displaystyle R}{|}}{C}HCH_2SO_2\overset{\overset{\displaystyle R}{|}}{C}HCH_2SO_2]_n-$$

Telomerization

Vinyl polymerization reactions are known that are truly of the chain type, i.e., the termination step generates the radical that is the initiator. Examples are found among the halogenated methanes; when carbon tetrachloride is condensed with styrene in the presence of acetyl peroxide, the chief product is a polymer of the type $Cl(C_6H_5CHCH_2)_nCCl_3$.[39]

The mechanism that has been offered for the formation of this polymer consists of the following steps.

$$(CH_3COO)_2 \rightarrow CH_3\cdot + CO_2 + CH_3COO\cdot \qquad (A)$$
$$CH_3\cdot + CCl_4 \rightarrow CH_3Cl + \cdot CCl_3 \qquad (B)$$
$$C_6H_5CH{=}CH_2 + \cdot CCl_3 \rightarrow \underset{\overset{|}{C_6H_5}}{\cdot CHCH_2CCl_3} \qquad (C)$$

$$\underset{\overset{|}{C_6H_5}}{\cdot CHCH_2CCl_3} + C_6H_5CH{=}CH_2 \rightarrow \underset{\overset{|}{C_6H_5}\;\overset{|}{C_6H_5}}{\cdot CHCH_2CHCH_2CCl_3} \qquad (D)$$

The secondary free radicals formed in step D may unite with another molecule of styrene and by repetition of this process give rise to a polymeric free radical.

$$\underset{\overset{|}{C_6H_5}\;\overset{|}{C_6H_5}}{\cdot CHCH_2[CHCH_2]_nCCl_3}$$

The growth of the chain is terminated by reaction of the free radical with carbon tetrachloride.

$$\underset{\overset{|}{C_6H_5}\;\overset{|}{C_6H_5}}{\cdot CHCH_2[CHCH_2]_nCCl_3} + CCl_4 \rightarrow \underset{\overset{|}{Cl}\;\overset{|}{C_6H_5}}{C_6H_5CHCH_2[CHCH_2]_nCCl_3} + \cdot CCl_3$$

It will be noted that this polymer is not made up of a recurring structural unit but is of the type $X - (A)_n - Y$. Such polymers have become known as *telomers*, and the process by which they are produced is termed *telomerization*; the compound X—Y is called a *telogen*.

[39] M. S. Kharasch, E. V. Jensen, and W. H. Urry, *J. Am. Chem. Soc.*, **69**, 1100 (1947).

Condensation

Many olefinic compounds combine with radicals to yield new radicals that are too stable to attack a second molecule of the olefin, and the propagation step does not occur. Inhibiters fall in this class, of course. Such molecules may be employed to "trap" radicals; a reaction of this type has been realized in the photochlorination of benzene. The addition of chlorine to benzene to yield benzene hexachloride is well known as is the addition of chlorine to maleic anhydride to give α,α'-dichlorosuccinic anhydride. When chlorine is passed into a mixture of benzene and maleic anhydride, however, the reaction takes a different course; the chief product is α-phenyl-α'-chlorosuccinic anhydride. It would appear that the attack of benzene by a chlorine free radical gives a chlorocyclohexadiene radical, which is intercepted by a molecule of maleic anhydride.[40] Dehydrochlorination of the intermediate reaction product yields phenylmaleic anhydride.

Although the yield is only 30 to 35%, the availability of starting materials and the simplicity of the process make the route attractive.

Olefins have been condensed with paraffins also by a non-catalytic process by the use of high pressure (4500 pounds per square inch) and a temperature of about 500°. In contrast with catalytic alkylation the non-catalytic process effects alkylation of normal paraffins as well as of isoparaffins. The alkylation of isobutane with ethylene is the basis of a commercial process for making neohexane.

[40] G. G. Ecke, L. R. Buzbee, and A. J. Kolka, *J. Am. Chem. Soc.*, **78**, 79 (1956).

Similar results have been obtained by the use of homogeneous catalysts such as aliphatic halogenated compounds and nitro compounds. When isobutane is condensed with propylene by this method, the chief products are 2,2-dimethylpentane and triptane.

$$CH_3-\underset{\underset{CH_3}{|}}{\overset{\overset{CH_3}{|}}{C}}-CH_2CH_2CH_3 \qquad CH_3-\underset{\underset{CH_3}{|}}{\overset{\overset{CH_3}{|}}{C}}-\underset{\underset{CH_3}{|}}{CH}CH_3$$

2,2-Dimethylpentane   Triptane

Thermal alkylation of paraffins is thought to occur by way of free radicals. The condensation of propane with ethylene illustrates the mechanism. The first step is homolytic cleavage of propane to a mixture of radicals (R·)

$$R\cdot + CH_3CH_2CH_3 \rightarrow RH + CH_3\overset{\cdot}{C}HCH_3$$

$$\underset{CH_3}{\overset{CH_3}{\diagdown}}CH\cdot + CH_2{=}CH_2 \rightarrow \underset{CH_3}{\overset{CH_3}{\diagdown}}CHCH_2CH_2\cdot$$

$$\underset{CH_3}{\overset{CH_3}{\diagdown}}CHCH_2CH_2\cdot + CH_3CH_2CH_3 \rightarrow \underset{CH_3}{\overset{CH_3}{\diagdown}}CHCH_2CH_3 + CH_3\overset{\cdot}{C}HCH_3$$

23

Substitution reactions in the aliphatic series

Replacement of hydrogen in paraffinic compounds shows only a formal resemblance to the substitution reactions of the aromatic series. Halogenation, nitration, sulfonation, and other substitution reactions usually are effected in the paraffin and cycloparaffin series under conditions conducive to radical formation. The evidence for this type of mechanism is most convincing perhaps in halogenation.

Chlorination

Paraffins
Chlorination of paraffins, for example, is postulated to involve radicals and to take place by a chain reaction. The chlorination of ethane may be taken as an example. The chlorine atom is the chain carrier.

Initiation: $\qquad$ $Cl_2 + h\nu \rightarrow 2Cl\cdot$

Propagation: $\qquad$ $Cl\cdot + C_2H_6 \rightarrow C_2H_5\cdot + HCl$

$\qquad\qquad\qquad C_2H_5\cdot + Cl_2 \rightarrow C_2H_5Cl + Cl\cdot$

Ethane and chlorine react very rapidly at 132° in the presence of tetraethyllead, whereas without the catalyst no reaction occurs at this temperature. Also, the reaction ceases at once if a little oxygen is passed into the mixture to destroy the free radical.

Direct chlorination of paraffins is difficult to control and almost invariably produces a mixture. A commercial method has been developed, however, for controlling the chlorination of paraffins so that the product consists largely of monochloro derivatives. It is the jet process, in which preheated reactants are brought together at a temperature at which reaction is extremely rapid. The chlorination of methane, which cannot give rise to isomeric chlorides, is a commercial route to methyl chloride, methylene chloride, chloroform, and carbon tetrachloride.

A commercial process consists of the chlorination of a petroleum fraction made up chiefly of pentanes. The product contains the mono-chlorides primarily and is used to make the various amyl alcohols (p. 280).

Chlorination occurs normally with cycloparaffins; cyclopropane offers problems, however.

$$\underset{CH_2-CH_2}{\overset{CH_2}{\diagdown}} + Cl_2 \rightarrow \underset{CH_2-CHCl}{\overset{CH_2}{\diagdown}} + HCl$$

Chlorination is carried out most satisfactorily by the photochemical method. The reason for this preference is that the cyclopropyl chloride from the thermal process is contaminated with allyl chloride. Up to 550° (residence time 0.5 second) the isomerization of cyclopropane is unimportant. Cyclopropyl chloride, however, undergoes ring opening to a considerable extent at higher temperatures; hence the photochemical method yields a purer product.

Chlorination of spiropentane has been effected in a similar manner.[1]

$$\underset{H_2C}{\overset{H_2C}{\diagup}}\underset{CH_2}{\overset{CH_2}{\diagdown}}C\underset{CH_2}{\overset{CH_2}{\diagup}} + Cl_2 \rightarrow \underset{H_2C}{\overset{H_2C}{\diagup}}\underset{CH_2}{\overset{CHCl}{\diagdown}}C\underset{CH_2}{\overset{CH_2}{\diagup}} + HCl$$

Halogenation of aromatic hydrocarbons carrying side chains usually can be made to proceed on the ring or in the side chain by proper control of conditions. As has been stated, the presence of iron (ferric halide) or a similar "carrier" favors nuclear halogenation, whereas heat and light in the absence of the carrier cause lateral halogenation. By the photochemical process toluene may be chlorinated readily to give benzyl chloride and benzal chloride.

$$C_6H_5CH_3 \rightarrow C_6H_5CH_2Cl \rightarrow C_6H_5CHCl_2$$

At temperatures above 150° the formation of benzotrichloride is favored, reaching 83% at 160°. Another reagent for effecting chlorination is sulfuryl chloride, which is useful for aliphatic as well as aromatic compounds. Toluene undergoes peroxide-catalyzed chlorination by sulfuryl chloride to give benzyl chloride, benzal chloride, and benzotrichloride.[2]

[1] D. E. Applequist and G. F. Fanta, *J. Am. Chem. Soc.*, **82**, 6393 (1960).
[2] F. Morgan and P. J. Pengilly, *Chem. and Ind.*, 1440 (1960).

In the aliphatic series chlorination is carried out by boiling the compounds with sulfuryl chloride in the presence of a small amount of benzoyl peroxide. The peroxide presumably acts upon the sulfuryl chloride to generate chlorine atoms. The method is particularly useful for chlorination of side chains of compounds containing sensitive nuclei. Toluene gives benzyl chloride in nearly quantitative yields, and *m*-xylene is transformed into α-chloro-*m*-xylene in 80% yield. Ethylbenzene affords α-chloro-ethylbenzene in similarly high yield. Of special interest is *t*-butylbenzene, which gives β-chloro-*t*-butylbenzene in 70% yield.

If paraffins are treated with a mixture of chlorine and sulfur dioxide, under the influence of light, chlorination is not the major reaction. The process, known as the Reed reaction, brings about chlorosulfonation instead (p. 42).

Olefins

Although olefins normally combine additively with halogens in the liquid phase, substitution can be effected in the gas phase. In particular, halogenation occurs readily at an allyl position. When propylene and chlorine, for example, are preheated and mixed in a jet at 600°, allyl chloride is formed in yields of 82%.

$$CH_2{=}CHCH_3 + Cl_2 \xrightarrow{600°} CH_2{=}CHCH_2Cl + HCl$$

Isobutylene reacts with chlorine in this manner at temperatures as low as −50° to yield methallyl chloride. The conditions involved suggest that the reaction is ionic in type. It may occur in gaseous or liquid phase, requires no external activation, and is unaffected by the presence of oxygen. The following mechanism is consistent with existing experimental data.[3]

Olefins such as ethylene, and certain of its chlorination products, which have no hydrogen atoms at an allyl position, react with chlorine under certain conditions to give addition compounds. The reaction is of the chain type and is inhibited by traces of oxygen. Under such conditions benzene comes close to behaving as 1,3,5-cyclohexatriene; it combines with chlorine to give benzene hexachloride. In the photochemical addition of chlorine to chlorobenzene and to *o*-dichlorobenzene, in the presence of

[3] R. W. Taft, Jr., *J. Am. Chem. Soc.*, **70**, 3364 (1948).

iodine, partial addition products are formed. Thus, chlorobenzene gives rise to 1,3,4,5,6-pentachloro-1-cyclohexene.[4]

Ethers

The α-position of aliphatic ethers is attacked readily by electrophilic agents. It may be on the other hand that chlorine, for instance, attacks by the radical mechanism. Whatever the mechanism, the reaction proceeds readily. Ethyl ether, for example, reacts with chlorine at $-20°$ to yield α-chloroethyl ethyl ether.[5]

$$CH_3CH_2OCH_2CH_3 \rightarrow CH_3\underset{\underset{Cl}{|}}{C}HOCH_2CH_3$$

In a similar way dioxane is converted into 2,3-dichloro-1,4-dioxane. It is likely that the monochloro derivative loses a molecule of hydrogen chloride to yield dioxene, which then reacts additively with chlorine.

Methyl ether reacts with chlorine under carefully controlled conditions to give dichloromethyl ether in 60% yields. The reaction is catalyzed by light.[6]

$$CH_3OCH_3 + 2Cl_2 \rightarrow ClCH_2OCH_2Cl + 2HCl$$

Carbonyl compounds

Hydrogen atoms in a position *alpha* to a carbonyl group are replaced with varying degrees of readiness, depending on the functions attached to the carbonyl group. Whether the reaction is to be classed as ionic or radical is generally difficult to decide. Aldehydes, the most reactive members of the group, may react with halogens to yield the corresponding acyl halides as well as the α-halo aldehydes. The formation of acid halides is satisfactory only with aldehydes that have no α-hydrogen atom. An

[4] A. J. Kolka, H. D. Orloff, and M. E. Griffing, *J. Am. Chem. Soc.*, **76**, 1244 (1954).
[5] G. E. Hall and F. M. Ubertini, *J. Org. Chem.*, **15**, 715 (1950).
[6] O. Neunhoeffer and G. Schmidt, *Chem. Tech.* (*Berlin*), **10**, 103 (1958).

example is the chlorination of *o*-chlorobenzaldehyde to produce *o*-chloro-benzoyl chloride (OS I, 155; 72% yield).

$$\text{(ring)}\begin{smallmatrix}\text{CHO}\\\text{Cl}\end{smallmatrix} + Cl_2 \rightarrow \text{(ring)}\begin{smallmatrix}\text{COCl}\\\text{Cl}\end{smallmatrix} + HCl$$

Halogenation of simple esters is not often employed. Chloromethyl acetate can be produced in satisfactory yield, however, by treatment of methyl acetate with chlorine at low temperatures.[7]

$$CH_3CO_2CH_3 + Cl_2 \rightarrow CH_3CO_2CH_2Cl + HCl$$

The usual method of preparing compounds of this type, it should be pointed out, is to condense aldehydes with acid halides (p. 402).
Ethylene carbonate undergoes chlorination also.[8]

$$\begin{matrix}CH_2O\\|\qquad\;\;\diagdown\\\qquad\quad CO\; + \;Cl_2\; \rightarrow\\|\qquad\diagup\\CH_2O\end{matrix}\qquad\begin{matrix}ClCH{-}CO\\|\qquad\qquad\diagdown\\\qquad\qquad\; O\; + \;HCl\\|\qquad\quad\diagup\\CH_2CO\end{matrix}$$

Pyruvic acid gives chloropyruvic acid when treated with sulfuryl chloride at room temperature for 60 hours (OS **40**, 54; yield 98%).

$$CH_3COCO_2H + SO_2Cl_2 \rightarrow ClCH_2COCO_2H + SO_2 + HCl$$

Aliphatic acid chlorides, as has been stated (p. 136), undergo chlorination preferentially at the α-position. When the reaction is carried out with sulfuryl chloride in the presence of peroxides, however, chlorination occurs at the β- and γ-positions. By this method propionyl chloride gives the α- and β-chloro derivatives in yields of 40 and 60%, respectively. The behavior of sulfuryl chloride suggests a free radical mechanism.

$$CH_3CH_2COCl \xrightarrow{SO_2Cl_2} CH_3CHClCOCl \quad \text{and} \quad CH_2ClCH_2COCl$$

In photochlorination of butyric acid, the acid chloride, the nitrile, and the methyl ester the β-position is favored.[9] In valeryl chloride, however, the γ-position is attacked preferentially, while in caproyl chloride the δ-position is favored.[10]

Bromination

Because it is expensive bromine has not been exploited extensively. Bromination is qualitatively similar to chlorination. Allyl and methallyl

[7] A. R. Jones and W. J. Skraba, *Science*, **110**, 332 (1949).
[8] M. S. Newman and R. W. Addor, *J. Am. Chem. Soc.*, **75**, 1263 (1953).
[9] H. Magritte and A. Bruylants, *Bull. soc. chim. Belges*, **66**, 367 (1957).
[10] P. Smit and H. J. den Hertog, *Rec. trav. chim.*, **77**, 73 (1958).

bromides have been made by bromination of propylene and isobutylene, respectively, under conditions similar to those employed for producing the corresponding chlorine compounds.

$$CH_2{=}CHCH_3 + Br_2 \rightarrow CH_2{=}CHCH_2Br + HBr$$

$$\underset{\underset{\displaystyle CH_3}{|}}{CH_2{=}CCH_3} + Br_2 \rightarrow \underset{\underset{\displaystyle CH_3}{|}}{CH_2{=}CCH_2Br} + HBr$$

Benzyl bromide is produced by bromination of toluene. *p*-Bromobenzal bromide is made in high yields by treating *p*-bromotoluene with two moles of bromine at temperatures up to 150° under an unfrosted 150-watt tungsten lamp (OS II, 89).

Under similar conditions bromination of *p*-xylene gives $\alpha,\alpha,\alpha',\alpha'$-tetrabromo-*p*-xylene (OS III, 788; 55% yield).

Since the second halogen atom is introduced with more difficulty than the first, it is possible to stop at the benzyl stage. *p*-Nitrotoluene affords *p*-nitrobenzyl bromide in 59% yield when treated with one mole of bromine at 145 to 150° (OS II, 443).

The difficulty of attaching a second halogen atom to a carbon atom is illustrated by the behavior of *o*-xylene toward bromine; it yields first α-bromo-*o*-xylene and then α,α'-dibromo-*o*-xylene.

If an aromatic ring holds sensitizing groups such as hydroxyl or amino, only nuclear halogenation occurs. Even in the absence of a carrier, *p*-cresol reacts rapidly with bromine to give 2,6-dibromo-*p*-cresol.

Ethyl ether reacts with bromine in chloroform solution to give the diethyl acetal of dibromoacetaldehyde in 55% yield. It is presumed that the α-bromo ether is formed as an intermediate.[11]

$$CH_3CH_2OCH_2CH_3 \xrightarrow{Br_2} Br_2CHCH(OCH_2CH_3)_2$$

N-Bromosuccinimide

Although bromination at an allyl position ordinarily cannot be achieved with bromine in the liquid phase, it can be effected by a procedure, discovered by Wohl and developed by Ziegler (CR **43**, 271), which consists in treating the compound with a bromoamide or bromoimide, usually in boiling carbon tetrachloride. By the Wohl-Ziegler method, for example, cyclohexene yields 3-bromocyclohexene.[12]

Bromination of 2-heptene with N-bromosuccinimide is of particular interest since this olefin contains an allylic methyl group and an allylic methylene group. As would be predicted on theoretical grounds the methylene group is brominated preferentially; the product is 4-bromo-2-heptene (OS **38**, 8; yield 64%).

$$CH_3CH_2CH_2CH_2CH=CHCH_3 \rightarrow CH_3CH_2CH_2\underset{\underset{Br}{|}}{C}HCH=CHCH_3$$

Methyl crotonate and methyl β-methylcrotonate give the corresponding γ-bromo esters in high yields.

$$CH_3CH=CHCO_2CH_3 \rightarrow BrCH_2CH=CHCO_2CH_3$$

$$CH_3\underset{\underset{CH_3}{|}}{C}=CHCO_2CH_3 \rightarrow BrCH_2\underset{\underset{CH_3}{|}}{C}=CHCO_2CH_3$$

[11] K. Kratzl and K. Schubert, *Monatsh.*, **81**, 988 (1950).
[12] See H. J. Dauben, Jr., and L. L. McCoy, *J. Am. Chem. Soc.*, **81**, 4863 (1959).

A similar example is the preparation of ethyl α-(bromomethyl)cinnamate; the yield is 94%.[13]

$$C_6H_5CH=CCO_2C_2H_5 \rightarrow C_6H_5CH=CCO_2C_2H_5$$
$$| \qquad\qquad\qquad\qquad |$$
$$CH_3 \qquad\qquad\qquad\qquad CH_2Br$$

Other examples are the following.

$$C_6H_5CH=CHCH_3 \rightarrow C_6H_5CH=CHCH_2Br$$

$$C_6H_5 \qquad\qquad\qquad\qquad C_6H_5$$
$$\diagdown \qquad\qquad\qquad\qquad \diagdown$$
$$C=CHCH_3 \rightarrow \qquad\qquad C=CHCH_2Br$$
$$\diagup \qquad\qquad\qquad\qquad \diagup$$
$$C_6H_5 \qquad\qquad\qquad\qquad C_6H_5$$

$$C_6H_5 \qquad\qquad\qquad\qquad C_6H_5$$
$$\diagdown \qquad\qquad\qquad\qquad \diagdown$$
$$C=CHCH_2CH_3 \rightarrow \qquad\qquad C=CHCHCH_3$$
$$\diagup \qquad\qquad\qquad\qquad \diagup \qquad\qquad |$$
$$C_6H_5 \qquad\qquad\qquad\qquad C_6H_5 \qquad\quad Br$$

The presence of benzoyl peroxide promotes this type of reaction. Methyl sorbate under these conditions yields methyl ε-bromosorbate.

$$CH_3CH=CHCH=CHCO_2CH_3 \rightarrow BrCH_2CH=CHCH=CHCO_2CH_3$$

Bromination of ethyl 4-methyl-2-pentenoate, which contains a tertiary hydrogen atom in the allyl position, proceeds satisfactorily also when peroxides are present.[14]

$$CH_3 \qquad\qquad\qquad\qquad\qquad CH_3$$
$$| \qquad\qquad\qquad\qquad\qquad\qquad |$$
$$CH_3CHCH=CHCO_2C_2H_5 \rightarrow CH_3CCH=CHCO_2C_2H_5$$
$$| $$
$$Br$$

N-Bromosuccinimide is effective in side chain bromination also if employed with benzoyl peroxide. This procedure is especially valuable with compounds containing sensitive aromatic nuclei; bromination of 3-methylthiophene by this method, for example, gives 3-thenyl bromide (OS **33**, 96; 80% yield).

$$CH\text{---}CCH_3 \qquad CH\text{---}CCH_2Br$$
$$\| \quad\quad \| \qquad\rightarrow\qquad \| \quad\quad \|$$
$$CH \quad CH \qquad\qquad CH \quad CH$$
$$\diagdown \quad\diagup \qquad\qquad\qquad \diagdown \quad\diagup$$
$$S \qquad\qquad\qquad\qquad S$$

[13] W. F. Beech and N. Legg, *J. Chem. Soc.*, 2906 (1950).
[14] H. J. Dauben, Jr., and L. L. McCoy, *J. Org. Chem.*, **24**, 1577 (1959).

Dibromination of 2,3-dimethylnaphthalene is another example; the yield is 80%.[15]

With bromine, even in the absence of a carrier, one would expect only nuclear substitution in this case.

o,o'-Bitolyl can be converted into the dibromide in a similar way.

Oximes are sometimes formed by rearrangement of the corresponding nitroso compounds (p. 168) and in certain reactions behave as though they were in tautomeric equilibrium with the nitroso forms. The formation of 2-bromo-2-nitrosopropane by the action of bromine water on the oxime of acetone has already been mentioned (p. 549). By the use of N-bromo-succinimide as the brominating agent it has been possible to prepare α-bromonitrosocycloalkanes from the corresponding oximes. Subsequent oxidation and debromination provide a route to the nitro cycloalkanes; nitrocyclohexane, for example, can be made in 80% yield.[16]

Certain chloroamines have attracted attention because treatment with sulfuric acid converts them to pyrrolidines. N-Chlorodi-n-butylamine, for example, yields N-butylpyrrolidine (OS III, 159; 80% yield).

This unusual transformation has been ascribed to a free radical chain mechanism involving intramolecular transfer of hydrogen.[17]

[15] W. Wenner, *J. Org. Chem.*, **17**, 523 (1952).
[16] D. C. Iffland and G. X. Criner, *J. Am. Chem. Soc.*, **75**, 4047 (1953).
[17] E. J. Corey and W. R. Hertler, *J. Am. Chem. Soc.*, **82**, 1657 (1960).

Fluorination

Early studies indicated that fluorination of organic compounds proceeded with explosive violence. Later, procedures were developed by which direct fluorination could be controlled (CR **40,** 51). Apparently the fluorine radical is the reacting species in all cases. The method of direct fluorination with elemental fluorine has been modified so that it affords fluorinated products in excellent yields.[18]

Many fluorocarbons and their derivatives can be produced directly from organic compounds and hydrogen fluoride by a one-step electrolytic process carried out at low temperatures. An example is the formation of trifluoroacetic acid; the initial product, trifluoroacetyl fluoride, is readily hydrolyzed.[19]

$$(CH_3CO)_2O + 1OHF \rightarrow 2F_3CCOF + OF_2 + 8H_2$$

Teflon, a linear polymer formed by polymerization of tetrafluoroethylene, is essentially a fluorocarbon.

$$xCF_2{=}CF_2 \rightarrow -(CF_2CF_2)_x-$$

Kel-F, the polymer of chlorotrifluoroethylene, is similar. Viton is a linear copolymer of vinylidene fluoride and perfluoroethylene. These polymers are chemically inert and very resistant to heat.

Nitration

Paraffins and cycloparaffins yield nitro derivatives when subjected to prolonged treatment with dilute nitric acid. At low temperatures the reaction is too slow to be useful, and at high temperatures extensive oxidation occurs. Vapor-phase nitration of paraffins, on the other hand, affords several of the simplest nitroparaffins in satisfactory yields (CR **32,** 373). Nitration takes place satisfactorily only under conditions that suggest a free radical mechanism. The method involves momentary contact of the hydrocarbon with nitric acid at temperatures near 400°. Both pyrolysis and nitration occur. Ethane yields nitroethane and nitromethane, the product containing 73 and 27%, respectively, of these compounds. Propane gives rise to a mixture of nitromethane, nitroethane, 1-nitropropane, and 2-nitropropane, which are available in commercial quantities. The figures in parentheses indicate the percentage of the

---

[18] *Ind. Eng. Chem.*, **39,** 236–433 (1947).
[19] K. A. Kauck and A. R. Diesslin, *Ind. Eng. Chem.*, **43,** 2332 (1951).

components in the product. Yields, based on propane, do not exceed 40%.

$$CH_3CH_2CH_3 \xrightarrow[420°]{HNO_3} \begin{cases} CH_3NO_2 & \text{Nitromethane} & (9) \\ CH_3CH_2NO_2 & \text{Nitroethane} & (26) \\ CH_3CH_2CH_2NO_2 & \text{1-Nitropropane} & (32) \\ CH_3CHCH_3 & \text{2-Nitropropane} & (33) \\ \quad | \\ \quad NO_2 \end{cases}$$

n-Butane likewise yields a mixture of nitroparaffins. Nitromethane, nitroethane, 1-nitropropane, 1-nitrobutane, and 2-nitrobutane are isolated in 6, 12, 5, 27, and 50%, respectively, of the nitroparaffin product. Isobutane, pentane, and isopentane have been nitrated also. Methane is likewise susceptible to nitration in the vapor phase.

It may be mentioned that benzene can be nitrated by the vapor phase method. The product, nitrobenzene, is obtained also from toluene. Cycloparaffins appear to undergo nitration readily; cyclohexane, for example, gives the mononitro derivative.[20]

The fragmentation of paraffins suggests that nitroparaffins might be produced in a similar way from ethers, alcohols, ketones, acids, and other compounds containing aliphatic radicals. Experiment has verified this expectation. Methyl ether, for example, yields nitromethane, and ethyl ether gives both nitromethane and nitroethane. Nitromethane has been obtained also from ethanol and acetone. In fact, nitration of oxygen-containing compounds has been realized without fragmentation. Ethyl ether and propionic acid, to take two examples, yield ethyl β-nitroethyl ether and β-nitropropionic acid, respectively.[21]

$$CH_3CH_2OCH_2CH_3 \rightarrow CH_3CH_2OCH_2CH_2NO_2$$
$$CH_3CH_2CO_2H \rightarrow O_2NCH_2CH_2CO_2H$$

Nitric acid is capable of replacing an active hydrogen atom by a nitro group, as is illustrated by the behavior of anthrone; when treated with a mixture of fuming nitric acid and glacial acetic acid, it forms nitroanthrone (OS I, 390; 67% yield).

[20] G. B. Bachman and J. P. Chupp, J. Org. Chem., **21**, 655 (1956).
[21] H. B. Hass and D. E. Hudgin, J. Am. Chem. Soc., **76**, 2692 (1954).

Barbituric acid, which likewise is classed as an active methylene compound, yields nitrobarbituric acid under similar conditions (OS II, 440; 90% yield).

$$
\begin{array}{ccc}
NH\!-\!CO & & NH\!-\!CO \\
| \quad | & & | \quad | \\
CO \quad CH_2 + HNO_3 & \rightarrow & CO \quad CHNO_2 + H_2O \\
| \quad | & & | \quad | \\
NH\!-\!CO & & NH\!-\!CO
\end{array}
$$

The conversion of 2-nitropropane into 2,2-dinitropropane is a similar reaction. It is accomplished by passing an equimolecular mixture of the nitropropane and nitric acid (70%) at a pressure of 800 to 1200 pounds per square inch through a tube heated at 204 to 232°. If the contact time is limited, conversions of 11 to 14% are realized, with ultimate yields above 50%.[22]

Alkaline nitration can be effected satisfactorily by the action of alkyl nitrates on certain active methylene compounds. Phenylacetonitrile reacts with methyl nitrate in the presence of sodium ethoxide to give the sodium salt of the expected nitro compound. This reaction provides the preferred route to phenylnitromethane (OS II, 512).

$$
C_6H_5CH_2CN \xrightarrow[\text{NaOC}_2H_5]{\text{CH}_3ONO_2} \underset{CN}{C_6H_5C\!=\!NO_2Na} \xrightarrow[\text{H}_2O]{\text{NaOH}}
$$

$$
\underset{CO_2Na}{C_6H_5C\!=\!NO_2Na} \xrightarrow{\text{HCl}} C_6H_5CH_2NO_2
$$

The nitration step of this synthesis may be described as follows.

$$
\underset{CN}{C_6H_5CH} \quad N\!-\!OCH_3 \rightarrow \underset{CN}{C_6H_5CHNO_2} + \bar{O}CH_3
$$

Acetone cyanohydrin nitrate is a singularly effective reagent for nitration of active methylene compounds. With malonic ester, for example, it gives diethyl nitromalonate. The mechanism has been formulated as follows.[23]

$$
\begin{array}{ccc}
CO_2C_2H_5 & O \quad CH_3 & CO_2C_2H_5 \quad CH_3 \\
| & \uparrow \quad | & | \quad | \\
CH & N\!-\!O\!-\!C\!-\!CN \rightarrow & CHNO_2 + O\!=\!C + CN^- \\
| & \| \quad | & | \quad | \\
CO_2C_2H_5 & O \quad CH_3 & CO_2C_2H_5 \quad CH_3
\end{array}
$$

[22] W. I. Denton, R. B. Biship, E. M. Nygaard, and T. T. Noland, *Ind. Eng. Chem.*, **40**, 381 (1948).

[23] W. D. Emmons and J. P. Freeman, *J. Am. Chem. Soc.*, **77**, 4391 (1955).

Sulfonation

Sulfonation of aldehydes and ketones has been realized by use of the addition compounds formed when sulfur trioxide and dioxane are brought together in an inert solvent. Either the mono- or the diaddition product can be used.

$$O \quad O + SO_3 \rightarrow O \quad O{\cdot}SO_3 + SO_3 \rightarrow O_3S{\cdot}O \quad O{\cdot}SO_3$$

When treated with dioxane sulfotrioxide, acetophenone, acetomesitylene, and pinacolone, for example, form sulfonic acids that are isolated as sodium salts.[24]

$$C_6H_5COCH_3 \rightarrow C_6H_5COCH_2SO_3Na$$

$$CH_3 \qquad\qquad CH_3$$
$$CH_3{-}\langle\;\rangle{-}COCH_3 \rightarrow CH_3{-}\langle\;\rangle{-}COCH_2SO_3Na$$
$$CH_3 \qquad\qquad CH_3$$

$$(CH_3)_3CCOCH_3 \rightarrow (CH_3)_3CCOCH_2SO_3Na$$

Carboxylic acids having an α-methylene group react with sulfur trioxide to give α-sulfonation products. α-Sulfopalmitic acid, for example, can be prepared from palmitic acid in this way (OS 36, 83; yield 75%).

$$CH_3(CH_2)_{13}CH_2CO_2H + SO_3 \rightarrow CH_3(CH_2)_{13}\underset{\overset{|}{SO_3H}}{CH}CO_2H$$

Direct sulfonation of paraffins is possible but has not been developed on an industrial scale. More attractive processes for making alkylsulfonic acids and their derivatives have been discovered. In one of these, known as the Reed reaction, a mixture of chlorine and sulfur dioxide (or sulfuryl chloride) is allowed to react with paraffins under the influence of light. Sulfonyl chlorides are produced in high yield. The reaction is of the chain type and is thought to proceed in the following way.

$$Cl_2 \rightarrow 2Cl{\cdot}$$
$$RH + Cl{\cdot} \rightarrow R{\cdot} + HCl$$
$$R{\cdot} + SO_2 \rightarrow RSO_2{\cdot}$$
$$RSO_2{\cdot} + Cl_2 \rightarrow RSO_2Cl + Cl{\cdot}$$

[24] W. E. Truce and C. C. Alfieri, *J. Am. Chem. Soc.*, **72**, 2740 (1950).

24

Autoxidation

Oxidation that is brought about by molecular oxygen without any accompanying flame is sometimes called *autoxidation*. The over-all process is complex and usually leads to a mixture of products (CR **46**, 155; **61**, 563); it is generally agreed, however, that the first phase of autoxidation consists in the incorporation of a molecule of oxygen to form a peroxide.[1] The way in which molecular oxygen reacts will be better understood if it is remembered that it possesses paramagnetism, a property characteristic of free radicals.

One of the most instructive examples is the autoxidation of hexaphenylethane to triphenylmethyl peroxide; the reaction is rapid and quantitative.

$$(C_6H_5)_3C—C(C_6H_5)_3 + O_2 \rightarrow (C_6H_5)_3C—O—O—C(C_6H_5)_3$$

At first this transformation was formulated as dissociation of the ethane followed by combination of a molecule of oxygen with two triphenylmethyl radicals. A study of the reaction rates revealed, however, that formation of the peroxide is faster than dissociation of the ethane to triphenylmethyl. The following mechanism, which is based on the assumption that the reaction is of the chain type, provides a satisfactory explanation of the facts.

$$(C_6H_5)_3C—C(C_6H_5)_3 \rightleftharpoons 2(C_6H_5)_3C\cdot$$
$$(C_6H_5)_3C\cdot + \cdot O—O\cdot \rightarrow (C_6H_5)_3C—O—O\cdot$$
$$(C_6H_5)_3C—O—O\cdot + (C_6H_5)_3C—C(C_6H_5)_3 \rightarrow$$
$$(C_6H_5)_3C—O—O—C(C_6H_5)_3 + (C_6H_5)_3C\cdot$$

The formulation of autoxidation as a chain reaction is consistent with the observation that it is inhibited by antioxidants such as hydroquinone. This interpretation is borne out by the discovery that autoxidation of the hexaarylethane induces a chain oxidation of other compounds such as styrene and dimethylfulvene.

[1] G. A. Russell, *J. Chem. Education*, **36**, 111 (1959).

Peroxidation is a characteristic reaction of compounds containing CH, CH_2, or CH_3 groups, the rate of oxidation being favored by an increase in the reactivity of the C—H bond in question. In other words, the attack proceeds according to the rules laid down for other aliphatic substitution reactions.

Ethers

The hydroperoxides of simple ethers are high explosives, and for this reason it is never wise to distil an ether without making sure that it is free of peroxides. Peroxidation of ethyl ether is prevented by storage in the dark or by the presence of iron. Peroxidation of isopropyl ether, which is at least twice as fast as the peroxidation of ethyl ether, is not prevented by these means. The peroxide of high quality ether can be removed by an ion exchange resin, Dowex 1.[2]

Paraffinic Hydrocarbons

Oxygen attacks paraffinic hydrocarbons chiefly at a tertiary hydrogen atom if one is present. At 120° autoxidation of ethylcyclohexane is rapid and affects all the hydrogen atoms, the tertiary atom being the most reactive.[3] Similarly, decalin is attacked preferentially at a tertiary carbon atom.

Isobutane suffers attack at the tertiary carbon atom, yielding *t*-butyl hydroperoxide, *t*-butyl peroxide, and *t*-butyl alcohol. In the presence of hydrogen bromide as a catalyst oxidation proceeds readily at 155 to 165°. Straight chain paraffins higher than ethane are oxidized preferentially at a secondary carbon atom in the presence of hydrogen bromide, the principal products being ketones.[4] From *n*-butane, for example, methyl ethyl ketone is produced.

Formaldehyde, acetaldehyde, acetone, methanol, ethanol, and *n*-propyl alcohol are made similarly by the oxidation of saturated hydrocarbons.

In the liquid phase, especially when catalysts are present, the hydroperoxides generally decompose by what appears to be an ionic path. Thus

[2] R. N. Feinstein, *J. Org. Chem.*, **24**, 1172 (1959).
[3] J. Hoffman and C. E. Boord, *J. Am. Chem. Soc.*, **78**, 4973 (1956).
[4] F. F. Rust and W. E. Vaughan, *Ind. Eng. Chem.*, **41**, 2595 (1949).

the acid-catalyzed decomposition of a hydroperoxide gives rise to a carbonyl compound.

$$\begin{array}{c} R \\ \diagdown \\ \diagup CHOOH \\ R \end{array} \xrightarrow{H^+} \begin{array}{c} R \\ \diagdown \\ \diagup CHO{-}\overset{+}{O}H_2 \\ R \end{array} \rightarrow H_2O + \begin{array}{c} R \\ \diagdown \\ \diagup CHO^+ \\ R \end{array} \xrightarrow{-H^+} \begin{array}{c} R \\ \diagdown \\ \diagup C{=}O \\ R \end{array}$$

Alkalis, on the other hand, promote the formation of alcohols.

Side Chains

An alkyl side chain on an aromatic ring is attacked at the methylene or methinyl group next to the ring; the hydroperoxides of tetralin, ethylbenzene, p-xylene, cumene, diphenylmethane, indan, and octahydroanthracene are formed by autoxidation. Tetralin is particularly suited to the study of peroxidation because it reacts with oxygen in boiling carbon tetrachloride (b.p. 76°) to give the corresponding hydroperoxide in high yields. The evidence indicates that the reaction is of the chain type and that the 1-tetralyl radical is the chain carrier.

Higher paraffins can be oxidized to acids suitable for making soaps or synthetic fats. One of the chief difficulties in the transformation is that cleavage occurs at various points in the chain. This disadvantage is not encountered, of course, in the oxidation of simple cycloparaffins; cyclohexane can be converted into adipic acid in satisfactory yields.

As was noted in the case of tetralin, longer side chains may give alcohols and ketones. The oxidation of ethylbenzene with oxygen in the presence of manganese acetate provides a commercial route to acetophenone and

methylphenylcarbinol, which in turn may be dehydrated to styrene.[5]
Another example is the formation of methyl p-acetylbenzoate from methyl
p-ethylbenzoate (OS 32, 81; yield 60%).

Aromatic Rings

Vigorous oxidation may effect cleavage of aromatic rings; under suitable
conditions, however, phenol can be made from benzene.

$$2C_6H_6 + O_2 \rightarrow 2C_6H_5OH$$

Oxidation of benzene, carried out commercially by passing a mixture of
air and the hydrocarbon over a vanadium oxide catalyst at 450°, is the
principal source of maleic anhydride.

Oxidation of naphthalene to phthalic anhydride is effected by passing a
mixture of the hydrocarbon and air over vanadium pentoxide at 450 to
500°.

$$+ 9(O) \rightarrow \quad + 2CO_2 + 2H_2O$$

The pyridine ring in quinoline is more resistant to oxidation than the
homocycle; oxidation with permanganate destroys the benzenoid ring
producing quinolinic acid.

This oxidation has been effected electrolytically at a platinum electrode in
75% sulfuric acid; the yield of quinolinic acid is 77%.[6]

Similarly, quinoxaline yields 2,3-pyrazinedicarboxylic acid.

Olefins

Autoxidation of olefins occurs at the methylene group adjacent to the
double bond. Cyclohexene and 1-hexene, for example, give derivatives
with the hydroperoxide function at an allyl position.

[5] H. J. Sanders, H. F. Keag, and H. S. McCullough, *Ind. Eng. Chem.*, **45**, 2 (1953).
[6] M. Kulka, *J. Am. Chem. Soc.*, **68**, 2472 (1946).

$$\begin{array}{c} \text{CHOOH} \\ \diagup \qquad \diagdown \\ \text{CH}_2 \qquad \text{CH} \\ | \qquad || \\ \text{CH}_2 \qquad \text{CH} \\ \diagdown \qquad \diagup \\ \text{CH}_2 \end{array} \qquad\qquad \begin{array}{c} \text{CH}_3\text{CH}_2\text{CH}_2\text{CH} \!\!-\!\! \text{CH} \!=\!\! \text{CH}_2 \\ | \\ \text{OOH} \end{array}$$

n-Butenes, when mixed with air and passed over a vanadium pentoxide catalyst at 350°, yield maleic anhydride.

$$\begin{array}{c} \text{CH}\!-\!\text{CH}_3 \\ || \qquad\quad + 3\text{O}_2 \rightarrow \\ \text{CH}\!-\!\text{CH}_3 \end{array} \qquad \begin{array}{c} \text{CH}\!-\!\text{CO} \\ || \qquad\qquad \diagdown \\ \qquad\qquad\quad \text{O} + 3\text{H}_2\text{O} \\ || \qquad\qquad \diagup \\ \text{CH}\!-\!\text{CO} \end{array}$$

Many organic compounds having a chain of four or five carbon atoms can be oxidized to maleic anhydride in this way; furfural and crotonaldehyde are interesting examples.

Ethylene oxide can be made by passing a mixture of ethylene and air or oxygen over a silver catalyst at 200 to 350°. When ethylene is oxidized with air or oxygen in the presence of cupric chloride and palladium chloride, acetaldehyde is produced.

Aldehydes

Aldehydes undergo autoxidation when allowed to remain in contact with air or oxygen, the reaction being of the chain type. Benzaldehyde, for example, reacts to give perbenzoic acid. The reaction can be initiated by a free radical such as triphenylmethyl, which serves to generate the benzoyl radical.

$$(\text{C}_6\text{H}_5)_3\text{C}\cdot + \text{O}_2 \rightarrow (\text{C}_6\text{H}_5)_3\text{C}\!-\!\text{O}\!-\!\text{O}\cdot$$

$$(\text{C}_6\text{H}_5)_3\text{C}\!-\!\text{O}\!-\!\text{O}\cdot + \text{C}_6\text{H}_5\overset{\overset{\text{O}}{||}}{\text{C}}\text{H} \rightarrow (\text{C}_6\text{H}_5)_3\text{C}\!-\!\text{O}\!-\!\text{OH} + \text{C}_6\text{H}_5\overset{\overset{\text{O}}{||}}{\text{C}}\cdot$$

$$\text{C}_6\text{H}_5\overset{\overset{\text{O}}{||}}{\text{C}}\cdot + \text{O}_2 \rightarrow \text{C}_6\text{H}_5\overset{\overset{\text{O}}{||}}{\text{C}}\!-\!\text{O}\!-\!\text{O}\cdot$$

$$\text{C}_6\text{H}_5\overset{\overset{\text{O}}{||}}{\text{C}}\!-\!\text{O}\!-\!\text{O}\cdot + \text{C}_6\text{H}_5\overset{\overset{\text{O}}{||}}{\text{C}}\text{H} \rightarrow \text{C}_6\text{H}_5\overset{\overset{\text{O}}{||}}{\text{C}}\!-\!\text{O}\!-\!\text{OH} + \text{C}_6\text{H}_5\overset{\overset{\text{O}}{||}}{\text{C}}\cdot$$

Furfural is oxidized to 2-furoic acid by oxygen in the presence of a cuprous oxide-silver oxide catalyst (OS **36,** 36; 90% yield). Air oxidation of certain other aldehydes is carried out on a commercial scale. Acetic acid is prepared by oxidation of acetaldehyde obtained from acetylene; air is passed into the aldehyde at 70° in the presence of manganous acetate.

$$CH_3CHO + \tfrac{1}{2}O_2 \rightarrow CH_3CO_2H$$

Propionaldehyde gives propionic acid in 90% yield when oxidized with oxygen in liquid phase in the presence of manganese propionate.[7]

$$CH_3CH_2CHO + \tfrac{1}{2}O_2 \rightarrow CH_3CH_2CO_2H$$

Open-chain ketones can be oxidized in a similar way; when air is passed for a long time through an acetic acid solution of diethyl ketone, a mixture of acetic and propionic acids is produced. The reaction goes much more rapidly in the presence of manganous acetate.

Aliphatic aldehydes unite with olefins under the influence of peroxides or ultraviolet light to give ketones. For example, enanthaldehyde and diethyl maleate combine in the presence of benzoyl peroxide to give diethyl enanthylsuccinate (OS **34**, 51; yield 76%).

$$CH_3(CH_2)_5CHO + \underset{\underset{\displaystyle CHCO_2C_2H_5}{\|}}{CHCO_2C_2H_5} \rightarrow CH_3(CH_2)_5COCHCO_2C_2H_5$$
$$\underset{\displaystyle CH_2CO_2C_2H_5}{|}$$

Such reactions have been interpreted by assuming that the radical $R\!-\!C\!\!=\!\!O$ is the reactive species.[8]

[7] W. K. Langdon and E. J. Schwoegler, *Ind. Eng. Chem.*, **43**, 1011 (1951).
[8] M. S. Kharasch, W. H. Urry, and B. M. Kuderna, *J. Org. Chem.*, **14**, 248 (1949).

25

Reactions of organic halogen compounds with metals

The reactions of organic halogen compounds with metals may be of the free radical type, although the evidence does not always permit a definite classification of the change that occurs. The usual result is coupling of hydrocarbon radicals, and one explanation of the coupling postulates the formation of free radicals; this type of mechanism is known to be correct for the formation of hexaphenylethane from triphenylmethyl chloride and silver.

$$(C_6H_5)_3CCl + Ag \rightarrow (C_6H_5)_3C\cdot + AgCl$$

$$2(C_6H_5)_3C\cdot \rightarrow (C_6H_5)_3C-C(C_6H_5)_3$$

Wurtz Reaction

Coupling of two n-butyl radicals occurs when n-butyl bromide, for example, is treated with sodium; the product is n-octane.

$$2C_4H_9Br + 2Na \rightarrow C_4H_9-C_4H_9 + 2NaBr$$

This type of transformation, known as the Wurtz reaction, has been presumed to require the intermediate formation of an alkyl sodium (CR **35**,1).

$$RX + 2Na \rightarrow RNa + NaX$$

$$RNa + RX \rightarrow R-R + NaX$$

Support for this mechanism is seen in the observation that isovaleric acid can be obtained by the action of carbon dioxide on a reaction mixture of sodium and isobutyl bromide. Also, when 2-chloroöctane is coupled, the carbon atom holding chlorine undergoes inversion.[1]

[1] E. LeGoff, S. E. Ulrich, and D. B. Denny, *J. Am. Chem. Soc.*, **80**, 622 (1958).

Triphenylmethylsodium can be prepared by the action of sodium amalgam on triphenylmethyl chloride (OS II, 607).

The Wurtz reaction, used for the synthesis of symmetrical paraffins, also serves for the closure of cycloparaffin rings if the alkyl halide is replaced by a suitably constituted polymethylene halide. Cyclopropane was first made by Freund in 1881 by this method. In 1887 Gustavson discovered that zinc in the presence of a protonic solvent was much more effective. The commercial procedure consists of treatment of trimethylene chloride with zinc in the presence of sodium iodide and sodium carbonate.

$$
\begin{array}{c}
\quad CH_2Cl \\
CH_2 \\
\quad CH_2Cl
\end{array}
\; + \; Zn \; \rightarrow \;
\begin{array}{c}
\quad CH_2 \\
CH_2 \quad | \\
\quad CH_2
\end{array}
\; + \; ZnCl_2
$$

A method of synthesis of alkyl cyclopropyl ethers from ethers of glycerol α,γ-dibromohydrin likewise illustrates this type of closure.

$$
\begin{array}{c}
\quad CH_2Br \\
ROCH \\
\quad CH_2Br
\end{array}
\; + \; Mg \; \rightarrow \;
\begin{array}{c}
\quad CH_2 \\
ROCH \quad | \\
\quad CH_2
\end{array}
\; + \; MgBr_2
$$

This ring closure is noteworthy also because the two bromine atoms are in positions *beta* to the ether linkage and therefore relatively unreactive.

The method is useful with other substituted trimethylene bromides and gives a spectacular change with pentaerythrityl bromide; one product is spiropentane.

$$
\begin{array}{c}
BrCH_2 \quad CH_2Br \\
C \\
BrCH_2 \quad CH_2Br
\end{array}
\; + \; 2Zn \; \rightarrow \;
\begin{array}{c}
CH_2 \quad CH_2 \\
C \\
CH_2 \quad CH_2
\end{array}
\; + \; 2ZnBr_2
$$

The principal product (70% yield), however, is methylenecyclobutane.

$$
\begin{array}{c}
CH_2\!-\!\!-C\!=\!CH_2 \\
| \qquad | \\
CH_2\!-\!\!-CH_2
\end{array}
$$

The scope of this method of making cyclobutane derivatives has been extended by the discovery that 1,1,1-tri(bromomethyl)alkanes react with zinc to yield alkylidenecyclobutanes; the formation of ethylidenecyclo-butane is an example.[2]

$$\begin{array}{c} CH_2Br \\ | \\ CH_3CH_2CCH_2Br \\ | \\ CH_2Br \end{array} \rightarrow \begin{array}{c} CH_2-C=CHCH_3 \\ | \quad | \\ CH_2-CH_2 \end{array}$$

Coupling of halomethyl derivatives of aromatic compounds takes place with particular ease and provides a satisfactory route to symmetrical 1,2-diarylethanes. An ususual example is the conversion of α,α′-dibromo-o-xylene into the corresponding dibenzcycloöctadiene by the action of sodium. Under conditions of high dilution the yield of the eight-membered ring compound is 46%.[3]

$$2 \underset{}{\bigcirc}\hspace{-0.5em}\begin{array}{c} CH_2Br \\ CH_2Br \end{array} \xrightarrow{Na} \begin{array}{c} CH_2CH_2 \\ \bigcirc \quad \bigcirc \\ CH_2CH_2 \end{array}$$

Benzal chloride reacts with certain metals to give stilbene, presumably by coupling followed by dechlorination of stilbene dichloride. In a similar way benzophenone dichloride undergoes coupling when heated with powdered copper; the product is tetraphenylethylene (OS **31**, 104; 70% yield).

$$2(C_6H_5)_2CCl_2 + 4Cu \rightarrow (C_6H_5)_2C=C(C_6H_5)_2 + 4CuCl$$

Allylic chlorides also undergo coupling when treated with metals. A superior reagent for such couplings is nickel carbonyl. In general, the products from allylic chlorides are mixtures, the composition of which is the same for the two isomeric chlorides.[4] 1-Chloro-2-butene or 3-chloro-1-butene yields a mixture of 2,6-octadiene and 3-methyl-1,5-heptadiene.

$$CH_3CH=CHCH_2Cl \xrightarrow{Ni(CO)_4} \left\{ \begin{array}{c} CH_3CH=CHCH_2CH_2CH=CHCH_3 \\ and \\ CH_3CH=CHCH_2CHCH=CH_2 \\ | \\ CH_3 \end{array} \right\} \xleftarrow{Ni(CO)_4}$$

$$\begin{array}{c} CH_3CHCH=CH_2 \\ | \\ Cl \end{array}$$

[2] J. M. Derfer, K. W. Greenlee, and C. E. Boord, *J. Am. Chem. Soc.*, **71**, 175 (1949).
[3] A. C. Cope and S. W. Fenton, *J. Am. Chem. Soc.*, **73**, 1668 (1951).
[4] I. D. Webb and G. T. Borcherdt, *J. Am. Chem. Soc.*, **73**, 2654 (1951).

The ether group is the only one of the familiar functional groups that can be tolerated in Wurtz reactions. Halogenated esters, ketones, and nitriles, for example, cannot be used successfully because the metal attacks the carbonyl and nitrile functions also.

Fittig Reaction

A similar method was used by Fittig to couple two aromatic radicals, but the yields of biaryls were always low. The amount of biphenyl obtained from bromobenzene, for example, was only 5% of the theoretical amount. Although of extremely limited synthetic value, this reaction has aroused much interest because of the nature of the by-products that are isolated. The action of sodium on chlorobenzene produces benzene, biphenyl, o-terphenyl, p-terphenyl, triphenylene, and 2,2'-diphenylbiphenyl.

The Fittig method, applied to 2,2'-dibromobiphenyl, failed to yield biphenylene. This interesting hydrocarbon has been produced by the following sequence of changes.

The proof of structure consists in oxidation to phthalic acid and hydrogenation to biphenyl.[5]

Biphenylene is produced also by irradiation of 2,2-biphenylenemercury.[6]

Wurtz-Fittig Reaction

Although sodium is not satisfactory for coupling two aromatic radicals, it is useful in joining an aromatic radical to an alkyl radical. Treatment of a mixture of equimolecular amounts of n-butyl bromide and bromobenzene with sodium, for example, produces n-butylbenzene in 70% yield (OS III, 157). This transformation, known as the Wurtz-Fittig reaction, is satisfactory only with bromides. To account for the preferential formation of

[5] W. C. Lothrop, J. Am. Chem. Soc., 63, 1187 (1941).
[6] G. J. Fonken, Chem. and Ind., 716 (1961).

the unsymmetrical hydrocarbon it is assumed that the two bromides function in different ways; the following steps have been postulated.

$$C_6H_5Br + 2Na \rightarrow C_6H_5Na + NaBr$$

$$C_6H_5Na + BrC_4H_9 \rightarrow C_6H_5C_4H_9 + NaBr$$

This method serves also to produce linear α,ω-diarylalkanes; an example is the preparation of 1,6-diphenylhexane from bromobenzene and hexamethylene bromide.

$$2C_6H_5Br + Br(CH_2)_6Br + 4Na \rightarrow C_6H_5(CH_2)_6C_6H_5 + 4NaBr$$

Ullmann Method

Although the coupling of aryl radicals by sodium is not a useful reaction, many biphenyl derivatives are made conveniently by treatment of aryl halides with copper powder (CR **38**, 139). This method, developed by Ullmann, is illustrated by the synthesis of 2,2′,4,4′-tetramethylbiphenyl, which can be produced in 86% yield from 2,4-dimethyliodobenzene.

The halogen atom must be reactive, which is the reason iodo compounds commonly are employed. Good results can be obtained also with activated halogen derivatives such as o-chloronitrobenzene, which gives 2,2′-dinitrobiphenyl in 61% yield (OS III, 339).

Treatment of ethyl 4-iodo-3-nitrobenzoate with copper bronze in nitrobenzene gives diethyl 2,2′-dinitro-4,4′-biphenyldicarboxylate in 69% yield.

Unsymmetrical biaryls have been made also by the Ullmann procedure. Treatment of a mixture of equal amounts of two different aryl halides with copper would be expected to give the desired unsymmetrical biaryl accompanied by two symmetrical biaryls. In fact, the yields of unsymmetrical biaryls in such couplings are generally not high. Methyl o-bromobenzoate and o-iodonitrobenzene give methyl 2-nitro-2'-biphenylcarboxylate in a yield of only 20%.

Since the iodine atom is more reactive than the bromine atom, the biaryl is formed in a much higher yield (68%) if the halogen atoms are interchanged. One reason for the improved yield is that the nitro group is a more effective activating group than the carbomethoxyl group, offsetting the fact than an iodide is more reactive than a bromide.

Couplings are known in which the unsymmetrical biaryl is the sole product obtained; picryl chloride and iodobenzene yield only 2,4,6-trinitrobiphenyl, for example.

In mixed Ullmann reactions it appears that only one of the aryl halides is attacked by the condensing agent and that the optimum temperature for the condensation is just below that at which attack of the other aryl halide would begin.[7]

p-Quaterphenyl has been synthesized by applying Ullmann's procedure to 4-iodobiphenyl.

Similarly, 2,2'-diphenylbiphenyl is formed in 72% yield from 2-iodobiphenyl.

[7] J. Forrest, *J. Chem. Soc.*, 594 (1960).

Intramolecular condensations have been effected also; 1,8-diiodonaphthalene, for example, yields perylene.

Similarly 2,2'-diiodo-5,5'-dimethoxybibenzyl can be converted into the corresponding dimethoxydihydrophenanthrene.

Dehalogenation

Dehalogenation of 1,2-dihalogen compounds by the action of metals was discussed in Chapter 14. Replacement of halogen by hydrogen may be accomplished by such reducing agents as hydrogen iodide, zinc and acids, stannous chloride, and sodium arsenite. Cetyl iodide, for example, gives *n*-hexadecane in 85% yield when treated with zinc and hydrochloric acid (OS II, 320).

$$CH_3(CH_2)_{14}CH_2I \rightarrow CH_3(CH_2)_{14}CH_3$$

Symmetrical benzoins are reduced to the corresponding desoxybenzoins by treatment with tin and hydrochloric acid, and the reaction may proceed by way of desyl chloride. The preparation of desoxyanisoin is an example (OS **40**, 16; yield 92%).

The preparation of diphenylacetic acid from benzilic acid by the action of phosphorus and iodine (OS I, 224; 97% yield) presumably depends on the intermediate formation of the iodo derivative.

$$(C_6H_5)_2CCO_2H \rightarrow (C_6H_5)_2CCO_2H \rightarrow (C_6H_5)_2CHCO_2H$$
$$\quad\ \ OH \qquad\qquad\quad\ I$$

Bromoform and iodoform are reduced to methylene bromide (OS I, 357; 90% yield) and methylene iodide (OS I, 358; 97% yield), respectively, by sodium arsenite.

$$CHBr_3 + Na_3AsO_3 + NaOH \rightarrow CH_2Br_2 + Na_3AsO_4 + NaBr$$

$$CHI_3 + Na_3AsO_3 + NaOH \rightarrow CH_2I_2 + Na_3AsO_4 + NaI$$

Treatment of picryl chloride with hydrogen iodide produces 1,3,5-trinitrobenzene (p. 21) in 70% yield.[8]

Tin and hydrobromic acid serve to reduce 1,6-dibromo-2-naphthol to 6-bromo-2-naphthol (OS III, 132).

A convenient synthesis of allenes involves dechlorination of acetylenic chlorides. An example is the production of 3-methyl-1,2-butadiene from 3-methyl-1-butyne-3-ol by way of the chloride; the yield is 51%. The dechlorination, effected with lithium aluminum hydride, appears to require attack by hydride ion at the 1-position. This displacement is of the S_N2' type (p. 452).

Organometallic Compounds

Many organometallic compounds are prepared by the action of metals on alkyl or aryl halides. Diphenylmercury, for example, can be produced in 37% yield by treatment of bromobenzene with sodium amalgam (OS I, 228).

$$2C_6H_5Br + Na_2(Hg) \rightarrow (C_6H_5)_2Hg + 2NaBr$$

[8] A. H. Blatt and E. W. Tristram, *J. Am. Chem. Soc.*, **74**, 6273 (1952).

Most useful of the organometallic compounds are those containing magnesium, zinc, or lithium.

Grignard reaction

One of the most useful reactions of alkyl and aryl halides is with magnesium to form Grignard reagents. The usual preparative procedure, discovered by Grignard in 1900, is to bring the halide in contact with the metal in ethyl ether.[9] The role of the ether is to coordinate with the newly formed organomagnesium halide; formation of the etherate not only transports the organometallic compound away from the metal surface being corroded but also protects the organomagnesium compound from attack by the incoming organic halide. In the absence of the ether the newly formed magnesium compound would react with unchanged organic halide, and a Wurtz-type coupling would occur. Indeed the relative donor capacity (basicity) of the solvent and of the organic halide determines the extent to which coupling occurs.

The Grignard reagent continues to be represented by the formula RMgX in spite of evidence in favor of a more complicated structure.[10] The etherate appears to have the following spatial arrangement.[11]

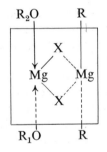

Methyl iodide, in spite of its relatively high cost, is used commonly to make the methyl reagent because it is the only methyl halide that is liquid at ordinary temperatures. Methyl bromide and methyl chloride (OS III, 696) give Grignard reagents in high yields, however. Certain chlorides are to be preferred; examples are very reactive chlorides such as t-butyl (OS I, 524), t-amyl, and benzyl (OS II, 47; OS I, 471). Low-molecular-weight secondary chlorides such as s-butyl (OS I, 361) are often used. Cyclohexyl chloride and bromide give the corresponding reagents in high yields (OS I, 186, 188). Satisfactory results are obtained also with primary chlorides

[9] See H. Rheinboldt, *J. Chem. Education,* **27,** 476 (1950).

[10] R. E. Dessy, G. S. Handler, J. H. Wotiz, and C. A. Hollingsworth, *J. Am. Chem. Soc.* **79,** 3476 (1957).

[11] A. Kirrman and R. Hamelin, *Compt. rend.,* **251,** 2990 (1960).

such as *n*-butyl (OS I, 363) and *n*-amyl. Usually, however, bromides are to be preferred (OS I, 306; OS II, 179, 406, 478, 602). In the aromatic series the bromides are used widely (OS I, 226, 550, 551).

Allyl and methallyl halides are too reactive to give Grignard reagents by the usual procedure; they yield coupling products instead. Allyl chloride, for example, gives biallyl in 65% yield (OS III, 121). This difficulty has been surmounted by slow addition of a dilute ether solution of allyl bromide to magnesium powder in large excess. Under these conditions allylmagnesium bromide can be made in 90% yields.

Allylmagnesium chloride is produced when an ether solution of allyl chloride is dropped slowly into a mixture of magnesium turnings and ether at ice-bath temperatures, with vigorous agitation. This reagent is insoluble in ether, but ether suspensions can be employed successfully in reactions.

3-Bromocyclohexene (p. 610) resembles the allyl halides in its behavior toward magnesium, readily undergoing coupling.

$$2\left\langle \begin{array}{c} \\ \end{array} \right\rangle Br + Mg \rightarrow \left\langle \begin{array}{c} \\ \end{array} \right\rangle - \left\langle \begin{array}{c} \\ \end{array} \right\rangle + MgBr_2$$

There are halides, on the other hand, that only react slowly with magnesium in ordinary ether. Conspicuous among them are the aryl chlorides, which react so sluggishly that specially activated magnesium and extended reaction periods are required.

A few aryl bromides likewise require special techniques when ethyl ether is employed. An example is bromomesitylene, which reacts slowly and often requires a catalyst (OS II, 360; III, 553). An effective catalyst is prepared by heating magnesium, containing 12% copper, with iodine (OS II, 361). Pentamethylphenyl bromide yields the corresponding Grignard reagent when the *entrainment method* is used. The procedure is to add a reactive halide such as ethyl bromide to the reaction mixture; the relatively rapid formation of ethylmagnesium bromide serves to promote the reaction of the aryl bromide with the metal, possibly by keeping the metal surface clean. The entrainment method permits the preparation of a Grignard reagent from 3-bromopyridine, ethyl bromide serving as the entrainment agent.[12]

Ethylene bromide has proved to be more effective as the entrainment agent than ethyl bromide; it has the advantage of reacting with the metal without forming a Grignard reagent.[13]

$$BrCH_2CH_2Br + Mg \rightarrow CH_2{=}CH_2 + MgBr_2$$

[12] J. P. Wibaut and H. G. P. van der Voort, *Rec. trav. chim.*, **71**, 798 (1952).
[13] D. E. Pearson, D. Cowan, and J. D. Beckler, *J. Org. Chem.*, **24**, 504 (1959).

Tetrahydrofuran is extremely useful in the preparation of Grignard reagents that are difficult to form in other solvents. Vinylmagnesium bromide, for example, may be made in yields of 95 to 97% by treating magnesium with vinyl bromide at 40 to 50° in this solvent. A trace of iodine, methyl iodide, or ethyl bromide may serve as an initiator. This method has been used successfully with many vinyl halides.[14] An apparatus has been developed for the continuous preparation of such reagents.[15]

Chlorobenzene and other aryl halides react without difficulty with magnesium in tetrahydrofuran to give the corresponding Grignard reagents. p-Chlorostyrene, in this solvent, yields p-vinylphenylmagnesium chloride. Carbonation of this reagent gives p-vinylbenzoic acid in 80% yield.[16]

$$CH_2{=}CHC_6H_4Cl \rightarrow CH_2{=}CHC_6H_4MgCl \rightarrow CH_2{=}CHC_6H_4CO_2H$$

In addition to tetrahydrofuran, 2-methyltetrahydrofuran, tetrahydropyran, dihydropyran, and ethyl tetrahydrofurfuryl ether can serve also.

A procedure for protecting the surface of the magnesium is to wash the metal with ether containing a small amount of paraffin. Iodine in the final wash serves to make the metal more active.[17]

Metal alkoxides are able to catalyze the reaction of magnesium with many organic halides in the absence of ether; chlorobenzene reacts with magnesium powder in the presence of small amounts of magnesium isopropoxide to give phenylmagnesium chloride in 93% yield.[18]

1,2-Dibromopropane reacts with magnesium to yield propylene; tetramethylene bromide, however, forms a di-Grignard reagent: $BrMg(CH_2)_4MgBr$(QR 11, 109). Similar behavior has been reported for several other polymethylene bromides.

The difference in reactivity of chlorine and bromine on the benzene ring is illustrated by the easy formation of p-chlorophenylmagnesium bromide. p-Dibromobenzene yields the mono- and dibromomagnesium derivatives.

[14] H. Normant, *Advances in Organic Chemistry*, Interscience Publishers, Inc., New York, Vol. II, p. 1, 1960.

[15] H. K. Reimschuessel, *J. Org. Chem.*, **25**, 2256 (1960).

[16] J. R. Leebrick and H. E. Ramsden, *J. Org. Chem.*, **23**, 935 (1958).

[17] F. S. Huber, *The Chemist Analyst*, **41**, 62 (1952).

[18] E. T. Blues and D. Bryce-Smith, *Chem. and Ind.*, 1533 (1960).

Organozinc compounds

Many organometallic compounds, other than Grignard reagents, are prepared by the action of metals on organic halides. Among the most important of these are the dialkylzincs, which played an extremely important role in organic chemistry before the discovery of the Grignard reagent and which continue to find use. A zinc-copper couple (OS II, 185) must be used to obtain good results. Bromides are not sufficiently reactive to serve, but iodides react vigorously. Replacement of part of the iodide by the corresponding bromide moderates the reaction and is economical. Diisopropylzinc, for example, is made in high yield by the interaction without solvent of zinc and a mixture of isopropyl bromide and isopropyl iodide.

$$2C_3H_7Br + 2C_3H_7I + 4Zn \rightarrow 2(C_3H_7)_2Zn + ZnBr_2 + ZnI_2$$

Diethylzinc is produced in an analogous way (OS II, 184; 84% yield). When zinc chloride is added to a Grignard reagent, the resulting mixture exhibits the properties of an organozinc compound. Organocadmium reagents are made in a similar way.

$$2RMgCl + CdCl_2 \rightarrow R_2Cd + 2MgCl_2$$

Organolithium compounds

Of the alkali metals only lithium has found extensive use because organometallic compounds containing other alkali metals decompose ethers too rapidly to be useful. Organolithium derivatives may be produced in much the same way as Grignard reagents. n-Butyllithium is formed in yields as high as 90% by treatment of n-butyl bromide with lithium in ethyl ether at about $-10°$. Perhaps the most valuable aryllithium compound is phenyllithium, prepared by the action of lithium on bromobenzene.

$$C_6H_5Br + 2Li \rightarrow C_6H_5Li + LiBr$$

Many halogen compounds that do not form Grignard reagents satisfactorily give lithium derivatives in high yields; an example is p-dimethylaminobromobenzene.

$$(CH_3)_2N\!\!\left\langle\!\!\bigcirc\!\!\right\rangle\!\!Br + 2Li \rightarrow (CH_3)_2N\!\!\left\langle\!\!\bigcirc\!\!\right\rangle\!\!Li + LiBr$$

Organolithium compounds of the aromatic series in general are conveniently made by halogen-lithium interconversion (OR **6**, 339). When *p*-bromochlorobenzene is treated with *n*-butyllithium, for example, the bromine and lithium atoms exchange places.

α-Bromonaphthalene and propyllithium react similarly.

This type of interchange is particularly valuable because it occurs with bromo compounds that contain hydroxyl, amino, carboxyl, and other groups. *o*-Bromophenol gives salicylic acid in satisfactory yield by the following sequence of reactions.

Interchange has been observed with other halogens and other metals, but its usefulness is due chiefly to the interchange of lithium and bromine. Interchange of lithium and iodine occurs when *p*-dimethylaminophenyllithium and iodobenzene are brought together; *p*-iododimethylaniline is formed in 54% yield.[19]

Cyclopropyl chloride reacts with lithium powder to give cyclopropyllithium, which reacts normally to yield various types of cyclopropyl compounds.[20] Nuclear metalation (OR **8**, 258) is greatly facilitated by the presence on the ring of *o,p*-directing groups, notably alkoxyl and amino. Anisole reacts readily with a wide variety of metal alkyls to yield *o*-derivatives; with phenyllithium the product is *o*-methoxyphenyllithium.

Another example is the conversion of the dimethyl ether of resorcinol into the 1,2,3-derivative.

[19] H. Gilman and L. Summers, *J. Am. Chem. Soc.*, **72**, 2767 (1950).
[20] H. Hart and J. M. Sandri, *Chem. and Ind.*, 1014 (1956).

When 2-methoxynaphthalene is treated with *n*-butyllithium, lithium takes the 3- rather than the 1-position.[21]

Metalation in general takes place predominantly in a position *ortho* to a substituent of the type OR, SR, or NR_2. Such reactions may be looked upon as the displacement of an acid from its salt by a stronger acid; the following compounds are arranged in increasing order of acidity (CR **35**, 9).

$$CH_3CH_3 < C_6H_6 < C_6H_5CH_3 < C_6H_5CH_2C_6H_5 < (C_6H_5)_3CH$$

Allyllithium is prepared most satisfactorily by the action of phenyllithium on allyltriphenyltin.[22]

$$(C_6H_5)_3SnCH_2CH{=}CH_2 + C_6H_5Li \rightarrow CH_2{=}CHCH_2Li + (C_6H_5)_4Sn$$

Vinyllithium can be made in a similar way from tetravinyltin or tetravinyllead and phenyllithium.[23] Preparation of this reagent from vinyl chloride or bromide and lithium metal has given trouble; satisfactory results are obtained, however, by use of lithium that contains about 2% of sodium with tetrahydrofuran as solvent.[24]

[21] S. V. Sunthankar and H. Gilman, *J. Org. Chem.*, **16**, 8 (1951).
[22] D. Seyferth and M. A. Weiner, *J. Org. Chem.*, **24**, 1395 (1959).
[23] E. C. Juenge and D. Seyferth, *J. Org. Chem.*, **26**, 563 (1961).
[24] R. West and W. H. Glaze, *J. Org. Chem.*, **26**, 2096 (1961).

26

Hydrogenation, hydrogenolysis, and dehydrogenation

The addition of molecular hydrogen to a multiple bond in the presence of a catalyst was discovered in 1897 by Sabatier, who effected hydrogenation of olefins in the presence of nickel. Since that time many other catalysts have come into use, and methods have been developed for the successful catalytic hydrogenation of almost every type of olefinic and acetylenic compound as well as aromatic rings. Aldehydes, ketones, esters, nitriles, and many other types of compounds have been hydrogenated also. In addition, much progress has been made in the search for conditions that permit selective hydrogenation, i.e., make possible hydrogenation of one type of reducible function without affecting others that might be present.

Under the conditions used for catalytic hydrogenation, bond cleavage may occur, leading to *hydrogenolysis*, a reaction that has found many applications. Many of the hydrogenation processes can be reversed by proper change of conditions. In its turn catalytic *dehydrogenation* has assumed an important position in synthesis as well as in degradation of natural products.[1]

Reduction by dissolving metals has been classified as a nucleophilic process (p. 545) because it occurs with carbonyl and cyano groups but not with simple olefins. The type of reduction to be discussed here, illustrated by the absorption of hydrogen by olefins on the surface of a transition metal, has the characteristics of a homolytic process; presumably the hydrogen is transferred from the metal as hydrogen atoms.

Catalytic Hydrogenation

Hydrogenation of unsaturated fats, an early industrial application of Sabatier's classic discovery, continues to be important; both edible and

[1] See L. M. Jackman, *Advances in Organic Chemistry*, Interscience Publishers, Inc., New York, Vol. II, p. 329, 1960.

nonedible fats are prepared in this way. Cyclohexane is made by the hydrogenation of benzene. Hydrogenation of naphthalene yields tetralin and decalin, which are useful solvents. Similarly, hexalin (cyclohexanol) is obtained from phenol. Technical "isoöctane" is produced in large quantities by hydrogenation of the condensation products of isobutylene and butylenes. The pure hydrocarbon, 2,2,4-trimethylpentane, is made by hydrogenation of the diisobutylenes.

$$
\underset{\underset{CH_3}{|}}{\overset{\overset{CH_3\ \ CH_3}{|\ \ \ \ |}}{CH_3CCH_2C}}\!=\!CH_2 \xrightarrow{\ H_2\ } \underset{\underset{CH_3\ \ CH_3}{|\ \ \ \ |}}{\overset{\overset{CH_3}{|}}{CH_3CCH_2CHCH_3}} \xleftarrow{\ H_2\ } \underset{\underset{CH_3\ \ CH_3}{|\ \ \ \ |}}{\overset{\overset{CH_3}{|}}{CH_3CCH}}\!=\!CCH_3
$$

Processes involving catalytic hydrogenation have been discovered for the production of liquid fuels. The Fischer-Tropsch method (p. 646) is an example. In the Bergius process crushed coal is dissolved in an equal weight of a heavy oil at 400° and subjected to catalytic hydrogenation. The heavy oil contains hydroaromatic compounds such as tetrahydronaphthalene, which serve as hydrogen carriers. Fuels are also made by hydrogenation of tars.

Reduction by ordinary chemical agents generally affords less satisfactory results than the catalytic method. Catalytic hydrogenation is easier to control and gives the product in relatively pure condition.

One concept of catalysis postulates the adsorption of the reactants individually on the surface of the catalyst, whereupon the reaction occurs (QR 3, 209). According to this theory a catalyst to be effective must adsorb and activate the reactants, must hold them in the proper ratio and space relationship, and must desorb the product.

Catalysts

The most useful catalysts for the hydrogenation of olefinic compounds are platinum, nickel, and copper-chromium oxide. The Adams method (OS I, 61, 463) employs platinum oxide and is effective at room temperature and low pressures for a wide variety of compounds. When more strenuous treatment is necessary, the high-pressure bomb is employed. An apparatus has been devised that makes it possible to measure the quantity of hydrogen absorbed, giving a method of estimating the amount of unsaturation.

Nickel on kieselguhr and Raney nickel generally are used at higher temperatures and pressures. The Raney catalyst is made by preparing an alloy of equal parts of nickel and aluminum and dissolving out the aluminum with sodium hydroxide. The degree of activity depends on the mode of preparation, and the catalysts are designated as W-4, W-6, etc., depending on the method employed. The most active type (W-6) is made by maintaining a hydrogen atmosphere over the catalyst throughout the washing operations (OS III, 176).

Raney catalyst W-2 is prepared by allowing a nickel-aluminum alloy (ca. 50%) to react with sodium hydroxide (OS III, 181).

$$NiAl_2 + 6NaOH \rightarrow Ni + 2Na_3AlO_3 + 3H_2$$

The alloy in contact with sodium hydroxide can serve as a reducing agent; it reduces sodium cinnamate to sodium hydrocinnamate. Deuterated Raney nickel has been prepared also.

Raney nickel is especially useful in hydrogenation of phenolic compounds such as phenol, resorcinol, and catechol. In the presence of this catalyst and at temperatures from 120 to 150°, the corresponding hydroxy cyclohexanes are formed in high yields. Phenols can be converted into the corresponding cyclohexanones by partial hydrogenation; presumably the resulting enol undergoes ketonization. This type of reaction has been postulated, for example, in the production of cyclohexanone by hydrogenation of phenol.

Catalytic hydrogenation of 2-naphthol produces 2-tetralone. In the presence of alkali partial hydrogenation may occur almost exclusively, affording a useful method for the preparation of the corresponding cyclohexanone derivatives. An example is the synthesis of dihydroresorcinol, or 1,3-cyclohexanedione, by hydrogenation of resorcinal in the presence of Raney nickel and sodium hydroxide (OS III, 278); the yield is 95%.

A similar result has been obtained with pyrogallol; with a mixture of one mole of alkali and one mole of pyrogallol the uptake of hydrogen ceases abruptly after one mole has been absorbed. The dihydro derivative is a stable enediol.[2]

[2] B. Pecherer, L. M. Jampolsky, and H. M. Wuest, *J. Am. Chem. Soc.*, **70**, 2587 (1948).

In long conjugated systems terminated by carbonyl groups, conjugate addition of hydrogen may involve the ends of the system. 1,2-Dibenzoylethylene yields a dienol, evidence for its existence being that 2,5-diphenylfuran is formed under conditions that leave the saturated diketone unchanged.

$$C_6H_5\overset{O}{\overset{\|}{C}}-CH=CH-\overset{O}{\overset{\|}{C}}C_6H_5 \xrightarrow{H_2} C_6H_5\overset{OH}{\overset{|}{C}}=CH-CH=\overset{OH}{\overset{|}{C}}C_6H_5 \longrightarrow$$

$$\begin{array}{c} CH\!\!-\!\!\!-\!\!CH \\ \overset{\|}{}\quad\quad\overset{\|}{} \\ C_6H_5C\quad\quad CC_6H_5 \\ \diagdown\quad\diagup \\ O \end{array}$$

A highly hindered analog containing mesityl groups gives a stable diol.

$$\underset{\underset{Mes}{|}}{Mes}\overset{O}{\overset{\|}{C}}C=CH\underset{\underset{Mes}{|}}{C}H=\overset{O}{\overset{\|}{C}}CMes \xrightarrow{H_2} \underset{\underset{Mes}{|}}{Mes}\overset{OH}{\overset{|}{C}}=C-CH=CH-\underset{\underset{Mes}{|}}{C}=\overset{OH}{\overset{|}{C}}CMes$$

The platinum oxide catalyst may serve in the reduction of carbonyl compounds to the corresponding alcohols as in the conversion of 3,5-dimethoxybenzaldehyde into 3,5-dimethoxybenzyl alcohol.

Nitriles can be hydrogenated satisfactorily with nickel as in the synthesis of decamethylenediamine from sebaconitrile (OS III, 229; 80% yield).

$$(CH_2)_8\overset{\diagup CN}{\underset{\diagdown CN}{}} + 4H_2 \xrightarrow[Ni]{NH_3} (CH_2)_8\overset{\diagup CH_2NH_2}{\underset{\diagdown CH_2NH_2}{}}$$

In a similar way phenylacetonitrile gives β-phenethylamine (OS III, 720; 87% yield). Another example is the manufacture of hexamethylenediamine from adiponitrile.

$$(CH_2)_4\overset{\diagup CN}{\underset{\diagdown CN}{}} + 4H_2 \xrightarrow{NH_3} H_2N(CH_2)_6NH_2$$

In the hydrogenation of nitriles, a side reaction leads to the formation of secondary amines. The presence of ammonia retards this side reaction, presumably because ammonia combines preferentially with the imine.

A superior method of hydrogenating nitriles employs acetic anhydride in the presence of a Raney metal catalyst and a basic cocatalyst such as sodium acetate. The amine is obtained as the N-acetyl derivative, which can be hydrolyzed to the amine.[3]

One of the most versatile catalysts is copper-chromium oxide, prepared by heating copper ammonium chromate at $350°$.[4] It is active not only for hydrogenation of olefinic and acetylenic compounds but also for carbonyl compounds. With it ethyl cinnamate may be converted into 3-phenyl-1-propanol in one operation.

$$C_6H_5CH{=}CHCO_2C_2H_5 \rightarrow C_6H_5CH_2CH_2CH_2OH$$

Copper-chromium oxide is used widely in the hydrogenation of esters (OR **8**, 1). Diethyl adipate affords hexamethylene glycol in 90% yield when this catalyst is employed (OS II, 325).

$$(CH_2)_4 \begin{array}{l} CO_2C_2H_5 \\ \\ CO_2C_2H_5 \end{array} \rightarrow HO(CH_2)_6OH$$

The effectiveness of Raney nickel on the one hand and of copper-chromium oxide on the other is well illustrated by the industrial process for hydrogenation of furfural.[5] Furfuryl alcohol is produced at $175°$ and 1000 to 1500 pounds per square inch in the presence of 1 to 2% of copper-chromium oxide catalyst. By merely changing the catalyst to Raney nickel, or better by using a mixture of the two catalysts, furfural can be transformed to tetrahydrofurfuryl alcohol.

Raney nickel makes possible practically quantitative conversion of 2,3-dihydropyran into tetrahydropyran (OS III, 794).

[3] F. E. Gould, G. S. Johnson, and A. F. Ferris, *J. Org. Chem.*, **25**, 1658 (1960).

[4] T. W. Riener, *J. Am. Chem. Soc.*, **71**, 1130 (1949).

[5] B. H. Wojcik, *Ind. Eng. Chem.*, **40**, 210 (1948).

This reaction has become important because of the discovery that 2,3-dihydropyran can be made from tetrahydrofurfuryl alcohol (p. 182).

The copper-chromium oxide catalyst also permits opening of the ring of tetrahydrofurfuryl alcohol to produce pentamethylene glycol (OS III, 693; 47% yield).

Hydrogenation of phenanthrene to 9,10-dihydrophenanthrene can be effected also with the copper-chromium oxide catalyst (OS **34**, 31; 77% yield). One advantage of the copper-chromium oxide catalyst is its relative insensitiveness to catalyst poisons. Platinum catalysts are more sensitive to such impurities than is nickel; copper-chromium oxide catalysts require no special precaution as to the purity of materials.

The most suitable solvents for use with nickel or copper-chromium oxide catalysts are ethyl alcohol, dioxane, ether, and methylcyclohexane. It is unsafe to use nickel with dioxane except at low temperatures; this solvent undergoes cleavage and may explode above 175°. Copper-chromium oxide, however, may be employed safely with dioxane. With platinum catalysts it is possible also to use acidic solvents such as glacial acetic acid.

Temperature, pressure of hydrogen, purity of reactants, activity of the catalyst, and alkalinity (or acidity) of the reaction medium are interdependent variables affecting the rate of hydrogenation.

Ruthenium, as the dioxide or on a carrier, is superior for the hydrogenation of nitrogen bases such as pyridine. Piperidine can be made in this way in quantitative yields at moderate temperatures and pressures.

Selectivity

The commonest example of selective hydrogenation is the saturation of olefinic linkages without altering ester groups or other oxygen-containing functional groups. Unsaturated esters are readily transformed into the corresponding saturated esters. The more difficult problem of effecting hydrogenation without involving the olefinic linkages has been solved, also, in a large number of instances. By employing zinc-chromium oxide at 300° it is possible to convert *n*-butyl oleate into oleyl alcohol, 1-octadecanol being formed in only small amounts.

$$CH_3(CH_2)_7CH{=}CH(CH_2)_7CO_2C_4H_9 \rightarrow$$
$$CH_3(CH_2)_7CH{=}CH(CH_2)_7CH_2OH$$

That zinc compounds inhibit hydrogenation of olefinic bonds is further exemplified by reduction of cinnamaldehyde to cinnamyl alcohol by treatment with hydrogen in the presence of a platinum catalyst containing zinc and ferrous salts. Ferrous salts are known to accelerate hydrogenation of carbonyl groups.

$$C_6H_5CH{=}CHCHO + H_2 \xrightarrow[Fe^{++},\,Zn^{++}]{Pt} C_6H_5CH{=}CHCH_2OH$$

Both palladium (OS III, 685) and Raney nickel can be used to reduce acetylenic compounds to the corresponding olefins. Since these catalysts are excellent for hydrogenation of olefins to saturated compounds, it is necessary to discontinue the introduction of hydrogen when the olefin has been formed. Raney iron serves to effect selective reduction of triple bonds in the presence of double bonds, which are not attacked in the presence of this catalyst. This type of differential hydrogenation can be accomplished also by use of a palladium-on-calcium carbonate catalyst, a method that is especially useful for the following type of transformation.

$$-CH{=}CHC{\equiv}CCH{=}CH- \ \rightarrow \ -CH_2{=}CHCH{=}CHCH{=}CH-$$

As has been mentioned (p. 545), hydrogenation of acetylenes over Raney nickel gives *cis*-olefins. The *cis*-forms of all the straight-chain hexenes and octenes, for example, have been made in this way. Similarly, *cis*-2-butene-1,4-diol has been made from 2-butyne-1,4-diol; the yield is 80%.[6]

$$HOCH_2C{\equiv}CCH_2OH + H_2 \ \rightarrow \ \begin{array}{c} HOCH_2CH \\ \| \\ HOCH_2CH \end{array}$$

Influence of pressure

Variations in pressure may affect the course of hydrogenation profoundly, as is illustrated by the hydrogenation of ethyl stearate at 250° in the presence of copper-chromium oxide. At 200 to 300 atmospheres 1-octadecanol is obtained in nearly quantitative yield; at 120 atmospheres the alcohol is accompanied by octadecyl stearate, presumably formed from octadecanal by a Tischenko type (p. 556) of reaction.

$$C_{17}H_{35}CO_2C_2H_5 \ \rightarrow \ C_{17}H_{35}CHO \ \rightarrow \ C_{17}H_{35}CH_2OH$$
$$2C_{17}H_{35}CHO \ \rightarrow \ C_{17}H_{35}CO_2CH_2C_{17}H_{35}$$

Such a reaction would be favored by low pressure, since the aldehyde (hydrogen acceptor) would be present in relatively higher porportion than hydrogen; few if any hydrogen atoms would be adsorbed between adjacent aldehyde molecules, thus favoring the reaction of aldehyde molecules with one another.

Sebacoin, when hydrogenated at 150° at a pressure of 135 atmospheres in the presence of copper chromite, gives a mixture of the *cis*(52% yield)- and *trans*(32% yield)-forms of 1,2-cyclodecanediol (OS **36**, 12).

$$(CH_2)_8 \begin{array}{c} C{=}O \\ | \\ CHOH \end{array} \ \rightarrow \ (CH_2)_8 \begin{array}{c} CHOH \\ | \\ CHOH \end{array}$$

[6] C. S. Marvel and C. H. Young, *J. Am. Chem. Soc.*, **73**, 1066 (1951).

In general high pressure is to be recommended when it is desired to avoid condensation reactions, these being favored by low concentration of hydrogen on the catalyst surface. High pressures are useful also in the hydrogenation of highly hindered esters to overcome the shielding effect of the branched chains on active centers of the catalyst. An example is the reduction of ethyl pivalate to neopentyl alcohol.

$$(CH_3)_3CCO_2C_2H_5 \rightarrow (CH_3)_3CCH_2OH$$

Amount of catalyst

A high ratio of catalyst to hydrogen acceptor (100 to 150% by weight) is effective in lowering the temperature of reaction with hydrogen and makes possible hydrogenations that do not take place otherwise. β-Hydroxy esters, which normally yield primary alcohols, give 1,3-glycols when massive amounts of catalyst are taken.

$$RCHCH_2CO_2C_2H_5 \xrightarrow[200°]{\substack{5\% \text{ copper-}\\ \text{chromium oxide}}} RCH_2CH_2CH_2OH$$
$$\overset{|}{OH}$$

$$RCHCH_2CO_2C_2H_5 \xrightarrow[125°]{\substack{150\% \text{ copper-}\\ \text{chromium oxide}}} RCHCH_2CH_2OH$$
$$\overset{|}{OH} \qquad\qquad\qquad\qquad \overset{|}{OH}$$

Another example is the reduction of methyl laurate to 1-dodecanol, which proceeds satisfactorily (80 to 90% yield) at 150° in the presence of 150% of copper-chromium oxide; no reduction occurs even at 200 to 210° when only 5% of the catalyst is present.

Reduction of α-amino esters to α-amino alcohols likewise takes place readily at low temperatures (25 to 100°) in the presence of 150% by weight of nickel.

Nitro compounds

Catalytic reduction is used widely to make primary amines from nitro compounds. An example is the synthesis of 2-amino-p-cymene from 2-nitro-p-cymene (OS III, 63; 90% yield). The catalyst of choice is Raney nickel.

In a similar way 2,6-diaminobenzoic acid is made from 6-nitroanthranilic acid.[7]

$$O_2N \underset{}{\overset{CO_2H}{\bigcirc}} NH_2 + 3H_2 \xrightarrow{Ni} H_2N \underset{}{\overset{CO_2H}{\bigcirc}} NH_2 + 2H_2O$$

Raney nickel serves in the reduction of *m*-nitrobenzaldehyde dimethylacetal to *m*-aminobenzaldehyde dimethylacetal (OS III, 59; yield 78%).

$$\underset{NO_2}{\bigcirc}CH(OCH_3)_2 + 3H_2 \xrightarrow{Ni} \underset{NH_2}{\bigcirc}CH(OCH_3)_2 + 2H_2O$$

Catalytic hydrogenation of oximes produces the corresponding primary amines. Secondary amines are formed also, presumably by reduction of an addition product of the primary amine and the oxime.

$$R_2C{=}NOH + R_2CHNH_2 \rightarrow \underset{R_2CHNH}{\overset{}{R_2C{-}NHOH}} \rightarrow (R_2CH)_2NH$$

As with nitriles (p. 641) the side reaction may be suppressed by conducting the hydrogenation in the presence of ammonia; reduction of the addition product of ammonia to the oxime yields the desired primary amine.

$$R_2C{=}NOH \xrightarrow{NH_3} R_2C\overset{\displaystyle NHOH}{\underset{\displaystyle NH_2}{\Big\langle}} \longrightarrow R_2CHNH_2$$

Hydrogenation of diethyl isonitrosomalonate over palladium produces diethyl aminomalonate (OS **40**, 24).

$$HON{=}C(CO_2C_2H_5)_2 \rightarrow H_2NCH(CO_2C_2H_5)_2$$

Methanol process

The production of methanol by hydrogenation of carbon monoxide made this alcohol cheap and also furnished in commercial quantities a number of alcohols that were previously rare and expensive. The process consists in the treatment of carbon monoxide with hydrogen in the presence of a zinc chromite catalyst at about 450° and 3000-pound pressure.

$$CO + 2H_2 \rightarrow CH_3OH$$

[7] C. M. Moser and T. Gompf, *J. Org. Chem.*, **15**, 583 (1950).

The formation of traces of higher alcohols is difficult to suppress; it has been suggested that in the presence of alkali a Guerbet type of reaction (p. 655) takes place. By addition of alkali metal or iron salts to the catalyst, formation of the higher alcohols is favored; they are prepared in quantity in this way. The chief products of the methanol process are the following alcohols.

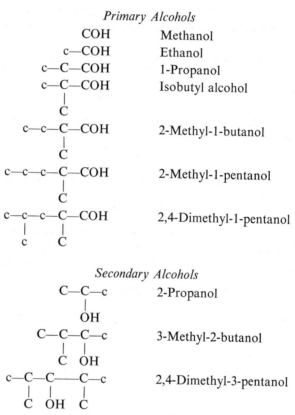

Primary Alcohols

COH	Methanol
c—COH	Ethanol
c—C—COH	1-Propanol

c—C—COH
      |
      C
	Isobutyl alcohol

c—c—C—COH
        |
        C
	2-Methyl-1-butanol

c—c—c—C—COH
          |
          C
	2-Methyl-1-pentanol

c—c—c—C—COH
   | |
   c   C
	2,4-Dimethyl-1-pentanol

Secondary Alcohols

C—C—c
     |
    OH
	2-Propanol

C—C—C—c
    | |
    C OH
	3-Methyl-2-butanol

c—C—C——C—c
    | | |
    C OH C
	2,4-Dimethyl-3-pentanol

As is indicated by the use of capital and lower-case letters for carbon atoms, the more complex alcohols may be derived from the simple ones.

Fischer-Tropsch synthesis

The Fischer-Tropsch synthesis converts synthesis gas ($CO + 2H_2$) at pressures of 1 to 10 atmospheres into a hydrocarbon mixture consisting principally of normal paraffins and olefins.[8] One type of catalyst is made up chiefly of cobalt and operates best in the temperature range of 185 to 215°. The composition of the immediate product is such that it is unsuitable for

---

[8] H. H. Storch, *Ind. Eng. Chem.*, **37**, 340 (1945).

use as a high-grade fuel and must be reformed by cracking and dehydrogenation. Iron catalysts, reduced with hydrogen at 650 to 850°, furnish a product consisting chiefly of branched-chain hydrocarbons.

Oxo reaction

The synthesis of certain aldehydes is carried out by bringing together an olefin, carbon monoxide, and hydrogen in the presence of dicobalt octacarbonyl. Aldehyde formation occurs rapidly at 120 to 125° under a pressure of 100 to 150 atmospheres. Allylidene diacetate and ethyl acrylate give succindialdehyde-1,1-diacetate and β-carbethoxypropionaldehyde, respectively.

$$CH_2\!=\!CHCH(OCOCH_3)_2 \xrightarrow{[Co(CO)_4]_2} \begin{array}{c} CH_2CH(OCOCH_3)_2 \\ | \\ CH_2CHO \end{array}$$

$$CH_2\!=\!CHCO_2C_2H_5 \xrightarrow{[Co(CO)_4]_2} \begin{array}{c} CH_2CO_2C_2H_5 \\ | \\ CH_2CHO \end{array}$$

Styrene furnishes a mixture of α- and β-phenylpropionaldehydes.[9]

$$C_6H_5CH\!=\!CH_2 + CO + H_2 \rightarrow C_6H_5CH_2CH_2CHO \quad \text{and} \quad \begin{array}{c} C_6H_5CHCHO \\ | \\ CH_3 \end{array}$$

In the preceding examples of this reaction, usually known as the *oxo reaction*, the over-all result is the addition of a hydrogen atom and a formyl radical to an olefinic double bond, a change that has been called *hydroformylation*. It is to be noted, however, that ketone formation occurs also.

$$2RCH\!=\!CHR + CO + H_2 \rightarrow \begin{array}{c} RCH_2CHCOCHCH_2R \\ |\quad\quad | \\ R\quad\quad R \end{array}$$

The oxo reaction furnishes a route to alcohols since, after the initial reaction, it is possible to vent the carbon monoxide and hydrogenate the aldehyde in the presence of the original catalyst. An example is the preparation of 3,5,5-trimethylhexanol from 2,4,4-trimethyl-1-pentene.

$$\begin{array}{c} CH_3 \\ | \\ CH_3CCH_2C\!=\!CH_2 \\ |\quad | \\ CH_3\ CH_3 \end{array} \rightarrow \begin{array}{c} CH_3 \\ | \\ CH_3CCH_2CHCH_2CHO \\ |\quad\ | \\ CH_3\ CH_3 \end{array} \rightarrow$$

$$\begin{array}{c} CH_3 \\ | \\ CH_3CCH_2CHCH_2CH_2OH \\ |\quad\ | \\ CH_3\ CH_3 \end{array}$$

[9] L. A. Wetzel, C. H. McKeever, and C. L. Levesque, *J. Am. Chem. Soc.*, **72**, 4939 (1950).

The oxo reaction has been realized with many olefins and diolefins and is applicable to other classes of unsaturated compounds as well. An alcohol is changed to the next higher homolog in one step by treatment with synthesis gas in the presence of a cobalt catalyst under conditions resembling those employed in the oxo reaction. Homologation of *t*-butyl alcohol by this procedure gives isoamyl alcohol in 63% yield.[10]

$$\underset{\underset{CH_3}{|}}{\overset{\overset{CH_3}{|}}{CH_3-C-OH}} + 2H_2 + CO \rightarrow (CH_3)_2CHCH_2CH_2OH$$

Ethylene glycol is produced from carbon monoxide, formaldehyde, and hydrogen by a modification of the oxo process.

$$CH_2O + CO + 2H_2 \rightarrow \underset{CH_2OH}{\overset{CH_2OH}{|}}$$

A mechanism proposed for hydroformylation assumes reversible addition of carbon monoxide to alkylcobalt carbonylates $[RCo(CO)_4]$.[11]

Hydrogenolysis

Hydrogenolysis of halogen compounds can be effected with various catalysts; actually hydrogenation of halogen compounds usually is accompanied by dehalogenation. With palladized charcoal or the Adams catalyst, aliphatically bound halogen atoms are resistant to hydrogenolysis in acid or neutral media unless under the influence of adjacent unsaturation. Aromatically bound halogen is removed more readily, particularly if labilized by an amino group. An important example is the preparation of lepidine from 2-chlorolepidine (OS III, 519; 87% yield).

t-Butylation of *p*-bromophenol followed by debromination with Raney nickel-aluminum alloy and aqueous alkali produces *o-t*-butylphenol.

[10] I. Wender, R. Levine, and M. Orchin, *J. Am. Chem. Soc.*, **71**, 4160 (1949).
[11] D. S. Breslow and R. F. Heck, *Chem. and Ind.*, 467 (1960).

By use of massive amounts of Raney nickel catalyst it is possible to effect hydrogenolysis of aryl p-toluenesulfonates; the products are the corresponding aromatic hydrocarbon and nickel p-toluenesulfonate. A method is thus provided for making hydrocarbons from phenols.[12] Substituted phenols also undergo this type of change. An example is the transformation of methyl salicylate to methyl benzoate.

$$2 \left[\underset{\text{OSO}_2\text{C}_7\text{H}_7}{\overset{\text{CO}_2\text{CH}_3}{\bigcirc}} \right] + \text{H}_2 + \text{Ni} \rightarrow 2 \left[\overset{\text{CO}_2\text{CH}_3}{\bigcirc} \right] + (\text{C}_7\text{H}_7\text{SO}_2\text{O})_2\text{Ni}$$

Benzyl ethers undergo catalytic hydrogenolysis (OR **7**, 263) (debenzylation) with platinum at room temperature or with nickel at 100°. An example is the cleavage of benzyl phenyl ether.

$$\bigcirc\text{CH}_2\text{O}\bigcirc + \text{H}_2 \xrightarrow{\text{Ni or Pt}} \bigcirc\text{CH}_3 + \bigcirc\text{OH}$$

Hydrogenolysis of the carbobenzoxy group (p. 325) is utilized in the Bergmann dipeptide synthesis, the final step of which is removal of this protecting group.

$$\underset{\overset{|}{\text{NHCO}_2\text{CH}_2\text{C}_6\text{H}_5}}{\text{RCHCONHCHCO}_2\text{H}} + \text{H}_2 \xrightarrow{\text{Pd-on-C}}$$

$$\underset{\overset{|}{\text{NH}_2}}{\overset{\text{R}}{\text{RCHCONHCHCO}_2\text{H}}} + \text{C}_6\text{H}_5\text{CH}_3 + \text{CO}_2$$

Debenzylation of acylmalonic esters is one step in a ketone synthesis. An example is the formation of heptadecan-8-one from dibenzyl n-octylmalonate and n-octoyl chloride; the yield is 91%.[13]

$$\underset{\overset{|}{\text{CO}_2\text{CH}_2\text{C}_2\text{H}_5}}{\overset{\text{CO}_2\text{CH}_2\text{C}_6\text{H}_5}{\text{CH(CH}_2)_7\text{CH}_3}} \rightarrow \underset{\overset{|}{\text{CO}_2\text{CH}_2\text{C}_6\text{H}_5}}{\overset{\text{CO}_2\text{CH}_2\text{C}_6\text{H}_5}{\text{CH}_3(\text{CH}_2)_6\text{COC(CH}_2)_7\text{CH}_3}} \rightarrow \text{CH}_3(\text{CH}_2)_6\text{CO(CH}_2)_8\text{CH}_3$$

[12] G. W. Kenner and M. A. Murray, *J. Chem. Soc.*, S178 (1949).
[13] R. E. Bowman, *J. Chem. Soc.*, 325 (1950).

The benzohydryl group is, of course, still more readily removed by hydrogenolysis. The benzohydryl ester of phenylacetic acid, when treated with hydrogen in the presence of a palladium-on-charcoal catalyst, gives phenylacetic acid and diphenylmethane.[14]

$$C_6H_5CH_2CO_2CH(C_6H_5)_2 + H_2 \rightarrow C_6H_5CH_2CO_2H + (C_6H_5)_2CH_2$$

Benzylamine and dibenzylamine are resistant to hydrogenolysis; but tertiary amines containing one benzyl radical are readily hydrogenolyzed. In fact, this cleavages provides a superior route to pure secondary amines as in the preparation of di-*n*-hexylamine.[15]

$$C_6H_5CH_2NH_2 \longrightarrow C_6H_5CH_2N(C_6H_{13})_2 \xrightarrow{H_2} (C_6H_{13})_2NH$$

Debenzylation of thio ethers provides an indirect method of replacing halogen with the thiol function; the formation of 6,8-dimercaptoöctanoic acid from ethyl 6,8-dibromoöctanoate is an example.[16]

$$\underset{\underset{Br}{\mid}}{CH_2}\underset{\underset{Br}{\mid}}{CH_2CH}(CH_2)_4CO_2C_2H_5 \xrightarrow[\substack{(2)\ KOH \\ (3)\ H_2O}]{(1)\ C_6H_5CH_2SNa}$$

$$\underset{\underset{C_6H_5CH_2S}{\mid}}{CH_2}\underset{\underset{SCH_2C_6H_5}{\mid}}{CH_2CH}(CH_2)_4CO_2H \xrightarrow[\text{liq. NH}_3]{Na} \underset{\underset{SH}{\mid}}{CH_2}\underset{\underset{SH}{\mid}}{CH_2CH}(CH_2)_4CO_2H$$

2,5-Dimethylhydroquinone is prepared by debenzylation of the phenolic Mannich base, 2,5-*bis*(dimethylaminomethyl)hydroquinone.

It has long been known that Hofmann's exhaustive methylation method does not open the heterocyclic ring of 1,2,3,4-tetrahydroquinoline. Cleavage does occur when the quaternary base is treated with sodium amalgam. This ring opening, known as the Emde reaction, is improved when Raney nickel is employed as the reducing agent.

Hydroxyl compounds in which the hydroxyl group is easily replaced readily undergo hydrogenolysis. Alcohols of the benzyl type, for example,

[14] E. Hardegger, Z. El Heweihi, and F. G. Robinet, *Helv.Chim. Acta*, **31**, 439 (1948).

[15] H. King and T. S. Work, *J. Chem. Soc.*, 1307 (1940).

[16] L. J. Reed and H.-Y. Niu, *J. Am. Chem. Soc.*, **77**, 416 (1955).

are hard to prepare by catalytic hydrogenation of the corresponding esters because of the difficulty of interrupting the process at the alcohol stage. A similar problem exists in the hydrogenation of substituted malonic esters; with copper-chromium oxide these yield chiefly substituted propyl alcohols instead of the expected 1,3-glycols. It is known, moreover, that 1,3-glycols undergo hydrogenolysis to propanols. For example, 1,3-cyclohexanediol gives cyclohexanol at 200° over copper-chromium oxide. Glycerol likewise loses one hydroxyl group, yielding propylene glycol. The peculiar ease with which 1,3-glycols suffer hydrogenolysis suggests that β-hydroxy carbonyl compounds, in which the hydroxyl group is labile, may be intermediates. An important advance in the catalytic reduction of esters over copper-chromium oxide was made when it was discovered that massive amounts of catalyst make it possible to interrupt the hydrogenation at the alcohol stage (p. 644).

It may be pointed out that hydrogenolysis of glycerol to propylene glycol is not desirable, since the glycol is made cheaply from propylene (p. 280). Hydrogenolysis of the secondary hydroxyl group, in the other hand, would give the relatively expensive trimethylene glycol. Fortunately this transformation can be brought about by a fermentation process.

When Raney nickel-aluminum alloy is added to a solution of furylacrylic acid in sodium hydroxide, a mixture of γ-n-propylbutyrolactone and β-(tetrahydrofuryl)propionic acid is produced (OS III, 742). Formation of the lactone could result from hydrogenolysis of the ring of the propionic acid followed by lactone formation.

Hydrogenolysis of terminal epoxides is influenced by experimental conditions. 1,2-Epoxydecane, in the presence of Raney nickel, yields mostly 1-decanol; if small amounts of sodium hydroxide are present, however, 2-decanol is the chief product.

Styrene oxide yields phenethyl alcohol exclusively with Raney nickel even when sodium hydroxide is present.[17]

$$C_6H_5CH\overset{O}{\overbrace{\quad\quad}}CH_2 + H_2 \rightarrow C_6H_5CH_2CH_2OH$$

In a similar way indene oxide furnishes 2-indanol.

One of the most interesting examples of this type of ring opening is the catalytic hydrogenolysis of 2,2-dimethylethylenimine to give *t*-butylamine (OS III, 148).

Primary alcohols undergo chain hydrogenolysis when treated with hydrogen at 250° under a pressure of 3000 pounds per square inch in the presence of Raney nickel. *n*-Heptadecane, for example, is made in 90% yield from 1-octadecanol by this procedure.[18]

$$CH_3(CH_2)_{15}CH_2CH_2OH + 2H_2 \rightarrow CH_3(CH_2)_{15}CH_3 + CH_4 + H_2O$$

Dehydroxymethylation under these conditions has served to produce various hydrocarbons. Cyclobutylcarbinol, for example, gives cyclobutane in 75% yield.[19]

As might be expected, this type of hydrogenolysis occurs much more readily when debenzylation is required; phenethyl alcohol is cleaved to toluene when treated with Raney nickel under relatively mild conditions. It is proposed that the aldehyde, produced by dehydrogenation, undergoes decarbonylation.[20]

[17] M. S. Newman, G. Underwood, and M. Renoll, *J. Am. Chem. Soc.*, **71**, 3362 (1949).
[18] A. K. Doolittle and R. H. Peterson, *J. Am. Chem. Soc.*, **73**, 2145 (1951).
[19] H. Pines, H. G. Rodenberg, and V. N. Ipatieff, *J. Am. Chem. Soc.*, **75**, 6065 (1953).
[20] J. A. Zderic, W. A. Bonner, and T. W. Greenlee, *J. Am. Chem. Soc.*, **79**, 1696 (1957).

Desulfurization

Removal of sulfur from a compound can be effected usefully by hydrogenolysis in the presence of an active Raney nickel catalyst. Actually the only hydrogen required is that adsorbed on the catalyst during its preparation. This behavior of sulfur compounds has been made the basis of a method of making aldehydes by way of thiol esters. When treated with Raney nickel, these esters undergo hydrogenolysis to give aldehydes (OR **8**, 229). Ethyl thiolpropionate, for example, yields propionaldehyde.

$$CH_3CH_2\overset{\overset{\displaystyle O}{\|}}{C}SCH_2CH_3 + 2H_2 \rightarrow CH_3CH_2CHO + H_2S + C_2H_6$$

Mercaptals and mercaptols are desulfurized also, yielding the hydrocarbons corresponding to the carbonyl compounds from which they were formed. This hydrogenolysis reaction provides a way, therefore, of reducing aldehydes and ketones to the hydrocarbon stage. Benzophenone, for example, yields diphenylmethane.

$$\begin{array}{c} C_6H_5 \\ \diagdown \\ \diagup \quad C{=}O \\ C_6H_5 \end{array} \xrightarrow{C_2H_5SH} \begin{array}{c} C_6H_5 \quad SC_2H_5 \\ \diagdown \diagup \\ C \\ \diagup \diagdown \\ C_6H_5 \quad SC_2H_5 \end{array} \xrightarrow[Ni]{H_2} C_6H_5CH_2C_6H_5$$

The method has found use in the reduction of α- and β-keto esters to the corresponding desoxy compounds, a transformation for which the Clemmensen and Wolff-Kishner methods have not proved to be generally applicable. An example is the reduction of ethyl benzoylacetate to ethyl hydrocinnamate; the yield is 77%.[21]

$$C_6H_5COCH_2CO_2C_2H_5 \rightarrow C_6H_5CH_2CH_2CO_2C_2H_5$$

When applied to ketoketene dimers (p. 700), this procedure affords a route to symmetrically substituted cyclobutane hydrocarbons.[22]

It has been employed also to reduce diketones to monoketones. 1,9-Cyclohexadecanedione, for example, gives cyclohexadecanone by way of its monoethylenedithioketal.[23]

$$\begin{array}{c} (CH_2)_7 \\ \diagup \quad \diagdown \\ CO \quad CO \\ \diagdown \quad \diagup \\ (CH_2)_7 \end{array} \rightarrow \begin{array}{c} CH_2S \quad (CH_2)_7 \\ | \diagup \quad \diagdown \\ C \quad CO \\ | \diagdown \quad \diagup \\ CH_2S \quad (CH_2)_7 \end{array} \rightarrow \begin{array}{c} (CH_2)_7 \\ \diagup \quad \diagdown \\ CH_2 \quad CO \\ \diagdown \quad \diagup \\ (CH_2)_7 \end{array}$$

[21] M. S. Newman and H. M. Walborsky, *J. Am. Chem. Soc.*, **72**, 4296 (1950).
[22] H. M. Walborsky and E. R. Buchman, *J. Am. Chem. Soc.*, **75**, 6339 (1953).
[23] A. T. Blomquist, J. Prager, and J. Wolinsky, *J. Am. Chem. Soc.*, **77**, 1804 (1955).

Rosenmund reduction

Hydrogenolysis of acid chlorides by the method of Rosenmund has been employed in the synthesis of aldehydes (OR **4**, 362). The usual catalyst is palladium deposited on barium sulfate (OS III, 685); an example is the reduction of 2-naphthoyl chloride to 2-naphthaldehyde (OS III, 626).

$$2-C_{10}H_7COCl + H_2 \rightarrow 2-C_{10}H_7CHO + HCl$$

Mesitaldehyde can be produced in a similar fashion (OS III, 551).

It is noteworthy that the hydrogenolysis of the —COCl group can be accomplished satisfactorily by the Rosenmund procedure even when certain other reducible groups are in the molecule. *p*-Nitrobenzaldehyde and cinnamaldehyde, for example, can be made from the corresponding chlorides in yields of 91 and 60%, respectively.

Dehydrogenation

Alcohols

One of the classical routes to aldehydes and ketones consists in dehydrogenation of the corresponding alcohols. In industrial practice catalytic dehydrogenation is generally carried out over silver or copper at about 300°. Formaldehyde, the simplest member of the class, is manufactured chiefly by passing methanol through a hot silver gauze; a limited amount of air is admitted to oxidize a large part of the hydrogen; this oxidation generates the heat required for the reaction.[24] Dehydrogenation of ethanol is one of the principal ways of making acetaldehyde.[25] Of great importance is the production of acetone by dehydrogenation of isopropyl alcohol. Similarly, cyclohexanone is made by the dehydrogenation of cyclohexanol, the usual catalyst being copper. *n*-Butyraldehyde, isobutyraldehyde, and methyl ethyl ketone are other examples of the many compounds that are manufactured by the catalytic method.

When allyl alcohol is passed over copper at 200 to 300°, hydrogen migrates to give propionaldehyde. In order to obtain acrolein it is necessary to introduce oxygen to destroy the hydrogen. This method, applied to

[24] R. N. Hader, R. D. Wallace, and R. W. McKinney, *Ind. Eng. Chem.*, **44**, 1508 (1952).

[25] J. M. Church and H. K. Joshi, *Ind. Eng. Chem.*, **43**, 1804 (1951).

methallyl alcohol, produces methacrolein in yields of 95%; the optimum temperature is 300 to 350°.[26] Catalytic dehydrogenation of ethylene glycol yields glyoxal.

$$\begin{array}{c} CH_2OH \\ | \\ CH_2OH \end{array} + O_2 \rightarrow \begin{array}{c} CHO \\ | \\ CHO \end{array} + 2H_2O$$

Dehydrogenation of alcohols to aldehydes has been proposed as a step In the *Guerbet reaction*, which takes place when an alcohol is heated with the corresponding sodium alkoxide at 250° under pressure. A branched chain primary alcohol is formed by the elimination of sodium hydroxide, the hydrogen atom being taken from the methylene group adjacent to the carbinol group.

$$RCH_2CH_2OH + RCH_2CH_2ONa \rightarrow \begin{array}{c} RCHCH_2OH \\ | \\ CH_2CH_2R \end{array} + NaOH$$

The steps in the Guerbet reaction appear to be dehydrogenation of the alcohol, followed by aldolization, crotonization, and hydrogenation. The transformation is facilitated by the presence of a catalyst containing copper chromite.[27]

Under suitable conditions benzyl alcohol benzylates normal primary alcohols as well as cyclohexanol.[28] Many other examples could be cited of the use of alcohols as alkylating agents, such as the formation of N,N'-diethylbenzidine by heating benzidine with Raney nickel in ethanol. Presumably acetaldehyde is formed, then the Schiff base, and finally the diamine (OS **36**, 21; 67% yield).

$$H_2NC_6H_4C_6H_4NH_2 \xrightarrow{CH_3CHO} CH_3CH=NC_6H_4C_6H_4N=CHCH_3 \xrightarrow{H_2}$$
$$CH_3CH_2NHC_6H_4C_6H_4NHCH_2CH_3$$

Methylation of ammonia and amines, effected at high temperatures in the presence of a copper chromium oxide catalyst, may proceed by way of formaldehyde. The preparation of methylamine is an example. Dimethyl- and trimethylamine are formed also, but by use of ammonia in excess the primary amine can be prepared in 80% yields.

$$CH_3OH + NH_3 \rightarrow CH_3NH_2 + H_2O$$

Suitably constituted dialdehydes undergo the Cannizzaro reaction to yield lactones. β-Methyl-δ-valerolactone, for example, is produced in

[26] J. M. Church and L. Lynn, *Ind. Eng. Chem.*, **42**, 768 (1950).
[27] M. N. Dvornikoff and M. W. Farrar, *J. Org. Chem.*, **22**, 540 (1957).
[28] E. F. Pratt and D. G. Kubler, *J. Am. Chem. Soc.*, **76**, 52 (1954).

47% yield by treating β-methylglutaraldehyde with aqueous alkali.[29] The same lactone is formed by heating 3-methyl-1,5-pentanediol with hydrogen in the presence of copper chromite (OS **35**, 87; 95% yield). Presumably the diol is dehydrogenated to the dialdehyde, which then goes to the lactone.

$$
\begin{array}{ccc}
\underset{\displaystyle CH_3CH}{\overset{\displaystyle CH_2CH_2OH}{\diagup\diagdown}} & \underset{\displaystyle CH_3CH}{\overset{\displaystyle CH_2CHO}{\diagup\diagdown}} & \underset{\displaystyle CH_3CH}{\overset{\displaystyle CH_2CO}{\diagup\diagdown}}O \\
CH_2CH_2OH & \rightarrow\ CH_2CHO & \rightarrow\ CH_2CH_2
\end{array}
$$

The use of oxygen to remove hydrogen, mentioned in connection with the manufacture of formaldehyde from methanol (p. 654), has proved to be particularly helpful in the carbohydrate series because primary alcohol groups are oxidized in preference to secondary (*Angew.*, **69**, 600).

Isomerization by redistribution of hydrogen

Release of hydrogen followed by its reabsorption at a different site, as in the isomerization of allyl alcohol to propionaldehyde, recalls the tendency of olefinic bonds to migrate under dehydrogenation conditions. β-Olefins, for example, are formed from α-olefins at 35 to 150° in the presence of reduced cobalt or nickel. Generally the rearrangement transforms the olefin into a more stable isomer.

In a similar way a diene in which the double bonds are isolated may rearrange to a conjugated diene. Biallyl (p. 632), for instance, rearranges to 2,4-hexadiene at 250° in the presence of an aluminum oxide-chromium oxide catalyst.

$$CH_2{=}CHCH_2CH_2CH{=}CH_2 \xrightarrow{\overset{Cr_2O_3}{Al_2O_3}} CH_3CH{=}CHCH{=}CHCH_3$$

Bimethallyl rearranges more readily than does biallyl.

$$\underset{\underset{CH_3}{\displaystyle |}}{CH_2{=}CCH_2}\underset{\underset{CH_3}{\displaystyle |}}{CH_2C{=}CH_2} \xrightarrow{\overset{Cr_2O_3}{Al_2O_3}} \underset{\underset{CH_3}{\displaystyle |}}{CH_3C{=}CHCH}\underset{\underset{CH_3}{\displaystyle |}}{{=}CCH_3}$$

Paraffins

Remarkable processes have been worked out for dehydrogenating *n*-butane; it gives 1-butene and 2-butene, and these in turn yield 1,3-butadiene. Isoprene can be made in quantity by dehydrogenation of isopentane. Neohexane gives *t*-butylethylene.

$$(CH_3)_3CCH_2CH_3 \rightarrow (CH_3)_3CCH{=}CH_2$$

[29] R. I. Longley, Jr., W. S. Emerson, and T. C. Shafer, *J. Am. Chem. Soc.*, **74**, 2012 (1952).

Styrene is made by pyrolysis of ethylbenzene in the presence of a chromia-alumina catalyst at temperatures in the neighborhood of 600°.

$$C_6H_5CH_2CH_3 \rightarrow C_6H_5CH\!=\!CH_2 + H_2$$

Vinylnaphthalenes may be produced from ethylnaphthalenes in a similar manner, the yields being as high as 90%.[30]

Aromatization

One of the most interesting developments in the petroleum field is the production of aromatic hydrocarbons from normal paraffins by a combination of dehydrogenation and cyclization. When the paraffin is passed over chromic oxide and alumina at 500° and 1 atmosphere the corresponding aromatic hydrocarbon is obtained in high yield. *n*-Heptane, for example, goes to toluene in 90% yield.

Aromatization occurs with those paraffins and monoolefins that have six carbon atoms, at least five of which are in a straight chain. If a compound can yield several different aromatic hydrocarbons, the product consists chiefly of an aromatic ring bearing one methyl group and the remaining carbon atoms in excess of six in one normal chain.

Dehydroaromatization is effected also with platinized alumina; with this catalyst 1,1-dimethylcyclohexane, for example, gives chiefly *o*-xylene.[31]

Aromatization of heptane and methylcyclohexane over stainless steel gauze has been conducted in such a way as to permit the isolation of a whole series of partially dehydrogenated products. Methylcyclohexane, for example, gives methylcyclohexenes and methylcyclohexadienes as well as toluene.[32]

[30] J. E. Nickels and B. B. Corson, *Ind. Eng. Chem.*, **43**, 1685 (1951).
[31] H. Pines and T. W. Greenlee, *J. Org. Chem.*, **26**, 1052 (1961).
[32] E. Gil-Av, J. Shabtai, and F. Steckel, *Chem. and Ind.*, 1055 (1960).

Hydroaromatic compounds

Hydroaromatic compounds can be dehydrogenated to the corresponding aromatic compounds; the usual procedure is to heat the compound with a metal such as palladium or platinum. Tetralin is dehydrogenated to naphthalene by heating with palladium-on-charcoal at 180°.

Colloidal platinum and palladium are the most useful catalysts for dehydrogenation on a laboratory scale. Invariably the activity of these metals is increased if they are supported on charcoal or asbestos, which appear to play an important role in determining the course of the reaction.

Liquids that are not too low boiling may be dehydrogenated simply by heating them with the catalyst; to prevent a reversal of the reaction and to furnish an inert medium the reaction is usually run in an atmosphere of carbon dioxide or nitrogen. Advantage is gained by passing carbon dioxide gas through the mixture to remove hydrogen. Also, it is helpful to maintain the reaction mixture in a state of vigorous ebullition, which aids in dislodging hydrogen from the active surface of the catalyst. In one method, the dehydrogenation is carried out in the presence of benzene in a high-pressure hydrogenation apparatus; hydrogen from the hydro-aromatic compound is taken up by the benzene, which forms cyclohexane.[33] By this method bicyclohexyl gives biphenyl in almost quantitative yields.

An important example of this method is the last step in the synthesis of hexahelicene in which hydrogen transfer to benzene is accomplished over 5% rhodium-on-alumina at 300°.[34]

Hexahelicene

Triphenylene may be formed by dehydrogenation of dodecahydro-triphenylene (p. 519).

[33] H. Adkins and L. G. Lundsted, *J. Am. Chem. Soc.*, **71**, 2964 (1949).
[34] M. S. Newman and D. Lednicer, *J. Am. Chem. Soc.*, **78**, 4765 (1956).

Dehydrogenation is often accompanied by other changes such as disproportionation, rearrangement, and elimination of groups. In spite of these weaknesses, however, it has proved to be a valuable tool in the determination of structure.

Aromatization of hydroaromatic compounds has been accomplished by use of bromine, sulfur, selenium, and quinones such as chloranil. A reagent that effects dehydration as well as dehydrogenation is triphenyl-methyl perchlorate.[35]

Dehydrogenation is facilitated by the presence of unsaturated linkages because of the enhanced reactivity of the hydrogen atoms of adjacent methylene groups. When certain olefinic compounds are heated in the presence of a hydrogenation catalyst, they undergo disproportionation to the corresponding dienes and paraffinic compounds; cyclopentene yields a mixture of cyclopentadiene and cyclopentane. The disproportionation can be effected at elevated temperatures in the presence of catalysts such as vanadium pentoxide.

The tendency to undergo disproportionation of this type is at a maximum with partially hydrogenated aromatic compounds because of the high degree of stability of the aromatic rings. Cyclohexene, for example, in the presence of chromia goes to a mixture of cyclohexane and benzene at temperatures below 100°. Di- and tetrahydrobenzenes also undergo disproportionation in the presence of platinum or palladium to yield mixtures of cyclohexane and benzene.

Dehydrogenation may be accompanied by other changes that may be necessary for aromatization to occur. Thus seven- and eight-membered rings may undergo diminution to six-membered rings. In this connection it is pertinent to mention that the synthesis of azulenes, highly conjugated hydrocarbons, can be effected by dehydrogenation of partially hydrogenated azulenes. 2-n-Propylazulene, for example, has been made in this way.[36]

Sulfur reacts with hydrocarbons to produce hydrogen sulfide, carbon disulfide, and complex sulfurized derivatives in addition to olefins (CR 39, 219). Thiophene and its homologs can be made by the interaction of sulfur and paraffins; if n-butane is used, thiophene is obtained in satisfactory yields. The reactants are preheated separately to about 600° and introduced rapidly through a mixing nozzle into a reaction tube at 600°

[35] W. Bonthrone and D. H. Reid, Chem. and Ind., 1192 (1960).
[36] P. A. Plattner, Z. Fürst, and K. Jirasek, Helv. Chim. Acta, 29, 740 (1946).

Evidence that unsaturated compounds are intermediates is the fact that, by recycling the unsaturated products, the conversion to thiophene may be increased to as much as 50%. It is well known, moreover, that butadiene and its derivatives yield thiophene and thiophene derivatives when heated with sulfur. An example is the preparation of 3-methylthiophene from isoprene.

Dehydrocyclization

Dehydrocyclization is the intramolecular loss of hydrogen from an aromatic or hydroaromatic compound to form a new compound with a greater number of rings. Many examples of this type of ring closure are known (CR **53**, 353); the formation of naphthalene from o-divinylbenzene is an example.[37]

$$
\underset{\text{CH=CH}_2}{\overset{\text{CH=CH}_2}{\bigcirc}} \rightarrow \bigcirc\bigcirc + H_2
$$

This ring closure was observed in the dehydrogenation of a mixture of diethylbenzenes to the corresponding divinylbenzenes. The conditions are similar to those employed in producing styrene from ethylbenzene (p. 657). The conversion of o-divinylbenzene into naphthalene is practically quantitative under these conditions.

When the triene, $\bigcirc$—CH=CH—$\bigcirc$, is heated at 350° in the presence of palladinized charcoal, phenanthrene is formed.

n-Butylbenzene may be dehydrocyclized by heating to 500° over a chromia catalyst; the product, naphthalene, is obtained in yields as high as 50% per pass.[38]

$$
\bigcirc\text{CH}_2\text{CH}_2\text{CH}_2\text{CH}_3 \rightarrow \bigcirc\bigcirc
$$

The formation of phenanthrene from 2,2'-dimethylbiphenyl by treatment with sulfur is another example.[39]

$$
\underset{\bigcirc-\bigcirc}{\overset{\text{CH}_3\ \text{CH}_3}{}} + 2S \rightarrow \bigcirc\bigcirc\bigcirc + 2H_2S
$$

A somewhat different type of dehydrogenation is exemplified by the synthesis of biphenyl by passing benzene through a hot pipe. Similar

[37] H. Hopff and H. Ohlinger, *Ber.*, **76**, 1250 (1943).
[38] W. J. Mattox and A. V. Grosse, *J. Am. Chem. Soc.*, **67**, 84 (1945).
[39] W. F. Short, H. Stromberg, and A. E. Wiles, *J. Chem. Soc.*, 319 (1936).

changes occur intramolecularly; an example is the formation of fluoro-anthane from 1-phenylnaphthalene.[40]

$$\rightarrow \qquad + H_2$$

This ring closure is similar to that discovered by Scholl.

o-Methylated diarylmethanes yield anthracenes when pyrolyzed; o-benzyltoluene, for example, gives anthracene in high yield.[41]

$$\rightarrow \qquad + 2H_2$$

Scholl reaction

In the Scholl reaction ordinarily an aroyl derivative of an aromatic hydrocarbon loses hydrogen and undergoes ring closure when heated with aluminum chloride; an example is the formation of benzanthrone from 1-benzoylnaphthalene.

$$\xrightarrow[\substack{150° \\ 2.5 \text{ hours}}]{AlCl_3} \qquad CO + H_2$$

The formation of phenanthrenequinone from benzil also falls in this category.

$$\rightarrow \qquad + H_2$$

[40] M. Orchin and L. Reggel, *J. Am. Chem. Soc.*, **69**, 505 (1947).
[41] L. A. Errede and J. P. Cassidy, *J. Am. Chem. Soc.*, **82**, 3653 (1960).

27

Decarbonylation and decarboxylation

Loss of carbon monoxide from a carbonyl compound and of carbon dioxide from a carboxylic acid often is produced by heating alone, which suggests a radical mechanism.

Decarbonylation

Loss of carbon monoxide is characteristic of ethoxalyl derivatives made by the condensation of active methylene compounds with diethyl oxalate; the products are substituted malonic esters. Diethyl methylmalonate, for example, can be made in nearly theoretical yields from ethyl ethoxalyl-propionate in this way (OS II, 279).

$$CH_3CH\begin{smallmatrix}CO_2C_2H_5\\COCO_2C_2H_5\end{smallmatrix} \xrightarrow{\text{heat}} CH_3CH\begin{smallmatrix}CO_2C_2H_5\\CO_2C_2H_5\end{smallmatrix} + CO$$

The condensation product of ethyl stearate and diethyl oxalate undergoes decarbonylation to give diethyl cetylmalonate in 71% yield (OS 34, 13).

$$C_{17}H_{35}CO_2C_2H_5 \rightarrow C_{16}H_{33}\underset{COCO_2C_2H_5}{CHCO_2C_2H_5} \rightarrow C_{16}H_{33}CH(CO_2C_2H_5)_2$$

Diethyl phenylmalonate is produced in a similar manner (OS II, 288) in 85% yields.

$$C_6H_5CH_2CO_2C_2H_5 + \begin{smallmatrix}CO_2C_2H_5\\ | \\ CO_2C_2H_5\end{smallmatrix} \rightarrow C_6H_5\underset{COCO_2C_2H_5}{CHCO_2C_2H_5} \rightarrow$$

$$C_6H_5CH(CO_2C_2H_5)_2$$

In certain cases loss of carbon monoxide by ethoxalyl compounds is promoted by addition of powdered soft glass.[1]

Diethyl dimethyloxalacetate boils at 230° at atmospheric pressure and does not undergo decarbonylation.

$$\begin{array}{c} CH_3 \\ | \\ C_2H_5O_2C-C-COCO_2C_2H_5 \\ | \\ CH_3 \end{array}$$

Even more striking is the thermal stability of alkoxalylmethanetricarboxylic esters. The methyl ester, for example, boils at 285 to 286° without evolving carbon monoxide.

$$\begin{array}{c} CO_2CH_3 \\ | \\ CH_3O_2CCCOCO_2CH_3 \\ | \\ CO_2CH_3 \end{array}$$

Thermal decarbonylation occurs with such compounds as diphenyl tri- and tetraketones.

$$C_6H_5COCOCOCOC_6H_5 \xrightarrow{-CO} C_6H_5COCOCOC_6H_5 \xrightarrow{-CO} C_6H_5COCOC_6H_5$$

By C^{14} tracer studies it has been established that in the decarbonylation of diphenyl triketone the central carbonyl group is lost.[2]

Diethyl diketosuccinate gives carbon monoxide and diethyl mesoxalate at 125°. The latter yields diethyl oxalate at 180°.

$$\begin{array}{c} CO_2C_2H_5 \\ | \\ CO \\ | \\ CO \\ | \\ CO_2C_2H_5 \end{array} \xrightarrow[125°]{-CO} \begin{array}{c} CO_2C_2H_5 \\ | \\ CO \\ | \\ CO_2C_2H_5 \end{array} \xrightarrow[180°]{-CO} \begin{array}{c} CO_2C_2H_5 \\ | \\ CO_2C_2H_5 \end{array}$$

In the compounds that lose carbon monoxide it is to be noted that the carbonyl group to be eliminated is held loosely because of electron impoverishment of the adjacent atoms. This observation applies likewise to acetylenic aldehydes, which are known to lose carbon monoxide when heated. Phenylpropiolaldehyde, for example, yields carbon monoxide and phenylacetylene.

$$C_6H_5C{\equiv}CCHO \rightarrow C_6H_5C{\equiv}CH + CO$$

[1] W. E. Bachmann, J. W. Cole, and A. L. Wilds, *J. Am. Chem. Soc.*, **62**, 824 (1940).

[2] J. D. Roberts, D. R. Smith, and C. C. Lee, *J. Am. Chem. Soc.*, **73**, 618 (1951).

Many decarbonylations occur under conditions that suggest ionic or radical intermediates. A number of carboxylic acids lose carbon monoxide when treated with concentrated sulfuric acid; the decomposition of formic acid is an example.

$$HCO_2H + H_2SO_4 \rightarrow CO + OH_3^+ + HSO_4^-$$

This type of decomposition is exhibited also by triphenylacetic acid, which yields the relatively stable triphenylmethyl carbonium ion.

$$(C_6H_5)_3CCO_2H + 2H_2SO_4 \rightarrow (C_6H_5)_3C^+ + OH_3^+ + 2HSO_4^- + CO$$

α-Hydroxy acids behave in a similar manner, yielding aldehydes or ketones; citric acid, for example, gives acetonedicarboxylic acid (OS I, 10; 90% yield).

$$
\begin{array}{c}
CH_2CO_2H \\
| \\
HOCCO_2H \\
| \\
CH_2CO_2H
\end{array}
\xrightarrow[0°]{\text{fuming } H_2SO_4}
\begin{array}{c}
CH_2CO_2H \\
| \\
CO \\
| \\
CH_2CO_2H
\end{array}
+ CO + H_2O
$$

When carbonyl compounds are decomposed photochemically carbon monoxide is produced. Photolysis of acetone, for example, yields carbon monoxide together with varying amounts of methane and ethane.[3]

Decarboxylation

Many carboxylic acids undergo loss of carbon dioxide when heated, the net result being decarboxylation or the replacement of a carboxyl group by a hydrogen atom (Gould, 346). A similar result is achieved by heating salts of acids with caustic alkalis. Thermal decomposition of salts often leads to the formation of ketones accompanied by carbonates.

It is to be expected that a carboxyl group held by an active methylene group will be lost easily. The decarboxylation of malonic, acetoacetic, and cyanoacetic acids are familiar examples.

$$
\underset{\text{HOC}}{\overset{O}{\|}}\!\!-\!\!CH_2\underset{}{\overset{O}{\|}}COH \rightarrow CO_2 + CH_3\underset{}{\overset{O}{\|}}COH
$$

$$
\underset{\text{HOC}}{\overset{O}{\|}}\!\!-\!\!CH_2\underset{}{\overset{O}{\|}}CCH_3 \rightarrow CO_2 + CH_3\underset{}{\overset{O}{\|}}CCH_3
$$

$$
\underset{\text{HOC}}{\overset{N}{\|}}\!\!-\!\!CH_2C\equiv N \rightarrow CO_2 + CH_3C\equiv N
$$

[3] W. Davis, Jr., *J. Am. Chem. Soc.*, **70**, 1867 (1948).

The formation of nitromethane from nitroacetic acid is another illustration (OS I, 401).

$$\underset{\substack{\| \\ \text{O}}}{\text{HOC}}\text{---}\text{CH}_2\text{N}{=}\text{O} \rightarrow \text{CO}_2 + \text{CH}_3\text{N}{=}\text{O}$$
$$\downarrow \qquad\qquad\qquad\qquad \downarrow$$
$$\text{O} \qquad\qquad\qquad\qquad \text{O}$$

A useful generalization is that decarboxylation of acids is facilitated by a multiple linkage in the β,γ-position; in other words, loss of carbon dioxide is to be expected of compounds of the type $Y{=}XCH_2CO_2H$. Of these the β-keto acids are the most important.

Decarboxylation has many practical applications; the conversion of an alkyl halide to the corresponding alkyl- or dialkylacetic acid by the malonic ester method is illustrative. It requires decarboxylation of the intermediate malonic acid. Examples are the preparation of β-methyl-valeric acid (OS II, 416) and pelargonic acid (OS II, 474).

$$\underset{\substack{| \\ \text{CH}_3}}{\text{CH}_3\text{CH}_2\text{CHBr}} \rightarrow \underset{\substack{| \\ \text{CH}_3}}{\text{CH}_3\text{CH}_2\text{CHCH(CO}_2\text{H)}_2} \rightarrow \underset{\substack{| \\ \text{CH}_3}}{\text{CH}_3\text{CH}_2\text{CHCH}_2\text{CO}_2\text{H}}$$

$$\text{CH}_3(\text{CH}_2)_5\text{CH}_2\text{Br} \rightarrow \text{CH}_3(\text{CH}_2)_5\text{CH}_2\text{CH(CO}_2\text{H)}_2 \rightarrow \text{CH}_3(\text{CH}_2)_7\text{CO}_2\text{H}$$

Acids of this group usually can be decarboxylated at temperatures below 150°.

The elimination of carbon dioxide from such acids may involve the formation of a *quasi* six-membered ring (p. 678). The decarboxylation of acetoacetic acid, for example, may be formulated as follows, the enol form of acetone being produced.

If such an enol is not possible, decarboxylation does not occur readily.

Evidence has been presented in support of the hypothesis that the relative ease with which α,β-unsaturated carboxylic acids undergo decar-boxylation is due to rearrangement reversibly to the corresponding

β,γ-isomers—acids that would be expected to be thermally unstable and, like β-keto acids, break down by way of a cyclic transition state.[4]

$$\text{(cyclic transition state)} \rightarrow RCH_2CH=CH_2 + CO_2$$

Isodehydroacetic acid, which has a highly conjugated system of double bonds, loses carbon dioxide when heated with copper powder at 230 to 235°. The yield of 4,6-dimethylcoumalin is 87% (OS **32**, 57).

$$\text{(isodehydroacetic acid structure)} \rightarrow \text{(4,6-dimethylcoumalin structure)} + CO_2$$

Cleavage of certain phenolic acids is understandable since they may tautomerize to β-keto acids. Also, the theory that the Kolbe reaction is reversible is consistent with the observation that the phenolic acids that are produced by the Kolbe method readily undergo thermal decarboxylation. It thus appears that the factors that facilitate introduction of the carboxyl group make for a corresponding ease of decarboxylation of the product. Naphthoresorcinol, for example, is produced in 56% yield by boiling an aqueous solution of 1,3-dihydroxy-2-naphthoic acid for 2 hours (OS III, 637).

$$\text{(1,3-dihydroxy-2-naphthoic acid structure)} \rightarrow \text{(naphthoresorcinol structure)} + CO_2$$

3-Hydroxyquinoline is produced by heating 3-hydroxycinchoninic acid in boiling diethyl succinate (OS **40**, 54).

$$\text{(3-hydroxycinchoninic acid structure)} \rightarrow \text{(3-hydroxyquinoline structure)} + CO_2$$

Because of the ease with which it may be introduced and subsequently removed, the carboxyl group may be employed to stabilize the ring for

[4] R. T. Arnold, O. C. Elmer, and R. M. Dodson, *J. Am. Chem. Soc.*, **72**, 4359 (1950).

purposes of substitution. For example, resorcinol, which is too sensitive to be brominated directly, can be converted into β-resorcylic acid, which undergoes bromination satisfactorily. Decarboxylation of the bromo acid gives 4-bromoresorcinol (OS II, 100); the yield is 92%, based on the β-resorcylic acid.

A somewhat similar scheme makes possible the synthesis of 2,6-dichlorophenol in satisfactory yields. Ethyl p-hydroxybenzoate is chlorinated, and the ester group is then removed (OS III, 267). The decarboxylation, effected by heating the acid with dimethylaniline, affords the dichlorophenol in 91% yield.

It is noteworthy also that, during nitration, aromatic acids of this type are prone to suffer replacement of the carboxyl group by the nitro group. An example is the preparation of 2,4,6-trinitroanisole by the action of a mixture of nitric and sulfuric acids on anisic acid.

Decarboxylation is facilitated by m-directing groups in o- or p-positions, as is illustrated by the decarboxylation of 2,4,6-trinitrobenzoic acid (p. 21). Excellent results are obtained by the use of copper or copper salts as catalysts. The commercial process for making benzoic acid from phthalic acid is another example.

The reaction is catalyzed by a small amount of copper phthalate.

Another example is the synthesis of furan from 2-furoic acid (OS I, 274; 78% yield). A superior synthesis of furan is to heat furfural with alkalis, thus effecting oxidation and decarboxylation in sequence. The acid is decarboxylated when heated at its boiling point (200 to 205°). Furan is obtained in better yields by heating a solution of the carboxylic acid and quinoline (b.p. 238°) under reflux in the presence of a small amount of copper sulfate. Similarly when 5-bromofuroic acid is heated in boiling quinoline in the presence of copper-bronze, 2-bromofuran forms in 75% yield.

When diarylacetic acids, however, are heated with copper in quinoline, anomalous results are obtained; the corresponding symmetrical tetra-arylethanes are produced. Diphenylacetic acid, for example, yields 1,1,2,2-tetraphenylethane.[5]

In the pyridine series the carboxyl groups in the 2- and 4-positions are more readily lost than those in the 3-position. Decarboxylation of pyridinepolycarboxylic acids, therefore, provides a useful route to nicotinic acid and its derivatives. When quinolinic acid is heated in boiling cyclo-hexanol, nicotinic acid is formed in 90% yields.

Thermal decarboxylation of certain carboxylic acids in the presence of carbonyl compounds may produce carbinols; when quinaldinic acid is heated at 175° for 2 hours in a large excess of benzophenone, diphenyl-2-quinolylcarbinol is formed.[6]

It has been suggested that a modified cyanide ion is an intermediate and that the condensation is analogous to cyanohydrin formation.

Cinnamic acid may be decarboxylated to styrene by the application of heat (OS I, 440; 41% yield). Advantage has been taken of this behavior in the preparation of substituted styrenes also (CR **45**, 359). Styrenes are obtained in satisfactory yields by heating the acids in boiling quinoline in

[5] G. Webber and F. Maggio, *Ann. chim. (Rome)*, **50**, 1438 (1960).
[6] M. R. F. Ashworth, R. P. Daffern, and D. L. Hammick, *J. Chem. Soc.*, 809 (1939).

the presence of copper powder. An example is *m*-nitrostyrene, which is made in a yield of 59% by heating *m*-nitrocinnamic acid at 185 to 195° in quinoline in the presence of copper powder (OS **33**, 62). In a similar way *cis*-stilbene is produced in a yield of 65% by heating a solution of α-phenylcinnamic acid in quinoline to which a small amount of copper chromite has been added (OS **33**, 88).

$$\begin{array}{c} C_6H_5CH \\ \| \\ C_6H_5CCO_2H \end{array} \rightarrow \begin{array}{c} C_6H_5CH \\ \| \\ C_6H_5CH \end{array} + CO_2$$

Pyrolysis of Salts

Possibly in these reactions it is the copper salt that undergoes cleavage. If so, such salts behave very differently from those of the alkaline-earth group. If salts of these metals are heated alone, decarboxylation of a different type occurs. Two molecules are condensed to an aldehyde or ketone, a carbonate being eliminated. A simple illustration is the conversion of calcium acetate to acetone by heating.

$$(CH_3CO_2)_2Ca \rightarrow CH_3COCH_3 + CaCO_3$$

The same result is achieved more satisfactorily by a vapor-phase reaction. Acetone is formed when acetic acid is passed through a hot tube containing manganous oxide.

$$2CH_3CO_2H \xrightarrow{MnO} CH_3COCH_3 + CO_2 + H_2O$$

Presumably the acetic acid reacts in the form of manganous acetate. Only a small amount of the oxide is required, since manganese acetate is regenerated by the action of the acid on the manganese carbonate.

Thermal decomposition of calcium benzoate yields benzophenone. Formates likewise undergo this type of pyrolysis; zinc formate produces formaldehyde.

$$Zn(OCHO)_2 \rightarrow CH_2O + ZnCO_3$$

It is to be noted that for ketones this method is successful with the higher acids as well. Stearone, for example, can be made by heating magnesium stearate at 350 to 360° (OS **33**, 84; yield 87%).

$$(C_{17}H_{35}CO_2)_2Mg \rightarrow C_{17}H_{35}COC_{17}H_{35} + MgO + CO_2$$

The method is useful for certain unsymmetrical ketones. When a mixture of acetic and phenylacetic acids is passed over thorium oxide at 430 to 450°, benzyl methyl ketone is formed in 65% yield (OS II, 389).

Similarly, ethyl phenethyl ketone is formed from propionic and hydro-cinnamic acids (OS II, 391).

$$CH_3CH_2CO_2H + C_6H_5CH_2CH_2CO_2H \rightarrow$$
$$CH_3CH_2COCH_2CH_2C_6H_5 + CO_2 + H_2O$$

A large excess of the low-molecular-weight acid is taken in order to convert the more expensive acid as completely as possible into the unsymmetrical ketone.

Aromatic acids may be used also; when a solution of o-ethylbenzoic acid in acetic acid is passed at 450° through a tube filled with thorium oxide on pumice, o-ethylacetophenone is obtained in 74% yield.[7]

In this connection mention should be made of the curious behavior of sodium formate; when heated rapidly to 360° it gives hydrogen and sodium oxalate.

$$2HCO_2Na \rightarrow \begin{matrix} CO_2Na \\ | \\ CO_2Na \end{matrix} + H_2$$

Volatile acids may be converted into the corresponding aldehydes by passing a mixture of the acid with formic acid over manganous oxide.

$$RCO_2H + HCO_2H \xrightarrow{MnO} RCHO + H_2O + CO_2$$

The same result can, of course, be brought about by destructive distillation of a mixture of the calcium salts of the acids.

$$(RCO_2)_2Ca + (HCO_2)_2Ca \rightarrow 2RCHO + 2CaCO_3$$

Suitably constituted dibasic acids form cyclic ketones. Adipic acid, for example, when heated at 285 to 295° with barium hydroxide yields cyclopentanone.

$$\begin{matrix} CH_2CH_2CO_2H \\ | \\ CH_2CH_2CO_2H \end{matrix} \rightarrow \begin{matrix} CH_2CH_2 \\ | \quad \diagdown \\ \quad \quad CO + H_2O + CO_2 \\ | \quad \diagup \\ CH_2CH_2 \end{matrix}$$

Actually, one mole of adipic acid is converted into cyclopentanone in 80% yield by about $\frac{1}{20}$ mole of barium hydroxide (OS I, 192). Lead salts of acids have been found to give the corresponding ketones in yields as high as 90%.

[7] W. Winkler, *Chem. Ber.*, **81**, 256 (1948).

This method served in the early syntheses of large rings; thorium oxide is a better catalyst than barium or calcium bases for the closure of such rings.

Pyrolysis of Anhydrides

Another ring closure method was developed by Blanc, who found that slow distillation of the anhydrides of certain dibasic acids produces cycloalkanones. The anhydrides are formed by heating the acids with acetic anhydride. Only a little cycloheptanone can be produced in this way, and even for cyclopentanone and cyclohexanone the yields do not exceed 50%. Alkyl groups have a remarkable effect on the yields, as is shown by the following examples, in all of which the yields are nearly quantitative.

$$
\begin{array}{ll}
\begin{array}{l}
CH_2\!\!-\!\!CH_2 \\
\;|\qquad\quad\diagdown \\
\;|\qquad\qquad CO \\
\;|\qquad\quad\diagup \\
CH_2\!\!-\!\!CHCH_3
\end{array}
&
\begin{array}{l}
CH_2\!\!-\!\!CH_2 \\
\;|\qquad\quad\diagdown \\
\;|\qquad\qquad CO \\
\;|\qquad\quad\diagup \\
CH_3CH\!\!-\!\!CH_2
\end{array}
\\[3em]
\begin{array}{l}
CH_2\!\!-\!\!C(CH_3)_2 \\
\;|\qquad\qquad\diagdown \\
\;|\qquad\qquad\;\; CO \\
\;|\qquad\qquad\diagup \\
CH_2\!\!-\!\!CH_2
\end{array}
&
\begin{array}{l}
CH_3CH\!\!-\!\!CH_2 \\
\;|\qquad\qquad\diagdown \\
\;|\qquad\qquad\;\; CO \\
\;|\qquad\qquad\diagup \\
CH_3CH\!\!-\!\!CH_2
\end{array}
\end{array}
$$

As a rule the presence of alkyl groups, particularly the *gem*-methyl group $[(CH_3)_2C]$, enhances the tendency of a chain to undergo cyclization. These results are summarized in what is known as the *Blanc rule*, which states that, when adipic acids or pimelic acids are heated with acetic anhydride and then distilled (at about 300°), cycloalkanones are formed, whereas succinic acids and glutaric acids under similar conditions yield cyclic anhydrides. This rule has served frequently in determining the constitution of dibasic acids of the hydroaromatic series. It is not always valid, however; sometimes when the two carboxyl groups are attached to different rings a seven-membered anhydride forms.

Replacement of the carboxyl group by hydrogen in saturated acids is illustrated by the synthesis of methane by pyrolysis of sodium acetate. However, the method is not suitable for the preparation of ethane or its higher homologs.[8] It has proved to be more useful in the aromatic series.

[8] T. S. Oakwood and M. R. Miller, *J. Am. Chem. Soc.*, **72**, 1849 (1950).

28

Molecular reactions

The reactions that have been discussed up to this point have been classified, often tentatively, as polar or radical by reference to the mechanisms
that have been proposed for them. It is recognized, however, that these two
categories do not embrace all known reactions; a third species, important
in organic chemistry, is the molecular reaction. In transformations of
this sort, also called four-center reactions, the atoms of the reactant or
reactants undergo change without electron pairing or unpairing and
without formation or destruction of ions. Four or more key atoms are
involved and, in the transition state, each simultaneously forms a new bond
and breaks an old one. From this description it is to be expected that such
reactions will be little affected by the conditions that promote or oppose
polar and radical processes. They should not possess the characteristics of
chain reactions and should not be catalyzed by light or by acids or bases.

Claisen Rearrangement

An interesting type of molecular reaction is the rearrangement, known as
the Claisen rearrangement, that certain aryl ethers undergo when heated
(OR **2**, 1). The simplest example is the isomerization of allyl phenyl ether
to 2-allylphenol. The four atoms of the side chain and two of the ring are
assumed to form a *quasi* ring of six members; the formation of the phenol
can then occur by the electron migration indicated by three curved arrows.

672

This migration may be pictured as taking place in a clockwise or counter-clockwise fashion. The immediate product, the keto form of 2-allylphenol, rearranges at once to the phenol. The ketone, of course, also has the possibility of existing in a *quasi* ring, which would permit the return of the electrons to their original positions. The rearrangement, in fact, has been shown to be reversible.

Once again it makes no difference whether the electron shift proceeds in a clockwise or counter-clockwise manner.

The change fulfills the requirement of the molecular type of reaction also in that no catalyst is necessary. For simple allyl aryl ethers that have boiling points not far above 200°, the method is to boil the compound until a constant boiling point is reached. The presence of substituents can be tolerated; *o*-eugenol, for instance, is made in 90% yield by rearrangement of guaiacol allyl ether (OS III, 418).

The rearrangement of crotyl phenyl ether is especially informative because the migrating group undergoes isomerization.

This phenomenon, known as inversion, is practically invariable in the rearrangement to the *o*-position.

Migration to the *p*-position is also observed; *o*-acetamidophenyl allyl ether, for example, yields both the *o*- and *p*-allyl phenols.

The rearrangement of allyl β-naphthyl ether is interesting because only migration to the 1-position is observed.

The allyl ether of 2,6-dihydroxynaphthalene also undergoes rearrangement involving entry of allyl groups in 1-positions. The allyl ether of this product is stable, however; no 1-positions are available.

Stable

Here again it is apparent that the 3-position does not behave as a true *o*-position (OR **2**, 13).

Rearrangement of allyl aryl ethers, induced by Lewis acids, is evidently a polar reaction involving the allyl carbonium ion. A striking example is the isomerization of allyl mesityl ether to 3-allylmesitol in the presence of boron chloride; the reaction is rapid at 10°, and the yield is 96%.[1]

Although the uncatalyzed rearrangement has been used chiefly in the aromatic series, it is known to occur also with aliphatic compounds. An example is the rearrangement of the allyl ether of ethyl acetoacetate to ethyl α-allylacetoacetate.

[1] P. Fahrni, A. Habich, and H. Schmid, *Helv. Chim. Acta*, **43**, 448 (1960).

If the migrating group is cinnamyl, inversion is observed and the product is ethyl α-phenylallylacetoacetate.

$$OCH_2CH{=}CHC_6H_5 \qquad C_6H_5CHCH{=}CH_2$$
$$CH_3C{=}CHCO_2C_2H_5 \rightarrow CH_3COCHCO_2C_2H_5$$

Allyl ethers of enols of ketones rearrange to the corresponding allyl ketones; when allyl isopropenyl ether, for example, is passed through a tube heated to 255°, it is isomerized almost quantitatively to allylacetone.

$$OCH_2CH{=}CH_2$$
$$CH_3C{=}CH_2 \qquad \rightarrow CH_2{=}CHCH_2CH_2COCH_3$$

Such allyl ethers are obtained by acid-catalyzed cracking of the appropriate diallyl ketals and can be caused to rearrange without being isolated. The diallyl ketal from cyclohexanone, for instance, gives 2-allylcyclohexanone in 98 % yield.[2]

One theory proposed to account for the p-rearrangement involves two allylic shifts, the first of which produces a cyclohexadienone. Evidence of the formation of such an intermediate has been found in the rearrangement of allyl 2,6-dimethylphenyl ether.[3]

[2] N. B. Lorette and W. L. Howard, *J. Org. Chem.*, **26**, 3112 (1961).
[3] H. Conroy and R. A. Firestone, *J. Am. Chem. Soc.*, **75**, 2530 (1953).

This mechanism is in accord with the fact that inversion is not noted in the p-rearrangement; inversion presumably occurs in each of the two steps and thus gives the normal product (Gould, 143).

The second step of the Claisen rearrangement is from carbon to carbon and may properly be classed as a Cope rearrangement.

N-Allylanilines do not undergo the Claisen rearrangement; an exception is N-allyl-1-naphthylamine, which gives 2-allyl-1-naphthylamine.[4]

Cope Rearrangement

A typical example of the Cope rearrangement is the thermal conversion of ethyl (1-methylpropenyl)allylcyanoacetate into ethyl (1,2-dimethyl-4-pentenylidene)cyanoacetate.

Similar rearrangements occur in the malonic ester and malononitrile series; an example of the first type is the transformation of diethyl allyl-propenylmalonate into diethyl (2-methyl-4-pentenylidene)malonate.

[4] S. Marcinkiewicz, J. Green, and P. Mamalis, *Chem. and Ind.*, 438 (1961).

In the malononitrile series allyl-1-cyclohexenylmalononitrile is easily transformed into 2-allylcyclohexylidenemalononitrile.

$$
\underset{\overset{|}{\text{CH}_2\text{CH}=\text{CH}_2}}{\underset{|}{\overset{\text{CN}}{\overset{|}{\text{C}}}}}\!\!\diagdown_{\text{CN}} \quad \rightarrow \quad \underset{\text{CH}_2\text{CH}=\text{CH}_2}{=}\overset{\text{CN}}{\underset{\text{CN}}{\text{C}}}
$$

In both the Claisen and the Cope rearrangements the change is intramolecular and of the first order. Another point of similarity is that, in the Cope reaction also, the allyl group may undergo inversion during the rearrangement. In the rearrangement of diethyl crotylisopropenylmalonate and ethyl crotyl(1-methylpropenyl)cyanoacetate inversion of the crotyl group is observed.

$$
\begin{array}{c}
\text{CH}_3 \\
| \\
\text{CH}_2\!\!=\!\!\text{C} \qquad \text{CO}_2\text{C}_2\text{H}_5 \\
\diagdown \quad \diagup \\
\text{C} \\
\diagup \quad \diagdown \\
\text{CH}_3\text{CH}\!\!=\!\!\text{CHCH}_2 \qquad \text{CO}_2\text{C}_2\text{H}_5
\end{array}
\quad \rightarrow \quad
\begin{array}{c}
\text{CH}_3 \quad \text{CO}_2\text{C}_2\text{H}_5 \\
| \qquad \diagup \\
\text{CH}_2\text{C}\!\!=\!\!\text{C} \\
| \qquad \diagdown \\
\qquad \text{CO}_2\text{C}_2\text{H}_5 \\
\text{CH}_3\text{CHCH}\!\!=\!\!\text{CH}_2
\end{array}
$$

$$
\begin{array}{c}
\text{CH}_3 \\
| \\
\text{CH}_3\text{CH}\!\!=\!\!\text{C} \qquad \text{CN} \\
\diagdown \quad \diagup \\
\text{C} \\
\diagup \quad \diagdown \\
\text{CH}_3\text{CH}\!\!=\!\!\text{CHCH}_2 \qquad \text{CO}_2\text{C}_2\text{H}_5
\end{array}
\quad \rightarrow \quad
\begin{array}{c}
\text{CH}_3 \quad \text{CN} \\
| \qquad \diagup \\
\text{CH}_3\text{CH}\!-\!\text{C}\!\!=\!\!\text{C} \\
| \qquad \diagdown \\
\qquad \text{CO}_2\text{C}_2\text{H}_5 \\
\text{CH}_3\text{CHCH}\!\!=\!\!\text{CH}_2
\end{array}
$$

The rearrangement of certain allylamine oxides appears to be similar to those just described; an intramolecular mechanism has been proposed.

$$
\begin{array}{c}
\text{CH}_3 \\
| \\
\text{C}_6\text{H}_5\text{N}\!\longrightarrow\!\text{O} \\
| \qquad \vdots \\
\text{CH}_2 \quad \text{CHCH}_3 \\
\diagdown \quad \diagup \\
\text{CH}
\end{array}
\quad \rightarrow \quad
\begin{array}{c}
\text{CH}_3 \\
| \\
\text{C}_6\text{H}_5\text{N}\!\longrightarrow\!\text{O} \\
| \qquad | \\
\text{CH}_2 \quad \text{CHCH}_3 \\
\diagdown \quad \diagup \\
\text{CH}
\end{array}
$$

Pyrolysis of Esters

Another reaction that may be of the molecular type is the pyrolysis of certain esters (CR **60**, 431); the products are the carboxylic acid and an olefin derived from the alkoxyl group. It has been suggested that pyrolysis of such esters goes by way of a *quasi* six-membered ring.

$$
\begin{array}{c}
\text{H} \\
\text{O} \quad \text{CHR} \qquad \text{OH} \quad + \text{CHR} \\
\text{RC} \quad \text{CH}_2 \quad \rightarrow \quad \text{RC} \qquad \text{CH}_2 \\
\text{O} \qquad\qquad \text{O}
\end{array}
$$

An example of this type of transformation is the preparation of acrylic acid from ethyl acrylate (OS III, 30).

$$CH_2{=}CHCO_2CH_2CH_3 \;\rightarrow\; CH_2{=}CHCO_2H + CH_2{=}CH_2$$

The reaction is general for esters so constituted that the production of an olefin by pyrolysis is possible; it furnishes a practical method of making olefins. Acetates are usually employed as raw materials. The process is spectacular with esters of certain alcohols, such as pinacolyl alcohol, which suffer chain rearrangement when dehydrated with acids (p. 186). Pinacolyl acetate decomposes thermally to give *t*-butylethylene.

$$
\begin{array}{c}
\text{OCOCH}_3 \\
| \\
(CH_3)_3CCHCH_3 \quad \rightarrow \quad (CH_3)_3CCH{=}CH_2 + CH_3CO_2H
\end{array}
$$

Dehydration of 2,2-dimethylcyclopentanol is accomplished also without skeletal rearrangement by pyrolysis of the acetate at 525°; 3,3-dimethyl-cyclopentene is produced in 88% yield.[5]

$$
\begin{array}{ccc}
\text{CH}_3 & \text{OCOCH}_3 & \\
& | & \text{CH}_3 \\
& \quad \rightarrow & \quad + CH_3CO_2H \\
\text{CH}_3 & & \text{CH}_3
\end{array}
$$

In the preparation of 1,4-pentadiene from 1,5-pentanediol it is necessary to pyrolyze the diacetate rather than the diol itself, since in the latter case isomerization of the product to piperylene takes place (p. 303).

At 575° the diacetate gives 1,4-pentadiene in 71% yield (OS **38**, 78). The acetate of 4-penten-1-ol, which is obtained as a by-product, also yields 1,4-pentadiene when pyrolyzed. It is therefore considered to be an intermediate product in the pyrolysis of the diacetate.

$$CH_3CO_2CH_2CH_2CH_2CH_2CH_2OCOCH_3 \;\rightarrow$$

$$CH_3CO_2CH_2CH_2CH_2CH{=}CH_2 \;\rightarrow\; CH_2{=}CHCH_2CH{=}CH_2$$

[5] C. F. Wilcox, Jr., and M. Mesirov, *J. Org. Chem.*, **25**, 1841 (1960).

Pyrolysis of acetates of substituted α-phenethyl alcohols has served to produce the corresponding styrenes (CR **45**, 353). 3,4-Dichlorostyrene, for example, is formed by pyrolysis of the acetate of 3,4-dichlorophenyl-methylcarbinol.

One way of introducing an ethylenic bond is to acetoxylate with lead tetraacetate and then subject the acetate to decomposition. The synthesis of indone from indanone is an example.[6]

Ethyl lactate cannot be dehydrated satisfactorily. It is possible, however, to effect this change indirectly, i.e., by pyrolysis of the acetyl derivative. This type of change furnishes a route to industrially important esters of acrylic acid; the formation of ethyl acrylate is an example.

$$CH_3CHCO_2C_2H_5 \xrightarrow{\text{heat}} CH_2{=}CHCO_2C_2H_5 + CH_3CO_2H$$
$$\overset{|}{O}COCH_3$$

Acrylonitrile is made from acetaldehyde cyanohydrin by way of the acetate.

The benzoate of crotonaldehyde cyanohydrin behaves in an interesting way, yielding 1-cyano-1,3-butadiene.

$$\overset{OCOC_6H_5}{\overset{|}{CH_3CH{=}CHCHCN}} \xrightarrow{575°} CH_2{=}CHCH{=}CHCN + C_6H_5CO_2H$$

Pyrolysis of 1,4-di(acetoxymethyl)-1-cyclohexene gives 1,4-dimethylene-2-cyclohexene.[7]

[6] C. S. Marvel and C. W. Hinman, *J. Am. Chem. Soc.*, **76**, 5435 (1954).
[7] W. J. Bailey and R. Barclay, Jr., *J. Am. Chem. Soc.*, **81**, 5393 (1959).

$$\underset{\underset{CH_2OCOCH_3}{|}}{\overset{\overset{CH_2OCOCH_3}{|}}{\bigcirc}} \quad \xrightarrow{490°} \quad \underset{\underset{CH_2}{||}}{\overset{\overset{CH_2}{||}}{\bigcirc}}$$

t-Amyl acetate, when heated at 400°, decomposes according to the Hofmann rule (p. 302), yielding 2-methyl-1-butene (74%); at 225°, however, the Saytzeff rule (p. 295) is obeyed, the chief product (58%) being 2-methyl-2-butene.[8]

$$\underset{\overset{|}{CH_3}}{CH_3C}{=}CHCH_3 \quad \xleftarrow{225°} \quad \underset{\underset{OCOCH_3}{|}}{\overset{\overset{CH_3}{|}}{CH_3C}}CH_2CH_3 \quad \xrightarrow{400°} \quad \underset{\overset{|}{CH_3}}{CH_2}{=}CCH_2CH_3$$

The dehydration of alcohols by heating with boric acid or anhydride appears to be similar, involving the decomposition of boric esters. However, the reaction proceeds at temperatures much lower than those required for pyrolysis of acetates. Olefins have been prepared also by pyrolysis of methyl alkyl sulfites.[9] The pyrolysis of alkyl carbonates likewise has been used for the production of olefins.[10]

In connection with the pyrolysis of esters, it will be remembered that formates are capable of undergoing a different type of change. The classical synthesis of allyl alcohol from glycerol and formic acid is an example. The monoformate decomposes into the alcohol, water, and carbon dioxide (OS I, 42; 47% yield).

$$\underset{\overset{|}{OH}}{HOCH_2CHCH_2OCHO} \rightarrow CH_2{=}CHCH_2OH + CO_2 + H_2O$$

Also when heated with oxalic acid, glycerol is transformed to allyl alcohol. In fact, this procedure provides a general method of converting a 1,2-glycol into the corresponding olefin.[11]

Chugaev method
Another indirect method of dehydrating alcohols is to heat the methyl

$$\overset{\overset{S}{||}}{}$$

alkyl xanthates, $ROC{-}SCH_3$, formed by condensing sodium alkoxides

---

[8] W. J. Bailey and W. F. Hale, *J. Am. Chem. Soc.*, **81**, 647 (1959).
[9] G. Berti, *J. Am. Chem. Soc.*, **76**, 1213 (1954).
[10] J. L. R. Williams, K. R. Dunham, and T. M. Laakso, *J. Org. Chem.*, **23**, 676 (1958).
[11] H. Wynberg and A. Kraak, *J. Am. Chem. Soc.*, **83**, 3919 (1961).

with carbon disulfide and treating the resulting xanthates with methyl iodide. The conversion of pinacolyl alcohol into *t*-butylethylene is an example.

$$\underset{\substack{|\\(CH_3)_3CCHONa}}{CH_3} \xrightarrow{CS_2} \underset{\substack{|\quad\;\;\|\\(CH_3)_3CCHOCSNa}}{CH_3\;\;S} \xrightarrow{CH_3I}$$

$$\underset{\substack{|\quad\;\;\|\\(CH_3)_3CCHOCSCH_3}}{CH_3\;\;S} \xrightarrow{heat} (CH_3)_3CCH{=}CH_2 + COS + CH_3SH$$

A *quasi* six-membered ring is postulated here also.[12]

$$\rightarrow (CH_3)_3CCH{=}CH_2 + CH_3SH + COS$$

There is good evidence that the Chugaev and acetate methods, in contrast to the *trans*-elimination observed in general, bring about *cis*-elimination. A few exceptions to this generalization have been encountered in cyclic systems.[13] Both methods follow predominantly the Hofmann rule in certain reactions and the Saytzeff rule in others. A logical explanation of these results would appear to be that elimination proceeds in such a way as to give the olefin that is more stable thermodynamically.[14]

Pyrolysis of β-hydroxy olefins

Pyrolysis of β-hydroxy olefins proceeds in such a way as to give an olefinic compound and an aldehyde or ketone and can be formulated as involving a *quasi* six-membered ring. An example is the thermal decomposition of 4-ethyl-1-phenyl-1-hexen-4-ol to allylbenzene and diethyl ketone.

$$\xrightarrow{500°} C_6H_5CH_2CH{=}CH_2 + (C_2H_5)_2C{=}O$$

The classical example of this type of pyrolysis is the conversion of ricinoleic acid into *n*-heptaldehyde and undecylenic acid.

[12] R. F. W. Bader and A. N. Bourns, *Can. J. Chem.*, **39,** 348 (1961).
[13] F. G. Bordwell and P. S. Landis, *J. Am. Chem. Soc.*, **80,** 2450 (1958).
[14] R. A. Benkeser and J. J. Hazdra, *J. Am. Chem. Soc.*, **81,** 228 (1959).

$$CH_3(CH_2)_5CHCH_2CH{=}CH(CH_2)_7CO_2H \ \rightarrow$$
$$\overset{|}{OH}$$

$$CH_3(CH_2)_5CHO + CH_2{=}CH(CH_2)_8CO_2H$$

It is interesting that fusion with alkali cleaves the molecule at a different point, yielding 2-octanol and a salt of sebacic acid.

$$CH_3(CH_2)_5CHCH_2CH{=}CH(CH_2)_7CO_2H \xrightarrow{\text{NaOH}}$$
$$\overset{|}{OH}$$

$$CH_3(CH_2)_5CHCH_3 \quad \text{and} \quad (CH_2)_8 \overset{\displaystyle CO_2Na}{\underset{\displaystyle CO_2Na}{\Big\langle}}$$
$$\overset{|}{OH}$$

The hydrogen atom at the 12-position plays no important part in the pyrolysis; methyl 12-methylricinoleate breaks down to give 2-octanone and methyl undecylenate.[15]

$$\overset{OH}{\underset{CH_3}{\overset{|}{CH_3(CH_2)_5\overset{|}{C}CH_2CH{=}CH(CH_2)_7CO_2CH_3}}} \ \rightarrow$$

$$CH_2{=}CH(CH_2)_8CO_2CH_3 + CH_3(CH_2)_5COCH_3$$

If the carbon-carbon bond undergoing fission is an appropriate element of a cyclic structure, the reaction provides a method of extending carbon chains. For example *trans*-(1′-*cis*-octenyl)cyclopentanol yields *trans*-tridecen-5-al.[16]

$$\rightarrow CH_3(CH_2)_5CH_2CH{=}CH(CH_2)_3CHO$$

[15] W. J. Gensler and C. B. Abrahams, *J. Org. Chem.*, **26**, 249 (1961).
[16] R. T. Arnold and G. Smolinsky, *J. Am. Chem. Soc.*, **82**, 4918 (1960).

Pyrolysis of Amine Oxides

The oxides of tertiary amines decompose when heated to give olefins and derivatives of hydroxylamine (OR **11**, 361). This method of elimination has the advantage over the Hofmann exhaustive methylation procedure in that it is less likely to give rearranged olefins. In the degradation of N-methylpiperidine to a pentadiene, for example, if the second step is brought about by pyrolysis of the N-oxide of 5-pentenyldimethylamine, 1,4-penta-diene is obtained in 61 % yield.[17]

$$CH_2{=}CHCH_2CH{-}CH_2 \quad \rightarrow \quad CH_2{=}CHCH_2CH{=}CH_2$$
$$\overset{|}{H} \quad \overset{|}{N(CH_3)_2}$$
$$\overset{|}{O}$$

Diels-Alder Reaction

Reactions of the molecular type occur also between molecules. The condensation of olefinic compounds with butadienes to give cyclohexenes, known as the *Diels-Alder diene reaction*, is an important example (CR **31**, 319; **61**, 537; *Angew.* **72**, 219). The combination of butadiene and maleic anhydride is illustrative.

$$
\begin{array}{ccc}
CH_2 & & CH_2 \\
HC & CH{-}CO & HC \quad CH{-}CO \\
 & \quad\quad O \rightarrow & \quad\quad O \\
HC & CH{-}CO & HC \quad CH{-}CO \\
CH_2 & & CH_2
\end{array}
$$

In these condensations the ethylenic compounds are known as *dieno-philes*, the product formed from the diene and the dienophile being spoken of as the *adduct*. Although maleic anhydride is the dienophile most frequently employed (OR **4**, 1), many others are known (OR **4**, 60). Acrolein, for example, may function in this way.

$$
\begin{array}{ccc}
CH_2 & & CH_2 \\
HC & CHCHO & HC \quad CHCHO \\
HC & + \quad CH_2 \rightarrow & HC \quad CH_2 \\
CH_2 & & CH_2
\end{array}
$$

[17] A. C. Cope and C. L. Bumgardner, *J. Am. Chem. Soc.*, **79**, 960 (1957).

In a similar manner cinnamaldehyde condenses with butadiene to give 2-phenyl-1,2,3,4-tetrahydrobenzaldehyde.[18] When acrylic acid is used the product is cyclohexene-4-carboxylic acid. It is noteworthy that the same compound is obtained from butadiene and β-propiolactone. The reaction with the lactone is catalyzed by potassium carbonate, which is known to aid polymerization of the lactone to the polyester and to assist in the pyrolysis of the polymer to give acrylic acid. The yield of cyclohexene-4-carboxylic acid from the lactone is 96%.[19]

Quinone ethylene linkages that are not part of an aromatic nucleus may be compared with that of maleic anhydride in degree and type of reactivity. The condensation of benzoquinone with isoprene illustrates a general reaction of quinones and dienes.

1,4-Naphthoquinone has been employed in the identification of dienes (OR **5**, 150). Its reaction with 2,3-dimethyl-1,3-butadiene is illustrative; the yield is 96%.

Although Diels-Alder reactions like others of the molecular type do not require a catalyst, certain of them, as mentioned previously (p. 7), are

[18] E. D. Bergman and J. Klein, *J. Org. Chem.*, **23**, 512 (1958).
[19] T. L. Gresham, J. E. Jansen, and F. X. Werber, *J. Am. Chem. Soc.*, **76**, 609 (1954).

affected by the presence of aluminum chloride. Similar effects have been observed with stannic chloride, boron fluoride, and other Lewis acids.[20]

Olefinic dienophiles

In addition to acrolein, benzoquinone, naphthoquinone, and maleic anhydride a large number of other olefinic compounds can serve as dienophiles. In most of these the ethylenic linkage is activated by a substituent. Under suitable conditions, however, simple olefins may likewise combine with dienes. At 200° and 200 to 400 atmospheres ethylene unites with 1,3-butadiene, for example, to yield cyclohexene.

The activating group may be nitro as is shown by the condensation of 1,3-butadiene with β-nitrostyrene.

1-Nitro-1-alkenes behave in a similar way; the simplest member, nitroethylene, combines with bi-1-cyclohexen-1-yl to give dodecahydro-9-nitrophenanthrene.[21]

Indene, an interesting dienophile, provides a route to fluorene.

[20] G. I. Fray and R. Robinson, *J. Am. Chem. Soc.*, **83**, 249 (1961).
[21] N. L. Drake and C. M. Kraebel, *J. Org. Chem.*, **26**, 41 (1961).

Vinylene carbonate (p. 296) offers a way to arrive at *cis*-diols; the condensation with 2,3-dimethyl-1,3-butadiene is an example.[22]

$$
\begin{array}{c}
CH_3C{=}CH_2 \\
| \\
CH_3C{=}CH_2
\end{array}
+
\begin{array}{c}
CH{-}O \\
\diagdown \\
\diagup \quad C{=}O \\
CH{-}O
\end{array}
\rightarrow
\begin{array}{c}
CH_3 \\
CH_3
\end{array}
\bigcirc
\begin{array}{c}
{-}O \\
{-}O
\end{array}
C{=}O
\rightarrow
\begin{array}{c}
CH_3 \\
CH_3
\end{array}
\bigcirc
\begin{array}{c}
OH \\
OH
\end{array}
$$

The fact that the six-membered adduct is cyclohexene or a substituted cyclohexene demonstrates that this type of olefin cannot act as a dienophile under ordinary conditions. It is therefore significant that cyclopentenes do serve as dienophiles under such conditions. This behavior is another indication that the ethylenic bond introduces strain into the five-membered ring.

Yields in diene reactions are frequently very high. In fact, the reaction has been used as the basis of a method for the quantitative estimation of butadiene. The determination is carried out by passing the gas to be analyzed through molten maleic anhydride and measuring the volume of gas absorbed.

An unusually reactive dienophile is tetracyanoethylene (*Angew.* **73**, 520), which combines with butadiene rapidly in the cold to give the Diels-Alder adduct in nearly quantitative yield.[23]

$$
\begin{array}{c}
CH_2 \\
\parallel \\
HC \\
| \\
HC \\
\parallel \\
CH_2
\end{array}
+
\begin{array}{c}
C(CN)_2 \\
\parallel \\
C(CN)_2
\end{array}
\rightarrow
\begin{array}{c}
CH_2 \\
HC \quad\quad C(CN)_2 \\
\parallel \quad\quad\quad | \\
HC \quad\quad C(CN)_2 \\
CH_2
\end{array}
$$

The electron density at the double bond of tetracyanoethylene is very low and is responsible for the ease of formation of pi-complexes with aromatic compounds. Compounds such as tetracyanoethylene are known as pi-acids. Another example is cyananil, which gives a deep-red complex with benzene.[24]

$$
\begin{array}{c}
O \\
\parallel \\
NC \quad\quad CN \\
\bigcirc \\
NC \quad\quad CN \\
\parallel \\
O
\end{array}
$$

[22] M. S. Newman and R. W. Addor, *J. Am. Chem. Soc.*, **77**, 3789 (1955).

[23] W. J. Middleton, R. E. Heckert, E. L. Little, and C. G. Krespan, *J. Am. Chem. Soc.*, **80**, 2783 (1958).

[24] K. Wallenfels and G. Bachmann, *Angew. Chem.*, **73**, 142 (1961).

Acetylenic dienophiles

Compounds containing a carbon-carbon triple bond may serve as dienophiles also; the adduct in these cases are cyclohexadiene derivatives. Ethyl propiolate, for example, combines with 1,2-dimethylenecyclohexane to produce the expected bicyclic ester.[25]

The addition of diethyl acetylenedicarboxylate to 1,4-*bis*(4-phenyl-butadienyl)benzene gives an adduct, which by hydrolysis, oxidation, and decarboxylation yields *p*-quinquephenyl (OS **40,** 85).

Dienic dienophiles

Dienes, of course, can serve also as dienophiles and are thus capable of undergoing self-condensation to yield cyclohexene derivatives. 1,3-Butadiene gives 4-vinylcyclohexene, for example.

1,5-Cyclooctadiene, which is formed also, can be made in 10% yield by dimerization of butadiene at high temperature (270°) and pressure in the presence of the polymerization inhibitor hydroquinone.[26]

[25] W. J. Bailey and H. R. Golden, *J. Am. Chem. Soc.*, **75,** 4780 (1953).
[26] K. Ziegler and H. Wilms, *Ann.*, **567,** 1 (1950).

$$\text{(diagram: two CH}_2\text{-CH}_2 \text{ units with HC and CH bridges} \rightarrow \text{cyclooctatetraene-like ring)}$$

Bridged adducts

By the use of cyclic dienes, bridged adducts may be obtained; the addition of maleic anhydride to cyclopentadiene is an example.

$$\text{(diagram: cyclopentadiene} + \text{maleic anhydride} \rightarrow \text{bridged adduct)}$$

The reactions with cyclopropene and vinyl acetate are similar.

$$\text{(diagram: cyclopentadiene} + \text{cyclopropene} \rightarrow \text{bridged bicyclic adduct)}$$

$$\text{(diagram: cyclopentadiene} + \text{CH}_2\text{=CHOCOCH}_3 \rightarrow \text{bridged adduct)}$$

Generally the olefinic bond of the adduct is not sufficiently reactive to serve as a dienophile; exceptions are noted with certain adducts of cyclo-pentadiene that, like monocyclic cyclopentene derivatives undergo second-ary addition. The behavior of vinyl acetate is typical; by suitable changes in the experimental conditions, the secondary adduct may be made the chief product.[27]

$$\text{(diagram: cyclopentadiene} + \text{bicyclic OCOCH}_3 \text{ adduct} \rightarrow \text{tricyclic OCOCH}_3 \text{ product)}$$

[27] K. Alder and H. Rickert, *Ann.*, **543**, 1 (1939).

Benzyne is capable of serving as a dienophile with cyclic dienes. When
o-bromofluorobenzene is treated with magnesium in the presence of anthracene, triptycene is obtained.[28]

A similar reaction has been observed with furan.

Non-cyclic dienes do not form such adducts; apparently benzyne does
not survive long enough to permit open-chain dienes to assume the requisite
cis-like arrangement that the cyclic dienes possess.[29]

Other dienophiles

Although olefinic and acetylenic compounds of great variety can serve
as dienophiles, the reaction is not limited to them. Nitriles, for example,
combine with dienes at moderately high temperatures to form pyridine
derivatives. Benzonitrile and butadiene gave 2-phenylpyridine, presumably
by way of the dihydro derivative.

With suitable catalysts the yield of 2-phenylpyridine is as high as 60%.

Formaldehyde reacts with 2-methyl-1,3-pentadiene in a similar way,
yielding a cyclic ether.

[28] G. Wittig and E. Benz, *Tetrahedron*, **10**, 37 (1960).
[29] J. F. Bunnett, *J. Chem. Education*, **38**, 278 (1961).

Sulfur dioxide can function as a dienophile, the products being cyclic sulfones. Isoprene, for example, combines with sulfur dioxide in the following way (OS III, 499; 82% yield).

$$CH_2=CH-\underset{\underset{CH_3}{|}}{C}=CH_2 + SO_2 \rightarrow$$

Diethyl azodicarboxylate combines with 1,3-butadiene to give a typical Diels-Alder adduct.

$$CH_2=CH-CH=CH_2 + \underset{NCO_2C_2H_5}{\overset{NCO_2C_2H_5}{\|}} \rightarrow$$

This dienophile reacts with cyclopentadiene in a similar way.

The nitroso group serves as a dienophile also; nitrosobenzene and cyclopentadiene, for example, combine in the Diels-Alder manner.[30]

The diene

The diene component may be almost any compound containing a conjugated system of multiple carbon-to-carbon linkages such as isoprene, 2,3-dimethyl-1,3-butadiene, or 1,3-cyclohexadiene. So general is the reaction, in fact, that it has been used as a test for the presence of a conjugated diene system in a molecule. As might be expected, the diene condensation fails with 4-methyl-1,3-pentadiene (I), the product being a copolymer. Apparently a methyl group that projects in the direction of approach of the diene to the dienophile opposes normal condensation.

[30] G. Kresze and G. Schulz, *Tetrahedron*, **12**, 7 (1961).

trans-Piperylene (II), for example, undergoes the diene condensation with maleic anhydride, whereas the *cis*-isomer (III) does not yield a cyclic product.

1,2-Dimethylenecyclobutane combines with maleic anhydride normally to yield a cyclobutene derivative.[31]

In the case of certain ketene acetals the diene may be replaced by two molecules of the olefinic compound. Reaction of ketene diethylacetal with maleic anhydride gives 3,5-diethoxy-1,6-dihydrophthalic anhydride, presumably formed from the initial adduct by loss of ethanol.[32]

[31] A. T. Blomquist and J. A. Verdol, *J. Am. Chem. Soc.*, **77**, 1806 (1955).
[32] S. M. McElvain and H. Cohen, *J. Am. Chem. Soc.*, **64**, 260 (1942).

Aromatic "dienes"

The bonds of aromatic systems may serve as dienes also. Anthracene condenses with dienophiles, including maleic and fumaric esters. It is noteworthy that dimethyl maleate yields a *cis*-compound, whereas dimethyl fumarate gives a *trans*-derivative.

These results illustrate the rule that the diene combines with the double bond of the dienophile in the *cis*-manner.

Condensation is possible also with conjugated systems made up of an ethylenic side chain and a bond of an aromatic ring. The condensation of α-vinylnaphthalene with maleic anhydride is an example.

Naphthalene itself and certain of its alkyl derivatives form Diels-Alder adducts when heated at 100° for 24 hours with 30 moles of maleic anhydride.

A monocyclic aromatic compound that undergoes the Diels-Alder reaction is hydroquinone, which combines with maleic anhydride in the 1,4-manner.[33]

Hexafluoro-2-butyne, a very powerful dienophile, reacts with durene to give a derivative of barrelene.[34]

[33] R. C. Cookson and N. S. Wariyar, *Chem. and Ind.*, 915 (1955).

[34] C. G. Krespan, B. C. McKusick, and T. L. Cairns, *J. Am. Chem. Soc.*, **83**, 3428 (1961).

$$F_3CC{\equiv}CCF_3 + \underset{\underset{\displaystyle CH_3}{|}}{\overset{\overset{\displaystyle CH_3}{|}}{\underset{CH_3}{\bigcirc}CH_3}} \rightarrow$$

Barrelene itself has attracted attention because of the possibility of conjugation of the three double bonds.[35]

Diene analogs

The diene function may be exercised by systems containing hetero-atoms. Reactions of this type occur with α,β-unsaturated aldehydes; the formation of the cyclic dimer of acrolein is an example.

$$\begin{matrix} HC{=}CH_2 \\ | \\ HC{=}O \end{matrix} + \begin{matrix} CH_2 \\ \| \\ CHCHO \end{matrix} \rightarrow \quad$$

Another illustration is the condensation of acrolein with methyl acrylate.

$$\begin{matrix} HC{=}CH_2 \\ | \\ HC{=}O \end{matrix} + \begin{matrix} CH_2 \\ \| \\ CHCO_2CH_3 \end{matrix} \rightarrow \quad$$

Vinyl ethers combine with α,β-unsaturated carbonyl compounds in a similar way; the reaction mixture is heated at 200° for 12 hours. The condensation of crotonaldehyde with methyl vinyl ether is an example (OS **34**, 29; 57% yield).

$$\begin{matrix} CHCH_3 \\ \| \\ HC \\ | \\ HC \\ \| \\ O \end{matrix} + \begin{matrix} CH_2 \\ \| \\ CHOCH_3 \end{matrix} \rightarrow \quad$$

Addition of methyl acrylate to dehydroindigo occurs when the reactants are heated in a sealed tube.

[35] H. E. Zimmerman and R. M. Paufler, *J. Am. Chem. Soc.*, **82**, 1514 (1960).

$$+ \ CH_2{=}CHCO_2CH_3 \ \rightarrow$$

In dehydroindigo the diene system is terminated by nitrogen atoms.

Reversibility

Condensation of ethylene with butadiene to form cyclohexene is a reversal of the pyrolysis of cyclohexene in the preparation of butadiene (p. 581). It would appear then that, by suitable alteration of the conditions, the diene reaction may be made to proceed in either direction. In this instance it is to be noted that high pressure favors the condensation and low pressure the reverse, as would be expected if the process is reversible.

In a similar way 1,3-butadiene may be regenerated from its dimer, 4-vinylcyclohexene, by heat.

$$\rightarrow \ 2CH_2{=}CHCH{=}CH_2$$

Reversal of the Diels-Alder reaction has been reported in a number of other instances, perhaps the most striking of which occurs with the adduct from maleic anhydride and a fulvene. The fulvene obtained from cyclohexanone and cyclopentadiene, like fulvenes in general, is highly colored, but the adduct is colorless making it possible to tell when the reaction is complete. Although the condensation is rapid at room temperature, the adduct dissociates with extreme ease. Its solutions develop the bright yellow fulvene color rapidly at the temperature of the steam bath.

A method of purifying anthracene is based on its condensation with maleic anhydride; the purified adduct is reconverted into anthracene and maleic anhydride by sublimation. 1,3-Butadiene can be purified in a similar way. The condensation of dienes with sulfur dioxide (p. 690) has likewise been found to be reversible. Pyrolysis of the adduct from sulfur dioxide and isoprene, for example, regenerates the original reactants.

$$CH{=\!\!=}CCH_3 \atop \underset{\underset{SO_2}{\diagdown\diagup}}{CH_2 \quad CH_2} \longrightarrow SO_2 + CH_2{=}CH{-}\underset{\underset{CH_3}{|}}{C}{=}CH_2$$

Extrusion of sulfur dioxide from certain cyclic sulfones that cannot form a diene furnishes a way of forming four-membered carbocycles. An example is the conversion of the tetroxide of symmetrical tetrahydrodithiophene into the corresponding benzodicyclobutene.[36]

The reaction of ethylene with dicyclopentadiene to form norbornylene evidently depends on previous dissociation of dicyclopentadiene to cyclopentadiene (OS **37**, 65; yield 71%).

Another example of thermal breakdown of a cyclohexene to butadiene and a dienophile is the formation of vinylidene cyanide from 4,4-dicyanocyclohexene.[37]

[36] M. P. Cava, A. A. Deana, and K. Muth, *J. Am. Chem. Soc.*, **82**, 2524 (1960).
[37] A. E. Ardis, S. J. Averill, H. Gilbert, F. F. Miller, R. F. Schmidt, F. D. Stewart, and H. L. Trumbull, *J. Am. Chem. Soc.*, **72**, 3127 (1950).

The Diels-Alder condensation of two molecules of hexachlorocyclo-pentadiene with naphthalene gives an adduct that can undergo such reactions as nitration and bromination. Subsequent reversal of the diene condensation produces 2-substituted naphthalenes in satisfactory yields. The synthesis of 2-nitronaphthalene is an example.[38]

The adduct formed from cyclopentadiene and maleic anhydride can be converted into the corresponding imide, which decomposes thermally to yield maleimide.[39]

Epoxidation of *p*-quinones of the benzene series by alkaline hydrogen peroxide does not occur directly but can be accomplished by way of Diels-Alder adducts. The adduct prepared from *p*-benzoquinone and cyclopentadiene, for example, is epoxidized readily; pyrolysis of the epoxy compound gives the epoxy derivative of 2-benzoquinone in high yield.[40]

[38] A. A. Danish, M. Silverman, and Y. A. Tajima, *J. Am. Chem. Soc.*, **76**, 6144 (1954).

[39] P. O. Tawney, R. H. Snyder, R. P. Conger, K. A. Leibbrand, C. H. Stiteler, and A. R. Williams, *J. Org. Chem.*, **26**, 15 (1961).

[40] K. Alder, F. H. Flock, and H. Beumling, *Chem. Ber.*, **93**, 1896 (1960).

Aromatization of adducts

Many Diels-Alder adducts can be changed to the corresponding aromatic compounds by ordinary methods of dehydrogenation. In some instances it is sufficient to carry out the condensation in the presence of nitrobenzene, which serves as the dehydrogenating agent. Oxygen may be used as the aromatizing agent also. Dehydrogenation of the adduct from 1,4-naphthoquinone and 2,3-dimethyl-1,3-butadiene, for example, can be effected by passing air through its alkaline solution (OS III, 310). The over-all yield of 2,3-dimethylanthraquinone, based on the quinone, is 96%.

A way of obtaining fully aromatized anhydrides is to employ dichloromaleic anhydride and subject the adduct to dehydrohalogenation.

Furans give oxygen-bridged adducts that can be dehydrated to the corresponding aromatic compounds. An example is the synthesis of 3,6-dimethylphthalic anhydride from α,α'-dimethylfuran and maleic anhydride.

Carbonyl bridge compounds (CR **37**, 209), formed when cyclopentadienones are employed, are aromatized by loss of hydrogen and carbon monoxide. When chloromaleic anhydride is the dienophile, carbon monoxide and hydrogen chloride are lost by the adduct. Thus, tetraphenylphthalic anhydride is formed by heating tetraphenylcyclopentadienone with chloromaleic anhydride for an hour in boiling bromobenzene.

The synthesis of pentaphenylbenzene from tetraphenylcyclopentadienone and phenylacetylene involves only the loss of carbon monoxide; the yield is 66%.[41]

Analogous condensations

Maleic anhydride reacts with various olefins in a manner that appears to be similar to that observed with dienes; the production of a ring cannot occur, however. An example is the formation of allylsuccinic anhydride from propylene and maleic anhydride.

$$CH_3CH{=}CH_2 + \begin{matrix} CH{-}CO \\ \| \quad\quad \diagdown \\ \quad\quad\quad O \\ \| \quad\quad \diagup \\ CH{-}CO \end{matrix} \rightarrow \begin{matrix} CH_2{=}CHCH_2CH{-}CO \\ | \quad\quad\quad \diagdown \\ \quad\quad\quad\quad\quad O \\ | \quad\quad\quad \diagup \\ CH_2{-}CO \end{matrix}$$

The condensation takes place at 220 to 230° and 110 atmospheres.

A similar reaction occurs when a mixture of allylbenzene and maleic anhydride is heated 22 hours under reflux in o-dichlorobenzene; γ-phenyl-allylsuccinic anhydride is produced in 47% yield (OS **31**, 85).

$$C_6H_5CH_2CH{=}CH_2 + \begin{matrix} CH{-}CO \\ \| \quad\quad \diagdown \\ \quad\quad\quad O \\ \| \quad\quad \diagup \\ CH{-}CO \end{matrix} \rightarrow \begin{matrix} C_6H_5CH{=}CHCH_2CH{-}CO \\ | \quad\quad\quad \diagdown \\ \quad\quad\quad\quad\quad O \\ | \quad\quad\quad \diagup \\ CH_2{-}CO \end{matrix}$$

[41] J. J. Dudkowski and E. I. Becker, *J. Org. Chem.*, **17**, 201 (1952).

Similar condensations have been effected with olefins and α,β-unsaturated nitriles.[42] Combination of isobutylene with acrylonitrile gives 5-methyl-5-hexenonitrile in 49 % yield. The course of the reaction has been formulated in the following manner.

A reaction closely related to the Diels-Alder is the uncatalyzed condensation of methylenecyclohexane and some of its derivatives with formaldehyde to yield the corresponding β-cyclohexenylethyl alcohols. When methylenecyclohexane, for example, is heated for 4 hours at 200 to 205° with paraformaldehyde in a sealed tube, 2-(Δ^1-cyclohexenyl)ethanol is produced in 70 % yield.

This type of reaction, which has been applied to methylenecyclopentane also,[43] differs from the Prins reaction (p. 157) not only in being uncatalyzed but also in that the ethylenic bond migrates during the reaction.

Formation of Four-Membered Rings

The formation of six-membered cycloalkenes and eight-membered cyclo-alkadienes suggests that self-addition of unsaturated compounds might produce rings of still other sizes. In particular, combination of an olefinic compound with another to produce a cyclobutane derivative may be included in this category. Sterically less favored than the formation of cyclo-hexenes, it has nevertheless been realized in many instances (Angew., **72**, 4).

[42] C. J. Albisetti, N. G. Fisher, M. J. Hogsed, and R. M. Joyce, *J. Am. Chem. Soc.*, **78**, 2637 (1956).

[43] R. T. Arnold, R. W. Amidon, and R. M. Dodson, *J. Am. Chem. Soc.*, **72**, 2871 (1950).

1,3-Butadiene, in fact, forms not only six- and eight-membered rings but a four-membered ring as well. When heated at 150° under a pressure of 100 atmospheres it dimerizes to form small amounts of *trans*-1,2-divinylcyclo-butane.[44]

$$2CH_2=CHCH=CH_2 \rightarrow \begin{array}{c} CH_2-CHCH=CH_2 \\ | \qquad | \\ CH_2-CHCH=CH_2 \end{array}$$

The dimerization of keto ketenes to cyclobutanediones has long been known; the behavior of diphenylketene is illustrative.

$$2(C_6H_5)_2C=C=O \rightarrow \begin{array}{c} (C_6H_5)_2C-C=O \\ | \qquad | \\ O=C-C(C_6H_5)_2 \end{array}$$

α,β-Unsaturated ethers unite with diphenylketene in the 1,2-manner; 2,3-dihydropyran is an example.[45]

Cycloaddition occurs when certain unsaturated esters and enamines combine; the products are cyclobutylamines. An example is the condensation of diethyl maleate and N,N-dimethylisobutenylamine.[46]

Allene, when passed over glass beads at 500 to 510°, dimerizes to 1,2-dimethylenecyclobutane.[47]

$$2CH_2=C=CH_2 \rightarrow \begin{array}{c} CH_2-C=CH_2 \\ | \qquad | \\ CH_2-C=CH_2 \end{array}$$

This type of reaction has been encountered with certain fluorinated olefins also. Tetrafluoroethylene, for example, not only dimerizes to octafluorocyclobutane but also combines with other olefinic substances to form cyclobutane rings. Its reactions with acrylonitrile and butadiene are illustrative.[48]

[44] H. W. B. Reed, *J. Chem. Soc.*, 685 (1951).

[45] C. D. Hurd and R. D. Kimbrough, Jr., *J. Am. Chem. Soc.*, **82**, 1373 (1960).

[46] K. C. Brannock, A. Bell, R. D. Burpitt, and C. A. Kelly, *J. Org. Chem.*, **26**, 626 (1961).

[47] A. T. Blomquist and J. A. Verdol, *J. Am. Chem. Soc.*, **78**, 109 (1956).

[48] D. D. Coffman, P. L. Barrick, R. D. Cramer, and M. S. Raasch, *J. Am. Chem. Soc.*, **71**, 490 (1949).

$$CF_2{=}CF_2 + CH_2{=}CHCN \rightarrow \begin{array}{c} CF_2{-}CF_2 \\ |\qquad | \\ CH_2{-}CHCN \end{array}$$

$$CF_2{=}CF_2 + CH_2{=}CHCH{=}CH_2 \longrightarrow$$

$$\begin{array}{c} CF_2{-}CF_2 \\ |\qquad | \\ CH_2{-}CH{-}CH{=}CH_2 \end{array} \xrightarrow{C_2F_4} \begin{array}{c} CF_2{-}CF_2 \;\; CF_2{-}CF_2 \\ |\qquad |\qquad |\qquad | \\ CH_2{-}CH{-}CH{-}CH_2 \end{array}$$

An interesting feature of these reactions is that addition of tetrafluoro-ethylene to acrylonitrile and to butadiene occurs more readily than does cyclodimerization of the fluorinated olefin. It seems possible that the two olefinic molecules that combine to give a cyclobutane derivative may have different functions analogous to those of dienes and dienophiles in the typical Diels-Alder reaction.

As in the Diels-Alder reactions, the rings formed may be heterocyclic; the addition of diphenylketene to benzoquinone in a synthesis of fuchsone illustrates this behavior. Ketenes react with many conjugated olefinic substances in this manner.

Benzyne dimerizes to a four-membered ring compound, biphenylene (p. 626); this hydrocarbon is produced in 24% yield by treatment of o-bromo-fluorobenzene with lithium amalgam.[49]

[49] G. Wittig and L. Pohmer, *Chem. Ber.*, **89**, 1334 (1956).

Cycloaddition occurs also when benzyne is produced in the presence of very reactive olefins such as bicyclo[2,2,1]-heptene.[50]

Phenanthrene combines with maleic anhydride under the influence of ultraviolet radiation to form a cyclobutane derivative.[51]

Photo-dimerization

Cyclobutane derivatives can be made also by irradiation of certain olefinic substances (CR **51**, 1). The mechanism of such photo-dimerization reactions, presumably different from that of thermal cycloaddition, may involve radicals. A very old example is the conversion of cinnamic acid into α-truxillic acid by exposure to sunlight.

A similar behavior has been observed with methylenemalonic esters. Hydrolysis of the dimers and decarboxylation of the resulting tetracarboxylic acid produce 1,3-cyclobutanedicarboxylic acid.

Under the influence of ultraviolet light dimethyl fumarate in the solid state undergoes dimerization to *cis*, *trans*, *cis*-1,2,3,4-tetracarbomethoxy-cyclobutane.[52]

[50] H. E. Simmons, *J. Am. Chem. Soc.*, **83**, 1657 (1961).
[51] D. Bryce-Smith and B. Vickery, *Chem. and Ind.*, 429 (1961).
[52] G. W. Griffin, A. F. Vellturo, and K. Furukawa, *J. Am. Chem. Soc.*, **83**, 2725 (1961).

$$2 \quad \begin{array}{c} CH_3O_2C \quad H \\ | \qquad | \\ C{=}C \\ | \qquad | \\ H \quad CO_2CH_3 \end{array} \quad \rightarrow \quad \begin{array}{c} CH_3O_2C \\ CH_3O_2C \\ \end{array} \diagdown \begin{array}{c} CO_2CH_3 \\ CO_2CH_3 \end{array}$$

Photo-oxides

Conjugated dienes and polyenes take up molecular oxygen rapidly under the influence of ultraviolet light or slowly in diffuse light to yield peroxides, often called *photo-oxides*, produced by the addition of the oxygen to the ends of the diene system. The reaction is formally of the Diels-Alder type, oxygen playing the role of dienophile. An example is the formation of ascaridole; it is naturally occurring and can be made from α-terpinene by photo-oxidation in the presence of a sensitizer such as chlorophyll.

Ascaridole is sufficiently stable to be distilled.

In the presence of methylene blue, α-phellandrene gives a similar peroxide in 52 % yield.[53]

Similar endoperoxides have been prepared in the steroid series as well as from 1,3-cyclohexadiene and cyclopentadiene.

Photo-oxides that contain a peroxide bridge in a 1,4-position, called transannular peroxides, are known also in the aromatic series. Aromatic hydrocarbons containing the basic resonating system of 9,10-diphenyl-anthracene form photo-oxides that are dissociated by heat to give the original hydrocarbon and oxygen. Perhaps the most striking of these is rubrene peroxide, the peroxide of 5,6,11,12-tetraphenylnaphthacene (CR **28,** 367).

[53] G. O. Schenck, K. G. Kinkel, and H.-J. Mertens, *Ann.*, **584,** 125 (1953).

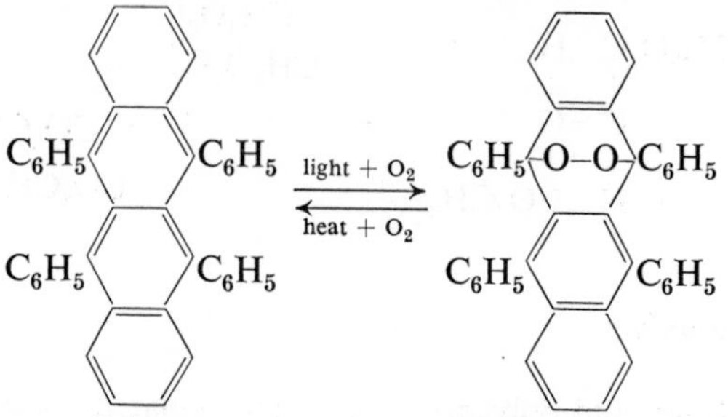

C_6H_5 C_6H_5 $\xrightarrow{\text{light} + O_2}$ C_6H_5—O—O—C_6H_5

C_6H_5 C_6H_5 $\xleftarrow{\text{heat} + O_2}$ C_6H_5 C_6H_5

Rubrene   Rubrene peroxide

Anthracene and its derivatives that do not have aryl substituents at each of the *meso*-carbon atoms may form peroxides in ultraviolet light, but such peroxides are not dissociated by heat to form the original reactants. 9-Methoxy-10-phenylanthracene, for example, is converted into the corresponding peroxide in 85% yield.[54]

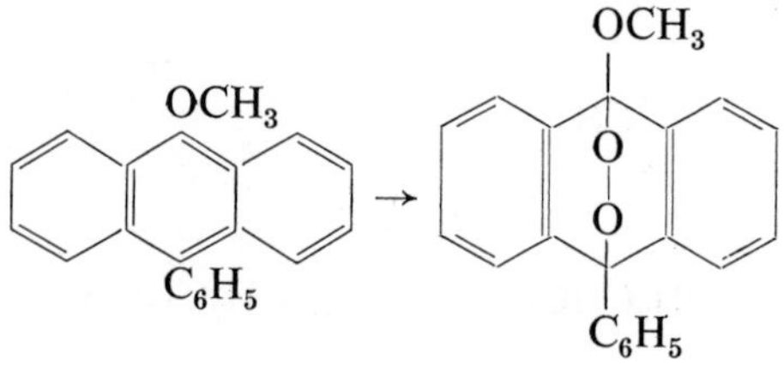

OCH_3

OCH_3 $\rightarrow$ O

C_6H_5 O

C_6H_5

1,3-Dipolar Addition

The addition of phenyl azide to strained olefins to form five-membered triazole rings illustrates *1,3-dipolar addition*; the azide represents the *1,3-dipole* and the olefin the *dipolarophile*. This type of addition may proceed by a concerted mechanism and would thus fall between the Diels-Alder closure of six-membered rings and the dimerization of olefinic compounds to produce four-membered rings.

An example is the addition of phenyl azide to the Diels-Alder adduct from cyclopentadiene and diethyl azodicarboxylate (p. 690).

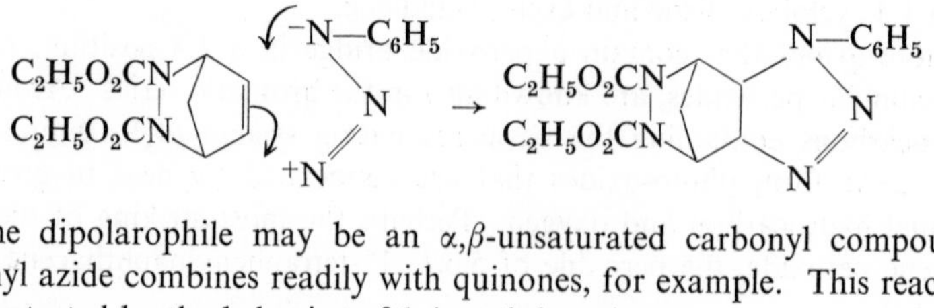

$C_2H_5O_2CN$ $-N—C_6H_5$ $N—C_6H_5$

$C_2H_5O_2CN$ N $\rightarrow$ $C_2H_5O_2CN$ N

$+N$ $C_2H_5O_2CN$ N

The dipolarophile may be an α,β-unsaturated carbonyl compound; phenyl azide combines readily with quinones, for example. This reaction is illustrated by the behavior of 1,4-naphthoquinone.

[54] C. Dufraisse, A. Etienne, and J. Rigaudy, *Compt. rend.*, **226**, 1773 (1948).

The 1,3-dipoles may be aliphatic diazo compounds, which combine with olefinic and acetylenic substances to yield, respectively, pyrazolines and pyrazoles. Addition occurs more readily if the double bond is conjugated with a carbonyl group. For example, unsaturated esters such as those of maleic, fumaric, and crotonic acids react with diazomethane to produce alkyl pyrazolinecarboxylates. Diethyl maleate and diethyl fumarate give the same pyrazoline:

In 2-cyano-2'-biphenylyl azide the nitrile group is able to function as a dipolarophile.[55]

The Addition of Carbenes to Olefins

As was mentioned earlier (p. 268), it has been postulated that alkalis act upon chloroform to produce dichlorocarbene. Striking confirmation of this theory is the discovery that, in the presence of chloroform and sodium hydroxide, unsaturated compounds take up the group CCl_2 to form dichlorocyclopropane derivatives (Angew., **73**, 161). An example is the behavior of cyclohexene.[56]

[55] P. A. S. Smith, J. M. Clegg, and J. H. Hall, *J. Org. Chem.*, **23**, 524 (1958).
[56] W. von E. Doering and A. K. Hoffmann, *J. Am. Chem. Soc.*, **76**, 6162 (1954).

Similarly isobutylene gives 1,1-dichloro-2,2-dimethylcyclopropane.

$$CH_3 \quad \overset{:CCl_2}{\underset{C=CH_2}{\diagdown}} \rightarrow \quad CH_3 \quad CCl_2$$

If 1,2-dimethylpropenyllithium is used with methylene chloride, the product is 2,3,3-trimethylcyclopropenyllithium; hydrolysis produces 1,3,3-trimethylcyclopropene.[57]

A convenient method of generating dichlorocarbene is treatment of an ester of trichloroacetic acid with an alkali metal alkoxide. 2-Oxa-7,7-dichloronorcarane can be made in 75% yield by treating ethyl trichloroacetate with sodium methoxide in the presence of 2,3-dihydropyran.

Methylene, formed by pyrolysis of ketene or diazomethane, is believed to have its electrons paired; by collision with inert gas molecules it is changed to a diradical, i.e., it passes from the singlet to the triplet state (Gould, 751).[58]

$$\overset{H}{\underset{H}{\mid}} C: \rightarrow \overset{H}{\underset{H}{\mid}} \cdot C \cdot$$

The argument in favor of the intermediate formation of carbenes in the production of cyclopropane derivatives from olefins has been strengthened by the observation that in the presence of bromoform and base the cis- and trans-2-butenes react stereospecifically. The cis- and trans-olefins yield the respective cis- and trans-1,1-dibromo-2,3-dimethylcyclopropanes.[59]

[57] G. L. Closs and L. E. Closs, *J. Am. Chem. Soc.*, **83**, 1003 (1961).

[58] F. A. L. Anet, R. F. W. Bader, and A.-M. Van der Auwera, *J. Am. Chem. Soc.*, **82**, 3217 (1960); D. B. Richardson, M. C. Simmons, and I. Dvoretzky, *J. Am. Chem. Soc.*, **82**, 5001 (1960); H. M. Frey, *J. Am. Chem. Soc.*, **82**, 5947 (1960).

[59] P. S. Skell and A. Y. Garner, *J. Am. Chem. Soc.*, **78**, 3409 (1956).

$$
\begin{array}{ccc}
\underset{H}{\overset{CH_3}{\diagdown}}C=C\underset{CH_3}{\overset{H}{\diagup}} & \rightarrow & \text{(1,1-dibromo-2,3-dimethylcyclopropane)}
\end{array}
$$

Dibromo- and dichlorocarbenes combine with butadiene to give the corresponding 1,1-dihalo-2-vinylcyclopropanes.[60]

$$
CH_2=CH-CH=CH_2 \quad \underset{:CCl_2}{\overset{:CBr_2}{\diagup\diagdown}}
$$

$$
\begin{array}{c}
CBr_2 \\
\diagup\diagdown \\
CH_2-CHCH=CH_2
\end{array}
$$

$$
\begin{array}{c}
CCl_2 \\
\diagup\diagdown \\
CH_2-CHCH=CH_2
\end{array}
$$

Carbene itself reacts with ethylene to give cyclopropane.[61]

$$
CH_2 + CH_2=CH_2 \rightarrow \begin{array}{c} CH_2 \\ \diagup\diagdown \\ CH_2-CH_2 \end{array}
$$

The addition of carbenes to olefinic compounds thus has provided a useful route to cyclopropane derivatives (Angew., **72**, 4).

When the nitroso derivative of 2,2-diphenylcyclopropylurea is treated with bases in the presence of 2-butenes, spiropentanes are formed; presumably 2,2-diphenylcyclopropylcarbene is an intermediate.[62]

$$
(C_6H_5)_2C\underset{CH_2}{\overset{\diagup\diagdown}{}}CN_2 \xrightarrow{-N_2} (C_6H_5)_2C\underset{CH_2}{\overset{\diagup\diagdown}{}}C: + CH_3CH=CHCH_3 \longrightarrow
$$

$$
\begin{array}{c}
CH_3CH-CHCH_3 \\
\diagdown\diagup \\
C \\
\diagup\diagdown \\
(C_6H_5)_2C-CH_2
\end{array}
$$

The formation of the spiranes from *cis*- and *trans*-2-butenes appears to be stereospecific.

Chlorocarbene is produced by treating methylene chloride with methyllithium. It attacks phenoxide ion, and the product undergoes ring expansion to yield tropone.[63]

[60] R. C. Woodworth and P. S. Skell, *J. Am. Chem. Soc.*, **79**, 2542 (1957).

[61] H. M. Frey, *J. Am. Chem. Soc.*, **79**, 1259 (1957).

[62] W. M. Jones, *J. Am. Chem. Soc.*, **82**, 6200 (1960).

[63] G. L. Closs and L. E. Closs, *J. Am. Chem. Soc.*, **83**, 599 (1961).

When methyllithium is added to a boiling solution of benzene in methylene chloride, 7-methylcyclohepta-1,3,5-triene is formed; chlorocarbene might react with benzene to form a bicyclic intermediate, which could decompose to tropylium chloride. Methylation of this salt would give the observed product.[64]

Stereospecific addition of carbene occurs also when olefins are heated with methylene iodide in the presence of a zinc-copper couple; cyclohexene yields norcarane.[65]

Although the mechanism of this way of adding carbene seems to be different from the others mentioned, this method has proven to be useful. Other examples are the cyclopropyl derivatives obtained by heating 1,5-cyclöoctadiene, 2,5-norbornadiene, and 4-vinylcyclohexene with methylene iodide and a zinc-copper couple.[66]

[64] G. L. Closs and L. E. Closs, *Tetrahedron Letters*, No. 10, 38 (1960).

[65] H. E. Simmons and R. D. Smith, *J. Am. Chem. Soc.*, **80**, 5323 (1958).

[66] S. D. Koch, R. M. Kliss, D. V. Lopiekes, and R. J. Wineman, *J. Org. Chem.*, **26**, 3122 (1961).

When ethynyldimethylcarbinyl chloride is treated with potassium t-butoxide in the presence of styrene a cyclopropane derivative is obtained that corresponds to the addition product of styrene and the carbene $(CH_3)_2C{=}C{=}C{:}$.[67]

$$CH_3{-}\underset{\underset{Cl}{|}}{\overset{\overset{CH_3}{|}}{C}}{-}C{\equiv}CH \xrightarrow{(CH_3)_3COK} (CH_3)_2C{=}C{=}C{:}$$

$$(CH_3)_2C{=}C{=}C{:} + C_6H_5CH{=}CH_2 \rightarrow \underset{C_6H_5CH{-}\!\!-\!\!{-}C{=}C{=}C(CH_3)_2}{\overset{CH_2}{\triangle}}$$

Phenylchlorocarbene combines with the dimethyl acetal of phenyl ketene to give the dimethyl ketal of diphenylcyclopropenone. The ketone is formed by hydrolysis of the acetal.[68]

$$C_6H_5CH{=}C\underset{OCH_3}{\overset{OCH_3}{\diagdown}} \xrightarrow{:CClC_6H_5} \underset{C_6H_5C}{\overset{C_6H_5C}{\diagdown}}\!\!C\!\!\underset{OCH_3}{\overset{OCH_3}{\diagup}} \longrightarrow \underset{C_6H_5C}{\overset{C_6H_5C}{\triangle}}C{=}O$$

Chloromethyl phenyl ether reacts with n-butyllithium to give lithium-chloromethyl phenyl ether, which undergoes α-elimination to yield phenoxycarbene. The carbene can be trapped in the usual way by olefins such as isobutylene.[69]

$$C_6H_5O{-}\underset{\underset{H}{|}}{\overset{\overset{Li}{|}}{C}}{-}Cl \xrightarrow{-LiCl} C_6H_5O\overset{..}{C}H \xrightarrow{(CH_3)_2C{=}CH_2} \underset{CH_2}{\overset{}{(CH_3)_2C\!\!-\!\!\!-\!\!\!-CHOC_6H_5}}$$

A nitrogen analog of carbene, an azene, has been proposed as an intermediate in the formation of 2,4,9-trimethylcarbazole from 2-azido-2′,4′,6′-trimethylbiphenyl.[70]

[67] H. D. Hartzler, *J. Am. Chem. Soc.*, **81**, 2024 (1959).
[68] R. Breslow, R. Haynie, and J. Mirra, *J. Am. Chem. Soc.*, **81**, 247 (1959).
[69] U. Schöllkopf and A. Lerch, *Angew. Chem.*, **73**, 27 (1961).
[70] G. Smolinsky, *J. Am. Chem. Soc.*, **83**, 2489 (1961).

α-Azidostyrene undergoes pyrolysis to give 2-phenylazirine, presumably by way of the azene.[71]

$$
\underset{\substack{C_6H_5 \quad\quad N_3}}{\overset{\substack{CH_2 \\ \| \\ C}}{}} \;\rightarrow\; \left[\underset{\substack{C_6H_5 \quad\quad N:}}{\overset{\substack{CH_2 \\ \| \\ C}}{}} \;\leftrightarrow\; \underset{\substack{C_6H_5 \quad\quad N\cdot}}{\overset{\substack{CH_2 \\ | \\ C}}{}} \right] \;\rightarrow\; C_6H_5C \!\!=\!\!\!=\!\! N: \overset{CH_2}{}
$$

Insertion Reactions

Carbene attacks carbon-hydrogen bonds indiscriminately producing the corresponding methyl derivatives; pentane, for example, yields a mixture of *n*-hexane, 2-methylpentane, and 3-methylpentane in the proportions corresponding to nearly random attack. The insertion of the methylene group between hydrogen and carbon may be formulated in a way similar to the ring-forming molecular reactions.

$$
\begin{array}{c}
CH_3CH_2 \\
\diagdown \\
C\!\!-\!\!-\!\!H \\
\diagup \\
CH_3CH_2 \quad H
\end{array}
\;
\overset{:CH_2}{}
\;\rightarrow\;
\begin{array}{c}
CH_3CH_2 \\
\diagdown \\
CHCH_3 \\
\diagup \\
CH_3CH_2
\end{array}
$$

Ethyl ether, in a similar way, yields ethyl *n*-propyl ether and ethyl iso-propyl ether in a ratio that differs little from that corresponding to indiscriminate attack.[72]

$$
CH_3CH_2OCH_2CH_3 \;\rightarrow\; CH_3CH_2OCH_2CH_2CH_3
$$
$$
\underset{CH_3}{CH_3CH_2OCHCH_3}
$$

When diazoacetic esters are decomposed by irradiation in cyclopentane or cyclohexane, the carbalkoxycarbene produced combines with the cyclo-paraffin to give a saturated ester. The behavior of ethyl diazoacetate in cyclohexane is illustrative.[73]

$$
N_2CHCO_2C_2H_5 \xrightarrow{\text{light}} N_2 + H\!\!-\!\!\ddot{C}\!\!-\!\!CO_2C_2H_5
$$

$$
H\!\!-\!\!\ddot{C}\!\!-\!\!CO_2C_2H_5 + \bigcirc \;\rightarrow\; \bigcirc\!\!CH_2CO_2C_2H_5
$$

[71] G. Smolensky, *J. Am. Chem. Soc.*, **83**, 4483 (1961).

[72] See W. von E. Doering, L. H. Knox, and M. Jones, Jr., *J. Org. Chem.*, **24**, 136 (1959).

[73] W. von E. Doering and L. H. Knox, *J. Am. Chem. Soc.*, **78**, 4947 (1956).

A carbene intermediate has been proposed for the dehydrohalogenation of neoalkyl halides by strong bases to produce cyclopropane derivatives. An example is the formation of 1,1-dimethylcyclopropane by the action of sodium; α-elimination of hydrogen chloride would produce a carbene, which could form a ring by intramolecular insertion.[74]

Primary alkyl chlorides that have hydrogen in the γ-position give varying amounts of the corresponding cyclopropane derivatives when treated with sodium or potassium or their alkyl derivatives.[75]

When 7,7-dibromobicyclo[4,1,0]heptane is treated with methyllithium it is converted into the corresponding carbene, which undergoes an intramolecular insertion reaction to form a bicyclobutane derivative.[76]

[74] L. Friedman and J. G. Berger, *J. Am. Chem. Soc.*, **83**, 500 (1961).

[75] W. Kirmse and W. von E. Doering, *Tetrahedron*, **11**, 266 (1960).

[76] W. R. Moore, H. R. Ward, and R. F. Merritt, *J. Am. Chem. Soc.*, **83**, 2019 (1961).

Author index

Subject index

746